Recent Mammoth titles

The Mammoth Book of Weird News
The Mammoth Book of Undercover Cops
The Mammoth Book of Antarctic Journeys
The Mammoth Book of Muhammad Ali
The Mammoth Book of Best British Crime 9
The Mammoth Book of Conspiracies
The Mammoth Book of Lost Symbols
The Mammoth Book of Nebula Awards SF
The Mammoth Book of Steampunk
The Mammoth Book of New CSI
The Mammoth Book of Gangs
The Mammoth Book of SF Wars
The Mammoth Book of One-Liners
The Mammoth Book of Best New SF 25
The Mammoth Book of Jokes 2
The Mammoth Book of Street Art
The Mammoth Book of Ghost Stories by Women
The Mammoth Book of Irish Humour
The Mammoth Book of Unexplained Phenomena
The Mammoth Book of Best British Crime 10
The Mammoth Book of Combat
The Mammoth Book of Dark Magic
The Mammoth Book of Angels and Demons
The Mammoth Book of New Sudoku
The Mammoth Book of Zombies
The Mammoth Book of Covert Ops
The Mammoth Book of the Rolling Stones
The Mammoth Book of Prison Breaks
The Mammoth Book of Time Travel SF
The Mammoth Book of Westerns

THE MAMMOTH

Quiz Book

Nick Holt

ROBINSON

Constable & Robinson Ltd.
55–56 Russell Square
London WC1B 4HP
www.constablerobinson.com

First published in the UK by Robinson,
an imprint of Constable & Robinson Ltd., 2013

A copy of the British Library Cataloguing in
Publication Data is available from the British Library

ISBN: 978-1-47210-588-2 (paperback)
ISBN: 978-1-47210-622-3 (ebook)

Printed and bound in the UK

1 3 5 7 9 10 8 6 4 2

Contents

CONTENTS

CONTENTS

INTRODUCTION

This is a tricky quiz book. I make no apologies for that. Easy quiz books are boring – especially for people who do a lot of quizzes – and these are exactly the sort of people likely to buy this quiz book. I've set a target for each quiz, for beginners and hardcore quizzers – some of the beginner targets are as low as 40 per cent so getting 6/10 can be a cause for celebration rather than dejection. There's one point per question unless otherwise indicated.

I've divided the book into sections of eight quizzes, each section containing two General Knowledge rounds and a series of more specialist rounds. The main topics for these rounds are history, geography, trivia, arts and books, TV, movies, rock and pop, sport and science, with various headings for specific subjects within these areas. These rounds are tougher – unless you are particularly good at that subject. I included science so my nephews – who are all scientists – don't moan at me. They got some wrong when I tested them, which made me really happy. *Schadenfreude* – there's a question about that in the book.

I've tried to make the questions interesting, and tried (probably unsuccessfully in some places) to erase the kind of question that makes a quiz book irksome, like 'Who was top scorer in the Premier League in 2003–4?' Not only do questions like that date a book terribly, but they are lazy – they seem easy but actually no one remembers what they were doing eight or ten years previously, except in TV police programmes where cold case units persuade witnesses to remember every detail of something that happened a decade earlier. Hopefully some of the questions will get a 'Gosh, I didn't know that!' or 'Oh, is that what happened!'

To that end there are a few list questions and multi-part questions to get you scratching your heads – I've taken a leaf out of David Gentle's excellent *On the Tip of My Tongue* – a quiz book which I'm prepared to concede is almost as good as this one (except for the title, which is rubbish – I'm a bit of a Ronseal man when it comes to book titles: if it's a quiz book call it *The So-and-So Quiz Book*, not *Diversions for the Inquiring Mind* or some such pseudo-literary claptrap).

There are a lot of pop culture questions. Again, no apologies, there is enough highbrow stuff to satisfy the culture snobs. The great thing about sport and pop culture questions is that they're a leveller – education is irrelevant to knowledge of sport, films or music, it's all about passion and experience. They are also subjects that throw up lists and statistics more readily than academic study. One caveat – there is very little on reality TV (one quiz). This is purely personal – I hate the stuff and couldn't even bring myself to research it with any enthusiasm.

There are also a number of mix-and-match quizzes. I've given you (for example) ten names and ten films and asked you to match the star to the film – these are fun and frustrating; just when you think you've cracked it you realize you've ended up with Brad Pitt in *Honey, I Shrunk the Kids*. (He wasn't.)

If you want to use the quizzes at a pub or school or social club feel free, I can't stop you. But I would ask that you take the book along, come clean about your source and encourage everyone to buy a copy. Then I get my 1.5p or whatever it is – only joking, dear publisher.

If you think you've spotted an error, then please . . . actually, no, on second thoughts, don't. Just get over it: we all make mistakes.

Enjoy. Get frustrated, certainly, possibly even a teensy bit angry. But still enjoy. Then I'll know it was a good quiz.

Quiz 1. General Knowledge

Straightforward twenty general knowledge questions, one point for each correct answer

Part 1

1   What term is given to the formal union between two people of the same sex in the UK, coined to avoid the controversy surrounding the use of the word 'marriage'?

2   For what inappropriate act was Prince Harry in the news in January 2005?

3   The Group Areas Act came into force on 27 April 1950. By what name is the Act better known?

4   The Velocipede was a nineteenth-century prototype of what?

5   What is the capital of the Bahamas, accounting for *c.*75 per cent of its population?

6   What name is given to a sheet of paper 17 in by 13½ in?

7   Agent Provocateur is a leading brand in the design and sales of what commodity?

8   Approximately what percentage of global methane emissions is caused by flatulent farm animals; is it 2 per cent, 14 per cent or 33 per cent?

9   In November 1997 a furore broke out over a donation of £1 million to the Labour Party by which businessman and Formula 1 entrepreneur?

10   In 2005 Margaret Thatcher's son, Mark, admitted to financial involvement in an attempted coup in which country? (a) Somalia (b) Equatorial Guinea (c) Mali

Part 2

11 'You turn if you want to. The lady's not for turning.' Who uttered these famous words in Brighton in 1980?

12 Dendochronology is the study of what?

13 The founder of the Yellow Cab Company in 1915 in Chicago was also the founder of a famous car rental company. What was his name?

14 What denomination is the largest banknote in the Bank of England's internal banking system? (a) £1,000 (b) £100,000 (c) £100 million

15 What euphemistic term is used by the US military to cover civilian deaths occurring as a result of military action?

16 Which is Britain's oldest Sunday newspaper, published for the first time in 1791?

17 Yuri Gagarin's first manned space flight was launched from within which post-Soviet country?

18 What does a haematologist study?

19 Which Welsh town was devastated by the collapse of a coal slag heap in 1966, leaving over 100 children dead?

20 With which internet phenomenon is Mark Zuckerberg associated?

Total Points: 20. Targets: Novice 10 Pro 15. Your Score:

Quiz 2. Movies

Just a straightforward twenty questions on movie history – 1 point for each answer

Part 1

1   Which Python contributed twelve cameos to their movie, *Life of Brian*?
2   Who played the title role, a whistle-blower on the tobacco industry, in *The Insider* (Michael Mann, 1999)?
3   Who played the title role of Hal in the 2001 Farrelly brothers comedy, *Shallow Hal*?
4   Which British actor died whilst still filming his supporting role in Ridley Scott's *Gladiator*?
5   Yuen Woo-ping choreographed the fights in *Crouching Tiger, Hidden Dragon* (2000); what high-octane American movie benefited from his work the previous year?
6   Susanne Christian had a small role at the end of Kubrick's *Paths of Glory*; what larger role did he find for her afterwards?
7   In which iconic European movie does Marcello Mastroianni follow a seductive Anita Ekberg into the Trevi Fountain in the centre of Rome?
8   Who played the wild and unruly Alex in *A Clockwork Orange*, and what was the name given to his gang? (2 pts)
9   Whose media organization tried to block the release of *Citizen Kane*, believing it to be a satire on their operation?
10 *Animal Crackers*, *Horse Feathers* and *Go West* all starred which movie combination?

Part 2

11 Which gangster movie was the Coen brothers' 1984 debut?

12 What kind of films does Hayao Miyazaki make?

13 With which studio do we most readily associate the directors Alexander Mackendrick and Charles Crichton?

14 *Catch Me If You Can* (2002) was based on the real-life story of which con-man?

15 Norman Hudis wrote the first few scripts and Talbot Rothwell took over for the rest of the series for which comedy film franchise?

16 What type of cars play a major role in the 1969 heist movie *The Italian Job*? In what other type of transport does the climax to the film take place? (2 pts)

17 Who plays the chat-show host who is the subject of Robert De Niro's obsession in Scorsese's *The King of Comedy* (1983)?

18 Tom Hanks talks to his volleyball; what's the film?

19 Which actor was born on 6 July 1946 to an Italian-American father and a half-Russian, half-French mother, with permanent paralysis to the left side of his face after a birthing accident?

20 Which two actresses have portrayed Clarice Starling in movies based on Thomas Harris's Hannibal Lecter series? (2 pts)

Total Points: 23. Targets: Novice 17 Pro 22. Your Score: [   ]

Quiz 3. Writers

Ten general questions on writers, and a multi-part teaser to finish. 1 point for each answer and five in total for the teaser

Part 1

1   True or false? Miguel de Cervantes, the author of *Don Quixote*, was once held captive for five years by Barbary pirates.
2   Which writer's modest house can be visited at Chawton, near Winchester?
3   In which city did the poet John Keats die?
4   Who lived at 17 Gough Square, London (off Fleet Street) in the mid-eighteenth century?
5   Which author died in 2008, seven years after his magnum opus takes place?
6   What was the name of the 1930s literary set who used to meet in the Eagle and Child pub in Oxford?
7   What does the 'P' stand for in P. D. James?
8   Agatha Christie also wrote romances; under which name?
9   To which famous poet was Elizabeth Barrett, herself a significant poet, happily married for fifteen years?
10 What connects Margaret Drabble and A. S. Byatt?

Teaser

11 Which school was attended by writers C. S. Forester, Raymond Chandler and P. G. Wodehouse?
12 What name is given to alumni of that school?
13 What were the main characters invented by these three writers? (3 pts)

Total Points: 15. Targets: Novice 6 Pro 11. Your Score:

Quiz 4. Wildlife

Twenty general questions on mammals, birds, insects and any other kind of wildlife

Part 1

1   Which bird is also known as the halcyon bird, a harbinger of calm and prosperity?

2   By what name is the dangerous aquatic life-form called the Physalia better known?

3   Giraffes, alligators and dolphins all share what nomenclature for male and female adults?

4   A yaffle is the old name for which kind of bird?

5   The Sargasso Sea is the source and breeding ground of various species of which kind of fish, whose migratory patterns remain an enigma?

6   Which mammal was rendered extinct by 1936 after the government introduced a cull in response to the farming lobby?

7   Octopi, squid and cuttlefish are all parts of which class of animals within the mollusc phylum?

8   The impala is a mammal unique to which continent?

9   The guillemot is a species of which group of sea birds?

10 A tapping or ticking noise in the rafters of old buildings in the summer is a likely indicator of the presence of *Xestobium rufovillosum*; what is its common name?

Part 2

11 What name is given to the majority of North American species of the creature known as a hare in Britain?

12 Which type of snake is responsible for 82 per cent of snakebite fatalities in the US?

13 A troglobite is a creature that cannot survive outside which natural environment?

14 The North American muskellunge is the largest of the Esox family of fish, better known by which more common name?

15 The Sirenia (sea cows) are aquatic mammals; three of the surviving species are manatees; what is the other? (a) platypus (b) dugong (c) basilisk

16 What kind of creature is a narwhal and to which region is it exclusively native?

17 Which of these is a member of the Pantherinae or big cat sub-family: cougar, cheetah, jaguar, ocelot?

18 The wombat and the possum belong to which sub-class of mammals?

19 A creature belonging to the species *canis lupus* is usually called what?

20 Adonis Blue, Essex Skipper and Purple Hairstreak are all species resident to the UK of which creature?

Total Points: 20. Targets: Novice 8 Pro 15. Your Score:

Quiz 5. Military History

Ten straight questions and a Mix and Match grid

Part 1

1   1 August 1990 saw 100,000 Iraqi troops invade which neighbouring state, sparking off the first Gulf War?
2   What was sunk by HMS *Conqueror* in 1982?
3   On 19 August 1968, Soviet tanks rolled into which country?
4   Which much romanticized but militarily inept action took place during the Battle of Balaclava in 1854?
5   In which city was Archduke Franz Ferdinand assassinated on 27 June 1914, an event which led directly to the start of World War I?
6   Which legendary German fighter pilot was shot down and killed on 20 April 1918?
7   The naval Battle of Gravelines is usually known by which two-word term?
8   Which Roman legion was believed to have been destroyed by Pictish warriors in Scotland in about AD 117?
9   Which two independent Dutch states fought the Boer Wars against the British? (2 pts)
10 What name was given to the South Vietnam forces that fought against the US and with the Communists in the Vietnam War?

Part 2

Mix and Match: Match the battle to the wider campaign or war during which it took place

1. Battle of the Bulge (aka Ardennes Offensive), 1944–5; 2. Battle of Inkerman, 1854; 3. Battle of Poitiers, 1356; 4. Relief of Mafeking, 1900; 5. Battle of el Ebro, 1938; 6. Battle of Leipzig, 1813; 7. Battle of Bosworth Field, 1485; 8. The Tet Offensive, 1968; 9. Six-Day War, 1967; 10. Battle of Marston Moor, 1644

a. Spanish Civil War; b. Napoleonic Wars; c. Crimean War; d. Wars of the Roses; e. English Civil War; f. Second Boer War; g. Arab–Israeli Wars; h. World War II; i. Hundred Years War; j. Vietnam War

Your Workings:

Total Points: 21. Targets: Novice 8 Pro 16. Your Score:

Quiz 6. General Sport

Twenty quick-fire questions

Part 1

1   Who once described trying to beat Phil Taylor at darts as like trying 'to eat candy floss in a wind tunnel'?

2   In which sport might you get a Naeryo followed by a Jireugi ap?

3   Who won the high jump gold medal at the 1968 Olympics and established a new style that remains the principle method for the discipline today?

4   What name is given to the rapid form of skiing slalom race, where the accent is on speed rather than technical proficiency?

5   If you watched Poole Pirates against Peterborough Panthers, what sport would you be watching?

6   Which is the only one of the four golf tournaments that make up the Majors to be held at the same venue every year?

7   The first Winter Olympics held in the US were at Lake Placid; in which state and which mountain range is this resort? (2 pts)

8   Which sport is commenced (and re-started) with a bully-off?

9   In 2012 Lewis Hamilton announced he was leaving McLaren to drive for which other Formula 1 team?

10 What was the national stadium for the French football and rugby union teams prior to the building of the Stade de France for the 1998 World Cup?

Part 2

11   Who was declared the Sportsman of the Century in 1999 by both the prestigious US magazine *Sports Illustrated* and the BBC?

12   Who was Secretary of the FA from 1934 until 1962, and then President of FIFA to 1974?

13   Which country is regarded as the primary practitioner of the game of polo?

14   How many cards will be on the table at the end of a game of Texas Hold 'Em if there are four players and all stay in the game until the showdown?

15   Which medieval French fortified city gives its name to a popular strategy tile game?

16   In a game of snooker a sequence of balls potted that reads red-black-red-black-red-pink-red-brown-red will score how many points?

17   What did Aroldis Chapman do at a world record speed of 105 mph in 2010? (a) pitch a baseball (b) hurl a javelin (c) ride a bobsleigh

18   What does MCC stand for, in a cricketing context?

19   What lends its name to a score of two below par for a particular golf hole?

20   What was used for the first time at Wimbledon in 1971 to prevent matches over-running?

Total Points: 21. Targets: Novice 8 Pro 16. Your Score:

Quiz 7. Births, Deaths and Marriages

Ten straight questions plus ten vaguely cryptic questions about folks who shuffled off this mortal coil in 2012

Part 1

1   Who were married at Canongate Kirk in Edinburgh on 30 July 2011?
2   Which two rock stars enjoyed brief marriages to Pamela Anderson? (2 pts)
3   Which former professional footballer owns and runs restaurants with his wife, actress Leslie Ash?
4   Jane Asher has been the partner of illustrator Gerald Scarfe since 1971; with which pop star did she have a five-year relationship in the 1960s?
5   George Harrison's first wife, model Patti Boyd, left him when she fell in love with which other musician?
6   Little Pixie Geldof was the third daughter of Bob Geldof and Paula Yates; what are the names of her two elder sisters? (2 pts)
7   What connects Sonny Bono and Gregg Allman of the Allman Brothers Band in the marital stakes?
8   Actress Jane Wyman was married to which US President?
9   After the divorce of Gordon Sumner from Irish actress Frances Tomelty, who became the second Mrs Sumner?
10 Andre Agassi married which other tennis player in 2001?

Part 2

11 She will always love us.
12 First man on the moon.
13 Harry met Sally but Julie never met Julia in this screenwriter's work.
14 Writer of classic sci-fi including *Fahrenheit 451*.
15 He couldn't take his eyes off of her.
16 This Irish writer lit a penny candle and had a circle of friends.
17 Ridley's younger brother was a *Top Gun*.
18 This singer was 'Hot Stuff' in the 1970s.
19 First Monkee to go.
20 Burt Bacharach's preferred lyricist.

Total Points: 22. Targets: Novice 11 Pro 18. Your Score:

Quiz 8. General Knowledge

Another twenty general knowledge questions

Part 1

1 Steve Chen, Chad Hurley and Jawed Karim were jointly responsible for the development of which internet phenomenon?

2 Tanqueray is a brand synonymous with which spirit?

3 Under what name did Charles Dodgson write a famous children's classic?

4 Which early Greek academic was the first to have recorded his studies of different animals and their anatomy and physiology?

5 What reopened on 9 June 1854 in south London, having been moved from its initial site in Hyde Park?

6 How did Henri Paul die in 1997?

7 As of 1 July 2007, what could you no longer do in a public house in England?

8 In which county were the *Poldark* series of novels by Winston Graham set?

9 Britain's first public library, Chetham's Library, was established in 1653 in which city?

10 Which fast-food bore the brunt of Jamie Oliver's disapproval in 2005, and promptly saw sales increase by up to a third?

Part 2

11 Who was subjected to an Islamic fatwa for his allegedly blasphemous work, *The Satanic Verses*?

12 What was the middle name of Wolfgang Mozart?

13 The song 'You'll Never Walk Alone' was written by Rodgers and Hammerstein for which musical?

14 What is the study of right and wrong and moral ambiguities?

15 Which George Bernard Shaw play would later provide the basis for the musical, *My Fair Lady*?

16 What is the art of stuffing animals for preservation?

17 What were banned by the Byzantine Emperor Theodosius in AD 393 having been part of Greek culture for over a thousand years?

18 Which Amazonian model and actress was married to Sylvester Stallone in 1985–7?

19 In which country, in 2001, were twelve British plane-spotters arrested and held on suspicion of spying?

20 If you dialled +33 at the start of an international call, which country would you be ringing?

Total Points: 20. Targets: Novice 10 Pro 15. Your Score: [   ]

Answers Quizzes 1–8

Quiz 1. General Knowledge

1. Civil partnership; 2. Dressing as a Nazi at a fancy-dress party; 3. Apartheid; 4. A bicycle; 5. Nassau; 6. Foolscap; 7. Lingerie; 8. 14 per cent; 9. Bernie Ecclestone; 10. (b) Equatorial Guinea; 11. Margaret Thatcher; 12. Tree rings; 13. (John D.) Hertz; 14. (c) £100 million (it is known as a Titan); 15. Collateral damage; 16. *Observer*, 17. Kazakhstan; 18. Blood; 19. Aberfan; 20. Facebook

Quiz 2. Movies

1. Michael Palin; his roles included the ex-leper scrounger, a boring prophet, a kindly centurion in the crucifix queue and Pontius Pilate; 2. Russell Crowe; 3. Jack Black; 4. Oliver Reed; 5. *The Matrix*; 6. His wife; 7. *La Dolce Vita*; 8. Malcolm McDowell; Droogs; 9. William Randolph Hearst; 10. Marx Brothers; 11. *Blood Simple*; 12. Animation; he is the jewel in the crown of Studio Ghibli, the Japanese animation company; 13. Ealing; 14. Frank Abagnale Jr; 15. *Carry On . . .*; 16. Mini Coopers; a coach; 17. Jerry Lewis; 18. *Cast Away*; 19. Sylvester Stallone; 20. Jodie Foster and Julianne Moore

Quiz 3. Writers

1. True. It took five years for the ransom to be raised. Cervantes had already lost a hand fighting the Turks at the Battle of Lepanto; 2. Jane Austen; 3. Rome; 4. Dr Samuel Johnson; 5. Arthur C. Clarke; 6. The Inklings; 7. Phyllis; 8. Mary Westmacott; 9. Robert Browning; 10. Sisters; 11. Dulwich College, London; 12. Old Alleynians; 13. Hornblower, Philip Marlowe, Jeeves and Wooster

Quiz 4. Wildlife

1. Kingfisher; 2. Portuguese Man o' War; 3. Cow and bull; 4. Woodpecker; 5. Eel; 6. Tasmanian Tiger; 7. Cephalopods; 8. Africa, specifically the southeastern part; 9. Auks; 10. Deathwatch beetle; 11. Jackrabbit; 12. Rattlesnakes; 13. A cave; a troglophile can survive outside the environment and a trogloxene (such as a bat) uses the cave simply as a home; 14. Pike; 15. Dugong; 16. It is a whale (related to the beluga whale) and it lives in the Arctic Ocean; 17. The jaguar; along with lions, tigers and leopards it makes up the big cat sub-family (all the others belong in felidae with the domestic cat and the lynxes; the creatures referred to as simply black panthers are either leopards or jaguars with black pigmentation); 18. Marsupials; 19. A wolf, specifically a grey wolf; 20. Butterfly

Quiz 5. Military History

1. Kuwait; 2. *General Belgrano*; 3. Czechoslovakia; 4. The Charge of the Light Brigade; 5. Sarajevo; 6. Baron von Richthofen (The Red Baron); 7. Spanish Armada; 8. IX Hispana or

Ninth Legion (many historians no longer believe this to have been the case; although the legion's fate remains historically uncertain, some of the senior officers reappear in historical annals at a later date); 9. Orange Free State and Transvaal Republic; 10. Viet Cong; Mix and Match: 1, h; 2, c; 3, i; 4, f; 5, a; 6, b; 7, d; 8, j; 9, g; 10, e

Quiz 6. Sport

1. Sid Waddell; 2. Taekwondo (that would be an axe-like kick followed by a front punch in Korean terminology); 3. Dick Fosbury; 4. Super G; 5. Speedway; 6. US Masters at Augusta National; 7. Adirondack Mountains in New York State; 8. Hockey, both field and ice; 9. Mercedes; 10. Parc des Princes, home to Paris St Germain; 11. Muhammad Ali; 12. Sir Stanley Rous; 13. Argentina; 14. 13 (two hole cards for each player, the three community cards that make up the flop, the fourth community card [turn] and the fifth [river]); 15. Carcassonne; 16. 29 (1–7–1–7–1–6–1–4–1); 17. (a) Pitch of a baseball in the US major leagues; 18. Marylebone Cricket Club, the original administrators of cricket and the England XI (they also hold the copyright to the laws of the game); 19. Albatross; 20. The tie break (initially the tie-break only came into effect if a set went to 8-8, but this was reduced to 6-6 in 1979)

Quiz 7. Births, Deaths and Marriages

1. Zara Phillips and Mike Tindall; 2. Tommy Lee (of Motley Crüe) and Kid Rock; 3. Lee Chapman; 4. Paul McCartney; 5. Eric Clapton; 6. Fifi Trixibelle and Peaches Honeyblossom; 7. They were both married to Cher; 8. Ronald Reagan; 9. Trudie Styler; Gordon Sumner is Sting; 10. Steffi Graf; 11. Whitney Houston; 12. Neil Armstrong; 13. Nora Ephron; 14. Ray Bradbury; 15. Andy Williams; 16. Maeve Binchy; 17. Tony Scott; 18. Donna Summer; 19. Davy Jones; 20. Hal David

Quiz 8. General Knowledge

1. YouTube; 2. Gin; 3. Lewis Carroll; 4. Aristotle; 5. The Crystal Palace; 6. He was the driver of the car in which Princess Diana and Dodi Al Fayed were killed; 7. Smoke a cigarette; 8. Cornwall – there is still a Poldark mine near Helston; 9. Manchester; 10. Turkey Twizzlers; 11. Salman Rushdie; 12. Amadeus; 13. *Carousel*; 14. Ethics; 15. *Pygmalion*; 16. Taxidermy; 17. The original Olympic games; 18. Brigitte Nielsen; 19. Greece; 20. France

Quiz 9. General Knowledge

Straightforward mix of twenty questions

Part 1

1   What opened at Anaheim, California, in 1955?

2   Which listings magazine was first published in 1923, costing tuppence?

3   Ursuline, Carmelite and Theatine are all orders of what?

4   On 4 October 1936, 200 walkers set off for London from which northeast town in protest at continued unemployment?

5   Where is the shopping avenue called Rodeo Drive? (a) Las Vegas (b) Beverly Hills (c) Hong Kong?

6   Robert Walpole became the first politician to take residence at which address in 1735?

7   The term bhp is used when describing the power of a motor vehicle; for what does it stand?

8   The world's longest pier was destroyed by fire in 1976 in which English town?

9   Who led a mutiny aboard a British sailing vessel in 1789?

10 If a Durex is a contraceptive in Britain, what is it in Australia?

11 Where in the UK are £100 banknotes used?

12 Which luxury car manufacturer produced a model called a Camargue?

13 What was the fate of Saint Dorothea? (a) she was burned at the stake by the Picts (b) she was beheaded by the Romans (c) she was cast into a snake pit by the Egyptians

14 Which former European leader died in a cell in The Hague in 2006?

15 Where was the body of George Mallory found on 2 May 1999, 75 years after he went missing?

Part 2

16 After Chinese in its various forms, what are the five most commonly spoken languages in the world? (5 pts)

Total Points: 20. Targets: Novice 10 Pro 15. Your Score:

Quiz 10. Rock and Pop

Ten straight questions, then a Name the Band quiz

Part 1

1 Who replaced Keith Moon as the drummer with The Who after Moon's death in 1978?

2 What connects Bob Dylan and Deadmau5, as diverse a pair of artists as is imaginable? (1 pt for one detail, 2 pts for more)

3 Which punk foursome consisted of John Cummings, Tom Erdelyi, Douglas Colvin and Jeffry Hyman?

4 Who was the singer, now a deep-voiced DJ, who fronted Manfred Mann in 1962–6? Who replaced him in the band? What instrument did Manfred himself play? (3 pts)

5 What was the 1976 No. 1 hit in the UK for Reg Dwight and Pauline Matthews?

6 'Something New' was the appropriately titled comeback single from which pop act in 2012? (It wasn't that new . . .)

7 Parlophone, Chrysalis and Mute were all labels owned by which music industry giant prior to its sale in 2012?

8 Jim Jarmusch's 1996 documentary *Year of the Horse* records a tour by which major artist and his band, Crazy Horse?

9 Who is the only *X Factor* judge to have presided over every series?

10 Seventies funk band Rufus was the start of which singer's successful career?

Part 2

We give you the line-up, you give us the name of the band

11 Lauryn Hill, Wyclef Jean, Pras Michel

12 Neil Finn, Paul Hester, Nick Seymour

13 Beyoncé Knowles, Kelly Rowland, Michelle Williams

14 Kurt Cobain, Dave Grohl, Krist Novoselic

15 Michael McCary, Nathan Morris, Wanya Morris, Shawn Stockman

16 Billie Joe Armstrong, Tre Cool, Mike Dirnt, Jason White

17 Geoff Barrow, Beth Gibbons, Adrian Utley

18 Mike Diamond, Adam Horowitz, Adam Yauch (Mike D, Ad-man, MCA)

19 Maxi Jazz, Rollo, Sister Bliss

20 Keith Duffy, Stephen Gately, Mikey Graham, Ronan Keating, Shane Lynch

Total Points: 23. Targets: Novice 9 Pro 17. Your Score:

Quiz 11. Computer Science

Cobol or cobblers? How much do you know?

Part 1

1 What name is given to a Google search that yields only a single result?
2 Who directed the launch video for the Apple Macintosh, aired during the Super Bowl in 1984?
3 What did Apple launch in 2003 to support the 2001 launched iPod?
4 What does the computer acronym RAM stand for?
5 Who, in 2001, overtook Compaq as the largest supplier of home-use PCs?
6 In 2002 PayPal became a subsidiary of which other online specialist?
7 What acronym does Microsoft use for its online and internet service provider?
8 What are Baidu, Bing and Yahoo!?
9 What size file is 1,000 Megabytes?
10 What purpose do the ICPA serve in the online world?

Part 2

11 Which university was Mark Zuckerberg attending when he devised Facebook with the help of his roommates?
12 'You Have 0 Friends', a parody of Facebook, was an episode of which TV comedy programme?
13 What is the web browser, a popular alternative to Google, run by the Mozilla Corporation?
14 In January of which year was Windows Vista released to the public, five years after its predecessor?
15 For what does the acronym IT stand?
16 Which company had the second highest share of the tablet computer market in 2012, after Apple?
17 What was the official launch name for the fourth generation iPad (or iPad4)?
18 What is 'flaming' in internet terminology?
19 What is the most common operating system for non-Apple mobile phones? What is the core system in use behind that? (2 pts)
20 What was the early computer prototype Colossus used for in the 1940s, and on whose theories was the enormous machine based? (2 pts)

Total Points: 22. Targets: Novice 7 Pro 17. Your Score:

Quiz 12. Media

Media matters (or does it?). Twenty questions on the folks who tell us what to think

Part 1

1   Which radio station employed Andy Gray and Richard Keys after they were sacked by Sky?

2   What returned to the newsagents in 1979 after nearly a year out of circulation due to industrial action?

3   Live broadcasts were transmitted from where for the first time on 8 June 1975?

4   'Vorsprung durch Technik' is the advertising slogan of which car manufacturer?

5   Who is 'your flexible friend' according to the advertisements?

6   A private company owned by which individual bought Mirror Group from Reed International in 1984?

7   Who was the former News International employee appointed as Director of Communications for David Cameron at No. 10? Why did he resign in 2011? (2 pts)

8   By what name was the *Guardian* newspaper known until 1959?

9   *Good Housekeeping, Cosmopolitan* or *Heat*: which has the biggest circulation according to early 2012 figures?

10 Which music channel launched in 1981 by playing 'Video Killed the Radio Star'?

Part 2

11   In the media, what does the term 'red top' describe?

12   Who made an ad for her own scent, Heat, that was deemed too provocative for pre 7.30 viewing in the US?

13   Paul Dacre is the editor of which daily tabloid newspaper?

14   In September 2011 Jill Abramson was appointed editor of which highly prestigious American publication, the first woman to be handed the post?

15   The Pollard Review was set up in the wake of which 2012 scandal?

16   Who was the editor of the Conservative mouthpiece the *Spectator* from 1999 to 2005?

17   Which newspaper, a relaunch of the earlier *Daily Worker*, has been the organ of the British Communist Party since 1966?

18   The *Globe* (owned by the New York Times Company) and the *Herald* (est. 1846, but now a tabloid) are the main print organs of which US city? (a) Los Angeles (b) Boston or (c) Philadelphia

19   What was established in 1946 as a successor to the Ministry of Information and handled all government advertising campaigns (e.g. forces recruitment and anti-smoking) and dissemination of policy until its disbandment in 2011?

20   Which company featured a talking toucan in many of their ads? And what is that company's famous logo? (2 pts)

Total Points: 22. Targets: Novice 9 Pro 17. Your Score:

Quiz 13. Crime Movies

Crime doesn't pay – unless you happen to make an Academy Award winning movie about it . . .

Part 1

Mix and Match: match the policeman to the movie in which his character is played by the actor named

1. Harry Callahan; 2. Virgil Tibbs; 3. Axel Foley; 4. FBI Agent Melvin Purvis; 5. Martin Riggs; 6. Sergeant Neil Howie; 7. Frederick Abberline; 8. Vincent Hanna; 9. Popeye Doyle; 10. Sergeant Gerry Boyle

a. *Lethal Weapon* (Mel Gibson, 1987); b. *Heat* (Al Pacino, 1995); c. *Public Enemies* (Christian Bale, 2009); d. *From Hell* (Johnny Depp, 2001); e. *The French Connection* (Gene Hackman, 1971); f. *The Guard* (Brendan Gleeson, 2011); g. *Magnum Force* (Clint Eastwood, 1973); h. *The Wicker Man* (Edward Woodward, 1973); i. *Beverly Hills Cop* (Eddie Murphy, 1984); j. *In the Heat of the Night* (Sydney Poitier, 1967)

Your Workings:

Part 2

You wanna get these right or you might just wake up next to a horse's head . . .

1   *The Godfather* was released in 1972; who played the title role, and who directed the movie? (2 pts)

2   Which two rivals does the Don's younger son assassinate in *The Godfather* to prove himself a worthy member of the mob? Who won an Oscar as his friend and advisor, the Don's adopted son, Tom Hagen? (3 pts)

3   What is the name of the family at the centre of *The Godfather* movies, and who has taken over the running of the family business by the second movie (1974)? (2 pts)

4   Who plays the second wife of the new Don in *The Godfather: Part II*? And who plays his father, the original Godfather, as a young man in a series of flashbacks? (2 pts)

5   When was the third *Godfather* movie released: 1977, 1980 or 1990? Who were the director's sister and daughter, who both had major roles in the movie? (3 pts)

Total Points: 22. Targets: Novice 9 Pro 17. Your Score:

Quiz 14: Olympic Games

Ten basic questions about the Olympic Games and a multi-part tester

Part 1

1 Which Finnish runner won double gold in the men's 5,000 metres and 10,000 metres in both 1972 and 1976 Olympic Games, with the aid of steroids which would later be banned?

2 Who won an astonishing triple of men's 5,000 metres, 10,000 metres and marathon in the Olympic Games of 1952? In which event did his wife also win a gold medal? (2 pts)

3 Which Soviet sprinter won both the 100 metres and 200 metres at the 1972 Olympic Games? Why would Russia have not won these medals in modern times? (2 pts)

4 Which French ski resort hosted the first Winter Olympics in 1924? (a) Aveyron (b) Chamonix or (c) Val d'Isere?

5 Greek post-office worker Spyridon Louys was the first winner of which famous event at the first modern Olympic Games in 1896?

6 What was seen for the first time in an Olympic swimming pool when Duke Kahanamoku won the 100 metres freestyle at the 1912 Olympics?

7 Which two countries contested a violent Olympic water polo semi-final at the 1956 games which left blood in the water and sparked fights in the audience? (2 pts)

8 What was the reason behind the boycott of the 1976 Olympics by twenty-six African nations? (Extra point for more detail)

9 Which piece of equipment let Daley Thompson down when attempting to defend his Olympic title in Seoul in 1988?

10 Michael Johnson won an unusual double by winning which two events at the 1996 Olympics? Who was the Frenchwoman who matched his feats in the women's events that year? (3 pts)

Part 2

11 Who won the first women's singles title at the Olympics when the sport returned to competition in 1988? Which sporting pin-up did she beat in the final? Miloslav Mečíř won the men's event for Czechoslovakia. Which British entrant did Mečíř beat along the way? Which country's Davis Cup team does he captain (at time of writing)? Which sixteen-year-old American woman beat the holder at the next Olympics in 1992? (5 pts)

Total Points: 20. Targets: Novice 8 Pro 15. Your Score:

Quiz 15. Books

Nothing tricky, just twenty straight questions

Part 1

1 The character of private eye Philip Marlowe, memorably portrayed on screen by Humphrey Bogart, was created by which American author?

2 *Marabou Stork Nightmares* was the less successful follow-up to which well-received debut novel?

3 Who is eligible for the Orange prize for fiction?

4 'Orr was crazy and could be grounded. All he had to do was ask; and as soon as he did, he would no longer be crazy and would have to fly more missions.' What is being described?

5 Who used popular novel writing, in works such as *Sybil* and *Tancred*, as a means to further his political policies in the nineteenth century?

6 In which year was the first Harry Potter book published, was it 1993, 1997 or 2000? And which publisher released the book? (2 pts)

7 Charles Frazier's *Cold Mountain* is set during which conflict?

8 What was Khaled Hosseini's 2007 follow up to *The Kite Runner*?

9 Whose 2000 debut, *White Teeth*, won eight literary awards, including the Whitbread prize?

10 Who wrote the well-received 2003 debut novel, *The Time Traveller's Wife*?

Part 2

11 Which novel charts the decline of the marriage of Dick and Nicole Driver?

12 Hemingway's *For Whom the Bell Tolls* is set during which conflict?

13 Gussie Fink-Nottle features in which series of comic novels?

14 Which twentieth-century English novel spawned the phrase, 'Big Brother Is Watching You'?

15 The Art of War is a masterwork by which Chinese martial philosopher?

16 What are *Zagat, Harden's* and *Gault and Millau* all examples of?

17 What epic history by Edward Gibbon was completed in 1788?

18 Which great Victorian novel by which writer was subtitled *A Tale of Manchester Life*? (2 pts)

19 What was Stephen Crane's 1895 epic about the American Civil War?

20 Stephen King's *Dark Tower* series was loosely inspired by a poem by which nineteenth-century author?

Total Points: 22. Targets: Novice 9 Pro 17. Your Score:

Quiz 16. General Knowledge

Fifteen straight questions and a multi-part tester; there's a *Phil*osophical air to this one

Part 1

1   In the Iron Age (roughly 800–500 BC), which group of city-states lay to the south of the Kingdom of Israel and included the city of Gaza within its territory? (It is a regular enemy to Israel in the Bible)

2   Who sprang to fame as a restless young mod in *Quadrophenia*, later turned up in *EastEnders*, but only had a short-lived TV dancing career?

3   Who is the most recent Brazilian driver to win the Formula 1 Brazilian Grand Prix?

4   Who was the BBC Sports Personality of the Year in 2006?

5   Who is the sporting twin of the man who captained Everton in the 2009 FA Cup final against Chelsea? (Careful . . .)

6   Which Dickens' novel has Philip Pirrip as its main protagonist?

7   Which US golfer won his first Major (the US Masters) in 2004, has since won three more, and has played on nine consecutive US Ryder Cup teams to 2012?

8   What name is given to the obstructive parliamentary art of talking for so long that a Bill is unable to be put through?

9   Which public figure was born on the Greek island of Corfu on 10 June 1921?

10 Sam Spade, Private Eye, is the most famous creation of which US thriller writer?

11 Who is Prince William's sister-in-law?

12 What great but eventually disastrous undertaking was launched by King Philip II of Spain in 1588?

13 What is the name given to the act of giving away money?

14 Who has been a team captain on *Never Mind the Buzzcocks* since the show began in 1996?

15 Phil Silvers, the US actor, is best known for which long-running TV role?

Part 2

16 In which US State is the city of Philadelphia? What took place in a sports stadium in the city on 13 July 1985? Old established baseball franchise the A's (Athletics) moved to which city from Philly in 1968? Who directed the film named after the city in 1993? And who won Academy Awards for Best Actor and Best Original Song at the following year's Oscar ceremony? (6 pts)

Total Points: 21. Targets: Novice 11 Pro 16. Your Score:

Answers Quizzes 9–16

Quiz 9. General Knowledge

1. Disneyland; 2. *Radio Times*; 3. Nuns; 4. Jarrow (The Jarrow Marches); 5. (b) Beverly Hills, California; 6. 10 Downing Street; 7. Brake horse power; 8. Southend-on-Sea; 9. Fletcher Christian; 10. Sticky tape; 11. Scotland; 12. Rolls-Royce; 13. (b) she was beheaded by the Romans; 14. Slobodan Milošević; 15. Mount Everest; 16. Spanish, English, Arabic, Hindi and Bengali

Quiz 10. Rock and Pop

1. Kenney Jones, previously with the Small Faces; 2. Zimmerman (Dylan's birth name was Robert Zimmerman, Deadmau5's was Joel Zimmerman); 3. The Ramones (Johnny, Tommy, Dee Dee and Joey respectively); 4. Paul Jones; Mike d'Abo; keyboards; 5. 'Don't Go Breaking My Heart' (they are the real names of Elton John and Kiki Dee); 6. Girls Aloud; 7. EMI; 8. Neil Young; 9. Louis Walsh; 10. Chaka Khan; 11. Fugees; 12. Crowded House; 13. Destiny's Child; 14. Nirvana; 15. Boyz II Men; 16. Green Day (White became an official member after 13 years as touring member and session support); 17. Portishead; 18. Beastie Boys; 19. Faithless; 20. Boyzone

Quiz 11. Computer Science

1. Googlewhack; 2. Ridley Scott; 3. iTunes; 4. Random Access Memory; 5. Dell; 6. eBay; 7. MSN; 8. Internet search engines; 9. Gigabyte; 10. They are the Internet Consumer Protection Agency; 11. Harvard; 12. *South Park*; 13. Firefox; 14. 2007; 15. Information Technology; 16. Samsung; 17. iPad with retina display; 18. Sending or posting offensive messages; 19. Android; Linux; 20. Cracking German codes; Alan Turing

Quiz 12. Media

1. talkSPORT; 2. *The Times*; 3. House of Commons; 4. Audi; 5. Access; 6. Robert Maxwell; 7. Andy Coulson (he was implicated in the phone hacking scandal at the *News of the World*); 8. *Manchester Guardian*; 9. *Good Housekeeping* (it sells over 400,000 copies per issue; *Cosmopolitan* is between 350–400,000, *Heat c.*325,000); 10. MTV; 11. Tabloid newspapers; 12. Beyoncé; 13. *Daily Mail*; 14. *New York Times*; 15. It was an investigation headed by Nick Pollard, former, head of Sky News, into the BBC's handling of the Jimmy Savile affair; 16. Boris Johnson; 17. *Morning Star*; 18. (b) Boston (the *Globe*, although twenty-six years younger than its rival, boasts an impressive twenty-one Pulitzer Prizes); 19. Central Office of Information (COI, it was one of a number of government departments axed during the cuts following the 2010 election); 20. Guinness; a harp

Quiz 13. Crime Movies

Mix and Match: 1, g; 2, j; 3, i; 4, c; 5, a; 6, h; 7, d; 8, b; 9, e; 10, f; 1. Marlon Brando; Francis Ford Coppola; 2. Sollozzo and McCluskey; Robert Duvall; 3. Corleone, Michael Corleone; 4. Diane Keaton; Robert De Niro; 5. 1990; Talia Shire is Coppola's sister, Sophia Coppola his daughter (Shire was an accomplished actress, but future director Sophia was a car-crash as Mary Corleone)

Quiz 14. Olympic Games

1. Lasse Viren; 2. Emil Zátopek of Czechoslovakia; javelin; 3. Valery Borzov; Borzov was Ukrainian not Russian; 4. (c) Chamonix; 5. Marathon; 6. Modern freestyle (or front crawl) swimming; 7. USSR and Hungary (the games came two months after the Soviet invasion of Hungary); 8. A New Zealand rugby tour of South Africa in contravention of agreements regarding sanctions against apartheid; 9. His pole snapped during the pole vault; 10. 200m and 400m; Marie-José Pérec; 11. Steffi Graf; Gabriela Sabatini; Jeremy Bates; Slovakia (where Mečíř was born); Jennifer Capriati

Quiz 15. Books

1. Raymond Chandler; 2. Irvine Welsh's *Trainspotting*; 3. Women writers, writing in English; 4. *Catch 22* (Joseph Heller); 5. Benjamin Disraeli; 6. 1997; Bloomsbury; 7. US Civil War; 8. *A Thousand Splendid Suns*; 9. Zadie Smith; 10. Audrey Niffenegger; 11. *Tender Is the Night* by F. Scott Fitzgerald; 12. The Spanish Civil War, where Hemingway himself was a protagonist; 13. The Jeeves and Wooster novels of P. G. Wodehouse; 14. *Nineteen Eighty-Four* (George Orwell); 15. Sun Tzu; 16. Restaurant guides; 17. *The History of the Decline and Fall of the Roman Empire*; 18. *Mary Barton* by Mrs Gaskell; 19. *The Red Badge of Courage*; 20. Robert Browning ('Childe Rolande')

Quiz 16. General Knowledge

1. Philistine Pentapolis (five city-states); 2. Phil Daniels played Jimmy in *Quadrophenia*, Kevin Wicks in *EastEnders* and exited *Strictly Come Dancing* in the first round in 2008; 3. Felipe Massa; 4. Zara Phillips; 5. Netball international Tracey Neville is the twin sister of Phil Neville (brother Gary is two years older); 6. *Great Expectations*; 7. Phil Mickelson; 8. Filibuster; 9. Prince Philip; 10. Dashiell Hammett; 11. Pippa Middleton; 12. Spanish Armada; 13. Philanthropy; 14. Phil Jupitus; 15. *Sergeant Bilko*; 16. Pennsylvania; Live Aid (US version); Oakland; Jonathan Demme; Tom Hanks and Bruce Springsteen

Quiz 17. General Knowledge

Part 1

1   What is the name of the country house on the Isle of Wight bought as a retreat by Queen Victoria and Prince Albert in 1845?

2   In which British National Park can the old cottage owned by the poet William Wordsworth be found?

3   What is the new name for what used to be John Hanning Speke Airport in Liverpool?

4   Who opened a store in New York in 1879, selling goods for only five cents?

5   Who was voted in as Russia's President in the country's first elections after the dismantling of the Communist state on 12 June 1991?

6   In 1909 Louis Blériot, a Frenchman, became the first aviator to cross which stretch of water?

7   Who won a second term as Prime Minister after a narrow election victory in 1951?

8   What connects the voting systems in Australia, Singapore and Turkey?

9   What was the name of the oil tanker which ran aground off the coast of Alaska in 1989?

10 Which long-established business institution in London allowed women in for the first time in 1973?

Part 2

11 The Gorbals is a famous working-class area of which city?

12 For what is the town of Whitstable in Kent best known?

13 In which country was human rights campaigner Ken Saro-Wiwa executed in 1995?

14 Which charity was launched by Bryn and Emma Parry in 2007 to help wounded soldiers with their recovery?

15 Where did Flight 19, which consisted of five US bombers on a training run, disappear in 1945?

16 In which Olympic sport might you get a double axel or a triple Salchow?

17 For what is movie director Gerald Thomas chiefly remembered?

18 The Tim Tam, a popular snack biscuit in Australia, was based on which equally popular British biscuit?

19 Where is the valuable Celtic manuscript *The Book of Kells* on display?

20 What is the most obvious connection between the English towns of Uttoxeter, Redcar, Pontefract and Market Rasen?

Total Points: 20. Targets: Novice 10 Pro 15. Your Score:

Quiz 18. Sci-Fi Movies

Science fiction – double feature

Part 1

1   What is the name of the villain in the first *Superman* movie (1980) played by Gene Hackman?

2   Which British comic actor played Scotty, the engineer aboard the *Enterprise* in *Star Trek* (2009)? And which Aussie was cast as the bad guy, Nero? (2 pts)

3   Who made Ray Bradbury's classic novel *Fahrenheit 451* into a movie in 1966?

4   In 2005 both Steven Spielberg and Peter Jackson revisited classic sci-fi stories for their major movies; what were the two films? (2 pts)

5   'Serve the trust. Protect the innocent. Uphold the law.' Whose mantra?

6   Which classic sci-fi movie concerns the invention of a beautiful robot by a scientist called Rotwang?

7   In which movie did David Bowie appear as Jareth the Goblin King?

8   What is Mad Max's surname? And who leads the gang that kill his family and ignite his revenge in the first film in the franchise? (2 pts)

9   Who played the obsessive character at the centre of *Close Encounters of the Third Kind* (1977)?

10 *Planet of the Apes* (1968); *Beneath the Planet of the Apes* (1970); MISSING (1971); *Conquest of the Planet of the Apes* (1972); MISSING (1973). Which two films in the original franchise are missing? (2 pts)

Part 2

11   Who made the 1989 underwater sci-fi chiller *The Abyss*?

12   If Sharon Stone betrayed an amnesiac Arnold Schwarzenegger in Paul Verhoeven's 1990 version, who betrayed who in the 2012 version under Len Wiseman's direction? (2 pts)

13   Who starred as a tough female tracker in a straight-to-video 1987 sci-fi film *Cherry 2000*, which has ascended to cult status?

14   What was the 1982 film starring Jeff Bridges as a computer software programmer battling to escape from being trapped inside his own programme?

15   The 2013 *Star Trek* film (*Star Trek into Darkness*) brings the number of films in the official franchise up to eight, twelve or sixteen?

16   What was the name of Duncan Jones's 2009 feature debut, and which actor carried the film almost single-handedly? (2 pts)

17   Who remade *Solaris* in 2002 and who took the lead role? Which Russian director made the original thirty years earlier? Which Polish writer wrote the source novel? (4 pts)

18   *Escape from New York* (1981), *The Thing* (1982) and *Big Trouble in Little China* (1986) are all escapist melodramas involving which director/star combination? (2 pts)

19   Which comic book hero provided a big break for Mexican director Guillermo del Toro in 2004? What was the subtitle of the follow-up, released in 2008? (2 pts)

20   Who was *The Invisible Man* in James Whale's 1933 film? And on whose story was the film based? (2 pts)

Total Points: 32. Targets: Novice 13 Pro 24. Your Score: [   ]

Quiz 19. TV

Some straight questions and a multi-parter to finish

Part 1

1 Who drove a car called the General and what type of vehicle was it? (2 pts)
2 Which TV series was an adaptation of Stephen Ambrose's real account of the work of a paratroop regiment?
3 What was the title of Alan Bennett's acclaimed series of monologues, written for TV in 1987 and published the following year?
4 *Boardwalk Empire*, the US TV drama, is set in which city?
5 What is the name of the Mayor of Springfield in TV series *The Simpsons*?
6 From which former Soviet state does Sacha Baron Cohen's Borat character purport to come?
7 Who was the prime mover behind the anarchic satirical show of the late 1990s, *The Saturday Night Armistice*? ·
8 Where was Michael Grade working when he was called the 'pornographer-in-chief' by right-wing journalist Paul Johnson?
9 Who connects *Surprise, Surprise* with *Blind Date*?
10 By what name are TV double act Dave Myers and Simon King better known?
11 If William H. Macy in the US is emulating David Threlfall in the UK, what is the show?
12 *Business Baazigar* is India's version of which popular UK TV show?
13 What first did Jacqui Oatley achieve in 2007?
14 Which TV entertainer and chat-show host once used the stage name The Joan Collins Fan Club?
15 Which British actor won a Golden Globe and an Emmy for his work in the HBO drama series *Homeland*?

Part 2

16 Who were the four stars of the first series of *Not the Nine O'Clock News* in 1981? And who came in to replace whom the following year? (5 pts)

Total Points: 21. Targets: Novice 8 Pro 16. Your Score:

Quiz 20. Geography

Places to go, things to see. A straight round and a quick-fire list round

1   Which river flows through Paris?
2   What is the administrative capital of South Africa? Which is the country's most populous city? And where is the judicial system centred? (3 pts)
3   Muscat is the capital city of which Arabian Sultanate?
4   Upolu and Sava'i are the largest of the islands making up which nation?
5   The Sierra Madre is a range of hills in which country?
6   Where would you find the Beaufort Sea, Franz Josef Land and the Fram Basin?
7   What is the southern region of Spain, taking in the cities of Seville, Granada and Malaga?
8   The Dodecanese and the Cyclades are island groups belonging to which country in which sea? (2 pts)
9   Which is the only country with a coastline on both the Red Sea and the Persian Gulf?
10 What is the Canadian state to the far northwest of the country, forming the majority of the border with Alaska?

Part 2

We've listed the name of a country and its biggest city by population (which is not necessarily the capital); we want you to name the second biggest city in the country.

11 Germany (Berlin)
12 Italy (Rome)
13 Ireland (Dublin)
14 Canada (Toronto)
15 Brazil (São Paolo)
16 Sweden (Stockholm)
17 Egypt (Cairo)
18 India (Mumbai)
19 Great Britain (London)
20 Japan (Tokyo)

Total Points: 23. Targets: Novice 9 Pro 17. Your Score:

Quiz 21. British Politics

Some questions on British politics and current affairs rather than strictly history
– although technically, it's all history, innit?

Part 1

1   What connects the governments formed by David Lloyd George in 1916 and
    David Cameron in 2010?

2   In which year did the Sex Discrimination Act become law: 1953, 1966 or
    1975?

3   David Cameron is the UK's third left-handed Prime Minister. Who were the
    other two (both twentieth century)? (2 pts)

4   Who stood down as Chancellor of the Exchequer in 1947 after admitting
    leaking budget information to a journalist? Who succeeded him in the
    Labour administration? (2 pts)

5   What cabinet post did Winston Churchill hold between 1924 and 1929?

6   Which former Conservative minister was appointed to oversee the handing
    back of Hong Kong to China in the 1990s?

7   Which political party was formed as the result of a merger of two smaller
    parties in 1934, with Alexander MacEwan as its first leader?

8   What are the three biggest sources of government income in the UK? (3 pts)

9   Who are Miriam González Durántez, Samantha Sheffield and Justine
    Thornton?

10 Who was Conservative MP for Falmouth in 1992–7?

Part 2

11   What position was Lib-Dem leader Nick Clegg given in the coalition government his party formed with the Conservatives in 2010?

12   In 1957, the government announced what change to the constituency of the House of Lords?

13   Who was the first black cabinet minister at Westminster?

14   Who brought to table the Private Member's Bill which led to the 1967 Abortion Act?

15   Who became Conservative MP for Louth in Lincolnshire in 1969? (a) Margaret Thatcher (b) Jeffrey Archer or (c) Boris Johnson

16   Who served four separate terms as Prime Minister in the nineteenth century? Who was his main adversary in the opposition party in the early years of his leadership? (2 pts)

17   Which unpopular measure by the Conservative government in 1989 sparked riots in most major British cities? (Please give official name and common name)

18   Who was Member of Parliament for Caernarvon Boroughs for fifty-five years from 1890 until his death just before the end of World War II?

19   Of the 650 MPs elected at the 2010 election, how many serve constituencies in England: 435, 501 or 533?

20   Who is the current (April 2013) UKIP Member of the European Parliament for South East England?

Total Points: 25. Targets: Novice 10 Pro 19. Your Score:

Quiz 22. Rugby Union

Sixteen straight questions and a multi-part one on the oval ball for fifteen good men and true (mostly)

Part 1

1 What creature gives its name to the South African Rugby Union team? What kind of animal is it? (2 pts)

2 If the Tigers beat the Scarlets, who would be playing? (2 pts)

3 Which was the southernmost town in New Zealand to host a match in the 2011 Rugby World Cup?

4 Which side beat New Zealand in a three-match series in late 2011, winning two and drawing the third match?

5 What nickname has been given to the 1924 touring New Zealand side, who won every one of their thirty-two matches?

6 Who played their home club games at Twickenham when the stadium was opened in 1909? What is the name of their new home, once a training ground? (2 pts)

7 Which two men share the distinction of captaining an Irish Grand Slam winning side (in 1948 and 2009 respectively)? (2 pts)

8 What strip do the Barbarians wear (shirts/shorts/socks)? (3 pts)

9 What was unusual about France's Grand Slam win in the 1977 Five Nations? (a) they selected four different half-back combinations (b) they selected the same XV for every match (c) they played all their games away from home as their Paris ground was under renovation

10 Who beat Will Carling's team in a memorable Grand Slam decider in 1990?

Part 2

11 Who won the Heineken Cup in 2011 and 2012 but failed to make it past the group stage in 2013?

12 Which New Zealander mowed through England's defence to score four tries in the Rugby World Cup semi-final in 1995?

13 Since the play-offs were introduced to Premier League rugby union in England, how many times have the side finishing top of the league also lifted the trophy? Which team has topped the league four times but never won the title? (2 pts)

14 How did David Campese publicly admit he was wrong after predicting Australia would beat England in the 2003 Rugby World Cup final?

15 Who has scored a record 277 points in Rugby World Cup football? And who scored a record for a single tournament, with 126 in the first ever competition in 1987? (2 pts)

16 Who holds the current record (in January 2013) for rugby union test caps with 139?

17 Who (in January 2013) holds the record for the most career points in the Five/Six Nations tournament? Who scored the most points in a single match and in a single season in 2001? Who has scored the most tries (twenty-five)? Which side has the most Grand Slam titles (twelve)? (4 pts)

Total Points: 28. Targets: Novice 11 Pro 21. Your Score:

Quiz 23. Costume Drama

More TV and movies, this time all frills and frou-frou

Part 1

1   *Braveheart* (1995) starring Mel Gibson featured the highly coloured account of which historical figure? Who directed the film? (2 pts)

2   Who set pulses racing emerging out of the mist in a wet shirt as Mr Darcy in *Pride and Prejudice* (1995)?

3   What is the name of the family at the centre of *Downton Abbey*, and what is the title of the family patriarch played by Hugh Bonneville? (2 pts)

4   Who was the young star of the 2001 adventure *A Knight's Tale*? And who was the other up-and-coming star who stole most of his scenes as poet Geoffrey Chaucer? (2 pts)

5   Who mutinied against Charles Laughton (1935), Trevor Howard (1962) and Anthony Hopkins (1984) respectively, in their roles as Captain Bligh in film versions of *The Mutiny on the Bounty*? (3 pts)

6   'I'm Spartacus' has become an oft-repeated refrain and the scene from Kubrick's 1960 movie has been much parodied; who did play Spartacus, and who won an Academy Award in a supporting role? (2 pts)

7   What was French director Louis Malle's first Hollywood production, a period piece set in a nineteenth-century brothel?

8   What was the 2012 TV drama set in a northern department store in the 1870s?

9   Which couple played Cleopatra and Mark Antony in an epic (and very costly) 1963 version of the story? (2 pts)

10 *The Crucible* (Nicholas Hytner, 1996) starring Daniel Day-Lewis was scripted by which playwright from his own 1953 work? What is the setting for the piece? (2 pts)

Part 2

11   What connects Katharine Hepburn in a George Cukor film in 1933 to Winona
     Ryder in a Gillian Armstrong film in 1994?

12   Which 'bad boy' of Hollywood had an early major role in *The Name of the
     Rose* as a monk's apprentice alongside Sean Connery as Brother William of
     Baskerville (a monk with a Scots accent)?

13   What were the two films made in the 1960s starring Peter O'Toole as King
     Henry II of England? (2 pts)

14   *Bright Star* was a 2009 film about the life of which romantic poet? Which
     actor played the poet? (2 pts)

15   *1492: Conquest of Paradise* (Ridley Scott, 1992) was an epic about the
     exploits of which adventurer? Who played the lead role? (2 pts)

16   What connects Keith Michell, Ray Winstone and Jonathan Rhys Meyers?
     (Extra point for more details)

17   What was the title of a 1961 epic about an eleventh-century warrior called
     Rodrigo Diaz de Vivar, and who played Rodrigo in the film? (2 pts)

18   Who played Abraham Lincoln in a 2013 biopic of the President's final
     months? Who is oddly cast as Lincoln's wife, Mary Todd? (2 pts)

19   In which decade was the TV drama *When the Boat Comes In* set, and who
     played the lead character, Jack Ford? (2 pts)

20   Which Pakistan-born actor first made his mark as Hari Kumar in the 1984
     Granada costume drama, *The Jewel in the Crown*?

Total Points: 35. Targets: Novice 14 Pro 26. Your Score: [   ]

Quiz 24. General Knowledge

Another twenty questions

Part 1

1   Which performer invented the flying trapeze act in the nineteenth century and lends his name to a garment suitable for that activity?

2   Which wartime pin-up insured her legs for $1 million?

3   What is the term for a text picture or symbol such as :-) made from standard characters?

4   What word is given to a series of spans or arches enabling passage of a road across a lower road or river valley?

5   D*face, Miss Van and JR are all exponents of what?

6   In which German city did the post-war trials of the Nazis accused of war crimes take place?

7   *Dead Famous* and *Past Mortem* are mysteries by which novelist and comedian?

8   Which comic strip, the creation of Charles M. Schulz, was published in 1950 for the first time?

9   Peter Cook, who died in 1995, formed a famous comic partnership with which other performer?

10 Which terrorist organization was responsible for the massacre of Israeli athletes at the Munich Olympics in 1972?

Part 2

11   What does the prefix 'par' mean in the word Paralympics?

12   Many cars are now fitted with a GPS navigational system; what does GPS stand for?

13   The Plimpton 322 is a clay tablet unearthed from Babylonian ruins; what is the subject matter? (a) mathematical equations (b) a history of the Babylonian kings (c) a sex manual, a prototype *Kama Sutra*

14   In 2005 artist Gianni Motti displayed and then sold a bar of soap made – allegedly – from the aftermath of a liposuction operation on which famous Italian?

15   How is deoxyribonucleic acid generally better known?

16   A collection of fifty tales rewritten by Philip Pullman in 2012 celebrated which literary bicentenary?

17   What famous legal case was brought by thirteen-year-old Jordan Chandler in August 1993?

18   Who became Australia's first woman Prime Minister?

19   Which film director released an album called *Crazy Clown Time* in 2011? (a) Quentin Tarantino (b) David Lynch (c) Woody Allen

20   How did Sir Guy of Gisborne end up as a dwarf?

Total Points: 20. Targets: Novice 10 Pro 15. Your Score:

Answers Quizzes 17–24

Quiz 17. General Knowledge

1. Osborne House; 2. Lake District; 3. (Liverpool) John Lennon; 4. Frank W. Woolworth; 5. Boris Yeltsin; 6. English Channel; 7. Sir Winston Churchill; 8. It is compulsory to vote; 9. Exxon Valdez; 10. London Stock Exchange. 11. Glasgow; 12. Oysters; 13. Nigeria; 14. Help for Heroes; 15. Bermuda Triangle; 16. Figure skating (half point only for ice skating); 17. As the director of over thirty *Carry On* films; 18. McVitie's Penguin; 19. Trinity College Dublin; 20. All have racecourses

Quiz 18. Sci-Fi Movies

1. Lex Luthor; 2. Simon Pegg; Eric Bana; 3. Francois Truffaut; 4. *War of the Worlds* (Spielberg) and *King Kong* (Jackson); 5. *Robocop*; 6. Fritz Lang's *Metropolis*; 7. *Labyrinth*; 8. Rockatansky; Toecutter; 9. Richard Dreyfuss (the story goes that he virtually had to stalk Spielberg to get the part after various big box office names turned it down); 10. *Escape from the Planet of the Apes* and *Battle for the Planet of the Apes*; 11. James Cameron; 12. Kate Beckinsale played Colin Farrell's false wife in the 2012 version of *Total Recall*; 13. Melanie Griffith; 14. *Tron*; 15. Twelve (there have been six original *Star Trek* movies, four *Next Generation* movies and two recent alternate timeline movies); 16. *Moon*; Sam Rockwell; 17. Steven Soderbergh; George Clooney; Andrei Tarkovsky; Stanislav Lem; 18. John Carpenter and Kurt Russell; 19. *Hellboy*; *Hellboy II – The Golden Army* was the full title of the sequel; 20. Claude Rains; H. G. Wells

Quiz 19. TV

1. *The Dukes of Hazzard*; Dodge Charger; 2. *Band of Brothers*; 3. *Talking Heads*; 4. Atlantic City; 5. Joe Quimby; 6. Kazakhstan; 7. Armando Iannucci; 8. Channel 4; 9. Cilla Black, who presented both; 10. *The Hairy Bikers*; 11. *Shameless*; 12. *The Apprentice*; 13. She was the first woman to commentate on a game on *Match of the Day*; 14. Julian Clary; 15. Damien Lewis; 16. Rowan Atkinson, Chris Langham, Mel Smith and Pamela Stephenson; Griff Rhys-Jones replaced Langham

Quiz 20. Geography

1. River Seine; 2. Pretoria; Johannesburg; Bloemfontein; 3. Oman; 4. Samoa; 5. Mexico; 6. Arctic Ocean; 7. Andalucia; 8. Greece; The Aegean; 9. Saudi Arabia; 10. Yukon Territory; 11. Hamburg; 12. Milan; 13. Cork; 14. Montreal; 15. Rio de Janeiro; 16. Gothenburg; 17. Alexandria; 18. Delhi; 19. Birmingham; 20. Yokohama

Quiz 21. British Politics

1. Both were coalitions; 2. 1975; 3. Winston Churchill; Jim Callaghan; 4. Hugh Dalton; Stafford Cripps; 5. Chancellor of the Exchequer; 6. Chris Patten; 7. Scottish National Party (SNP); 8. Income tax, national insurance, value added tax (VAT); 9. The wives of the three main party

leaders, as of January 2013 (Clegg, Cameron and Miliband respectively); 10. Sebastian Coe; 11. Deputy Prime Minister; 12. Admission of women peers; 13. Paul Boateng, Chief Secretary to the Treasury in 2002; 14. Sir David Steele; 15. (b) Jeffrey Archer; 16. William Gladstone; Benjamin Disraeli (answers must be the right way round); 17. Community Charge, generally known as the Poll Tax; 18. David Lloyd George; 19. 533 (there are fifty-nine in Scotland, forty in Wales and eighteen in Northern Ireland); 20. Nigel Farage, the leader of UKIP

Quiz 22. Rugby Union

1. Springbok; a type of gazelle (antelope is fine); 2. Leicester and Llanelli; 3. Invercargill; 4. England's Women's XV; 5. The Invincibles; 6. Harlequins; The Stoop; 7. Jackie Kyle and Brian O'Driscoll; 8. Black and white hoop shirts, black shorts and the socks of their current club; 9. (b) they played the same side in every match under captain Jacques Fouroux; 10. Scotland (their slow, menacing march out to the pitch was a highlight they haven't matched since); 11. Leinster; 12. Jonah Lomu; 13. Five; Gloucester; 14. He wore a sandwich board stating he was wrong on a crowded shopping street; 15. Jonny Wilkinson; Grant Fox; 16. George Gregan of Australia (Richie McCaw is the most likely current player to catch him); 17. Ronan O'Gara; Jonny Wilkinson; Brian O'Driscoll; England

Quiz 23. Costume Drama

1. William Wallace; Gibson directed himself; 2. Colin Firth; 3. Crawley; Rt Hon. Robert, Earl of Grantham; 4. Heath Ledger; Paul Bettany; 5. Clark Gable, Marlon Brando and Mel Gibson were the three Fletcher Christians; 6. Kirk Douglas; Peter Ustinov; 7. *Pretty Baby*; 8. *The Paradise*; 9. Elizabeth Taylor and Richard Burton; 10. Arthur Miller; the setting is the Salem Witch Trials in Massachusetts in the late seventeenth century; 11. They both played Jo in *Little Women*; 12. Christian Slater; 13. *Becket* (1964) and *The Lion in Winter* (1968) (O'Toole was nominated for an Academy Award for both roles, as was Richard Burton for playing Thomas à Becket and Katharine Hepburn for playing Eleanor of Aquitaine in *The Lion in Winter* – only Hepburn won; O'Toole was nominated eight times in all, but never won Best Actor); 14. John Keats; Ben Whishaw; 15. Christopher Columbus; Gerard Depardieu; 16. They have all played King Henry VIII in a TV series (Michell in the classic 1970 series *The Six Wives of Henry VIII*, Winstone in a 2003 ITV two-parter and Rhys Meyer in *The Tudors*; 17. *El Cid*; Charlton Heston; 18. Daniel Day-Lewis was Lincoln in the biopic of the last weeks of his life, and Sally Field (eleven years older than Day-Lewis) played Mary Todd (nine years younger than Lincoln); 19. 1920s, James Bolam; 20. Art Malik

Quiz 24. General Knowledge

1. Jules Léotard; 2. Betty Grable; 3. Emoticon; 4. Viaduct; 5. Street art; 6. Nuremberg; 7. Ben Elton; 8. Peanuts; 9. Dudley Moore; 10. Black September; 11. 'Beside' or 'alongside' (it is not a reference to paralysis as is often imagined); 12. Global Positioning System; 13.

Mathematics; 14. Silvio Berlusconi (the soap sold for $18,000); 15. DNA; 16. The publication, in 1812, of the Brothers Grimm's first anthology of tales; 17. Accusations of abuse by Michael Jackson; 18. Julia Gillard; 19. (b) David Lynch (it was er . . . unusual); 20. Richard Armitage, who played Gisborne in the primetime BBC series *Robin Hood*, then played Thorin Oakenshield in *The Hobbit*

Quiz 25. General Knowledge

Part 1

1   If you were at a milonga, what would you most likely be doing?
2   In Australia 11 November is Remembrance Day, in the US it is Veterans Day; how is it known in the UK?
3   Which country supplies about 40 per cent of the tea drunk in the UK?
4   Who was the South African journalist whose work was dramatized by Richard Attenborough in the film *Cry Freedom*?
5   Roughly how long is the Grand Canyon: 46 miles, 123 miles or 277 miles?
6   Which artist bought Toddington Castle in Gloucestershire for £3 million in 2005?
7   Which TV chef swam the Channel, aged sixteen?
8   Which athlete became the youngest ever recipient of an MBE in the 2009 New Year's Honours list?
9   What did Howard Carter and the Earl of Carnarvon (George Herbert) discover in 1922?
10 What was the name of the hurricane which caused devastation in New Orleans in 2005?

Part 2

11 What started with a Sergeant in 1958?
12 What is the name of the horse in Michael Morpurgo's *War Horse*?
13 Which mobile phone rival lost a court case for passing off brought by Apple in the US in 2012?
14 The source of the River Nile is in which hilly African country?
15 What is unusual about the baseball card and stats for Bo Obama?
16 What term is given to media photographers who follow and even hound well-known public figures?
17 What is the artistic discipline of Gustav von Aschenbach in Visconti's film version of *Death in Venice* (1971)? And how does this differ from the book? (2 pts)
18 Who is the alter-ego of fictional character Bruce Wayne?
19 What are Razer Onxa and Razer Sabertooth?
20 Where is the Northern Ireland Assembly based?

Total Points: 21. Targets: Novice 11 Pro 16. Your Score:

Quiz 26. Westerns

Gunslingers and gorgeous gals in Wild West movies

Part 1

1   Who stars as the malevolent killer Joe Erin opposite Gary Cooper in *Vera Cruz* (1954)?

2   Which Wild West personality connects Jean Arthur, Jane Russell, Ellen Barkin and Robin Weigert? And who played probably the most famous incarnation of that character in a 1953 film? (2 pts)

3   What was the 1969 musical comedy western starring Clint Eastwood (his only musical role), and who was his male co-star, equally unsuited to a singing role as he showed when he growled his way through 'Wandrin' Star'? (2 pts)

4   Which director, more usually associated with horror movies, made the 1995 western *The Quick and the Dead*? Who played the female gunslinger amidst a starry cast? (2 pts)

5   The 1968 Euro-western *Shalako* featured which star as a rough-and-ready guide taking a party of wealthy travellers through Indian country? Which French bombshell co-starred as an arrogant countess? (2 pts)

6   What connects the role allotted to Clint Eastwood in Sergio Leone's *The Good, the Bad and the Ugly* with the one Leone gave to Charles Bronson in *Once Upon a Time in the West*?

7   Who plays the American drifter-pianist in the bleak western parable *Bring Me the Head of Alfredo Garcia*? In which other Sam Peckinpah western did he also take a leading role? (2 pts)

8   *Winchester '73* was a famous western starring James Stewart; to what is the title a reference?

9   Grace Kelly made her screen debut in 1951 in *Fourteen Hours*. Which western released in the following year saw her in a starring role for the first time?

10 Who plays the flawed anti-hero on the trail of missing relatives in *The Searchers*? Which Native American tribe have abducted his nieces? (2 pts)

Part 2

11 What is the name of the gang in *Butch Cassidy and the Sundance Kid*? Where do they go when they are chased out of the US? What song is playing when Newman is riding the bicycle? Who wrote the tune? How many people does Butch shoot in the film? (5 pts)

12 After *Cimarron* in 1931, only two westerns (released only two years apart in 1991 and 1993) have won the Academy Award for Best Picture; both also won Best Director, and both director-stars were nominated for Best Actor. What were the movies and who were the two stars? Who won Best Supporting Actor for the later movie? (5 pts)

Total Points: 26. Targets: Novice 10 Pro 20. Your Score:

Quiz 27. Discoveries and Inventions

Let's discover how inventive you can be with your answers

Part 1

1   Where, in 1984, was the skeleton of Nariokotome Boy found, a link to *Homo erectus*, the precursor of *Homo sapiens*? (a) Kenya (b) Alaska (c) Siberia

2   What nationality connects the inventors of the Rubik's Cube and the biro?

3   Who developed the V-2 rocket during World War II, technology which eventually transferred to the US and was at the core of its space programme?

4   In 1608 two Dutchmen, Lippershey and Janssen, almost simultaneously crafted which important ocular device?

5   The credit for the invention of calculus is a disputed area between the German scientist Leibniz and which British scholar?

6   What was the chemical compound dichlorodiphenyltrichloroethane (DDT) used for after its discovery just before World War II, prior to its banning in the developed world in the 1970s?

7   John Harrington installed the first recorded instance of what at Richmond Palace in 1591? (a) bay window (b) dumb waiter (c) flushing toilet

8   Calder Hall in Cumbria was the first what in the UK?

9   What was Lucius Paciolus's (or Luca Pacioli's) contribution to the life of accountants everywhere in 1495?

10 Dmitri Mendeleev conceived it in 1866 and Primo Levi named his 1975 collection of stories after it; what is it?

Part 2: some famous firsts

11   Who developed the first telegraphic code and lends his name to it still?

12   Which US statesman and scientist produced the first bifocal lens in 1780?

13   Louis Daguerre was the first to commercially achieve what?

14   George Thomas Morton, in 1887, conducted the first (a) appendectomy (b) lobotomy (c) birth by Caesarean section?

15   How did Percy Spencer's 1945 invention make meal-time quicker once it was rolled out commercially?

16   What did Nicolas Conté produce in 1795? (They are still manufactured in his name.)

17   Dennis Amiss was the first high-profile international cricketer to use which piece of equipment in the 1970s?

18   Harrods installed the first example of what new technology in the UK in 1898?

19   Vinyl records are coming back into fashion, but in which year did Emil Berliner, founder of Deutsche Gramophone, first produce a playable flat disc recording: 1888, 1904 or 1922?

20   Whitcomb L. Judson made getting dressed easier in 1890/91 when he developed the precursor of what everyday item?

Total Points: 20. Targets: Novice 8 Pro 15. Your Score:

Quiz 28: History

No tricks, twenty straight questions

Part 1

1   Who was elected as the first woman President of the Irish Republic in 1990?

2   Where did a Marxist coup lead to an American invasion in 1983?

3   Down House in Kent was opened to the public in 2009 because which famous person had lived there? (a) Winston Churchill (b) P. G. Wodehouse (c) Charles Darwin

4   Who became Britain's youngest Prime Minister, aged only twenty-four, in 1783?

5   What is the name of the city-state created in 1929 within the city of Rome?

6   In 1572, French Catholics completed a massacre which became known by what name, a reference to the saint associated with 23 August, the date of the event?

7   Where did an English force, especially the Welsh bowmen, defeat a (numerically) vastly superior French and Genoese army on 25 August 1386?

8   Who sacked Rome in AD 410 and 455 respectively? (2 pts)

9   On 24 April 1983, German magazine *Stern* published the first instalment of which controversial work?

10 Who was Lord High Admiral of the British Fleet when they beat off the Spanish Armada in 1588?

Part 2

11   Which poet and activist organized the flight of over 2,000 Republican refugees to Chile at the end of the Spanish Civil War? (a) Che Guevara (b) Pablo Neruda (c) Salvador Allende

12   Kublai Khan moved his capital to Kanbaliq; what is the modern name for Kanbaliq and what was Kublai Khan's former capital, immortalized in an English poem? (2 pts)

13   Which French city was home to a number of antipopes, set up in opposition to Rome in the fourteenth century? (a) Toulouse (b) Nice (c) Avignon

14   Where, specifically, did the fire at Gresford in North Wales take place in 1934, with the loss of 265 lives?

15   King Hussein bin Talal ruled which country for forty-seven years from 1952 until his death in 1990?

16   In which African country did the Mau Mau rebel against English colonial occupation in 1952?

17   The Great Arab Revolt, a general Middle Eastern uprising supported by the allied powers of World War I, led to the break up and partition of which centuries-old empire?

18   Where did the Confederates surrender in 1865, officially ending the American Civil War? Which two generals were involved on either side? (3 pts)

19   To which island was Napoleon Bonaparte exiled after abdicating as Emperor of France in 1814?

20   Whose regime in Cambodia was formally ended in January 1979?

Total Points: 24. Targets: Novice 10 Pro 18. Your Score:

Quiz 29. Fashion and Photography

Just point and click (or something like that)

Part 1

1   What was different about Spencer Tunick's 2005 photograph of 1,700 people outside the Sage in Gateshead?

2   What iconic American design was first marketed by New Era in the 1950s?

3   Marilyn Monroe, Ali MacGraw, Catherine Deneuve, Vanessa Paradis and Kate Moss have all been the face of which French parfumerie?

4   Who is the artistic director of the house of Chanel?

5   Who, in 1966, first marketed paper dresses sold in envelopes?

6   What is the material, similar to suede, but using the outer side of the cattle hide not the inner?

7   In which city was the Benetton company founded in 1965? (a) Milan (b) Treviso (c) Parma

8   Who would wear a chasuble?

9   In which year did a number of high-profile photographers form the collective Magnum: 1929, 1947 or 1965?

10 Gerda Taro and her lover, Endre Friedmann, were both war photographers. What name did they give to the fictitious photographer who represented their collaborative work? (a) Brassat (b) Man Ray (c) Robert Capa

Part 2

11 What was the subject of a famous 1976 poster shot that became an iconic image for the card and poster retailer Athena two years later?

12 Which of these is the most accurate description of a farthingale? (a) a pair of silk trousers worn under a dress (b) a veil worn during a period of mourning (c) a hooped frame worn to spread skirts

13 Designer John Galliano was dismissed as head of which fashion house after a well-publicized anti-Semitic outburst in a Paris bar?

14 Where would one wear a Homburg or a Glengarry?

15 Which celebrity designer was the creative head of Chloé in 1997–2001?

16 They make other things, but for what are the fashion house Jimmy Choo best known?

17 In a 2005 poll for Harvey Nichols on iconic fashion items, which three classics were in the top three? (The answers are general as opposed to brand specific – numbers four, five and six, for example, were flares, cowboy boots and platform shoes.) (3 pts)

18 Who, by opening his Rive Gauche chain of stores, led the major fashion houses into the realm of prêt-a-porter design?

19 Which cities are regarded as the 'big four' amongst fashion capitals of the world? (4 pts)

20 'It's all gone celebrity, hasn't it? Celebrity, looks, fashion. If I see another picture of Gwyneth Paltrow I think I'll put my head down the toilet.' Which venerable photojournalist, subject of a 2013 documentary, is a little disillusioned with his industry?

Total Points: 25. Targets: Novice 10 Pro 19. Your Score:

Quiz 30. Premier League

Twelve questions on the Premier League and some multi-part teasers

Part 1

1   Between 1997 and 2012, twenty players were sent off in Merseyside derbies; which two players, one from each side, have been sent off twice in the fixture? (2 pts)

2   Blackpool surprised pundits by winning their first ever Premier League match 4–0 away from home in August 2010; who were their incompetent opponents on the day?

3   Who made 310 consecutive Premier League appearances between 2004 and 2012?

4   Who has scored in the Premier League for Coventry, Newcastle, Blackburn, Liverpool, West Ham and Manchester City?

5   Which team picked up a Premier League record eight yellow cards in a match against QPR on October 2012?

6   Who scored injury-time goals for Manchester City to seal a dramatic last-gasp Premier League title from their rivals across the city? (2 pts)

7   Why were four teams relegated from the Premier League in 2004–5?

8   Who were relegated in 2002–3 with a record high total (for a twenty-team division) of forty-two points?

9   What were the lowest Premier League finishes for Manchester United and Arsenal under Alex Ferguson and Arsène Wenger, prior to the 2012–13 season? (2 pts)

10 Which Finnish former international made his 500th appearance in English football in 2012–13 and his 400th in the Premier League? Which of his countrymen played over 300 games for Liverpool? (2 pts)

11 Who was the first Latvian player to star in the Premier League (he remains the only player from Latvia to make any real impact), scoring over forty goals in over a hundred games for Southampton?

12 Bolton Wanderers boasted two former Champions League winners from Real Madrid in their ranks in 2004–5; who were they? (2 pts)

Part 2

13   Nottingham Forest had which three men as manager during their relegation season of 1996–7? (3 pts)

14   Which three players have been sent off eight times in their Premier League careers (as of January 2013)? (3 pts)

15   What was Arsenal's all-English back five that underpinned their first Premier League title in 1998? (5 pts)

16   Which three strikers have scored fifteen goals in a Premier League season for Middlesbrough? (Tip: one of them is English – if you get this you're either a Boro fan or you need to get out more) (3 pts)

Total Points: 31. Targets: Novice 12 Pro 23. Your Score: [   ]

Quiz 31. Sherlock Holmes

The game is afoot: fifteen straight questions and a multi-parter (I'd make a gag about it being elementary except you Sherlock fans would point out that Holmes's most famous phrase is a misquote)

1   In which magazine were most of the Sherlock Holmes stories first published?
2   Who was the housekeeper at 221b Baker Street?
3   What is the location for Conan Doyle's *The Hound of the Baskervilles*?
4   What is the name of the elder brother of Sherlock Holmes? At which club do the two tend to meet? (2 pts)
5   *A Study in Scarlet*, the first of Conan Doyle's four full-length Sherlock Holmes novels, features the first fictional use of what object as a tool of crime-solving?
6   Which was Conan Doyle's final book of short stories about Holmes, written between 1921 and 1927?
7   What is the name of Sherlock's nemesis in the first volume of stories, and where does the final showdown between the two take place? (2 pts)
8   Who was 'that woman' who outwits Holmes in one of the earlier stories, and what is the story in which she appears? (2 pts)
9   In 'The Adventure of the Speckled Band', what is the speckled band?
10 What is the name given to the street urchin gang who occasionally assist Holmes in searches through London's underworld?
11 Which story, the first in the second volume of short stories, *The Memoirs of Sherlock Holmes*, concerns the disappearance of a winning racehorse?
12 Which Holmes story concerns the coded messages between Mrs Elsie Cubitt and Abe Slaney, an American gangster and acquaintance from her past life?
13 Which policeman appears most frequently in the Holmes stories (thirteen times), from the first work (*A Study in Scarlet*) to the story set in 1902, 'The Adventure of the Three Garridebs'?
14 What is the criminal profession of the title character in 'The Adventure of Charles Augustus Milverton'?
15 How does Conan Doyle subtly refer to a member of the royal family in the title of one of the stories in *The Case-Book of Sherlock Holmes*?
16 If Basil Rathbone, Jeremy Brett, Robert Downey Jr and Benedict Cumberbatch are Holmes, who are the five (not a typo) Watsons? (5 pts)

Total Points: 23. Targets: Novice 9 Pro 17. Your Score:

Quiz 32. General Knowledge

All these have connections to a Christopher, a Christine, a Chris or suchlike

Part 1

1   Who was the only British track and field athlete to win a medal at both the Beijing and London Olympic Games?

2   Actor Christopher Timothy is best known for which role in a popular country TV drama in the late 1970s?

3   Who is the central protagonist in the York Mystery Plays cycle?

4   Which Bulgarian footballer and European Cup winner (with Barcelona) was known as El Pistolero (The Gunslinger)?

5   How many full-length (i.e. not including collections of short stories) detective novels did Agatha Christie write: forty-four, sixty-six or eighty-eight?

6   Which British Olympic gold medallist, the forerunner of the great British cycling teams of the twenty-first century, was the first Olympic winner to ride the carbon fibre 108 time trial bicycle developed by Lotus?

7   What was the 2009 film that featured Christoph Waltz as a deranged German colonel, a role that won him an Academy Award as Best Supporting Actor?

8   Where was the popular British athlete Kriss Akabusi born, he of the permanent smile?

9   Which former England cricketer was given a thirteen-year prison sentence for drug-smuggling in 2008?

10 Who co-stars with Jackie Chan in the *Rush Hour* films?

Part 2

11 Which poet, part of the Pre-Raphaelite movement and sister to one of the movement's leading painters, wrote the words to the carol 'In the Bleak Midwinter'?

12 Who made her name in Hollywood as the malevolent Wednesday in *The Addams Family* movie?

13 Which heiress died in Buenos Aires in 1988 aged thirty-seven after four failed marriages and a life in the glare of the media?

14 What was the name of Christina Aguilera's 1999 single that rocketed her to stardom as a teenager, reaching no. 1 in the US and UK?

15 Who was hunting deer in 1978, the King of New York in 1990 and one of seven psychopaths in 2012?

16 Who took time off from discovering America to direct the first two Harry Potter movies?

17 To which other tennis star was Chris Evert married in 1979 (and divorced from eight years later)? With which singing star and actor did she have a high-profile affair that put a strain on the marriage? (2 pts)

18 Who is the lead singer of Coldplay? In which English city was he brought up? (2 pts)

19 Who did Chris Eubank box in a 1993 super middleweight unification fight the promoters billed as Judgement Day?

20 Which children's show helped launch the careers of Chris Tarrant and Lenny Henry, amongst others?

Total Points: 22. Targets: Novice 11 Pro 17. Your Score: ☐

Answers Quizzes 25–32

Quiz 25. General Knowledge

1. Dancing the tango; 2. Armistice Day; 3. Kenya; 4. Donald Woods; 5. 277 miles; 6. Damien Hirst; 7. Antony Worrall Thompson; 8. Paralympic swimmer Ellie Simmonds; 9. The tomb of Tutankhamen; 10. Katrina; 11. The *Carry On* . . . films; 12. Joey; 13. Samsung; 14. Uganda; 15. Bo isn't a baseball star, he is the US President's family dog; 16. Paparazzi; 17. He is a composer; in Thomas Mann's novella, von Aschenbach is a writer; 18. Batman; 19. State of the art controllers for game consoles; 20. Stormont, Belfast

Quiz 26. Westerns

1. Burt Lancaster; 2. All played Calamity Jane (Wiegert in the TV series *Deadwood*; Doris Day played Jane in the 1953 musical); 3. *Paint Your Wagon*; Lee Marvin; 4. Sam Raimi; Sharon Stone; 5. Sean Connery (complete with Scots accent); Brigitte Bardot; 6. Neither character is given a name; 7. Warren Oates; *The Wild Bunch*; 8. A rifle; 9. *High Noon*; 10. John Wayne; Comanche; 11. Hole-in-the-Wall Gang; Bolivia; 'Raindrops Keep Falling on My Head'; Burt Bacharach; None; 12. *Dances with Wolves* (Kevin Costner, 1990) and *Unforgiven* (Clint Eastwood, 1992); Gene Hackman

Quiz 27. Discoveries and Inventions

1. Near Lake Turkana in Kenya (it was found by Kamoya Kimeu, a Kenyan archaeologist); 2. Hungarian; 3. Werner Von Braun; 4. Telescope; 5. Isaac Newton; 6. Insecticide; 7. Flushing lavatory; 8. Atomic power station; 9. Double-entry bookkeeping; 10. The Periodic Table; 11. (Samuel) Morse; 12. Benjamin Franklin; 13. A method of developing photographs; 14. (a) he performed the first appendix removal; 15. It was the microwave oven; 16. A graphite pencil; 17. A protective helmet while batting; 18. An escalator; 19. 1888 (he was marketing them commercially by the mid-1890s); 20. The zip fastening (it was called a clasp-lock at the time but had the same mechanism as a modern zip)

Quiz 28. History

1. Mary Robinson; 2. Grenada; 3. (c) Charles Darwin; 4. William Pitt the Younger; 5. Vatican City; 6. St Bartholomew's Day Massacre; 7. Crécy; 8. Visigoths and Vandals; 9. 'The Hitler Diaries', eventually exposed as a fake; 10. Lord Howard of Effingham (1st Earl of Nottingham); 11. Pablo Neruda; 12. Beijing; Xanadu; 13. Avignon; 14. In a pit/colliery; 15. Jordan; 16. Kenya (the Mau Mau rebels continued the struggle for the next decade, although the capture of their leader in 1956 ended the overt rebellion); 17. Ottoman Empire; 18. Appomatox Court House; Ulysses S. Grant and General Robert E. Lee; 19. Elba; 20. Pol Pot

Quiz 29. Fashion and Photography

1. They were all naked; 2. Baseball cap; 3. Chanel; 4. Karl Lagerfeld; 5. Paco Rabanne; 6. Nubuck; 7. (b) Treviso; 8. A priest; it is the long outer garment worn whilst presiding over Mass; 9. 1947 (Cartier-Bresson was among the founders); 10. Robert Capa; 11. Tennis girl (the image shows a girl walking towards the net with a racket in one hand and scratching her exposed backside with the other); 12. (c) from the fifteenth to the seventeenth centuries women (and the odd chap, most likely) wore these frames or a hooped petticoat under their skirts to give them volume; 13. Dior; 14. On your head, or heid in the case of the Scottish Glengarry; 15. Stella McCartney; 16. Shoes; 17. Miniskirt, jeans, little black dress; 18. Yves Saint-Laurent; 19. London, New York, Milan and Paris; 20. Don McCullin

Quiz 30. Premier League

1. Steven Gerrard and Phil Neville; 2. Wigan Athletic; 3. Brad Friedel; 4. Craig Bellamy; 5. West Ham (the game was far from violent and the cards probably had more to do with fussy refereeing than excessive foul play); 6. Edin Dzeko and Sergio Aguero; 7. The league was being reduced from twenty-two to twenty teams to ease fixture congestion (only two, instead of the usual three, would earn promotion from the second tier); 8. West Ham United (Bolton were two points above them); 9. 3rd (Man Utd) and 4th (Arsenal); 10. Jussi Jääskeläinen; Sami Hyppia; 11. Marian Pahars; 12. Ivan Campo and Fernando Hierro (Campo played for Bolton for a few years, but Hierro came for a swansong season at 36 years of age); 13. Frank Clark, Stuart Pearce (temporary player-manager) and Dave Bassett; 14. Duncan Ferguson, Patrick Vieira and Richard Dunne; 15. David Seaman, Lee Dixon, Nigel Winterburn, Tony Adams and Steve Bould; 16. Paul Wilkinson (1992–3), Fabrizio Ravanelli (1996–7) and Hamilton Ricard (1998–9) (2 pts each for Wilkinson and Ricard)

Quiz 31. Sherlock Holmes

1. The Strand; 2. Mrs Hudson; 3. Dartmoor; 4. Mycroft; The Diogenes Club; 5. The magnifying glass; 6. *The Case-Book of Sherlock Holmes*; 7. Professor Moriarty; Reichenbach Falls; 8. Irene Adler; 'A Scandal in Bohemia' (contrary to some popular depictions, she does not reappear, nor does she provide any romantic interest for Holmes); 9. A snake (it is used to terrify and kill by the villain, who induces it to crawl along the heating pipes); 10. The Baker Street Irregulars – an early Holmes fan club took the name for their society; 11. 'Silver Blaze'; 12. 'The Dancing Men'; 13. Inspector Lestrade; 14. He is a master blackmailer (the Granada complete Holmes retitled the story thus in its adaptation); 15. The Illustrious Client; 16. Nigel Bruce (Rathbone); Edward Hardwicke and David Burke (Brett); Jude Law (Downey); Martin Freeman (Cumberbatch)

Quiz 32. General Knowledge

1. Christine Ohuruogu; 2. He played vet James Herriot in the TV series based on Herriot's own books; 3. Jesus Christ; 4. Hristo Stoichkov; 5. Sixty-six (and fifteen short-story volumes); 6. Chris Boardman; 7. *Inglourious Basterds*; 8. London (Paddington); 9. Chris Lewis; 10. Chris Tucker; 11. Christina Rossetti; 12. Cristina Ricci; 13. Christina Onassis; 14. 'Genie in a Bottle'; 15. Christopher Walken; 16. Christopher Columbus; 17. John Lloyd; Adam Faith (Evert and Lloyd reconciled briefly but were divorced a couple of years later); 18. Chris Martin; Exeter; 19. Nigel Benn; 20. *Tiswas*

Quiz 33. General Knowledge

Identify the answer from the following clue

Part 1

1 Athos, Porthos, Aramis
2 Balthazar, Casper, Melchior
3 Larry, Moe, Curly
4 Hale-Bopp
5 The Cape Doctor
6 Elfmeter
7 Hildegard von Bingen
8 Ronald, O'Kelly, Rudolph, Ernie, Marvin
9 Beatrix Kiddo
10 Kate Middleton

Part 2

11 Karen O
12 Uluru
13 Srinivasaraghavan Venkataraghavan
14 Shahada, salat, zakat, sawm and hajj
15 Ω
16 Parentheses
17 Mensuration
18 Bernie Taupin
19 Frances Ethel Gumm
20 Omega Pharma Quick-Step

Total Points: 20. Targets: Novice 10 Pro 15. Your Score: [   ]

Quiz 34. Kings and Queens

Monarchs but not necessarily of England

Part 1

1   Roughly how much of his ten-year reign did Richard I spend in England: six months, one year or three years?

2   Which English king died in January 1066?

3   Who was executed at Fotheringay Castle in 1587 and which English king was born there 135 years earlier? (2 pts)

4   Which of these was *not* a king of France of the Carolingian dynasty: Charles the Bald, Charles the Fat, Charles the Lazy or Charles the Simple?

5   By what name, presumably a reference to his florid appearance, was King William II of England commonly known? And how did he die? (2 pts)

6   William Cecil, Lord Burghley, was the principal adviser to which monarch?

7   Which Hanoverian king enjoyed the longest rule of England to that date? And did it last forty-five, fifty or sixty years? (2 pts)

8   Who was installed as king of Spain by his brother and ruled from 1808 to 1813?

9   Who was the leader of the Welsh forces who rebelled repeatedly against King Henry IV of England?

10 What is the official London residence of the Prince of Wales, and what is the name of his privately owned Gloucestershire estate? (2 pts)

Part 2

We give you a monarch, you give us the country they rule(d) and the century in which their reign happened (2 pts each)

11 Ivan the Terrible

12 Louis XVI of Bourbon

13 Queen Beatrix

14 Robert the Bruce

15 Henry (III) of Valois

16 Philip II of Habsburg

17 Gustav VI Adolf

18 Catherine the Great

19 Theodosius

20 Prince Albert II

Total Points: 34. Targets: Novice 14 Pro 26. Your Score:

Quiz 35. Comedy Movies

Funny stuff, ha ha ha

Part 1

1 *God Bless America* was a 2012 movie made by which comic film-maker and actor? In which movie franchise did he make his name? (2 pts)

2 Who play Shaun's mum and stepdad in *Shaun of the Dead*? And what was the TV show made by director Edgar Wright and Simon Pegg? (3 pts)

3 Apart from his mockery of Hitler as Adenoid Hynkel, what part was played by Chaplin in his own *The Great Dictator* (1940)? The character Napolini in the same film was a parody of which other political figure? (2 pts)

4 Who or what is the 'baby' mentioned in the title of the 1938 comedy *Bringing Up Baby*?

5 What 1990s cult movie spawned fan festivals involving vast consumption of White Russian cocktails? What are the two main ingredients of a White Russian? (3 pts)

6 What is the subtitle of Stanley Kubrick's 1964 satire of the military, *Dr Strangelove*?

7 *The Jerk*, *The Man with Two Brains*, *Dead Men Don't Wear Plaid* and *All of Me* are collaborations between which star and director? (2 pts)

8 Who play the body-swap mother and daughter in *Freaky Friday* (2003)? (2 pts)

9 Kareem Abdul-Jabaar features as a co-pilot in the hit 1980s comedy *Airplane!* For what was he better known?

10 Which film concerns the declaration of war by Freedonia against neighbouring Sylvania?

Part 2

A couple of multi-part questions on silly 1990s comedies

11 What are the full titles of the three Austin Powers movies? Who played both Powers and his nemesis, Dr Evil? Who appeared as Dr Evil's son, Scott? (5 pts)

12 What four games do Bill and Ted play against Death (and win) in *Bill and Ted's Bogus Journey*? Which classic European film is the scene spoofing? (5 pts)

Total Points: 28. Targets: Novice 11 Pro 21. Your Score: [   ]

Quiz 36. Science

Twenty straight questions on geeky stuff

Part 1

1 What typically makes up between 0.5 per cent and 3 per cent of the dry weight of tobacco?

2 Which component of the limbic system processes human emotions and memories?

3 By what name is N-acetyl-5-methoxytryptamine better known?

4 Which head of the Lyceum in Athens published *Historia Plantarum*, the first serious treatise on botany?

5 If an apricot is dried, its carbohydrate content rises from 13 per cent to (a) 25 per cent (b) 38 per cent or (c) 67 per cent?

6 Whose binomial theorem applied mathematics to gambling games and developed the notion of betting odds?

7 What is the drawback to superconductors that makes them largely unviable for commercial use?

8 Carrots are good for your eyesight: true or false (with explanation)?

9 In which state did a massive volcanic eruption occur in the US at Mount St Helens in 1980, with fifty-seven lives lost, despite a comprehensive evacuation programme?

10 What are *Eagle, Intrepid, Antares, Falcon, Orion* and *Challenger*?

Part 2

11   What fraction is denoted decimally as 0.2727 recurring?

12   Which science deals with the measurement and calibration of the earth and its surface and gravitational field? (a) geologics (b) geodetics (c) genomonics

13   What do the initials USB stand for in computer science?

14   What is the hard, set polymer used in old-fashioned telephones and electrical insulators?

15   What name is given to the elementary particle believed to have been finally identified at CERN in 2012?

16   Who discovered oxygen before Joseph Priestley and chlorine before Humphry Davy, but failed to publish and never got the credit?

17   The modern branch of mathematics called algebra came to the West from which area?

18   What was the profession of Edwin Hubble in Pasadena in the 1920s?

19   What, after oxygen, is the second most common component of the earth's crust? (a) iron (b) carbon or (c) silicon

20   What is the third most common gas in the earth's atmosphere after Nitrogen and Oxygen? (a) carbon dioxide (b) argon (c) helium

Total Points: 20. Targets: Novice 6 Pro 15. Your Score:

Quiz 37. Sci-Fi and Fantasy

Just a big Mix and Match. Confusing? Good, it's meant to be

Mix and Match: you have ten science-fantasy authors, ten novels (all the first in a series), ten series of novels and ten main cast characters. All you have to do is match them up (1 pt each for novel, series and character)

1. Steven Eriksson; 2. Stephen Donaldson; 3. Robert Jordan; 4. Raymond E. Feist; 5. David Eddings; 6. Terry Pratchett; 7. George R. R. Martin; 8. Joe Abercrombie; 9. Robin Hobb; 10. Trudi Canavan

a. *Game of Thrones* (1996); b. *The Magicians' Guild* (2001); c. *The Blade Itself* (2006); d. *Lord Foul's Bane* (1977); e. *Magician* (1982); f. *The Colour of Magic* (1983); g. *Assassin's Apprentice* (1995); h. *Gardens of the Moon* (1999); i. *Pawn of Prophecy* (1982); j. *The Eye of the World* (1990)

i. *The Riftwar Saga*; ii. *Discworld*; iii. *The Wheel of Time*; iv. *A Song of Ice and Fire*; v. *The Farseer Trilogy*; vi. *Malazan Book of the Fallen*; vii. *The Belgariad*; viii. *The First Law Trilogy*; ix. *The Black Magician*; x. *The First Chronicles of Thomas Covenant, the Unbeliever*

Q. Aunt Pol; R. Whiskeyjack; S. Rand al'Thor; T. Tyrion Lannister; U. Sonea; V. Logen Ninefingers; W. Foamfollower; X. Prince Verity; Y. Pug; Z. Rincewind

Total Points: 30. Targets: Novice 12 Pro 23. Your Score:

Quiz 38. Golf

Fifteen straight questions and a multi-part question. Fore!

Part 1

1   Which three British golfers all hit the world no. 1 spot in 2011 or 2012? (3 pts)

2   Who, in 2011, became the all-time leading points scorer in the Solheim Cup?

3   If the Golden Bear beat the Great White Shark by one stroke, who has just beaten who? (2 pts)

4   Which Australian golfer won five Open Championships between 1954 and 1965?

5   Who, in 1969, was the first British winner of the Open Championship for eighteen years?

6   Which three British players won four consecutive Masters tournaments between them from 1988 to 1991? (3 pts)

7   Who, in 1999, went down the eighteenth at the Open Championship needing a six for the title and blew it, taking a seven and committing himself to a play-off? What was the venue and who was the eventual winner, from a record ten shots back going into the last round? (3 pts)

8   Who was youngest when they won their first Major: Seve, Tiger or Rory?

9   Which European player was the dominant figure on the ladies professional golf circuit around the turn of the century, winning ten Major titles, the most by any player in the modern era?

10 Which golf scoring system scores a player three points for a birdie, and carries a minimum score of zero points for a poor hole, irrespective of whether the hole is scored at two over par or seven over par?

Part 2

11   What is the common name given to the championship golf course known formally as the Royal Liverpool Golf Club?

12   Who was the first British player to win both the Open Championship and the US Open?

13   A matchplay contest between the Big Easy and Boom Boom; who would we be watching? (2 pts)

14   At what age is a player permitted to join the Seniors Tour?

15   Which European player holds the record for most Ryder Cup appearances (eleven) and most points earned (twenty-five)?

16   Which five players have won the most money in their careers on the US PGA Tour? (Hint: there are three Americans, and prize money has escalated, so it is likely that all five are recent, but have had time to accumulate earnings) (5 pts)

Total Points: 28. Targets: Novice 11 Pro 21. Your Score: ☐

Quiz 39. Plants

Fifteen straight questions

Part 1

1   What is the correct name for the shrub or small tree commonly called a California lilac?

2   Cork, cinnamon, quinine and aspirin are all developed from what part of a plant?

3   What distinguishes ferns from the angiosperm group, which includes the vast majority of the world's fauna?

4   Marigolds, chrysanthemums and dahlias all belong to which family of flowers?

5   The malus genus of trees comprises thirty to thirty-five species more commonly known by what name?

6   What is the tree, native to China and with useful medicinal properties, that is the only remaining species of a once widely represented group?

7   What is the more usual English name for the herb sometimes called cilantro?

8   Which of radish, leek, garlic or chive is an *Allium*, a member of the onion genus?

9   Cedars, cypresses, junipers, larches and yews are all types of which division of plants?

10   In which part of the world did the tomato originate? (a) the Americas (b) Japan (c) India

11   What is the root, a member of the nightshade family and similar in appearance to a parsnip, the ingestion of which causes hallucinations and even madness according to popular mythology?

12   Hydrangeas are native to which part of the world? (a) China and Southeast Asia (b) North America (c) South Africa

13   Which genus of tree comes in Lebanon, Atlas and Cyprus varieties?

14   What group of plants (example: agaves) have unusually thickened stems or leaves to enable them to store moisture in dry climates?

15   What hellish name is sometimes given to the *Phallus impudicus*, the stinkhorn fungus?

Total Points: 15. Targets: Novice 6 Pro 11. Your Score:

Quiz 40. General Knowledge

Nothing complicated (apart from the odd tricky question . . .)

Part 1

1 What connects Hadrian's Wall, the standing stones at Avebury, Ironbridge Gorge and Kew Gardens?

2 The Treaty of Paris, signed by the British government in 1783, recognized what?

3 Which English city boasts the renovated Albert Docks as a visitor attraction?

4 Why specifically might you stay at Keukenhof, near Noordwijk, in the Netherlands?

5 Which Chancellor was forced to pull Britain out of the Exchange Rate Mechanism in Europe to protect the falling pound in 1992?

6 For which novel was Salman Rushdie awarded the Booker Prize?

7 What now-familiar event was first presented at the Queen's Hall, London, by Henry Wood in 1895?

8 Which famous French mime artist, born 21 March 1923, died in 2007?

9 Which Olympic sport started life as a training exercise for the Norwegian Army? Which two disciplines are involved? (3 pts)

10 Who or what connects Richard Curtis to Clement Freud?

Part 2

11   The ancient town of Syracuse was on which modern island? Which famous mathematician was born there in *c.*290 BC? (2 pts)

12   DJ Mike Read, disgraced former Tory MP Neil Hamilton (and ubiquitous wife, Christine) and actress Joan Collins are all paid-up members of which political party?

13   What type of shape is made by curling wire around a cylindrical object?

14   Who has more ribs (assuming a full set), a woman or a man?

15   If one owned a few Aberdeen Angus, what would one's job most likely be?

16   Who conducted the first eight symphonies composed by Gustav Mahler, between 1888 and 1907?

17   A statistic from 2009 – how many official vineyards were registered in England: 94, 202 or 416?

18   For what have Snoop Dogg, Naomi Campbell, Gerard Depardieu and David Hasselhoff all been arrested? (Additional point for extra details)

19   Who was the ex-footman to the Queen and butler to Princess Diana, supposedly her 'rock' and confidant, but not averse to making a few quid out of his royal connections?

20   What industrial development did Alfred Yarrow move from London to Glasgow in 1906–8?

Total Points: 24. Targets: Novice 12 Pro 18. Your Score:

Answers Quizzes 33–40

Quiz 33. General Knowledge

1. The Three Musketeers; 2. The Three Wise Men; 3. The Three Stooges; 4. A comet that passed close to the earth in 1997; 5. A bracing southeasterly wind that blows across Cape Town; 6. A penalty kick in German (penalty spot is c.11 metres from goal-line, elf is eleven in German); 7. Twelfth-century abbess and composer of polyphonic choral music; 8. The Isley Brothers; 9. The avenger in *Kill Bill*; 10. Prince William's wife. 11. Lead singer of the Yeah Yeah Yeahs; 12. Freestanding plateau in the Australian outback, sacred to the Aboriginals (formerly called Ayers Rock); 13. Indian spin bowler, usually known simply as Venkat, who played fifty-seven tests between 1965 and 1983 (he became a top class umpire after retiring as a player); 14. The Five Pillars of Islam; 15. The capital and small case form of the letter Omega, the last letter in the Greek alphabet; 16. The posh word for round brackets ( ); 17. The measurement of geometric figures; 18. The lyricist who co-wrote Elton John's hits; 19. Birth name of Judy Garland (no wonder she changed it); 20. Belgian cycling team Mark Cavendish joined after leaving Team Sky in 2012

Quiz 34. Kings and Queens

1. Six months; 2. Edward the Confessor; 3. Mary, Queen of Scots; Richard III; 4. Charles the Lazy (the last Carolingian king does bear the epithet 'lazy' but he was Louis V); 5. William Rufus; shot by an arrow whilst out hunting; 6. Elizabeth I, in the first part of her reign; 7. George III was on the throne for sixty years (although he was barking for the last bit); 8. Joseph Bonaparte (brother of Napoleon, half a point for Bonaparte); 9. Owain Glyndŵr; 10. Clarence House; Highgrove; 11. Russia, sixteenth; 12. France, eighteenth; 13. Netherlands, twentieth/twenty-first; 14. Scotland, fourteenth; 15. France, sixteenth; 16. Spain, sixteenth; 17. Sweden, twentieth; 18. Russia, eighteenth; 19. Rome, fourth; 20. Monaco, twenty-first

Quiz 35. Comedy Movies

1. Bobcat Goldthwait; *Police Academy*; 2. Penelope Wilton and Bill Nighy; *Spaced*; 3. A Jewish barber; Mussolini; 4. A leopard; 5. *The Big Lebowski*; vodka and Kahlua (or any coffee liqueur); 6. Or How I Learned to Stop Worrying and Love the Bomb; 7. Steve Martin and Carl Reiner; 8. Jamie Lee Curtis and Lindsay Lohan; 9. As a star performer in NBA basketball; 10. *Duck Soup*; 11. *Austin Powers: International Man of Mystery*, *Austin Powers: The Spy Who Shagged Me* and *Austin Powers in Goldmember*; Mike Myers; Seth Green; 12. Battleships, Cluedo, table football, twister; Bergman's *The Seventh Seal*, in which the hero Knight plays Death at chess

Quiz 36. Science

1. Nicotine; 2. Amygdala; 3. Melatonin; 4. Theophrastus; 5. 67 per cent – it seems high, but it is logical when you consider most fruit and vegetables have high water content and by removing it everything else increases; 6. Blaise Pascal; 7. They only operate at extremely cold temperatures – well below even the coldest air temperature; 8. Carrots are a source of retinal, which helps the eye absorb light energy (it needs constant replenishment; carrots won't make eyesight sharper but will improve ocular health); 9. Washington State; 10. The six lunar modules to carry astronauts to the moon's surface; 11. 3/11 (three-elevenths); 12. (b) geodetics (Struve's geodetic arch is a series of survey points across ten countries that helped accurately measure the meridian of the earth: it took thirty years for the project to be completed); 13. Universal Serial Bus; 14. Bakelite; 15. Higgs Boson (or Higgs particle); 16. Swedish scientist Karl Scheele (called Hard Luck Scheele by Isaac Asimov); 17. The Arabic world, where it was known as *al-jabr*; 18. Astronomer; he was based at the Mount Wilson Observatory and used the vast Hooker telescope to expand our knowledge of the universe; 19. (c) silicon; 20. (b) argon; carbon dioxide is fourth and helium sixth after neon

Quiz 37. Sci-Fi and Fantasy

Mix and Match: 1 Erikson, h, vi, R; 2 Donaldson, d, x, W; 3 Jordan, j, iii, S; 4 Feist, e, i, Y; 5 Eddings, i, vii, Q; 6 Pratchett, f, ii, Z; 7 Martin, a, iv, T; 8 Abercrombie, c, viii, V; Hobb, g, v, X; Canavan, b, ix, U

Quiz 38. Golf

1. Luke Donald, Rory McIlroy and Lee Westwood; 2. Laura Davies; 3. Jack Nicklaus beat Greg Norman; 4. Peter Thomson; for the first four Thomson didn't have to compete against the best Americans, who never turned up, but his win in 1965 was against a field that included Nicklaus, Palmer and many other fine players; 5. Tony Jacklin; 6. Sandy Lyle (1988), Nick Faldo (1989 and 1990), Ian Woosnam (1991); 7. Jean Van de Velde; Carnoustie, Paul Lawrie; 8. Tiger Woods was twenty-one and three months, Ballesteros and McIlroy had just turned twenty-two; 9. Annika Sörenstam; 10. Stableford; 11. Hoylake; 12. Harry Vardon; 13. Ernie Els and Fred Couples; 14. Fifty; 15. Nick Faldo; 16. Tiger Woods, Phil Mickelson, Vijay Singh, Jim Furyk and Ernie Els

Quiz 39. Plants

1. *Ceanothus*; 2. Tree bark; quinine is cinchona bark, while aspirin is derived from willow bark; 3. Ferns reproduce via spores rather than carpels and stamens; 4. Asteraceae (accept aster or daisy family); 5. Apples (it includes domestic apples as well as various species of wild apple); 6. Ginkgo; 7. Coriander; 8. Radish is from the brassica family – the onions are all types of amaryllis; 9. Conifers (bonus point for Pinophyta); 10. It was brought

back to Europe from the Americas by the Spanish and spread from there (the tomato belongs to the largely poisonous nightshade family); 11. Mandrake; 12. China and South-east Asia (the plants available in Europe are only a small cross-section of the genus found in Asia); 13. Cedar; 14. Succulents; 15. Devil's Candlestick (or Devil's Horn).

Quiz 40. General Knowledge

1. All are designated World Heritage Sites; 2. American independence; 3. Liverpool; 4. To see the tulips; 5. Norman Lamont; 6. *Midnight's Children*; 7. Promenade Concert, or Prom; 8. Marcel Marceau; 9. Biathlon; cross-country skiing and shooting; 10. Emma Freud (she is the mother of Curtis's three children and Freud's daughter); 11. Sicily; Archimedes; 12. UKIP; 13. Helix; 14. Neither, both have twelve; 15. Farmer (they are a breed of cattle); 16. Mahler himself; 17. 416; 18. In-flight or airport misbehaviour (Snoop and his posse started a mini riot, Campbell threw a major hissy at the pilot, Depardieu had a wee in first class and the Hoff was so nuked he could barely stand, allegedly); 19. Paul Burrell; 20. His shipyard

Quiz 41. General Knowledge

Part 1

1   Why did the wrestling authorities change their name from the World Wrestling Federation to the World Wrestling Entertainment?

2   Scone Palace is closest to which Scottish town or city? (a) Perth (b) Dundee (c) Edinburgh

3   'Ich bin ein Berliner.' Who uttered these famous words in a speech in Berlin on 25 June 1963?

4   To which post was Hilary Clinton appointed in Barack Obama's first administration in 2009?

5   Meg Whitman spent more than any other person in the history of US politics on her campaign to become Governor of California in 2010; who beat her in the polls? Of which company is Whitman CEO? (2 pts)

6   Under what name do we know musician, actor, writer, etc., Ben Drew?

7   By what English name do we know the Ponte dei Suspiri, which spans the Rio Palazzo in Venice?

8   According to a 1976 theory (but still debated) how many colours are required to provide a clear map of political boundaries of any given region?

9   What is made up of the Mishnah and the Gemara?

10 In 1822 the poet Shelley drowned in his own boat; what was the name of the boat, taken from the title of a poem by his friend, Byron?

Part 2

11 Which has the biggest population, Denmark, Austria or Ireland?

12 Which has the biggest population, Japan, the Philippines or Mexico?

13 Which has the biggest population, Argentina, France or South Korea?

14 Which has the biggest population, Jamaica, Kuwait or New Zealand?

15 Which has the biggest population, Bulgaria, Hungary or Serbia?

16 Which has the biggest population, Iceland, Malta or Luxembourg?

17 Which has the biggest population, Mongolia, Norway or Peru?

18 Which has the biggest population, Bangladesh, Pakistan or Russia?

19 Which has the biggest population, Egypt, Democratic Republic of Congo or South Africa?

20 Which has the biggest population, Germany, Ukraine or United Kingdom?

Total Points: 21. Targets: Novice 11 Pro 16. Your Score: [   ]

Quiz 42. Musicals

Song and dance movies and shows – feel free to sing along; ten straight questions and a match 'em up

Part 1

1   What is the street in the heart of New York that intersects Broadway and lent its name to a 1980 musical?

2   Who won an Academy Award for her support work in the 2002 musical *Chicago*? Who polished up his dance moves as Billy Flynn? (2 pts)

3   Which rock singer starred as Velma Von Tussle in the original 1988 film of *Hairspray*, and which actress star took the role in the later (2007) musical version? (2 pts)

4   Which two musically trained stars were cast as Valjean and Fantine in the 2013 film version of *Les Misérables*? (2 pts)

5   What was the role for which Liza Minnelli won her only Academy Award? And what is the name of the rich playboy who seduces both Minnelli and her co-star Michael York in the film? (2 pts)

6   What was the 1983 musical based on a French play of 1973 about a drag club and its owner, Georges?

7   Who played the Demon Barber in the 2007 film of *Sweeney Todd*? What was the type of shop owned by his landlady, Mrs Lovett? (2 pts)

8   Who had great fun, if not great voices, as the trio of possible fathers of Meryl Streep's daughter in the 2008 film of the musical *Mamma Mia!*? (3 pts)

9   For all the success of *The Phantom of the Opera* on stage, the 2004 film version of the show was not loved by the critics; who took the part of the Phantom?

10 Who played Deena in the 2006 film version of *Dreamgirls* and who won an Academy Award in the support role of Effie? (2 pts)

Part 2

Mix and Match: match the song to the musical from which it comes

1. 'Bewitched, Bothered and Bewildered'; 2. 'Happy Talk'; 3. 'My Favourite Things'; 4. 'There's No Business Like Show Business'; 5.'The Lady Is a Tramp'; 6. 'Follow the Yellow Brick Road'; 7. 'Who Wants to Be a Millionaire?'; 8. 'Getting to Know You'; 9. 'Oh What a Beautiful Mornin''; 10. 'Luck Be a Lady'

a. *The Sound of Music*; b. *The Wizard of Oz*, c. *Guys and Dolls*; d. *Pal Joey*, e. *Oklahoma!*; f. *Babes in Arms*; g. *The King and I*; h. *Annie Get Your Gun*; i. *South Pacific*; j. *High Society*

Your Workings:

Total Points: 28. Targets: Novice 11 Pro 21. Your Score:

Quiz 43. Around Britain

Finding your way round Britain . . . or not, in my dear wife's case . . . ten straight questions and two multi-parters

Part 1

1   Which two southeastern towns make up the Cinque ports with Dover, Hastings and Romney? (2 pts)

2   Which inland lake to the west of Belfast is Ireland's largest inland body of water?

3   What is the name of the strip of water between the northeastern tip of mainland Scotland at John o'Groats and the Orkney Islands? (a) North Minch (b) Moray Firth (c) Pentland Firth (d) Colin Firth

4   Bangor and Caernarfon both lie on which narrow stretch of water? What lies on the other side? (2 pts)

5   Which English cathedral city also houses the Church of St Martin, the country's oldest church and the Abbey of St Augustine? (a) York (b) Canterbury (c) Winchester

6   Hawick, Kelso, Jedburgh and Melrose are all towns in which administrative region?

7   The remains of which abbey, destroyed in Henry VIII's dissolution, lies in Studley Royal Park in North Yorkshire?

8   What is the oldest motorway in Britain? And which northern town did the first stretch by-pass? (2 pts)

9   Where might you enjoy Nemesis, Oblivion, Rita and Th13teen?

10 Rising in the Cambrian Mountains in Wales, the River Severn flows through which three county towns before discharging into the sea via the Bristol Channel? (Bristol is not a county town.) (3 pts)

Part 2

11 The Lake District lies within which large English county? What were the old names of the two counties which once roughly made up this area? What is the largest town in the county? And which is the largest body of water in the Lake District? (5 pts)

12 Worcestershire is bordered by which five counties or administrative regions? (5 pts)

Total Points: 25. Targets: Novice 10 Pro 19. Your Score:

Quiz 44. Horror Movies

Quick, behind the sofa, it's the horror movie section; this is a tricky round and most of the films are old classics rather than modern slasher thrill-rides

Part 1

1   Don Siegel in 1956 and Philip Kaufman in 1976 directed two versions of which classic horror movie?

2   Who directed the low-budget horror classic *The Evil Dead* in 1981? What was the name of the main protagonist, played by Bruce Campbell? (2 pts)

3   Who starred in the defining 1958 Hammer Horror version of *Dracula* as the urbane but terrifying Count, and who played his nemesis, Van Helsing? (2 pts)

4   What was the compendium chiller movie made in 1945 at Ealing with Alberto Cavalcanti, Charles Crichton, Basil Dearden and Robert Hamer each directing a segment?

5   Which 1974 Tobe Hooper slasher movie had to wait twenty-five years to get a rating from the British Board of Film Classification?

6   Deborah Kerr is a governess who looks after two monstrous children, Flora and Miles, in a disturbing 1960s creepy classic; Jack Clayton directs — what's the movie?

7   What was Hideo Nakata's 1998 horror classic, remade by Gore Verbinski in 2002?

8   What was the voyeuristic 1960 chiller that was greeted with such opprobrium that it hampered director Michael Powell's career?

9   What was Elsa Lanchester's most famous role, in a James Whale directed film of 1935?

10 Which later-to-be-very-famous New Zealand director made the 1992 gross-out horror-comedy *Braindead*?

Part 2

11   Carl Theodor Dreyer's *Vampyr* (1932) was based on stories by which nine-teenth-century Irish writer of ghost stories? (a) M. R. James (b) J. Sheridan Le Fanu (c) Bram Stoker

12   What was Tomas Alfredson's 2008 film, a bleak contemporary account of a vampire's existence set in a small town in Sweden?

13   What is the name of the possessed girl played by Linda Blair in *The Exorcist*?

14   Which film features Joe Turkel as Lloyd, a polite but sinister barman, and Lisa and Louise Burns as the young Grady twins?

15   Who makes an appearance as the Prince of Darkness in Neil Jordan's *The Company of Wolves* (1984)? (a) David Hemmings (b) Christopher Lee (c) Terence Stamp

16   Who is the first victim of the psychotic killer in *Halloween*?

17   What was Kathryn Bigelow's 1987 cult movie about a blood-drinking family travelling across America?

18   Who remade *The Fly* in 1986 and who took the lead role? (2 pts)

19   Which cult horror movie is set on the Scottish island of Summerisle?

20   Which star, the film's biggest name, is carved up in the opening sequence of Wes Craven's *Scream* (1996)?

Total Points: 23. Targets: Novice 9 Pro 17. Your Score: [   ]

Quiz 45. Books

Have you read these modern classics? Let's hope so or you won't do very well

Part 1

1 Which modern American writer won the Pulitzer Prize for *The Road* (2006)? What was his 2005 work made into an Academy Award winning film by the Coen brothers? (2 pts)

2 Who is the object of Jay Gatsby's desire in *The Great Gatsby*?

3 Who wrote the exuberant 1973 comedy *Rubyfruit Jungle*?

4 Which 1951 Graham Greene novel charts an affair between a novelist and a married woman, and has twice been made into a movie?

5 What is L. P. Hartley's major work from 1953, a tale of forbidden love during a turn-of-the-century summer?

6 Which modern masterpiece concerns the late-in-life reunion between Florentino Ariza and Fermina Daza?

7 Which city provides the setting for Henry Miller's *Tropic of Cancer* (1934)?

8 Which semi-autobiographical novel written by one of a group of upper-class sisters concerns the lives of the Radlett sisters?

9 J. G. Ballard's wartime novel *Empire of the Sun* is set in which city during World War II?

10 What is the name of Jaroslav Hašek's 'Good Soldier' in his 1923 comic masterpiece?

Part 2

11 What was the 1948 war novel that made Norman Mailer's reputation aged only twenty-six?

12 Whose first novel, *Burmese Days*, uses the author's own experience as a serviceman during World War II?

13 Alan Paton's *Cry, the Beloved Country* is about the travails of which country?

14 Who wrote the oft-adapted 1984 ghost story, *The Woman in Black*?

15 In which decade was Robert M. Pirsig's *Zen and the Art of Motorcycle Maintenance* published?

16 *The Bonfire of the Vanities* is set in which US city?

17 'If you really want to hear about it, the first thing you'll probably want to know is where I was born, and what my lousy childhood was like, and how my parents were occupied before they had me, and all that David Copperfield kind of crap.' These are the opening lines to which twentieth-century classic?

18 Which two novels by D. H. Lawrence concern the lives and loves of the Brangwen family in the north of England? (2 pts)

19 'What's it going to be then, eh?' is the first line of which provocative work by Anthony Burgess, later made into a provocative film by Stanley Kubrick?

20 *Brighton Rock*, *The Quiet American* and *The Honorary Consul* were all written by which British novelist?

Total Points: 22. Targets: Novice 9 Pro 17. Your Score:

Quiz 46. Cricket

Time to don the harlequin cap and thrash a few boundaries

Part 1

1 Which three counties have never finished bottom of the County Championship since 1895 when the contest increased to fourteen teams? (In modern times, bottom means bottom of Division 2) (3 pts)

2 What was Geoff Allott's 'achievement' whilst playing for New Zealand against South Africa in 1999?

3 Who scored 364 for England against Australia in 1938, an individual test match record that stood for twenty years? Who broke the record against Pakistan in 1958? Which Pakistani batsman had already scored a triple hundred earlier in the same series? (3 pts)

4 Brian Lara made his two highest scores (400 not out and 375) against the same team on the same ground; which team, which ground? (2 pts)

5 Who was the youngest English player to score a test century? And the oldest? (2 pts)

6 Greg Chappell, in 1981, notoriously instructed his brother, Tim, to bowl underarm to prevent his side conceding a six to lose a one-day match off the last ball. Who was the opposition?

7 Which erudite cricketer's 1985 book, *The Art of Captaincy*, became a self-improvement classic?

8 Which England captain once walked out to bat but forgot to take his bat with him?

9 In which city is the Wankhede Stadium?

10 Which future England stalwart and captain went on a tour to the West Indies in 1990, broke his wrist playing tennis and waited another three years for his test debut?

Part 2

11 Which pair put on a massive fifth-wicket partnership to turn round a test match against Australia in 2001, winning the game after following on 274 runs behind? (2 pts)

12 Which two Australian players featured in their World Cup victories of 1987 and 1999? (2 pts)

13 Who scored 167 not out, England's highest ever individual one-day score, against Australia in a one-day international in 1993?

14 'I'm not orthodox, I don't live by "the rules".' Which cricketing legend did Ricky Gervais namecheck in this David Brent speech from *The Office*?

15 Who is England's heaviest test run-scorer (1,713 runs) of those who never scored a test match hundred? And who heads the list for all countries with over 3,000 runs? (2 pts)

16 Which is the largest capacity cricket ground in India?

17 Which England cricket captain was fired in 1977 over his involvement with Kerry Packer's commercial cricket circus?

18 How many balls did Yuvraj Singh take to reach fifty against England in the Twenty20 World Cup match in 2007? Which bowler did he flog for six sixes in one over?

19 Who won the first inter-county Twenty20 Cup in 2003?

20 Which Indian batsman became the first player to pass 10,000 runs in test cricket in 1987?

Total Points: 29. Targets: Novice 12 Pro 22. Your Score:

Quiz 47. Theatre

Two for the stalls please – a straight ten questions and a playwright Mix and Match

Part 1

1   *The Voysey Inheritance* and *Waste*, both revived in the noughties, are plays written by which dramatist a century before?

2   What are the names of the two tramps in Samuel Becket's *Waiting for Godot*? (2 pts)

3   17 March 1982 saw the Attorney-General close an obscenity trial, with the National Theatre in the dock. Who brought the case to court?

4   Harold Pinter's *Betrayal*, first performed in 1978, chronicles his affair in the 1960s with which high-profile broadcaster?

5   Which farce about an amateur production of another farce opened at the Lyric Hammersmith in 1982 and ran in the West End for four years?

6   Who wrote *Shopping and F*******, one of the most contentious plays of the 1900s, mainly for its attention-seeking title?

7   In what capacity has Cicely Berry earned plaudits for her work with the Royal Shakespeare Company?

8   In 2011 James Purefoy and Sienna Miller starred in a play called *Flare Path* in the West End; who wrote this rarely performed piece?

9   What was originally known as the Royal Victoria Hall and Coffee Tavern, located near Waterloo Station?

10 *Look Back in Anger* by John Osborne, written in 1956, gave rise to a rash of gritty, realist dramas which came to be known by which generic term?

Part 2

Mix and Match: match these twenty-first century plays to the writers

1. *Clybourne Park*; 2. *The History Boys*; 3. *God of Carnage*; 4. *Democracy*; 5. *Enron*; 6. *Jerusalem*; 7. *August, Osage County*; 8. *Black Watch*; 9. *Port*; 10. *Vincent in Brixton*

a. Lucy Prebble; b. Alan Bennett; c. Tracy Letts; d. Bruce Norris; e. Nicholas Wright; f. Gregory Burke; g. Michael Frayn; h. Simon Stephens; i. Jez Butterworth; j. Yasmina Reza

Your Workings:

Total Points: 21. Targets: Novice 8 Pro 16. Your Score:

Quiz 48. General Knowledge

Straight and narrow

Part 1

1   Ferrari donated a Testarossa to which 1980s TV series because they were appalled at the show using a cheap copy to masquerade as a Ferrari in the early programmes?

2   In 1983, Microsoft announced the first release of which cornerstone product?

3   William Joyce was executed in 1946 as a wartime traitor. By what name was he better known to the British public?

4   In 2005 Mark Felt, ninety-one, revealed a role he had carried earlier in his life. What was that role? (a) he was Churchill's body double (b) he was the fifth Soviet mole in MI6 (c) he was the FBI whistle-blower known as Deep Throat

5   Frenchman Baron Pierre de Coubertin was the driving force behind what sporting contest in the late nineteenth century?

6   Which Hollywood star made his directorial debut at the age of seventy-five with the 2012 film, *Quartet*?

7   *Dandelion Mind* and *Part Man, Part Troll* were live shows by which comedian?

8   Where in California is the hottest spot in the USA?

9   Which two books of the Bible list the Ten Commandments? (2 pts)

10 What were Henry Olonga and Andy Flower mourning with their black armbands in the 2003 Cricket World Cup?

Part 2

11   The Manchester Ship Canal links that city to which other in the northwest?

12   'The Devil's Picture Book' was the name given to what by the seventeenth-century Puritans?

13   What is the mathematical name for a defined point on a curve?

14   Which member of a famous Cambridge spy ring defected to the Soviet Union in 1963?

15   What connects Mayfair, London, with the Rue de la Paix in Paris and the Boardwalk in Atlantic City, New Jersey?

16   How did Valegro strike Gold in 2012?

17   Nureyev in Paris in 1961, Makarova in London in 1972 and Baryshnikov in New York in 1974, all with the Kirov Ballet; what's the connection?

18   Who have been the last three MPs for the Cheshire constituency of Tatton? (3 pts)

19   On 12 September 1982, the trial of Lindy Chamberlain for the murder of her own daughter began in Australia; what was her defence?

20   Who played with the Yardbirds, John Mayall's Bluesbreakers and Cream before enjoying a hugely successful solo career?

Total Points: 23. Targets: Novice 12 Pro 17. Your Score: [.]

Answers Quizzes 41–48

Quiz 41. General Knowledge

1. They lost a court case brought by the World Wildlife Fund which prevented them from using the initials WWF; 2. (a) Perth; 3. John F. Kennedy; 4. Secretary of State (Foreign Affairs to us); 5. Jerry Brown; Hewlett Packard; 6. Plan B; 7. Bridge of Sighs; 8. Four (the map theorem of Appel and Haken was a very boring document including 700 pages of handwritten calculations); 9. The Talmud, the Jewish holy book; 10. *Don Juan*; 11. Austria, with just over eight million (Denmark has *c.*5.5, Ireland 4.6); 12. Japan (126 million), with Mexico on 112.5 million and Philippines just under 100 million; 13. France has over sixty-four million inhabitants, densely populated South Korea has just under fifty million and Argentina over forty million; 14. New Zealand has *c.*4.3 million people, both the others have *c.*2.8 million; 15. Hungary has ten million inhabitants, the other two just over seven million (even if Serbia's claim to Kosovo is recognized that only adds another 1.8 million; 16. Luxembourg's 500,000 tops the other two; 17. This isn't even close: Mongolia and Norway have less than eight million between them, Peru has nearly thirty million; 18. Pakistan has over 180 million people, crowded Bangladesh 156 million and Russia just under 140 million; 19. Egypt has eighty million inhabitants, Congo seventy million and South Africa fifty million; 20. Germany has over eighty million inhabitants, Britain just over sixty million and Ukraine about forty-five million

Quiz 42. Musicals

1. *42nd Street*; 2. Catherine Zeta-Jones; Richard Gere; 3. Debbie Harry and Michelle Pfeiffer (the film wasn't strictly a remake – John Waters' 1988 film boasted a snappy soundtrack and was later made into a musical and the 2007 film was a version of the musical); 4. Hugh Jackman and Anne Hathaway; 5. Sally Bowles; Maximilian; 6. *La Cage aux Folles*; 7. Johnny Depp; a meat pie shop (Sweeney's victims are recycled into pies in the shop below the salon); 8. Pierce Brosnan, Colin Firth and Stellan Skarsgård; 9. Gerard Butler; 10. Beyoncé Knowles; Jennifer Hudson; Mix and Match: 1, d; 2, i; 3, a; 4, h; 5, f; 6, b; 7, j; 8, g; 9, e; 10, c

Quiz 43. Around Britain

1. Hythe and Sandwich; 2. Lough Neagh; 3. Pentland Firth; the Minches are in the Hebrides, the Moray Firth is on the east coast leading in to Inverness, and Colin Firth is an award-winning actor; 4. Menai Straits; Isle of Anglesey (Ynys Mon); 5. (b) Canterbury; 6. Scottish Borders; 7. Fountains Abbey; 8. M6; Preston; 9. Alton Towers; 10. Shrewsbury, Worcester and Gloucester; 11. Cumbria; Cumberland and Westmoreland; Carlisle; Lake Windermere; 12. Shropshire, West Midlands, Warwickshire, Gloucestershire and Herefordshire

Quiz 44. Horror Movies

1. They directed the two versions of *Invasion of the Body Snatchers*; 2. Sam Raimi, Ash; 3. Christopher Lee and Peter Cushing; 4. *Dead of Night*; 5. *The Texas Chainsaw Massacre*; 6. *The Innocents*; 7. *Ringu* (*The Ring*); 8. *Peeping Tom*; 9. *Bride of Frankenstein*; 10. Peter Jackson; 11. (b) J. Sheridan Le Fanu; 12. *Let the Right One In*; 13. Regan; 14. *The Shining*; 15. (c) Terence Stamp; 16. His older sister, Judith, seen killed in a flashback at the start of the movie; 17. *Near Dark*; 18. David Cronenberg; Jeff Goldblum; 19. *The Wicker Man*; 20. Drew Barrymore

Quiz 45. Books

1. Cormac McCarthy; *No Country for Old Men*; 2. Daisy (Buchanan); 3. Rita Mae Brown; 4. *The End of the Affair*; 5. *The Go-Between*; 6. *Love in the Time Of Cholera* (Gabriel García Márquez); 7. Paris; 8. Nancy Mitford's *The Pursuit of Love*; 9. Shanghai; 10. Švejk; 11. *The Naked and the Dead*; 12. George Orwell; 13. South Africa; 14. Susan Hill; 15. 1970s; 16. New York; 17. *The Catcher in the Rye* by J. D. Salinger; 18. *The Rainbow* and *Women in Love*; 19. *A Clockwork Orange*; 20. Graham Greene

Quiz 46. Cricket

1. Lancashire, Middlesex and Surrey; 2. The slowest (seventy-seven balls) nought in test-match history; 3. Len Hutton; Gary Sobers; Hanif Mohammad; 4. England, St John's, Antigua; 5. Denis Compton, aged twenty in 1938; Jack Hobbs, aged forty-six in 1929; 6. New Zealand; 7. Mike Brearley; 8. Bob Willis; 9. Mumbai, India; 10. Nasser Hussain; 11. V. V. S. Laxman and Rahul Dravid; 12. Steve Waugh and Tom Moody; 13. Robin Smith; 14. Ian Botham; 15. John Emburey; Shane Warne; 16. Eden Gardens in Kolkata; 17. Tony Greig; 18. Twelve; Stuart Broad; 19. Surrey; 20. Sunil Gavaskar

Quiz 47. Theatre

1. Harley Granville Barker; 2. Vladimir and Estragon; 3. Mary Whitehouse, protesting about brutal scenes of homosexual rape in Howard Brenton's *The Romans in Britain*; 4. Joan Bakewell; 5. *Noises Off* by Michael Frayn; 6. Mark Ravenhill; 7. She is the RSC's voice and diction coach; 8. Terence Rattigan; 9. The Old Vic; 10. Kitchen sink drama; Mix and Match: 1, d; 2, b; 3, j; 4, g; 5, a; 6, i; 7, c; 8, f; 9, h; 10, e

Quiz 48. General Knowledge

1. *Miami Vice*; 2. Windows; 3. Lord Haw-Haw, the voice of 'Germany calling'; 4. (c) he was Deep Throat, the FBI informant at the heart of the Watergate scandal; 5. The modern Olympic Games; 6. Dustin Hoffman; 7. Bill Bailey; 8. Death Valley; 9. Exodus and Deuteronomy; 10. The death of democracy in Zimbabwe; 11. Liverpool; 12. Playing cards; 13. Cusp; 14. Kim Philby; 15. They are all the highest priced squares in traditional versions of

the game Monopoly; 16. He was the horse ridden by double gold medal winner Charlotte Dujardin at the London Olympics; 17. They all defected to the West; 18. Neil Hamilton held it for the Conservative Party from 1983 to 1997, when he was defeated by Martin Bell on an anti-corruption ticket. Bell stood down in 2001 and current Chancellor of the Exchequer, George Osborne, won back this naturally Tory seat (it is the most affluent in the north of England); 19. That a dingo took the baby (she was found guilty but later vindicated and freed); 20. Eric Clapton

Quiz 49. General Knowledge

Part 1

1 *Carry On Cabbie* (1963) was an early placement opportunity for a motor company in the movies; what type of cars made up the Glamcab fleet in the movie?

2 Which news reporter came to public notice during the 1980 Iranian Embassy siege? Who was the policeman guarding the embassy who became one of the hostages? (2 pts)

3 What do Cresswell Crags in England, Altamira in Spain and Pech Merle in France have in common?

4 What was unique about Dr John Sentamu's appointment as Archbishop of York in 2005?

5 What is represented by the Latin words '*Citius, Altius, Fortius*', and how do they translate into English? (2 pts)

6 What is the bizarre dance style introduced, originally as satire, by Korean pop star Psy?

7 What milestone was shared by Elton John, David Bowie, Mick Fleetwood of Fleetwood Mac and Meat Loaf in 2012?

8 Which two states share a border with Florida? (2 pts)

9 In which city was the Plymouth Brethren founded by Reverend John N. Darby in 1827? (a) Boston (b) Dublin (c) Plymouth

10 Who headbutted the competition director during the 1986 UK Snooker Championships?

Part 2

11   Who murdered her husband Agamemnon on his return from the siege of Troy, and who was his son who avenged his death? (2 pts)

12   Armistice Day, 11 November, commemorates the end of which conflict?

13   Why would it be wrong to shout 'bravo' after a performance by, say, Maria Callas or Cecilia Bartoli?

14   What is the second largest city in Greece, after Athens?

15   What is the modern word for a phrase, style or action that spreads through a culture from person to person by word of mouth (or, more commonly, by fixation on something received via modern media)?

16   Chris Evans bought his then-wife Billie Piper a Ferrari; why was it a pointless gesture?

17   Who was the author of the 1687 treatise *Principia Mathematica*, one of the most fundamental texts in the development of modern science?

18   Who provided the guitar solo on Michael Jackson's hit single, 'Beat It'? And who did the honours on 'Give in to Me' off the *Dangerous* album? (2 pts)

19   From what post did former US military officer David Petraeus resign in November 2012 after admitting to an extra-marital affair?

20   A fourteen-year-old boy was given a five-match ban by his football league for (a) turning up to a game under the influence of alcohol (b) scoring a goal and revealing a T-shirt saying 'Mr. Shaw [his teacher] wears a wig' (c) when cautioned by the referee he gave his name as Santa Claus?

Total Points: 25. Targets: Novice 13 Pro 19. Your Score:

Quiz 50. Kids' TV

Fourteen straight questions and a *Wacky Races* teaser

Part 1

1 What is the name of the bulldog that beats up Tom in the original *Tom and Jerry* cartoons?

2 For which drama role is Dani Harmer best known? Which author created the character? (2 pts)

3 What is the setting for the US children's sitcom, *The Suite Life of Zack and Cody*? What is the job of Zack and Cody's mum, Carey? (2 pts)

4 What is the name of the life-size fairground doll that provides the 'love interest' in children's drama series *Worzel Gummidge*, and who portrayed her in the series from 1979–81? (2 pts)

5 Who, along with statisticians Ross and Norris McWhirter, was the original presenter of *Record Breakers* when it first aired in 1972? For what else are the McWhirter twins mainly remembered? (2 pts)

6 What are the 'Big Three' network broadcasting channels for children in the US? (3 pts)

7 Who was a presenter on *Blue Peter* from December 1997 to January 2008, comfortably the longest stint of the modern era?

8 Apart from being dogs, what connects Scooby Doo, Astro (from *The Jetsons*) and Muttley?

9 Who fought a constant battle against MAD, led by the evil Dr Claw?

10 Mr Llewellyn, Mrs Keele, Mr McNab, Mr Robson, Mrs Bassinger and Miss Gayle have all held which fictional post?

11 In the classic kids' series, *The Magic Roundabout*, what kinds of creature were Brian and Ermintrude respectively? (2 pts)

12 Who owns a talking backpack and a monkey called Boots?

13 What is Pingu and where does he live? (2 pts)

14 Which anthropomorphic aardvark appeared on TV for the first time in 1996? Who sings the show's theme tune, 'Believe in Yourself'? (2 pts)

Part 2

15 What number was Dick Dastardly's car in *Wacky Races*? Who drove the Compact Pussycat? Which two characters sit in the Arkansas Chuggabug? What is the name of the Ant Hill Mob's car, and how many of them are there, all sitting in the front seat? (6 pts)

Total Points: 29. Targets: Novice 12 Pro 22. Your Score:

Quiz 51. Myths and Legends

Some straight questions and a Nordic teaser

Part 1

1   Who was the son of Jocasta and Laius?

2   Azazel, Seirizzim and Apollyon are alternative names for what?

3   Who is the Hound of Ulster, one of the major figures of Irish legend?

4   A faun is a hybrid between a man and what animal?

5   Helen of Troy was semi-immortal; who was her mortal sister, and who was her lover, favoured by the Goddess Aphrodite, who abducted her and started the Trojan War? (2 pts)

6   Which sailor made seven trips in his vessel according to a famous Middle Eastern folk tale?

7   The Strait of Messina, as it is now known, offered which twin perils when Odysseus encountered it on his way home from Troy? (2 pts)

8   Who was the mother goddess of Egyptian mythology and who was both her husband and brother? (2 pts)

9   Which land, according to mythology, was once ruled by the Tuatha Dé Dannan?

10 Who was the sixth-century bard who played a central role in many of the best-known Welsh myths and legends?

Part 2

11 Who was the god of the vine? (Either the Greek or Roman name is fine.) What race were his loyal followers? (2 pts)

12 Who was the Norman knight often portrayed as the primary accomplice of the Sheriff of Nottingham in versions of the Robin Hood tales?

13 A gryphon (modern spelling 'griffin') is a hybrid of which two fearsome creatures? (2 pts)

14 What is the cannibalistic spirit that features in the mythology of the Algonquin tribes of North America?

15 How many tasks did King Eurystheus give to Heracles at the gods' behest, in punishment for his murder of his own family in a fit of madness? (1 extra point for a bit of detail)

16 Who is the leader of the gods in Norse mythology? With what is he often depicted on his shoulder? Where does he bring half the heroes who fall in battle, and who escort them? For which final confrontation is he preparing them? (5 pts)

Total Points: 26. Targets: Novice 10 Pro 10. Your Score:

Quiz 52. Science

Straightforward quiz. Unlike science, which I have never found straightforward

Part 1

1   Roughly what proportion of their DNA do humans and chimpanzees share: 77 per cent, 92 per cent or 98.5 per cent?

2   In which field did Austrian monk Gregor Mendel's study of plants lead to major breakthroughs?

3   What name is given to a biological process that sets itself naturally to a twenty-four-hour cycle?

4   What was the occupation of the Greek scientist Galen, whose work was at the forefront of thinking in his field for over 1,000 years?

5   E200+ numbers are preservatives and most E400+ numbers are emulsifiers and stabilizers, but what are E100+ numbers?

6   What was the primary objective of the alchemists of the middle ages, whose early experiments with metals and minerals were the forerunner of chemistry?

7   In the classic atom model, do the electrons orbit the nucleus or does the nucleus encase the agitated electrons?

8   Which side of the brain would be mostly used to evaluate whether a new wardrobe fits into the space available in a bedroom?

9   Which scientific theory postulates that subatomic particles are tiny one-dimensional loops?

10 What was the name of the spaceship from which the final lunar landing took place and in which year was it? (2 pts)

Part 2

11   What is the SI unit of thermodynamic temperature?

12   What imperial measurement is equal to 0.028 of a cubic metre?

13   What is the square root of 225?

14   Rayleigh scattering accounts for which everyday phenomenon?

15   Why would someone suffering from trypanophobia have reason to resent Charles Pravaz for his 1835 contribution to medical science?

16   Broca's area in the human brain is responsible for which function?

17   If circle A is placed within a larger circle B, what is the term for the space between the circumference of A and the circumference of B?

18   In Einstein's famous theory E=mc2, what does the 'c' represent?

19   Before Dolly, the cloned sheep, there were Megan and Morag; in what way was Dolly unique?

20   In which three scientific disciplines are Nobel Prizes awarded? (3 pts)

Total Points: 23. Targets: Novice 7 Pro 17. Your Score:

Quiz 53. TV Cops

Mainly straight questions with one multi-parter

Part 1

1   *Elementary* was a 2012 US TV show based around the Sherlock Holmes stories; where is it set and who plays Watson to Jonny Lee Miller's Holmes? (2 pts)

2   What was the name of Bergerac's dodgy ex-father-in-law in the long-running TV series? What is the setting for the series? (2 pts)

3   Who created the fictional detective Adam Dalgliesh, and which two actors have portrayed him on UK TV? (3 pts)

4   Which actress had the *Gentle Touch* between 1980 and 1984?

5   Who is DS James Hathaway and who plays him on TV? (2 pts)

6   Which series (three seasons, cancelled by Fox in 2011) starred Tim Roth as a psychoanalyst helping various law enforcement agencies?

7   Who played Agatha Christie's Marple in 1984–92? And which two actresses have embraced the role in the ITV revivals since 2004? (3 pts)

8   What crime drama was created by Steven Bochco and David Milch and set in a fictional 15th Precinct in Manhattan?

9   Which gritty Scottish drama has been made for thirty years? Which actor's death in 1994 required a change of focus? (2 pts)

10 Who is the BBC's wartime detective, played by Michael Kitchen? What is the role in his team of Samantha Stewart, and who plays her? (3 pts)

Part 2

11 Who was gloriously moustachioed as *Magnum PI* for most of the 1980s?

12 Which series stars amateur sleuth and writer Jessica Fletcher? Who played the role for twelve years, earning a record number of Golden Globe nominations in the process? (2 pts)

13 Who played a pair of gardening sleuths in *Rosemary and Thyme* from 2003 to 2007? (2 pts)

14 Which two historic cases formed the basis of the first two series of *Whitechapel*? (2 pts)

15 Which big screen actor returned to the TV to play the head of a missing persons unit in *Without a Trace* (2002–9)?

16 What are the five spin-offs from the long established US crime show, *Law and Order*, which ran for twenty years before ending in 2010? (5 pts)

Total Points: 33. Targets: Novice 13 Pro 25. Your Score: [   ]

Quiz 54. Sport

Part 1

1 Mike Powell set a world record in which athletics discipline that remains unbroken (as of April 2013)? Whose twenty-three year-old record did he break? (2 pts)

2 The next Rugby World Cup is to be held in England in 2015; where is the tournament after that taking place, the first time it will be hosted by one of the minor rugby powers?

3 The traditional Claret Jug is the trophy awarded to the winner of which annual sporting event?

4 The Amateur Open Championship is a match-play golf tournament. The 1984 final saw an eighteen-year-old Spanish player beat an up-and-coming Scot; who were the players? (2 pts)

5 Aintree hosts the Grand National; which three courses host the Welsh National, the Scottish National and the Irish National? (3 pts)

6 Which Welshman, a former postman and miner, won the world snooker title at the first attempt in 1979?

7 Who was the Austrian-born Luxembourg skier who won a record five World Cup titles between 1985 and 1993?

8 Which US golfer holds the record for most Ladies PGA Major wins (fifteen between 1937 and 1958)?

9 Which great batter and celebrity husband holds the Major League baseball record for most consecutive hits?

10 Which famous American businessman won sailing's America's Cup with *Courageous* in 1977?

Part 2

11   What do Wolverhampton and Warrington have in common?

12   How many minutes does a lacrosse match last? How many players on each side? What is the goal called in lacrosse? (3 pts)

13   Which three rugby league sides did Alex Murphy lead to victory in the Challenge Cup as a player? (3 pts)

14   Which snooker legend also played top-level Aussie Rules Football for a decade, as well as being a champion surfer?

15   Which former Wimbledon champion was ordained as a minister in Perth in 1991?

16   Who was the first President of the Women's Tennis Association, formed in 1973?

17   In which sport did Heather McKay dominate the women's game for two decades in the 1960s and 1970s?

18   What are the four international boxing federations? (4 pts)

19   What is the awkward handicap that snooker player Peter Ebdon has to overcome every time he goes to the table?

20   Kristan Bromley and Shelley Rudman both compete in which sport for Britain? What else is notable about these two athletes? (2 pts)

Total Points: 32. Targets: Novice 13 Pro 24. Your Score:

Quiz 55. Scandals

Tittle-tattle and trivia – fourteen questions and a rather complicated teaser on various public scandals

Part 1

1 Which leading UK politician sued the Move in 1967 when a single portrayed him in bed with a woman who was not his wife? What was the single? (2 pts)

2 Who resigned from the government after admitting an affair with society girl Christine Keeler?

3 Which former politician was cleared of the murder of Norman Scott on 21 June 1979? What position did he hold in British politics? (2 pts)

4 Who conducted the inquiry into the phone-hacking scandal at the News International-owned *News of the World*?

5 Who drove a car off a bridge near Chappaquiddick Island, Massachusetts, in 1969, killing his female passenger, Mary Jo Kopechne?

6 Who was the intern with whom President Bill Clinton had 'improper relations' during his second term in office?

7 Which Labour MP attempted to fake his own death in 1974 amidst the pressure of personal financial ruin?

8 The Westland Affair briefly threatened Margaret Thatcher's government in 1986; who broke ranks and resigned from the cabinet? What did the Westland company manufacture? (2 pts)

9 Who was the alleged lover of Diana, Princess of Wales, involved in the 'Squidgygate' tapes exposed by the media in 1992?

10 What was the insensitive act which buried the career of Labour spin doctor Jo Moore in 2001?

11 Which government scientist was found dead in a field in 2000, giving rise to the Hutton Report?

12 Which newspaper broke open the scandal over MPs' misuse of their expenses system, and in which year did the story break? Whose moat was cleaned at the taxpayers' expense? (3 pts)

13 Which twenty-two year-old actor was the subject of the first widely distributed tape of 'celebrity sex' in 1986?

14 What headline, described by Paddy Ashdown as 'dreadful but brilliant', did the *Sun* dream up when they ran a story about an affair between the former Liberal Democrat leader and his secretary?

Part 2

15   Which three Director-Generals of the BBC have resigned under political and
     media pressure since 1983? (3 pts for the names and 3 pts for the details)

Total Points: 25. Targets: Novice 10 Pro 18. Your Score: _____

Quiz 56. General Knowledge

Back to good old General Knowledge: fifteen straight questions and a teaser

Part 1

1 Which papal name has been used most often? (a) Benedict (b) Pius (c) Clement

2 Crna Gora, the local name for the country we call Montenegro, translates as what?

3 Which specialist hospital for children admitted its first patient in 1852?

4 Antigua is part of which Caribbean island group?

5 Which year saw the first Paralympics held in conjunction with the Olympics?

6 Whose album, *Beacon*, was one of the surprise indie hits in the 2012 album charts?

7 Who is the famous father of furniture designer David Linley?

8 If Mashhad, Isfahan and Tabriz are the second, third and fourth largest cities in this country, what is the biggest?

9 Who was the messenger of God who gifted the Qur'an to Muhammad?

10 Who was the former Wimbledon Men's singles champion humbled by Billie Jean King in a 1973 'Battle of the Sexes' grudge match?

Part 2

11 Emma, Lady Hamilton, who died in 1815, was most famous as the mistress of which historic figure?

12 Who married Michael Douglas in a lavish wedding in New York in 2000?

13 By what name is the military commander Sir Arthur Wellesley best remembered?

14 Which two instruments would properly accompany a flamenco dance? (2 pts)

15 Marc (Soft Cell) Almond, Bob Geldof, Donny Osmond, Sting, Eddie van Halen; who is the oldest and who is the baby of the group? (2 pts)

16 Ellen Johnson Sirleaf became the first democratically elected female leader of which African country in 2005? Who did she beat in the run-off for the Presidency? Where did she attend university? What is the capital city of her country? Where does this city get its name? (5 pts)

Total Points: 22. Targets: Novice 11 Pro 17. Your Score: ☐

Answers Quizzes 49–56

Quiz 49. General Knowledge

1. Ford Consul Cortinas (Ford Cortinas is accepted); 2. Kate Adie; PC Trevor Lock; 3. All sites of cave paintings; 4. He became Britain's first black archbishop; 5. The Olympic motto: 'Faster, Higher, Stronger'; 6. Gangnam; 7. All turned pensionable age at sixty-five; 8. Alabama and Georgia; 9. (b) Dublin; 10. Alex Higgins; 11. Clytemnestra, his wife; Orestes, who killed his mother and was haunted by it afterwards; 12. World War I; 13. Bravo is the masculine form – the done thing is to shout 'brava' to a female singer; 14. Thessaloniki; 15. Meme; 16. She couldn't drive; 17. Isaac Newton; 18. Eddie van Halen; Slash; 19. Director of the CIA (the scandal broke as a result of an FBI investigation – given their rivalry I'm sure the Feds found it all very amusing); 20. (c) he gave his name as Santa Claus (John Terry was banned for four matches for use of the term 'black c***' – compare and contrast)

Quiz 50. Kids' TV

1. Spike; 2. Tracy Beaker; Jacqueline Wilson; 3. The Tipton Hotel in Boston; she is a performer in the hotel nightclub; 4. Aunt Sally; Una Stubbs; 5. Roy Castle; developing *The Guinness Book of Records*; 6. Disney Channel, Nickelodeon and Cartoon Network; 7. Konnie Huq; 8. They were all voiced by the same actor, Don Messick; 9. Inspector Gadget; 10. Head Teacher at Grange Hill; 11. A snail and a cow; 12. Dora the Explorer; 13. He is a penguin and lives at the South Pole (of course he does – where else would a penguin live?); 14. Arthur; Ziggy Marley (and the Melody Makers); 15. Double Zero (00); Penelope Pitstop; Luke and Blubber Bear; the Bulletproof Bomb; and there are seven gangsters

Quiz 51. Myths and Legends

1. Oedipus; 2. The devil in Christian mythology; 3. Cuchulain (various spellings); 4. Goat; 5. Clytemnestra; Paris; 6. Sinbad; 7. Scylla, a monster, and Charybdis, a whirlpool; 8. Isis and Osiris; 9. Ireland; 10. Taliesin; 11. Dionysus (Greek) or Bacchus (Roman); the satyrs; 12. Guy of Gisborne; 13. It has the talons, head and wings of an eagle and the body of a lion; 14. Wendigo; 15. Ten (or twelve if the two for which he received assistance are included); 16. Odin; two ravens (Thought and Memory); Valhalla, the Valkyries; Ragnarok

Quiz 52. Science

1. 98.5 per cent; this statistic, arrived at by King and Wilson, established the rough date of the split between chimps and *Homo sapiens*; 2. Genetics or heredity; 3. Circadian rhythm; 4. A physician (doctor); 5. Colorants; 6. To find or create the Philosopher's Stone; 7. The electrons orbit the nucleus; 8. Right side, which deals with most spatial issues; 9. String theory (not that I fully understood the explanation I was offered);

10. *Apollo 17* in 1972; 11. Kelvin; 12. A cubic foot; 13. Fifteen; 14. The blue appearance of daytime sky and the reddening at night; 15. He invented the hypodermic syringe (trypanophobia is fear of needles or medical procedures involving injection); 16. Speech and articulation; 17. Annulus; 18. The speed of light; 19. She was cloned from an adult cell, whereas Megan and Morag were cloned from embryo cells; 20. Physics, chemistry and physiology or medicine

Quiz 53. TV Cops

1. New York; Lucy Liu; 2. Charlie Hungerford; Jersey; 3. P. D. James; Roy Marsden on ITV and more recently Martin Shaw on the BBC; 4. Jill Gascoigne as DI Maggie Forbes; 5. He is Lewis's sidekick and is played by Laurence Fox; 6. *Lie to Me*; 7. Joan Hickson; Geraldine McEwan and Julia McKenzie; 8. *NYPD Blue*; 9. *Taggart*; Mark McManus; 10. DCS Christopher Foyle (*Foyle's War*); she is Foyle's driver and is played by Honeysuckle Weeks; 11. Tom Selleck; 12. *Murder, She Wrote*; Angela Lansbury; 13. Felicity Kendal and Pam Ferris; 14. Jack the Ripper and the Kray Twins; 15. Anthony LaPaglia; 16. Law and Order: Special Victims Unit, Criminal Intent, Trial by Jury, the UK version, Los Angeles

Quiz 54: Sport

1. Long jump; Bob Beamon; 2. Japan; 3. (British) Open (Golf) Championship; 4. José María Olazábal and Colin Montgomerie; 5. Chepstow, Ayr and Fairyhouse; 6. Terry Griffiths; 7. Marc Girardelli; 8. Patty Berg; 9. Joe Di Maggio, 1941; 10. Ted Turner; 11. Both have teams known as the Wolves (Wolverhampton Wanderers in football and Warrington Wolves in rugby league); 12. Sixty minutes (thirty minutes per half); twelve; pocket; 13. St Helens, Leigh and Warrington; 14. Eddie Charlton; 15. Margaret Court; 16. Billie Jean King; 17. Squash; 18. WBA, WBO, WBC and IBF; 19. He is colour blind; 20. Skeleton (a form of luge); they are married to one another

Quiz 55. Scandals

1. Harold Wilson; 'Flowers in the Rain'; 2. John Profumo; 3. Jeremy Thorpe; Leader of the Liberal Party; 4. Lord Leveson; 5. Edward Kennedy (it ended his hopes of running for President; he was given a two-month suspended sentence for leaving the scene of the crime); 6. Monica Lewinsky; 7. John Stonehouse; 8. Michael Heseltine; helicopters; 9. James Gilbey; 10. She suggested it might be a good time to 'bury' some unwanted bad news at the time of the 9/11 attacks in New York; 11. David Kelly; 12. *Daily Telegraph*; 2009; Douglas Hogg; 13. Rob Lowe; 14. Paddy Pantsdown (in the end everyone emerged rather well; Ashdown beat the *Sun* to the punch and announced the affair himself, his wife remained resolute and his former lover declined to cash in with a newspaper story); 15. Alasdair Milne resigned in 1987 as Margaret Thatcher's government tried to bring the corporation to heel; Greg Dyke resigned in 2003 in the wake of the conduct of BBC

journalists exposed by the Hutton Enquiry (Dyke was not directly involved); George Entwistle resigned in 2012 over the failure to screen a Jimmy Savile exposé and an erroneous accusation of wrongdoing aimed at a political grandee

Quiz 56. General Knowledge

1. (a) Benedict (sixteen times, compared to fourteen for Clement and twelve for Pius); 2. Black Mountain, same as Montenegro in Venetian; 3. Great Ormond Street; 4. Leeward Islands; 5. 1960 in Rome; 6. Two Door Cinema Club; 7. Lord Snowdon, the photographer; 8. The country is Iran, so the answer is Tehran; 9. Archangel Gabriel; 10. Bobby Riggs; 11. Horatio, Admiral Lord Nelson; 12. Catherine Zeta-Jones; 13. He became the Duke of Wellington, who was a prime mover in the defeat of Napoleon; 14. Guitar and castanets; 15. Sting sneaks it as the oldest, by three days from Sir Bob, while Marc Almond is the office junior, two years younger than Eddie and Donny; 16. Liberia; former footballer George Weah; Harvard, US; Monrovia; named after James Monroe, fifth President of the US (Liberia began as a colony of freed American slaves, who adopted a US-style democracy as their political framework in the nineteenth century

Quiz 57. General Knowledge

Johnny This and That round – a mixed bag of twenty questions all with a theme, know what I mean, John?

Part 1

1 Who became President of the United States by default when Kennedy was assassinated?

2 Who wrote and recorded the original version of 'Johnny B. Goode'?

3 Which two Johans were the inspirational players in the Netherlands side which reached the 1974 World Cup final? (2 pts)

4 'Jean Genie', released November 1972 and a no. 2 hit in the UK, was the lead single from which David Bowie album, released the following year?

5 Under what name was Scarlett Johansson born in November 1984?

6 Who wrote the *Earth's Children* series of novels, beginning with *Clan of the Cave Bear* (1980)?

7 Which French philosopher and novelist and all-round twentieth-century misery guts hypothesized that hell is other people?

8 In which story is Jean Valjean the main protagonist? Who wrote the novel? (2 pts)

9 Who is the only man to have both ridden and trained 100 winners in a National Hunt season?

10 Who carded a 63, the lowest final round to win a major, when he won the 1973 US Open after starting last day in twelfth place?

Part 2

11 In his lifetime Johann Sebastian Bach was recognized less as a composer but regarded highly as a practitioner of which instrument?

12 What position did Barry John play for Wales and the Lions before his surprise retirement in 1972, only twenty-seven years old?

13 The 1968 album *Gris Gris*, a trippy blues-Cajun hybrid, was the work of which artist, born Malcolm 'Mac' Rebennack in 1940?

14 Who played mountain man Jeremiah Johnson in the 1972 film directed by Sydney Pollack?

15 Chelsea and England centre-half John Terry has played for the club all his career except for six matches on loan to which club as a youngster? (a) Millwall (b) West Ham (c) Nottingham Forest

16 Juan Carlos I became King of Spain officially in 1975, two days after whose death?

17 Who proved a bad buy at £28.1 million for Manchester United in 2001, and a worse one for £15 million for Chelsea two years later?

18 What epithets were accorded the Russian rulers Ivan III and Ivan IV? What relation were they to each other? (3 pts)

19 What was the title of Mozart's opera first performed in 1787 about a legendary fictional seducer?

20 Jean Grey is a fictional character who features in which series of graphic novels and films?

Total Points: 24. Targets: Novice 12 Pro 18. Your Score:

Quiz 58. Action Heroes

Simply identify who played these kick-ass roles

Part 1

1 John McClane in *Die Hard* (1988)
2 The Bride in *Kill Bill* (2003)
3 Rambo in *First Blood* (1982)
4 Jason Bourne in *The Bourne Identity* (2002)
5 Max in *Mad Max* (1979)
6 Casey Ryback in *Under Siege* (1992)
7 James Bond in *Goldeneye* (1995)
8 Sonja in *Red Sonja* (1985)
9 Neo in *The Matrix* (1999)
10 James Bond in *Live and Let Die* (1973)

Part 2

11 Hit Girl in *Kick-Ass* (2010)
12 Xander Cage in *xXx* (2002)
13 Samantha Caine/Charly Baltimore in *The Long Kiss Goodnight* (1996)
14 Jason Bourne in *The Bourne Legacy* (2012)

Part 3

15 Robin Hood in *Robin Hood* (1922), *The Adventures of Robin Hood* (1938), *Robin and Marian* (1976), *Robin Hood: Prince of Thieves* (1991), *Robin Hood: Men in Tights* (1993) and *Robin Hood* (2010) (6 pts)

Total Points: 20. Targets: Novice 8 Pro 15. Your Score:

Quiz 59. Astronomy

More science, this time spacey-wacey, timey-wimey stuff, as Doctor Who once called it. Just fifteen straight questions for you to get wrong this time

1   If earth is 1 Astronomical Unit away from the sun, roughly how many AUs away is Neptune?

2   What was Cape Canaveral in Florida called between 1963 and 1973?

3   Which dormant volcano in Hawaii houses a number of astronomical devices and telescopes?

4   In 1965, Cosmonaut Alexei Leonov became the first man to do what?

5   How many moons does the planet Mars have?

6   What was the name of the Soviet space shuttle launched in February 1986?

7   Which factual TV programme has had the longest run with a single presenter; and who was the presenter? (2 pts)

8   Who was launched into space aboard the Russian satellite *Sputnik II*?

9   Who continued Newton's exploratory work into the paths of comets around the turn of the seventeenth century?

10 What was the name of the first US station, launched by NASA in 1973?

11 In 1990 the shuttle *Discovery* was launched into space with what famous piece of equipment aboard?

12 What is the earth's only planetary satellite?

13 Sinus Iridum sounds rather prosaic, but this lunar feature has which more romantic English name?

14 In which city was Mission Control for the *Apollo* moon landings based?

15 *Luna 3* (1959) was launched by the Soviet Space programme and brought back the first pictures of what celestial vista?

Total Points: 16. Targets: Novice 6 Pro 12. Your Score:

Quiz 60. Religion

Belief systems of different denominations: some straight, some probably veering towards heretical (let's face it, one believer's religion is de facto another's heresy)

Part 1

1   Who was the founder of the Franciscan order of monks? In which month is his feast day? (2 pts)

2   What is the principal religion of Hungary?

3   The Temple of the Tooth (Kandy, Sri Lanka) claims to house which legendary dental relic?

4   In which modern-day country was Mother Teresa born? (a) India (b) Macedonia (c) Montenegro

5   Who was the first Christian martyr, stoned to death in *c*.AD 35? (a) St Dunstan (b) St Asaph (c) St Stephen

6   Who became the first black leader of the Anglican Church in South Africa in 1986?

7   Who, in biblical mythology, is the leader of the angels and the armies of heaven?

8   Which religious leader made a first visit to Britain in 1973?

9   Also known as Twelfth Night, what Christian festival is celebrated on 6 January?

10 What proportion of the world's Islamic worshippers are Sunni Muslims: 59 per cent, 70 per cent or 84 per cent? What other sect allows for nearly 90 per cent of the balance? (2 pts)

Part 2

11   What name is given to an Islamic group involved in a jihad or struggle?

12   Which is the only gospel to recount the tale of the Three Wise Men visiting the baby Jesus?

13   Which famous actress converted to Judaism in 1959 (aged twenty-seven) after being brought up as a Christian Scientist?

14   At what age do girls and boys reach bar mitzvah in Judaism? (2 pts)

15   Córdoba (Argentina), St Trinidad de Paraná (Paraguay), Chiquitos (Bolivia) and Santa María la Mayor (Argentina) are all evidence of the influx of which religious order to South America in the sixteenth century?

16   The Veda is the world's oldest scripture; to adherents of which religion is it sacred?

17   Although the Christian Orthodox Church has no official senior leader, the prelate of which See is unofficially regarded as first amongst equals, due to the See's position in the establishment of the faith?

18   Whose story is told in Genesis 4:1 to 4:16?

19   Noah, Jacob, Samson, Jonah; which of these biblical characters is not also considered an Islamic prophet?

20   Who led the Israelites at the Battle of Jericho? In which territory did the city lie? (2 pts)

Total Points: 24. Targets: Novice 10 Pro 18. Your Score:

Quiz 61. Bestselling Books

Twenty straight questions on books that hit the charts

Part 1

1   Which author created the action hero Dirk Pitt?

2   *The Host* was the first adult novel by which bestselling author for older children?

3   Lisbeth and Blomqvist are the main protagonists in which bestselling Scandinavian thriller?

4   What was John Grisham's profession before he became a bestselling writer?

5   Which author, best known for children's books, wrote *And Another Thing*, part six of *A Hitchhiker's Guide to the Galaxy*?

6   In which classic popular novel of the 1960s, one of the pioneering pieces of sex-and-shopping fiction, does Neely flush her rival's wig down the toilet? Who was the author? (2 pts)

7   What was Tracey Chevalier's second novel?

8   *The Da Vinci Code* (2003) was the book that made Dan Brown a multi-million-selling novelist, but what was the book, published three years earlier, that first featured the symbologist Robert Langdon?

9   *The Guns of Navarone* and *Ice Station Zebra* are amongst the bestsellers written by which adventure writer, at his peak in the 1960s and 1970s?

10   What was Colleen McCullough's 1977 bestseller that became a hugely successful TV mini-series six years later?

Part 2

11   Who adapted his own spy thriller *Restless* for the BBC dramatization in 2012?

12   *The Knife of Never Letting Go* is the first in which sci-fi trilogy for older kids (and adults as the themes are serious and the narrative complex)? Who wrote the books? (2 pts)

13   Who went *Behind the Scenes at the Museum* for her prize-winning 1995 debut? What is the name of the private investigator who is the main protagonist in four later – highly successful – novels? (2 pts)

14   Which MP wrote the 1994 bestseller *A Parliamentary Affair*, a mildly ironic title considering she conducted one with a former Prime Minister?

15   What connects Kay Scarpetta and Richard Sharpe?

16   Who made his commercial breakthrough with *The Lost Continent: Travels in Small-Town America*? What was his book about travelling through Britain, published six years later in 1995? (2 pts)

17   Who had her first novel published in 1983, aged seventy-one, and followed it the next year with the hugely successful *The Camomile Lawn*?

18   The film *The Running Man* was based on a novel by Richard Bachman; who is Richard Bachman?

19   Who wrote *The Thirty-Nine Steps* and a host of other buccaneering boys' own adventures in the first half of the twentieth century?

20   Who published his first novel, *Waverley*, anonymously in 1814, and continued that anonymity for a number of years, despite being the first British novelist to enjoy an international reputation?

Total Points: 24. Targets: Novice 10 Pro 18. Your Score: [   ]

Quiz 62. Boxing

Fifteen straight questions and one multi-parter on the noble art

Part 1

1   Which boxing trainer, who died in 2012, trained a record forty-one world champion fighters?

2   Who beat Lennox Lewis in 1994, a fight which caused Lewis to re-evaluate his career and step on to become world champion?

3   If the Bronx Bull fought the Brown Bomber in a fantasy boxing match, who would be in the ring? (2 pts)

4   Who, in 1956, was the youngest fighter to become heavyweight champion of the world?

5   Who flew into London Olympia on a 'magic carpet' to fight Vuyani Bungu in 2000?

6   Which German boxer did Joe Louis defeat in a politically laden heavy-weight contest in 1938?

7   Who beat John L. Sullivan to win the world heavyweight championship in 1892?

8   Whose career as a heavyweight saw him retire unbeaten with a 49–0 count in his favour?

9   Which middleweight boxer was imprisoned in 1966 on a questionable charge of murder?

10 Which heavyweight boxer broke Muhammad Ali's jaw in a 1973 fight in San Diego?

11 What is the name of Rocky's trainer in the *Rocky* movies?

12 Which relative novice became world heavyweight champion when he outpointed Muhammad Ali in 1978? Who beat him for the WBA title later the same year? (2 pts)

13 By what nickname was Thomas Hearns most commonly known in boxing circles?

14 Which great boxer did Sugar Ray Leonard defeat in 1987 to win the world middleweight title after a three-and-a-half year retirement?

15 How many rounds did Mike Tyson take to finish off Frank Bruno in Las Vegas in 1989?

Part 2

16 Who fought the Rumble in the Jungle in 1974? In which country did the fight take place? Who was the promoter whose efforts brought the two fighters together? How many rounds did the fight last? (5 pts)

Total Points: 22. Targets: Novice 9 Pro 17. Your Score:

Quiz 63. Alter Egos

A straight quiz about people who use pen-names, initials or names other than their own

Part 1

1 By what name was Martha Jane Canary-Burke better known in America?

2 What was artist L. S. Lowry's full name? (a) Lawrence Stephen Lowry (b) Lionel St John Lowry (c) Lancelot Sheridan Lowry

3 Gordon is actually Gordon Brown's second given name; what is his first? (a) James (b) Angus or (c) Gavin?

4 Under what name did Richard Hope-Weston work as a deep-voiced Radio 1 DJ with a penchant for hard rock?

5 Kathleen Brien, born in Peckham 1989, is better known by which moniker?

6 By what name was Margaretha 'Margreet' Zelle, executed by the French in 1917, better known?

7 What name did Walker Smith Jr adopt on account of his sweet right hand?

8 Angelo Siciliano, a Sicilian-born US citizen, changed his name to what in 1922, in order to market his body-building programme? What was the name of the programme, which was used and endorsed by many champion boxers and weightlifters including Rocky Marciano? (2 pts)

9 If William Cody had a fantasy shoot-out with Henry McCarty, who would we be watching? (2 pts)

10 Bette Davis had a long-running feud with Lucille LeSueur, better known as whom?

Part 2

11   Cathleen Collins, as she was born, got 'ten' times the attention under which acting and modelling name?

12   What connects Eric Bana, Mark Ruffalo and Givanildo Vieira de Souza?

13   Who was the 'crazy' country singer, born Virginia Hensley, who died, aged only thirty, in 1963?

14   Which media mogul was born Jan Ludwig Hoch in the Czech Republic in 1923?

15   Under what name did Alecia Moore release her debut album *Can't Take Me Home* in 1999?

16   Under what name did Ellen June Hovick become famous for taking her clothes off?

17   Amandine Dudevant and Mary Ann Evans both wrote using the same man's first name; what were their pseudonyms? (2 pts)

18   Joyce Frankenberg became a Bond girl using which name, borrowed from one of Henry VIII's wives?

19   Under what name did Samuel Langhorne Clemens become a revered American literary figure?

20   Chester Burnett became a blues legend under what apposite name?

Total Points: 23. Targets: Novice 12 Pro 18. Your Score:

Quiz 64. General Knowledge

Mixed Bag again – fifteen straight questions and a teaser

Part 1

1   *The Fellowship of the Ring* was only the second highest grossing film of 2001; it was eclipsed by the start of which other film franchise?

2   Who was set free in 1991 after five years in captivity in the Lebanon?

3   The *Harrisburg Examiner* conducted the first what during the 1824 US Presidential election?

4   The world's largest castle is found in which European city, a popular tourist destination?

5   Where in London were the 1908 Olympic Games held?

6   Who, in 2012, got the sack just after delivering the ultimate prize to his employers?

7   Who is the politician mother of pop singer Jess Mills?

8   What is the second biggest city in Pakistan and the capital of the Punjab territory?

9   If the Black Monks are the Benedictines, who are the White Monks?

10   Which phrase came into the sporting lexicon from Brad Gilbert's 1993 account of how he used mental strength and discipline to beat more talented opponents?

Part 2

11   If it was Ink-Butter-Monkey in World War I, what would it be today? (3 pts)

12   In which city did gas escape from a Union Carbide plant and kill 2,000 people (as well as poisoning countless others) in 1984?

13   Girondins is a name given to inhabitants of which French city, which stands at the estuary known as La Gironde, where the rivers Garonne and Dordogne both spill into the sea?

14   Which Australian author has twice won the Booker Prize, most recently with *The True History of the Kelly Gang*?

15   Hanna-Barbera Productions was established in 1957; under whose auspices was William Hanna and Joseph Barbera's earlier work produced? (a) Disney (b) MGM (c) Warner Brothers

16   What was Richard O'Brien's 1975 musical, which opened at the Royal Court Theatre Upstairs in 1973 and became a global cult? Which part did O'Brien himself play in the movie of the show? Which song from the show became a party dance classic? What was the less successful 1981 follow-up, made directly as a movie? Which TV show did O'Brien present in 1990–93? (5 pts)

Total Points: 22. Targets: Novice 11 Pro 17. Your Score:

Answers Quizzes 57–64

Quiz 57. General Knowledge

1. Lyndon B. Johnson; 2. Chuck Berry; 3. Cruyff and Neeskens; 4. *Aladdin Sane*; 5. Scarlett Johansson (this is *not* a typo, though they no doubt appear elsewhere in the book); 6. Jean M. Auel; 7. Jean-Paul Sartre; 8. *Les Misérables* by Victor Hugo; 9. Jonjo O'Neill; 10. Johnny Miller; 11. The organ; 12. Fly-half (or outside half; no. 10); 13. Dr John (bonus point for Dr John the Night Tripper); 14. Robert Redford; 15. (c) Nottingham Forest – he was on West Ham's books as a kid but never played for the first team; 16. General Franco; 17. Juan Sebastián Verón; 18. The Great and The Terrible; grandfather/grandson; 19. *Don Giovanni*; 20. *X-Men*; she is the empath played by Famke Janssen in the movie series

Quiz 58. Action Heroes

1. Bruce Willis; 2. Uma Thurman; 3. Sylvester Stallone; 4. Matt Damon; 5. Mel Gibson; 6. Steven Seagal; 7. Pierce Brosnan; 8. Brigitte Nielsen; 9. Keanu Reeves; 10. Roger Moore; 11. Chloë Grace Moretz; 12. Vin Diesel; 13. Geena Davis; 14. Jeremy Renner; 15. Douglas Fairbanks; Errol Flynn; Sean Connery; Kevin Costner; Cary Elwes; Russell Crowe

Quiz 59. Astronomy

1. 30 (30.06 to be precise); 2. Cape Kennedy; 3. Mauna Kea; 4. Spacewalk; 5. Two; 6. *Mir*; 7. *The Sky at Night*; Patrick Moore; 8. Laika, a dog; 9. Edmund Halley; 10. *Skylab*; 11. Hubble Telescope; 12. The moon; 13. Bay of Rainbows; 14. Houston, TX; 15. Images of the far side of the moon

Quiz 60. Religion

1. St Francis of Assisi; October; 2. Roman Catholic; 3. The left canine tooth of Buddha; 4. Macedonia; 5. (c) St Stephen; 6. Archbishop Desmond Tutu; 7. Michael; 8. Dalai Lama; 9. Epiphany; 10. About 84 per cent of the Muslim world is Sunni; Shi'ite; 11. Mujahideen; 12. Matthew; 13. Elizabeth Taylor; 14. Twelve (girls) and thirteen (boys); 15. Jesuit Brotherhood; 16. Hinduism; 17. Patriarch of Constantinople; 18. Cain and Abel; 19. Samson; 20. Joshua; Canaan

Quiz 61. Bestselling Books

1. Clive Cussler; 2. Stephenie Meyer; 3. Stieg Larsson's *The Girl Who Played with Fire*; 4. A lawyer (unsurprising, given the subject matter of his books); 5. Eoin Colfer; 6. *Valley of the Dolls* by Jacqueline Susann; 7. *Girl with a Pearl Earring*; 8. *Angels and Demons*; 9. Alistair MacLean; 10. *The Thorn Birds*; 11. William Boyd; 12. *Chaos Walking*; Patrick Ness; 13. Kate Atkinson; Jackson Brodie; 14. Edwina Currie; 15. Cornwell; Patricia writes the Scarpetta forensic crime books, while Bernard created the nineteenth century military

hero Sharpe; 16. Bill Bryson; *Notes from a Small Island*; 17. Mary Wesley; 18. Stephen King; 19. John Buchan; 20. Walter Scott (Scott did not wish to compromise his reputation as a premier poet by being associated with popular novels)

Quiz 62. Boxing

1. Manny Steward; 2. Oliver McCall; 3. Jake La Motta and Joe Louis; 4. Floyd Paterson; 5. Naseem Hamed; 6. Max Schmeling; 7. 'Gentleman' Jim Corbett; 8. Rocky Marciano; 9. Rubin Carter; 10. Ken Norton; 11. Mickey Goldmill; 12. Leon Spinks; Ali in a re-match; 13. 'The Hitman' Hearns; 14. Marvin Hagler; 15. Five; 16. Muhammad Ali and George Foreman; Zaire (now Democratic Republic of Congo); Don King; Ali knocked out Foreman in the eighth round

Quiz 63. Alter Egos

1. Calamity Jane; 2. (a) the most prosaic of the three – he was Lawrence Stephen (life would have been tough in Salford with a name like Lancelot Sheridan); 3. James; 4. Tommy Vance; 5. Katy B; 6. Mata Hari; 7. Sugar Ray Robinson; 8. Charles Atlas; dynamic tension; 9. Buffalo Bill v. Billy the Kid; 10. Joan Crawford; 11. Bo Derek; 12. The Hulk (Bana and Ruffalo have both played him in movies whilst de Souza plays football under the name Hulk); 13. Patsy Cline; 14. Robert Maxwell; 15. P!nk; 16. Gypsy Rose Lee; 17. George; George Sand and George Eliot; 18. Jane Seymour; 19. Mark Twain; 20. Howlin' Wolf – although Chester Burnett would have made a darned fine blues name in itself

Quiz 64. General Knowledge

1. Harry Potter; 2. John McCarthy; 3. Opinion poll; 4. Prague; 5. White City; 6. Roberto Di Matteo, fired as Chelsea manager six months after they won the Champions League; 7. Tessa Jowell; 8. Lahore; 9. Cistercians; 10. Winning ugly; 11. India-Bravo-Mike; 12. Bhopal; 13. Bordeaux; 14. Peter Carey; 15. (b) MGM (they had already made the classic Tom and Jerry shorts, and formed their own studio, with Columbia's backing, after MGM closed down its animation division); 16. *The Rocky Horror Show*; Riff-raff; 'Time Warp'; *Shock Treatment*; *The Crystal Maze*

Quiz 65. General Knowledge

Ten simple questions and a knotty section to finish

Part 1

1   What was Howard Shore's contribution to *The Lord of the Rings* film trilogy?
2   Which famous university was founded in New Haven, Connecticut, in 1701?
3   What political party was founded in Dublin by Arthur Griffith in 1905?
4   What are the two races in Rwanda, whose old enmity has caused so much suffering? (2 pts)
5   What do the five rings of the Olympic movement symbolize?
6   Grafton. Chandos. Sanders. Janssen. What are we babbling about?
7   What did Vivienne Westwood forget when she went to Buckingham Palace to collect her OBE?
8   Who, at the 2008 MTV awards, described George W. Bush, then US President, as 'retarded' and said if he were in England, Bush 'wouldn't be trusted with the scissors'?
9   Who is the other great Tibetan Lama alongside the Dalai Lama?
10 Who was the first female sportsperson to earn over $100,000 in a year or season?

Part 2

Solve some or all of the first five clues and work out the connection . . .
11 Who played rock star Jim Morrison in the movie about the Doors?
12 Who played a fictional singer bearing a remarkable similarity to David Bowie in *Velvet Goldmine*?
13 Who played a serial killer in a car in Tarantino's Grindhouse movie, *Death Proof*?
14 What was the album Paul Simon made in South Africa with assorted African session musicians including Ladysmith Black Mambazo?
15 Who starred as Jack Singer in the 1992 romantic comedy *Honeymoon in Vegas*?
16 What's the connection linking the answers to Part 2? (5 pts according to the amount of detail given)

Total Points: 21. Targets: Novice 11 Pro 16. Your Score: ▢

Quiz 66. Movies

All you have to do is make the connection between the different parts of the clue (sorry, that makes it sound easy – it isn't)

Part 1

1 Roberto Rossellini and *The Big Sleep*
2 *Apocalypse Now* and *Lost in Translation*
3 The film noir classics *The Postman Always Rings Twice* and *Double Indemnity*.
4 Amy Heckerling's *Clueless* (1995) and Ron Howard's *Moonstruck* (1987)
5 Franklin J. Schaffner (classic, 1968) and Tim Burton (turkey, 2001)
6 Fay Wray (1933); Jessica Lange (1976); Naomi Watts (2005)
7 Academy Award nominated films *Amadeus* and *Sleuth*
8 Hitchcock's *The Birds* and Roeg's *Don't Look Now*
9 Henry Travers in *It's a Wonderful Life* and Cary Grant in *The Bishop's Wife*
10 Dick Powell (1944) and Robert Mitchum (1975)

Part 2

11 Jim Carrey, Pamela Anderson, Michael J. Fox and Neve Campbell
12 *Buffy the Vampire Slayer* and *The Avengers*
13 *Halloween* and *Psycho*
14 *CSI: Las Vegas* and Hannibal Lecter
15 The 2012 films *Untouchable, Rust and Bone* and *The Sessions*
16 Joy Division and Jack Kerouac
17 Robert De Niro in a 1980 Scorsese boxing movie and Renée Zellweger in a 2001 box office smash-hit chick-flick
18 Robbie Coltrane in 1990 to Shirley MacLaine in 1969 to Whoopie Goldberg in 1992 to Deborah Kerr in 1947
19 Alain Delon in 1960, Matt Damon in 1999 and John Malkovich in 2002
20 *The Piano, From Here to Eternity* and *Chariots of Fire*

Total Points: 20. Targets: Novice 10 Pro 15. Your Score:

Quiz 67. Backing Bands

Easy-peasy, we give you a backing group, you tell us who's the one with their name at the top of the posters

1 The Dap-Kings
2 The Machine
3 The Dakotas
4 The Diamonds
5 The Mothers of Invention
6 E-Street Band
7 The Shadows
8 The Crickets
9 The Attractions
10 Crazy Horse
11 The Banshees
12 The Vandellas
13 The Range
14 The Imposters
15 The Bad Seeds
16 The High Flying Birds
17 The Bunnymen
18 The Magnetic Zeros
19 The Heartbreakers
20 The Maytals

Total Points: 20. Targets: Novice 8 Pro 15. Your Score:

Quiz 68. Geography

Ten straight questions on demographics and directions and a few that need multiple answers

Part 1

1 Name the four countries bordering Greece (although Greece will not recognize the name of one of them). (4 pts)
2 Which is the most northerly of these eastern seaside towns: Scarborough, Bridlington, Hartlepool or Redcar?
3 Which is the furthest west: Exmoor, Bodmin Moor or Dartmoor?
4 Which is the greater land mass: Iran, Mongolia or Kazakhstan?
5 Afghanistan, Nepal, Uzbekistan, Bangladesh; which of these is not entirely landlocked?
6 Which is the most northerly major Russian city, situated to the northwest of the country?
7 Which is closest to New York: Washington DC, Philadelphia or Boston?
8 What connects Gabon, Uganda, Indonesia, Ecuador and Brazil?
9 Which is furthest north: Gloucester, Worcester or Leicester?
10 Which is furthest north: Kidderminster, Leicester, Norwich or Aberystwyth?

Part 2

Multi-parters (remember, only five answers can be given, no grape shot)
11 Name the five countries that border Ethiopia. (5 pts)
12 Romania has five neighbours; name them. (5 pts)
13 Laos is bordered by which five other Asian countries? (5 pts)

Total Points: 28. Targets: Novice 11 Pro 21. Your Score: [   ]

Quiz 69. US Politics

Twenty questions on the mass of contradictions that is the United states (some are quite contemporary, more current affairs than history)

Part 1

1   In 1997, who was sworn in as the United States first female Secretary of State?

2   What did Anna Chapman (New York), Richard and Cynthia Murphy (New Jersey) and Michael Zottoloi (Seattle) have in common?

3   Who made a speech in West Virginia in 1950 that prompted the anti-communist witch-hunt in the US?

4   Where did US-sponsored rebels land in an attempt to overthrow Fidel Castro in 1961?

5   Who was the outspoken leader of the US Teamsters Union who went missing in 1975?

6   Which former US Civil War general was voted in as President in 1869 and served for two terms until 1877?

7   In which state was Barack Obama born? And in which state was he a Senator from 2005 to 2008? (2 pts)

8   True or false: apart from George W. Bush, all the US Presidents since 1974 have been left-handed?

9   Which US President initiated the policy of detente (a peaceful stand-off with the Soviet Union rather than the outright hostility of the cold war) and also ended US involvement in the Vietnam War?

10   How many seats are there in the US House of Representatives: 365, 435 or 520?

Part 2

11 Which two former Presidential candidates still have seats in the US Senate (at the end of 2012)? (2 pts)

12 Who succeeded Abraham Lincoln as US President after his assassination in 1865?

13 Whose death in the middle of a fourth term in the twentieth century prompted the Twenty-Second Amendment which restricted Presidents to two terms in office?

14 Which Democrat, in 1893, was the first and only US President to return to office after being voted out four years previously?

15 What scuppered the presidency of Herbert Hoover only months after he took office in 1929?

16 Which US President presented the country with a New Deal, incorporating labour groups, ethnic groups and liberal intellectuals as legitimate parts of a Democratic coalition alongside traditional white-collar supporters?

17 Who was Governor of California in 1967–75? Who served in that post from 1975–83 and, most unusually, returned to the office in 2011? Which adopted US citizen did he succeed in 2011? (3 pts)

18 Who was the industrialist who stood as an independent against both Bush Sr and Clinton in 1992, with a former admiral, James Stockdale, as his Vice Presidential nomination?

19 What name was given to the 1922–3 scandal whereby federal oil reserves were sold off for personal gain by the Secretary of the Interior, Albert Fall? Who was President at the time? (2 pts)

20 What was the name of the motorist beaten by police in 1992, an event which precipitated the Los Angeles riots?

Total Points: 25. Targets: Novice 10 Pro 19. Your Score:

Quiz 70. Football

Twenty (sort of) straightforward questions on the Beautiful Game (ha!)

Part 1

1   Which all-time-great was one of two players to receive a red card when the system was first introduced in 1976? Which Hull City player was the other, less well-known recipient? (2 pts)

2   Who scored both goals in the final as Manchester United lifted Alex Ferguson's first European trophy in 1991? Who were their opponents? Which European club did the scorer later join? (3 pts)

3   Who had the last laugh after being sacked by Preston North End in December 2010 and how? (2 pts)

4   Who was banned from European fixtures for headbutting Tottenham coach Joe Jordan in a heated Champions League fixture in 2011?

5   He played in the French Cup final for Nantes in 2000, scoring twice, then had spells at Lens, Newcastle, Manchester City and Wigan Athletic; who is he?

6   When the survivors of the 1958 Munich air crash travelled by plane next, it was to play for United against Milan in the semi-final of the European Cup; how were they greeted by the Milan supporters?

7   For which five Premier League clubs has Nicolas Anelka plied his trade? (5 pts)

8   Who was the last English striker to be Premier League top scorer, in 1999–2000? (Tip: it wasn't Alan Shearer.) Which club was this striker playing for that season? (2 pts)

9   What connects Henning Berg, Kolo Touré, Nicolas Anelka and Gaël Clichy? Which two players are missing from this exclusive list? (3 pts)

10 What do Joey Beauchamp, David Unsworth and Didi Hamann have in common? (2 points for a bit of explanation)

Part 2

11   Who won two FA Cups at the beginning of the last century, winning the two matches by an aggregate score of 10–0?

12   Which Scottish side joined the Scottish League in 2002, climbed quickly to the Scottish Premier League, reached the Scottish Cup final, then promptly went into liquidation when their sugar daddy withdrew support?

13   Prior to 2012–13, when it has to happen again, who were the only Scottish club to finish in the top two of the SPL apart from Celtic and Rangers?

14   Who were the first non-Premier League side for twenty-three years to knock Manchester United out of the FA Cup in 2010? Who scored the only goal of the game? (2 pts)

15   What connects Rotherham United in 1961 and Bradford City in 2012?

16   Which four current players (as of January 2013) have scored over fifty goals for their country? (Hint: all are nearing the end of their careers.) (4 pts)

17   With which Dutch club was Ruud Gullit playing before his move to AC Milan in 1987?

18   Who captained the Wales side against England aged only twenty in 2011?

19   Whilst Spurs bought Ardiles and Villa after the 1978 World Cup, Birmingham City invested less successfully in which of their compatriots? (He even started a fight with one of their own fans!)

20   Who are the top two scorers (by a huge distance) in the history of the SPL? (2 pts)

Total Points: 37. Targets: Novice 15 Pro 28. Your Score: [   ]

Quiz 71. Costume Drama

A mix of questions on big and small screen trips back in time

Part 1

1 Which screen legend made an appearance as Martha Levinson, Hugh Bonneville's mother-in-law, in *Downton Abbey*?

2 In which language was the 1976 Derek Jarman film *Sebastiane* recorded?

3 What was the name of Martin Scorsese's film about the violent underworld in New York during the US Civil War? What was the name of Daniel Day-Lewis's fearsome character? (2 pts)

4 What is the setting for David Lean's 1965 epic *Dr Zhivago*?

5 The cast included Judi Dench, Michael Gambon, Francesca Annis, Alex Jennings, Imelda Staunton and Julia Sawalha; what was the classic TV series? From whose novels was it adapted? (2 pts)

6 *Pride and Prejudice* (1995); *The Way We Live Now* (2001); *North and South* (2004); *Little Dorrit* (2008); which of these was not adapted for TV by Andrew Davies?

7 Which 1967 TV series, shown in twenty-six parts, is regarded as having paved the way for the Sunday evening costume drama?

8 Who directed the lengthy 2004 film about the life of Alexander the Great with Colin Farrell in the title role? And who starred in an earlier 1956 version of Alexander's story? (2 pts)

9 Cornwall provided the setting for which popular 1970s TV drama? And who adapted the work from his own novels? (2 pts)

10 What crimes is Johnny Depp's character investigating in the 2001 Victorian melodrama *From Hell*?

Part 2

Two multi-part questions to finish

11   Who plays Lucy's (Helena Bonham Carter) aunt-cum-chaperone, Charlotte, in *A Room with a View* (1985)? The virtues of which range of guide books does she readily extol? Who does she witness kissing Lucy? Who plays the clergyman to whom Lucy is forcibly engaged? In which city do the final romantic scenes take place? (5 pts)

12   In the 1970s Edward Fox played King Edward VIII in *Edward and Mrs Simpson*, a much-praised TV drama. Who played Wallis? And which two actors played Edward in *The King's Speech* and in Madonna's 2012 movie version, *W.E.*? Which part did Edward Fox play in *W.E.*? And who was Wallis Simpson in this version? (5 pts)

Total Points: 24. Targets: Novice 10 Pro 18. Your Score:

Quiz 72. General Knowledge

Another potpourri to stretch the mind and the memory

Part 1

1　Where are we most likely to encounter the skin irritant capsaicin?

2　Where is Sir Christopher Wren, the architect of St Paul's Cathedral, buried?

3　For what is Sheikh Mansour bin Zayed Al Nahyan best known in the UK?

4　What change to the postal service was initiated in 1968? (a) first and second class (b) franking for business mail (c) automated sorting

5　Which has the longer distance as a recorded men's world record: the discus or the hammer?

6　Which venerable American newsman disappeared off the networks after he failed to substantiate a 'scoop' about President George W. Bush's Army record?

7　According to George MacDonald Fraser's comic historical novel, *Flashman at the Charge*, what precipitates the reckless charge towards the Russian cannon? (a) the tearing of a pair of trousers (b) a fart (c) a champagne bottle uncorking

8　Angers, Blois, Nantes, Orléans and Saumur all lie on which French river?

9　Which Archbishop of Canterbury drew up the *Book of Common Prayer*?

10　*Open* was a controversial and bestselling 2009 autobiography by which major American sportsman?

Part 2

11 What was the name of the supergroup formed by Bob Dylan, George Harrison, Jeff Lynne, Roy Orbison and Tom Petty? What role did Jim Keltner have? (2 pts)

12 In 1979, which former art advisor to the Queen was named as the fourth man in the Cambridge spy ring which included Burgess, Maclean and Philby?

13 Members of which Russian pop act were imprisoned in 2012 for 'hooliganism' while voicing displeasure at Vladimir Putin's government?

14 Georgia and Russia fell out over which region in 2008?

15 What kind of building is the preserved Tower of Hercules at the seaport of La Coruña in Galicia, Spain?

16 What connects Glyndebourne Festival of Opera with Peter Jackson's *The Lord of the Rings* film trilogy?

17 For what type of writing is M. R. James best known?

18 Abba had nine no. 1 hit singles in the UK; which was the only one to top the Billboard Hot 100 chart in the US as well?

19 The French animation classic *Le Manège Enchanté* was screened in the UK as what? Who rewrote the scripts in a knowing, adult way that ensured the programme's enduring cult status? (2 pts)

20 The plane carrying the Manchester United team crashed in 1958 bringing them back from a European Cup quarter-final against which side?

Total Points: 22. Targets: Novice 11 Pro 17. Your Score:

Answers Quizzes 65–72

Quiz 65. General Knowledge

1. He wrote the musical score; 2. Yale; 3. Sinn Fein; 4. Tutsi and Hutu; 5. The five main populated continents of the world; 6. They are the names given to various portraits alleged to be of William Shakespeare; 7. Her knickers; 8. Russell Brand; 9. The Panchen Lama; 10. Billie Jean King; 11. Val Kilmer; 12. Jonathan Rhys Meyers; 13. Kurt Russell; 14. Graceland; 15. Nicolas Cage; 16. Elvis (Kilmer appears as an Elvis-like ghost in *True Romance*; Rhys Meyers played Elvis in a successful US mini-series; Russell made an Elvis biopic with John Carpenter; Simon's album shares its name with Elvis's mansion; Cage won his girl by sky-diving dressed in an Elvis costume in the movie

Quiz 66. Movies

1. Ingrid Bergman was married to Rossellini and starred in *The Big Sleep*; 2. Coppola (Francis Ford directed *Apocalypse Now* while daughter Sofia directed *Lost in Translation*); 3. Both based on novels by James L. Cain; 4. Cher is the name of Alicia Silverstone's character in *Clueless* and Cher stars as Loretta in *Moonstruck*; 5. *Planet of the Apes*; 6. They all played Ann Darrow in versions of *King Kong*; 7. The Shaffer twins (Peter Shaffer based the *Amadeus* screenplay on his own stage play, and Anthony did the same with *Sleuth*); 8. Taken from Daphne du Maurier stories; 9. Both play angels who have come down to earth; 10. Both played Philip Marlowe in adaptations of Chandler's *Farewell, My Lovely*; 11. They are all Canadian; 12. Joss Whedon, creator of *Buffy*, directed the 2012 movie *Marvel Avengers Assemble* and has been booked for a follow-up; 13. Jamie Lee Curtis (*Halloween*) is the daughter of Janet Leigh (*Psycho*); 14. William Petersen, who played Gil Grissom in *CSI* and also Will Graham in *Manhunter*, the agent who put Hannibal Lecter in jail; 15. All have central characters with severe physical disabilities; 16. Sam Riley played Ian Curtis in the biopic *Control* and Sal Paradise in the movie of Kerouac's *On the Road*; 17. Both actors piled on the pounds for their roles in *Raging Bull* and *Bridget Jones's Diary*; 18. Nuns (Coltrane in *Nuns on the Run*, MacLaine in *Two Mules for Sister Sara*, Goldberg in *Sister Act* and Kerr in *Black Narcissus*); 19. They all played Tom Ripley; 20. Each film's most famous scene takes place on a beach

Quiz 67. Backing Bands

1. Sharon Jones; 2. Florence (Welch); 3. Billy J. Kramer; 4. Marina; 5. Frank Zappa; 6. Bruce Springsteen; 7. Cliff Richard; 8. Buddy Holly; 9. Elvis Costello; 10. Neil Young; 11. Siouxsie (Sioux); 12. Martha Reeves; 13. Bruce Hornsby; 14. Elvis Costello (again); 15. Nick Cave; 16. Noel Gallagher; 17. Echo; 18. Edward Sharpe; 19. Tom Petty; 20. Toots

Quiz 68. Geography

1. Turkey; Albania; Bulgaria; Macedonia; 2. Hartlepool; 3. Bodmin Moor in Cornwall (the other two are in Devon); 4. Kazakhstan; 5. Bangladesh has a coast on the Bay of Bengal; 6. Murmansk; 7. Philadelphia; 8. All lie on the equator; 9. Leicester; 10. Norwich; 11. Somalia, Kenya, Sudan, Djibouti, Eritrea; 12. Ukraine, Moldova, Hungary, Serbia, Bulgaria; 13. China, Vietnam, Cambodia, Thailand, Burma

Quiz 69. US Politics

1. Madeleine Albright; 2. They were part of the Russian spy-ring uncovered by the FBI in 2010; 3. Senator Joseph McCarthy; 4. Bay of Pigs; 5. Jimmy Hoffa; 6. Ulysses S. Grant; 7. Hawaii; Illinois; 8. False (Jimmy Carter was also right-handed; Reagan, Bush Sr, Clinton and Obama are all left-handed; 9. Richard Nixon; 10. 435, a number which is legally enshrined (the seats are proportioned equally across the states according to population, but each state must have at least one seat); 11. John McCain (Rep – Arizona); John Kerry (Dem – Massachusetts); 12. Andrew Jackson, a Democrat (Jackson was the leader of the War Democrats who helped Lincoln win the 1864 election on a ticket of non-appeasement towards the Confederate South; the main Democrat leadership was pro-peace and recon-ciliation); 13. Franklin D. Roosevelt; 14. Grover Cleveland (he counts twice in the numbering of Presidents, as the twenty-second and twenty-fourth incumbent; 15. The Wall Street Crash; 16. Franklin D. Roosevelt; 17. Ronald Reagan; Jerry Brown; Arnold Schwarzenegger; 18. Ross Perot; 19. Teapot Dome Scandal (so named because the oil was under a rock formation shaped like a teapot); Warren G. Harding; 20. Rodney King

Quiz 70. Football

1. George Best, David Wagstaffe; 2. Mark Hughes; Barcelona; also Barcelona; 3. Darren Ferguson; his new club, Peterborough (also his old club) won promotion to the Championship where they replaced relegated Preston; 4. Gennaro Gattuso of Milan; 5. Antoine Sibierski; 6. They were pelted with vegetables; 7. Arsenal, Liverpool, Manchester City, Bolton Wanderers, Chelsea; 8. Kevin Phillips, Sunderland; 9. They have all won Premier League winners' medals with two different clubs; Carlos Tévez and Ashley Cole; 10. They all signed for clubs but never played a game (Beauchamp signed for West Ham but got homesick, bless him, and went back to Swindon; Unsworth signed for Aston Villa, but thought better of it; while Hamann signed for Bolton but then signed for Manchester City the next day – a tribunal awarded Bolton a transfer fee); 11. Bury (they beat Southampton, then a non-league side, 4–0 in 1900 and then thrashed Derby 6–0 five years later; times have been tougher since); 12. Gretna; 13. Heart of Midlothian in 2005–6; 14. Leeds United; Jermaine Beckford; 15. Both reached the League Cup final whilst playing in the lowest division of the league; 16. Miroslav Klose (Germany); Didier Drogba (Côte d'Ivoire); Robbie Keane (Ireland); Samuel Eto'o (Cameroon); 17. PSV Eindhoven; 18. Aaron Ramsey; 19. Alberto Tarantini; 20. Kris Boyd and Henrik Larsson

Quiz 71. Costume Drama

1. Shirley MacLaine; 2. Latin; 3. *Gangs of New York*; Bill 'The Butcher' Cutting; 4. The Russian Revolution and its aftermath; 5. *Cranford*; Mrs Gaskell; 6. *North and South* was adapted by Sandy Welch; 7. *The Forsyte Saga* (it was shown in the week and repeated on Sunday evenings, garnering record audiences for a serious TV drama); 8. Oliver Stone; Richard Burton; 9. *Poldark*; Winston Graham; 10. The Jack the Ripper murders; 11. Maggie Smith; Baedeker's; George Emerson (Julian Sands); Daniel Day-Lewis; Florence; 12. Cynthia Harris; Guy Pearce and James D'Arcy; Edward's father, King George V; Andrea Riseborough

Quiz 72. General Knowledge

1. In the seeds of chilli peppers; 2. St Paul's Cathedral; 3. The owner of Manchester City; 4. (a) distinction between first and second class; 5. Jürgen Schult's discus record is 74.08 metres, but Yuri Sedykh threw the hammer 86.74 metres; 6. Dan Rather; 7. (b) Flashman farts and Lord Cardigan mistakes it for an enemy attack; 8. Loire; 9. Thomas Cranmer during the reign of Henry VIII after the schism from the Church of Rome; 10. Andre Agassi; 11. The Traveling Wilburys; he was the drummer but didn't appear as an 'official' member of the band until the third recording session; 12. Sir Anthony Blunt; 13. Pussy Riot; 14. South Ossetia; 15. A lighthouse; formerly known as the Farum Brigantium, the lighthouse was built by the Romans; 16. The London Philharmonic Orchestra provide the instrumentation for both; 17. Ghost stories; 18. 'Dancing Queen'; 19. *The Magic Roundabout*; Eric Thompson; 20. Red Star Belgrade (not Bayern Munich; the plane was merely refuelling at Munich airport)

Quiz 73. General Knowledge

To be *frank*, we're giving away points here (that's a clue, by the way, it's in italics)

Part 1

1   Who had a no. 1 hit in the UK with their debut single 'Relax' in 1983?

2   Which great German footballer was known as *Der Kaiser* for his authority and imperious manner?

3   Who was the film director, especially adept at social comedy, behind the 1930s classics *It Happened One Night* and *Mr Smith Goes to Washington*?

4   What was the 1996 'misery memoir', an account of a squalid and miserable childhood, that became a bestseller for Irishman Frank McCourt?

5   What is the name of the main character, played by Tim Curry, in the cult musical film *The Rocky Horror Picture Show*?

6   Which legendary entertainer was known as Ol' Blue Eyes?

7   What was the gothic novel conceived by Mary Shelley when she was living in Geneva in 1816 and published two years later?

8   Who is the only Italian female to win a Grand Slam singles title in tennis?

9   Who was Britain's first £1 million footballer?

10 On which racecourse did Frankie Dettori go 'through the card', winning all seven of the day's races in September 1996?

Part 2

11   Who sailed for adventure and profit in the ship the *Golden Hinde*?

12   When Ken Livingstone was voted in as Mayor of London on a rebel ticket in 2000, who was the official Labour Party candidate?

13   Which abrasive Scottish comedian left the panel of *Mock the Week* rather than agree to tone down his act?

14   Who stars as Fran Kubelik in *The Apartment*, opposite Jack Lemmon?

15   Who left north London for his home city of Barcelona in 2011?

16   Who was given a diary for her thirteenth birthday in 1942?

17   Which football character is the uncle of England international Frank Lampard?

18   St Francis of Assisi is *not* a patron saint of which of the following groups? (a) stowaways (b) beggars (c) the environment (d) animals

19   Which famous American architect designed the Guggenheim Museum in New York?

20   Which tragic figure was portrayed by Jessica Lange in a 1982 movie, a role which earned the actress an Academy Award nomination?

Total Points: 20. Targets: Novice 10 Pro 15. Your Score:

Quiz 74. Name the Album

We give you some tracks, you tell us the album. If you're reading the quiz out loud and wish to make it harder, leave out the third track listed as it is a bit of a giveaway for anyone who knows their musical onions; these are all albums from the 1990s and 2000s (the oldies section comes later)

Part 1

1   'Rumour Has It', 'He Won't Go', 'Someone Like You' (2010)
2   'God's Cop', 'Bob's Yer Uncle', 'Kinky Afro' (1990)
3   'Weather to Fly', 'Starlings', 'One Day Like This' (2008)
4   'Nightblindness', 'Sail Away', 'Babylon' (1998)
5   'Black Star', 'Fake Plastic Trees', 'Street Spirit (Fade Out)' (1995)
6   'Lego House', 'Small Bump', 'Drunk' (2011)
7   'Are We the Waiting', 'Give Me Novocaine', 'Boulevard of Broken Dreams' (2004)
8   'I'm Your Villain', 'Walk Away', 'Do You Want To' (2005)
9   'Some Unholy War', 'Tears Dry on Their Own', 'Rehab' (2006)
10 'Numb', 'It Could Be Sweet', 'Glory Box' (1994)

Part 2

11 'Runaway', 'Bloodbuzz Ohio', 'Terrible Love' (2010)
12 'Hell of a Life', 'Monster', 'All of the Lights' (2010)
13 'Trouble', 'Shiver', 'Yellow' (2000)
14 'Don't Stop the Rock', 'Setting Sun', 'Block Rockin' Beats' (1997)
15 'The Thaw', 'Trumpet or Tap', 'Stingin' Belle' (2013)
16 'Star Me Kitten', 'Man on the Moon', 'Everybody Hurts' (1992)
17 'Gangster Tripping', 'Praise You', 'Right Here, Right Now' (1998)
18 'Turn Me On', 'Nightingale', 'Don't Know Why' (2002)
19 'Night Time', 'Basic Space', 'Heart Skipped a Beat' (2009)
20 'Suitcase', 'My Kind of Love', 'Next to Me' (2012)

Total Points: 20. Targets: Novice 8 Pro 15. Your Score: [   ]

Quiz 75. Human Body

A straight twenty questions on physiognomy and features

Part 1

1   Which two bones make up the lower arm, between the elbow and wrist? (2 pts)
2   What are the three types of muscle? (3 pts)
3   What is the fluid that protects joints, as most joints are comprised of two imperfectly connected bones?
4   Where is the muscle called the trapezius found?
5   What are the three types of vertebrae? (3 pts)
6   What are the small bones found in both the feet and the hands?
7   Folic acid, used in the body to promote cell division and create red blood cells, is part of which vitamin group?
8   Where in the body are the corticosteroids that provide the body's natural anti-inflammatories produced?
9   What are the four basic types of tissue in animals? (4 pts)
10 What would an Ishihara test hope to establish?

Part 2

11 In what part of the body are the human vocal chords found?
12 What was the significance of the finding of simian bones in a cave near Düsseldorf in 1856?
13 What part of the body has a protective layer called the sclera?
14 What are the four types of tooth in a human mouth? (Half a point each)
15 What could a woman not do without a Fallopian tube?
16 What is the fluid that surrounds, bathes and nutrifies cells in the body? And what carries excess of it around the body and feeds it back into the blood supply? (2 pts)
17 Which would provide the most protein per 100 g: roast chicken, grilled bacon or tinned tuna?
18 What is the term applied when an organ protrudes through the protective cavity around it, often causing discomfort or pain?
19 What part of the body has four parts; ascending, descending, transverse and sigmoid?
20 What is the longest (and widest) nerve in the human body, running from the lower back through the buttock into the legs?

Total Points: 30. Targets: Novice 12 Pro 23. Your Score:

Quiz 76. History

A mixed bag of historical titbits

Part 1

1 Achaemenid, Parthian and Sassanid are all dynastic empires of which long-lasting ancient power?

2 What is the name given to the amphitheatre in the centre of Rome begun during the rule of the Emperor Vespasian?

3 Which school of philosophy, founded in the third century BC by Zeno of Citium, tells us that sound judgement and upright behaviour are the key to eradicating negativity?

4 Ashoka the Great ruled the Maurya Empire for much of the third century BC; which modern country did his empire encompass?

5 What name was officially given to the Kingdom of Serbs, Croats and Slovenes in 1929?

6 Which significant historical event took place by Senlac Ridge in Sussex?

7 What was the council called by Pope Paul III to counter the growth of Protestantism?

8 What did Scottish nationalists steal back from Westminster Abbey on Christmas Day 1950?

9 Which former hero of the Boer Wars became the first Prime Minister of the newly formed Union of South Africa in 1910? Who did he take prisoner when capturing a military train in 1899? (2 pts)

10 Salvador de Bahia was the original colonial capital of what is now Brazil; it was also the first place to hold a market selling what to the American continent?

Part 2

11 The Principality of Antioch and the Counties of Edessa and Tripoli were three of the states set up by which invading force in the thirteenth century? What was the fourth and most significant of these states? (2 pts)

12 Which European statesman was the first to introduce old age pensions in 1889?

13 In which English cathedral is the early English chronicler the Venerable Bede buried?

14 What was the more common name given to the Local Defence Volunteers in World War II?

15 The nineteenth and twentieth dynasties of Ancient Egypt, which saw the empire at the peak of its power, included only pharaohs carrying which name?

16 Which social and educational organization for ladies came into being on 19 February 1897?

17 Where in South Africa did the police massacre over fifty unarmed civilians in 1960?

18 After seizing control of Egypt in 1952, the military coup installed General Muhammad Naguib as the nation's first President; which former ally brought about Naguib's downfall in 1956?

19 Which port, which changed hands between England and France on many times during its medieval history, lies on the mouth of the River Seine on the English Channel?

20 Who was the powerful Anglo-French baron who led the revolt against King Henry III and became effective ruler of England between 1263 and 1265? Near which Cotswold town was he killed in battle? (2 pts)

Total Points: 23. Targets: Novice 9 Pro 17. Your Score: _____

Quiz 77. Fine Art and Architecture

Ten straight questions and a Mix and Match section

Part 1

1   Which London college was home to *Freeze*, an exhibition of student art organized by Damien Hirst in 1988? (a) Royal Holloway (b) Goldsmiths (c) Imperial

2   Where was the 2011 Turner Prize exhibition held, the first time it had been located outside London?

3   Which architectural masterpiece was officially opened in San Francisco on 26 May 1937?

4   Who submitted a urinal to a New York exhibition of modern art in 1915?

5   Whose painting, *Adele Bloch-Bauer I*, was sold for $135 million in New York in June 2006?

6   In 1987, a world record £27 million was paid at Sotheby's for *Irises*, a work by which artist?

7   The Clore Gallery, part of the Tate in London, houses a fine collection of paintings by which English master?

8   The Colossus at Rhodes was considered one of the Seven Wonders of the Ancient World; who or what was the subject matter of the Colossus?

9   What are the three original Greek orders of architecture? (3 pts)

10 Emile Zola's *L'Oeuvre* ended his friendship with which painter, whose depiction in the book was distinctly unflattering? (a) Cézanne (b) Degas (c) Picasso

Part 2

Mix and Match: match the painter to the work

1. Edward Burne-Jones; 2. John Constable; 3. Salvador Dalí; 4. Edgar Degas; 5. Frans Hals; 6. Dante Gabriel Rossetti; 7. Jean Renoir; 8. Diego Velázquez; 9. Pablo Picasso; 10. Piet Mondrian

a. *Beata Beatrix*; b. *Dedham Vale*; c. *Broadway Boogie Woogie*; d. *Persistence of Memory*; e. *Moulin de la Galette*; f. *The Rokeby Venus* (properly, *The Toilet of Venus*); g. *King Cophetua and the Beggar Maid*; h. *L'Absinthe*; i. *Guernica*; j. *The Laughing Cavalier*

Your Workings:

Total Points: 22. Targets: Novice 9 Pro 17. Your Score:

Quiz 78. Horse Racing

The Sport of Kings; twenty questions on horses and riders, both on the flat and over fences

Part 1

1 Which jockey earned his first Derby win aged thirty-six aboard Authorized in 2007?

2 Who was the first amateur rider for thirty years to win the Cheltenham Gold Cup when he rode Long Run to victory in 2011?

3 What connects the 1973 Grand National winner, Red Rum, to the 2011 winner, Ballabriggs? (Extra detail for 2 pts)

4 Which of Sheikh Mohammed's horses emulated the great Mill Reef in winning the Derby, the King George VI and Queen Elizabeth Stakes and the Prix de l'Arc de Triomphe in the same year (1995)?

5 The 1,000 Guineas and the Oaks are open exclusively to which kind of horse?

6 What nickname is given to the third day of the five-day Royal Ascot meeting? And what is the key Group 1 race run that day? (2 pts)

7 In which year was Diomed the first winner of the Epsom Derby: 1780, 1845 or 1902?

8 Which Irish racecourse hosts all the premier flat races, including the Irish 2000 Guineas, Irish Derby and Irish St Leger?

9 Which horse won the 1981 Epsom Derby by a record ten lengths and who was the nineteen-year-old jockey on board? (2 pts)

10 Which great Australian rider was Champion Jockey four times, including a hat-trick in 1961–3, and rode his first Derby winner (Santa Claus), aged fifty, in 1964?

Part 2

11 What race is the highlight of the French racing season in October? Over which course is it run? (2 pts)

12 The Aintree Festival in April includes seven Grade 1 races; what is notably not amongst them?

13 Which Paul Nicholls trained horse won the Cheltenham Gold Cup at the first attempt in 2008? Who was the previous year's winner, also trained by Nicholls, who was beaten into second place? What happened the following year? (3 pts)

14 Who won his first Grand National aboard Don't Push It in 2010? What other prize was he given at the end of the year, a unique achievement for a jockey? (2 pts)

15 Which Paddy Mullins trained horse, the best mare in jump-racing history, won the Champion Hurdle in 1984 and the Gold Cup in 1986, a unique double? Which famous jump jockey, now a trainer of note, rode her to both victories? (2 pts)

16 What first was achieved by the jockey of the third-placed horse, Seabass, at the 2012 Grand National?

17 Which 2012 Gold Cup winner was killed at the Grand National the following month, renewing calls for increased safety or the abandonment of the race?

18 Which durable horse entered six Grand Nationals, finishing five, including a win in 1986, a second place in 1989 and two fourths?

19 In which city is Churchill Downs racecourse and what famous race is held there each year? (2 pts)

20 Which three jockeys have each won three Derby races in the last twenty years (1993–2012)? (3 pts)

Total Points: 31. Targets: Novice 12 Pro 23. Your Score:

Quiz 79. Children's Books

Fifteen questions and a multi-parter

Part 1

1 *I Will Not Ever Never Eat a Tomato* was the first book featuring which child characters? Who is the author of the series? (2 pts)

2 Fleshlumpeater and Childchewer are characters from which Roald Dahl book?

3 Which classic for older children, set in World War II, concerns the inhabitants of Druid's Bottom?

4 Which enduring classic by J. M. Barrie began life as a stage play in 1904?

5 Which nineteenth-century social reformer wrote the children's tale *The Water Babies*?

6 What was Fungus the Bogeyman's job in Raymond Briggs's picture story?

7 Who is the author of the famous story, *The Night Before Christmas*, traditionally read to children on Christmas Eve?

8 Whose diary did Jeff Kinney start in 2008?

9 What was Roger Hargreaves's contribution to the pantheon of children's literature?

10 What is the setting for Rosemary Sutcliff's 1954 classic, *The Eagle of the Ninth*?

Part 2

11 Which author returned to World War I, the scene of his greatest triumph, for his 2003 prize-winning book, *Private Peaceful*?

12 *Catching Fire* (2008) was the follow-up to which international bestseller?

13 Who is Eoin Colfer's teenage criminal genius?

14 *The Jolly Postman* was a 1986 classic composed by which wife and husband team?

15 Which, from the following list, were the first two books in the perennial *Horrible Histories* series? (a) *Awesome Egyptians* (b) *Groovy Greeks* (c) *Rotten Romans* (d) *Terrible Tudors* (e) *Vile Victorians* (2 pts)

16 What is the name of the boat in *Treasure Island* and who is its new owner? What is the curse that 'kills' Billy Bones and to whose treasure does his map lead? What is Long John Silver's job aboard ship before the mutiny? (5 pts)

Total Points: 22. Targets: Novice 9 Pro 17. Your Score: ☐

Quiz 80. General Knowledge

Twenty quick-fire questions

Part 1

1 Why is someone suffering from panophobia probably having a really bad time?
2 With what is the name Stanley Gibbons associated?
3 Which new legal body opened officially on 1 October 2009?
4 Who was found in a cellar in Tikrit in 2003?
5 Which Australian sporting icon was the first woman to swim the 100 metre freestyle in less than a minute?
6 Which Prime Minister's wife sold 75,000 copies of her *Selected Poems*?
7 What physical problem did Martin Sheen have to overcome whilst shooting *Apocalypse Now*? (a) a bout of malaria (b) a heart attack (c) partial amnesia after a fall
8 The marine life rich archipelago of Papahanaumokuakea lies within whose administration? (a) Papua New Guinea (b) Samoa (c) US state of Hawaii
9 Nicola, Highland Burgundy and Mr Little's Yetholm Gypsy are all types of what?
10 What passed from Jaap Stam to Laurent Blanc to Cristiano Ronaldo?

Part 2

11 In which movie is the Holy Hand Grenade of Antioch a secret weapon?
12 Who did Charles Darwin replace on the £10 note in 2000?
13 What is the more common English name for Il Ridotto?
14 Which alternative calendar to our Gregorian one begins in 622?
15 What connects the golfer Gary Player to country music legend Johnny Cash?
16 James Dean; Marilyn Monroe; Rudolph Valentino; River Phoenix; Jean Harlow; Heath Ledger. All died young, but who lived longest and who died at the youngest age? (2 pts)
17 What does the MGM studio use as the centrepiece of its logo?
18 In 1908 Allison Cargill was the first (a) suffragette to be imprisoned (b) girl guide (c) woman to be recorded as wearing trousers?
19 At which famous London restaurant did Jamie Oliver cut his teeth en route to stardom?
20 The first America's Cup, run in 1851, was a contest to sail around which island?

Total Points: 21. Targets: Novice 11 Pro 16. Your Score: [   ]

Answers Quizzes 73–80

Quiz 73. General Knowledge

1. Frankie Goes to Hollywood; 2. Franz Beckenbauer; 3. Frank Capra; 4. *Angela's Ashes*; 5. Frank N. Furter; 6. Frank Sinatra; 7. *Frankenstein*; 8. Francesca Schiavone; 9. Trevor Francis; 10. Ascot; 11. Sir Francis Drake; 12. Frank Dobson; 13. Frankie Boyle; 14. Shirley MacLaine; 15. Cesc Fàbregas (Cesc is a shortening of Francesc, the Catalan variant on Francesco); 16. Anne Frank; 17. Harry Redknapp (Harry married the sister of Frank's father, also Frank); 18. Beggars; 19. Frank Lloyd Wright; 20. Frances Farmer

Quiz 74. Name the Album

1. *21*, Adele; 2. *Pills 'n' Thrills and Bellyaches*, Happy Mondays; 3. *The Seldom Seen Kid*, Elbow; 4. *White Ladder*, David Gray; 5. *The Bends*, Radiohead; 6. *+*, Ed Sheeran; 7. *American Idiot*, Green Day; 8. *You Could Have It So Much Better*, Franz Ferdinand; 9. *Back to Black*, Amy Winehouse; 10. *Dummy*, Portishead; 11. *High Violet*, The National; 12. *My Beautiful Dark Twisted Fantasy*, Kanye West; 13. *Parachutes*, Coldplay; 14. *Dig Your Own Hole*, Chemical Brothers; 15. *Opposites*, Biffy Clyro; 16. *Automatic for the People*, REM; 17. *You've Come a Long Way, Baby*, Fatboy Slim; 18. *Come Away with Me*, Norah Jones; 19. *XX*, xx; 20. *Our Version of Events*, Emeli Sandé

Quiz 75. Human Body

1. Ulna and radius; 2. Skeletal, cardiac and smooth; 3. Synovia or synovial fluid; 4. Base of the skull; 5. Cervical, thoracic and lumbar; 6. Phalanges; 7. Folic acid is B9; 8. Adrenal cortex; 9. Epithelial, connective, muscular and nervous; 10. The degree of colour-blindness in the subject; 11. Larynx; 12. It was Neanderthal man; 13. The eye (it is the opaque, milky fluid which protects the sensitive working parts); 14. Incisor, canine, molar, premolar; 15. Give birth (the tube carries the egg from the ovary to the uterus); 16. Interstitial fluid; the lymphatic system; 17. Tuna, with *c.*28 g of protein per 100 g, compared to *c.*19 g for chicken and even less for bacon; 18. Hernia; 19. Colon; 20. Sciatic nerve

Quiz 76. History

1. Persia; 2. Colosseum; 3. Stoic; 4. India (and other parts of the Indian subcontinent); 5. Yugoslavia; 6. Battle of Hastings; 7. Council of Trent; 8. Stone of Scone; 9. Louis Botha; Winston Churchill; 10. Slaves; 11. The knights of the First Crusade (accept Crusaders); Kingdom of Jerusalem; 12. Bismarck, the German Chancellor; 13. Durham; 14. Home Guard; 15. Rameses; 16. Women's Institute; 17. Sharpeville; 18. (Gamel Abdal) Nasser, who became President until his death in 1970; 19. Le Havre; 20. Simon de Montfort; Evesham

Quiz 77. Fine Art and Architecture

1. Goldsmiths; 2. Baltic, Gateshead; 3. Golden Gate Bridge; 4. Marcel Duchamp; 5. Gustav Klimt; 6. Vincent van Gogh; 7. J. M. W. Turner; 8. The Titan, Helios; 9. Doric, Ionian and Corinthian; 10. (a) Paul Cézanne; Mix and Match: 1, g; 2, b; 3, d; 4, h; 5, j; 6, a; 7, e; 8, f; 9, i; 10, c

Quiz 78. Horse Racing

1. Frankie Dettori; 2. Sam Waley-Cohen; 3. McCain; Red Rum was trained by Ginger, Ballabriggs by son Donald; 4. Lammtarra; 5. Three-year-old thoroughbred fillies (three-year-olds will do for the point); 6. Ladies Day; Ascot Gold Cup; 7. 1780 (it is one of the oldest prestige events in sport); 8. Curragh; 9. Shergar; Walter Swinburn; 10. Scobie Breasley; 11. Prix de l'Arc de Triomphe; Longchamp; 12. Grand National; the National is a Grade 3 race (it's attraction is a spectacle and test of stamina as it is the longest graded race of the season); 13. Denman: Kauto Star; the positions were reversed (Denman went on to finish second twice more); 14. A. P. McCoy; BBC Sports Personality of the Year; 15. Dawn Run; Jonjo O'Neill; 16. She was Katie Walsh, and the first female jockey to ride a placed horse in the race; 17. Synchronised; 18. West Tip; 19. Louisville, home of the Kentucky Derby; 20. Kieren Fallon, Michael Kinane and Johnny Murtagh

Quiz 79. Children's Books

1. Charlie and Lola; Lauren Child; 2. *The BFG* by Roald Dahl; 3. *Carrie's War* by Nina Bowden; 4. *Peter Pan*; 5. Charles Kingsley; 6. Lavatory attendant; 7. Clement Moore; 8. *Diary of a Wimpy Kid*; 9. *Mr Men* and *Little Miss*; 10. Roman Britain (specifically a journey over Hadrian's Wall into Scotland); 11. Michael Morpurgo, author of *War Horse*; 12. *The Hunger Games*; 13. Artemis Fowl; 14. Janet and Allan Ahlberg; 15. (a) *Awesome Egyptians* and (d) *Terrible Tudors*, both published in 1993; 16. *Hispaniola*; Squire Trelawney; the Black Spot; Captain Flint; ship's cook

Quiz 80. General Knowledge

1. They're afraid of everything; 2. Stamp collecting; 3. Supreme Court of the United Kingdom; 4. Saddam Hussein; 5. Dawn Fraser; 6. Mary Wilson; 7. He suffered a (fortunately relatively minor) heart attack; 8. (c) Hawaii; 9. Potato; 10. A house in Cheshire; 11. *Monty Python and the Holy Grail*; 12. Charles Dickens; 13. Venice Carnival; 14. The Islamic calendar; 15. They both earned the nickname 'The Man in Black' for their preference for black garb; 16. Monroe reached thirty-six to be the oldest; Phoenix was only twenty-three; 17. A lion; 18. (b) she was the first sworn member of the new girl guides; 19. River Café; 20. Isle of Wight

Quiz 81. General Knowledge

More questions on your knowledge of things which are generally known

Part 1

1 Which concoction of gin, lemon, sugar and soda was named after a Victorian London barman?

2 The island of Trinidad and Tobago is situated off the coast of which South American country?

3 How did Monty, Holly and Willow perform in front of millions of viewers in the summer of 2012?

4 16 October 1902 saw the first of which brand of motor car roll off the production line in Detroit?

5 Who made his TV debut during a 1970 0–0 draw between Liverpool and Chelsea?

6 What does the P. J. stand for in Mercury-award winning artist P. J. Harvey's moniker?

7 What was the value in modern money of the old coin called a crown?

8 What three things does an incoming US President take an oath to do to the US Constitution at his inauguration ceremony? (3 pts)

9 What was the name of the German parliament building burned down in 1933?

10 Who was the Florentine thinker, born 1469, whose political treatises made his name synonymous with a certain style of political manoeuvring?

Part 2

11   The Entente Cordiale of 1904 was an agreement to protect mutual interest against German aggression made between which two countries? Which other country made the alliance a Triple Entente in 1907? (3 pts)

12   What was found under a building site in Colchester in 2005? (a) a stash of gold, hidden by Royalist sympathizers in the English Civil War (b) remains of a Roman chariot-racing arena (c) the body of a man missing for forty-three years who was an assumed victim of the Kray twins

13   Which two Middle Eastern countries fought a protracted war in the 1980s that saw at least 500,000 deaths on each side before peace was agreed in 1988? (2 pts)

14   Which senior position was held by the poet John Donne? (a) Queen's physician (b) Dean of St Paul's (c) Lord Mayor of London

15   Which popular song has four verses, each ending 'And sent him homeward / Tae think again'?

16   From which five countries does Britain import most products? Which of these is not amongst the top five countries who buy British exports? (6 pts)

Total Points: 26. Targets: Novice 13 Pro 20. Your Score:

Quiz 82. Factual TV

Twelve questions on factual TV and a couple of multi-parters

Part 1

1 What was the title of David Attenborough's 2001 exploration of life under the oceans?

2 With which bucolic programme would you associate the team of John Craven, Michaela Strachan and Ben Fogle?

3 'Don't have nightmares' is the advice given at the end of every episode of which TV show?

4 Which series, hosted by Gareth Malone, started in 2006? What was the angle to the 2011 series that produced a bestselling album? (2 pts)

5 Who originally presented and gave his name to *Newsround*, a factual news programme for children? In which decade was it first broadcast? (2 pts)

6 For doing what on TV is Barry Norman best known?

7 As of January 2013 which two women share the anchor role on the show *Loose Women*? (2 pts)

8 Who went *Pole to Pole* and *Around the World in Eighty Days*?

9 Which current affairs programme screened the famous 1995 Martin Bashir interview with Diana, Princess of Wales?

10 Who taught us *How to Look Good Naked* on Channel 4?

Part 2

11 Who was a junior lawyer in 1996–7 and a teacher from 2001–3 before becoming a zombie-bashing cop in 2010? What are the three shows involved? (4 pts)

12 Who was the original frontperson for *Top Gear* in its first incarnation as a rather dull car magazine programme? Which channel briefly snapped up the programme when the BBC dropped it in 2001? What is the name of the feature where a celebrity does a timed lap of the *Top Gear* test circuit in a saloon car? What is the name of the white-clad 'mystery' test driver? (4 pts)

13 What are the surnames of the presenting double-act Richard and Judy? Which ITV programme, launched in 1988, first gave them major exposure? What was the role on the programme of energetic Fred Talbot? (4 pts)

Total Points: 25. Targets: Novice 10 Pro 19. Your Score:

Quiz 83. Movie Quotes

Part 1

1 'When you marooned me on that God forsaken spit of land, you forgot one very important thing, mate.' What had they forgotten and who's the actor? (2 pts)

2 'You're gonna need a bigger boat!' They did. What was the movie?

3 In which film noir does the narrator reflect: 'How could I have known that murder can sometimes smell like honeysuckle?'

4 'My name is Inigo Montoya; you killed my father. Prepare to die.' Which movie and which actor? (2 pts)

5 'We're on a mission from God.' Who were?

6 'She was as cute as lace panties, a redhead' and 'It was a blonde; a blonde to make a Bishop kick a hole in a stained glass window' are observations from which character in which movie? (2 pts)

7 'Cancel the kitchen scraps for lepers and orphans. No more merciful beheadings. And call off Christmas.' Who's getting mean in the face of adversity? (Character, actor, film) (3 pts)

8 'You can leave in a taxi. If you can't leave in a taxi you can leave in a huff. If that's too soon, you can leave in a minute and a huff.' Typical madness from which classic cinema comedy team? And the film? (2 pts)

9 In *Bill and Ted's Excellent Adventure*, what does Ted reply when asked, 'Who was Joan of Arc?'

10 'I'm not bad – I'm just drawn that way.' Which sassy cartoon lady said this?

Part 2

11   'Mother . . . what's the phrase . . . isn't quite herself today.' Which actor in
     which part comes across all nut-job in which classic scary movie? (3 pts)

12   MAN: 'No man can be friends with a woman that he finds attractive. He
     always wants to have sex with her.' WOMAN: 'So you're saying that a man
     can be friends with a woman he finds unattractive?' MAN: 'No. You pretty
     much want to nail them too.' Who are talking (actors as well as characters)
     in which film? (5 pts)

13   Which iconic line did Greta Garbo utter in *Grand Hotel*?

14   In which movie does Humphrey Bogart say, 'Play it again, Sam'?

15   'There is no spoon.' In which 1990s classic adventure are we treated to this
     preposterous piece of cod philosophy?

16   'Above all things I believe in love. Love is like oxygen. Love is a many-
     splendored thing. Love lifts us up where we belong. All you need is love.'
     Which actor in which film? (2 pts)

17   'When you absolutely, positively got to kill every motherf***** in the room,
     accept no substitutes.' What is Samuel L. Jackson describing and in which
     movie? (2 pts)

18   'Achilles only had his heel – I have an Achilles body.' A typically self-depre-
     cating line from which screenwriter cum actor cum director?

19   'A census taker once tried to test me. I ate his liver with some fava beans
     and a nice Chianti.' Which actor as which character in which movie? (3 pts)

20   'Toto, I have a feeling we're . . .' How does Dorothy's line end in *The Wizard
     of Oz*?

Total Points: 36. Targets: Novice 14 Pro 27. Your Score:

Quiz 84. Medical Science

Just fifteen straight questions

Part 1

1   What is the common name for the H5N1 strain of the influenza virus, which caused widespread panic in 1997 and still carries pandemic threat, despite relatively few instances of fatality?

2   In which city is the Queen's Medical Centre, the biggest hospital in Britain? (a) Liverpool (b) Glasgow (c) Nottingham

3   By what name is the relatively minor affliction known as hypermetropia better known?

4   What is the more popular name for laparoscopic surgery?

5   The bacterial disease listeriosis, which can cause onset of meningitis, is most usually contracted by eating what?

6   Why might you take sodium bicarbonate?

7   Pop singer Anastacia, former US President Dwight D. Eisenhower and former King of France Louis XIII have all suffered from which debilitating bowel disorder?

8   The Medical Research Council issued a report indicating the perils of which social habit in June 1957?

9   Who was the discoverer of penicillin, born 5 August 1881?

10 What was Edward Jenner's lifesaving contribution to medical science, made initially in 1796?

11 Hypertension is the correct term for what common disorder?

12 What 'wonder drug' was first marketed by the German pharmaceutical company Bayer in 1897 (and under its current name in 1899)?

13 Which wonder drug was initially named 'isletin', after its derivation?

14 The immunosuppressor cyclosporine revolutionized what aspect of medical science in the 1970s?

15 Apoptosis is the controlled manner in which the body manages what?

Total Points: 15. Targets: Novice 5 Pro 11. Your Score: [   ]

Quiz 85. Business

Who bought what and when and why and for how much

Part 1

1 Who paid $1.65 billion for YouTube in 2006?

2 Which retailer opened its first railway station outlet in Euston station in 1848?

3 What name was given to the policy of printing money to enrich banks' capital during the financial meltdown of 2008?

4 The first Habitat store opened in London in 1964; which designer and entrepreneur founded the stores?

5 In January 2009, which country's Prime Minister, Geir Haarde, became the first to step down over the world financial crisis?

6 What did Jeff Bezos start in a Seattle garage in the 1990s?

7 What percentage of the world's motor vehicle production takes place in the UK (2010 stats): 1.6 per cent, 4.1 per cent or 9.5 per cent?

8 Which airport is the busiest to be situated on an island?

9 In which city did Joseph Cadbury set up his chocolate-making company? And what was the name of the 'model village' in which he housed them? (2 pts)

10 What was founded in an Abbey Road Baptist church in 1874? What is it now part of? (2 pts)

Part 2

11 Entrepreneur Howard Schultz published the tale of his success in 2010; what was the company he built to earn his fortune?

12 Which distinctive organic chocolate company was acquired by Cadbury in 2005? And which even larger US conglomerate subsumed Cadbury's in 2009? (2 pts)

13 What was the world's first credit card, launched in 1950?

14 What is the business name given to the fundraising method whereby a project is advertised online, inviting contributions in exchange for potential return, from numerous random sources?

15 Which Devon town hit the headlines in 2012 when local residents persuaded the council to reject an application by Costa Coffee to open a store in the town, arguing that the high street was better off without major branded stores? (a) Totnes (b) Dartmouth (c) Tiverton

16 What are the five biggest oil-producing countries in the world? (5 pts)

Total Points: 23. Targets: Novice 9 Pro 17. Your Score:

Quiz 86. Rock and Pop

Just general questions

Part 1

1   Which two Queen albums took their titles from Marx Brothers movies? (2 pts)

2   Whose debut album *An Awesome Wave* won the 2012 Mercury Prize?

3   In what subject does Queen guitarist Brian May have a PhD?

4   Kele Okereke is the front man on which UK rock band?

5   With which instrument would you associate Billy Cobham, Hal Blaine and Sly Dunbar?

6   Which former member of Roxy Music and long-time collaborator of Talking Heads' David Byrne produced the second Heads album, *More Songs about Buildings and Food*?

7   Kamaljit Singh Jhooti records under which more familiar name? What was his Billboard chart-topping US debut single? (2 pts)

8   How much did the 1975 video for Queen's massive no. 1 hit 'Bohemian Rhapsody' cost: £1,500, £4,500, £15,000 or £45,000?

9   What change did Genesis undergo between *The Lamb Lies Down on Broadway* (1974) and *A Trick of the Tail* (1976)? (2 pts)

10 What city connected the pop rock band Cheap Trick and Bob Dylan in 1978–9?

Part 2

11 Who was the only artist to have the biggest selling album of the year twice in the 1980s, and what were the albums? (3 pts)

12 The same is true of the 2000s; which artist had the biggest album of both 2001 and 2003 but has experienced a sharp commercial decline since? What were the albums? (3 pts)

13 Charlie Dore's 'Pilot of the Airwaves' was an appropriate choice of track to be the last played on which pirate radio station?

14 Which *X Factor* winner had the last UK no. 1 single of 2012 and stayed top of the charts in the first week of the new year?

15 Who died youngest: Bob Marley, John Lennon or Elvis Presley?

16 What were Culture Club's two 1980s no. 1 singles? And what was Boy George's 1987 solo debut, a cover, which also went to no. 1? Who had a no. 1 hit single in the UK thirteen years previously with the same song? And for which band (his own) did David Gates write the song, including it on their 1972 album, *Baby, I'm a Want You*? (5 pts)

Total Points: 27. Targets: Novice 11 Pro 20. Your Score:

Quiz 87. Sport

All sorts of fun and games, with a brain-and-memory-stretcher at the end (not that stretchy really, just a list . . .)

Part 1

1. When choosing their name for one-day games, did Leicester County Cricket Club choose the association football or rugby football route?

2. In 1984, which was the only Warsaw Pact country to ignore the boycott and send a team to the Los Angeles Olympics?

3. Which great British Olympian had the Christian names Francis Morgan, but used neither?

4. What was founded in 1932 at Griffith Park, Los Angeles by English character actor C. Aubrey Smith? (a) Hollywood Bowls Club (b) Los Angeles Polo Club (c) Hollywood Cricket Club

5. Which two countries compete for the Bledisloe Cup, and in which sport? (3 pts)

6. Which New Zealand side has won the southern hemisphere Super Rugby tournament the most times (seven)?

7. What was Bobby Jones the last person to receive as winner of the Open Championship in 1927?

8. For what is Belmont Park a major sporting venue in the US? (a) horse racing (b) baseball (c) women's soccer

9. Stephen Hendry v. Ronnie O'Sullivan, 1997, Liverpool. O'Sullivan pulled back from 8–2 down to level at 8–8. What happened in the deciding frame?

10. Who, in 1995, became the first athlete to hold both the 5,000 metres and 10,000 metres world records?

Part 2

11. Which ten British drivers have won the Formula 1 World Driver's Championship? (10 pts)

Total Points: 22. Targets: Novice 9 Pro 17. Your Score: ☐

Quiz 88. General Knowledge

Take it away

Part 1

1   What phrase came into the American lexicon as a result of the Second Gulf War military strategy?

2   Which author 'predicted' the *Apollo* moon landing in an 1865 story?

3   Why, in 2009, did 154 people have Mr Chesley Sullenberger to thank for their lives?

4   What major change in British public life came into effect on 15 February 1971?

5   What do the weightlifters Yossef Romano, David Berger and Ze'ev Friedman and wrestlers Eliezer Halfin and Mark Slavin have in common?

6   Which of these UK place names does *not* exist? (a) Pimple, Cornwall (b) Thong, Kent (c) Crackpot, North Yorks (d) Nasty, Herts

7   On 8 July 1982, Michael Fagan was arrested for breaking and entering which building?

8   The late Honoretta Pratt was the first to undergo what process in 1769?

9   What new hot drink did Nestlé successfully introduce to the market in 1937?

10 Which serving Prime Minister captained a winning British Admiral's Cup team in the running of the famous yacht race in 1971?

Part 2

11 Which sporting icon died in 1995, aged thirty, and has a statue in a Southport shopping street?

12 What was the name of the aeroplane in which Charles Lindbergh (born 1902) became the first man to make a solo flight across the Atlantic in 1927?

13 Where in England does the annual Festival of Nine Lessons and Carols take place on Christmas Eve?

14 What is the musical heritage of the lead singer of I Blame Coco?

15 Which actor/comedian rowed in the 1980 University Boat Race?

16 Who played drums on the original 1984 Band Aid single, 'Do They Know It's Christmas?' Who sang the opening line? Who mimed Bono's line on *Top of the Pops* as the ever-shaded one couldn't make it? Who produced the record and which voguish producer remixed it for the ubiquitous 12 in version? (5 pts)

Total Points: 20. Targets: Novice 10 Pro 15. Your Score:

Answers Quizzes 81–88

Quiz 81. General Knowledge

1. Tom Collins; 2. Venezuela; 3. They were the Queen's corgis who appeared on screen when Daniel Craig appeared as 007 to escort Her Majesty to the Opening Ceremony of the Olympic Games; 4. Cadillac; 5. John Motson; 6. Polly Jean; 7. 25p (five shillings); 8. Preserve, protect and defend; 9. Reichstag; 10. Niccolò Machiavelli; 11. United Kingdom and France; Russia; 12. (b) Roman arena (there was evidence of horse tackle as well as a fully formed arena); 13. Iran and Iraq; 14. He was a cleric and was appointed Dean of St Paul's in 1621; 15. 'Flower of Scotland', the unofficial Scottish National Anthem; 16. Germany, USA, China, Netherlands, France; China is only ninth in the exports list

Quiz 82. Factual TV

1. *Blue Planet*; 2. *Countryfile*; 3. *Crimewatch UK*; 4. *The Choir*, where Malone teaches a newly formed choir to perform; the 2011 series took a group of military wives and turned them into a choir (sympathy for the women during the Afghanistan campaign took the programme to new audience levels and their single became Christmas no. 1 ahead of the ubiquitous *X Factor* winner); 5. John Craven; 1972; 6. Reviewing films on the BBC – he presented *Film 72* and subsequent series until 1998; 7. Carol Vorderman and Andrea McLean; 8. Michael Palin; 9. *Panorama*; 10. Gok Wan (didn't work for me, I'm afraid . . .); 11. Andrew Lincoln; *This Life*, *Teachers* and *The Walking Dead*; 12. Angela Rippon; Channel 5 (the show was renamed *5th Gear*); 'Star in a Reasonably Priced Car'; the Stig; 13. Madeley and Finnigan; *This Morning*; he presented the weather on a huge relief map floating in Liverpool docks

Quiz 83. Movie Quotes

1. The next line is 'I'm Captain Jack Sparrow' – so Johnny Depp was the actor; 2. *Jaws*; 3. *Double Indemnity*; Walter Neff (Fred MacMurray) adds a hindsight voiceover to this darkest of movies; 4. *The Princess Bride*; Mandy Patinkin as the aforementioned master swordsman, Inigo Montoya (for those who give a hoot, it's my favourite film); 5. Jake and Elwood (John Belushi and Dan Aykroyd) in *The Blues Brothers*; 6. Philip Marlowe in *Farewell, My Lovely*; 7. Alan Rickman as the Sheriff of Nottingham in *Robin Hood: Prince of Thieves*; 8. Marx Brothers (Groucho, specifically); *Duck Soup*; 9. 'Noah's wife?'; 10. Jessica Rabbit (voiced by Kathleen Turner) in *Who Framed Roger Rabbit?*; 11. Anthony Perkins as Norman Bates in *Psycho*; 12. Billy Crystal as Harry and Meg Ryan as Sally in *When Harry Met Sally*; 13. 'I want to be alone'; 14. None. The actual quote from *Casablanca* is 'If she can stand it, I can. Play it!' (The scene, with Bogart and the piano player is a reprise of an earlier scene where Ingrid Bergman requests a song from Sam); 15. *The Matrix*; 16. Ewan McGregor in *Moulin Rouge*; 17. An AK-47 (accept semi-automatic or machine gun) in

Jackie Brown; 18. Woody Allen; 19. Anthony Hopkins as Hannibal Lecter in *The Silence of the Lambs*; 20. '. . . not in Kansas anymore'.

Quiz 84. Medical Science

1. Avian flu or bird flu; 2. (c) Nottingham (QMC is a teaching hospital, part of the Nottingham University Hospitals NHS Trust); 3. Long-sightedness; 4. Keyhole surgery; 5. Unpasteurized soft cheese; it is particularly dangerous for pregnant women; 6. As an antacid to combat stomach acidity; 7. Crohn's disease; 8. Smoking; 9. Alexander Fleming; 10. Smallpox vaccination; 11. High blood pressure; 12. Aspirin; 14. Transplants (cyclosporine dampens the immune system, allowing the receiving body time to 'accept' the transplanted organ or skin graft); 15. Cell death (and consequent replenishment)

Quiz 85. Business

1. Google; 2. WHSmith; 3. Quantitative easing; 4. Sir Terence Conran; 5. Iceland; 6. Amazon; 7. 4.1%; 8. London Heathrow; 9. Birmingham; Bourneville; 10. Abbey National (it was then the Abbey Road and St John's Wood Mutual Benefit Building Society); Santander; 11. Starbucks; 12. Green and Black's; Kraft (now Mondelez International); 13. Diners' Club; 14. Crowdfunding; 15. (a) Totnes; 16. Russia, Saudi Arabia, United States, Iran, China

Quiz 86. Rock and Pop

1. *A Night at the Opera* and *A Day at the Races*; 2. Alt-J; 3. Astrophysics; 4. Bloc Party; 5. Percussion or drums; 6. Brian Eno; 7. Jay Sean; 'Down'; 8. £4,500; 9. Peter Gabriel left and was replaced on vocals by drummer Phil Collins (from thereon the band pursued a softer, more commercial sound rather than the experimental theatrics of the Gabriel era); 10. They both played at the Budokan arena in Japan in 1978 and released an album called '. . . *at Budokan*' the following year; 11. Michael Jackson; *Thriller* and *Bad*; 12. Dido; *No Angel* and *Life for Rent*; 13. Radio Caroline; 14. James Arthur; 15. Elvis was forty-two, Lennon was forty but Marley was only thirty-six years old; 16. 'Do You Really Want to Hurt Me?' and 'Karma Chameleon'; 'Everything I Own'; Ken Boothe; Bread

Quiz 87. Sport

1. Association (they are Leicester Foxes, not Leicester Tigers); 2. Romania; 3. Daley Thompson (Daley came from his third name, Ayodélé, from his Nigerian father); 4. (c) Hollywood Cricket Club; 5. Australia and New Zealand; rugby union; 6. (Canterbury) Crusaders; 7. The original Claret Jug (after that a replica was given to the winner while the original remained on display at St Andrews); 8. (a) Horse racing; 9. Hendry won with a maximum 147 break; 10. Haile Gebrselassie; 11. Jenson Button (2009); Jim Clark (1963 and 1965); Lewis Hamilton (2008); Mike Hawthorn (1958); Damon Hill (1996); Graham Hill

(1962 and 1968); James Hunt (1976); Nigel Mansell (1992); Jackie Stewart (1969, 1971 and 1973); John Surtees (1964)

Quiz 88. General Knowledge

1. Shock and awe; 2. Jules Verne; 3. He was the pilot who landed an aircraft safely on the Hudson River after both engines failed; 4. Decimalization; 5. They were murdered by terrorists, along with six coaches, during the Munich Olympic games; 6. Pimple, Cornwall; 7. Buckingham Palace (he got into the Queen's bedroom); 8. Cremation; 9. Instant coffee; 10. Ted Heath; 11. Red Rum; 12. *The Spirit of St Louis*; 13. King's College Chapel in Cambridge; 14. She is Coco Sumner, daughter of Sting and Trudie Styler; 15. Hugh Laurie; 16. Phil Collins; Paul Young; Paul Weller; Midge Ure and Trevor Horn

Quiz 89. General Knowledge

A straight ten and then a few linked clues

Part 1

1   In which city did Roger Bannister break the four-minute-mile barrier for the first time in 1954?

2   Which American patriot, born on New Year's Day, 1735, was immortalized in a poem by Henry Wadsworth Longfellow?

3   True or false: the recent Pope, Benedict XVI, is the first German to have held the office?

4   Where in 1984 did Indian troops storm a Sikh holy place? And what was the major consequence of that event which happened later that year? (2 pts)

5   Sebastian Coe was Chairman of the 2012 London Olympic bid team, but which other former Olympic medallist was his deputy? (a) Steve Ovett (b) Alan Pascoe (c) Linford Christie

6   If you were studying Stanislavski, what subject would you be learning?

7   How come Barry Stoller gets £40 every time *Match of the Day* is screened?

8   How many serving dukes are there in the British Isles: (a) 14 (b) 31 (c) 88? (We don't mean the formal appellation 'in the peerage of the United Kingdom', but legal dukes, whatever the origin of their title, still living and in possession of said title.)

9   What runs from Chicago to Los Angeles?

10 During which race did Ellen MacArthur become the fastest woman to sail round the planet in 2001? How old was she at the time? (2 pts)

Part 2

11 Who is the presenter of intellectual quiz *QI*?

12 Who was the lead singer with heavy metal band Black Sabbath during their halcyon years?

13 Who wore *Crocodile Shoes* on TV in 1994?

14 Who was the face of the BBC antiques show, *Bargain Hunt*?

15 Who returned to *EastEnders* in 2003 after supposedly dying fourteen years previously?

16 What's the link between the answers for Part 2?

Total Points: 18. Targets: Novice 9 Pro 14. Your Score:

Quiz 90. Name the Band

We give you the members, you just give us the name of the band, all prominent this century

Part 1

1. Chris Edwards, Christopher Karloff, Tom Meighan, Sergio Pizzorno
2. Tom Fletcher, Danny Jones, Harry Judd, Dougie Poynter
3. Martie Maguire, Natalie Maines, Emily Robison
4. Freddie Cowan, Arnie Hjorvar, Pete Robertson, Justin Young
5. Jesse Carmichael, Matt Flynn, Adam Levine, Mickey Madden, James Valentine
6. Matt Berninger, Aaron Dessner, Bryce Dessner, Bryan Devendorf, Scott Devendorf
7. Guy Garvey, Richard Jupp, Craig Potter, Mark Potter, Pete Turner
8. Frank Iero, Ray Toro, Gerard Way, Mikey Way
9. Cheryl Cole, Nadine Coyle, Sarah Harding, Nicola Roberts, Kimberley Walsh
10. Dane Auerbach, Patrick Carney
11. Niall Horan, Zayn Malik, Liam Payne, Harry Styles, Louis Tomlinson
12. Matthew Bellamy, Dominic Howard, Christopher Wolstenholme
13. Roma Madley Croft, Oliver Sim, Jamie Smith
14. Dean Fertita, Jack Lawrence, Alison Mossheart, Jack White
15. Nathan Connolly, Gary Lightbody, Jonny Quinn, Tom Simpson, Paul Wilson

Part 2

A bit harder, we miss out one key member of the band, and this time you have to name both the band *and* the missing member (2 pts per question)

16. MISSING, David Keuning, Mark Stoerner, Ronnie Vannucci
17. Ted Dwane, Ben Lovett, Winston Marshall, MISSING
18. MISSING, Nikolai Fraiture, Albert Hammond Jr, Fabrizio Moretti, Nick Valensi
19. Christopher Bear, MISSING, Daniel Rossen, Chris Taylor
20. Jamie Cook, Matt Helders, Nick O'Malley, MISSING

Total Points: 25. Targets: Novice 19 Pro 19. Your Score: [￼]

Quiz 91. Food and Drink

Pretty straightforward if you know your jus from your juice and your drizzle from your drivel

Part 1

1   If you went to the US and were served zucchini and mashed rutabaga with your chicken, what would you be eating? (2 pts)

2   Who first came to prominence hosting a BBC cookery programme, *Family Fare*?

3   What is the term used for pasta cooked, as the Italians like it, slightly firm to the bite?

4   What is the name of Darina Allen's cookery school based on her organic farm in Cork?

5   Which variety of potato is used by the vast majority of Britain's fish and chip shops?

6   What invention of Italo Marcioni made eating a summer seaside treat walking along the promenade much easier in 1896?

7   Which distilled beverage is made from the blue agave plant?

8   *Toast* was the account of the early years of which food writer?

9   What is the clarified butter used as a base oil in Indian cooking?

10   What was the name of the culinary magazine launched by Martha Distel in 1895?

Part 2

11   If Amaretto is a liqueur flavoured with almond, with what is Frangelico flavoured?

12   Crêpe Suzette is a pancake finished with caramelized sugar, juice, zest and butter over which alcohol is poured and set alight; what kind of alcohol would normally be used?

13   Which is the watery part remaining when milk is separated?

14   Alice Waters is the chef at which prestigious Californian restaurant?

15   What is wrong with the instruction: 'to soften the dried apricots, masticate them in a shallow dish of amaretto'?

16   Mascarpone and Ricotta are two Italian soft cheeses; what is the principal difference between the two?

17   If a children's party in the US served potato chips, pastries, cotton candy and cookies, what would kids at an identical party in the UK be eating? (4 pts)

Total Points: 21. Targets: Novice 8 Pro 16. Your Score: ⬚

Quiz 92. World War II

Twenty straight questions on the global conflict

Part 1

1   In 1939, the Soviet Union invaded which country while attention was diverted to events in central Europe?

2   In which month of which year did the Japanese bomb Pearl Harbor? In which US state does Pearl Harbor lie? (2 pts)

3   Which two countries signed the Molotov–Ribbentrop Pact in August 1939? (2 pts)

4   Which monastery was the scene of a brutal and costly episode in the Allied push through Italy in early 1944?

5   Who became known as 'The Few', after a speech by Churchill praising their contribution to the war effort?

6   Operation Husky (9–10 July, 1943) saw the Allied forces seize control of which strategically crucial island in the Mediterranean?

7   A secret meeting between Churchill and Roosevelt in Newfoundland in 1941 led to the signing of which Allied accord?

8   Sword; Omaha; Gold; Orange; Juno; Eagle; Utah: which two of these were not names designated to beaches assaulted during the 1944 Normandy landings? (2 pts)

9   Which French city was the location of the German surrender on 7 May 1945?

10 The German Operation Typhoon was a major offensive launched with the intention of securing which city? (a) Paris (b) Kiev (c) Moscow

Part 2

11 Churchill has been condemned by many post-war historians for a torrid bombing campaign against which German city in 1945, with the tide of the war already turned firmly in favour of the Allies?

12 22 June 1941 saw the start of Operation Barbarossa; what was it?

13 The *Anschluss*, formally declared on 12 March 1938, was the union of which two countries? (2 pts)

14 Where in Italy did Allied forces land on 22 January 1944?

15 In 1942, the entire population of which country were awarded the George Cross for bravery for their resistance during World War II?

16 Which Libyan city was under siege by the Germans and their allies for 240 days in 1941?

17 What was the area of Czechoslovakia ceded to the Germans at the 1938 Munich agreement, and later used as a springboard for German annexation of the rest of Czechoslovakia?

18 HMS *Exeter*, HMS *Achilles* and HMS *Ajax* took on which German ship in a naval battle off the coast of South America in September 1939? What name has been given to the encounter, and in which harbour did the German battleship seek sanctuary? (3 pts)

19 Neville Chamberlain resigned as Prime Minister in May 1940 shortly after the Allied retreat from which occupied country?

20 Which British sovereign territory surrendered to the Japanese on Christmas Day 1941? And which primary Allied base fell in February 1942? (2 pts)

Total Points: 27. Targets: Novice 11 Pro 20. Your Score:

Quiz 93. Movies

Just a general mish-mash (but nothing about *M*A*S*H*)

Part 1

1   Why is Bill Murray's character (Bob) in Tokyo in the movie *Lost in Translation* (2003)?

2   In the French New Wave's most successful film, Jeanne Moreau's character (Catherine) falls in love with two men, Jules and Jim. Who directed the 1962 movie? (a) Jean Cocteau (b) Jean-Paul Godard (c) François Truffaut

3   What was designed by Cedric Gibbons and made out of twenty-four carat gold by George Stanley, weighs 8½ pounds and stands 1 ft 1½ in tall?

4   If Martha Vickers as Carmen Sternwood and Dorothy Malone as a bookstore assistant are the minor flirtations, who was the major love interest? And what is the movie? (2 pts)

5   In which language was *Crouching Tiger, Hidden Dragon* filmed?

6   On what date is the Frank Capra classic *It's a Wonderful Life* set?

7   Who took the part of Mr Pink in Tarantino's *Reservoir Dogs*, a role the director had reportedly earmarked for himself?

8   Which novelist adapted *Pride and Prejudice* for Joe Wright's movie version? (a) Emma Thompson (b) Deborah Moggach (c) Hilary Mantel

9   Which electronic band composed all the music for *Tron: Legacy* in 2010? (a) Daft Punk (b) Chemical Brothers (c) Kraftwerk

10 Who plays corrupt sheriff Hank Quinlan in Orson Welles's *Touch of Evil* (1958)?

11 As well as being a B-movie horror film of some panache, *The Blob* (1958) also saw an early star turn by which Hollywood icon?

12 What is the name of the vegetation assessor that becomes the object of the hero's affection in *WALL-E*?

13 Which pair of real-life brothers (including first names) play the titular roles in *The Fabulous Baker Boys* (1989)? And what is the name of the alluring singer for whom they both fall, played by Michelle Pfeiffer? (3 pts)

14 Who stars as the perfect, over-achieving Tracy Flick in *Election* (1999), Alexander Payne's 1999 film about high-school jealousies?

Part 2

Six questions and a tricky connection to solve

15   Who got tetchy when British critics ridiculed his English accent in Ridley
     Scott's 2010 *Robin Hood*?

16   *A Bronx Tale* (1993) was the directorial debut of which Hollywood star?

17   Who was the I in *I Am Legend*?

18   In 1999 Gwyneth Paltrow won an Academy Award in a role in *Shakespeare
     in Love* that demanded she spent much of the film pretending to be a man;
     who replicated this feat the following year, and in which film?

19   Who won an Oscar nomination for his portrayal of American activist
     Malcolm X?

20   What are the five related movies (with similar subject matter) that connect
     these five stars? (5 pts)

Total Points: 27. Targets: Novice 14 Pro 20. Your Score: ☐

Quiz 94. World Cup

A straight quiz on football's biggest circus

Part 1

1   In the 2010 World Cup final, referee Howard Webb handed out nine yellow cards to Dutch players; who got two and was sent off?

2   In 1982 Sheikh Fahd al-Sabah ran on to the pitch in a World Cup match to protest against the award of a goal against his team. Which two sides were playing? What happened to the Sheikh in 1990? (3 pts)

3   Which two sides, neither of whom made it past the group stages, did Pelé predict would contest the 2002 World Cup final? (2 pts)

4   Which five nations have won most games at the World Cup finals? (Hint: England dropped to sixth in 2010.) (5 pts)

5   Which four nations have won the Women's World Cup since it started in 1991 (six tournaments)? (4 pts)

6   Which two sides beat England and subjected them to a humiliating early exit when they first played in the World Cup finals in 1950? (2 pts)

7   Who are the only two teams to win the World Cup final on penalties? And which three teams have eliminated England by the same method? (5 pts)

8   Who was the Scottish manager who paid for his hubris and pre-tournament predictions with an embarrassing early exit in 1978? Who beat a complacent Scots side in their opening match? Who scored twice as the players nearly redeemed themselves with a superb 3–2 win over the Dutch in the last game? (3 pts)

9   Who scored the goal that enabled the Republic of Ireland to beat Italy at the 1994 World Cup finals? Who was their manager for this and the 1990 tournament, when they also reached the knockout phase? (2 pts)

10 Who is the only player to have scored a goal for Italy in the World Cup finals and also played in the Premier League?

Part 2

11 Who was manager of the Republic of Ireland when Roy Keane had a hissy fit and walked out prior to the 2002 World Cup finals? Who missed a penalty in their knockout match against Spain, and who scored a nerveless one in the last minute to force extra time? (3 pts)

12 Who, aged forty, was the oldest World Cup winning captain?

13 Who has played most World Cup finals matches (seventeen) for England?

14 When was the last time an England World Cup squad featured only players playing in the English leagues?

15 Which three members of the England World Cup squad from 2010 were travelling to their third World cup tournament? (3 pts)

16 Which two members of England's 1986 World Cup squad were playing for AC Milan at the time? (2 pts)

17 Which two clubs had more than one player in England's World Cup final winning team? (2 pts)

18 Who, in 1962, was the first man to be picked for an England World Cup finals squad whilst playing abroad? Which club side did he play for? (2 pts)

19 Who were the two teenagers picked in England's 2006 World Cup squad? And which two members of the Euro 2012 squad probably had to ask their parents' permission? (4 pts)

20 Geoff Hurst remains the only man to score a hat-trick in a World Cup final; which three players since 1966 have scored twice in a single final? (3 pts)

Total Points: 50. Targets: Novice 20 Pro 38. Your Score:

Quiz 95. Alter Egos

By other names shall ye know them . . .

Part 1

1 By what name do we know the actor Richard Jenkins, born in Wales in 1925 and deceased in Switzerland in 1984?

2 Actress Kate Hardie derives her surname from both her parents' last names; the 'Har' came from her mother, Jean Hart, so who was her comedian cum naturalist father? And which well-known photographer was Kate's husband in 1995–8? (2 pts)

3 Under what name did Bristol-born Archibald Leach earn Hollywood stardom?

4 By what name is the US politician born as William Blythe better known?

5 What is K. T. Tunstall's first name? (a) Kate (b) Kim (c) Kelly

6 Which all-girl band used the stage names T-Boz, Left Eye and Chilli?

7 Brian Warner got his stage name from combining a tragic actress with a cult leader; who is he?

8 Caryn Johnson became a stand-up comic and referenced a joke-shop staple with which stage name?

9 Which Academy Award winning British actress was born Julia Elizabeth Wells in 1935?

10 Why did David Cornwell have to publish under the pseudonym John le Carré?

Part 2

11   Virginia McMath is dancing in a Hollywood movie with Frederick Austerlitz; who are we watching? (2 pts)

12   Which comedian, film director and actor, born into the Konigsberg family in 1935, used a variation of his first name as his surname when he started his professional career?

13   Acton, Currer and Ellis Bell were pseudonyms for which three famous literary sisters? (Please include first names.) (3 pts)

14   Lynne Stringer and Maurice Micklewhite shared the same stage surname; who are they? (2 pts)

15   What name, far more suitable to his profession, did Shirley Crabtree adopt in his capacity as a sportsman and TV entertainer?

16   Michael Lubowitz's Earth Band wouldn't have had much of a ring to it so he changed his stage name to what?

17   Edson Arantes do Nascimento. You've heard of him, but by what name?

18   *Sketches by Boz* is the first published work by which literary great? And under what pseudonym did Hablot Knight Browne illustrate many of his books? (2 pts)

19   Frederick Dannay and Manfred B. Lee were a writing team who published crime novels under which name?

20   Who was behind the outrageous TV personality Lily Savage?

Total Points: 26. Targets: Novice 13 Pro 21. Your Score:

Quiz 96. General Knowledge

Solve the (occasionally mildly cryptic) clues and identify these people, all of whom died in 2012 – their age at the time of their death is given in brackets where applicable

1   'Don't panic, Mr Mainwaring . . .' (92)
2   Norah's dad (92)
3   Beastie MCA (47)
4   Clouseau's boss (95)
5   Chelsea manager 1967–74 (82)
6   She'd rather have gone blind (73)
7   Emmanuelle (60)
8   Winger known as 'The Swerve' (65)
9   Soapy Texan bad guy (81)
10 He was *Where the Wild Things Are* (83)

Part 2

11 TV's Mr Astronomy (89)
12 His quartet Took Five (91)
13 He wanted to tell you a story and get you to singalong (89)
14 He taught you to *Learn Guitar in a Day* (91)
15 Three time Golden Cuban boxer (60)
16 Directed a classic comedy film about a piece of wood (89)
17 Stormin' Norman, Gulf Warrior (78)
18 Won an Oscar for *Marty* (95)
19 I'll have a vowel . . . (83)
20 The voice of darts (72, not 180 alas)

Total Points: 20. Targets: Novice 10 Pro 15. Your Score: [   ]

Answers Quizzes 89–96

Quiz 89. General Knowledge

1. Oxford; 2. Paul Revere; 3. True (there have only been four non-Italian Popes, apart from a few Frenchmen when the Papacy was disputed); 4. Golden Temple at Amritsar; assassination of Indira Gandhi by her Sikh bodyguards; 5. (b) Alan Pascoe; 6. Acting or drama; 7. He wrote the theme tune; 8. There are thirty-one (eleven England, seven Scotland, two Great Britain, two Kingdom of Ireland, nine UK); 9. Route 66; 10. Vendée Globe; 24; 11. Stephen Fry; 12. Ozzy Osbourne; 13. Jimmy Nail; 14. David Dickinson; 15. Dirty Den (Leslie Grantham); 16. They have all served time in jail

Quiz 90. Name the Band

1. Kasabian; 2. McFly; 3. Dixie Chicks; 4. The Vaccines; 5. Maroon 5; 6. The National; 7. Elbow; 8. My Chemical Romance; 9. Girls Aloud; 10. The Black Keys; 11. One Direction; 12. Muse; 13. The xx; 14. The Dead Weather; 15. Snow Patrol; 16. The Killers (Brandon Flowers); 17. Mumford and Sons (Jason Mumford); 18. The Strokes (Julian Casablancas); 19. Grizzly Bear (Ed Droste); 20. Arctic Monkeys (Alex Turner)

Quiz 91. Food and Drink

1. Courgettes and mashed swede (and chicken, obviously); 2. Delia Smith; 3. Al dente; 4. Ballymaloe; 5. Maris Piper; 6. Ice-cream cone; 7. Tequila (also mezcal); the infamous worm is the larva of a moth which feeds on the agave; 8. Nigel Slater; 9. Ghee; 10. Le Cordon Bleu; 11. Hazelnut; 12. Grand Marnier (any orange flavoured liqueur would substitute); 13. Whey; 14. Chez Panisse; 15. The word masticate means to chew and is inappropriate here – the word should be macerate; 16. Mascarpone is a cream cheese, ricotta is a whey cheese (made from the whey left over after conventional cheese production, and suitable for people with milk allergy but not lactose intolerance); 17. Crisps, cakes, candy floss and biscuits

Quiz 92. World War II

1. Finland; 2. December 1941; Hawaii (on the island of Oahu); 3. Soviet Union and Germany (it was a pact of non-aggression that allowed both powers to invade agreed territories); 4. Monte Cassino; 5. The RAF pilots at the Battle of Britain; 6. Sicily; 7. Atlantic Charter; 8. Orange and Eagle (Sword and Gold were assaulted by British infantry, Juno by Canadian forces and Utah and Omaha by the US infantry, who took heavy casualties at Omaha); 9. Rheims; 10. Moscow (it was a three-pronged attack repulsed by rapid Soviet deployment of extra manpower from the East); 11. Dresden; 12. German invasion of the Soviet Union; 13. Germany and Austria; 14. Anzio; 15. Malta; 16. Tobruk; 17. Sudetenland; 18. *Graf Spee*; Battle of River Plate, Montevideo; 19. Norway; 20. Hong Kong; Singapore

Quiz 93. Movies

1. He is an actor shooting an advert for whiskey; 2. François Truffaut; 3. The Oscar statuette; 4. Lauren Bacall as Vivian Rutledge, opposite Bogart in *The Big Sleep*; 5. Mandarin Chinese; 6. Christmas Eve; 7. Steve Buscemi; 8. (b) Deborah Moggach; 9. (a) Daft Punk; 10. Welles plays the part himself; 11. Steve McQueen; 12. EVE; 13. Jeff Bridges and Beau Bridges; Susie Diamond; 14. Reese Witherspoon; 15. Russell Crowe; 16. Robert De Niro; 17. Will Smith; 18. Hilary Swank (in *Boys Don't Cry*); 19. Denzel Washington; 20. The connection is boxing (Crowe in *Cinderella Man*; De Niro in *Raging Bull*; Smith in *Ali*; Swank in *Million Dollar Baby*; Washington in *Hurricane*; all except Crowe won Oscar nominations at least)

Quiz 94. World Cup

1. Johnny Heitinga; 2. France and Kuwait (the referee upheld the claim that the Kuwaitis were distracted by a whistle and disallowed the goal; France were 3–1 up and won 4–1); he was killed in the First Gulf War by Iraqi troops; 3. Argentina and France; 4. Brazil, Germany, Italy, Argentina and Spain; 5. United States (1991 and 1999); Norway (1995); Germany (2003 and 2007); Japan (2011); 6. Spain and United States (the US won 1–0 but sections of the England press assumed the result was a misprint and reported the score as 10–1 to England); 7. Brazil in 1994 and Italy in 2006; Germany in 1990, Argentina in 1998 and Portugal in 2006; 8. Ally McLeod; Peru; Archie Gemmill (his second goal was inspired, one of the great goals in World Cup history); 9. Ray Houghton; Jack Charlton; 10. Dino Baggio, who played nine games on loan at Blackburn in 2003 (huge respect to anyone who got this); 11. Mick McCarthy; Ian Harte; Robbie Keane; 12. Dino Zoff (Italy, 1982); 13. Peter Shilton; 14. Not long ago – it was 2010; 15. David James, Ashley Cole and Joe Cole; 16. Ray Wilkins and Mark Hateley; 17. West Ham (Moore, Hurst, Peters) and Manchester United (Charlton and Stiles); 18. Gerry Hitchens of Inter Milan (2 pts); 19. Aaron Lennon and Theo Walcott; Alex Oxlade-Chamberlain and Jack Butland; 20. Mario Kempes (Argentina, 1978); Zinedine Zidane (France, 1998) and Ronaldo (Brazil, 2002)

Quiz 95. Alter Egos

1. Richard Burton; 2. Bill Oddie; Rankin; 3. Cary Grant; 4. Bill Clinton (Clinton was actually his stepfather's name); 5. (a) Kate; 6. TLC; 7. Marilyn Manson (not sure he would have reached the same level of notoriety as Brian Warner . . .); 8. Whoopi Goldberg; 9. Julie Andrews; 10. Because he was a diplomat and not allowed to publish under his own name; 11. Ginger Rogers and Fred Astaire; 12. Woody Allen, born Allan Konigsberg; 13. Anne, Charlotte and Emily Brontë; 14. Marti Caine and Michael Caine; 15. He was the wrestler, Big Daddy; 16. Manfred Mann; 17. Pelé; 18. Charles Dickens; Phiz; 19. Ellery Queen (the name was also used for a leading character in many of the books); 20. Paul O'Grady

Quiz 96. General Knowledge

1. Clive Dunn; 2. Ravi Shankar; 3. Adam Yauch; 4. Herbert Lom; 5. Dave Sexton; 6. Soul singer Etta James; 7. Sylvia Kristel; 8. Mervyn Davies; 9. Larry Hagman; 10. Maurice Sendak; 11. Patrick Moore; 12. Dave Brubeck; 13. Max Bygraves; 14. Bert Weedon; 15. Teófilo Stevenson; 16. Eric Sykes; 17. Norman Schwarzkopf; 18. Ernest Borgnine; 19. Bob Holness; 20. Sid Waddell

Quiz 97. General Knowledge

Who said that? (Come on, own up . . .)

Part 1

1 'The only genius with an IQ of 60.' Which great post-war writer on which 1960s cultural icon? (2 pts)

2 'There are three kinds of lies: lies, damned lies and statistics.' Who was Mark Twain quoting when he recorded this pithy summary?

3 'Please don't call me arrogant, but I'm European Champion and I think I'm a special one.' Who?

4 'You can over-communicate; we're over-communicating piffle. You don't need to tell everyone you've just had a crap or hear that Sarah Brown isn't eating veal.' Janet Street-Porter on what topic?

5 'When the President does it, that means it's not illegal.' Who is justifying himself to whom? (2 pts)

6 'I am satisfied that the diaries are authentic.' Who regretted saying this about what? (They weren't.) (2 pts)

7 'There is no light so perfect as that which shines from an open fridge door at 2 a.m.' Which food writer?

8 'Mr Gladstone addresses me as though I were a public meeting.' Who was taking offence?

9 'I don't really class myself as a footballer. I call myself an entertainer.' Which footballer?

10 'Come, friendly bombs, and fall on Slough! / It isn't fit for humans now.' Which Poet Laureate?

11 'Margaret Thatcher says she has given the French President a piece of her mind – this is not a gift I would receive with alacrity.' Which opposition wit?

12 'I can't see the sense in it really. It makes me a Commander of the British Empire. They might as well make me a Commander of Milton Keynes – at least that exists.' Which comedian and writer is a little baffled by the British honours system?

13 'You were a right old slapper in the seventies, weren't you?' Which feminist icon is feeling the rough end of Mrs Merton's tongue?

14 'He couldn't bowl a hoop downhill.' A typically churlish dismissal of Ian Botham by which former player turned commentator?

15 'Rock 'n' roll is not just music. You're selling an attitude, too. Take away the attitude and you're just like anyone else. The kids need a sense of adventure and rock 'n' roll gives it to them.' Which pop guru and entrepreneur?

Total Points: 18. Targets: Novice 7 Pro 14. Your Score: [   ]

Quiz 98. Sci-Fi Movies

To boldly go – twenty questions on science-fiction films

Part 1

1   What is the name of the Jonathan Pryce character in Terry Gilliam's bizarre satire, *Brazil*? And what is the occupation of Tuttle (Robert De Niro)? (2 pts)

2   'But he's just a raggedy-man!' Who is dismissing whom in which movie? (2 pts)

3   Johnny Rico, Dizzy Flores and Sugar Watkins are all characters in which high-octane 1997 sci-fi action movie? Who made the film? (2 pts)

4   What was the 1955 Hammer Horror sci-fi chiller, essentially a remake of a 1953 TV series, the first adult sci-fi series on the BBC?

5   What are the names of Marty's parents in the *Back to the Future* trilogy? (2 pts)

6   Who played Superman in the 1980s film versions, and which British actor was cast in the 2013 reboot? (2 pts)

7   Who stars in *Westworld* (1973) as a creepy robotic gunslinger?

8   What was David Lynch's flawed but somehow mesmerizing take on a classic sci-fi novel by Frank Herbert?

9   In the two remakes of the *Planet of the Apes* franchise (Tim Burton, 2001, and Rupert Wyatt, 2011), which actors took the role made famous by Charlton Heston in the 1968 original? (2 pts)

10   What name is given to the psychics who forewarn the police department when a crime will take place in *Minority Report*? Who plays Agatha, the most potent of the three psychics? (2 pts)

Part 2

11   Which two actors have played Spider-Man in Hollywood versions of the story in the twenty-first century? (2 pts)

12   In which decade was the original Godzilla (or Gojira, if you're feeling pretentious) movie made? Which city is the monster devastating in the movie? (2 pts)

13   *La Jetée* was an experimental twenty-eight minute sci-fi film made in 1962 by Chris Marker; what was it called when Terry Gilliam remade it as a full-length film with Bruce Willis in 1995? And what film starring Willis in 2012 adopted the same premise, with a time-travelling investigator? (2 pts)

14   What was the seminal 1951 sci-fi film with an inquisitive alien called Klaatu and his robot-minder, Gort?

15   Who connects the 1971 sci-fi virus-thriller film *The Andromeda Strain* with the 1978 medical-horror-suspense film *Coma*?

16   What was the 1981 sci-fi thriller, inspired by *High Noon* and starring Sean Connery as a policeman investigating murders on an isolated mining planet?

17   What was the 'curse' commonly ascribed to the *Star Trek* films by fans, and how was it broken? (2 pts)

18   Who is the CEO of InGen in a 1993 sci-fi thriller directed by Steven Spielberg, and what does the company do? (2 pts)

19   Leeloominaï Lekatariba Lamina-Tchaï Ekbat De Sebat (known simply as Leeloo, and played by Milla Jovovich); who looks after her when she falls on to his taxi, and in which 1997 Luc Besson film? (2 pts)

20   Which star, who had a major comic renaissance in the 1980s, played the heroic Commander Adams in *Forbidden Planet* (1956)? And who played his love interest, the alien, Altaira Morbius? (2 pts)

Total Points: 34. Targets: Novice 14 Pro 26. Your Score: [   ]

Quiz 99. Books

They do furnish a room (according to Anthony Powell)

Part 1

1   The John Galsworthy novels *A Man of Property*, *In Chancery* and *To Let* are commonly known by which collective name?

2   Roger Corman made seven films based on the stories of which Gothic master?

3   Who wrote a story about a proud cockerel called Chaunticleer, and who is the narrator of the story? (2 pts)

4   In which decade was *Whitaker's Almanack* first published: 1860s, 1890s or 1930s?

5   Who embarks on a long challenge with the aid of his 'mate' Passepartout?

6   In Alexandre Dumas' *The Three Musketeers*, who is the young man who helps the musketeers and from what part of France, regarded with disdain by the Parisians, does he come? (2 pts)

7   *Don't Fall Off the Mountain* (1970) and *Dancing in the Light* (1986) are books which combine autobiography and spiritual musings by which Hollywood star?

8   The 2009 Booker winner *Wolf Hall* concerned the life of which historical figure? Who wrote it? What was the 2012 follow-up which, uniquely for a sequel to a previous winner, won the same prize? (3 pts)

9   What connects the historical romancers, Jean Plaidy, Victoria Holt and Philippa Carr?

10 Who had *An Awfully Big Adventure* in 1989?

Part 2

11 Who or what was the subject matter of *Shout!*, biographer Philip Norman's exhaustive 1981 work which he updated in 1996?

12 What is the only completed book by Alain-Fournier, and why was he unable to complete more? (2 pts)

13 What was Mike Wilks's intricate art book, published in 1988, and sold as a competition for readers to enter having studied the images in the book?

14 Which classic book, written by whom, revolves around a lengthy court case, Jarndyce v. Jarndyce? (2 pts)

15 Who took over sponsorship of the Whitbread Book Awards from 2006?

16 The Big Read was a public poll in the UK in 2004 to find the nation's favourite books; fifteen of the top twenty were by British authors. Which were the four American books in the top twenty, and which was the only mainland European novel? (5 pts)

Total Points: 26. Targets: Novice 10 Pro 20. Your Score:

Quiz 100. Gardening

Time for the urban flat-dwellers to twiddle their thumbs and leave it to those whose fingers are green

Part 1

1   Where is the Royal Horticultural Society's own garden to be found?

2   In which country are the Keukenhof Gardens, the largest flower garden in the world open to the public?

3   Who was BBC *Gardeners' World*'s longest serving lead presenter?

4   Absolutely Fabulous, Moulin Rouge, Great Expectations, Sunset Boulevard; which of these has not been awarded the rose of the year prize by Roses UK?

5   What is the Japanese art of growing miniature trees?

6   Garden designer Gertrude Jekyll was a key player in which artistic movement around the turn of the nineteenth century? Which architect was her most frequent collaborator? (2 pts)

7   *Dear Friend and Gardener*, published 1998, detailed the correspondence between Christopher Lloyd and which other prominent garden writer?

8   Which garden flowers caused a brief obsession amongst enthusiasts that saw prices of the flowers rise to the cost of semi-precious stones in the first half of the seventeenth century?

9   Who was the English property developer who left a bequest that helped create a gardening institute in Merton Park, Surrey, where the scientists developed a compost that still bears his name?

10   A fruit tree trained to grow only laterally so it stands flat against a wall or on a border is described by what word?

Part 2

Mix and Match: gardener's question time – match the Latin name to the common name of these familiar plants

1. Impatiens; 2. Galanthus; 3. Narcissus; 4. Helianthus; 5. Dianthus; 6. Althea; 7. Papaver; 8. Syringa; 9. Pyracantha; 10. Antirrhinum

a. Sunflower; b. Lilac; c. Hollyhock; d. Busy Lizzie; e. Snapdragon; f. Daffodil; g. Firethorn; h. Poppy; i. Sweet William; j. Snowdrop

Your Workings:

Total Points: 21. Targets: Novice 8 Pro 16. Your Score:

Quiz 101. Military Encounters

General knowledge – no, really, your knowledge of generals and other things military is being tested

Part 1

1   The Battle of Bunker Hill, fought 16 June 1775, was part of which wider conflict?

2   Which former trading station was the scene of a heroic rearguard action by 150 troops during the Zulu wars?

3   A dragoon is (a) a light cavalryman (b) a siege engine or (c) a member of the French Head of State's household guard?

4   Hannibal was eventually defeated by which Roman general at the Battle of Zama during the Second Punic War in *c.*202 BC? (a) Pompey (b) Marcus Aurelius (c) Scipio

5   What was the name given to the British force sent to France at the start of World War II?

6   Which city was besieged by German forces and their allies for 872 days in 1941–2?

7   The first day of which 1916 engagement saw the heaviest British casualties of any single day in the history of warfare?

8   Who led the German Sixth Army's assault on Stalingrad in 1942?

9   Antietam, Chickamauga and Shiloh were all battles during which brutal conflict?

10 The Battle of the Ebro was the biggest single conflict in which twentieth-century conflict?

Part 2

11   Where did the Allied forces, mainly US, direct their first counter-offensive in the Pacific in August 1942?

12   Where, in 1896, did the British fleet regain control in a conflict that lasted thirty-eight minutes after a rebellious Sultan opened fire on the Royal Navy?

13   What connects socialist politician Tony Benn, children's author Roald Dahl, jockey and author Dick Francis and actor Peter Sellers?

14   The independence of which country was established by a war that lasted from 1821 to 1828, when it ultimately defeated Turkey, but only with help from Britain, Russia and France?

15   What was the politically ideological wing of the German Army, which effectively became the fourth limb of the Wehrmacht alongside the Army, Navy and Air Force?

16   The Battle of Bosworth (1485) ended which thirty-year conflict?

17   Who defeated who at the Battle of Dien Bien Phu in May 1954? (2 pts)

18   What name is given to the campaign by the allied forces (mainly British assisted by guerrillas from the occupied countries) to oust Napoleon's armies from Spain and Portugal?

19   Which Crusade included the Battle of Jaffa (1192) and who led the Christian forces against Saladin? (2 pts)

20   How long did hostilities in the first Gulf War last: forty-three days, six months or fourteen months?

Total Points: 22. Targets: Novice 9 Pro 17. Your Score:

Quiz 102. Rock and Pop

All sorts, for all ages, so bring the family

Part 1

1   *Seasons of My Soul* was the 2010 debut album of which singer?

2   Bjorn Again were one of the first tribute bands to be successful in their own right; to which act were they an homage?

3   Who had a surprise hit with the soundtrack from the blaxploitation movie, *Shaft*, replete with wah-wah guitar and stealthy rhythms?

4   Whose song 'Lightning Bolt' from his eponymous UK no. 1 debut album (to be released later the same year) was played as Usain Bolt warmed up for the 100 metres Olympic final in 2012?

5   What song did the Beatles pen for *Our World*, a live global broadcast (the first of its kind) in 1967?

6   Who, in 2012, matched Beyoncé's feat of two years previously and won six Grammy awards in one night?

7   Who broke the hearts of Scouting for Girls according to their 2007 song?

8   Brian Wilson's co-writer on most of the songs on the classic Beach Boys album *Pet Sounds* was Tony Asher; for what kind of musical composition was Asher best known?

9   What was Jean-Michel Jarre's breakthrough third album, which went to no. 2 in the UK album chart? Who was his British actress-girlfriend (later wife) who provided the photography for the cover? (2 pts)

10 Who was the producer who made instant stars of Frankie Goes to Hollywood and what was the label on which the debut album and early singles were released? (2 pts)

Part 2

11   Chris Frantz and Tina Weymouth collaborated on an experimental album (it included the track 'Wordy Rappinghood') in 1981 that would influence funk and hip-hop artists over the next three decades; what was the name under which they recorded and which band was their 'full-time' job? (2 pts)

12   Who duetted with Australian singer-songwriter Nick Cave on the disturbing 'Where the Wild Roses Grow' from his *Murder Ballads* album?

13   Whose 2010 album *Fearless* made her the youngest recipient of the Grammy award for the Best Album of the Year?

14   At what age did Kurt Cobain, Jimi Hendrix, Jim Morrison and Amy Winehouse all die, regarded by some (very silly) people as some sort of divine conspiracy?

15   In a *Rolling Stone* list of 100 Greatest Singers in rock and pop history, only one woman featured in the top ten, but she was at no. 1 – who was she? (Tip: *Rolling Stone* is steeped in history and tradition and pretension, so it isn't going to be Madonna.) Which Brit topped a separate list of singers who fronted bands? (Sorry, Liam, same applies.) (2 pts)

16   Which five brothers made up the Jackson 5? (5 pts)

Total Points: 24. Targets: Novice 10 Pro 18. Your Score:

Quiz 103. TV Drama

From both sides of the Atlantic

Part 1

1 Who played the First Lady to Martin Sheen's President in *The West Wing*?

2 Which US TV series starred Mary-Louise Parker as a middle-class mum who starts dealing dope to support her children's lifestyle?

3 Who played the bitter married couple at the centre of the black comedy *At Home with the Braithwaites*? (2 pts)

4 Which popular TV character referred genially to his wife as 'she who must be obeyed'?

5 What was the 1976 drama, scripted by Andrea Newman from her own novel, that set the tabloids chattering and tongues wagging with intimations of incest, part of a smorgasbord of illicit desire and infidelity?

6 Teri Hatcher, Marcia Cross, Felicity Huffman and Eva Longoria are all what?

7 *Longford* (2006) concerned the efforts of Labour peer Lord Longford (Jim Broadbent) to have which historical figure released on parole? Who played the prisoner with chilling accuracy? (2 pts)

8 Aiden Gillen and Charlie Hunnam both starred in which groundbreaking Channel 4 drama of 1999? What part did Gillen play in *The Wire*? And which US drama has featured Hunnam as a lead character since 2008? (3 pts)

9 Which 1970s drama started with Captain Webster selling the *Charlotte Rose*, a seagoing vessel?

10 What is unconventional about the regular appearances of Richard Jenkins as Nathaniel Fisher Sr in *Six Feet Under*?

Part 2

11 What was the powerful drama set in a Japanese prisoner-of-war camp for women? Who gave the performances of their careers as the courageous Rose and chippy Blanche? (3 pts)

12 What connects Jaime Murray and Kelly Adams?

13 *Band of Gold*, *Playing the Field* and *Fat Friends* were all the work of which writer? What was the setting for *Playing the Field*? (2 pts)

14 What was the 2001 TV film about the meeting at which a committee of Nazi officials matter-of-factly come up with the 'Final Solution'? Who played Heydrich and Eichmann, the architects of the plan? (3 pts)

15 What role did John Hurt reprise from thirty-four years earlier in the 2009 drama *An Englishman in New York*?

16 What was Alex Haley's slave drama, screened in the 1970s and still one of the most-watched dramas in US TV history?

17 Who are Fiona, Lip, Ian and Liam?

18 Which US drama series is based in New Orleans in the aftermath of the devastation caused by Hurricane Katrina? What is the profession of Antoine Batiste, played by Wendell Pierce (Bunk in *The Wire*)? (2 pts)

19 What was the presidential sounding name of the Sheriff (Michael Ontkean) in *Twin Peaks*?

20 What sort of health centre did Peter Davison run on the campus of Lowlands University in the 1980s?

Total Points: 30. Targets: Novice 12 Pro 23. Your Score:

Quiz 104. General Knowledge

Part 1

1 John Eric Bartholomew and Ernest Wiseman; who are they?

2 How did Glaswegian John Smeaton become a national hero in 2007?

3 What was the name of the old Roman fertility festival celebrated on 13–15 February? (a) Lunalia (b) Lupercalia (c) Lycanthropia

4 Vladimir Ilyich Ulyanov died in 1924. By what name is he more commonly known?

5 Jürgen Hingsen of Germany was the great rival to which British superstar, but never managed to beat him in one of the big events?

6 Why has Aretha Franklin not toured outside the US since 1983?

7 What are the Moai?

8 What was held for the first time in 1453? (Everything afterwards was an anti-climax.)

9 Which spice comes from the stigmas of a species of crocus and is the most expensive spice to buy due to the intensiveness of farming it?

10 Who manufactured the sports car racer the Sebring Sprite?

Part 2

11 Which of these American place names does *not* exist? (a) Boring, Oregon (b) Hygiene, Colorado (c) Pigsbreath, Idaho (d) Hell, Michigan

12 On 14 July 1789, a Paris mob stormed which symbol of aristocratic repression?

13 What is the name given to the effect whereby a tiny change in the initial conditions of a prognosis produces a wildly different end result?

14 The longest river in Canada, the Mackenzie, flows northeast into which body of water?

15 What product is the main UK import from Norway? (a) dry ice (b) gas (c) fish

16 Who narrated *Bagpuss* and how many episodes were made: twelve in two series, thirteen in one series, or eighteen in three series?

17 *And Smith must score . . .* has become the ironic title of a fanzine for which club?

18 Which famous actor was known as 'Little Spartacus' at school?

19 Which glamorous actress/singer was born Holly Vukadinovic?

20 In 1999 a naked man assaulted and injured eleven people in a south London church. With what did he assault them?

Total Points: 20. Targets: Novice 10 Pro 15. Your Score:

Answers Quizzes 97–104

Quiz 97. General Knowledge

1. Gore Vidal on Andy Warhol; 2. Benjamin Disraeli, quoted in Mark Twain's autobiography, 1924.; 3. José Mourinho in his first press conference as Chelsea manager (he has been proved right); 4. Janet Street-Porter is having a pop at the Twitter phenomenon; 5. Richard Nixon, 1977, explaining away his actions during Watergate to David Frost in a famous interview; 6. Hugh Trevor-Roper in *The Times*, 1983, talking about the 'Hitler Diaries' (his reputation was shot); 7. Nigel Slater; 8. Queen Victoria on her least favourite Prime Minister; 9. George Best; 10. John Betjeman, 'Slough' (1937); 11. Denis Healey; 12. Spike Milligan (he isn't the only one); 13. Germaine Greer; 14. Fred Trueman, who could never abide the thought that anyone might even be half as good as he was (Botham broke his test wickets record for England); 15. Malcolm McLaren

Quiz 98. Sci-Fi Movies

1. Sam Lowry; air-conditioning engineer; 2. Aunty Entity (Tina Turner, either will do) on Max in *Mad Max Beyond Thunderdome*; 3. *Starship Troopers*; Paul Verhoeven; 4. *The Quatermass Xperiment* (if written answers, award a bonus for spelling *Xperiment* without the 'e' at the beginning); 5. George and Lorraine; 6. Christopher Reeve; Henry Cavill; 7. Yul Brynner; 8. *Dune* (to be watched if only for Sting, who gives a great comedy performance without meaning to); 9. Mark Wahlberg and James Franco; 10. Precogs; Samantha Morton; 11. Tobey Maguire and Andrew Garfield; 12. 1950s (1954 to be precise); Tokyo; 13. *Twelve Monkeys*; *Looper*; 14. *The Day the Earth Stood Still*; 15. Michael Crichton (*The Andromeda Strain*, directed by Robert Wise, was taken from a Michael Crichton book; Crichton himself directed *Coma*, an adaptation of a book by Robin Cook); 16. *Outland*; 17. The 'curse' was that odd numbered films would be rubbish (step forward *Star Trek V: The Final Frontier*) and even numbered films of good quality (*Star Trek II: The Wrath of Khan* is still revered by the fan-base); the sequence was broken by *Star Trek: Nemesis* (no. 10) which was bad, and the 2009 re-boot, which was excellent; 18. John Hammond (accept Richard Attenborough, who plays the part); they are the company whose genetic research has recreated dinosaurs in *Jurassic Park*; 19. Bruce Willis (as Korben Dallas); *The Fifth Element*; 20. Leslie Nielsen; Anne Francis

Quiz 99. Books

1. *The Forsyte Saga*; 2. Edgar Allan Poe; 3. Chaucer, it is 'The Nun's Priest's Tale' from *The Canterbury Tales*; 4. 1860s (1868 to be precise) by J. Whitaker and Sons, who continued publishing until 1997; 5. Phineas Fogg in *Around the World in Eighty Days*; 6. D'Artagnan; Gascony; 7. Shirley MacLaine; 8. Thomas Cromwell; Hilary Mantel; *Bring Out the Bodies*; 9. They are all the same person, (Eleanor Hibbert); 10. Beryl Bainbridge; 11. The Beatles; 12. *Le Grande Meaulnes*; he died in World War I; 13. *The Ultimate Alphabet*; 14. *Bleak*

House by Charles Dickens; 15. Costa Coffee (Costa is a subsidiary of Whitbread, and was felt to be a brand which more closely matched a literary prize); 16. No. 6 was *To Kill a Mockingbird* by Harper Lee; no. 11 was *Catch-22* by Joseph Heller; no. 15 was *The Catcher in the Rye* by J. D. Salinger; no. 18 was *Little Women* by Louisa May Alcott; the European work was no. 20, *War and Peace* by Leo Tolstoy

Quiz 100. Gardening

1. Wisley, near Woking, Surrey; 2. Netherlands (near Lisse, in a country park); 3. Geoff Hamilton; 4. Moulin Rouge; the others won in 2010, 2001 and 1997 respectively; 5. Bonsai; 6. Arts and Crafts Movement; Sir Edwin Lutyens; 7. Beth Chatto; 8. Tulips; 9. John Innes; 10. Espalier; Mix and Match: 1, d; 2, j; 3, f; 4, a; 5, i; 6, c; 7, h; 8, b; 9, g; 10, e

Quiz 101. Military Encounters

1. American War of Independence; 2. Rorke's Drift; 3. (a) light cavalryman (it originally meant a mounted infantryman, but evolved into a horse soldier); 4. Scipio, who was known afterwards as Scipio the African; 5. The British Expeditionary Force (the term had been used during World War I); 6. Leningrad (now St Petersburg); 7. Battle of the Somme (19,240 British dead); 8. General Paulus (towards the end when German defeat was inevitable, Hitler promoted Paulus to Field-Marshal and reminded him no German Field-Marshal had ever surrendered; Paulus still surrendered); 9. US Civil War; 10. Spanish Civil War; 11. Guadalcanal; 12. Zanzibar; 13. All served in the RAF during World War II (Benn, in spite of pacifist leanings, fought in the East, Dahl and Francis were airmen, and Sellers was a ground corporal); 14. Greece; 15. Waffen-SS; 16. The Wars of the Roses; 17. The Vietnamese under Ho Chi Minh defeated the French colonial army; Vietnam was divided into North and South, an unsatisfactory arrangement which led to the next conflict in the following decade; 18. Peninsular War; 19. Third; Richard Lionheart; 20. Forty-three days (Iraq was ill-equipped to resist a UN backed twenty-nine nation expeditionary force)

Quiz 102. Rock and Pop

1. Rumer; 2. Abba; 3. Isaac Hayes; 4. Jake Bugg; 5. All You Need Is Love; 6. Adele; 7. Children's TV presenter, Michaela Strachan; 8. Writing advertising jingles; 9. *Oxygène*; Charlotte Rampling; 10. Trevor Horn; Zang Tuum Tumb (ZTT will do); 11. Tom Tom Club; Talking Heads; 12. Kylie Minogue (the track gave the prolific Cave his only UK top twenty hit in a thirty-year career (as of April 2013); 13. Taylor Swift; 14. Twenty-seven; 15. Aretha Franklin; Robert Plant; 16. Jackie, Tito, Jermaine, Marlon and Michael

Quiz 103. TV Drama

1. Stockard Channing; 2. *Weeds*; 3. Amanda Redman and Peter Davison; 4. Rumpole in John Mortimer's *Rumpole of the Bailey*; 5. *Bouquet of Barbed Wire*; 6. *Desperate*

Housewives; 7. Myra Hindley (the Moors Murderer); Samantha Morton; 8. *Queer as Folk*; Tommy Carcetti (Councilman and later Mayor of Baltimore); *Sons of Anarchy*; 9. *The Onedin Line* (the buyer is James Onedin); 10. The character is dead, and only appears in flashbacks or hallucinations; 11. *Tenko*; Stephanie Beacham and Louise Jamieson; 12. They played Stacie Monroe and Emma Kennedy, the two female con-artists in *Hustle*; 13. Kay Mellor; a women's football team; 14. *Conspiracy*; Kenneth Branagh and Stanley Tucci; 15. Quentin Crisp; 16. *Roots*; 17. Some of the Gallagher children in *Shameless*; 18. *Tremé*; a trombonist (accept jazz musician); 19. Harry S. Truman; 20. *A Very Peculiar Practice*

Quiz 104. General Knowledge

1. Morecambe and Wise; 2. He was the 'have-a-go' baggage-handler who tackled fleeing terrorists at Glasgow airport; 3. (b) Lupercalia; 4. Lenin; 5. Daley Thompson; 6. She has a fear of flying after a turbulent short flight; 7. Giant headed statues on Easter Island; 8. The Lord Mayor's Show; 9. Saffron; 10. Austin-Healey; 11. Pigsbreath, Idaho; 12. The Bastille; 13. The Butterfly Effect – it is an aspect of scientific chaos theory; 14. Arctic Ocean; 15. (b) gas, most of it via the massive Langeled Pipeline which connects to the Humber estuary; 16. Oliver Postgate; there were only thirteen, all broadcast in one series in 1974; 17. Brighton and Hove Albion (he didn't score, they drew and subsequently lost the 1983 FA Cup final replay 4–0 to Manchester United); 18. Michael Douglas; 19. Holly Valance; 20. Samurai sword

Quiz 105. General Knowledge

Words, words, words

Part 1

1 Which word, now with a more general meaning of stuff or equipment, meant, in medieval times, a married woman's possessions over which she held personal sway independently from her husband?

2 If you are an expert in zymurgy, in what profession are you likely to be working?

3 In bygone days, if someone were molly, half-rinsed or inked, what condition were they in?

4 What is the difference between the words biennial and biannual?

5 If an unpardonable sin is a mortal sin, what is a lesser one called?

6 What phrase for an idyllic period stems from a mythical bird that calmed the elements?

7 Fiction with a high degree of verisimilitude would be most likely to (a) depict the actual world (b) depict a parallel and alternative world similar to the actual world or (c) present itself as actual truth and conceal the fictive element?

8 What word means both the jargon used by a profession or clique and a deviation at an angle from a plane, but is negative with an apostrophe?

9 Slander and libel; which is verbal, which is written?

10 What is the meaning of the French import to our vocabulary, legerdemain?

Part 2

11 What connects a bowyer and a fletcher?

12 What English term came about as a corruption of the Hindustani word *bilayati*, meaning 'abroad'?

13 The words assassin, leviathan, syrup, sequin and kiosk have all come into English from which region?

14 If one nation unilaterally declares war on another, what are the circumstances?

15 Which German word in use in English encapsulates the idea of deriving pleasure from the misfortune of others?

16 Which nine words make up around 25 per cent of the English written language between them? (1 pt for getting five words, 2 for six etc., up to 5 pts for all nine)

Total Points: 20. Targets: Novice 10 Pro 15. Your Score:

Quiz 106. Rock and Pop

Bits and bats, this and that

Part 1

1   Which folk singer, who died aged twenty-six in 1974, left behind three albums which were largely ignored for the next twenty years until his reputation enjoyed a renaissance in the early 1990s?

2   The 1964 single 'Zoot Suit/I'm the Face' by the High Numbers was the precursor to which highly successful career?

3   What were the second and third albums from Olly Murs, which both went straight to no. 1 in the UK on release in 2011 and 2012? (2 pts)

4   Who was the longstanding producer and friend of John Peel?

5   *Call Me* and *I'm Still in Love with You* are classic albums from which soul legend? (a) Ben E. King (b) Marvin Gaye (c) Al Green

6   Which 1960 song changed the fortunes of singer Ernest Evans (better known by his stage name Chubby Chekker) and started a short-lived dance craze? What was the 1961 follow-up that revived the craze? (2 pts)

7   Which legendary rock band formed initially to honour contractual touring obligations for the Yardbirds?

8   In 2011 the Waterboys released an album with lyrics taken from the poems of which twentieth-century great?

9   What was John Lydon's first project after the disbandment of the Sex Pistols?

10 Which 1980s and 1990s glam-metal crossover band was fronted by Perry Farrell and featured Dave Navarro on guitar?

Part 2

11 *Introducing the Hardline According to* . . . who in 1987?

12 What connects Fela Kuti, the Verve, the Clash and Blur?

13 Who was the singer with bluesy 1960s band Big Brother and the Holding Company? (a) Janis Joplin (b) Joan Baez (c) Grace Slick

14 Who provided the artwork evoking the Paris riots of 1968 and the work of Jackson Pollock for the Stone Roses' 1989 debut album?

15 Which American singer's 1986 album brought the South African singing group Ladysmith Black Mambazo to a wider audience?

16 Norman Cook morphed into Fatboy Slim when he left which 1980s pop band?

17 Which French DJ and producer enjoyed his first no. 1 in the UK as a lead artist aged forty-one in 2009 with 'When Loves Takes Over'?

18 Which Welsh singer had the bestselling album of 2008 but has failed to match that success since? What was the album? (2 pts)

19 What was the American version of Band Aid and what was their hit single? (2 pts)

20 What was Fleetwood Mac's 1979 follow-up (a double LP) to their multi-platinum-selling 1976 effort, *Rumours*?

Total Points: 24. Targets: Novice 10 Pro 18. Your Score:

Quiz 107. Geography

Ten straight questions and a get-your-thinking-caps-on teaser

Part 1

1   The Swedish port of Malmö lies across a narrow strip of the Baltic Sea from which capital city?

2   Which recently independent African country has Juba as its capital city? (a) Djibouti (b) South Sudan (c) Lesotho

3   The city of Palermo is the capital of which territory?

4   Zabid, the hottest city on earth, is found in which country? (a) Yemen (b) Ecuador (c) Pakistan

5   What are Uruguay's two neighbours? (2 pts)

6   What are the four traditional provinces of Ireland? Which is the most populous? (5 pts)

7   Which country has governance of the Mediterranean island of Corsica?

8   What is the mountainous region of France situated south of the city of Clermont-Ferrand? Which industrial giant has its origins in that city? (2 pts)

9   The Pyrénées form a natural border between which two countries? (2 pts)

10 What name is given to the stretch of coastline in West Africa with the Ivory Coast to the west and the Slave Coast to the east?

Part 2

11 Which are the biggest islands in each of the six major continents: Asia, Africa, Europe, North America, South America, Oceania? (6 pts)

Total Points: 23. Targets: Novice 9 Pro 17. Your Score: ⬚

Quiz 108. Food and Drink

Let your tummy do the thinking (I usually do!)

Part 1

1   Who was the chef at the Savoy Hotel who designed the Peach Melba for Dame Nellie Melba, the opera star?

2   Which beer was released from a Bangalore brewery for the first time in 1989?

3   Campylobacter is the most common what in the UK?

4   Who opened a small chocolate shop in Bull Street, Birmingham, in 1824?

5   What name do the Japanese give to edible raw fish?

6   Kecap manis is a sweetened Indonesian variant on which key condiment in Eastern cuisine?

7   Marcus Wareing's restaurant in St Pancras Station is named after which Victorian architect?

8   A beef stew called goulash is the national dish of which European country?

9   Which famous food emporium is found at 181 Piccadilly, London?

10 What is a toque?

Part 2

11 Which of these peppers is graded as the hottest: jalapeno, tabasco or Scotch bonnet?

12 Mortagne-au-Perche in France hosts a celebration of which culinary treat every March? (a) foie gras (b) snails (c) black pudding

13 Torrontes is a signature white wine from which country?

14 What was the name of the first TV cookery series presented by Nigella Lawson?

15 What were Spangles, Texan and Pacers, and what fate did they share?

16 What name is given to the base of sugar syrup and egg yolks used to make a mousse?

17 Something cooked in a pouch of foil or parchment is described as cooked how?

18 DOC is the term applied to Italian wines where the point of origin has been verified (DOCG if it is verified and guaranteed); what is the French equivalent?

19 A wine made in Hunter Valley would be from where? (Be specific) (2 pts)

20 Where does Manchego cheese come from, and from what is it made? (2 pts)

Total Points: 22. Targets: Novice 9 Pro 17. Your Score:

Quiz 109. Children's Books

Kids' literature of yesteryear (Part 1) and yesterday (Part 2)

Part 1

1   A Blue Plaque to which famous children's author can be found at 207 Hook Road, Chessington, Surrey?

2   If Thomas was blue, what colour were James and Gordon? (2 pts)

3   Frederick Marryat's *The Children of the New Forest* is set as which war draws to a close?

4   Who was the author of *101 Dalmatians*, and what was the title of the sequel? (2 pts)

5   Who penned the classic early Victorian adventure for boys, *The Coral Island*?

6   The 1845 work, *A Book of Nonsense*, was a work of children's poems by which celebrated limerick-writer?

7   What kind of creature is Aslan in the Narnia tales of C. S. Lewis?

8   Which story, later a successful animated movie, was E. B. White's first published children's story?

9   In Enid Bagnold's *National Velvet*, what is the sporting achievement accomplished by Velvet's mother?

10 What was P. L. Travers's 1934 bestselling children's book, the first in a series about her most popular character? In which decade was the last of this series written? (2 pts)

Part 2

11 Who has a 'horse' called Blackjack and a 'dog' called Mrs O'Leary?

12 *The Bad Beginning*, where Violet, Klaus and Sunny are sent to live with Count Olaf, is the start of what?

13 Which new Sir (January 2013) is famous for his illustrations to Roald Dahl's stories as well as his own writing and illustration?

14 Who created the imaginative girl-in-care, Tracy Beaker?

15 Axel Scheffler drew *The Gruffalo*, but who wrote the stories? What post was she awarded in 2011? (2 pts)

16 Who created teenage spy Alex Rider?

17 Valkyrie Cain is the assistant in chief to which supernatural detective?

18 Who is the teenage heroine of *Angus, Thongs and Full-Frontal Snogging*, the first in a series of 'Confessions . . .' written by Louise Rennison?

19 *Wolves* (2005) and *Little Mouse's Big Book of Fears* (2008) both won which award for writer/illustrator Emily Gravett?

20 If *Rodrick Rules* was the second and *The Third Wheel* the seventh and most recent, what were the first and sixth? (2 pts)

Total Points: 25. Targets: Novice 10 Pro 19. Your Score:

Quiz 110. Name the Team

We give you a sporting team from a famous contest and you fill in the gaps. No football – they're elsewhere

Part 1

1. The England cricket team that won the miraculous Headingley Test of 1981: Gooch; Boycott; MISSING; Gower; MISSING; Willey; Botham; MISSING; MISSING; Old; MISSING (batting order) (5 pts)

2. The England team that won the 2003 Rugby World Cup final: Lewsey; MISSING; Greenwood; MISSING (sub: Catt 79); Cohen; Wilkinson; MISSING; Dallaglio; MISSING; Hill (Sub: Moody 93); Kay; Johnson; Vickery (sub: MISSING 86); Thompson; Woodman (in formation) (5 pts)

3. The Welsh team that clinched the 1976 Five Nations Grand Slam with a 19–13 victory over a very strong French team: MISSING; G. Davies; Gravell; MISSING; John Williams; MISSING; Edwards; M. Davies; Taylor; Evans; David; Wheel; Martin; MISSING; MISSING; Faulkner (in formation) (5 pts)

4. The 1985 Ryder Cup team that won back the trophy from the US in 1985: Ballesteros (Spa); MISSING (Sco); Canizares (Spa); Clark (Eng); MISSING (Eng); Langer (Ger); MISSING (Sco): Pinero (Spa); Rivero (Spa); Torrance (Sco); MISSING (Eng); MISSING (Wal); Captain: Jacklin (alphabetical order) (5 pts)

5. The West Indies team that beat England in the second Cricket World Cup final in 1979: Greenidge; MISSING; Richards; MISSING; MISSING; King; Murray; MISSING; MISSING; Holding; Croft (batting order) (5 pts)

6. The Australian team that completed a 5–0 whitewash of West Indies in January 2001: MISSING; Hayden; Langer; M. Waugh; S. Waugh; MISSING; MISSING; Gillespie; Miller; MISSING; MISSING (batting order) (5 pts)

7. The US team that won the 2008 Ryder Cup: Campbell; MISSING; Curtis; MISSING; Holmes; Kim; MISSING; MISSING; Mickelson; Perry; Stricker; MISSING; Captain: Azinger (alphabetical order) (5 pts)

8. The England XV that started the momentous victory over the All Blacks in 2012: MISSING; Ashton; MISSING; Barritt; Brown; Farell; MISSING; Corbisiero; MISSING; Cole; Launchbury; Parling; Wood; MISSING; Morgan (in formation) (5 pts)

9. The England XI that annihilated Australia in the final two Tests of the 2010–11 Ashes series: Strauss; Cook; MISSING; Pietersen: MISSING: Bell; MISSING; Bresnan; MISSING; MISSING; Anderson (batting order) (5 pts)

10. The 2012 Ryder Cup team that came back on the last day to retain the trophy: Colsaerts (Bel); MISSING (Eng); Garcia (Spa); Hanson (Swe); Kaymer

(Ger); MISSING (Sco); MISSING (Nir); McIlroy (Nir); Molinari (Ita); Poulter (eng); MISSING (Eng); Westwood (Eng); Captain: MISSING (alphabetical order) (5 pts)

Total Points: 50. Targets: Novice 20 Pro 38. Your Score:

Quiz 111. Doctor Who

Who's who? A straight quiz on the Doctor(s) and his companions

Part 1

1   Who played the eighth Doctor, but only for one made-for-TV movie in 1996?

2   Where was Torchwood located in the spin-off series from *Doctor Who*? Who was in charge? (2 pts)

3   What was Gwen Cooper's job before she joined the Torchwood team? In which *Doctor Who* episode did actress Eve Myles appear, a fact referred to in a later episode when the Doctor and Rose recognize her similar appearance? (2 pts)

4   Charles Dickens; Vincent van Gogh; Jane Austen; William Shakespeare; Agatha Christie: which of these has *not* appeared in an episode of the modern-era *Doctor Who* (up to March 2013)?

5   Who starred as 'the other Doctor' in 'The Next Doctor' (Christmas, 2008), a brave man with amnesia trying to save the people of London?

6   What connects Camille Coduri, Adjoa Andoh and Jacqueline King during David Tennant's tenure as the Doctor?

7   What was the Christmas special that first teamed the Doctor with Donna Noble?

8   What is the name of the pleasure liner in 'The Voyage of the Damned'? What is the waitress called (played by Kylie Minogue) who helps the Doctor save earth? Where does she end up? (3 pts)

9   Which foes of the Doctor are first encountered in the episode 'Blink'? And who had a leading role as Sally Sparrow? Who wrote this episode? (3 pts)

10 Where did the battle for Amy's child take place in 'A Good Man Goes to War'? Who is the Sontaran commander who repays a debt to the Doctor by helping him? What name is given to Amy's child in the episode and who does she turn out to be? Who are the creepy opponents working for Madame Kovarian in the battle? (5 pts)

Part 2

11 What guise does the warlike facet of Rory's character tend to take?

12 Which companion of an earlier Doctor returns in 'School Reunion' and as a major ally in 'The Stolen Earth'? What is the name of her son? (2 pts)

13 Which two actors played the Master in the three-part story at the end of the third series since *Doctor Who*'s return? In what guise does he gain control of the United Kingdom? (3 pts)

14 Who was in the thick of it in 'The Fires of Pompeii' as sculptor Lucius Caecilius?

15 What is the name of the Dalek sect that has taken over Manhattan in 'Daleks in Manhattan'?

16 Who played the desperate President of the Time Lords in 'The End of Time', the two-parter which saw the transition from David Tennant as the Doctor to Matt Smith?

17 Who was the ditzy blonde who accompanied Jon Pertwee's Doctor, often seen climbing sheer rockfaces in heels and a mini-skirt and being not much use (apart from picking locks)?

18 One series of *Doctor Who* concerned the Doctor's trial by the Time Lord council; which Doctor was involved?

19 What was Tom Baker's Doctor's distinctive piece of attire? And for what human foodstuff did he have something of a fetish? (2 pts)

20 What is the name of the Dalek home planet and which other species lived there until the two started a war that resulted in Dalek supremacy? (2 pts)

Total Points: 35. Targets: Novice 14 Pro 26. Your Score:

Quiz 112. General Knowledge

Part 1

1   According to Stephen R. Covey, how many habits do highly effective people have?
2   Which explorer discovered the source of the Nile at Lake Victoria? (a) Livingstone (b) Gordon (c) Speke
3   Which river runs through the heart of Glasgow?
4   What is the more common name for chiromancy?
5   What was the nickname of the tennis superstar of the 1950s, Maureen Connolly?
6   Which comic actor hosted the Academy Awards ceremony on seven occasions in the 1960s?
7   The Statue of Coatlicue is an example of the art of which culture?
8   Which newspaper was the first to launch a colour supplement in 1962?
9   Something cooked *al forno* in Italy would be cooked how?
10 Which Australian cricket ground traditionally hosts a test match (cricket) starting on Boxing Day?

Part 2

11 In 2013 Nicolás Maduro became president of which country after securing the narrowest of election victories? Who was his charismatic and occasionally controversial predecessor? (2 pts)
12 Who died in a prison cell in Port Elizabeth, South Africa, on 11 September 1977?
13 What is the ratio of an individual's mental age to his or her actual age multiplied by 100?
14 The Darling River, the longest single river on the Australian land mass at just over 3,000 km, runs a further 750 km after merging with which other river?
15 If listed by assets, what is the largest US bank?
16 The Archies, who had a no. 1 hit with 'Sugar, Sugar', were a cartoon band created for which successful animated series?
17 Which South African cricketer's career was ended by match-fixing scandals before his life ended prematurely in a plane crash?
18 In what discipline did Rowan Atkinson graduate?
19 What is the profession of Camilla Parker-Bowles's son, Tom?
20 Who landed by air at Lord's cricket ground in 2008, but was in jail awaiting trial by the end of the following year?

Total Points: 21. Targets: Novice 11 Pro 16. Your Score: ⬚

Answers Quizzes 105–112

Quiz 105. General Knowledge

1. Paraphernalia; 2. Brewing (it is the branch of chemistry dealing with fermentation); 3. Drunk; 4. Biennial is every two years, biannual is twice every year; 5. Venal; 6. Halcyon days; 7. (c) verisimilitude can best be described as the semblance or likelihood of truth; 8. Cant, which becomes can't; 9. Slander is verbal, libel written; 10. Sleight of hand or trickery; 11. Arrows; the name bowyer would once have meant a bow-maker or seller, while a fletcher was an arrow-maker; 12. Blighty, as a reference to a missed home country; 13. Middle East (or Western Asia); 14. They do not have support or sanction from any other power or authority; 15. *Schadenfreude*; 16. the, of, and, to, it, you, be, have, will

Quiz 106. Rock and Pop

1. Nick Drake; 2. The Who (they released the single before changing their name back to the Who and releasing 'I Can't Explain' later that year; 3. *In Case You Didn't Know* (2011) and *Right Place, Right Time*; 4. John Walters; 5. (c) Al Green; 6. 'The Twist'; 'Let's Twist Again'; 7. Led Zeppelin; 8. W. B. Yeats; 9. Public Image Ltd (PIL); 10. Jane's Addiction; 11. Terence Trent D'Arby; 12. The Good, the Bad and the Queen (the band was made up of ex-Fela drummer Tony Allen, Simon Tong, the Verve guitarist, Clash bassist Paul Simonon and Blur's Damon Albarn); 13. (a) Janis Joplin; 14. The band's guitarist John Squire; 15. Paul Simon's *Graceland*; 16. The Housemartins; 17. David Guetta; 18. Duffy; *Rockferry*; 19. USA for Africa; 'We Are the World'; 20. *Tusk*

Quiz 107. Geography

1. Copenhagen; 2. (b) South Sudan; 3. The island of Sicily; 4. (a) Yemen; 5. Brazil and Argentina; 6. Connaught, Leinster, Munster and Ulster; Leinster, largely because Dublin lies within its borders; 7. France, where it is known as Corse; 8. Massif Central; Michelin; 9. France and Spain; 10. Gold Coast; 11. Borneo (Asia); Madagascar (Africa); Great Britain (Europe); Greenland (North America); Tierra del Fuego (South America); New Guinea (Oceania).

Quiz 108. Food and Drink

1. Auguste Escoffier; 2. Cobra; 3. Food poisoning bacteria; 4. John Cadbury; 5. Sashimi; 6. Soy sauce; 7. (Sir) Gilbert Scott; 8. Hungary; 9. Fortnum and Mason; 10. A tall white chef's hat; 11. Scotch bonnet; 12. (c) black pudding; 13. Argentina; 14. *Nigella Bites*; 15. All forms of confectionery discontinued in the 1980s; 16. *Pâte à bombe*; 17. *En papillote*; 18. AC or *appellation contrôlée* (the system, designed to protect the integrity of the wine-growing regions, was introduced in France in 1952; Italy followed suit in 1963); 19. Australia (specifically New South Wales for a bonus point); 20. Spain (la Mancha); sheep's milk

Quiz 109. Children's Books

1. Enid Blyton; 2. Red and green (in Revd W. Awdry's *Thomas the Tank Engine* series); 3. The English Civil War; 4. Dodie Smith; *Starlight Barking*; 5. R. M. Ballantyne; 6. Edward Lear; 7. Lion; 8. *Stuart Little*; 9. Swimming the channel; 10. *Mary Poppins*; 1980s (1988; Travers was born Helen Lyndon Goff in Australia in 1899 and died in 1996); 11. Percy Jackson, the hero of Rick Riordan's modern tales of Olympian gods; 12. *A Series of Unfortunate Events* (Lemony Snicket); 13. Quentin Blake; 14. Jacqueline Wilson; 15. Julia Donaldson; Children's Laureate; 16. Anthony Horowitz; 17. Skulduggery Pleasant in the books by Irish writer Derek Landy; 18. Georgia (Anne) Nicholson; 19. Kate Greenaway Award (for children's illustration); 20. *The Diary of a Wimpy Kid* by Jeff Kinney; no. 6 was called *Cabin Fever*.

Quiz 110. Name the Team

1. Brearley; Gatting; Taylor; Dilley; Willis; 2. Robinson; Tindall; Dawson; Back; Leonard; 3. J. P. R. Williams; Fenwick, Bennett, Price, Windsor; 4. Brown; Faldo; Lyle; Way; Woosnam; 5. Haynes; Kallicharran; Lloyd; Roberts; Garner; 6. Slater; Ponting; Gilchrist; MacGill; McGrath; 7. Cink; Furyk; Leonard; Mahan; Weekley (Woods was injured); 8. Goode; Tuilagi; Ben Youngs; Toby Youngs; Robshaw; 9. Trott; Collingwood; Prior; Swann; Tremlett; 10. Donald; Lawrie; McDowell; Rose; Olazabal

Quiz 111. Doctor Who

1. Paul McGann; 2. Cardiff; Captain Jack Harkness; 3. She was a policewoman; 'The Unquiet Dead' (accept 'the one with Charles Dickens'); 4. Jane Austen; 5. David Morrissey (reunited with David Tennant, with whom he starred in *Blackpool*); 6. They play the mothers of his companions; Rose, Martha and Donna; 7. 'The Runaway Bride'; 8. *Titanic*; Astrid Peth; as a constellation; 9. The Weeping Angels; Carey Mulligan; Steven Moffat; 10. Demon's Run; Strax; Melody, she is River Song; the Headless Monks; 11. A Roman centurion, a reference to the Pandorica story, where he reappears as a Roman after seemingly being lost; 12. Sarah-Jane Smith; Luke; 13. Derek Jacobi and John Simm; as Prime Minister Harold Saxon; 14. Peter Capaldi; 15. The Cult of Skaro; 16. Timothy Dalton; 17. Jo Grant (Katy Manning); 18. Colin Baker; 19. A scarf; jelly babies; 20. Skaro; the Thals

Quiz 112. General Knowledge

1. Seven; 2. John Speke; 3. Clyde; 4. Palm reading; 5. Little Mo; 6. Bob Hope; 7. Aztec; 8. *Sunday Times*; 9. Baked in an oven; 10. Melbourne (MCG); 11. Venezuela; Hugo Chávez; 12. Steve Biko; 13. His or her IQ, as devised by the psychologist William Stern in 1912; 14. River Murray; 15. JP Morgan Chase; 16. *Scooby Doo*; 17. Hansie Cronje; 18. Electrical engineering; 19. Food writer; 20. Sir Allan Stanford

Quiz 113. General Knowledge

Part 1

1   What is the name of the Rothschild house built near Aylesbury to display his art collection and house his spectacular wine collection?

2   In 1994, what legislative change promised more revenue for retail stores?

3   The former MP for Falmouth and Camborne (1992–7), born 28 September 1956, is better known for his prowess in other areas. Who is he?

4   Which country is the world's leading arms exporter?

5   What connects the Winter Olympics of 1932 with a 1999 monster movie?

6   Which band might you get if you mixed two-thirds of a spaghetti western and Helen Mirren's Oscar turn?

7   Whose endorsement of *From Russia with Love* saw US sales of Ian Fleming's novels soar in the early 1960s? (a) Muhammad Ali (then Cassius Clay) (b) John F. Kennedy (c) Frank Sinatra

8   Mrs Alice Stebbins Wells, in 1910, became the first female member of (a) the State Congress of California (b) Pebble Beach Golf Club, CA (c) the Los Angeles Police Department?

9   What would the French and the Italians respectively call a starter? (2 pts)

10 Which side have lost the most FA Cup finals (eight) to 2012? And which side have lost all four they have reached? (2 pts)

Part 2

11 Who succeeded François Mitterrand as President of France in 1995?

12 What begins in a field near Kemble in Gloucestershire?

13 Which book was cleared for UK publication in 1988, despite government attempts to have it quashed?

14 What do Mo Mowlam, Kate Winslet and J. K. Rowling have in common? (a) they all left school with no qualifications (b) they were all head girl at school (c) they were all home-schooled

15 Who was the BBC Director-General at the centre of the Savile child abuse row in 2012?

16 Who are the four Welsh players to have appeared in a European Cup final? And the only one from Northern Ireland? (5 pts)

Total Points: 22. Targets: Novice 11 Pro 17. Your Score:

Quiz 114. TV Soaps

A very clean quiz about soap . . .

Part 1

1   Who was murdered during a break-in at Mike Baldwin's factory in *Coronation Street* in 1978?

2   What was the boat built by Jerry, Ray and Len that sank in a 1972 episode of *Coronation Street*?

3   What was the name of the baby poisoned by David Platt (with Ecstasy) in *Coronation Street* in 2005?

4   Who was Jez Quigley trying to murder when he suffered a punctured lung in hospital in *Coronation Street* in 2000?

5   What was the name of Ken Barlow's wife who was killed in *Coronation Street* in 1971 and how did she die? (2 pts)

6   Who created the Channel 4 soap, *Brookside*, and who was the head of Channel 4 who commissioned the series? (2 pts)

7   What was the name of the 'soap within a soap' in *Brookside* that used the programme's original working title? (a) 'The Close' (b) 'Huyton Sound' (c) 'Meadowcroft Park'

8   Which soap ramped up the pulling power by casting Hollywood veterans Charlton Heston and Barbara Stanwyck as the head of the household and his tough-cookie sister? From which other soap was it a spin-off? (2 pts)

9   To whom did Emily Nugent first get engaged before calling off the wedding? Which two husbands did she eventually marry? (3 pts)

10 Which two actors were the only ones who appeared throughout the entire thirteen-year run of *Dallas*? (2 pts)

Part 2

11   How did the network explain the apparent resurrection of Bobby Ewing in *Dallas*, when Patrick Duffy reconsidered his decision to leave the show?

12   Which three British actresses had leading roles as glamorous older women in *Dynasty*? (3 pts)

13   Which five surnames has Pat (Pam St Clement) sported in *EastEnders*? (5 pts)

14   Which of Carol Jackson's four children has David Wicks for a father? And which of them married Ricky Butcher? (2 pts)

15   Which *EastEnders* family head has been married to Masood Ahmed and the abusive Yusef Khan?

16   What connects Sharon Crossthwaite in *Emmerdale* with the Di Marco family in *EastEnders*?

17   Which soap character's stepchildren are a wheelchair-bound cad and a lesbian vet? What happened to her husband, Frank? By what mode of transport did she leave the show in 1999? (3 pts)

18   What part was played by Eric Porter in the 1960s and Damien Lewis in the 2000s?

19   What was set up by the Australian Seven Network as a rival to Ten Network's *Neighbours* in 1988?

20   Which pop stars played Nina Tucker and Beth Brennan respectively in *Neighbours*? (2 pts)

Total Points: 36. Targets: Novice 14 Pro 27. Your Score: ☐

Quiz 115. Chiller Movies

Psychopaths and sickos, thrills and chills

Part 1

1. Which influential and controversial 1970s thriller starring Clint Eastwood featured a serial killer called Scorpio?
2. Who play a predatory femme fatale and the FBI agent tracking her down in the 1987 thriller *Black Widow*? (2 pts)
3. Who starred in *The Assassin* (*Point of No Return* in the US), a remake of the 1990 French thriller *Nikita*? Who directed the original *Nikita*? (2 pts)
4. Which French 1950s pin-up played the mistress of a school head teacher who conspires with his wife to bump him off in Clouzot's noir thriller *Les Diaboliques*? Who, unsurprisingly, also wanted to option the rights on the psycho-chiller novel which provides the plot? (2 pts)
5. Who plays the repellent Mason Verger in *Hannibal* (2001) and what fate does he meet? (2 pts)
6. Who plays Mrs Woodhouse in the 1969 chiller *Rosemary's Baby*, and who is it suggested fathered her unborn child? (2 pts)
7. What name is given to a plot device, used especially in thrillers, which gives a lead character a drive and purpose that often appears out of proportion with life off-screen?
8. The French thriller *Ne le Dis à Personne* was made by Guillaume Canet; which bestselling US novel by which author was it based on? (2 pts)
9. What was the 1987 film starring Charles Dance and Greta Scacchi concerning the 1941 Happy Valley murder, a scandal centred around ex-pat Brits in Kenya?
10. What was the 1983 conspiracy film about a Russian policeman (William Hurt) who investigates some grisly Moscow murders? Which British playwright wrote the screenplay from Martin Cruz Smith's novel? (2 pts)

Part 2

11 Who stars as the hit-man Jackie in the 2012 noir thriller *Killing Them Softly*? Who also appears as an unstable and self-indulgent colleague who Jackie arranges to have arrested? (2 pts)

12 Who brought Robert Harris's novel *The Ghost* to the screen in 2010, and who played British Prime Minister Adam Lang as a barely concealed portrait of Tony Blair? (2 pts)

13 *Presumed Innocent* was a 1990 film starring Harrison Ford and based on which practising attorney's debut novel? Who played Ford's dead colleague around whose murder the plot is wrapped? (2 pts)

14 Who starred as Harry Palmer in the 1965 film version of Len Deighton's first spy novel, *The Ipcress File*, and in two follow-ups? What was Harry's name in the original novel? (2 pts)

15 Who played the ex-Army Sergeant turned terrorist who plants a bomb on a bus in *Speed* (1994)? Who replaced Keanu Reeves as the hero for the sequel, *Speed 2*? (2 pts)

16 Who face off as Agent Frank Horrigan and assassin Mitch Leary in the 1993 thriller *In the Line of Fire*? (2 pts)

17 *Manhunter* was the first movie to feature which famous character? Who played him and who directed the film? Who plays retired agent Will Graham, and what name is given to the serial killer he is chasing? (5 pts)

Total Points: 34. Targets: Novice 14 Pro 26. Your Score:

Quiz 116. Computer Science

Part 1

1 What was the affordable 8-bit home computer released by Sinclair Research in 1982?

2 The Mac OSX system is based on which core operating system?

3 What was the company formed by Steve Jobs when he temporarily parted company with Apple in 1985? Who bought the company in 1996? (2 pts)

4 Who replaced Steve Jobs as CEO of Apple shortly before Job's death in 2011?

5 What name is given to the southern section of the Bay Area of San Francisco, dominated by technological industries?

6 In which Californian city can the headquarters of Hewlett Packard be found? (a) Sacramento (b) San Diego (c) Palo Alto

7 Who produced the Presario, an entry product which led to the company briefly enjoying a position as the world's leading PC manufacturer?

8 What was the new search engine released by Google in December 2008?

9 If a computer file is labelled .tif, what is the most likely content?

10 Napster was the first high-profile example of what type of file sharing, deemed illegal by the authorities of many countries?

Part 2

11 Which international company acquired Myspace in 2005? And which pop star was the high-profile face of a 2011 buyout of the declining company? (2 pts)

12 What was the 2001 release of Windows that sought to combine the home and business uses of the product?

13 The Dell Corporation, founded in 1984 by Michael Dell, is based where? (a) Silicon Valley, California (b) Miami Dade, Florida (c) Round Rock, Texas

14 What is the minimum data transfer rate required to qualify as a 4G network? (a) 40 mbps (megabytes per second) (b) 100 mbps (c) 1 gbps (gigabyte per second)

15 Which technology company makes the modems and transceivers for Apple iPhones?

16 Who were the co-founders of Microsoft in 1975? How old was the younger and more famous of the two at the time? In which Southern US city was the company started? In which state is its current base? (5 pts)

Total Points: 22. Targets: Novice 7 Pro 17. Your Score:

Quiz 117. Terrorism

One man's freedom fighter is another man's terrorist; twenty questions on the use of premeditated murder as a political argument

Part 1

1   Who was the Conservative MP and shadow Northern Ireland secretary killed by a car bomb at the House of Commons in 1979?

2   Which terrorist group blew up the West German embassy in Stockholm in 1975?

3   Where in Northern Ireland did a bomb kill eleven people at a Remembrance Day service in 1987?

4   Who was found murdered on 8 May 1978, eight weeks after his kidnap by the Red Brigade group of Italian terrorists?

5   In 2000, the last prisoners of the Troubles in Northern Ireland walked free from which prison?

6   In the aftermath of the attack on the World Trade Center in 2001, what name was given to the site where the twin towers once stood?

7   Which co-founder of the *Guinness Book of Records* was murdered outside his home in London by the IRA in 1975?

8   In which year were the London bombings of 7 July? What number bus was hit by a bomb that day? In which London square was it at the time? What was the fatality count from the bombings? (Allow two either way.) (4 pts)

9   What capital city was bombed by US airplanes as a reprisal for terrorist attacks in April 1986?

10 Which cousin of the Queen was killed aboard his boat by an IRA bomb in 1979?

Part 2

11   Where were three IRA members shot by security forces in 1988?

12   Who, on 13 March 1991, were freed after sixteen years in prison when their convictions for acts of terrorism were quashed?

13   Who was the leader of the conspiracy to blow up Parliament in 1605 that led to the celebration of 5 November as Bonfire Night?

14   Where did Israeli commandos rescue over 100 hostages in a surprise raid in 1976?

15   The Palestinian group that took members of the Israeli Olympic team hostage at the Munich Games in 1982 demanded the release of the leaders of which terrorist group, as well as Palestinians held in Israeli jails?

16   The terrorist organization ETA fight for the autonomy for which region?

17   Irish gangster John Traynor was arrested in 2010 for the high-profile murder, fourteen years previously, of which campaigning journalist?

18   Which terrorist organization (or freedom fighters, depending on perspective) was formed by Velupillai Prabhakaran in 1972?

19   Who were the US-backed rebels in Nicaragua in the 1980s and what was the name given to the left-wing government they were trying to undermine? (2 pts)

20   Who was the US Defense Secretary in the War Cabinet formed by George W. Bush in response to the 9/11 attacks?

Total Points: 24. Targets: Novice 10 Pro 18. Your Score:

Quiz 118. Olympic Games

Heroes and sporting history

Part 1

1   Who coached the Great Britain men's and women's football teams at the 2012 Olympics? (2 pts)

2   There were twelve track cycling events held in the velodrome; how many of the twelve were won by Team GB? Who was the unlucky member of the track team not to win a medal of any colour? (2 pts)

3   Prior to Usain Bolt, who was the last man to win the sprint double of 100 metres and 200 metres? Where would his winning time have placed him in the 2012 100 metres final? (2 pts)

4   Who was the Dutch mother-of-two who won more gold medals than any other athlete at the 1948 Olympic Games?

5   Who remains Namibia's only Olympic medallist, having won silver medals in the men's 100 metres in 1992 and 1996?

6   Which was the first Olympic Games attended by the Soviet Union as a communist power?

7   Women competed in the modern Games for the first time in 1900, in five events. Which of these was *not* one of the five: archery, croquet, equestrian, golf, sailing, tennis?

8   Which two gold medal-winning athletes are celebrated in the film *Chariots of Fire*? In which two other events did they also win medals? What happened when the two raced each other? (5 pts)

9   Wilma Rudolph overcame what crippling childhood disorder to win three sprint gold medals for the USA at the 1960 Olympics?

10 In 1972, competing in his third Olympics, Alan Pascoe finally won a silver medal in the 400 metres hurdles; true or false?

Part 2

Mix and Match: all these sports people are former Olympic athletes who provided commentary for the BBC at London 2012; match the pundit to his or her sport

1. Leon Taylor; 2. Andy Jameson; 3. Chris Boardman; 4. Gail Emms; 5. Dan Topolski; 6. Helen Reeves; 7. Pippa Funnell; 8. Stephanie Cook; 9. Brendan Foster; 10. Lennox Lewis

a. Badminton; b. Equestrian; c. Athletics; d. Canoeing; e. Diving; f. Cycling; g. Modern Pentathlon; h. Boxing; i. Swimming; j. Rowing (10 pts)

Your Workings:

Total Points: 27. Targets: Novice 11 Pro 20. Your Score:

Quiz 119. Myths and Legends

Ten mixed questions and ten on the Arthurian cycle

Part 1

1   What was the curse Apollo put on the seer, Cassandra?

2   Whose *Le Morte d'Arthur* is regarded as the grandfather of the modern versions of the Arthurian cycle?

3   Who drowned swimming the Hellespont trying to reach his Hero?

4   Which French writer created the idea of the fairy tale with his translations and reworkings of old folk stories in the seventeenth century?

5   Who completed the quest for the Golden Fleece in Greek mythology? What was the name of the boat in which he sailed? (2 pts)

6   What was the seat of the High Kings of Ireland in that country's mythological tales?

7   Theseus married Hippolyta; of which race was she the queen?

8   By what names were the Roman goddess of the hunt, Diana, and the messenger boy, Mercury, known to the Greeks? (2 pts)

9   In Greek mythology, who gave fire to mankind and what kind of creature was he? (2 pts)

10   'Which creature walks on four legs in the morning, two legs in the afternoon and three legs in the evening?' Who waylaid travellers to Thebes with this riddle in Greek mythology, and what was the correct answer given by Oedipus to lift the curse? (2 pts)

Part 2

11   King Arthur is buried, according to some versions, under the ruins of which abbey?

12   Who is the real son of Sir Ector and therefore Arthur's foster-brother and later his Seneschal at Camelot?

13   Who is the 'pure knight' who is allowed to fulfil the Quest for the Holy Grail? Who is his father? (2 pts)

14   Which knight accompanies Arthur when he throws his sword back into the water as he nears his death after the last battle?

15   Where does the final battle between Arthur and Mordred's forces take place?

16   What is the name of the sword which is delivered to Arthur by the Lady of the Lake?

17   Which of Gawain's brothers is portrayed in most versions of the Arthurian cycle as a conspirator with Mordred against the king and his allies? (a) Gareth (b) Gaheris (c) Agravain

18   In *Le Morte d'Arthur*, which knight, a cousin of Sir Lancelot, is prepared to joust for Guinevere's honour, but is saved from doing so by Lancelot's return?

19   Who is the half-sister of Morgana-le-Fay, also a half-sister of Arthur who is married to King Lot of Orkney? (In some versions it is she, not Morgana, who incestuously seduces Arthur and bears Mordred.)

20   The knights Perceval and Geraint are from which corner of Arthur's kingdom?

Total Points: 25. Targets: Novice 10 Pro 19. Your Score:

Quiz 120. General Knowledge

Dead straight

Part 1

1   Who once heckled the Pope at the European Parliament, denouncing him as the Antichrist?

2   Colchis, the mythical location of the Golden Fleece, was situated in which modern-day country? (a) Greece (b) Georgia (c) Montenegro

3   Joseph Ratzinger was elected to which key world position in 2005?

4   How many fluid ounces make up a pint?

5   Which East German skater was described by *Time* magazine as 'the beautiful face of socialism'?

6   2005 saw the launch (briefly) of *Daddy Cool*, a musical based on the songs of which 1970s chart band?

7   Terry Gilliam, director of *Brazil*, was formerly a member of which comedy team?

8   The first sex change operation in 1952 was performed by (a) Dr Hamburger (b) Dr Bratwurst or (c) Dr Enchillada?

9   Which historic boat was damaged by a fire caused (in all likelihood) by a vacuum cleaner malfunction in 2007?

10 Who converted billionaire Paul Getty to cricket watching, leading to Getty's purchase of *Wisden Cricketers' Almanack* in 1993?

Part 2

11   The Ogaden region is a territory in dispute between which two nations? (2 pts)

12   Where in Australia did Englishman Arthur Phillip land in 1788?

13   What scientific phenomenon is being demonstrated by a dog reacting with eagerness to the opening of a cupboard that he knows contains his food?

14   The Mississippi-Missouri is the longest river in the US; which of the two is the longer before they merge to run for a further 2,000 km? Into which body of water do they empty and which city stands at the delta? Which city stands at the confluence of the two rivers in Missouri State? (4 pts)

15   What was housed in the British Museum for nearly 250 years before moving to a new site in St Pancras in 1997?

16   *Rosie and Jim, Teletubbies* and *In The Night Garden* were all produced by which children's TV company?

17   What first did the Arsenal v. Portsmouth fixture in December 2009 achieve, which had the sportswriters bemoaning the future of the national football team?

18   Which actor-singer appeared in a video for 'That's the Way Love Goes' by Janet Jackson?

19   In 2012 Fay Maschler celebrated forty years working for the London *Evening Standard* in which capacity?

20   Where in Britain did a lone gunman kill sixteen schoolchildren in 1996?

Total Points: 24. Targets: Novice 12 Pro 18. Your Score:

Answers Quizzes 113–120

Quiz 113. General Knowledge

1. Waddesdon Manor; 2. Legalization of Sunday trading; 3. Sebastian Coe; 4. United States; 5. Lake Placid was the host resort for the games and the title (and location) of the movie; 6. The Good, the Bad and the Queen; 7. (b) John F. Kennedy listed it as one of his favourite books; 8. (c) She joined the LAPD; 9. Hors d'oeuvres and antipasto; 10. Everton; Leicester City; 11. Jacques Chirac; 12. River Thames; 13. *Spycatcher*, 14. (b) they were all head girls at school; 15. George Entwistle; 16. Terry Yorath (Leeds, 1975); Joey Jones (Liverpool, 1977); Ian Rush (1984 and 1985); Ryan Giggs (1999, 2008, 2009, 2011); Northern Ireland's Martin O'Neill (Nottingham Forest, 1980) (Jonny Evans made the bench for Manchester United in 2009 but never got on the field)

Quiz 114. TV Soaps

1. Ernest Bishop; 2. Shangri-La; 3. Bethany; 4. Steve McDonald; 5. Val; she was electrocuted by a hairdryer; 6. Phil Redmond; Jeremy Isaacs; 7. (c) Meadowcroft Park; 8. *The Colbys*; *Dynasty* (it was originally billed as *Dynasty II – The Colbys*); 9. Leonard Swindley; Ernie Bishop and Arnie Swain; 10. Larry Hagman (as JR) and Ken Kercheval (as Cliff Barnes); 11. They pretended the previous series was an elaborate sequence of events dreamed by Bobby's wife, Pamela; 12. Joan Collins (Alexis); Stephanie Beacham (Sable); Kate O'Mara (Caress); 13. Harris, Beale, Wicks, Butcher and Evans; 14. Bianca; also Bianca; 15. Zainab Masood; 16. Louise Jamieson, who played Sharon and also played Rosa di Marco; 17. Kim Tate, the arch-bitch in *Emmerdale*; he died of a heart attack when Kim 'came back from the dead'; in a helicopter; 18. Soames Forsyte in *The Forsyte Saga*; 19. *Home and Away* (Seven had commissioned *Neighbours* but canned it after a slow start); 20. Delta Goodrem and Natalie Imbruglia

Quiz 115. Chiller Movies

1. *Dirty Harry*; 2. Teresa Russell and Debra Winger; 3. Bridget Fonda; Luc Besson; 4. Simone Signoret; Alfred Hitchcock; 5. Gary Oldman; he is eaten by wild boars he has bred for that purpose; 6. Mia Farrow; the Devil; 7. MacGuffin; 8. *Tell No One* by Harlan Coben; 9. *White Mischief*; 10. *Gorky Park*; Dennis Potter; 11. Brad Pitt; James Gandolfini; 12. Roman Polanski; Pierce Brosnan; 13. Scott Turow; Greta Scacchi; 14. Michael Caine; he doesn't have one (Deighton deliberately made the character mysterious, but this device did not translate to film); 15. Dennis Hopper; Jason Patric; 16. Clint Eastwood and John Malkovich; 17. Dr Hannibal Lecter (or Lecktor); Brian Cox, Michael Mann directed; William Petersen; the Tooth Fairy

Quiz 116. Computer Science

1. ZX Spectrum; 2. Unix; 3. NeXT Inc; Apple; 4. Tim Cook; 5. Silicon Valley; 6. (c) Palo Alto; 7. Compaq; 8. Google Chrome; 9. Digital image (TIFF is an alternative compression format to JPEG); 10. Peer-to-Peer or P2P; 11. News Corporation; Justin Timberlake; 12. Windows XP; 13. Round Rock, Texas; Dell is the world's third biggest PC manufacturer and employs over 100,000 people worldwide; 14. 100 mbps; 15. Qualcomm; 16. Bill Gates and Paul Allen; Gates was twenty; Albuquerque; Washington (Redmond)

Quiz 117. Terrorism

1. Airey Neave; 2. Baader-Meinhof Gang; 3. Enniskillen; 4. Aldo Moro; 5. The Maze; 6. Ground Zero; 7. Ross McWhirter; 8. 2005; no. 30; Tavistock Square; 52; 9. Tripoli, Libya; 10. Lord Louis Mountbatten; 11. Gibraltar; 12. The Birmingham Six; 13. Robert Catesby; 14. Entebbe airport, Uganda; 15. Baader-Meinhof Group or Red Army Faction; 16. Basque region of Spain; 17. Veronica Guerin; 18. Tamil Tigers; 19. Contras; Sandinista (Frente Sandinista de Liberación Nacional); 20. Donald Rumsfeld

Quiz 118. Olympic Games

1. Stuart Pearce and Hope Powell; 2. Nine; Jess Varnish (disqualified in the women's team sprint with Victoria Pendleton); 3. Carl Lewis (he ran the first sub-ten-second Olympic 100 metres without the benefit of a rarefied atmosphere); in 2012 the time would have placed him eighth, ahead of only Asafa Powell, who pulled a hamstring; 4. Fanny Blankers-Koen (her achievements blew away any notions that mothers with children could not achieve sporting distinction); 5. Frankie Fredericks; 6. 1952, Helsinki; 7. Archery; 8. Harold Abrahams (100 metres) and Eric Liddell (400 metres); Liddell won bronze in the 200 metres, Abrahams was part of the silver medal 4 x 100 metres relay team; they never raced each other; 9. Polio; 10. False (he did win his silver medal, but as the anchor of the 4 x 400 metres relay team; Mix and Match: 1, e; 2, i; 3, f; 4, a; 5, j; 6, d; 7, b; 8, g; 9, c; 10, h

Quiz 119. Myths and Legends

1. She would prophesy accurately, but no one would believe her; 2. Sir Thomas Malory; 3. Leander; 4. Charles Perrault; 5. Jason; *Argo*; 6. Tara; 7. Amazons; 8. Artemis and Hermes; 9. Prometheus; he was a Titan; 10. The Sphinx; the answer is man; 11. Glastonbury; 12. Sir Kay; 13. Sir Galahad; Sir Lancelot; 14. Sir Bedivere; 15. Camlann Field; 16. Excalibur; 17. (c) Agravain; 18. Sir Bors de Ganis; 19. Morgause; 20. Wales

Quiz 120. General Knowledge

1. Revd Ian Paisley; 2. (b) Georgia; 3. Pope (Benedict XVI); 4. Twenty; 5. Katarina Witt; 6. Boney M; 7. Monty Python; 8. It was Dr Christian Hamburger who made George into Christine; 9. *Cutty Sark* (it has now been repaired at a cost of over £40 million and is back

on show at its berth in Greenwich); 10. Mick Jagger; 11. Ethiopia and Somalia; 12. Botany Bay; 13. A Pavlovian response; 14. Missouri; Gulf of Mexico, New Orleans; St Louis; 15. British Library; 16. Ragdoll; 17. No English players started the game; 18. Jennifer López; 19. Restaurant critic; 20. Dunblane, Scotland

Quiz 121. General Knowledge

Part 1

All the events in this first section happened in 1980 (it was a busy year)

1   Who was elected Prime Minister of Zimbabwe?
2   Riots broke out in the St Paul's area of which English city after a typically heavy-handed police intervention?
3   Nigel Short, at fourteen years of age, became the youngest person to achieve Master status – at what?
4   In January 1980, six US citizens escaped from Tehran posing as Canadians; which 2012 film dramatized these events?
5   Josip Tito died, aged eighty-two, after twenty-seven years as head of which state?
6   1980 saw one of the great Wimbledon finals as Bjorn Borg of Sweden won his fifth consecutive title (it would be his last); which US player, now a commentator, did he beat in a five-set thriller?
7   Ian Curtis was found hanged in his bedroom; of which band was he the lead singer?
8   Which political party dropped the acknowledgement of equal rights for women at its 1980 conference?
9   Who led the strikes at the Gdansk shipyards in Poland that would eventually lead to the country's independence from communist domination?
10 Which English team won the European Cup (what is now the Champions League, but back then open only to actual winners of their national league or the holders of the trophy) for the second consecutive year? Which other English club did they beat along the way? (2 pts)

Part 2

A couple of multi-parters (but nothing to do with 1980)

11 A legionary based in Britain was forced to flee Camulodunum when the Iceni attacked; he joined his new legion at Verulamium, and they marched down to fortify Isca Dumnoniorum via Aquae Sulis. On his retirement he bought a farm near Eboracum where he saw out his days. Translate into modern geography. (5 pts)
12 What are the four main national US network TV channels? What was the fifth large channel created by the merger of UPN and Warner in 2006? (5 pts)

Total Points: 21. Targets: Novice 11 Pro 16. Your Score: [   ]

Quiz 122. Sci-Fi TV

Part 1

1 Which 1962 sci-fi series about a computer-generated wonder-woman made a star of Julie Christie?

2 Which series finds the protagonists struggling against the Goa'uld, the Replicators and the Ori?

3 Which sci-fi series is set aboard a space station during a time of peace between humanity and the alien Minbari, with whom they had previously been at war?

4 Who is the Chief Navigator aboard the USS *Enterprise*?

5 Who is Captain Jonathan Archer? Which former time-traveller played him on TV? (2 pts)

6 The actor who played Commander Adama in the original 1970s *Battlestar Galactica* is referenced in which later sci-fi show as the name of a major character?

7 What was the pioneering 1950s sci-fi show about the work of the British Rocket Group created by BBC in-house writer Nigel Kneale?

8 Which remorseless enemy is introduced as the 'big bad' during the second series of *Star Trek: Next Generation*?

9 What was the Channel 5 sci-fi/horror drama screened in 2000 and 2001, consisting of a series of separate stories linked by a twist in the final episode of the series?

10 How many episodes of the original *Star Trek* series were made: 79, 153 or 202?

Part 2

11   NCC 1701: explain.

12   Who is the Deputy Commander of the *Galactica* in the modern remake of *Battlestar Galactica*? What number is the strapping blonde cylon played by Tricia Helfer? Which British actor plays Gaius Baltar, the victim of her mind games? (3 pts)

13   What, in the world of TV sci-fi, were Zen, Orac and Slave?

14   What was the Australian sci-fi show set aboard a living ship captained (sort of) by John Crichton, a lost-in-space human astronaut? What was the title of the mini-series that tied up the series' loose ends after it was cancelled before a planned fifth season could be made? (2 pts)

15   What was Joss Whedon's 'western in space' series, inexplicably cancelled after one (unfinished) series? Who was the show's charismatic star? How would the ship's engineer, Kaylee, describe a decision to renew the show? (3 pts)

16   What happened to Lieutenants Starbuck and Boomer between the original 1970s series of *Battlestar Galactica* and the noughties remake?

17   What was the follow-up to *Stargate SG-1* launched in 2004, seven years after the start of the parent show? And what was the animated series launched in 2002? (2 pts)

18   Who is the captain of the *Voyager* in the *Star Trek* spin-off *Star Trek: Voyager*? And who leads the rebels she is pursuing, eventually becoming her deputy in a new alliance? (2 pts)

19   Which TV show detailed the planned invasion of earth by an alien force called the Visitors? What did they want from the earth? (2 pts)

20   Who is the head of Warehouse 13, where all the dangerous artefacts collected by the government are kept and 'controlled'? With which sister show does this series occasionally cross over? (2 pts)

Total Points: 30. Targets: Novice 12 Pro 23. Your Score:

Quiz 123. Tourist Attractions

Twenty straight questions about tourist destinations

Part 1

1　Which nation boasts the most World Heritage Sites within its borders?

2　South Africa's Blue Train connects which two cities? (2 pts)

3　The USA designated its first National Park in 1872 across Idaho, Montana and (principally) Wyoming. What is its name?

4　What is the island to the north of Venice known for its glass-making?

5　What is the northeastern county of Northern Ireland, and what is the World Heritage Site on its northern coast? (2 pts)

6　What is the principal language of Brazil?

7　In which US state does Mount Rushmore stand? (a) Washington (b) South Carolina (c) South Dakota

8　In which country are the Ajanta Caves with their amazing murals?

9　Where, in 1682, did Louis XIV move his family home? And to what use was the old palace put? (2 pts)

10　Calakmul in Mexico, Quirigua in Guatemala and Copan in Honduras are all preservation sites reflecting which civilization?

Part 2

11 The nature-rich Galapagos Islands, so influential on Darwin's work, are 500 miles off the coast of which country, which administers the islands?

12 In which city is Independence Hall, where the US Declaration of Independence was signed and the constitution drawn up?

13 In which city can you find Temple Mount, the Wailing Walls and the Dome of the Rock?

14 Which German city houses the oldest cathedral in northern Europe, where German kings were crowned throughout the middle ages? (a) Cologne (b) Leipzig (c) Aachen

15 Who lived in the palace at Schönbrunn, Vienna, until 1918?

16 The Plantin-Moretus Museum in Antwerp houses Europe's finest collection of what? (a) Jurassic fossils (b) medieval printing equipment and works (c) farm equipment, machinery and literature

17 Alexander Gardens is a public park lying to the west of which famous Moscow edifice?

18 The Acropolis (constructed fifth century BC) sits on hill overlooking which European city?

19 A palace built by the Roman Emperor Diocletian saw the beginning of which coastal city in modern-day Croatia?

20 Malta is the biggest of the islands which make up the state of Malta; what is its more rural neighbour, the second biggest island in the archipelago?

Total Points: 23. Targets: Novice 9 Pro 17. Your Score:

Quiz 124. History

All sorts, everywhere, every when

Part 1

1   Which volcano erupted in 1906, causing huge damage and over 100 deaths in the city of Naples?

2   What was the major cultural contribution of the Pharaoh Khufu (2589–2566 BC)?

3   Julius Caesar defied the ruling Senate in 49 BC by marching his army across which river?

4   What was the philosophical work written by Lao Tzu around the sixth century BC that has remained an influence on Chinese ethical and religious thinking through to modern times?

5   Whose rebel army threw the Spanish out of Venezuela in 1821?

6   Who was beheaded on 18 May 1536? And which relation of hers was released from the Tower of London eighteen years later to the day? (2 pts)

7   How or why did ten days go missing in 1582?

8   What became legal tender for food on 1 January 1955?

9   What is referred to by various names including Long, Short, Useless, Rump and Barebones in studies of seventeenth-century English history?

10 Which nation revolted against Spanish occupation in 1572, commencing a struggle that was only ended by the 1648 Peace of Munster, which acknowledged their independence?

Part 2

11   Which empire, led by which charismatic general, conquered a vast part of Europe (Hungary, most of the Ukraine, much of Germany and Poland and parts of the Balkans) in the fifth century, before the empire dissolved just as quickly after the death of the leader?

12   In which city in 1979 were over ninety people taken hostage in the US embassy?

13   For what is Englishman Nicholas Breakspear best remembered?

14   Who was the President of Egypt who was assassinated at a military parade in 1981?

15   When did the Civil Rights Act become law, establishing people of all colours as US citizens: 1866, 1899 or 1928?

16   When did Israel seize control of the Old City of Jerusalem: 1948, 1967 or 1996?

17   By what name was Ho Chi Minh City known prior to and during the Vietnam War?

18   The powerful English nobleman Richard Neville (1428–71) is better known by which nickname for his activity during the Wars of the Roses?

19   Which mathematician and mystic was Court Astrologer under Elizabeth I, having incurred her sister Mary's wrath by forecasting that Elizabeth would become Queen?

20   The Battle of Waterloo took place in 1815; but did it take place in the pouring rain in April, freezing cold in February or pleasant weather in June?

Total Points: 21. Targets: Novice 8 Pro 16. Your Score:

Quiz 125. Shakespeare

Bardy stuff

Part 1

1   Much of *Henry V* takes place before and after which major battle in English history?

2   Who, in Shakespeare's history cycle, is referred to as the 'She-Wolf of France'?

3   What 'play within a play' is enacted by the rustic workmen in *A Midsummer Night's Dream*?

4   Valentine and Proteus are the title characters of which Shakespeare play?

5   What are the names of the pair of central sparring lovers in *Much Ado About Nothing*? (2 pts)

6   Which history play is believed by many academics to have been a collaboration between Shakespeare and another dramatist? Who was the other writer? (2 pts)

7   What was the name of the theatre troupe for whom Shakespeare wrote many of his plays? Who was the leader of the troupe who took most of the plum parts? (2 pts)

8   By what name is Henry IV known in *Richard II*, before he seizes the throne? Who was his father? (2 pts)

9   What were the names of Shakespeare's twin children? (a) Judith and Hamnet (b) Romeo and Juliet (c) Juliet and Hamlet

10 What are the names of the two companions of Rosalind when she is banished by the cruel Duke and flees to the Forest of Arden? (2 pts)

Part 2

11 Who does the Duke of Vienna leave in charge when he takes a 'sabbatical' in *Measure for Measure*? And whose body does this deputy covet? (2 pts)

12 The Prince of Aragon and the Prince of Morocco choose badly, while Bassanio chooses well; what is the prize?

13 In which play does a character wake up next to the headless body of her dead stepbrother?

14 Who is King Lear's eldest daughter, and who is her husband, one of the few left standing at the end of the play? (2 pts)

15 Which play by Tom Stoppard takes two minor characters from *Hamlet* and puts them centre stage?

16 Which of Shakespeare's plays is set during the Trojan War?

17 How many sonnets did Shakespeare write: thirty-two, ninety or 154?

18 In which play, the most violent in the canon, does one character have her hands cut off and her tongue cut out, while another is forced to eat her own sons in a pie?

19 How many plays cover the cycle of the Wars of the Roses?

20 Whose wife was Calpurnia?

Total Points: 27. Targets: Novice 8 Pro 20. Your Score:

Quiz 126. Champions League

A tribute in quiz form to the UEFA Champions League, where an occasional game of football interrupts the mad dash for buckets of cash

Part 1

1   2000 saw the first European Cup final between two sides from the same country; which two? (2 pts)

2   Which three clubs have won the European Cup more than four times up to 2012? (3 pts)

3   Liverpool and AC Milan met in the European Cup final in 2005 and 2007; who were the managers of the two clubs on both occasions? (2 pts)

4   Which overseas coach brought Barcelona their first European Cup success in 1992?

5   Who was the first Englishman to play for an overseas side in a European Cup final and for which team? (2 pts)

6   Who is the only Scottish player to get on the pitch during a European Cup final over the last twenty years (1993–2012)?

7   Who are the only two uncapped (at the time) English players to have appeared in a Champions League final (i.e. since the competition changed name in 1992–3)? (2 pts)

8   Who is the only English player to have scored in two separate European Cup finals (up to 2012)?

9   Which two English players have appeared in European Cup finals for two different clubs? (2 pts)

10 Dimitar Berbatov has come on as a substitute in a European Cup final for which two clubs? (2 pts)

Part 2

11 Who were the first team from Eastern Europe to contest a European Cup final in 1965–6? And who were the second, and first (and only one thus far) to win twenty years later? (2 pts)

12 Which is the only club in the Champions League era (since 1993) to have lost two European Cup finals without ever winning the trophy?

13 Who are the only finalists from the Champions League in the twenty-first century who did not play in their country's top division in 2012–13?

14 Who knocked out reigning English champions Leeds United in the 1992–3 European Cup, the final year of straight knockout?

15 Who scored the penalty that earned Celtic a 2–1 win over Spartak Moscow in December 2012 and saw them reach the knockout stage of the Champions League for the first time in five years? Who were the other two teams in a far-from-easy group? (3 pts)

16 Which four clubs are the only ones from their respective countries to win the European Cup (to 2012)? Which of these teams won their only final? (5 pts)

17 Ernst Happel was the first ccach to win the European Cup twice, in 1970 and 1983, with two separate clubs; which clubs? For which country was Happel a star, so much so they named their national stadium after him? Who matched his feat in 2001, winning with Bayern Munich after guiding Borussia Dortmund to victory four years previously? And with which two clubs did José Mourinho show that perhaps he really is a 'Special One' in 2004 and 2010? Who added his name to this august list in 2013 and with which two clubs did he achieve the feat? (9 pts)

Total Points: 40. Targets: Novice 16 Pro 30. Your Score: [   ]

Quiz 127. True Crime

The evil that men do (and women, but less often)

Part 1

1   Notorious gangster Al Capone was prosecuted not for extortion and murder, but for which white-collar crime?

2   Where did Major Nidak Malik Hasan shoot forty-two people in November 2009, killing thirteen?

3   What was the name of the cult led by Charles Manson? (a) The Brotherhood (b) The Family (c) The Passion

4   Who went missing on 8 February 1983?

5   Steve Wright terrorized women in which English town before his arrest and conviction in 2008? What was his occupation? (2 pts)

6   What did Mohammad Aamer, Mohammad Asif and Salman Butt do?

7   Who was convicted and hanged in 1962 for a murder and separate rape on the A6 the previous year (a forty-year campaign for the verdict to be quashed ended when the killer's body was exhumed in 2002 and DNA tests proved his guilt)?

8   Which murderer was arrested aboard the SS *Montrose* in 1910 after the ship's captain suspected him and his co-traveller of not being who they said they were?

9   By what name is the fugitive from justice John Bingham better known? For whose murder was he wanted for twenty-five years? (2 pts)

10 An investigation into the death of Kathleen Grundy in 1998 eventually led to the prosecution and conviction of which mass-murderer? In which prison did he hang himself in 2004? (2 pts)

Part 2

11   The manipulative John Bunting and his accomplice Robert Wagner were responsible for a series of killings in South Australia known by what name?

12   Who was convicted, in 2009, of the imprisonment and rape of his own daughter for twenty-four years in Austria?

13   Which former companion of Joan of Arc was convicted and hanged for the murder of around 400 children in 1440?

14   What is the generic name for the organized crime families in Naples and surrounding Campania?

15   By what name was Donald Neilson, who killed four people during armed robberies in the 1970s, known? Which young heiress was one of his victims? (2 pts)

16   What nickname was given to Beverley Allitt, a paediatric nurse who killed (at least) four babies in her care in 1991?

17   What did the FBI announce for the first time on 14 March 1950?

18   Who terrorized New York in 1976–7, instigating a huge police hunt for the man dubbed the 'Son of Sam' by the press?

19   Michigan was the first US state to abandon capital punishment (except for treason) – in which decade was this: 1840s, 1890s or 1930s?

20   Kenneth Lay, who died in 2006 before he could be sentenced, was convicted of ten counts of fraud or malpractice perpetrated while he was an executive of which company?

Total Points: 24. Targets: Novice 10 Pro 18. Your Score:

Quiz 128. General Knowledge

Part 1

1   Which country is governed by a body called the Knesset?

2   Which country voted to keep the British monarch as Head of State in 1999?

3   Who did Boris Yeltsin name as acting President when he resigned from the post in 1999?

4   How tall is the Statue of Liberty: 46 metres, 72 metres or 90 metres?

5   Whose nude pictures ensured the very first edition of *Playboy* magazine would sell every copy?

6   Which iconic film director made a 1968 film about the Rolling Stones, *Sympathy for the Devil*?

7   The first six Marx Brothers movies were made by which major Hollywood studio? (a) Universal (b) MGM (c) Paramount

8   What is Nikolai Lobachevsky known for? (a) devising a new form of geometry (b) winning the world chess championship a record number of times (c) being the first astronaut/cosmonaut to die in a take-off accident

9   What was the 1975 non-fiction work and the 1982 sex and shopping novel that were runaway bestsellers for Shirley Conran? (2 pts)

10 Which endurance test was started in 1923 in the south of France?

Part 2

11   For what 'offence' were US sprinters Tommie Smith and Bob Carlos sent home 'in disgrace' during the 1968 Olympics in Mexico?

12   American journalists and politicians adopted the offensive phrase 'cheese-eating surrender monkeys' to describe the French after their refusal to participate in the invasion of Iraq. What is the origin of this phrase?

13   Who or what connects the band Destiny's Child to the film *My Week with Marilyn*?

14   'Mine eyes have seen the glory of the coming of the Lord'; everyone knows the first line, but what is the title of the hymn? To the tune of which other anthem is it sung? (2 pts)

15   The Brahmans are the priest class of which religion?

16   Ivor Wood supervised the animation of *Postman Pat*, who wrote the scripts? And what is the name of the village where Pat works? (2 pts)

17   True or false: Jodie Marsh survived a difficult upbringing by her single father in Essex before carving out her modelling and celebrity career?

18   Which actress made over fifty adverts for British Telecom across a five-year period?

19   Richard Jones, bassist with the Feeling, is married to which pop diva?

20   Which American businesswoman and celebrity cookery writer served five months in prison for financial irregularities in 2004?

Total Points: 23. Targets: Novice 12 Pro 17. Your Score:

Answers Quizzes 121–128

Quiz 121. General Knowledge

1. Robert Mugabe (he seemed such a nice man at the time); 2. Bristol; 3. Chess; 4. *Argo*;
5. Yugoslavia; 6. John McEnroe (he had his revenge the following year and ended Borg's
era of domination); 7. Joy Division; 8. The US Republican Party, pressured by the religious
right; 9. Lech Wałęsa (Solidarity was recognized later that year and Wałęsa was voted in
as President in 1990); 10. Nottingham Forest; Liverpool – English champions from 1979;
11. He fled Colchester and rejoined the army at Hemel Hempstead; from there he marched
to Exeter via Bath before retiring to York; 12. ABC, CBS, NBC and Fox (the relative
newcomer, established in the 1980s); CW

Quiz 122. Sci-Fi TV

1. *A for Andromeda* (Christie was in such demand that the BBC were priced out of her
services for a second series so she was replaced by Susan Hampshire); 2. *Stargate SG-1*;
3. *Babylon* 5; 4. Mr Sulu; 5. He is the captain of the *Enterprise* in the prequel to *Star Trek*
set in the twenty-second century; Scott Bakula, star of *Quantum Leap*; 6. Angel; Lorne
Greene was the actor, and the green karaoke-loving demon in *Angel* calls himself Lorne; 7.
The *Quatermass* series; 8. The Borg; the Klingons had joined the Federation so a new evil
race was needed, and the Ferengi from the first series were just too silly; 9. *Urban Gothic*
(essential cult viewing); 10. Only seventy-nine, in three series (amazing how repeats can
alter one's perception); 11. It is the registration of the USS *Enterprise* in the original *Star
Trek* series; 12. Saul Tigh; Number Six; James Callis; 13. The three ship's computers in
Blake's 7, all voiced by Peter Tuddenham; 14. *Farscape*; *The Peacekeeper Wars*; 15. *Firefly*;
Nathan Fillion (now the star of *Castle*); Shiny; 16. They changed gender (both were male in
the earlier version); 17. *Stargate Atlantis*; *Stargate Infinity*; 18. Kathryn Janeway; Chako-
tay; 19. *V*; to harvest humans for food; 20. Artie (Nielsen); *(A Town Called) Eureka*

Quiz 123. Tourist Attractions

1. Italy; 2. Cape Town and Johannesburg; 3. Yellowstone; 4. Murano; 5. County Antrim;
Giants' Causeway; 6. Portuguese; 7. (c) South Dakota; 8. India; 9. Versailles; to house his
art collection, it was what is now the Louvre; 10. Mayan; 11. Ecuador; 12. Philadelphia;
13. Jerusalem (the old city); 14. (c) Aachen; 15. The Habsburg Emperors; 16. (b) It is an old
printworks and houses a collection of art, manuscripts and machinery related to the
industry; 17. Kremlin; 18. Athens; 19. Split; 20. Gozo

Quiz 124. History

1. Mount Vesuvius; 2. The building of the Great Pyramid at Giza; 3. Rubicon (hence the
phrase 'crossing the Rubicon' indicating that a point of no return has been passed; 4. *Tao*

Te Ching, the classic work of Taoism; 5. Simón Bolívar; 6. Anne Boleyn; her daughter Elizabeth (later Queen Elizabeth I); 7. In the shift to the new Gregorian calendar, ten days were missed to adjust the seasonal equinoxes to the right date; 8. Luncheon Vouchers; 9. Parliament; 10. Netherlands (including modern-day Belgium); 11. The Huns, led by Attila; 12. Tehran, Iran; 13. As the first (and only) English Pope (1154–9); 14. Sadat; 15. 1866, during the Presidency of Andrew Johnson; 16. 1967, during the Six-Day War; 17. Saigon; 18. Warwick the Kingmaker; 19. John Dee; 20. It was 17 June

Quiz 125. Shakespeare

1. Agincourt; 2. Margaret of Anjou; 3. Pyramus and Thisbe; 4. *The Two Gentlemen of Verona*; 5. Benedick and Beatrice; 6. *Henry VIII*; John Fletcher; 7. Lord Chamberlain's Men (they became the King's Men after James I came to the throne, so either is acceptable); Richard Burbage; 8. Bolingbroke; John of Gaunt; 9. (a) Judith and Hamnet; 10. Her cousin, Celia, and the clown, Touchstone; 11. Angelo; the novice (apprentice nun), Isabella; 12. The hand of the heiress, Portia, in *The Merchant of Venice*; 13. Cymbeline; Imogen wakes next to the corpse of Cloten (it's OK, they weren't close!); 14. Goneril, (Duke of) Albany; 15. *Rosencrantz and Guildenstern Are Dead*; 16. *Troilus and Cressida*; 17. 154 (he was a busy boy); 18. *Titus Andronicus*; 19. Eight (*Richard II*, *Henry IV* x 2, *Henry V*, *Henry VI* x 3, *Richard III*); 20. Julius Caesar

Quiz 126. Champions League

1. Real Madrid v. Valencia; 2. Real Madrid (nine), Milan (seven) and Liverpool (five); 3. Rafael Benítez and Carlo Ancelotti; 4. Johan Cruyff; 5. Kevin Keegan for Hamburg (against Nottingham Forest in 1980); 6. Paul Lambert (later a Premier League manager) played for Borussia Dortmund in 1996–7; 7. Jermaine Pennant (Liverpool, 2006–7); Ryan Bertrand (Chelsea, 2011–12, he was capped later the same summer); 8. Phil Neal (he scored a penalty in the 3–1 win against Borussia Mönchengladbach in 1977, and from open play against Roma in 1983–4, where he also scored in the successful penalty shoot-out); 9. Owen Hargreaves (Bayern Munich in 2001, Manchester United in 2008) and Ashley Cole (Arsenal in 2006, Chelsea in 2008 and again in 2012); 10. Bayer Leverkusen in 2002 and Manchester United in 2011; 11. Partizan Belgrade; Steaua Bucharest (they stifled Barcelona for two hours and won on penalties when Barca missed all four of their spot kicks); 12. Valencia in 2000 and 2001; 13. AS Monaco, beaten by Porto in the 2004 final; 14. Rangers; 15. Kris Commons; Barcelona (whom Celtic beat in a heroic display at Parkhead) and Benfica; 16. Celtic (Scotland); Steaua Bucharest (Romania); Olympique Marseille (France); Red Star Belgrade (Yugoslavia/Serbia); Red Star played one final and won (beating Marseille on penalties); 17. Feyenoord and Hamburg; Austria; Ottmar Hitzfeld; Porto and Internazionale of Milan; Jupp Heynckes; Real Madrid and Bayern Munich AIs

Quiz 127. True Crime

1. Tax evasion; 2. Fort Hood Army base, Texas (accept US army base); 3. (b) The Family; 4. Shergar; 5. Ipswich; fork-lift truck driver; 6. They were the Pakistani cricketers found guilty of match-rigging in 2010; 7. James Hanratty; 8. Dr Harold Crippen; it was the first time a radio was used to help catch a criminal; 9. Lord Lucan; his children's nanny, Susan Rivett (the nanny gets the point); 10. Harold Shipman; Wakefield; 11. The Snowtown Murders; 12. Josef Fritzl; 13. Gilles de Rais (he is believed to have been an inspiration for the character of Bluebeard); 14. Camorra; 15. The Black Panther; Lesley Whittle; 16. The Angel of Death; 17. The Ten Most Wanted list; 18. David Berkowitz (he killed six people); 19. 1840s (Rhode Island followed suit in 1852 and Wisconsin a year later); 20. Enron

Quiz 128. General Knowledge

1. Knesset is the Israeli Parliament; 2. Australia; 3. Vladimir Putin; 4. 46 metres; 5. Marilyn Monroe; 6. Jean-Luc Godard; 7. (c) Paramount (they defected to MGM after *Duck Soup* in 1933); 8. (a) Lobachevsky devised a form of non-Euclidean geometry in the early nineteenth century; 9. *Superwoman* and *Lace*; 10. Le Mans 24 Hour Race; 11. They gave a black-gloved black-power salute on the medal rostrum – and returned to a hero's welcome from the African-American equal rights campaigners; 12. Spoken by Willie the Groundskeeper in *The Simpsons*; 13. Destiny's Child includes a singer called Michelle Williams, coincidentally the name of the actress who portrayed Monroe in the movie; 14. 'Battle Hymn of the Republic' by Julia Ward Howe; 'John Brown's Body'; 15. Hinduism; 16. John Cunliffe; Greendale; 17. False (her father is a wealthy businessman and she went to a good school); 18. Maureen Lipman; 19. Sophie Ellis-Bextor; 20. Martha Stewart

Quiz 129. General Knowledge

Part 1

1   What illegal organization was founded in Tennessee in 1866?

2   Which remote island, known for birds and knitwear, was purchased by the National Trust for Scotland in 1954?

3   King George VI, the father of Queen Elizabeth II, died on 6 February 1952. Which earlier British monarch died on the same date in 1685?

4   What is the name of the beautiful gypsy girl beloved of Quasimodo in *The Hunchback of Notre Dame?* (a) Beatrice (b) Esmerelda (c) Celestine

5   What are the surnames of Edina and Patsy in *Absolutely Fabulous*? (2 pts)

6   What were the two principal fighter planes used by the RAF in the Battle of Britain? (2 pts)

7   In the movies, what is the significance of a star having a Bacon number of one?

8   For what are the two non-scientific Nobel Prizes awarded each year? (2 pts)

9   With what is Ted Avery (born Frederick Bean, 1908–80) associated?

10 In which two events do only women athletes compete at the Olympic Games? (2 pts)

Part 2

11 What would you build if you needed to take a man-made waterway like a canal over another waterway, like a river?

12 Who came between Penny Calvert and Wilnelia?

13 Who is the only star to win a Best Actress Oscar in a film directed by her husband?

14 What 'first' took place on the Isle of Man on 27 May 1907?

15 What were the biggest selling singles of the 1950s, 1960s, 1970s, 1980s, 1990s and 2000s? (6 pts)

Total Points: 24. Targets: Novice 12 Pro 18. Your Score:

Quiz 130. Movies

A general quiz about films

Part 1

1 Which 2009 prison drama saw North African French star Tahar Rahim make an immediate impact on the international movie scene?

2 Which 1967 film ended in a slow-motion shoot-out that would change the way violence was used in the movies for good?

3 What is wuxia? (a) a gravity-defying style of martial arts in East Asian cinema (b) the honour code of the Chinese triads (c) the Mexican term for what Western critics call spaghetti westerns

4 Which of these classics came first: Eisenstein's *Battleship Potemkin*, Fritz Lang's *Metropolis* or James Whale's *Frankenstein*?

5 Which pop group are the stars of Bob Rafelson's debut feature, *Head* (1968)?

6 Which effects pioneer created the Medusa monster for the original *Clash of the Titans* (1981)?

7 In cinema parlance, what is the BBFC?

8 Who plays the headmistress in *The Prime of Miss Jean Brodie* (1969)? (a) Maggie Smith (b) Celia Johnson (c) Diana Dors

9 The 59,000 square foot stage in Pinewood Studios, the biggest in Europe, was built at whose behest?

10 Which Hollywood studio has as its logo a statue of a woman holding a torch called Lady Liberty?

11 What was Steven Spielberg's first feature film? (Careful . . .)

12 Which 2001 anime feature remains Japan's highest grossing film world-wide? (a) *Akira* (b) *Spirited Away* (c) *Howl's Moving Castle*

13 Which short-lived star played new-girl-at-school Tai in the 1995 teen comedy *Clueless*?

14 *Knight and Day* was a massive flop in 2010; who co-starred alongside Tom Cruise?

Part 2

Five questions, all with a connection

15   What film saw Jim Carrey give a star-making turn as Stanley Ipkiss?

16   What was the gangster movie that saw Tom Hanks on the run from a relent-
     less but not very talkative assassin played by Jude Law?

17   Who directed the thriller *A History of Violence* starring Viggo Mortensen?

18   What was the cult 1968 sci-fi movie directed by Jane Fonda's husband,
     Roger Vadim?

19   What was the Hughes brothers 2001 movie starring Johnny Depp about the
     mystery surrounding the Jack the Ripper murders?

20   What's the link?

Total Points: 20. Targets: Novice 10 Pro 15. Your Score: [   ]

Quiz 131. Rock and Pop

A few general questions and a Mix and Match section

Part 1

1 *Third Strike* was a 2010 hit album for which British artist?
2 Them Crooked Vultures is a supergroup formed by John Paul Jones, Dave Grohl and Josh Homme; with which bands are the three associated? (There are two permissible answers for Grohl.) (3 pts)
3 Reggae singer Fred Hibbert is better known by what name?
4 *Real Life* was a 2006 breakthrough for which female backing singer, born Joan Wasser?
5 What, in 1952, became the first weekly newspaper to feature a singles chart?
6 As well as being Damon Albarn's girlfriend, Justine Frischmann had her own band at the height of Britpop; who were they?
7 Who is the only permanent member of Nine Inch Nails?
8 Whose first UK no. 1 single was a 1982 cover of a Supremes song?
9 *Innervisions* and *Fulfillingness' First Finale* were 1970s classics by which soul singer?
10 Who recorded the hit electro-pop album *Dare* in 1981? And which album were two former members of the band recording under the name Heaven 17 in the same studio? (2 pts)

Part 2

Mix and Match: match these metal muthas to the band for which they shout/sing/scream/rap

1. Rou Reynolds; 2. Jacoby Shaddix; 3. Simon Neil; 4. Till Lindemann; 5. Hayley Williams; 6. Zack De La Rocha; 7. Eva Spence; 8. Fred Durst; 9. Oli Sykes; 10. Corey Taylor

a. Bring Me the Horizon; b. Limp Bizkit; c. Rammstein; d. Rolo Tomassi; e. Paramore; f. Enter Shikari; g. Papa Roach; h. Biffy Clyro; i. Slipknot; j. Rage Against the Machine (10 pts)

Your Workings:

Total Points: 23. Targets: Novice 9 Pro 17. Your Score:

Quiz 132. TV

Some broad TV questions

Part 1

1 What connects *Judge John Deed* to *Inspector George Gently*?

2 Which legal series featured William Shatner as a slightly barking old Republican lawyer bonding with James Spader's rebellious liberal attorney?

3 Who played ditzy Alice and dim Hugo, so perfect for each other they were married? What was the show? (3 pts)

4 How was Mr Spock a hero in a show that had nothing to do with *Star Trek*?

5 What is the cult American TV series about a chemistry teacher who starts to manufacture drugs to help support his family when he is diagnosed with cancer?

6 What was the successful ITV drama screened first in 2004 that starred Caroline Quentin as a mother-of-two going through a messy split from her husband and trying to re-energize her life?

7 Who scooted around in a van called the Mystery Machine?

8 Long before *Outnumbered* Hugh Dennis and Claire Skinner (along with Simon Pegg, Mark Heap, Kevin Eldon and a host of other familiar TV faces) worked together on which spoof documentary series, conceived and made by Chris Morris?

9 Who were Sabrina Duncan, Jill Munroe and Kelly Garrett?

10 During transmission of an edition of *Celebrity Mastermind*, Ian Lavender took the familiar black chair and was asked his name; what did Rick Wakeman, the keyboard player and another contestant, shout from his seat?

Part 2

11   Which former nurse plays Alicia Florrick in *The Good Wife* (from 2009)?

12   What was the name of the housekeeper in *Father Ted* (played by Pauline McLynn) who had scarcely any lines but still became an oft-quoted cult comedy figure?

13   In which year was the BBC's flagship programme *Horizon* launched: 1964, 1969 or 1976?

14   Who plays the ambitious lawyer Martha Costello in the hit BBC drama *Silk*?

15   Which major long-running drama series came out of a hit 1970 movie directed by Robert Altman?

16   Why does the gentle TV whodunnit series *Death in Paradise*, which launched in 2012, provide heart-warming viewing for fans of 1990s cult sci-fi comedy, *Red Dwarf*?

17   Who is 'Mr Big', as played by Chris Noth? What is his proper name? (2 pts)

18   It's 2013 – thirty-eight years ago it was fourteen years ago: explain?

19   What was the name of Carter and Regan's boss in *The Sweeney*?

20   Who were the parents of the many Walton siblings and where did they live? (3 pts)

21   Who was the pilot of the massive air-freighter *Thunderbird 2*? What was the name of the drilling machine kept in the hold? Which other *Thunderbird* also launched from within *Thunderbird 2*? What was the colour of FAB1, Lady Penelope's Rolls-Royce car? And what was the name of her man-servant? (5 pts)

Total Points: 30. Targets: Novice 12 Pro 23. Your Score:

Quiz 133. Cars

One for the petrol-heads

Part 1

1   Lexus is the luxury car division of which giant motor company?

2   What became an obligatory aspect of road travel from 1 January 1921?

3   Designed in the 1930s in France, unveiled at a motor show in 1948 and universally derided, yet still a two-and-half-year waiting list built up in the first year of restricted production (materials were still scarce post-war); what is it?

4   What was Percy Shaw's 1933 contribution to road safety? (a) crash barriers (b) automated traffic lights (c) cats' eyes

5   Which car manufacturer introduced the MX-5 in 1989, a roadster that would challenge the British sports car manufacturers and which remains a popular and affordable option?

6   Which sports car, launched under the Chevrolet brand by General Motors in 1953, became the iconic rock 'n' roll cool car of the age? What name was the second generation of the model given after launch in 1962? (2 pts)

7   Who launched the Miura in 1966, the first so-called supercar?

8   Which US city is nicknamed Motor City due to the high concentration of automotive businesses there?

9   What was introduced as a deterrent to enhance road safety by Transport Minister Barbara Castle in 1967? (a) speed cameras (b) breathalysers (c) speeding tickets

10 Which brand of US car was the oldest in the country when it was phased out by General Motors in 2004 after 107 years?

Part 2

11 Which was the first mainstream family car to introduce (in 1977) turbo-injection to a 2-litre engine? (a) Ford Capri (b) Saab 99 (c) BMW 5-Series

12 Designer Colin Chapman was associated with which UK motor company?

13 What was the first number plate issued by the London authority to Lord Russell in 1903? (a) A1 (b) R1 (c) LON1?

14 Which new model, launched the previous year, did Ford expect to sell 100,000 units in 1965, and end up shifting over 650,000? (The model is still in production.)

15 *Car* magazine celebrated fifty years in 2012; what was the title of the publication on launch in 1962? (a) *Mini and Other Marques* (b) *Car and Mini Enthusiast* (c) *Small Car and Mini Owner*? Which sports car did the fiftieth anniversary edition acclaim as the best car of the last fifty years? (2 pts)

16 Which sports car manufacturer (now owned by the Volkswagen group, but still based in Molsheim, France) launched the reassuringly expensive Veyron in 2005?

17 What started as an E30 in 1986 and progressed through the E36, E46 to the 2009 E92, the current model?

18 How much did Afzal Khan pay for his F1 car registration at auction in 2008? (a) £115,000 (b) £440,000 (c) £1,100,000

19 Which motor company was founded by Giovanni Agnelli in 1899? In which football club do the family have a controlling interest? (2 pts)

20 One of the few success stories in car manufacturing in the UK in recent years is the UK plant making Japanese cars that was established in 1986 and became, in 2010, the first plant to make over 400,000 cars in a year; which company opened the plant, and where? (2 pts)

Total Points: 24. Targets: Novice 10 Pro 18. Your Score: [   ]

Quiz 134. Tennis

Serving up twenty straight questions about tennis

First Serve

1 How did Richard Rasking compete in the 1977 US Open ladies' singles championships?

2 Which female tennis player has won the most major singles titles (twenty-four)?

3 Which Grand Slam title eluded Pete Sampras?

4 Which two players contested three successive Wimbledon finals in 1988–90? (2 pts)

5 Who did Andre Agassi beat in the final for his only singles victory at Wimbledon?

6 Who was the Bounding Basque, a Frenchman who won Wimbledon in 1924 and 1926?

7 Before Rafael Nadal in 2008, who was the last Spanish player to win the Wimbledon Men's singles title, forty-two years previously?

8 Who partnered John Newcombe to twelve Grand Slam men's doubles titles?

9 Which two American players are the only two women to have beaten Steffi Graf in a Wimbledon ladies' singles final? (2 pts)

10 Who is the only French winner of a Wimbledon singles title since 1946?

Second Serve

11 Other than Americans, who were the last two players from the same country to win the ladies' and men's singles titles in the same year at Wimbledon? (2 pts)

12 Who knocked out both Roger Federer and Novak Djokovic at Wimbledon in 2010 en route to the final?

13 Which two countries won every Davis Cup played between 1946 and 1973? Who broke the hegemony in controversial circumstances in 1974? (3 pts)

14 France won the Davis Cup for the first time in fifty-nine years in 1991; which two left-handers made up their team in the final, both beating Pete Sampras? (2 pts)

15 Which three doubles pairings have won all four Grand Slam titles in the last twenty years? (3 pts, one per pairing)

16 From 2006 to 2012 all but two of the men's singles Grand Slam titles available were won by Federer, Nadal or Djokovic; who bucked the trend? (2 pts)

17 Who won most Grand Slam singles titles: Martina Hingis, Kim Clijsters or Justine Henin?

18 Pam Shriver won twenty-two Grand Slam titles; good player, Pam, but in what sense did she get lucky?

19 Who did Martina Navratilova beat five times in Wimbledon singles finals? And who were the only two players to beat Martina in a Wimbledon final? (3 pts)

20 Pete Sampras won seven out of eight Wimbledon titles between 1993 and 2000; who ambushed him in the quarter-final in 1996 and went on to win the title?

Total Points: 31. Targets: Novice 12 Pro 23. Your Score: ☐

Quiz 135. Trivia

What they did before they were famous . . .

Part 1

1   Who first made her name as a child star in *Lassie Come Home* and *Courage of Lassie*?

2   Who made a toothsome appearance as Jodie Foster's daughter in *Panic Room* prior to encountering teeth of a different kind in a bestselling movie franchise?

3   Which soon-to-be-megastar played a young boy in Stephen Spielberg's 1987 film, *Empire of the Sun*? From whose book was the film adapted? (2 pts)

4   Before her career as a stand-up comedian, Jo Brand was (a) a cleaner (b) a psychiatric nurse or (c) a primary school teacher?

5   Which massively successful band in the 1980s started out in the previous decade as the Café Racers? (a) INXS (b) Dire Straits (c) Spandau Ballet

6   Which major nineteenth-century artist gave up a career as a stockbroker to pursue his love of painting? (a) Claude Monet (b) Henri Toulouse-Lautrec (c) Paul Gauguin

7   What connects the child stars of *Billy Elliot* and *Thirteen*?

8   Which Hollywood great was part of a circus acrobatic duo called Lang and Cravat in the 1930s before an injury forced him to look at other means of making a living?

9   Which Hollywood actress was once a runner-up in the Miss USA contest and sixth in the Miss World pageant? (a) Demi Moore (b) Jennifer Aniston (c) Halle Berry

10 Which two unknowns, one American, one English, played Danny and Sandy in the original Broadway hit of *Grease* when it opened in London? (2 pts)

Part 2

Mix and Match: match the actor to the brand for which they appeared in a TV commercial long before finding fame in their profession (yes, we know there are only eight products listed – three of the celebs all worked for Burger King)

1. Brad Pitt; 2. Morgan Freeman; 3. Paul Rudd; 4. Meg Ryan; 5. Keanu Reeves; 6. Kate Winslet; 7. Ben Affleck; 8. Sarah Michelle Gellar; 9. Naomi Watts; 10. Anthony Head

a. Sugar Puffs; b. Burger King; c. Tampax; d. Kellogg's Corn Flakes; e. Nescafé Gold Blend; f. Pringles; g. Listerine; h. Nintendo (10 pts)

Your Workings:

Total Points: 22. Targets: Novice 11 Pro 17. Your Score:

Quiz 136. General Knowledge

Jo, Joey, Joseph, Joanna . . .

Part 1

1   Which actress married Val Kilmer in 1988 and divorced him in 1995?

2   Who is Josephine March?

3   *La Traviata* and *Rigoletto* are amongst the operas composed by which nine-teenth-century giant?

4   He entered Parliament as the MP for Leeds North East in 1956, served as a cabinet minister under Macmillan, Heath and Thatcher, and is regarded as one of the chief architects of the free-market economic policies that came to be known as 'Thatcherism'; who was he?

5   The Italian football arena formally called the Stadio Giuseppe Meazza is better known by what name?

6   What position did Joseph Goebbels hold in the Third Reich in 1933–45? (a) Air-Marshal of the Luftwaffe (b) Head of the Gestapo (c) Minister of Propaganda?

7   In which Academy Award-winning 1998 film did Joseph Fiennes play the lead role, without picking up a nomination himself?

8   Who was elected Vice President of the United States alongside Barack Obama in 2008?

9   With which band did guitarist and songwriter Joe Walsh enjoy his greatest commercial success?

10   *A Village Affair* caused a minor sensation on release in 1989 with its story about a rural lesbian affair; who wrote it?

Part 2

11   Which well-known pop song begins with the words, 'Jojo was a man who thought he was a loner . . .'?

12   Who was born Iosef Dzhugashvili in Georgia, Eastern Europe, in 1878?

13   Which multi-millionaire married Neil Murray in 2001, between the publication of her fourth and fifth books?

14   Prior to Heather Watson in 2012, who was the last British winner of a WTA (Women's Tennis Association) singles title, back in 1983?

15   Which Academy Award-winning actress was married to Paul Newman from 1958 until his death in 2008?

16   *The Evening Session*, an indie rock show on Radio 1 for much of the 1990s, was co-hosted by Steve Lamacq and which other DJ?

17   Josephine Baker, the American singing star, was a success at the Folies-Bergère in the 1920s with her 'Danse Sauvage', which featured her wearing an outfit made from: (a) miniature heads and teeth (b) bananas (c) grape vines?

18   Who won the TT Formula One world championship five consecutive times in 1982–6?

19   Josephine de Beauharnais is remembered as the first Empress of France and consort to Napoleon Bonaparte; what happened to her first husband?

20   Folk singer Joanna Newsom is unusual in popular music for being a virtuoso on what instrument?

Total Points: 20. Targets: Novice 10 Pro 15. Your Score: [   ]

Answers Quizzes 129–136

Quiz 129. General Knowledge

1. Ku Klux Klan; 2. Fair Isle; 3. Charles II; 4. (b) Esmerelda; 5. Monsoon and Stone; 6. (Hawker) Hurricane and (Supermarine) Spitfire; 7. They have appeared in a film with Kevin Bacon (in the game 'Six Degrees of Kevin Bacon', the Bacon number is how many steps it takes to link an actor to Kevin Bacon); 8. Literature and Peace; 9. He was a cartoonist (and voice actor) behind many of the great early Warner Bros. cartoons, including *Bugs Bunny*; 10. Synchronized swimming and rhythmic gymnastics; 11. An aqueduct; 12. Anthea Redfern (she was Bruce Forsyth's second wife); 13. Frances McDormand (her husband is Joel Coen); 14. TT Race; 15. 'Rock Around the Clock' (Bill Haley and His Comets); 'She Loves You' (The Beatles); 'Mull of Kintyre' (Wings); 'Do They Know It's Christmas?' (Band Aid); 'Candle in the Wind '97' (Elton John); 'Anything Is Possible/Evergreen' (Will Young – accept either)

Quiz 130. Movies

1. *A Prophet*; 2. *Bonnie and Clyde* (Arthur Penn shot the scene from multiple angles and then had it edited by Dede Allen into the finished product – an orgiastic synergy of violence and beauty that amazed and appalled critics); 3. (a) it is the form of aerial combat first introduced to the mainstream in *Crouching Tiger, Hidden Dragon*; 4. *Battleship Potemkin* was 1925, *Metropolis* two years later and *Frankenstein* in 1931; 5. Pop group the Monkees; 6. Ray Harryhausen; 7. British Board of Film Classification (the censors); 8. (b) Celia Johnson (Maggie Smith was a teacher at the school, not the head); 9. Cubby Broccoli, the producer of the Bond movies; 10. Columbia; 11. *Sugarland Express* (*Duel* is incorrect – it was a made-for-TV movie that had a limited theatrical release after being well-received on TV; *Sugarland Express* was the first film Spielberg made that was intended for cinema release); 12. (b) *Spirited Away*; 13. Alicia Silverstone; 14. Cameron Diaz (the film is so bad it may be destined to become a classic turkey); 15. *The Mask*; 16. *Road to Perdition*; 17. David Cronenberg; 18. *Barbarella*; 19. *From Hell*; 20. All these movies were based on comic strips

Quiz 131. Rock and Pop

1. Tinchy Stryder; 2. Jones was in Led Zeppelin, Homme is the head boy in Queens of the Stone Age and Grohl was in Nirvana and now fronts Foo Fighters; 3. He is Toots of Toots and the Maytals; 4. Joan as Policewoman; 5. *New Musical Express*; 6. Elastica; 7. Trent Reznor; 8. Phil Collins; 9. Stevie Wonder; 10. The Human League; Penthouse and Pavement; Mix and Match 1, f; 2, g; 3, h; 4, c; 5, e; 6, j; 7, d; 8, b; 9, a; 10, i

Quiz 132. TV

1. Both are played by Martin Shaw; 2. *Boston Legal* (the programme mixed great set-piece legal cases with the outrageous, near-surreal private lives of the various lawyers); 3.

Emma Chambers and James Fleet; *The Vicar of Dibley*; 4. Zachary Quinto, Spock in the recent *Star Trek* movie reboot, played Sylar in the TV sci-fi drama *Heroes*; 5. *Breaking Bad*; 6. *Life Begins*; 7. Scooby Doo and the gang; 8. *Brass Eye*; 9. The original *Charlie's Angels*; 10. 'Don't tell him, Pike!' (the wet-behind-the-ears private in *Dad's Army* was Lavender's defining role); 11. Julianna Margulies (she was the head nurse in *ER*); 12. Mrs Doyle; 13. 1964 and still going; 14. Maxine Peake; 15. *M*A*S*H*; 16. It provided the first major role for Danny John-Jules, who will forever be the Cat in *Red Dwarf*; 17. He is Carrie Bradshaw's prospective Mr Right in *Sex and the City*; his real name is John, as revealed in the final episode; 18. *Space: 1999* was first screened in 1975; 19. (DCI Frank) Haskins; 20. John and Olivia; the Blue Ridge Mountains (of Virginia); 21. Scott Tracy; The Mole; *Thunderbird 4*, the submarine; pink; (Aloysius) Parker

Quiz 133. Cars

1. Toyota; 2. Displaying a road tax disc on the windscreen; 3. Citroën 2-CV; 4. (c) cats' eyes; 5. Mazda; 6. Corvette; Sting Ray; 7. Lamborghini; 8. Detroit; 9. The breathalyser test; 10. Oldsmobile; 11. (b) Saab 99; 12. Lotus; 13. (a) A1; 14. Ford Mustang; 15. (c) *Small Car and Mini Owner*; Porsche 911; 16. Bugatti; 17. BMW M3 series; 18. £440,000; he stuck it on a Mercedes-Benz McLaren, which cost a lot less, at *c.*£250,000; 19. Fiat; Juventus; 20. Nissan; Sunderland

Quiz 134. Tennis

1. 'He' became a she – Renée Richards, and competed after winning a court case against the US Tennis Association; 2. Margaret Court; 3. French Open; 4. Stefan Edberg and Boris Becker; Edberg won in 1988 and 1990; 5. Goran Ivanisevic; 6. Jean Borotra; 7. Manuel Santana; 8. Tony Roche; 9. Martina Navratilova and Lindsay Davenport; 10. Amelie Mauresmo in 2006; 11. Michael Stich and Steffi Graf in 1991; 12. Tomas Berdych; 13. USA and Australia; South Africa (they won the final by a walk-over as India refused to play them); 14. Guy Forget and Henri Leconte (the match was played on clay courts to negate Sampras's power on grass, and Leconte, one of the great flair players, had one of 'those days' – the pair even beat Flach and Seguso, one of the top doubles pairings); 15. Bob and Mike Bryan; Todd Woodbridge and Mark Woodforde (accept the Woodies); Jacco Eltingh and Paul Haarhuis; 16. Juan Martin del Potro (2009) and Andy Murray (2012) both won the US Open; 17. Henin, with seven (Hingis won four, Clijsters three); 18. She was partnered by Martina Navratilova for twenty of those titles (she won one apiece with Natasha Zvereva and mixed partner Emilio Sanchez); 19. Chris Evert; Steffi Graf and Conchita Martínez; 20. Richard Krajicek

Quiz 135. Trivia

1. Elizabeth Taylor; 2. Kristen Stewart; 3. Christian Bale; J. G. Ballard; 4. (a) a psychiatric nurse; 5. (b) Dire Straits; 6. (c) Paul Gauguin; 7. Jamie Bell and Evan Rachel Wood were

married in 2012; 8. Burt Lancaster; 9. (c) Halle Berry; 10. Richard Gere and Elaine Paige; Mix and Match 1, f; 2, g; 3, h; 4, b; 5, d; 6, a; 7, b; 8, b; 9, c; 10, e

Quiz 136. General Knowledge

1. Joanne Whalley; 2. She is one of the main characters in *Little Women* by Louisa May Alcott; 3. Giuseppe Verdi; 4. Keith Joseph; 5. San Siro in Milan (Meazza was one of the first great stars to appear for both Milan clubs, who share the stadium); 6. (c) Minister of Propaganda; 7. *Shakespeare in Love*; 8. Joe Biden; 9. The Eagles; 10. Joanna Trollope; 11. 'Get Back', written by Lennon/McCartney, performed by the Beatles; 12. Joseph Stalin; 13. J. K. (Jo) Rowling; 14. Jo Durie; 15. Joanne Woodward; 16. Jo Wiley; 17. Bananas (artificial); 18. Joey Dunlop; 19. He was guillotined during the post-revolutionary Terror; 20. Harp

Quiz 137. General Knowledge

Part 1

1 Thirty-three miners were trapped underground in Chile in 2010; what were they mining for?

2 Where might you lie on the beach at Negril, climb Blue Mountain Peak or dive in the Ocho Rios reefs?

3 What nationality is UN Secretary-General Ban Ki-moon?

4 What happened to Jean Charles de Menezes, a Brazilian-born electrician working in London, on 22 July 2005?

5 Unusually for an East German, Katarina Witt was allowed to start a professional career; with which US Olympic gold medal winner did she form a famous dance partnership?

6 Who directed the 2006 movie *Glastonbury*, a tribute to the long-running rock festival?

7 Which cult 2009 comedy film featured a cameo by former world champion boxer Mike Tyson?

8 Which novelist advised the Post Office to adopt the French notion of a letter box, after studying postal problems on the Channel Islands in 1852? (a) Anthony Trollope (b) Charles Dickens (c) Emily Brontë?

9 What connects comedian Bill Bailey with rock band Guns N' Roses?

10 What was unique about the Australia v. England cricket match at Melbourne on 5 January 1971?

11 Which classic musical was adapted from a 1909 play by Ferenc Molnár?

12 Which anthemic song was written by Claude Rouget de Lisle in 1792?

13 How did Sheridan Smith emulate Reese Witherspoon?

14 What did John Major and John Prescott have in common when they left school?

Part 2

Answer the questions and then tie them together

15   Who was the Prime Minister who handed over power to the black majority in Rhodesia (now Zimbabwe)?

16   Who was UK TV's first high-profile female producer, who introduced *Doctor Who* to the schedule, alongside many other programmes?

17   Who was the psychiatrist who once made Geoffrey Boycott blub on the radio?

18   Who made up the *New Avengers* along with Patrick Macnee and Joanna Lumley?

19   Who founded Body Shop?

20   In which year did all these people die?

Total Points: 20. Targets: Novice 10 Pro 15. Your Score:

Quiz 138. Rock and Pop

Ten straight questions and a Name the Band section

Part 1

1   What dominates the front cover of the 1967 *The Velvet Underground & Nico* album?

2   By what name were the sisters Kim, Debbie, Joni and Kathy known as in their musical career?

3   Bruce Springsteen's album *We Shall Overcome* was a collection of covers and songs influenced by which songwriter and folk singer?

4   In 2003, who became Britain's only entry to score nil points in the Eurovision Song Contest? (a) Jemini (b) Jedward (c) Creme Brulee (d) Darius

5   What was the Cuban collective which enjoyed an international hit in collaboration with Ry Cooder?

6   On what instrument was 'Sneaky' Pete Kleinow of the Flying Burrito Brothers a pioneering practitioner? (a) pedal steel guitar (b) harmonica (c) electric mandolin

7   Who was the most famous member of 1970s cult pub rock band, the 101ers?

8   The successful independent British record label Bella Union was founded by two members (Robin Guthrie and Simon Raymonde) of which cult UK band?

9   Which promoter and composer wrote most of the songs on Meatloaf's *Bat Out of Hell*?

10 African music star Youssou N'Dour announced in 2012 that he would run for the presidency of which country?

Part 2

We give you the band members, you tell us under what name they achieved their fame

11   Lemmy, Fast Eddie Clarke, Phil Taylor

12   Tony Hadley, John Keeble, Gary Kemp, Martin Kemp, Steve Norman

13   Arabian Prince, DJ Yella, Dr Dre, Eazy E, Ice Cube

14   Jazzie B, Daddae, Nellee Hooper, Simon Law, Caron Wheeler

15   Brian Johnson, Phil Rudd, Cliff Williams, Malcolm Young, Angus Young

16   Tommy Lee, Mick Mars, Vince Neil, Nikki Sixx

17   Andy Fletcher, Dave Gahan, Martin Gore, Alan Wilder

18   David Byrne, Chris Frantz, Jerry Harrison, Tina Weymouth

19   Bob Dylan, George Harrison, Jim Keltner, Jeff Lynne, Roy Orbison, Tom Petty

20   Steven Adler, Duff McKagan, Axl Rose, Slash, Izzy Stradlin

Total Points: 20. Targets: Novice 8 Pro 15. Your Score: ☐

Quiz 139. Wildlife

Some questions about the natural world

Part 1

1   In the term *Equus burchelli* (the Linnaean term for a zebra), to what taxonomic groups do the two words, *Equus* (capitalized) and *burchelli* (lower case) belong? (2 pts)

2   If a male ass or donkey is a jack, what is the female called?

3   Which creature, believed extinct, was caught by South African fisherman Hendrik Goosens in 1938, and remains with us today?

4   How many digits does a squirrel have?

5   What name is given to the home of an otter?

6   How many breeds of snake can be found in the UK: four, six or twenty-two?

7   The order squamata has two sub-orders, sauria and serpentes – these two, in common parlance, are what? (2 pts)

8   What are the two main types of cartilaginous fish? (2 pts)

9   The next taxonomic division after the all-inclusive kingdom, animalia, is a phlyum; which phylum boasts the greatest number of species?

10 Char, smelt and grayling are all fish in which family?

Part 2

Conservationists categorize all animal species according to their viability; identify which category each of these creatures falls into from this list: least concern; vulnerable; near threatened; endangered; critically endangered; extinct

11 Giant panda

12 Black rhinoceros

13 Cheetah

14 Bald eagle

15 Quagga

16 Dingo

17 Western gorilla

18 Snow leopard

19 Polar bear

20 Walrus

Total Points: 23. Targets: Novice 9 Pro 17. Your Score:

Quiz 140. British Politics

Mostly from recent history

Part 1

1   Which Prime Minister announced his shock resignation on 15 March 1976?

2   Which two Scottish Liberal MPs were the House of Commons's youngest members when they joined in 1965 and 1983, aged twenty-six and twenty-three respectively? (2 pts)

3   In 1969, MPs voted for which major change to judicial law in the UK?

4   What short-lived initiative was launched by Prime Minister John Major in July 1991?

5   30 January 1965 saw the State Funeral of which famous leader?

6   Who lives at No. 11 Downing Street?

7   Which five men served as Chancellor of the Exchequer in the eighteen years of Conservative government from 1979 to 1997? (5 pts)

8   What was 0345 504030, seen on roads across Britain as part of a bizarre piece of legislation in 1992?

9   Who was the First Minister of Scotland when the Scottish Assembly first convened in 1999?

10   Who is the ceremonial door-keeper of the House of Lords who also serves as the monarch's attendant should he or she choose to visit?

Part 2

Mix and Match: match the high profile politician to the constituency they represent(ed)

1. Tony Blair; 2. Samuel Pepys; 3. Clement Freud; 4. David Cameron; 5. Margaret Thatcher; 6. David Owen; 7. Arthur Wellesley, 1st Duke of Wellington; 8. Jack Straw; 9. Charles Kennedy; 10. Alex Salmond

a. Ross, Skye and Lochaber and its antecedents; b. Plymouth Sutton/Plymouth Devonport; c. Witney, Oxfordshire; d. Blackburn, Lancashire; e. Would never countenance anything so common as being elected; f. Castle Rising and Harwich; g. Sedgefield, Co. Durham; h. Banff and Buchan; i. Finchley, North London; j. Isle of Ely, later N.E. Cambridgeshire

Your Workings:

Total Points: 25. Targets: Novice 10 Pro 19. Your Score:

Quiz 141. Books

My booky book quiz – scratch that, I'm sounding like Russell Brand . . . Here are twenty questions on well-known books

Part 1

1   Thomas Hardy's *Far from the Madding Crowd* takes its title from which famous poem, published 1751?

2   Which 1982 sci-fi film was based on a Philip K. Dick short story called 'Do Androids Dream of Electric Sheep'?

3   By what name is James Fenimore Cooper's hero Natty Bumppo generally addressed in the five books that feature him? Which is the best known (and second chronologically) of the five? (2 pts)

4   With which longstanding reference book is the name Brewers associated?

5   Which novel of Scottish derring-do concerns the adventures of Alan Breck and David Balfour?

6   Whose work details the adventures of Jack Aubrey and Stephen Maturin in the Royal Navy during the Napoleonic wars?

7   In which classic work for children can you find the 'great green greasy Limpopo river'?

8   Which German book was eventually published, having unsurprisingly opted against the original title, 'My Four and a Half Years of Struggle Against Lies, Stupidity and Cowardice'?

9   Who is the hero of the series of historical novels by George MacDonald Fraser, and from which earlier classic did he 'pinch' the character? (2 pts)

10   A lie told by Briony Tallis is at the heart of which prize-winning modern novel?

Part 2

11 What city is referred to in the title of Armistead Maupin's *Tales of the City* series?

12 What did Walter Scott call his house after he rebuilt the original farmhouse he bought?

13 *Colonel Sun*, the first James Bond novel written after Ian Fleming's death, was penned by Robert Markham, an acronym for which well-known author? (a) John le Carré (b) Kingsley Amis (c) Len Deighton

14 What was the name of the pig who assumes leadership of the animals in George Orwell's *Animal Farm*? And who was the ill-fated horse who represented the workers in the allegorical tale? (2 pts)

15 Margaret Atwood finally won the Booker Prize in 2000 for *Blind Assassin*; which of her three previous novels had made the shortlist but not won? (3 pts)

16 What was the first movie based on a novel by Stephen King?

17 What is the famous old bookstore found at 113–119 Charing Cross Road?

18 Johnston McCulley published a book about a hero called Don Diego Vega in 1919; by what name is that hero better known?

19 Anne Desclos released her bestselling book, an erotic novel, in 1954 under the pseudonym Pauline Reage; what was the book?

20 Who wrote *Underworld* (1997), widely regarded as one the great contemporary American novels?

Total Points: 25. Targets: Novice 10 Pro 19. Your Score:

Quiz 142. Sport

Different ones, all mixed up

Part 1

1   Which New Zealand cricketer was the first to pass 400 wickets in a test match career?

2   Who was the TeamSky rider who played second fiddle to Bradley Wiggins in the 2012 Tour de France, finishing second behind Wiggins and joining him on the podium?

3   Who broke the St Andrews course record with a first round sixty-three in the 2010 Open Championship?

4   In which sport was Fred Archer the premier practitioner of the Victorian era?

5   Argentinian Adolfo Cambiaso reached the pinnacle of which sport?

6   Who, in 2012, was Britain's highest paid sports star (salary only, not earnings)? And who pays his extravagant salary? (2 pts)

7   Who threw away a good crack at the 1968 Masters title when he signed for a four at the seventeenth hole after taking a three, leaving Bob Goalby as sole winner instead of forcing a play-off?

8   Which ice hockey legend is known simply as the Great One?

9   What indignity was heaped on South Africa's Caster Semenya after winning the women's 800 metres at the 2009 World Athletics Championships?

10 Which former South African rugby union star scored 392 tries in 408 games for rugby league club St Helens?

Part 2

11   Who was the driver at the centre of the 'deliberate crash' controversy which engulfed the Renault F1 team in 2009?

12   Which club did Martin Offiah join when he switched codes from rugby union to rugby league?

13   At which extreme athletic discipline was Britain's Chrissie Wellington an undisputed world no. 1 prior to her retirement in December 2012? (a) the Tour of Europe, a forty-four-day bike marathon (b) the Sahara Marathon (c) Ironman Triathlon (a 2.4 mile swim, a 112 mile cycle and a marathon around the volcanic hills of Hawaii)

14   How did Gunter Parche influence women's tennis in the 1990s?

15   Which former Formula 1 World Champion entered the 2010 World Rally Championship in a Red Bull Citroën?

16   What is the name of the famous polo club at Midhurst in Sussex?

17   Cricket in Sussex; rugby in Stockport; basketball in Sheffield. What's the connection?

18   Janette Brittin is (a) the leading scorer for England's women's hockey team (b) the leading run scorer for England women's cricket team (c) England's multiple world ladies' darts championship winner?

19   Which great American driver remains the only man to have won the Formula 1 driver's championship, the Indy 500 and the Daytona 500?

20   Which famous Welsh rugby player was also once a Wimbledon junior tennis champion?

Total Points: 21. Targets: Novice 8 Pro 16. Your Score:

Quiz 143. Poetry

Questions for you, answer if you know it / most of them are probably a poem or a poet

Part 1

1   *Lyrical Ballads* (1798) is credited with starting the Romantic movement amongst English poets; which two literary giants collaborated on the work? (2 pts)

2   Which famous European poet had the last name Aligheri?

3   What did the hard-up poet John Milton sell for £10 on 27 April 1667?

4   Who became England's first Poet Laureate in 1668?

5   Who turned down the job of Poet Laureate in 1984? Who accepted it? Who succeeded him in 1999? What was different about this accession? Who became the post's first female incumbent in 2009? (5 pts)

6   Which nineteenth-century American poet self-published *Leaves of Grass* in 1855, a major collection which was accused at the time of being obscene but now ranks as one of the great works of American literature?

7   Which very private American writer, born 1830, published very little during her lifetime, (the first complete edition of her work wasn't published until 1955), but was later heralded as a major nineteenth-century poet?

8   Oscar Wilde, James Joyce, W. B. Yeats and Samuel Beckett; all great Irish literary figures, all born in Dublin, all died abroad. Which one was not buried in France?

9   Which popular modern poet has written translations or versions of Homer's *Odyssey*, *Sir Gawain and the Green Knight* and *The Death of King Arthur*?

10 *The Hawk in the Rain*, *Gaudete* and *Birthday Letters* are collections by which major modern poet who died in 1998?

Part 2

We give you the opening lines (with one exception) and the date of ten poems, you (hopefully) give us the poet and the name of the poem (2 pts per question)

11   How do I love thee? Let me count the ways. / I love thee to the depth and breadth and height / My soul can reach (1850)

12   She walks in beauty, like the night / Of cloudless climes and starry skies (1814)

13   At once a voice arose / Among the bleak twigs overhead / In a full-hearted evensong / Of joy illimited (1900)

14   Season of mists and mellow fruitfulness / Close bosom-friend of the maturing sun (1819)

15   . . . but at my back I always hear, / Times winged chariot drawing near / And yonder all before us lie / Deserts of vast infinity (1650s)

16   Bent double, like old beggars under sacks, / Knock-kneed, coughing like hags, we cursed through sludge (1917)

17   Once upon a midnight dreary, while I pondered weak and weary, / Over many a quaint and curious volume of forgotten lore (1845)

18   Remember me when I am gone away, / Gone far away into the silent land (1862)

19   Half a league, half a league / Half a league onward / All in the valley of death / Rode the six hundred (1854)

20   I wandered lonely as a cloud / That floats on high o'er vale and hills (1802)

Total Points: 35. Targets: Novice 14 Pro 26. Your Score:

Quiz 144. General Knowledge

Part 1

1   Which more recent pop star holds the copyright to all of Buddy Holly's songs?

2   Which British designer was behind Apple's iMac, iPhone and iPod?

3   Golda Meir became which country's first female Prime Minister on 6 March 1969?

4   Which two books, made into celebrated films, make up Marcel Pagnols' *L'Eau des Collines*? (2 pts)

5   Which two Norwegian cities have played host to the Winter Olympics? (2 pts)

6   What did Richard Carlson advise us to do with the 'Small Stuff' in 1997?

7   In which movie field have both Donald Trumbull and his son Douglas both excelled?

8   Which scientist was the first woman to win a Nobel Prize of any sort? And what other unique record does she hold in the history of the prizes? (2 pts)

9   Under what name did Florence Nightingale Graham build a cosmetics empire in the first half of the twentieth century? (a) Max(ine) Factor (b) Elizabeth Arden (c) Patrice Lancôme

10 Winstrol and nadrolone are types of which kind of performance enhancing drugs?

Part 2

11 Who released a lamentable song called 'Ole Ola' during the build up to Scotland's infamous (and embarrassing) 1978 World Cup campaign?

12 Which 1972 British Museum exhibition remains the most-attended in British history?

13 What connects Audrey Tatou and Carl Barat of the Libertines?

14 In which country did the Latin dance cha-cha-cha originate?

15 Where did EMI buy a nine-bedroom house to convert into a London studio?

16 Which US TV series (and later film and game franchise) was developed from a Japanese series called *Super Sentai*?

17 Which movie director earned the enmity of men across the globe when he married Helen Mirren?

18 In the 1970s, who was sacked as host of BBC *Gardeners' World* after appearing in an advert on ITV?

19 Edith Bowman came to prominence in what occupation?

20 A rampaging gunman killed fourteen people in which Berkshire market town in 1987?

Total Points: 23. Targets: Novice 12 Pro 17. Your Score: ☐

Answers Quizzes 137–144

Quiz 137. General Knowledge

1. Copper; 2. Jamaica; 3. South Korean; 4. He was shot and killed as a suspected terrorist by police because he looked foreign and was wearing a rucksack; 5. Brian Boitano; 6. Julien Temple; 7. *The Hangover*; 8. Trollope (he worked as a surveyor for the Post Office and wrote novels in his spare time); 9. Axl Rose is the singer in Guns N' Roses and his real name is William Bailey; 10. First one-day international; 11. *Carousel*; 12. 'La Marseillaise', the French national anthem; 13. She played Elle Woods in the stage musical version of *Legally Blonde*; 14. No qualifications; 15. Ian Smith; 16. Verity Lambert; 17. Anthony Clare; 18. Gareth Hunt; 19. Anita Roddick; 20. 2006

Quiz 138. Rock and Pop

1. Banana; 2. Sister Sledge; 3. Pete Seeger; 4. Jemini; 5. Abbey Road; 6. Pedal steel guitar; 7. Joe Strummer in pre-Clash days; 8. Cocteau Twins; 9. Jim Steinman; 10. Senegal; 11. Motorhead; 12. Spandau Ballet; 13. NWA; 14. Soul II Soul; 15. AC/DC; 16. Motley Crüe; 17. Depeche Mode; 18. Talking Heads; 19. Traveling Wilburys; 20. Guns N' Roses

Quiz 139. Wildlife

1. Genus and species (the taxonomic system, developed by Linnaeus in the eighteenth century, names the genus, followed by the species; a genus may contain a number of species but the combination is unique); 2. Jenny; 3. Coelacanth; 4. Eighteen (four on each front foot, five on each back foot); 5. Holt; 6. Four (the grass snake, the adder and the smooth snake are native, while the biggest, the Aesculapian snake, has been imported and naturalized); 7. Lizards and snakes; 8. Sharks and rays (including skates); 9. Arthropoda (includes crustaceans, spiders, insects and numerous others – insects is incorrect); 10. Salmon; 11. Endangered; 12. Critically endangered; 13. Vulnerable; 14. Least concern; 15. Extinct; 16. Vulnerable; 17. Critically endangered; 18. Endangered; 19. Vulnerable; 20. Near threatened

Quiz 140. British Politics

1. Harold Wilson; 2. David Steel and Charles Kennedy; 3. Abolition of capital punishment; 4. Citizens Charter; 5. Winston Churchill; 6. Chancellor of the Exchequer; 7. Geoffrey Howe, Nigel Lawson, John Major (all under Margaret Thatcher); Norman Lamont, Kenneth Clarke (under Major); 8. The Cones Hotline (it was put there so motorists could call and complain about roadworks that serve no apparent purpose; a nice idea but entirely impractical); 9. Donald Dewar of the Scottish Labour Party (he sadly died in October the following year after less than eighteen months in office); 10. The Gentleman Usher of the Black Rod (Black Rod is fine); Mix and Match 1, g; 2, f; 3, j; 4, c; 5, i; 6, b; 7, e; 8, d; 9, a; 10, h

Quiz 141. Books

1. Thomas Gray's *Elegy Written in a Country Churchyard*; 2. *Blade Runner*; 3. Hawkeye; *The Last of the Mohicans*; 4. *Brewers Dictionary of Phrase and Fable*; 5. *Kidnapped* (Robert Louis Stevenson); 6. Patrick O'Brian; 7. *Just So Stories* (Rudyard Kipling); 8. Adolf Hitler's *Mein Kampf*; 9. Flashman; *Tom Brown's Schooldays*; 10. *Atonement* (Ian McEwan); 11. San Francisco; 12. Abbotsford; 13. (b) Kingsley Amis; 14. Napoleon; Boxer; 15. *The Handmaid's Tale*, *Cat's Eye* and *Alias Grace*; 16. *Carrie* (1976); 17. W. and G. Foyle Ltd, usually referred to as just Foyle's; 18. Zorro (Don Diego is the effete Spanish aristocrat, Zorro his masked alter ego); 19. *The Story of O*; 20. Don DeLillo

Quiz 142. Sport

1. Richard Hadlee; 2. Chris Froome; 3. Rory McIlroy (two players had scored sixty-two on the Old Course but the record books were reset when the course was lengthened significantly to counter modern equipment); 4. Horse racing (he was the leading jockey both on the flat and over jumps); 5. Polo; 6. Luol Deng, who plays in the NBA for the Chicago Bulls; 7. Roberto de Vicenzo; 'What a stupid I am,' was Roberto's take on the incident; 8. Wayne Gretzky; 9. She was asked to take a gender test; 10. Tommy Van Vollenhoven; 11. Nelson Piquet Jr; 12. Widnes; 13. (c) Ironman Triathlon (Wellington won the world championship in 2007 after only a year in competition, and had added the title in every year she has competed since); 14. He stabbed Monica Seles because she had usurped Steffi Graf as world no. 1 (Seles was never the same player while Parche walked free after a German court bungled his trial); 15. Kimi Raikkonen; 16. Cowdray Park; 17. Sharks (Sussex Sharks in one-day cricket, Sale Sharks play at Stockport's Edgeley Park ground, Sheffield Sharks are the city's basketball franchise); 18. (b) Janette was a cricketer who amassed 1,935 test runs at an average of just under fifty; 19. Mario Andretti; 20. J. P. R. Williams

Quiz 143. Poetry

1. William Wordsworth and Samuel Taylor Coleridge; 2. Dante; 3. The manuscript to *Paradise Lost*, his most famous work; 4. John Dryden; 5. Philip Larkin; Ted Hughes; Andrew Motion – it became a ten-year stipend rather than an until-death appointment; Carol Ann Duffy; 6. Walt Whitman; 7. Emily Dickinson; 8. Joyce is buried in Zurich, Switzerland, where he spent his last years; Wilde and Beckett are buried in Paris, Yeats in the south of France; 9. Simon Armitage; 10. Ted Hughes; 11. Sonnet 43 (accept Sonnet); Elizabeth Barrett Browning; 12. 'She Walks in Beauty'; George, Lord Byron; 13. 'The Darkling Thrush'; Thomas Hardy; 14. 'Ode to Autumn'; John Keats; 15. 'To His Coy Mistress'; Andrew Marvell; 16. 'Dulce et Decorum Est'; Wilfred Owen; 17. 'The Raven'; Edgar Allan Poe; 18. 'Remember'; Christina Rossetti; 19. 'The Charge of the Light Brigade'; Alfred, Lord Tennyson; 20. 'Daffodils'; William Wordsworth

Quiz 144. General Knowledge

1. Paul McCartney (through MPL Communications); 2. Jonathan Ive; 3. Israel; 4. *Jean de Florette* and *Manon des Sources*; 5. Oslo (1952) and Lillehammer (1994); 6. *Don't Sweat the Small Stuff*; 7. Special effects (Donald worked on *The Wizard of Oz* and *Star Wars* while Douglas worked on *Blade Runner, 2001: A Space Odyssey* and *Close Encounters*); 8. Marie Curie, in 1903, when she won the Nobel Prize for Physics; she later became the first (and thus far only) individual to win in two fields when she won the Chemistry prize in 1911; 9. Elizabeth Arden; 10. Anabolic steroids; 11. Rod Stewart; 12. Tutankhamen; 13. Dirty Pretty Things (Tatou starred in the 2002 film of that name and Barat used it as a band name after the break-up of the Libertines); 14. Cuba; 15. Abbey Road; 16. *Power Rangers* (bonus point for the title of the original series *Mighty Morphin Power Rangers*); 17. Taylor Hackford; 18. Percy Thrower; 19. Radio 1 DJ; 20. Hungerford

Quiz 145. General Knowledge

Includes one of your favourite Mix and Matches

Part 1

1 Which car manufacturer brought us the Boxster and the Cayman?

2 The jungles of Borneo are mostly within the borders of which country?

3 Who is the actress daughter of Tippi Hedren, star of Hitchcock's *The Birds*?

4 What was first aired on the BBC for the first time on 5 February 1924, and for the last time on the same date in 1990?

5 What name is given to the narrow strip of Mexico running south from Tijuana south of California

6 Which 2012 event became known as the Miracle of Medinah?

7 How many episodes of *The Muppets* were made: 120, 212 or 606?

8 Which two fugitives were shot and killed at a police road block in Louisiana on 22 May 1934?

9 Which famous painting was stolen from the Louvre in Paris on 20 August 1911?

10 Patrick O'Brien from County Cork is officially the tallest ever man in Britain and Ireland; was he seven foot eleven, eight foot one or eight foot five?

Part 2

Mix and Match: match the self-help book to its 'guru'

1. *How to Stop Worrying and Start Living*; 2. *The Power of Positive Thinking*; 3. *Awaken the Giant Within*; 4. *Emotional Intelligence*; 5. *The Road Less Travelled*; 6. *Think and Grow Rich*; 7. *Use Your Head*; 8. *The 7 Habits of Highly Effective People*; 9. *The Power of Now*; 10. *Feel the Fear and Do It Anyway*

a. Susan Jeffers; b. Anthony Robbins; c. Tony Buzan; d. Daniel Goleman; e. Eckhart Tolle; f. Stephen R. Covey; g. Dale Carnegie; h. Napoleon Hill; i. Dr Norman Vincent Peale; j. M. Scott Peck

Your Workings:

Total Points: 20. Targets: Novice 10 Pro 15. Your Score:

Quiz 146. Movie Directors

Part 1

We have listed four films – identify the director and state which film was the first to be released (2 pts per question)

1 *Notorious, The Birds, North By Northwest, Rebecca*
2 *Citizen Kane, The Magnificent Ambersons, The Lady from Shanghai, Touch of Evil*
3 *Ed Wood, Planet of the Apes, Edward Scissorhands, Mars Attacks!*
4 *Full Metal Jacket, Spartacus, The Shining, A Clockwork Orange*
5 *Nashville, The Player, M*A*S*H, Gosford Park*
6 *Witness, Gallipoli, Master and Commander, The Cars that Ate Paris*
7 *Fargo, Barton Fink, No Country for Old Men, O Brother, Where Art Thou?*
8 *The Terminator, Avatar, The Abyss, Titanic*
9 *Jaws, Close Encounters of the Third Kind, Saving Private Ryan, Schindler's List*
10 *Tess of the d'Urbervilles, Rosemary's Baby, Frantic, The Pianist*

Part 2

Read carefully: identify the director of three of the films in every group of four; identify the odd film out; now state who directed that film, bearing in mind it is one of the other ten directors who provide the initial answer to one of the other questions in this section (3 pts per question)

11 *The Wild Bunch, Bring Me the Head of Alfredo Garcia, Straw Dogs, My Darling Clementine*
12 *Bringing Up Baby, The Big Sleep, Bullets Over Broadway, The Dawn Patrol*
13 *The Private Life of Sherlock Holmes, Great Expectations, Bridge on the River Kwai, Dr Zhivago*
14 *Goodfellas, Scarface, The Age of Innocence, Shutter Island*
15 *Pale Rider, Pat Garrett and Billy the Kid, Mystic River, The Changeling*
16 *The Searchers, Lawrence of Arabia, The Quiet American, The Man Who Shot Liberty Valance*
17 *Out of Sight, The Doors, Erin Brokovich, Ocean's Eleven*
18 *Platoon, Wall Street, Heartbreak Ridge, Natural Born Killers*
19 *The Lost Weekend, Sunset Boulevard, The King of Comedy, Ace in the Hole*
20 *Manhattan, King of the Hill, Crimes and Misdemeanors, Sleeper*

Total Points: 50. Targets: Novice 20 Pro 38. Your Score:

Quiz 147. TV Sitcoms

Both old and new

Part 1

1 What is the name of the old-school, beleaguered Tory MP played by Roger Allam in the 2012 series of *The Thick of It*?

2 How are Russell Tovey and Sarah Solemani known together on TV?

3 Who played the middle-aged couple at the heart of the sitcom *As Time Goes By*? What is the name of their daughter, played by Moira Brooker? (3 pts)

4 Which hard-hitting comedy stars Joanna Scanlan, Jo Brand and Vicki Pepperdine? (They also wrote it.)

5 Which sitcom was set in a café in the French village of Nouvion?

6 What is the title of the sitcom starring Dylan Moran set in a secondhand bookshop? Who plays his hapless assistant, Manny? (2 pts)

7 Before owning Cheers bar, what was the profession of Sam Malone? (Be specific for 2 pts)

8 What are the character names of the three children in the hit comedy *Outnumbered*? Who plays the dreaded Aunt Angela? (4 pts)

9 Who were the four privates in the seven-man platoon that made up *Dad's Army*? (4 pts)

10 What was the name of the company that employed Reggie Perrin, and who was his boss? (2 pts)

Part 2

11 What was the follow-up to *Porridge*? Who is dating Fletcher's daughter Ingrid in the show? (2 pts)

12 In the space sitcom *Red Dwarf*, what is the deeply uncool alter ego of the immaculately dressed and hip ship's cat?

13 Who played Victor Meldrew's long-suffering wife, Margaret, in *One Foot in the Grave*? And which comedian wrote the show's theme? (2 pts)

14 What is the name of Del Boy's policeman nemesis (Jim Broadbent) in *Only Fools and Horses*?

15 What were the first names of Rigsby and Miss Jones in *Rising Damp*? (2 pts)

16 Who played Frank Spencer's exhausted wife Betty alongside Michael Crawford in the 1970s?

17 Wilfred Brambell and Harry H. Corbett carried which sitcom double-handed for twelve years?

18 After *Blackadder*, which sitcom (1995–6) was the next combination between writer Ben Elton and actor Rowan Atkinson?

19 Who are Polly Shearman and Major Gowen?

20 Who were the *Men Behaving Badly* and who created the show? (3 pts)

Total Points: 36. Targets: Novice 14 Pro 27. Your Score:

Quiz 148. Science

I hope you do better than I would have had I not looked up the answers . . .

Part 1

1 Carotene is an alternative name for which vitamin?

2 With which branch of science do we associate Murray Gell-Mann?

3 In 1912, the skull of which 'missing link' was presented to the public? (It was proved a fake some forty years later.)

4 Whose book, *Elements*, written *c.*300 BC, formed the basis for the study of geometry until the start of the twentieth century?

5 When people use the word alcohol, they usually mean which specific chemical compound with the formula C2H5OH?

6 What are the biological catalysts that convert substrates into products?

7 What is the expected value of a perfectly weighted dice roll?

8 Which of these does *not* describe the earth? (a) an oblate sphere (b) an ellipse (c) an oval

9 The SI unit of electricity, the volt, is named after (a) the 'variable oscillations of a length of tin', a test carried out by nineteenth-century scientists in Cambridge, (b) the Italian scientist who first demonstrated conclusively the electrical conductivity of metals or (c) the Dutch scientist who showed the transmission of lightning energy through metal rods?

10 What did Napoleonic troops discover in Egypt in 1799 that hugely increased understanding of Egyptian hieroglyphics?

Part 2

Give an explanation for what you see written down

11 C2H2

12 Ichthyosaur

13 Chandrayaan-1

14 C6H12O6

15 René Laennec

16 $4/3\varpi r^2$

17 Cartesian coordinate

18 Cis-1, 4-polyisoprene

19 Pathogen

20 Analgesic

Total Points: 20. Targets: Novice 6 Pro 15. Your Score:

Quiz 149. Kings and Queens

Twenty questions on monarchs – not necessarily of this country

Part 1

1   Who was the first Protestant to inherit the French throne, even if he did convert to Catholicism eventually?

2   Which English king had a favoured courtier called Piers Gaveston who infuriated the rest of the nobility? (a) Edward II (b) Richard II (c) George II

3   In 1301, Edward, heir to the throne (the future Edward II), became the first to hold which title, still in existence today?

4   Five of the early kings of which land were named Baldwin?

5   Which English king fathered more than twenty illegitimate children? (a) Henry I (b) Edward III (c) Henry VIII

6   What was the name of the ruling house of Italy from 1861 to 1946? (a) Savoy (b) Medici (c) Ragazza

7   Who was King of Scotland in 1040–57, succeeding Duncan I?

8   Which monarch died at one of her favourite residences, Osborne House on the Isle of Wight?

9   Which European ruling family provided Holy Roman emperors, Spanish monarchs and Austrian emperors, as well as kings of Bohemia, Aragon, Sicily, Germany and Castile, amongst other territories?

10   Who ascended the French throne in 1743, aged five, and ruled for seventy-two years? What is the nickname history has accorded him, a tribute to the prosperity of France in that period? (2 pts)

Part 2

11 Beaumaris, Harlech and Caernarfon are castles built by which English king as part of a plan to subdue the Welsh raiders in the late thirteenth century?

12 Which 1950s rocker was known affectionately as 'The King'?

13 Sarah Churchill, Duchess of Marlborough, for many years enjoyed a highly influential friendship with which English monarch?

14 What was the official residence of the Russian rulers from 1732 until their overthrow in 1917?

15 Who were the first and last monarchs of the house of Stuart? (2 pts)

16 Who was the Danish king who wrested control of England (except Wessex) from Edmund Ironside in 1016?

17 Richard II succeeded his grandfather Edward III to the throne as his father had predeceased Edward; by what name was his father known?

18 The current King of Spain, Juan Carlos, is a scion of which house, first ascending the throne in 1700 with Philip V?

19 King Zog I was ruler of which European country in 1928–39? Zog died in 1961; why was he unable to assume power in his country for the last twenty-two years of his life? (2 pts)

20 The house of Bernadotte have been the titular monarchs of which European country since 1818?

Total Points: 23. Targets: Novice 9 Pro 17. Your Score:

Quiz 150. Soundtracks

Twenty questions about soundtracks and movie songs

Part 1

1 How did defunct 1960s rock band the Troggs make a bundle of cash from the movie *Four Weddings and a Funeral*?

2 Music from which voguish (at the time) album was used with chilling effect in *The Exorcist*?

3 Who wrote the sharp jazz score to Jacques Demy's *Les Parapluies de Cherbourg* (*The Umbrellas of Cherbourg*) in 1964?

4 Bernard Herrmann provided movie scores; with which director's work is he most closely associated?

5 Which composer's music is used as a motif throughout Kubrick's *A Clockwork Orange*?

6 'Hell Hole', 'Big Bottom' and 'Stonehenge' all appear on the soundtrack to which 1984 movie?

7 Which composer provided the famous atmospheric scores for Sergio Leone's spaghetti western series?

8 Who wrote the taut musical scores for the John Carpenter movies *Assault on Precinct 13*, *Halloween* and *Escape from New York*?

9 Whose name appears on the soundtrack album to *True Grit* (1969) even though he only played and sang on two tracks?

10 What song does Doris Day sing in Hitchcock's *The Man Who Knew Too Much* (1956 version)?

Part 2

Three songs – all you need do is identify the movie soundtrack on which they appeared (the third is usually the 'gimme')

11 'Dancing in the Sheets' (Shalamar); 'The Girl Gets Around' (Sammy Hagar); 'Holding Out for a Hero' (Bonnie Tyler)

12 'Temptation' (New Order); 'Lust for Life' (Iggy Pop); 'Born Slippy' (Underworld)

13 'Girl You'll Be a Woman Soon' (Urge Overkill); 'Son of a Preacher Man' (Dusty Springfield); 'Jungle Boogie' (Kool and the Gang)

14 'Someday (I'm Coming Back)' (Lisa Stansfield); 'Even If My Heart Would Break' (Kenny G and Aaron Neville); 'I'm Every Woman' (Whitney Houston)

15 'Anyone Else But You' (Moldy Peaches); 'Superstar' (Sonic Youth); 'I'm Sticking with You' (Velvet Underground)

16 'Love Potion No. 9' (The Clovers); 'Get a Job' (Silhouettes); various other rock 'n' roll jukebox classics

17 'Joy to the World' (Three Dog Night); 'What's Going On' (Marvin Gaye); 'Ain't Too Proud To Beg' (Temptations)

18 'More Than a Woman' (Tavares); 'Disco Inferno' (Trammps); 'Night Fever' (Bee Gees)

19 'I'll Fly Away' (Gillian Welch and Alison Krauss); 'You Are My Sunshine' (Norman Blake); 'In the Jailhouse Now' (Soggy Bottom Boys)

20 'If You Leave' (OMD); 'Left of Center' (Suzanne Vega and Joe Jackson); 'Bring on the Dancing Horses' (Echo and the Bunnymen); but we've omitted the iconic lead song . . .

Total Points: 20. Targets: Novice 8 Pro 15. Your Score:

Quiz 151. Media

Some questions about the wicked world of media moguls

Part 1

1   As of 2009, where was the US ranked in the world's media freedom index: fourth, thirty-sixth or seventieth?

2   As of 2009, where was the UK ranked in the world's media freedom index: first, ninth or twenty-third?

3   Of the Twitter accounts with the most followers at the end of 2012, only one of the top six was *not* a pop star; was it (a) Sarah Palin (b) Mark Zuckerberg (c) Barack Obama?

4   Which newspaper was closed down in 2011 after the phone hacking scandal was exposed?

5   What is Alexander Lebedev's role in the British media?

6   Which free, hand-distributed publication, is the world's biggest circulation magazine?

7   What magazine, established in 1922, headed the US circulation lists until it was topped by *Better Homes and Gardens* in 2009?

8   What was the name of the state-owned international news agency of the Soviet Union?

9   Which daily British newspaper was first published by Lord Northcliffe in 1896? (a) *Daily Express* (b) *Guardian* (c) *Daily Mail*

10 Which ad agency's 'Labour Isn't Working' poster, showing a long queue at a dole office in 1978, was credited with being a major factor in the Conservative election victory in 1979?

Part 2

Mix and Match: match the celebrity to the brand for which they have famously advertised

1. Peter Kay; 2. Joan Collins; 3. David Beckham; 4. Gary Lineker; 5. Maureen Lipman; 6. Alan Whicker; 7. Holly Valance; 8. Daniel Craig as 007; 9. Ian Botham; 10. Henry Cooper

a. British Telecom; b. Cinzano; c. Omega watches; d. Brut; e. Fosters; f. Emporio Armani; g. Shredded Wheat; h. John Smith's Bitter; i. Barclaycard; j. Walker's Crisps

Your Workings:

Total Points: 20. Targets: Novice 8 Pro 15. Your Score:

Quiz 152. General Knowledge

Part 1

1　Where in China did the army massacre hundreds of unarmed civilians on 3 June 1989?

2　Which astronomer changed the face of astronomy in the fifteenth century by placing the sun at the centre of the universe, defying the prevailing Ptolemaic theories?

3　The castle of Kronborg in Helsingør on the Danish island of Zealand is the inspiration for which famous Danish castle?

4　What term was first used by Charles Burney in 1805 to encompass intimate compositions not intended for grand-scale performance in church or concert hall?

5　Which label manufactured hits for artists such as Diana Ross, Smokey Robinson, Martha Reeves and the Four Tops?

6　'He's blond, he's quick, his name's a porno flick.' About which popular over-seas player were the Arsenal fans singing?

7　What do Napoleon Bonaparte, Neil Armstrong, Barack Obama and Charlie Chaplin have in common?

8　What does the K stand for in J. K. Rowling?

9　Who was voted Mayor of Carmel, California, on 7 April 1986?

10　Which famous sailing vessel was blown up by French agents in Auckland Harbour in 1985?

Part 2

11   What and where are the Islas Malvinas? (2 pts)

12   The French Open tennis tournament is held at the Stade Roland Garros; for
      what was the man for whom the arena is named principally known? (a) he
      was a French revolutionary philosopher and pamphleteer (b) he was a
      pioneering aviator (c) he was the architect who redesigned the gardens at
      Versailles in the 1930s

13   In 2003 Ron Davies stood down from the Welsh Assembly after being
      accused of seeking clandestine gay sex; what did he claim he had been
      doing whilst 'out and about'? (a) badger watching (b) looking for a mobile
      phone he dropped whilst walking the dog (c) taking a walk whilst he fine-
      tuned a speech to the Assembly the next day?

14   Who was disengaged to Sienna Miller in 2005 after tangling with the
      nanny?

15   Who married Alex Curran, Emma Hadfield and Lisa Roughead on the same
      day, 16 June 2006? (3 pts)

16   How much did Paul McCartney's wedding ring for Linda Eastman cost: £12,
      £1,200 or £120,000?

17   Who was the star of the *Transformers* movies whose lurid private life made
      her a tabloid star?

18   Which hard-living Irish folk-rock singer attended the really rather posh
      Westminster School?

19   Which South American team did Pelé predict would win the 1994 World
      Cup? How far did they get? (2 pts)

20   By which year did Pelé predict, in 1980, that an African side would win the
      World Cup?

Total Points: 24. Targets: Novice 12 Pro 18. Your Score:

Answers Quizzes 145–152

Quiz 145. General Knowledge

1. Porsche; 2. Malaysia; 3. Melanie Griffith; 4. The pips from Greenwich; 5. Baja California; 6. The extraordinary last day comeback of the European Ryder Cup team at Medinah Golf Club; 7. Only 120 (the characters have lived on but the actual show ended in 1981 after a five-year run); 8. Bonnie (Parker) and Clyde (Barrow); 9. *Mona Lisa*; 10. He was 8 foot 1 (how different must his world have seemed); Mix and Match 1, g; 2, i; 3, b; 4, d; 5, j; 6, h; 7, c; 8, f; 9, e; 10, a

Quiz 146. Movie Directors

1. Alfred Hitchcock; *Rebecca* (1940); 2. Orson Welles; *Citizen Kane* (1941); 3. Tim Burton; *Edward Scissorhands* (1990); 4. Stanley Kubrick; *Spartacus* came out in 1962 (no, silly, not in that way . . .); 5. Robert Altman; *M*A*S*H* (1970); 6. Peter Weir; *The Cars that Ate Paris* (1974); 7. Coen brothers; *Barton Fink* (1991); 8. James Cameron; *The Terminator* (1984); 9. Steven Spielberg; *Jaws* (1975); 10. Roman Polanski; *Rosemary's Baby* (1968) was his first US hit; 11. Sam Peckinpah; the much earlier *My Darling Clementine* was directed by John Ford; 12. Howard Hawks; *Bullets Over Broadway* was Woody Allen; 13. David Lean; the Sherlock Holmes movie was by his contemporary, Billy Wilder; 14. Martin Scorsese; *Scarface* was Howard Hawks (yes it was, the original 1932 version – the later one was directed by Brian De Palma); 15. Clint Eastwood; *Pat Garrett and Billy the Kid* was Sam Peckinpah; 16. John Ford, who didn't direct *Lawrence of Arabia*, which was by David Lean; 17. Steven Soderbergh; *The Doors* was Oliver Stone; 18. Oliver Stone; Clint Eastwood directed *Heartbreak Ridge*; 19. Billy Wilder; *The King of Comedy* was Scorsese; 20. Woody Allen; *King of the Hill* was Steven Soderbergh

Quiz 147. TV Sitcoms

1. Peter Mannion; 2. *Him and Her* (Steve and Becky); 3. Judi Dench and Geoffrey Palmer; Judi (Judith); 4. *Getting On*; 5. *'Allo, 'Allo*; 6. *Black Books*; Bill Bailey; 7. Pitcher for the Boston Red Sox (just 1 pt for baseball player); 8. Jake, Ben and Karen; Samantha Bond; 9. Frazer (John Lawrie); Godfrey (Arnold Ridley); Pike (Ian Lavender); Walker (James Beck); 10. Sunshine Desserts; C.J.; 11. *Going Straight*; Godber (Richard Beckinsale); 12. Dwayne Dibley; 13. Annette Crosbie; Eric Idle; 14. DCI Roy Slater; 15. Rupert and Ruth; 16. Michele Dotrice; 17. *Steptoe and Son*; 18. *The Thin Blue Line*; 19. They are Polly and the Major in *Fawlty Towers* – their surnames are rarely used; 20. Martin Clunes and Neil Morrissey; Simon Nye

Quiz 148. Science

1. Vitamin A; 2. Quantum theory; 3. Piltdown Man; 4. Euclid; 5. Ethanol; 6. Enzymes; 7. 3.5 (if the dice were rolled a large number of times, the average of the rolls would most likely be

3.5); 8. The earth is not an oval, it is a flattened ellipse (oblate sphere); 9. Alessandro Volta, an Italian, proved that a stack of metal coins separated by moist card would provide and maintain a charge for a period of time; 10. Rosetta Stone; 11. Acetylene; 12. Underwater vertebrate that appeared around the same time as the dinosaurs; 13. First Indian lunar probe; 14. Glucose; 15. Nineteenth-century French physician who invented the stethoscope; 16. The volume of a sphere; 17. A point on a graph or chart, either 2D or 3D defined by its distance from perpendicular planes; 18. Latex, or natural rubber; 19. A biological agent or microorganism that causes disease or illness in the host body; 20. Painkiller

Quiz 149. Kings and Queens

1. Henri IV (Henri of Navarre); 2. Edward II; 3. Prince of Wales; 4. The Crusader Kingdom of Jerusalem; 5. Henry I (he used them cleverly to cement alliances); 6. (a) House of Savoy (a line intact from the eleventh century); 7. Macbeth; 8. Queen Victoria; 9. Habsburg; 10. Louis XIV; the Sun King; 11. Edward I; 12. Elvis Presley; 13. Queen Anne; 14. The Winter Palace in St Petersburg; 15. James I and Queen Anne; 16. Cnut (various spellings such as Knut, Knyt); 17. Edward; the Black Prince; 18. Bourbon; 19. Albania; the country was invaded by Italy in 1939 and became a communist state after the war; 20. Sweden

Quiz 150. Soundtracks

1. The Troggs song 'Love Is All Around', covered by Wet Wet Wet, was used as the film's signature tune and was at no. 1 on the UK singles chart for fifteen weeks; 2. *Tubular Bells* by Mike Oldfield; 3. Michel Legrand; 4. Alfred Hitchcock; 5. Beethoven; 6. *This Is Spinal Tap*; 7. Ennio Morricone; 8. Carpenter himself wrote the music, as he did for most of his films; 9. Glen Campbell; 10. 'Que Sera Sera'; 11. *Footloose*; 12. *Trainspotting*; 13. *Pulp Fiction*; 14. *The Bodyguard*; 15. *Juno*; 16. *American Graffiti*; 17. *The Big Chill*; 18. *Saturday Night Fever*; 19. *O Brother, Where Art Thou?*; 20. *Pretty In Pink*

Quiz 151. Media

1. Thirty-sixth; 2. Twenty-third; 3. Barack Obama; 4. *News of the World*; 5. He owns the *Independent*, *Independent on Sunday* and the London *Evening Standard*; 6. *Watchtower*; 7. *Reader's Digest*; 8. TASS (Telegraph Agency of the Soviet State); 9. *Daily Mail* (Northcliffe wielded enormous influence in the years around the first World War and he could justifiably claim to be the principal pioneer of the tabloid press); 10. Saatchi and Saatchi (they reprised the role for David Cameron in 2010); Mix and Match: 1, h; 2, b; 3, f; 4, j; 5, a; 6, i; 7, e; 8, c; 9, g; 10, d

Quiz 152. General Knowledge

1. Tiananmen Square, Beijing; 2. (Nicholas) Copernicus; 3. Elsinore in Shakespeare's *Hamlet*; 4. Chamber music; 5. Tamla Motown; 6. Emmanuel Petit; 7. All were or are

left-handed; 8. Nothing, it was invented at the behest of her agent; 9. Clint Eastwood; 10. Greenpeace's *Rainbow Warrior*; 11. Falkland Islands; they are in the South Atlantic; 12. He was a pioneering aviator, the first to fly solo across the Mediterranean (he was also the inventor of the forward-firing gun for aeroplanes); 13. (a) badger watching; 14. Jude Law; 15. Steven Gerrard, Gary Neville and Michael Carrick; 16. £12; 17. Megan Fox; 18. Shane McGowan; 19. Colombia; they were eliminated in the group stages; 20. 2000

Quiz 153. General Knowledge

Two lots of ten questions, the second with a twist

Part 1

1   What video game/phone app did David Cameron claim he enjoyed playing to help him relax?

2   Where would you find the zygomatic bones?

3   Who created the spy George Smiley?

4   French, Spanish and Italian all belong to which group of languages?

5   Who bought 3,500 trees and planted them in Carrifan Wildforest near Peebles, Scotland, to offset the carbon footprint of her bestselling album?

6   The 2011 Japanese anime movie *Arrietty* was based on which series of English children's books?

7   Who was the most famous son of the city of Qufu in Shangdong province in Eastern China?

8   Kenroku-en in Kanazawa, Koraku-en in Okayama and Kairaku-en in Mito are regarded as the three great examples of what in Japan? (a) pleasure gardens (b) Shogunate palaces (c) Buddhist temples

9   Who made the only watch to be worn on the moon?

10 Which famous song was composed by Arthur Sullivan of Gilbert and Sullivan fame? (a) 'God Save the Queen' (b) 'Onward, Christian Soldiers' (c) 'It's a Long Way to Tipperary'

Part 2

Ten questions with a connection

11   What was the proper given first name of the landscape garden designer Capability Brown?

12   Who, in 1812, was the only British Prime Minister to be assassinated?

13   Who played the lead role in the original stage production of Andrew Lloyd Webber and Tim Rice's 1978 musical *Evita*?

14   Which company operates the UK National Lottery?

15   What was Roxy Music's 1982 album, their eighth, notable for its drenched electronic sound and dreamy rhythms? It included the UK top ten single, 'More Than This'.

16   What was the name of the Rolls-Royce engine used in World War II airplanes like the Hawker Hurricane and the Spitfire?

17   In Hans Christian Andersen's story, what is the name of the boy Gerda rescues from the Snow Queen?

18   Which Royal Fleet Auxiliary landing and supply ship was sunk during the Falklands War by Argentine attack planes?

19   What is the highest peak of the hills which rise above the city of Edinburgh?

20   And, rather obviously, the connection?

Total Points: 20. Targets: Novice 10 Pro 15. Your Score:

Quiz 154. Comedy Movies

Movies that make us laugh, or not

Part 1

1   What two things does Bill Murray learn to do to win the heart of Andie MacDowell in *Groundhog Day* (1993)? (2 pts)

2   Which film capitalized on the controversy surrounding its release, adding 'so funny it was banned in Norway' as a strapline to the marketing campaign?

3   What is the name of the aristocratic family in *Kind Hearts and Coronets*? How many of the eight members of the family does Alec Guinness play? (2 pts)

4   Keanu Reeves got a big break as one of the slacker dudes in *Bill and Ted's Excellent Adventure*; but who played Bill to Keanu's Ted?

5   What is the name of the old lady who turns the tables on the gang of criminals in *The Ladykillers* (1955)? Who made a clumsy version of the film in 2004 with Tom Hanks in the lead? (2 pts)

6   Which comedy team of two wrote and directed the puppet comedy *Team America: World Police?* (2 pts)

7   Which movie features a musical act called Sweet Sue's Society Syncopators? What is the name of their singer and who plays her in the film? (3 pts)

8   In which film does Peter Graves (TV's Jim Phelps in *Mission Impossible*) ask a teenage boy if he's ever seen a grown man naked?

9   Which popular comedian took the lead in the very first *Carry On* movie, *Carry on Sergeant?* And Who [sic] played the sergeant of the title? (2 pts)

10 Who starred in and wrote the 2011 comedy hit *Bridesmaids*?

Part 2

Woody Allen, and his movies

11 Which Woody Allen movie represents his biggest box office hit?

12 *Manhattan Murder Mystery* (1993) saw Woody Allen reunited with which former muse and lover?

13 Which two actresses played 'her sisters' in Woody Allen's *Hannah and Her Sisters*? And who won an Academy Award as Hannah's husband, Elliot? (3 pts)

14 Which actress connects the three twenty-first-century Woody Allen films *Match Point, Scoop* and *Vicky Cristina Barcelona*?

15 In which 2011 Woody film did Owen Wilson play the lead in the style of Woody himself? Adrien Brody enjoyed a cameo as which iconic painter in the movie? (2 pts)

16 Allen has been nominated for twenty-three Academy Awards, fifteen as a writer; which film earned him his only acting nomination and his only Best Director award?

17 Who played ambitious playwright David Shayne in *Bullets Over Broadway* (1994)? Which British stalwart appeared as the leading man in the play-within-a-movie? (2 pts)

18 Who plays the artist Juan Antonio Gonzalo at the centre of the love triangle in *Vicky Cristina Barcelona*? Who shakes up the ménage still further as ex-wife Maria? (2 pts)

19 Which Woody Allen film has a character from a film come to life? And which real movie is playing in the film's closing scene? (2 pts)

20 Woody Allen is well-known for his love of jazz; what instrument does he play?

Total Points: 33. Targets: Novice 13 Pro 25. Your Score:

Quiz 155. Around Britain

How well do you know the British Isles?

Part 1

1   Rum, Eigg and Muck are some of the smaller islands in which group?
2   Chatsworth House, Ladybower Reservoir and the town of Bakewell all lie within which National Park, formed in 1951?
3   Which inlet of the North Sea has Edinburgh on its south bank and Kirkcaldy on the north bank?
4   Walsall; West Bromwich; Dudley; Solihull: which of these is *not* a borough within the administrative region of the West Midlands?
5   What were the two most common metals retrieved from the industrial mines in Cornwall and Devon? (2 pts)
6   What is the body of water, famous for sailing, between the south coast of Hampshire and the Isle of Wight?
7   The M8 connects which two major British cities? (2 pts)
8   The navigable wetland known as the Broads encompasses land in which two English counties? (2 pts)
9   Which northern city is actually a conglomeration of six separate towns, including Hanley, Burslem and Tunstall?
10 The port and airport of Stornoway are found on which Hebridean island? (a) Islay (b) Lewis (c) Barra

Part 2

11 Which northern city was the centre of England's steel industry – it is often referred to as 'steeltown'?
12 What are Hilton Park, Stafford, Keele and Sandbach?
13 The Tamar Bridge, opened in 1961, connects traffic between which two English counties? (2 pts)
14 England's busiest heritage railway operates in which area of outstanding beauty joining coastal Whitby to inland Pickering?
15 In which English county is the natural beauty spot called the Forest (or Trough) of Bowland to be found?
16 Which Oxfordshire town houses the impressive Blenheim Palace? The palace is the seat of which family? Which two architects were primarily responsible for its design and construction? And who laid out the land-scaped gardens? (5 pts)

Total Points: 24. Targets: Novice 10 Pro 18. Your Score: [   ]

Quiz 156. Rock and Pop

Part 1

1   Which producer was famous for the Wall of Sound production on many 1960s hits?

2   Richard Hawley received huge acclaim for his 2012 album *Standing at the Sky's Edge*; with which band did Hawley first come to prominence?

3   Chanteuse and songwriter Isobel Campbell was once part of which Scottish indie band?

4   Eddie Van Halen is remembered as the guitarist in the band Van Halen; but what was his brother Alex's contribution?

5   *All Hail the Queen* was a key rap record of the late 1980s; but who was the Queen in question?

6   Whose 2010 Circle tour was the year's biggest grossing tour by a rock or pop act?

7   Which festival first took place in Shepton Mallet in 1982?

8   Who was the guest female vocalist on Bobby Womack's 1984 classic soul album *The Poet II*? (a) Patti Smith (b) Patti LaBelle (c) Pat Benatar

9   Glenn Miller's 'Chattanooga Choo Choo' was the first record to be awarded what in 1941?

10 What was the dream-team of female country singers who teamed up for the 1987 release, *Trio*? (3 pts)

Part 2

11 Who is the only Spice Girl to have appeared on the BBC's music show, *Later . . . with Jools Holland*?

12 What was Michael Jackson's best-selling single in the UK?

13 Chris Blackwell is the founder of which record label, instrumental in the growth of interest in reggae music in the 1970s?

14 What was Massive Attack's 1991 debut, an album that set a standard for groovy, chilled music that the ensuing decade would struggle to match?

15 Which Oxford band released the successful power-pop debut *I Should Coco* when they were still teenagers in 1995

16 Who connects the American grunge acts Screaming Trees, Queens of the Stone Age and the Gutter Twins?

17 What was Amy Winehouse's rather candid debut album? Which year did it come out? (2 pts)

18 Which singer was dating Lance Armstrong from 2003–6?

19 Who sang backing vocals on Dire Straits' 'Money For Nothing' (and played the song with them at the Live Aid concert)?

20 Who were the two producers (they also played guitar and bass) behind the rhythmic disco sound of Chic and Sister Sledge in the late 1970s? (2 pts)

Total Points: 24. Targets: Novice 10 Pro 18. Your Score: [   ]

Quiz 157. Non-fiction Books

Part 1

1   Who wrote the 1974 bestseller *Dog Training My Way*?

2   What was the subject matter of the books which saw Paul Hollywood top the book charts in 2012 and 2013?

3   What was Ernest Gombrich's seminal 1950 work?

4   *My Family and Other Animals* was a famous memoir of whose upbringing on Corfu? Who riffed on the title and released an autobiography called *My Animals and Other Family* in 2012? (2 pts)

5   Who wrote the groundbreaking feminist work, *The Female Eunuch*, aged thirty-one, in 1970?

6   The 1995 bestseller, *Writing Home*, was the autobiography of which celebrated author?

7   Fitness guru David Marshall works and writes under which professional name?

8   Which non-fiction book by Edmund de Waal was a surprise bestseller in 2011?

9   Which entrepreneur entitled his autobiography *Losing My Virginity*?

10 What was the subject matter of Jack Reed's 1919 book, *Ten Days That Shook the World*, a sensation on release?

Part 2

11 What was the title of Dawn French's 2008 autobiography?

12 *In Patagonia* was the first book by which travel writer?

13 *The Journal of a Tour to the Hebrides* and *A Journey to the Western Islands of Scotland* are accounts by which two authors of their trip to Scotland? (2 pts)

14 What was the book of advice, slightly satirical and tongue-in-cheek, that Cynthia Heimel published for women in 1983?

15 Whose *Herbal*, first published in 1653, is still in print today?

16 Which book prize has been sponsored for a number of years by William Hill?

17 Which series of famous travel guides was launched in France in 1900?

18 Who wrote the exploration of consumerism in the 1990s, *No Logo*?

19 Chris Kyle's autobiography was one of the bestselling non-fiction books of 2012; what was his profession?

20 What was Malcolm Gladwell's bestselling 2005 book about instinct?

Total Points: 22. Targets: Novice 9 Pro 17. Your Score:

Quiz 158. Olympic Games

Part 1

1   At the opening ceremony for the Olympic Games, the teams parade in alphabetical order (in the language of the host nation), with which two exceptions?

2   What new feature of the Games in Mexico City in 1968 resulted in the withdrawal of many high-profile athletes?

3   Which three US cities have hosted the Summer Olympic Games? (3 pts)

4   Johnny Weissmuller, who would later play Tarzan in Hollywood movies, won six Olympic medals: five swimming golds and a bronze in which other discipline?

5   Who won light heavyweight gold in the Olympic boxing tournament in 1960? Why did he throw his medal in the Ohio River shortly afterwards? (2 pts)

6   Which Soviet gymnast was the darling of the arena in 1972? And who was a perfect ten (times seven) in 1976? (2 pts)

7   Which British Paralympian sprinter won the T34 100 metres and 200 metres for women at the 2012 Games?

8   A swimmer from Equatorial Guinea became a legend in the pool in Sydney in 2000 after a swim that took twice as long as the eventual gold medallist; who was he?

9   Which legendary female skater won the mixed pairs figure-skating gold medal in three consecutive Olympics from 1972 to 1980? Who was her most famous partner, who shared gold in 1976 and 1980? (2 pts)

10   Which Italian slalom expert won five Olympic medals, including three gold medals, in the slalom and giant slalom between 1988 and 1994?

Part 2

11   Which two great heavyweights won gold for the US at the 1964 and 1968 Olympic Games? (2 pts)

12   Simon Ammann of Switzerland is the only man to win which two (very similar) Winter Olympic events at two separate Games? What was unusual about the achievement? (2 pts)

13   Which GB athlete took his tally of Olympic gold medals in wheelchair racing to six at the 2012 Paralympics?

14   Which two British athletes won long jump gold medals at the 1964 Olympics? (2 pts)

15   Who is the only GB athlete to have won an Olympic medal in any of the three long-distance races for women: 5,000 metres, 10,000 metres and marathon?

16   GB's track and field team had a poor Olympics in 2004; who was the huge double gold medal-winning exception? And who picked up the only other individual medal in the women's heptathlon? (2 pts)

17   In 1980 sixty-two countries boycotted the Moscow Olympics in protest at what action by the Soviet government?

18   Who won the Olympic pentathlon and decathlon in 1912 only to be stripped of the medals for playing a season of semi-pro baseball?

19   Who was the Australian triple gold-medal swimmer banned by her own country's authorities for allegedly trying to steal an Olympic flag from outside the Imperial Palace in Tokyo in 1964?

20   In 1976, which GB swimmer broke an American monopoly in the men's swimming events?

Total Points: 29. Targets: Novice 12 Pro 22. Your Score:

Quiz 159. Natural Wonders

A section on the world's natural splendours

Part 1

1   The world's highest waterfall, Angel Falls, is found in which South American country?

2   Yemen and other desert countries are full of wadis; what is a wadi?

3   In which country and which mountain range is the 5,432 metre peak, Popocatépetl? (2 pts)

4   The tallest peak in North America is Mount McKinley; where can it be found?

5   What rises in the Rockies and runs into the Pacific Ocean at the Gulf of California? What is its most famous feature? (2 pts)

6   What is the small island (part of the Aeolian group) to the north of Sicily that houses one of the country's three active volcanoes? And what is the active volcano on the Sicilian mainland? (2 pts)

7   What was the supercontinent whose break-up formed the southern hemisphere as we know it now?

8   For what extraordinary feature is the Puerto Princesa National Park in the Philippines known?

9   What name is given to the light displays in the northern hemisphere caused by particle collision in the thermosphere?

10 Gullfoss and Dettifoss are spectacular waterfalls found in which European country?

Part 2

11 What is the height of Mount Everest, the world's highest mountain? (a) 4,990 metres (b) 8,848 metres (c) 10,115 metres

12 What are Santa María in Guatemala, Nyamuragira in the Democratic Republic of Congo and Lascar in Chile?

13 The Victoria Falls drop 108 metres and are part of the course of which river?

14 The Great Barrier Reef lies off the coast of which Australian state? And over how many thousands of square kilometres does it extend: 144, 210 or 344? (2 pts)

15 The harbour of which South American city is often cited as one of the Seven Natural Wonders of the World?

16 There are thirteen National Parks in England and Wales; where are the three Welsh ones? And what are the two Scottish Parks in addition to these thirteen? (5 pts)

Total Points: 24. Targets: Novice 10 Pro 18. Your Score: ⬜

Quiz 160. General Knowledge

Part 1

1   What name is given to a formal gathering of practising poets in Wales, now more commonly associated with a general arts festival?

2   What is the difference between skeleton and luge?

3   What was the name of the dog in the dog-food adverts featuring Clement Freud? What breed of dog were the various canine actors who portrayed this character? (2 pts)

4   What connects the England rugby team and Liberal Democrat minister Vince Cable?

5   When genetic fingerprinting was introduced in the mid-1980s, what proportion of death-row prisoners in the US were cleared of the crimes for which they were sentenced to death? (a) one in eight (b) one in twelve (c) one in twenty

6   What was the profession of Elizabeth Barrett, the wife of the Victorian poet Robert Browning?

7   What does M*A*S*H stand for in the title of the 1970 movie and subsequent hit TV series?

8   For 900 years the Great Copper Mountain in Falun provided over half of Europe's copper requirements; which nation reaped the economic benefits?

9   What name is given to the industrial area of Germany which includes the towns of Essen, Duisburg and Dortmund?

10 What was supposedly 300 cubits long, 50 cubits wide and 30 cubits high, and made from gopher wood?

Part 2

11 What is the English name for the Welsh song written by Evan and James James, 'Hen Wlad fy Nhadau'?

12 Ann Arbor is a neighbour and part of the same urban conglomerate as which major US industrial city? In which US state do both lie? (2 pts)

13 Boudin, gumbo and jambalaya are signature dishes of which cuisine? Which US state is the centre of this style of cooking? (2 pts)

14 Who, in 2009, was sentenced to 150 years in prison for running the biggest Ponzi scheme ever unveiled?

15 For what is one Robert Trent Jones best known? (a) inventing the Anti-Lock Braking System (b) designing prestigious championship golf courses (c) Commander-in-Chief of the US forces when they invaded Afghanistan

16 What are the given names of the five Spice Girls and what were their 'spicy' names? (10 pts)

Total Points: 28. Targets: Novice 14 Pro 21. Your Score:

Answers Quizzes 153–160

Quiz 153. General Knowledge

1. Angry Birds; 2. Cheeks; 3. John le Carré (in *Call for the Dead*); 4. Romantic; 5. K. T. Tunstall; 6. *The Borrowers* (Mary Norton); 7. Confucius; 8. (a) Gardens (they are the garden of six aspects, the garden of delayed pleasure and the shared garden); 9. Omega; 10. (b) 'Onward Christian Soldiers', words by the Reverend Sabine Baring-Gould (but you knew that, of course); 11. Lancelot; 12. Spencer Perceval (he was shot by John Bellingham, a disgruntled merchant); 13. Elaine Paige; 14. The Camelot Group; 15. *Avalon*; 16. Merlin; 17. Kay; 18. Sir Galahad; 19. Arthur's Seat; 20. All are names of people or places in the Arthurian myth cycle

Quiz 154. Comedy Movies

1. Make ice sculptures; speak French; 2. *Life of Brian*; 3. D'Ascoyne; eight; 4. Alex Winter; 5. Mrs Wilberforce; Coen brothers; 6. Trey Parker and Matt Stone; 7. *Some Like It Hot*, Sugar Kane, played by Marilyn Monroe; 8. *Airplane!*; 9. Bob Monkhouse; William Hart-nell, who would later become the first Doctor Who; 10. Kristen Wiig; 11. *Hannah and Her Sisters*; 12. Diane Keaton; 13. Barbara Hershey and Dianne Wiest; Michael Caine; 14. Scarlett Johansson appears in all three films; 15. *Midnight in Paris*; Salvador Dalí; 16. *Annie Hall*; 17. John Cusack; Jim Broadbent; 18. Javier Bardem; Penelope Cruz; 19. *The Purple Rose of Cairo*; *Top Hat*; 20. Clarinet

Quiz 155. Around Britain

1. Hebrides; 2. Peak District; 3. Firth of Forth; 4. West Bromwich; 5. Tin and copper; 6. The Solent; 7. Glasgow and Edinburgh; 8. Norfolk and Suffolk; 9. Stoke-on-Trent; 10. (b) Lewis; 11. Sheffield; 12. Motorway services on the M6 between Birmingham and Manchester; 13. Cornwall and Devon; 14. North Yorkshire Moors; 15. Lancashire; 16. Woodstock; the Churchill family, the Dukes of Marlborough; Nicholas Hawksmoor and Sir John Vanbrugh; Capability Brown

Quiz 156. Rock and Pop

1. Phil Spector; 2. Pulp; 3. Belle and Sebastian; 4. Drums; 5. Queen Latifah; 6. Bon Jovi; 7. WOMAD; 8. Patti LaBelle; 9. A gold disc; 10. Dolly Parton, Linda Ronstadt and Emmylou Harris; 11. Mel C; 12. 'Earth Song'; 13. Island Records; 14. *Blue Lines*; 15. Supergrass; 16. Mark Lanegan, who has played or sung with all of them, as well as carving out an idiosyn-cratic solo career – busy boy; 17. *Frank*, 2003; 18. Sheryl Crow (the era represents one of her weakest artistically, so presumably she wasn't sharing the stimulants); 19. Sting; 20. Bernard Edwards and Nile Rodgers

Quiz 157. Non-fiction Books

1. Barbara Woodhouse; 2. Baking; 3. *The Story of Art*; 4. Gerald Durrell; Clare Balding; 5. Germaine Greer; 6. Alan Bennett; 7. The Body Doctor; 8. *The Hare with the Amber Eyes*; 9. Richard Branson, founder and Chairman of Virgin; 10. The October Revolution in 1917, which he experienced at close quarters; 11. *Dear Fatty*; 12. Bruce Chatwin; 13. Dr Samuel Johnson and James Boswell; 14. *Sex Tips for Girls*; 15. Nicholas Culpeper; 16. Sports Book of the Year; 17. Michelin guides; 18. Naomi Klein; 19. He was a crack shot US Navy Seal – the book is *American Sniper*; 20. *Blink*

Quiz 158. Olympic Games

1. Greece, who always go first in honour of their contribution to the Olympic movement, and the host nation, who come out last so they don't steal attention from the others; 2. Systematic drug testing; 3. St Louis, Los Angeles (twice) and Atlanta; 4. Water polo; 5. Cassius Clay (accept Muhammad Ali reluctantly, he was still Clay at the time; he was refused service in a segregated restaurant in the US); 6. Olga Korbut; Nadia Comaneci; 7. Hannah 'Hurricane' Cockcroft; 8. Eric 'the Eel' (Mosambani); 9. (Irina) Rodnina; (Alexander) Zaitsev; 10. Alberto Tomba; 11. Joe Frazier (1964) and George Foreman (1968); 12. Normal hill and long hill ski jump (accept both ski jumps); there was an eight-year gap between the wins (he won in 2002 and 2010 and had a stinker in 2006); 13. Dave Weir; 14. Lyn Davies and Mary Rand; 15. Liz McColgan, silver in the 10,000 metres in 1988; 16. Kelly Holmes; Kelly Sotherton; 17. Invasion of Afghanistan (oh, the irony . . .); 18. Jim Thorpe (the IOC restored his medals in 1983, thirty years after his death); 19. Dawn Fraser; 20. David Wilkie in the 200 metres breaststroke

Quiz 159. Natural Wonders

1. Venezuela; 2. A dried-out river bed; 3. Mexico, Sierra Madre; 4. In Alaska, US; 5. Colorado River, the Grand Canyon; 6. Stromboli; Mount Etna; 7. Gondwana; 8. An underground river; 9. An aurora, the most spectacular of which is the aurora borealis; 10. Iceland; 11. (b) 8,848 metres; 12. Active volcanoes; 13. Zambezi; 14. Queensland; it covers approximately 344,000 square kilometres; 15. Rio de Janeiro; 16. Brecon Beacons, Pembrokeshire Coast and Snowdonia; Loch Lomond and the Trossachs and Cairngorms

Quiz 160. General Knowledge

1. Eisteddfod; 2. Skeleton is face down, head first, luge is face up, feet first (both are, of course, completely bonkers); 3. Henry; bloodhound – the breed was chosen to mimic Freud's own rather lugubrious expression; 4. Twickenham (it is the home ground of the England rugby team and Cable is MP for the constituency); 5. (a) one in eight (12.5 per cent); 6. She was also a poet; 7. Mobile Army Surgical Hospital; 8. Sweden; 9. The Ruhr; 10. Noah's Ark; 11. 'Land of My Fathers'; 12. Detroit; Michigan; 13. Cajun; Louisiana (it

was developed by French-speaking Canadian immigrants displaced in the colonial wars); 14. Bernie Madoff (a Ponzi is a pyramid scheme where the investors at the top cream off profit direct from new investments without actually reinvesting any of the capital to make it work); 15. (a) he is a golf course designer; 16. Victoria Adams (accept Beckham reluctantly; Posh Spice); Melanie Brown (Scary Spice); Emma Bunton (Baby Spice); Melanie Chisholm (Sporty Spice); Geri Halliwell (Ginger Spice)

Quiz 161. General Knowledge

Delving deeply into the dangerous world of Dave (and David, Davies, Davidson, etc.)

Part 1

1   Who became England's oldest international football debutant for fifty years when he came on as a substitute against Montenegro in October 2010?

2   Which former TV sports presenter was ridiculed after predicting the end of the world during an interview on Terry Wogan's show in 1991?

3   As what did the TV comedy channel Dave start life in 1998 before undergoing various rebranding exercises, becoming Dave in 2007?

4   Originally a federal retreat called Hi-Catoctin, and later known as Camp David, what name did President Roosevelt give the country retreat in Maryland when he refurbished it in 1942? (a) Xanadu (b) Lady Eleanor (c) Shangri-La

5   Who was the leader, self-styled the Lamb of God, of the Branch Davidian cult? Where was their base? (2 pts)

6   Who has played the title role in the BBC mystery series *Jonathan Creek* since the first episode in 1997?

7   Who was the first professional snooker player to earn £1 million from the game?

8   In July 2006 a court ruled that Jim Davidson (a) serve six months in jail for public order offences (b) be declared bankrupt after failing to keep up mortgage and maintenance payments (c) be given a suspended sentence for inciting racial disharmony?

9   Who connects *Great Expectations* (1946), *The Bridge on the River Kwai* (1957) and *Doctor Zhivago* (1965)?

10   What was the name of the musical sitcom that launched the career of David Cassidy?

Part 2

11 Whose career benefited from a partnership formed at Cambridge University with Robert Webb?

12 Who controversially signed for rugby league club Widnes in 1989 after winning thirty-seven caps as fly-half for Wales at rugby union?

13 Who signed as head coach and player for Barnet in League Two in 2012, taking sole charge of the team in December that year?

14 Which athlete, the poster girl of British swimming, won a silver medal at the 1980 Olympics before embarking on a successful career as a presenter and poolside interviewer with the BBC?

15 Who was the only African American member of the famous 'Rat Pack' group of entertainers in the 1950s and 1960s?

16 Brothers Ray and Dave Davies were the centre of which 1960s (and beyond) rock group?

17 In which century was St David, the patron saint of Wales, active: the third, sixth or tenth?

18 What is the name of the FBI special agent played by David Boreanaz in the popular TV crime drama *Bones*?

19 Who was Mulder to Gillian Anderson's Scully?

20 Who had a UK and US no. 1 hit single in 1976 with 'Don't Give Up On Us'?

Total Points: 21. Targets: Novice 11 Pro 16. Your Score:

Quiz 162. Costume Drama

Some straight questions and a Mix and Match section

Part 1

1   Which Irish freedom fighter was the subject of a 1996 biopic directed by Neil Jordan and starring Liam Neeson?

2   What was the 1970s TV drama (eight series in all) about the owners of a shipping company and their extended family?

3   The 2006 film *Amazing Grace*, starring Ioan Gruffudd, was a biopic of which historical figure and his campaign to end the slave trade?

4   Who won an Academy Award for his work as Mozart's nemesis Salieri in the 1984 film *Amadeus*? How many Academy Awards did the film win? One, four or eight? (2 pts)

5   Who played John Brown, the Scottish servant whose relationship with a bereaved Queen Victoria was explored in the 1997 film, *Mrs Brown*?

6   Who played the title role in the 1964 biopic of Archbishop Thomas à Becket? Who was King of England at the time, and who played him in the film? The actor who played the King had already made which memorable screen appearance? On which French writer's play was the film based? (5 pts)

7   Orson Welles in 1944, George C. Scott in 1970, William Hurt in 1996 and Michael Fassbender in 2011 all played which mysterious literary character?

8   *Farewell, My Queen* (*Les Adieux à la Reine*) was a 2013 box office hit in France about the last days of which French queen? Who played the same queen in a 2006 movie about her life by Sofia Coppola? (2 pts)

9   What was the title of Michel Hazanavicius's 2012 Academy Award winning homage to the age of silent cinema?

10 In 1973–4 Richard Lester directed an action comedy version of *The Three Musketeers*; who starred as the title characters and who put in twinkle-in-the-eye turns as baddies Cardinal Richelieu and Milady de Winter? (5 pts)

Part 2

Mix and Match: match the actor to the character to the costume drama (2 pts per question)

1. Keira Knightley; 2. Penelope Wilton; 3. Helena Bonham Carter; 4. Hannah Gordon; 5. Siân Phillips; 6. Amanda Redman; 7. Diana Rigg; 8. Anna Maxwell-Martin; 9. Kristin Scott-Thomas; 10. Jennifer Ehle

a. Livia Drusilla; b. Mrs Merdle; c. Lizzie Bennett; d. Lady Dedlock; e. Georgiana, Duchess of Devonshire; f. Elizabeth Boleyn (Anne's mum); g. Elizabeth Bowes-Lyon; h. Virginia, Viscountess Bellamy; i. Esther Summerson; j. Mrs Crawley

i. *The King's Speech* (2010); ii. *Bleak House* (1985); iii. *Bleak House* (2005); iv. *Downton Abbey* (2010–); v. *I, Claudius* (1976); vi. *Pride and Prejudice* (1995); vii. *Little Dorrit*; viii. *Upstairs Downstairs* (1971–5); ix. *The Other Boleyn Girl* (2008); x. *The Duchess* (2008)

Total Points: 40. Targets: Novice 16 Pro 30. Your Score:

Quiz 163. Pop Stars in the Movies

Simply identify which actor played the star in the named movie

Part 1

1   Tina Turner in *What's Love Got to Do With It?* (1993)
2   Ian Curtis in *Control* (2007)
3   Ian Dury in *Sex and Drugs and Rock and Roll* (2010)
4   Glenn Miller in *The Glenn Miller Story* (1953)
5   Joan Jett in *The Runaways* (2010)
6   Johnny Cash in *Walk the Line* (2005)
7   Jim Morrison in The Doors (1991)
8   Sid Vicious in *Sid and Nancy* (1986)
9   John Lennon in *Nowhere Boy* (2009)
10 Billie Holiday in *Lady Sings the Blues* (1972)
11 Elvis Presley in John Carpenter's Elvis (1979)
12 Ray Charles in *Ray* (2004)
13 Buddy Holly in *The Buddy Holly Story* (1978)
14 David Bowie in *Zoolander* (2001)
15 The six various fictional incarnations of Bob Dylan in *I'm Not There* (2007)
    (6 pts)

Total Points: 20. Targets: Novice 8 Pro 15. Your Score: [   ]

Quiz 164. Weather

A quiz about the weather – well, why not, it is meant to be the favourite topic of conversation amongst the British

1   In which decade did Vilhelm and Jacob Bjerknes (father and son) develop the idea of cyclonic fronts as the basis for meteorological forecasting?

2   What types of rays from the sun are absorbed by the earth's ozone layer, allowing life to develop and continue?

3   If there are cumulonimbus in the sky what weather should we expect?

4   What is the layer of earth's atmosphere that contains the ozone layer?

5   The meteorological sea area Fastnet lies (a) off the Hebridean coast of Scotland (b) to the east of England by the Humber estuary or (c) to the south of the Republic of Ireland?

6   In which year was *Tiros 1*, the first meteorological satellite launched: 1955, 1960 or 1967?

7   What is the difference between a cyclone, a hurricane and a typhoon?

8   In which century did Seleucus link tidal flow to the phase of the moon: tenth century BC, second century BC or sixth century AD?

9   When was daylight saving introduced in the UK? (a) 1775 (b) 1849 (c) 1916

10 In 1643 Evangelista Torricelli produced which aide to meteorological science? (a) weather vane (b) barometer (c) wind speed gauge

11 What speed (mph) does wind need to attain to be classed as gale force? (a) 33–7 (b) 39–46 (c) 64–72

12 In which decade did Benjamin Franklin establish that lightning conducted electricity: 1750s, 1790s or 1850s?

13 In which city is the UK Met Office based? (a) Exeter (b) Bath (c) Cardiff

14 What does a seismograph measure?

15 What name is given to a high speed wind flying at over 30,000 feet?

Total Points: 15. Targets: Novice 6 Pro 11. Your Score:

Quiz 165. History

Nothing sinister, just fifteen questions and a multi-parter

Part 1

1   King Ptolemy I, founder of the last dynasty of ancient Egypt, first ruled the country after being appointed by which conqueror?

2   Which country became the first to give women the vote in 1893?

3   Charles, the second Earl Grey, who lent his name to the tea of that name, was famous for a passionate affair with which society belle?

4   Who landed at Brixham Harbour in Devon in November 1688?

5   In which European city was the world's first university founded in the eleventh century?

6   Which trading company, founded 1602, sent the first Europeans to lay claim to the territory which is modern Indonesia?

7   What did the US Congress recommend be recited in schools in 1945?

8   Which three states, regarded as 'slave states' and southern in spirit, elected to remain within the original union during the US Civil War? (3 pts)

9   A civil war (1975–90) in which country pitted Christian Phalange militia against a Muslim alliance including the Druze and the PLO?

10 What was the name of the bodyguard of the Roman emperors?

Part 2

11 Who published the 'Zinoviev Letter' in 1924, and what was it? (2 pts)

12 The Frank family, written about in such detail in *Anne Frank's Diary*, lived in which occupied European city during World War II?

13 Which city was the first capital of the Russian Empire in the ninth century? (a) Novgorod (b) Omsk (c) St Petersburg

14 To what, in 1853, did Van Diemen's Land change its name? (a) Orange Free State (b) Tasmania (c) Borneo

15 Which were the two principal protagonists in the Peloponnesian War in Greece (431–404 BC)? Which historian left a detailed contemporary account of the war? (3 pts)

16 Who was the brother of Harold Godwinson who rebelled against Harold's rule in 1066? Who was the Norwegian king who allied with him? And where was their army defeated by Harold's forces? Where did William of Normandy's troops land, forcing Harold to march south before his forces were fully recovered? Where was William finally crowned after ending Saxon resistance? (5 pts)

Total Points: 25. Targets: Novice 10 Pro 19. Your Score:

Quiz 166. Premier League

Just six questions, but not just a single answer . . .

1   Which five Manchester United players have seven or more Premier League winner's medals? (Stats to the end of the 2011–12 season) (5 pts)

2   Apart from England, which five countries can boast more than five players who have won a Premier League winner's medal? (5 pts)

3   Which four players have scored five times in a single Premier League match? (4 pts)

4   Which four clubs have managed just a single season in the Premier League up to 2012–13? (4 pts)

5   Which two players have been top or joint-top scorer in the Premier League with two different clubs? What were the clubs involved? (Stats to the end of 2011–12 season) (6 pts)

6   Which six players were given an award for having made 500 Premier League appearances in the first twenty years of the competition? (Tip: all are British) (6 pts)

Total Points: 30. Targets: Novice 12 Pro 23. Your Score:

Quiz 167. Alter Egos

In the first part we give you a birth name and a clue, and we're looking for the pop star alter-ego; the second part is a Mix and Match

Part 1

1   Upwardly moving singer Yasmin Evans
2   Chill-out chick Florian Cloud Armstrong
3   Robyn Fenty preferred her middle name
4   Audrey Perry, country star with belief
5   Oscar nominee and big-voiced belter Dana Owens
6   Mathangi Arulpragasam initially
7   Christa Paffgen; ethereal, now deceased 1960s chanteuse
8   Stefani Germanotta, singer and fashionista
9   Unimpressed country singer Eileen Edwards
10 Multi-instrumentalist Natasha Khan

Part 2

Mix and Match: match the birthname to the alias of these rock and pop stars

1. Stuart Goddard; 2. Gordon Sumner; 3. Paul Hewson; 4. Brian Rankin; 5. Marvin Lee Aday; 6. Chaim Weitz; 7. Henry Deutschendorf Jr; 8. Declan McManus; 9. Vincent Furnier; 10. Terry Nelhams

a. Gene Simmons; b. Alice Cooper; c. Adam Faith; d. Sting; e. John Denver; f. Meat Loaf; g. Adam Ant; h. Bono; i. Hank Marvin; j. Elvis Costello

Your Workings:

Total Points: 20. Targets: Novice 10 Pro 16. Your Score:

Quiz 168. General Knowledge

Part 1

1   Which cartoon character first appeared in a children's section in a Belgian newspaper in 1929?

2   Who returned to Iran after a fourteen-year exile on 1 February 1979?

3   Which IRA member was voted MP for Fermanagh and South Tyrone on 9 April 1981?

4   Alec Issigonis was the designer of which iconic 1960s product, actually launched by its manufacturer in 1959?

5   Deborah Compagnoni is (a) an Italian model and former lover of Silvio Berlusconi (b) an Italian Green Party MP and mother of the children of footballer Roberto Baggio or (c) a gold medal Alpine skier married to the Chairman of Benetton?

6   What connects Eoghan Quigg, Steve Brookstein and Andy Abraham?

7   Who redeemed his 2012 failure at Royal Lytham with success at Augusta the following spring?

8   Knole House, the birthplace of Vita Sackville-West, is a country home on the edge of which Kent market town?

9   American entertainer Jack Benny's act relied in part on his ability to play which instrument, often deliberately badly, despite his proficiency?

10   What record was broken by nineteen-year-old Gertrude Ederle in 1926?

Part 2

11   Name the nine actors who play the Fellowship in the first of Peter Jackson's *The Lord of the Rings* films. Who played two roles in *The Two Towers*? (10 pts)

Total Points: 20. Targets: Novice 10 Pro 15. Your Score:

Answers Quizzes 161–168

Quiz 161. General Knowledge

1. Kevin Davies (Bolton Wanderers); 2. David Icke; 3. UK Gold Classics (accept UK Gold as the principle brand); 4. (c) Shangri-La, after the mythical mountain paradise; 5. David Koresh; Waco, Texas; 6. Alan Davies; 7. Steve Davis, six times world champion in the 1980s during the boom of snooker as a televised sport; 8. (b) Davidson, with four failed marriages behind him and an expensive house, found his declining income could not match his lifestyle; 9. David Lean; 10. *The Partridge Family*; 11. David Mitchell; 12. Jonathan Davies; 13. Edgar Davids; 14. Sharron Davies (Petra Schneider, who beat her in 1980, later admitted to being part of the East German doping system which defrauded sport in that era); 15. Sammy Davis Jr; 16. The Kinks; 17. Sixth century (he died a very old man in 589); 18. (Seeley) Booth; 19. David Duchovny (they are the lead characters in *The X-Files*); 20. David Soul

Quiz 162. Costume Drama

1. Michael Collins; 2. *The Onedin Line*; 3. William Wilberforce; 4. F. Murray Abraham; eight, including Best Picture and Best Director (Miloš Forman), Best Adapted Screenplay (Peter Shaffer from his own stage play) and four technical awards; 5. Billy Connolly; 6. Richard Burton; Henry II; Peter O'Toole; *Lawrence of Arabia*; Jean Anouilh; 7. Mr. Rochester in *Jane Eyre*; 8. *Marie-Antoinette*; Kirsten Dunst; 9. *The Artist*; 10. Oliver Reed, Richard Chamberlain and Frank Finlay; Charlton Heston and Faye Dunaway; Mix and Match 1, e, x; 2, j, iv; 3, g, i; 4, h, viii; 5, a, v; 6, b, vii; 7, d, ii; 8, i, iii; 9, f, ix; 10, c, vi

Quiz 163. Pop Stars in the Movies

1. Angela Bassett; 2. Sam Riley; 3. Andy Serkis; 4. James Stewart; 5. Kristen Stewart; 6. Joaquin Phoenix; 7. Val Kilmer; 8. Gary Oldman; 9. Aaron Taylor-Johnson; 10. Diana Ross; 11. Kurt Russell; 12. Jamie Foxx; 13. Gary Busey; 14. Bowie has a small cameo as himself; 15. Christian Bale, Cate Blanchett, Marcus Carl Franklin, Richard Gere, Heath Ledger and Ben Whishaw

Quiz 164. Weather

1. 1920s (the terms 'cold front' and 'warm front' were borrowed from military terminology from the recently ended World War I); 2. Ultra violet; 3. Thunderstorm; 4. Stratosphere; 5. (c) south of Ireland; 6. 1960; 7. None really (they are different names for the same type of tropical storm); 8. 2nd century BC (probably the 150s); 9. (c) 1916; 10. (b) Torricelli produced the first tube barometer; 11. 39–46 mph (anything above 73 mph is technically a hurricane); 12. 1750s (in 1751 Franklin conducted various dangerous experiments with conducting rods to prove his theories; he survived to continue working for almost forty

more years); 13. a) Exeter; 14. Earthquakes on the Richter scale, named after the inventor of that scale; 15. Jet stream

Quiz 165. History

1. Alexander the Great (Ptolemy was one of Alexander's principal trusted satraps or generals); 2. New Zealand; 3. Georgiana Cavendish, Duchess of Devonshire; 4. William of Orange and his army; 5. Bologna; 6. Dutch East India Company; 7. Pledge of Allegiance; 8. Missouri, Kentucky and West Virginia; 9. Lebanon; 10. Praetorian Guard (the term was also used for the household guard of other senior figures); 11. *Daily Mail* (it was a fake letter claiming that Ramsay MacDonald's Labour Party was in cahoots with Russian communists and seeking 'armed warfare'); 12. Amsterdam; 13. (a) Novgorod, or properly, Yeliky Novgorod; 14. (b) Tasmania, which became a self-governing colony two years later; 15. Athens and Sparta; Thucydides; 16. Tostig; Harold Hardrada; Stamford Bridge (no, not the Chelsea FC ground); Pevensey Bay; Westminster Abbey

Quiz 166. Premier League

1. Ryan Giggs (twelve), Paul Scholes (ten), Gary Neville (eight), Denis Irwin (seven) and Roy Keane (seven); 2. France (twenty-one); Netherlands (ten); Portugal (seven); Brazil (seven); Argentina (six); 3. Alan Shearer; Andrew Cole, Jermaine Defoe and Dimitar Berbatov; 4. Barnsley, Blackpool, Burnley, Swindon Town; 5. Alan Shearer (Blackburn and Newcastle); Jimmy Floyd Hasselbaink (Leeds and Chelsea); 6. Ryan Giggs, David James, Gary Speed, Frank Lampard, Emile Heskey, Sol Campbell

Quiz 167. Alter Egos

1. Yazz; 2. Dido; 3. Rihanna; 4. Faith Hill; 5. Queen Latifah; 6. MIA; 7. Nico; 8. Lady Gaga; 9. Shania Twain; 10. Bat for Lashes; Mix and Match 1, g; 2, d; 3, h; 4, i; 5, f; 6, a; 7, e; 8, j; 9, b; 10, c

Quiz 168. General Knowledge

1. Tintin; 2. Ayatollah Khomeini; 3. Bobby Sands; 4. British Motor Company's Mini; 5. (c) Compagnoni won gold in the Super G slalom in 1992 and the giant slalom in 1994 and 1998; she has three children with husband Alessandro Benetton; 6. They were all *X Factor* finalists; 7. Adam Scott (who won his first Major golf championship at the US Masters less than a year after blowing a healthy lead in the final stages of the 2012 Open); 8. Sevenoaks; 9. Violin; 10. Cross-channel swim (she was the first woman to complete the journey); 11. Sean Astin, Sean Bean, Orlando Bloom, Billy Boyd, Dominic Monaghan, Ian McKellen, Viggo Mortensen, John Rhys-Davies, Elijah Wood; Rhys-Davies also provided the voice of Treebeard

Quiz 169. General Knowledge

Who said what? Some quotes and their origins

1 'It's silly talking about how many years we will have to spend in the jungles of Vietnam when we could pave the whole country and put parking stripes on it and still be home by Christmas.' Which future President is getting it horribly wrong in 1965?

2 'Biologically and temperamentally . . . women were made to be concerned first and foremost with child care, husband care and home care.' Which childcare expert, now (thankfully) discredited?

3 'A woman's preaching is like a dog's walking on his hind legs. It is not done well; but you are surprised to find it done at all.' Which scholar and raconteur lived long enough ago that this comment seems less offensive than question 2?

4 'If your surname is Toblerone you should always take along an empty Toblerone chocolate box when attending interviews for office jobs. This would save your potential employer the expense of having to make a name plaque for your desk.' Sage advice from the pages of which magazine?

5 'She is the self-sufficient postmodern phenomenon. A masterpiece of controlled illusion.' Which writer's view of which performer? (2 pts)

6 'A lot of people say it's lack of vocabulary that makes you swear. Rubbish. I know thousands of words, but I still prefer "fuck".' Which sweary comedian?

7 'You get bunches of players like you do bananas, though that is a bad comparison.' A classic piece of nonsense, one of hundreds from which unwittingly hilarious pundit?

8 'Repartee, n. Prudent insult in retort. Practised by gentlemen with a constitutional aversion to violence, but a strong disposition to offend.' A typical example from which 1911 humorous work by whom? (2 pts)

9 Speaker A: 'I think you've forgotten who you're talking to.' Speaker B: 'An overweight, over-the-hill, nicotine-stained, borderline-alcoholic homophobe with a superiority complex and an unhealthy obsession with male bonding?' Speaker A: 'You make that sound like a bad thing.' A classic exchange from which two characters and from which TV show? (3 pts)

10 'A . . . is a person who writes a ten-thousand-word document and calls it a 'brief'.' Who is Franz Kafka castigating?

11 'If you hadn't run around so much, maybe you wouldn't have been so thirsty.' Mrs Merton to which star?

12 'That woman speaks eighteen languages, and can't say "No" in any of them.' Which 1920s female writer and wit?

13   '. . . is probably the most respectable form of lying.' What is, according to Patrick White in a *New York Times* interview?

14   'Christianity will go. It will vanish and shrink. I needn't argue about that. I'm right and I'll be proved right. We're more popular than Jesus now.' Who was talking about what phenomenon in 1966? (2 pts)

15   'Reading makes a full man, meditation a profound man, discourse a clear man.' Which American statesman and scientist?

Total Points: 20. Targets: Novice 8 Pro 15. Your Score:

Quiz 170. Chick Flicks

Flicks for chicks (and a guilty pleasure for the odd feller, I'm sure)

1   Who played Lloyd Dobler in Cameron Crowe's *Say Anything*, a 1989 teen romance?

2   Ben Affleck; Bradley Cooper; Jennifer Aniston; Ryan Gosling; Drew Barrymore; which of these was *not* in the 2009 rom-com *He's Just Not That into You*? The film was based on a self-help book, the title of which was taken from the snappy dialogue in which TV series? (2 pts)

3   *Pillow Talk*, *Lover Come Back* and *Send Me No Flowers* were a trio of hugely successful romantic comedies made between 1959 and 1964 and starring which onscreen couple? (2 pts)

4   In Scorsese's adaptation of *The Age of Innocence* (1993) Daniel Day-Lewis is torn between the woman he is due to marry and the passionate Countess he desires; who play the two women in the love triangle? (2 pts)

5   Who play the caddish Daniel Cleaver and the true love Mark Darcy in the film version of *Bridget Jones's Diary*? (2 pts)

6   Who plays *The Wedding Singer* in the film of that name (1998) and where is Drew Barrymore working when they first meet? (2 pts)

7   Who made her leading-lady debut (and won an Academy Award) as a flighty princess in William Wyler's *Roman Holiday* (1953)? What is the profession of the character played by co-star Gregory Peck? (2 pts)

8   Which 1957 romantic comedy reduces Meg Ryan to tears in which 1993 romantic comedy? Who are the male romantic leads in the two movies? (4 pts)

9   What was the 2000 Wong Kar-wai film, resonant of *Brief Encounter*, about an ill-fated affair between two lonely neighbours played by Tony Leung and Maggie Cheung?

10 Which cities provided the setting for *Before Sunrise* (1995) and *Before Sunset* (2004)? Who played the briefly connected couple in both movies? (4 pts)

11 Who is (eventually) the object of Heath Ledger's affection in *Ten Things I Hate About You* (1999)? On which Shakespeare play is the story (very) loosely based? (2 pts)

12 Who played sparring partners in nine movies, including *Woman of the Year* (1942), *Adam's Rib* (1949) and *Desk Set* (1957)? (2 pts)

13 Who – shockingly – at the time, flashed a stockinged leg at a passing car to hitch a ride in *It Happened One Night* (1934)? Who was her co-star, who daringly stripped down to (. . . wait for it . . .) his vest? (2 pts)

14   *Roxanne* was a 1987 romantic comedy directed by Fred Schepisi: for which star was it essentially a vehicle and on which classic tale was the story based, albeit with a cop-out happy ending? (2 pts)

15   Who directed the 1989 romantic comedy *When Harry Met Sally*? Which two stars did the film launch in to superstardom? Who wrote the script and who added some of the zippy one-liners? (5 pts)

Total Points: 35. Targets: Novice 14 Pro 26. Your Score:

Quiz 171. Geography

Some quick-fire questions and a couple of multi-parters

Part 1

1   What is the main port of Pakistan, looking out over the Arabian Sea?
2   The resorts of Dubrovnik and Split are in which old region of which modern country? (2 pts)
3   Asunción is the capital city of which South American country?
4   The Skagerrak Strait separates which two countries?
5   What and where is the Mariana Trench?
6   What is the county, containing a National Park with rolling hills, directly south of Dublin county in the Republic of Ireland?
7   If you live in Dhaka, and spend your taka, in which country do you live?
8   Ibiza, Mallorca and Menorca are the main three islands in which group? Which is the largest? What is the small sister island to Ibiza, situated to the south? (3 pts)
9   Which mountain range separates Georgia and Azerbaijan from Russia?
10 Burkina Faso, Mali, Benin, Niger; which of these has a coastline?
11 Which US state separates California from New Mexico?
12 The island of Hispaniola in the Caribbean has Haiti to the west and which country to the east?

Part 2

13 The River Danube passes through which four European capital cities? (4 pts)
14 The Peloponnese is a large peninsula separated from the mainland of which country by a large inlet of water called the Gulf of Corinth? The Gulf flows in from which larger body of water? What took place on the peninsula for 400 years from 800 to 400 BC? And which military city-state lies at the southern end of the peninsula? (4 pts)

Total Points: 23. Targets: Novice 9 Pro 17. Your Score: [   ]

Quiz 172. Light Entertainment

TV shows

Part 1

1   Who presented the first three series of *The X Factor*? Of which teen maga-
    zine was she formerly the editor? (2 pts)

2   Which pop guru persuaded a reluctant Robson Green and Jerome Flynn to
    record their rendition of 'Unchained Melody' and release it as a single?

3   Twenty-three year-old David Frost fronted a satirical programme with a cast
    that included Bernard Levin, Roy Kinnear, Willie Rushton and Cleo Laine;
    what was the programme?

4   In which year was *Top of the Pops* first shown on the BBC: 1964, 1967 or
    1971? Who wrote 'Whole Lotta Love', the most famous of its theme tunes,
    first used in 1972? (2 pts)

5   Which famous TV comedy duo started their show with the words 'Tonight,
    in a packed programme . . .' before listing various fictitious guests and
    attractions?

6   Who fronted the montage programme of out-takes and bloopers, *It'll Be
    Alright on the Night*, until his retirement in 2006?

7   Why were the team from Corpus Christi College, Oxford, forced to relin-
    quish the *University Challenge* title to their beaten opponents, Manchester
    University, in 2009?

8   Which artist made the most appearances on *Later . . . with Jools Holland* in
    the show's first twenty years?

9   What was Judith Keppel's first claim to fame as a TV contestant?

10 Which show launched the TV career of DJ Chris Evans, and what was his
    first solo show after leaving this format in 1994? (2 pts)

Part 2

11   Who presented the first seventeen series of *Never Mind the Buzzcocks*?

12   Which American TV legend served as a judge on *Britain's' Got Talent* in 2011?

13   Who are the only group to win *The X Factor*? Which song by Damien Rice was their first single, which inevitably went to no. 1 in the UK? What was their debut album, released in 2012? (3 pts)

14   What was the high-octane BBC2 show presented first by Jeremy Clarkson and then by Craig Charles?

15   Which TV game show found lugubrious writer Will Self cast as an unlikely team captain?

16   *Sale of the Century* made a household name out of which character actor and radio presenter?

17   Who make up the four-person judging panel on ITV's *Britain's Got Talent* for series six and seven in 2012 and 2013? (4 pts)

Total Points: 25. Targets: Novice 10 Pro 19. Your Score:

Quiz 173. Fashion and Photography

Snappy questions and a Mix and Match

Part 1

1 Which hairdresser designed the iconic Mary Quant bob in the 1960s?
2 For what are Theo Fennell, Lara Bohinc and Leo de Vroomen known?
3 In a famous Chanel poster of 2007, with what was Keira Knightley covering her naked breasts?
4 Who was the Italian fashion designer shot and killed outside his own house in Miami in 1997?
5 Which revealing item of clothing was launched in Paris on 4 July 1946?
6 What name is given to the wide sash worn from shoulder to opposite hip and usually holding a sword in ceremonial dress?
7 What is a billycock? (a) a wide-brimmed hat (b) a belt worn bandolier-style across the shoulders (c) a decorative codpiece worn by dandies
8 Who is the designer behind the New Look, the 'H' Line and the 'A' Line?
9 What was George Eastman's contribution to the arts? (a) the development of roll film to a mass market (b) the development of the Kodak camera (c) the development of the Brownie camera
10 By what name is photographer Arthur Fellig known professionally?

Part 2

Mix and Match: match the perfume to the house

1. L'Air du Temps; 2. No. 19; 3. Ysatis; 4. Obsession; 5. J'Adore; 6. Anais Anais; 7. Fame; 8. Brut; 9. Opium; 10. Heat

a. Yves St Laurent; b. Cacherel; c. Chanel; d. Christian Dior; e. Fabergé; f. Haus of Gaga/Coty; g. Beyoncé; h. Givenchy; i. Nina Ricci; j. Calvin Klein

Your Workings:

Total Points: 20. Targets: Novice 8 Pro 15. Your Score:

Quiz 174. London

We all know the world revolves around London – Londoners tell us often enough – so here's a quiz all about the Big Smoke (and before you all write in and complain, I love the place, I've lived there more than half my life)

Part 1

1   In which year was there a Great Smog in London, estimated to have caused around 4,000 deaths: 1864, 1926 or 1952?

2   Where in London would you find the Royal Naval College?

3   Which of these is *not* in Greenwich? (a) Royal Observatory (b) National Maritime Museum (c) Victoria and Albert Museum (d) *Cutty Sark*?

4   What was introduced in London on 16 February 2003?

5   How many Underground lines pass through King's Cross station?

6   What is the great mansion at the north end of Hampstead Heath?

7   What damaged properties in Kensal Rise, London, in July 2006?

8   What was launched on to the London streets in 1954, to a design by A. M. Durrant?

9   Where in London did rioting take place after clashes between spectators and police at an annual street festival in 1976?

10   Columbia Road Market is famous for selling which commodity?

Part 2

11   Richmond upon Thames; Hounslow; MISSING; Kensington and Chelsea;
     Westminster; City; MISSING; Newham. Following the Thames on the north
     side from west to east, which two boroughs fill in the gaps? (2 pts)

12   On the house of which romantic poet was London's first Blue Plaque erected
     in 1867?

13   Which was the first tunnel under the River Thames and which father-of-the-
     famous organized it's construction? (2 pts)

14   Who or what are Misty and Houdini, regular exhibits for visitors to London's
     Tate Modern gallery? (a) a pair of falcons who nest at the building (b) nick-
     names for the two chimneys atop the building (c) the ghosts of two workmen
     who died in the original construction of the building and are said to haunt
     the galleries

15   Which south London borough on the river has Richmond to the west and
     Lambeth to the east?

16   Which west London park was bought from the Rothschild family in 1926 by
     the boroughs of Acton and Ealing in 1925?

17   What connects *Das Kapital*, *Middlemarch* and *The Hitchhiker's Guide to the
     Galaxy*?

18   What connects the first Salvation Army rally in 1895, an indoor marathon in
     1909, the Eurovision Song Contest of 1968 and a 1995 Stephen Hawking
     lecture?

19   All distances to and from London are measured from which landmark?

20   Where did fierce fighting take place on 4 October 1936 between Oswald
     Mosley's fascist Blackshirts and their opponents?

Total Points: 22. Targets: Novice 9 Pro 17. Your Score:

Quiz 175. Golf

Twenty questions about the biennial locking of horns that is the Ryder Cup

Part 1

1   Which country will host the 2018 Ryder Cup, the first time the competition has been held there?

2   Which great US player was Ryder Cup captain for the first six matches?

3   Which Welshman captained the GB and Ireland team to a rare Ryder Cup victory in 1957?

4   Who sportingly conceded a putt to which opponent on the last green to halve their match in the 1969 Ryder Cup and consequently halve the overall contest 16–16? (2 pts)

5   What was the venue for the 1997 Ryder Cup, the first time Europe had played a home match outside the British Isles?

6   At Brookline in 1999 there was controversy when the US team celebrated a sensational putt by which golfer, trampling over the green in the process? Which golfer was his opponent, who still had a long putt to take the game to the next hole? (2 pts)

7   Who is the only US captain to win the Ryder Cup in the twenty-first century (up to and including the 2012 contest)?

8   Who clinched the 2010 Ryder Cup by closing out Hunter Mahan in the final, decisive singles match?

9   Which European player has won twelve of his fifteen Ryder Cup matches played thus far (including 2012), a phenomenal record in the modern era?

10 Who will be the two team captains for the 2014 Ryder Cup? Which course will host the tournament for the first time? (3 pts)

Part 2

11 Who was the European team captain when they wrested back the Ryder Cup in 1985, the first victory since 1957? Who sank the winning putt, and what was the venue that year? (3 pts)

12 In which year did the Great Britain and Ireland Ryder Cup team become the European Ryder Cup team: 1969, 1979 or 1985? Which two Spanish golfers made the team that year? (3 pts)

13 Which South Carolina course hosted the tempestuous 1991 Ryder Cup, nicknamed 'The War by the Shore' to reflect its over-competitive edge?

14 Who was the last Welshman to play in the Ryder Cup (2002) and who did he beat in his singles match, having only played one doubles game and lost? (2 pts)

15 Who were the brothers who played in the 2010 Ryder Cup?

16 Twenty-eight players from continental Europe have played in the Ryder Cup (including 2012); which two countries account for eighteen of these, with nine representatives each? (2 pts)

17 Who, in 2012, became the first player from his country to play in the Ryder Cup?

18 Who, in 2012, became the player with most appearances (and most matches played) on the US Ryder Cup team?

19 In the modern era (i.e. played most of his matches since Great Britain and Ireland became Europe), which US player has the best Ryder Cup record, with 21.5 points from thirty-four matches between 1977 and 1993?

20 Who has the best Ryder Cup record between the best three US golfers of the last twenty years: Jim Furyk, Phil Mickelson or Tiger Woods?

Total Points: 30. Targets: Novice 12 Pro 23. Your Score:

Quiz 176. General Knowledge

Part 1

1   Which Moroccan city stands over the Strait of Gibraltar on the African side?

2   In which year did 999 become the number for the emergency services: 1926, 1937 or 1947?

3   What was used in France for the last time on 9 September 1977?

4   Where in America did a new cathedral called the Cathedral of Our Lady of the Angels open in 2002?

5   Who won Olympic gold for Great Britain in the ice dance pairs competition at the 1984 Olympics? In which city? What music did they use? What was the date of the final? (4 pts)

6   What national symbol do Palestine and England have in common?

7   The NKVD was the precursor of which organization?

8   For what is the Dickin Medal, instigated in 1943, awarded?

9   Which historical figure's real surname was Schicklgrüber?

10 How did five become six in sport in 2000?

Part 2

11 Where is Eel Pie Island? Who opened up a recording studio using the name Eel Pie on the mainland nearby? (2 pts)

12 Composer Thomas Arne, born 1710, is best known for which populist anthem?

13 The term AIDS is an acronym for what full description of the disease?

14 What term is used for plucking a violin's strings with the fingers rather than using the bow?

15 Mary J. Blige, Missy Elliott, Fergie, Lauryn Hill, Alicia Keys; who is the oldest and who's the baby of the bunch? (2 pts)

16 Who or what is POTUS?

17 Who did Portia de Rossi marry in California on 16 August 2008?

18 Which pop star was actress Amanda Donohoe's first serious boyfriend?

19 Which actress made over $10 million from exercise videos?

20 What gemstone traditionally marks a fortieth wedding anniversary?

Total Points: 25. Targets: Novice 13 Pro 19. Your Score:

Answers Quizzes 169–176

Quiz 169. General Knowledge

1. Ronald Reagan; 2. Dr Benjamin Spock, 1979; 3. Samuel Johnson (I still visualize him as played by Robbie Coltrane in *Blackadder*); 4. *Viz* (it was my favourite of their splendid 'Top Tips' series); 5. Martin Amis, 1992, on Madonna; 6. Billy Connolly (1998) in the *Observer* magazine, 3 January 2010 (I'm ashamed to say I have the same proclivity . . .); 7. Kevin Keegan (at least he provided laughs unlike the po-faced dull shower on *Match of the Day* in recent years); 8. *The Devil's Dictionary* by Ambrose Bierce (1911); 9. Philip Glenister and John Simm exchange banter as Gene Hunt and Sam Tyler in *Life on Mars*; 10. Lawyers; 11. Alcoholic former footballer George Best; 12. Dorothy Parker; in Alexander Woollcott, *While Rome Burns* (1934); 13. Autobiography; 14. John Lennon talking about the Beatles success in New York (he was trying to be provocative – it worked); 15. Benjamin Franklin

Quiz 170. Chick Flicks

1. John Cusack; 2. Ryan Gosling wasn't in the movie (he was lucky); *Sex and the City*; 3. Doris Day and Rock Hudson; 4. Winona Ryder is the fiancée and Michelle Pfeiffer the Countess; 5. Hugh Grant and Colin Firth; 6. Adam Sandler; as a waitress at a wedding where he is singing; 7. Audrey Hepburn; Peck is a journalist looking for a scoop but falling in love instead; 8. *An Affair to Remember*; *Sleepless in Seattle*; Cary Grant and Tom Hanks; 9. *In the Mood for Love*; 10. Vienna and Paris; Julie Delpy and Ethan Hawke; 11. Julia Stiles; *The Taming of the Shrew*; 12. Katharine Hepburn and Spencer Tracy; 13. Claudette Colbert; Clark Gable; 14. Steve Martin; *Cyrano de Bergerac*; 15. Rob Reiner; Billy Crystal and Meg Ryan; Nora Ephron, Billy Crystal

Quiz 171. Geography

1. Karachi; 2. Dalmatia in Croatia; 3. Paraguay; 4. Norway and Denmark; 5. A trench in the Pacific Ocean believed to be the deepest anywhere; 6. Wicklow; 7. Bangladesh; 8. Balearic Islands; Mallorca; Formentera; 9. Caucasus; 10. Benin; 11. Arizona; 12. Dominican Republic; 13. Vienna (Austria); Bratislava (Slovakia); Budapest (Hungary) and Belgrade (Serbia); 14. Greece; Ionian Sea; Olympic Games; Sparta

Quiz 172. Light Entertainment

1. Kate Thornton; *Smash Hits*; 2. Simon Cowell; 3. *That Was the Week that Was*; 4. 1964; Led Zeppelin, although the version used was by CCS (sadly, the show's image will forever now be tainted by the knowledge of what Jimmy Savile was up to); 5. *The Two Ronnies*; 6. Denis Norden; 7. One of their team (Sam Kay) had already graduated from the college and was thus ineligible to play; 8. Paul Weller; 9. She was the first person to win £1,000,000 on *Who Wants to be a Millionaire?*; 10. *The Big Breakfast*; *Don't Forget Your*

Toothbrush (2 pts); 11. Mark Lamarr; 12. David Hasselhoff (he had previously done a stint on *America's Got Talent*); 13. Little Mix in 2011; 'Cannonball'; *DNA* (3 pts); 14. *Robot Wars*; 15. *Shooting Stars*, in its later incarnation; 16. Nicholas Parsons; 17. Simon Cowell; Amanda Holden; Alesha Dixon; David Walliams (4 pts)

Quiz 173. Fashion and Photography

1. Vidal Sassoon; 2. Jewellery; 3. A bowler hat; 4. Gianni Versace; 5. Bikini; 6. Baldric; 7. (a) a felt hat with a wide brim; 8. Christian Dior; 9. (a), (b) and (c) (they were all developed through the Eastman Kodak company, of which George was the founder and presiding genius); 10. Weegee; Mix and Match 1, i; 2, c; 3, h; 4, j; 5, d; 6, b; 7, f; 8, e; 9, a; 10, g

Quiz 174. London

1. 1952 (the result was the Clean Air Act of 1956 and the conversion of most homes away from fossil fuels; the problem now is traffic fumes as some London roads are over three times the recommended EU limit); 2. Greenwich; 3. (c) The V&A is in the borough of Kensington and Chelsea; 4. Congestion charge; 5. Six (Victoria, Piccadilly, Northern, Circle, Hammersmith and City and Metropolitan); 6. Kenwood House; 7. A tornado; 8. Routemaster bus; 9. Notting Hill; 10. Flowers; 11. Hammersmith and Fulham; Tower Hamlets; 12. Lord Byron; 13. Rotherhithe; Marc Brunel, father of Isambard; 14. (a) a pair of peregrine falcons who nest there; 15. Wandsworth; 16. Gunnersbury Park; 17. Highgate Cemetery; Karl Marx, George Eliot and Douglas Adams are all buried there; 18. All took place in the Royal Albert Hall; 19. Charing Cross, the monument in front of the railway station of that name; 20. Cable Street

Quiz 175. Golf

1. France (Le Golf National, Saint-Quentin-en-Yvelines, near Paris); 2. Walter Hagen; 3. Dai Rees; 4. Jack Nicklaus to Tony Jacklin; 5. Valderrama, Spain; 6. Justin Leonard; José María Olazábal; 7. Paul Azinger; 8. Graeme McDowell; 9. Ian Poulter; 10. Paul McGinley and Tom Watson (the oldest captain in the competition's history); Gleneagles Hotel, Scotland; 11. Tony Jacklin; Sam Torrance, The Belfry, Warwickshire; 12. 1979; Seve Ballesteros and Antonio Garrido; 13. Kiawah Island; 14. Phillip Price; Phil Mickelson; 15. Francesco and Edoardo Molinari; 16. Spain and Sweden; 17. Nicolas Colsaerts of Belgium (oddly, he is the only player from his country to have played in the Cup); 18. Phil Mickelson; 19. Lanny Wadkins (he was known as the Street Fighter for his combative matchplay ability); 20. They all have dreadful records (Furyk has a woeful 0.367 ratio of points to matches, Woods has 0.439 and Mickelson scrapes in as the best of a bad bunch with 0.447)

Quiz 176. General Knowledge

1. Tangier; 2. 1937; 3. Guillotine; 4. Los Angeles; 5. (Jayne) Torvill and (Christopher) Dean; Sarajevo; Ravel's 'Bolero'; Valentine's Day (14 February); 6. Both have St George as their

patron saint; 7. The KGB (it was the People's Commissariat for Internal Affairs); 8. Animal gallantry in service (it carries the message 'we also serve'); 9. Adolf Hitler; 10. Italy joined the northern hemisphere rugby elite to make the Five Nations into the Six Nations; 11. A small silt island on the River Thames near Twickenham; Pete Townshend but he sold it in 2008 (the island also holds a famous hotel which served as a top-class dance hall from 1957 to 1967; it later became a hippie commune before it burned down in odd circumstances in 1971); 12. 'Rule, Britannia'; 13. Acquired immunodeficiency syndrome; 14. Pizzicato; 15. Mary J. has just turned forty-two (January 2013) and is a few months older than Missy; Alicia is the baby at thirty-one (the other two are thirty-seven); 16. It is an acronym for the President of the United States; 17. Ellen DeGeneres; 18. Adam Ant; 19. Jane Fonda; 20. Ruby

Quiz 177. General Knowledge

Fifteen quickies and a slowie

Part 1

1   In Bram Stoker's novel, in which English seaside town did Dracula first land when he came to England?

2   Who was the lawyer who handled Princess Diana's divorce? Which later client fired him in the midst of another high-profile divorce case? (2 pts)

3   Which make of aircraft flew for the first time on 9 February 1969?

4   How many Scottish Cup finals of the last twenty years (1993–2012) have been contested between Celtic and Rangers?

5   To whom did thirty-year-old model Danielle Bux get married in 2009?

6   What were the Cornavii, the Ordovices, the Venicones and the Brigantes?

7   How many gallons of beer make up a firkin? So if 180 rugby players drink three pints each, how many firkins have they consumed? (3pts – 1 for the first question, 2 for the maths)

8   Who controlled most of the Indian subcontinent during the latter part of the seventeenth century and the first half of the eighteenth?

9   Which global catastrophe claimed an estimated seventy-five million lives?

10 Who shot Dixon of Dock Green?

Part 2

11 Herreys, Carola, Charlotte Nilsson and Loreen have been numbers 2, 3, 4 and 5; who were no. 1?

12 What are the names of the two main warders in *Porridge*, played by Fulton Mackay and Brian Wilde? (2 pts)

13 What was H. E. Bates popular 1958 work, later televised with David Jason and a young Catherine Zeta-Jones?

14 Which cause was benefited when Cliff Richard returned to the top of the charts with a re-recording of an old song accompanied by the cast of the hit comedy show *The Young Ones*? What was the song? (2 pts)

15 Where were the BBC's Pebble Mill studios?

16 What are the ten largest cities within the European Union? (10 pts)

Total Points: 30. Targets: Novice 15 Pro 23. Your Score:

Quiz 178. TV Doctors

There are a lot of them about, and it's amazing how often their patients are colleagues, friends, family and ex-lovers . . .

Part 1

1 Where did Mark Craig practise fictional medicine?

2 'I could make a better incision with a lawnmower' was a typically acid observation by which senior member of staff at *Holby City*?

3 Dr John Carter (played by Noah Wyle) was an intern at which fictional hospital?

4 What brand of medicine does the womanizing Guy Secretan (Stephen Mangan) practise in *Green Wing*?

5 Who plays the title role in the 2011 medical drama, *Monroe*?

6 Who plays the charismatic Tony Whitman in *Bodies*?

7 Who plays the medical doctor, Ray Langston, who decides to give up the day job and join the CSI team in Las Vegas?

8 Who played crime-solving doctor Mark Sloan in *Diagnosis: Murder*?

9 What was the name of Dr Finlay's housekeeper in *Dr Finlay's Casebook*?

10 Which ITV show revolved initially around a role written for Kevin Whately but carried on for another six years after his departure?

Part 2

11 Which former doctor turned bestselling novelist created the medical soap
    ER?

12 Who is Dr Jennifer Melfi?

13 Which comedienne co-stars as Chummy Browne in the popular BBC drama
    Call the Midwife? Who provides some narration for the series as an older
    version of Jenny, the lead character? (2 pts)

14 Which medical series starred Patrick Baladi and Max Beesley as a consult-
    ant and registrar who lock horns at South Central infirmary?

15 What was the specific profession of Sean McNamara and Christian Troy,
    the subjects of a US drama from 2003 until 2010?

16 Which series starred Jemma Redgrave as a female doctor battling sexism
    and poor conditions in a Victorian hospital?

17 Who played the TB ridden doctor struggling to help others while battling his
    own condition in the hard-edged western series *Deadwood*?

18 Which medical soap premiered in 1963 and clocked up 12,750 episodes
    (not a misprint, folks) in February 2013?

19 What are the names of the junior doctors played by Zach Braff and Sarah
    Chalke in *Scrubs*, whose on/off relationship is a central thrust of the show?
    (2 pts)

20 Which British actor, already successful as a comic performer in the UK,
    made himself a *House*hold name in the US?

Total Points: 22. Targets: Novice 9 Pro 17. Your Score: [   ]

Quiz 179. Geography

A potpourri of here and there, and a couple to ponder over

Part 1

1   Mount Vesuvius overlooks which modern Italian city?
2   Helsinki lies across the Gulf of Finland from which other Baltic capital city?
    And which major Russian city lies inland along the gulf? (2 pts)
3   What is the capital city of Slovenia, formerly part of the state of Yugoslavia?
4   A trip to Timbuktu would take you to which modern country?
5   Ukraine's only coastline is on which body of water?
6   What is the island off the coast of Donegal in the northwest of Ireland?
    (a) Clare Island (b) Craggy Island (c) Arranmore
7   Which European country shares its border with the most neighbours (nine)?
8   What and where is the region known as the Camargue? (2 pts)
9   Sumatra, Borneo, Sarawak and Java; which of these is *not* part of
    Indonesia?
10 Which island lies the other side of the Mozambique Channel from
    Mozambique?

Part 2

11 What are the seven Gulf states, the Middle Eastern countries with access
    to the Persian Gulf? (7 pts)
12 Which five administrative regions have a border with North Dakota (5 pts)

Total Points: 24. Targets: Novice 10 Pro 18. Your Score:

Quiz 180. Science

Mainly straightforward (if you happen to know anything about science)

Part 1

1   The chemical symbol Y denotes which uncommon metal?

2   What is the smallest possible y value in the function $y = x^2 + 1$?

3   By what name was the Italian mathematician Leonardo of Pisa known, after pioneering work introducing the Indian decimal system into the European trading world?

4   Of what, in 1798, did Henry Cavendish determine the weight to an accuracy within 2 per cent of the accepted modern figure?

5   What did Austrian monk Gregor Mendel use to explore his theories of inherited genetic characteristics?

6   In which decade did Paul Dirac first postulate the notion of antimatter?

7   Particle accelerators were first devised so scientists could reproduce what conditions?

8   What is the measure of electrical charge?

9   In 1984 Dan Shechtman and his team heated an alloy of manganese and aluminium and cooled it; what did they get that broke the 'laws' of science?

10 Which country heads the OECD list of worst offenders on both carbon dioxide emissions and pesticide use?

Part 2

11 If you place a bet on two horses in different races, one of £5 on a 6–1 shot and one of £8 on an 11–4 favourite, and both win, how much profit do you make on your £13?

12 Who used the development of electric currents to conduct experiments in the 1800s that deconstructed items like potash and soda to isolate the elements now known as potassium and sodium?

13 An absence of the SRY gene means what for a human being?

14 What was the title of Stephen Hawking's bestselling 1988 book, an attempt to explain astrophysics to the lay person?

15 What was the subject matter of Alhazen or ibn Al-Haytham's hugely influential 1021 work? (a) optics (b) circulation of the blood (c) geocentric universe

16 What were the five classifications of life proposed by Robert Whittaker in 1969? (5 pts)

Total Points: 20. Targets: Novice 6 Pro 15. Your Score:

Quiz 181. Transport

Some general stuff about getting from A to B (or not, in some cases)

Part 1

1   Which airship made its maiden flight in 1936 and exploded the following year, killing thirty-six?

2   In the same year as Lindbergh flew across the Atlantic, to where in the southern hemisphere did Lt Dick Bentley fly from London?

3   What independent airline launched the Skytrain service from Gatwick to JFK in 1977?

4   Which company started producing motorcycles out of Milwaukee, Wisconsin, in the first decade of the 1900s?

5   Which seaside town boasts the last remaining old-fashioned trams service?

6   Manganese Bronze Holdings, once the dominant manufacturer of British motorcycles, now runs just one plant out of Coventry manufacturing mainly which type of commercial vehicle? (a) London's black cabs (b) replica cars for movie stunts (c) road sweepers

7   London has the oldest underground rail service in the world, opened in 1863; which European city opened the second six years later? (a) Paris (b) Athens (c) Venice

8   The route of the first what went from Marylebone to Euston in 1829?

9   Where was the first commercial airport in London, developed from two existing aerodromes and opened in 1920?

10 Hartsfield-Jackson is the busiest airport in the world; in which southern US city is it located? Which (non-US) city is the second busiest? (2 pts)

Part 2

11   What connects Brig in Switzerland with Domodossola in Italy?

12   Now often misused as a description for any large passenger airline, the phrase 'jumbo jet' was initially coined for which new model of jet, launched commercially by Pan-Am in 1970?

13   P&O Ferries were established in London in the early nineteenth century; for what is P&O an abbreviation?

14   *Pyroscaphe*, built in Lyon, France, in 1783, was the first working example of what type of vessel?

15   What was the destiny of the Cunard flagship *Queen Mary*? (a) it is used by the royal family of Bahrain for private parties (b) it sits in dry dock in Miami and is used as a casino and pleasure park (c) it is a floating hotel, moored off Long Beach, California

16   What was the name of the Royal Navy vessel that fought at Trafalgar and was immortalized being towed to its last berth by J. M. W. Turner?

17   If *Nimrod* and *Quest* were the first and third, what was the second?

18   Europe's longest railway bridge, the Øresund Bridge (*c.*7850 metres, just under 5 miles), connects which two countries across a narrow strait? (2 pts)

19   If you went by train from Temple Meads to Lime Street and then on to Waverley, you would have visited which three cities? (3 pts)

20   In train parlance, what are Mogul, Baltic, Prairie and Mikado?

Total Points: 24. Targets: Novice 10 Pro 18. Your Score:

Quiz 182. World Cup

Some famous football World Cup line-ups listed, with a few players missing –
simply identify the names missing and we'll load you up with points

1   The England 1966 World Cup final team: Banks, Wilson, MISSING; Moore;
    Cohen; MISSING; Stiles; MISSING; MISSING; Hurst; MISSING (5 pts)

2   The England team that warmed the nation by beating Germany 5–1 in
    Munich in a 2001 World Cup qualifier: MISSING; Neville; MISSING; MISS-
    ING; Cole; Beckham; MISSING (sub: Carragher); Gerrard (sub: Hargreaves);
    Barmby (sub: McManaman); MISSING; Owen (5 pts)

3   The Brazil team that won the 1970 World Cup final: Felix; MISSING; Wilson
    Piazza; MISSING; Brito; MISSING; Gerson; Clodoaldo; MISSING; Pelé;
    MISSING (5 pts)

4   The England team that lost to Germany 3–2 in 1970 after leading 2–0:
    MISSING; Newton; Labone; Moore; MISSING; Ball; MISSING; Charlton
    (sub: MISSING, 70); Peters (sub: Hunter, 81); Lee, MISSING (5 pts)

5   The Italy team that won the 2006 final on penalties against France: MISS-
    ING; Zambrotta; Materazzi; MISSING; Grosso; Perotta (De Rossi, 61);
    MISSING; MISSING; Camoranesi (sub; Del Piero, 86); Toni, MISSING (sub:
    Iaquinta) (5 pts)

6   The Northern Ireland team that beat hosts Spain 1–0 in 1982, despite a
    cowardly referee giving every decision for the home team: MISSING;
    Nicholl (J); Nicholl (C); McLelland; MISSING; MISSING; McCreery; MISS-
    ING; Whiteside; MISSING; Hamilton (5 pts)

7   The Germany team that started when they stuffed England 4–1 in 2010 (and
    forget the disallowed goal, England were completely outplayed): MISSING;
    Boateng; MISSING; Friedrich; MISSING; Khedira; Schweinsteiger; MISS-
    ING; Müller; Podolski; MISSING (5 pts)

8   The France team that brought home the trophy in 1998: MISSING; MISS-
    ING; Desailly; MISSING; Lizarazu; Djorkaeff (sub: MISSING, 74); Deschamps;
    Petit; MISSING; Karembeu (sub; Boghossian, 55); Guivarc'h (sub: Dugarry,
    66) (5 pts)

9   The Ireland team that beat Italy in 1994: MISSING; Irwin; MSSING; Staun-
    ton; Babb; Phelan; MISSING; Townsend; Sheridan; Houghton (sub:
    MISSING); Coyne (sub: MISSING) (5 pts)

10 The England team (they played 5–3–1–1) that so nearly reached the 1990
    World Cup final: Shilton; Parker; MISSING; MISSING; Butcher (sub: Steven);
    Pearce; Gascoigne; MISSING; MISSING; MISSING; Lineker (5 pts)

Total Points: 50. Targets: Novice 20 Pro 38. Your Score: [   ]

Quiz 183. Births, Deaths and Marriages

Part 1

1   Which wedding was the marriage of Spice Girl and Goldenballs? (2 pts)

2   Vice Admiral Tim Laurence is the second (and current) husband of which British public figure?

3   Who was Carrie Fisher's mother and to which popular singer was Carrie married in 1983 (for a year)? (2 pts)

4   With which actress did Johnny Depp have a fourteen-year relationship (and two children) before it was called off in 2012?

5   To which actor and comedian is comedienne turned psychologist Pamela Stephenson married?

6   Which US comedian, who died aged 100 in 1996, was married to fellow entertainer Gracie Allen until her death in 1964? (He never remarried.)

7   Had Elvis still been alive in 2003, what relation would he have been to actor Nicolas Cage?

8   Renate Blauel had a somewhat farcical four-year marriage to which celebrity in the 1980s?

9   Philippe Junot, Stefano Casiraghi and Ernst August (Prince of Hanover) are the three husbands of which European royal?

10 Which two *Doctor Who* actors have married co-stars from the programme? (2 pts)

Part 2

11   Who was the Swedish-Italian actress who cavorted with various members of the Rolling Stones in the 1960s?

12   Who died youngest: John Keats, Emily Brontë or Christopher Marlowe?

13   To which other film star was Penélope Cruz married in 2010?

14   Tom Ravenscroft is a presenter on BBC 6 Music. Who was his more famous father?

15   Which British folk-singer and activist was married to pioneer theatre director Joan Littlewood and also to American singer Peggy Seeger, half-sister of Pete Seeger?

16   Which Middle Eastern dictator had an even more obnoxious son called Uday?

17   Who is the actress mother of Hollywood actress Kate Hudson?

18   Which rock star is married to the Somali-born model Iman?

19   Who had a five-year relationship with actor Rupert Friend, with whom she appeared in *Pride and Prejudice* in 2005?

20   Which actress earned a $100 million divorce settlement from Steven Spielberg after they split in 1989?

Total Points: 23. Targets: Novice 12 Pro 18. Your Score:

Quiz 184. General Knowledge

Wham bam, points in the bag

Part 1

1   In which country would you find the spectacular coastal area called Milford Sound?

2   Who joined the union on 3 January 1959?

3   Hundreds of people died in a chemical leak at a factory in which Indian city in 1984?

4   What is the title of Andrew Lloyd Webber's sequel to *The Phantom of the Opera*?

5   What was the profession of Eddie 'The Eagle' Edwards, who competed in the ski jump for Great Britain at the 1988 Olympics?

6   Who did you used to be able to contact by dialling Whitehall 1212?

7   Who were the oldest and youngest England managers at the time of their appointment? (Discount Walter Winterbottom, who wasn't a manager in the modern sense, having no control of team selection.) (2 pts)

8   Who was the showgirl at the centre of the Profumo affair in 1963? Whose government did the incident help bring down? What was Profumo's cabinet position? Which celebrity photographer took the famous photo of the showgirl astride a plywood chair? Who portrayed her in the 1989 film *Scandal* about the incident? (5 pts)

9   What connects actor Michael Douglas to Buster Keaton?

10   What is 106 metres for normal and 140 metres for large at the Winter Olympics?

Part 2

11   What does UNESCO stand for? (2 pts)

12   In which Cornish village would you expect to eat Stargazy Pie on Tom Bawcock's Eve to commemorate legendary events of this day?

13   The four emerging economic powers are denoted by the acronym BRIC. What does it stand for? (4 pts)

14   Boosey and Hawkes Ltd are major operators in which field?

15   Craig David, Olly Murs, Dizzee Rascal, Justin Timberlake, Will Young; who is reaching for the pension book and who is still in short pants? (In other words, who is the oldest and who the youngest?) (2 pts)

16   Which two bodies make up the US Congress? (2 pts)

17   What are the names of Barack and Michelle Obama's two daughters? (2 pts)

18   Which actor caught Emma Thompson's eye during the making of *Sense and Sensibility*?

19   Who is Gottfried Dienst?

20   Which rock star, born in Zanzibar in 1946, died in 1991, only a day after publicly announcing he was HIV positive?

Total Points: 32. Targets: Novice 16 Pro 24. Your Score:

Answers Quizzes 177–184

Quiz 177. General Knowledge

1. Whitby; 2. Anthony Julius; Heather Mills-McCartney; 3. Boeing 747; 4. Two (1999 and 2002, Rangers won both); 5. Gary Lineker; 6. They were British tribes around the time of the first Roman invasion; 7. Nine; 7.5 (there are 8 pints to a gallon, so 72 pints in a firkin, $3 \times 180 = 540$, divide by $72 = 7.5$); 8. Moghul Empire; 9. The Black Death in the fourteenth century; 10. Dirk Bogarde (George Dixon originated as a character in a 1949 film *The Blue Lamp*, where he is shot by a petty thief played by a young Bogarde); 11. ABBA (they are the Swedish acts who have won the Eurovision Song Contest); 12. Mr Mackay and Mr Barrowclough; 13. *The Darling Buds of May*; 14. It was the first Comic Relief single in 1986; 'Living Doll'; 15. Birmingham; 16. London, Berlin, Madrid, Rome, Paris, Hamburg, Budapest, Vienna, Warsaw, Bucharest

Quiz 178. TV Doctors

1. *St Elsewhere*; 2. Dr Anton Meyer; 3. *ER*; 4. He is an anaesthetist; 5. James Nesbitt; 6. Keith Allen; 7. Laurence Fishburne; 8. Dick Van Dyke; 9. Janet; 10. *Peak Practice*; 11. Michael Crichton; 12. She is the psychiatrist seen by Tony Soprano in *The Sopranos*; 13. Miranda Hart; Vanessa Redgrave; 14. *Bodies*; 15. Plastic surgeons (the programme is *Nip/Tuck*); 16. *Bramwell*; 17. Brad Dourif; 18. *General Hospital*; 19. J. D. (John Dorian) and Eliot (Reid); 20. Hugh Laurie

Quiz 179. Geography

1. Naples; 2. Tallinn; St Petersburg; 3. Ljubljana; 4. Mali; 5. Black Sea; 6. (c) Arranmore; Clare Island is further down off Co. Mayo and Craggy Island exists only in *Father Ted*; 7. Germany; Serbia has eight, including one (Kosovo) which it disputes; 8. Wetland region in the south of France; 9. Sarawak is part of Malaysia, and shares the same landmass as Borneo; 10. Madagascar; 11. Saudi Arabia, Kuwait, Iraq, Iran, Oman, United Arab Emirates and Qatar; 12. Montana, South Dakota, Minnesota, Manitoba, Saskatchewan (well, we didn't say states of the US, did we?)

Quiz 180. Science

1. Yttrium; 2. 1 (even if x is 0, $x^2 + 1$ still equals 1); 3. Fibonacci; 4. The earth; 5. Peas; Mendel conducted his experiments in the gardens at a monastery in Brno in the Czech Republic; 6. 1920s; 7. Those of the Big Bang; 8. Coulomb; 9. A quasicrystal (previously all solids were defined as glass or crystal, but this new form had a unique pentagonal structure; its durability has made it highly practicable for commercial use); 10. United States; 11. 52; 12. Humphry Davy; 13. It means the human is a she (the presence of the sex-determining region Y gene is the specific factor which leads to maleness in mammals); 14.

A Brief History of Time (From the Big Bang to Black Holes); 15. (a) He is regarded as a forerunner of all modern thinking on vision and optics; 16. Animals, plants, fungi, protists (microbes) and bacteria

Quiz 181. Transport

1. *Hindenburg*; 2. Cape Town; 3. Laker Airways, the company owned by Freddie Laker (the company collapsed in 1982 with record debts); 4. Harley-Davidson; 5. Blackpool; 6. (a) London taxis; 7. (b) Athens (the Paris Metro didn't open until 1900 by which time systems were in place in Budapest, Glasgow, Boston and Chicago; Venice would find it tricky to operate an underground system . . .); 8. Bus service; 9. Croydon; 10. Atlanta; Beijing (Heathrow vies for third spot with O'Hare airport, Chicago); 11. Simplon Tunnel; 12. Boeing 747; 13. The company was originally called the Peninsular and Oriental Steam Navigation Company; 14. A paddle steamer; 15. (c) it is indeed a floating hotel – complete with Steampunk Ball and Highland Games; 16. The (*Fighting*) *Temeraire*; 17. *Endurance* (they were the ships used for Shackleton's three expeditions to the South Pole); 18. Denmark and southern Sweden; 19. Bristol, Liverpool and Edinburgh; 20. Wheel configurations

Quiz 182. World Cup

1. Jack Charlton, Ball, Bobby Charlton, Peters, Hunt; 2. Seaman, Ferdinand, Campbell, Scholes, Heskey; 3. Carlos Alberto, Everaldo, Jairzinho, Rivelino, Tostao; 4. Bonetti, Cooper, Mullery, Bell, Hurst; 5. Buffon, Cannovaro, Gattuso, Pirlo, Totti; 6. Jennings, Donaghy (sent off – an outrageous decision), O'Neill, McIlroy, Armstrong; 7. Neuer, Mertesacker, Lahm, Ozil, Klose; 8. Barthez, Thuram, Lebouef, Vieira, Zidane; 9. Bonner, McGrath, Keane, McAteer, Aldridge; 10. Walker, Wright, Waddle, Platt, Beardsley

Quiz 183. Births, Deaths and Marriages

1. Victoria Adams and David Beckham; 2. Princess Anne; 3. Debbie Reynolds and Paul Simon; 4. Vanessa Paradis; 5. Billy Connolly; 6. George Burns; 7. Father-in-law (at the time Cage was married to Lisa Marie Presley); 8. Elton John (the marriage, it seems, was one primarily of cosmetic convenience for the star); 9. Princess Caroline of Monaco; 10. David Tennant married Georgia Moffett in 2011 and Tom Baker was married to former companion Lalla Ward; 11. Anita Pallenberg; 12. Keats was twenty-four (Marlowe was twenty-nine and Brontë thirty); 13. Javier Bardem; 14. John Peel; 15. Ewan MacColl (born James Miller); 16. Saddam Hussein; 17. Goldie Hawn; 18. David Bowie; 19. Keira Knightley; 20. Amy Irving

Quiz 184. General Knowledge

1. New Zealand; 2. Alaska became the forty-ninth state of the USA; 3. Bhopal; 4. *Love Never Dies*; 5. Plasterer (Edwards finished fifty-eighth and fifty-fifth in his two events – both being last place; opinion is divided as to whether his efforts were heroic or fatuous);

6. Scotland Yard; 7. Fabio Capello was sixty-two on his appointment in 2008, while Glenn Hoddle was only thirty-eight; 8. Christine Keeler; Harold Macmillan; Secretary of State for War; Lewis Morley; Joanne Whalley; 9. Another Michael Douglas with ambition to Hollywood stardom changed his name by adopting the silent star's surname and became Michael Keaton; 10. Ski jump (the distance is the K-point, a critical target point similar to the par on a golf hole); 11. United Nations Educational, Scientific and Cultural Organization; 12. Mousehole; 13. Brazil, Russia, India, China; 14. (Classical) Music publishers; 15. Will Young is thirty-three (as of January 2013), while Dizzee is twenty-eight (a few months younger than Olly; the other two are thirty-one); 16. House of Representatives and the Senate; 17. Malia and Sasha; 18. Greg Wise; 19. The Swiss referee who allowed Geoff Hurst's dodgy goal in the 1966 World Cup final; 20. Freddie Mercury

Quiz 185. General Knowledge

Part 1

1 Evan Williams, Jack Dorsey and Biz Stone. What did they do?

2 By what name are the historical rebel organization called Fists of Righteous Harmony more commonly known?

3 Artist Tom Keating (1918–84) was best known for which kind of work?

4 The 1992 Winter Olympics were held in Albertville – in which country is Albertville? And which head of state opened the Games? (2 pts)

5 What connects Angelina Jolie, Ian Botham and Bruce Dickinson of Iron Maiden? (a) they all own vineyards (b) they have all done charity walks for leukaemia (c) they have each got a pilot's licence?

6 Manchester (Central), Tameside, Stockport, Wigan, Trafford, Bury and Bolton are seven of the boroughs that make up Greater Manchester; what are the other three? (3 pts)

7 Whose nude pictures in 1998 led to only the second ever complete sell-out of an edition of *Playboy* magazine? (a) model Elle Macpherson (b) ice skater Katarina Witt (c) tennis star Anna Kournikova or (d) actress Sarah Michelle Gellar?

8 In fantasy role-playing games, which category of characters cannot fight with bladed weapons?

9 What title did Margaret Thatcher adopt when she received the inevitable peerage?

10 Which sporting figure's autobiography was entitled *Black, White and Gold*?

Part 2

11   What sport would you expect to watch at Whistling Straits?

12   According to the last comprehensive retail index, the average combined
     cost in 2007 of a dozen eggs, a pint of milk and a pint of beer was £5.13.
     What was it in 1971: 28p, 46p or £1.06?

13   What is the common name given to the personification of death with a
     hooded cloak and a scythe?

14   What was odd about Jack Dee fronting an ad campaign for John Smith's
     bitter?

15   Who were the last team from outside the Premier League to contest an FA
     Cup final (up to 2012)?

16   Whose famous photographs of the 1960s model Jean Shrimpton were
     featured on the front cover of the first *Sunday Times Magazine*? In which
     year in the 1960s did the issue appear? Which Burnley footballer was also
     on the cover? Who played Shrimpton and the photographer in the 2012 TV
     drama based on the shoot in Chelsea? (5 pts)

Total Points: 23. Targets: Novice 12 Pro 17. Your Score:

Quiz 186. Rock and Pop Singles

Chart-toppers and one-hit wonders – a selection on hit singles

Part 1

1   Whose song 'Drive' was their biggest international hit on its 1984 release? What gave it a push back up the charts a year later? (2 pts)

2   What were the first two no. 1 singles for the Police, both taken from their second album, *Regatta de Blanc*? (2 pts)

3   'Swing the Mood' was a composite track made up of clips of remixed rock 'n' roll tracks which became a 1989 UK No. 1 hit; under what artist's name was it released?

4   What was glam rock band Sweet's only UK no. 1 hit? And what was the name of their lead singer, he of the androgynous, long blond locks? (2 pts)

5   Since their debut single, 'Sound of the Underground', went straight to no. 1 in the UK, Girls Aloud had only two further no. 1s; what were they? (2 pts)

6   Which four artists collaborated on the 1995 Comic Relief chart-topper, 'Love Can Build a Bridge'? (4 pts)

7   Which 1986 movie took its title from a Psychedelic Furs song from five years earlier and made the song into a hit?

8   'This Town Ain't Big Enough for the Both of Us' was a classic 1974 hit by which quirky pop duo? From which album was it taken? (2 pts)

9   David Bowie has had five UK no. 1 hits, two of them collaborations with other artists; who were those artists? Which was the only Bowie song to reach no. 1 on both sides of the Atlantic? What was his other US no. 1, a track off the white soul album *Young Americans* that reached only no. 17 in Britain? And which single put back Bowie back in the UK top ten for the first time this century in 2013? (5 pts)

10 Who is the Canadian singer who had a massive 2011 hit with 'Call Me Maybe', reportedly on the back of a Justin Bieber tweet?

Part 2

In this part we name songs that have topped the chart twice and give you one of the performers – you name the other artist

11 'Mary's Boy Child': Harry Belafonte in 1957 and who in 1978?

12 'The Tide Is High': Blondie in 1980 and who in 2002?

13 'Somethin' Stupid': Frank and Nancy Sinatra in 1967 and who in 2001?

14 'Uptown Girl': Billy Joel in 1983 and who in 2001?

15 'You'll Never walk Alone': Gerry and the Pacemakers in 1963, the Crowd in 1985 and who in 1996?

16 'I Got You Babe': Sonny and Cher in 1965 and who in 1985?

17 'With a Little Help from My Friends': Joe Cocker in 1968, Sam and Mark with a ghastly 2004 version and who in 1988?

18 'Without You': Harry Nilsson in 1972 and which diva in 1994?

19 'Young Love': Tab Hunter in 1957 and who in 1973?

20 'Tragedy': Steps in 1999 but who with the original in 1979?

Total Points: 32. Targets: Novice 13 Pro 24. Your Score: [   ]

Quiz 187. Astronomy

Reach for the stars

1   What is the Nebula galaxy seen from the UK just above the square Pegasus constellation?

2   Which unit of measurement is equal to 3.26 light years?

3   What was the name of the Russian vessel launched in 1957, the first man-made object to orbit the earth?

4   'In space, no one can hear you scream.' So went the tagline for *Alien*. But is it true?

5   Who was left in the space capsule while Neil Armstrong and Buzz Aldrin walked on the moon?

6   Who published *On the Revolution of the Heavenly Spheres* in Nuremberg in 1543?

7   By what common name is the star cluster given the Greek name the Pleiades better known?

8   Prior to the implementation of the Gregorian calendar, whose calculations from *c.*130 BC formed the basis of the duration of the year and the seasons?

9   What was 'added' by scientist William Herschel to our solar system in 1781?

10 By what name is the star Alpha Canis Majoris sometimes known?

11 The Quadrantids, the Perseids and the Geminids are all regularly occurring what?

12 Titan, Phoebe, Janus and Prometheus are all satellites of which planet?

13 In space exploration terms, what are Scout, Taurus and Atlas in the US, Proton in the USSR, Long March in China and Ariane in Europe?

14 Who was the main presenter of the BBC coverage of the first *Apollo* moon landing? (a) Cliff Michelmore (b) Richard Dimbleby (c) Patrick Moore

15 What is the Blue Marble? (a) a crater on Mars (b) an unidentified shaded spot on the surface of Jupiter (c) a name given to a famous image of the earth from space

Total Points: 15. Targets: Novice 6 Pro 11. Your Score:

Quiz 188. History

Just a straightforward twenty mixed questions

Part 1

1   A castle was built near the fishing village of Edo in 1456; which modern city was in the first stages of its development?

2   In the USA, what was changed by a ratification to the twenty-sixth amendment on 30 June 1971? (a) confirmation of the right to bear arms (b) new laws on racial equality (c) change in the voting age

3   Who led the Gallic tribes in their resistance to Julius Caesar's Roman legions?

4   Who was Prime Minister when Britain joined the European Union?

5   The Soviet Union and seven other countries signed which mutual assistance treaty in 1955?

6   Who was the Scottish general, with his Coldstream Guards, who was instrumental in the restoration of Charles II as monarch in 1660?

7   What was the group, led by Robespierre, that dominated the revolutionary government and implemented the Reign of Terror in 1793–94?

8   What was the first perforated UK postage stamp, issued in 1854?

9   What name is given to 7 May to mark the unconditional surrender of the German Army at the end of World War II?

10 Which wars led to the secession of Hong Kong from China to Great Britain in 1842?

Part 2

11 To what was the Australian settlement of Palmerston renamed in 1911?

12 19 November 1975 saw the death of which European right-wing dictator after thirty-nine years in power?

13 Who was denounced by Soviet leader Nikita Khrushchev in a famous speech in 1956?

14 From where did Justinian I attempt to restore order to the 'new' Roman Empire?

15 In which modern country are Bukhara and Samarkand, both important stop-offs on the old Silk Road?

16 Who was the Archbishop of Krakow from 1963 to 1978?

17 The Edict of Expulsion by Edward I saw all Jews forcibly removed from England; the Edict stayed in place until it was formally removed by which English ruler?

18 By what name do we now know the Roman town of Lutetia?

19 Who was the Austrian Foreign Minister who coordinated the alliance against Napoleon in 1812–13?

20 Where did the army of King William III crush an attempt to reinstate the Catholic King James II on the throne of England and Scotland?

Total Points: 20. Targets: Novice 8 Pro 15. Your Score:

Quiz 189. Bible

A section on the Holy Book, especially the juicy mythology of the Old Testament

Part 1

1   Which two kings are beaten down at 'The Battle of the Kings' in the Book of Genesis? (2 pts)

2   Which biblical figure lived for 969 years?

3   Who sold his birthright to his brother Jacob for a mess of pottage (bowl of stew)?

4   Who was Jacob's wife and the mother of Joseph and Benjamin, his youngest sons?

5   What is the name of the officer of the Pharaoh who buys Joseph when he is sold into slavery by his jealous brothers?

6   The book of Exodus concerns the persecution of the sons of Israel (the Hebrew race) and their flight from which land?

7   Aaron throws down his rod before the Pharaoh and it becomes a serpent; the Pharaoh's magicians perform the same feat; what happens next?

8   What is the familiar biblical term for the bread which maintains the exiled Israelites in the desert for forty years in the Book of Exodus?

9   After Moses receives the Ten Commandments and the stone tablets on Mount Sinai, what is he instructed to build to house the Commandments?

10 Which book of the Bible details the laws God prescribes for the behaviour of his chosen people?

Part 2

11 Who is anointed by Samuel as the first King of Israel in the first book of Samuel?

12 Who is the wife of Uriah the Hittite with whom King David commits adultery? (a) Ruth (b) Bathsheba (c) Miriam. What is the name of their second son, after the Lord takes their first as penance? (2 pts)

13 Who was the wife of Ahab, whose name has become synonymous with wicked, scheming women?

14 Which of the psalms begins with the words, 'The Lord is my Shepherd . . .'?

15 What is the book of the Bible between Ecclesiastes and Isaiah which consists of a number of love poems narrated by a man and a woman?

16 In which language was the Gospel of St Matthew composed in *c.*70 AD?

17 The parable of the Good Samaritan appears in which of the four Gospels of the New Testament?

18 How many books of the Old Testament are there: eighteen, twenty-nine or thirty-nine?

19 What is the final book of the New Testament?

20 Where was Saul heading when he experienced his epiphany and conversion? And in which book of the New Testament is the story recounted? (2 pts)

Total Points: 23. Targets: Novice 9 Pro 17. Your Score:

Quiz 190. Motorsport

Chaps (mainly) driving, very fast, in cars and on bikes

Part 1

1   Who were the two Red Bull drivers in the thick of the action during the 2010–13 F1 seasons? (2 pts)

2   With which team did Michael Schumacher make a largely unsuccessful return to F1 in 2010? Who was the team's other driver, who did rather better? (2 pts)

3   Ayrton Senna died during practice for which Grand Prix?

4   Who won most Grands Prix: Stirling Moss, Jackie Stewart or Jim Clark?

5   The great racing driver Jim Clark was killed in an accident at which circuit in 1968?

6   Which newcomer to F1 was attacked by Ayrton Senna after having the temerity to overtake the maestro after Senna had already lapped him?

7   Which three tracks were used both in the first Formula 1 season of 1958 and fifty years later in 2008? (3 pts)

8   Who won the 2004 World Drivers' Championship in Formula 1 with a record thirteen Grand Prix victories?

9   In the rule change that came into force in 2006 in Formula 1, how many cars compete for pole position in the third and final round of qualifying?

10 Who won the inaugural Formula 1 World Drivers' Championship in 1951, and won four more later in the decade?

Part 2

11 Brabham; Lauda; Piquet; Prost; Senna: which of these drivers won the World Championship most times?

12 Who is the only man to have won world championships on a motorbike and in a F1 car?

13 Who won the 1993 Indy Car championship a year after winning the F1 championship?

14 From 2006 what has been the maximum engine capacity of a Formula 1 car: 2L, 2.4L or 3L?

15 Which Brazilian driver, who retired in 2011, holds the record for number of races started in Formula 1?

16 Who was F1's only posthumous World Champion? What nationality was he? At which circuit was he killed in practice? Which close friend of his had already been killed that season? Who presented the trophy to his wife, Nina? (5 pts)

Total Points: 24. Targets: Novice 10 Pro 18. Your Score: _____

Quiz 191. Arts and Culture

The high arts (classical music, opera, ballet) – ten straight questions and a Mix and Match

Part 1

1   Who performed all thirty-two of Beethoven's piano sonatas to a sold-out auditorium in London in 2008, his first appearance in the city since 1970?
2   How long was John Cage's 1952 piece, consisting of a fixed period of silence?
3   Which famous Handel oratorio had its first public performance in Dublin on 12 April 1742?
4   What is the lowest type of female voice in opera singing?
5   The Mariinsky Theatre in St Petersburg is home to which famous dance company?
6   Alina Ibragimova, born is Russia, educated mainly in the UK, is a virtuoso on which musical instrument?
7   Mark Elder restored which Manchester-based orchestra to its former eminence?
8   *Desert Island Discs* celebrated its seventieth anniversary in 2012; which classical piece had proved the most popular musical choice over those years? And which (different) composer had the most pieces chosen? (2 pts)
9   What was Beethoven's only opera?
10 Whose best-known work was his 1830 *Symphonie Fantastique*?

Part 2

Mix and Match: match the composer to his opera

1. Benjamin Britten; 2. Modest Mussorgsky; 3. Wolfgang Amadeus Mozart; 4. Henry Purcell; 5. Gaetano Donizetti; 6. Giacomo Puccini; 7. Richard Strauss; 8. Bedřich Smetana; 9. Pyotr Tchaikovsky; 10. Giuseppe Verdi

a. *The Bartered Bride*; b. *Dido and Aeneas*; c. *Lucia di Lammermoor*; d. *Eugene Onegin*; e. *La Traviata*; f. *Der Rosenkavalier*; g. *Boris Godunov*; h. *Don Giovanni*; i. *Peter Grimes*; j. *La Bohème*

Your Workings:

Total Points: 21. Targets: Novice 8 Pro 16. Your Score:

Quiz 192. General Knowledge

Part 1

1 Who, on 24 February 1920, became the first woman to speak in the British Parliament?

2 Cristina Kirchner was elected President of which South American country in 2007?

3 To what does the West Country term 'grockles' apply?

4 What is the title of Oscar Wilde's only novel?

5 Which two of these sports made their modern debut at the Winter Olympics of 1998? (a) curling (b) two-man skeleton (c) Nordic downhill (d) water-boarding (e) snowboarding (2 pts)

6 How many eggs or decorations should a simnel cake have?

7 In an article for the *Observer*, singer Rufus Wainwright selected his 'Top Ten Musical Gay Icons'. The list included only two men; who? And which diva, unsurprisingly given who was making the choices, topped the list? (3 pts)

8 In the eighteenth and nineteenth centuries, someone living in a rookery lived (a) on the top floor or attic of a building, (b) in a squalid slum area of a city, or (c) in a gypsy caravan?

9 By what name do we know Joel Chandler Harris, recounter of American stories for children?

10 Which of these is *not* featured at the Paralympics? (a) archery (b) badminton (c) fencing (d) sailing

Part 2

11   What is the name of the annual art fair opened in Regent's Park in 2003?

12   Which school of Greek philosophy favours intellectual detachment and rigour over emotion or spirit?

13   Who was Vladimir Putin's successor as President of Russia?

14   What is the alternative name of Psalm 51, which has been set to music by countless composers?

15   Which 1993 movie earned Bruce Springsteen an Academy Award for best movie song?

16   Which twentieth-century US President shared a surname with a twentieth-century British Prime Minister? (They were not contemporaries.)

17   Who was the famous grandson of pottery magnate Josiah Wedgwood?

18   Who married director James Cameron, after appearing in *Terminator 2*?

19   Actress Connie Fisher, born 16 June 1983, achieved instant stardom by winning a BBC talent show to win a part in which musical?

20   Which British singer was run over and killed by a speedboat in Mexico in 2000?

Total Points: 23. Targets: Novice 12 Pro 17. Your Score:

Answers Quizzes 185–192

Quiz 185. General Knowledge

1. Set up Twitter; 2. Boxers; 3. Forgeries or fakes; 4. France; François Mitterrand; 5. (c) they all have a pilot's licence (only Botham of the three has a vineyard and did the walks); 6. Oldham, Rochdale and Salford; 7. Katarina Witt; 8. Priests and clerics (this is historically accurate, as clerics were forbidden by the Bible to wield blades and so would fight with barred staffs and maces); 9. Baroness Thatcher of Kesteven; 10. Kelly Holmes; 11. It's an American golf course; 12. 46p (Milk rose by about seven times, eggs about eight and beer about seventeen); 13. The Grim Reaper; 14. Jack Dee is a teetotaller after encountering problems in the 1980s; 15. Cardiff City in 2008; 16. David Bailey; 1962; Jimmy McIlroy; Aneurin Barnard and Karen Gillan

Quiz 186. Rock and Pop Singles

1. The Cars; it was used as the backdrop to harrowing films of starving children during the Live Aid fundraising push; 2. 'Walking on the Moon' and 'Message in a Bottle'; 3. Jive Bunny (the memories still wake me up in a cold sweat); 4. 'Block Buster!' Brian Connolly; 5. 'I'll Stand By You' and 'The Promise'; 6. Cher, Chrissie Hynde, Neneh Cherry and Eric Clapton; 7. 'Pretty in Pink'; 8. Sparks; *Kimono My House*; 9. Queen ('Under Pressure') and Mick Jagger ('Dancing in the Street'; the Rolling Stones is incorrect, it was just Jagger); 'Let's Dance'; 'Fame'; 'Where Are We Now?'; 10. Carly Rae Jepsen; 11. Boney M; 12. Atomic Kitten; 13. Robbie Williams and Nicole Kidman; 14. Westlife; 15. Robson and Jerome; 16. UB40 with Chrissie Hynde; 17. Wet Wet Wet; 18. Mariah Carey; 19. Donny Osmond; 20. The Bee Gees

Quiz 187. Astronomy

1. Andromeda; 2. Parsec; 3. *Sputnik 1*; 4. Yes (no sound can be heard in a vacuum, and space is almost a perfect vacuum); 5. Michael Collins; 6. Nicolaus Copernicus; 7. Seven Sisters; 8. Hipparchus; 9. Uranus; 10. Sirius, the Dog Star; 11. Meteor showers; 12. Saturn; 13. Launch systems; 14. (a) Cliff Michelmore, with Moore and James Burke providing more technical back-up; 15. (c) the Blue Marble was taken by the crew of *Apollo 17* and is a remarkably beautiful and clear early picture of the surface of the earth

Quiz 188. History

1. Tokyo; 2. (c) change in the voting age from twenty-one to eighteen; 3. Vercingetorix; 4. Ted Heath; 5. Warsaw Pact; 6. General (George) Monck; 7. The Jacobins or Jacobin Club; 8. Penny red; 9. VE Day; 10. Opium Wars; 11. Darwin; 12. General Franco of Spain; 13. Stalin; 14. Constantinople (accept Byzantium); 15. Uzbekistan; 16. Karol Wojtyla, later Pope John Paul II; 17. Lord Protector, Oliver Cromwell; 18. Paris; 19. Metternich; 20. Battle of the Boyne in (Northern) Ireland

Quiz 189. Bible

1. Kings of Sodom and Gomorrah; 2. Methuselah; 3. Esau; 4. Rachel; 5. Potiphar; 6. Egypt; 7. Aaron's serpent-rod swallows the other serpents; 8. Manna from heaven; 9. The Ark of the Covenant; 10. Leviticus; 11. Saul; 12. (b) Bathsheba; Solomon; 13. Jezebel; 14. Psalm no. 23; 15. Song of Solomon; 16. Greek; 17. Luke; 18. Thirty-nine; 19. Revelation (deduct a half for 'Revelations'; award a bonus for the full title of 'The Revelation of St John the Divine'); 20. Damascus; Acts of the Apostles

Quiz 190. Motorsport

1. Mark Webber and Sebastien Vettel; 2. Mercedes; Nico Rosberg; 3. San Marino; 4. Jackie Stewart won twenty-seven (Clark won twenty-five, Moss sixteen); 5. Hockenheim; 6. Eddie Irvine; 7. Silverstone (Britain); Monza (Italy) and Spa-Francorchamps (accept Belgium); 8. Michael Schumacher; 9. Ten; 10. Juan Manuel Fangio of Argentina; 11. Alain Prost won four, all the others won three, although Senna may well have won more but for his premature death (Sebastien Vettel may overtake them, his win in 2012 was his third); 12. John Surtees; 13. Nigel Mansell; 14. 2.4L, previously it had been 3L; 15. Rubens Barrichello; 16. Jochen Rindt; Austrian; Monza; Piers Courage; Jackie Stewart

Quiz 191. Arts and Culture

1. Daniel Barenboim; 2. 4 min 33 secs (this amounts to 273 seconds, and Cage was making a connection with -273 °C, or absolute zero; 3. *Messiah*; 4. Contralto; 5. Kirov Ballet; 6. Violin; 7. Hallé; 8. Beethoven's *Ninth Symphony*; Mozart; 9. *Fidelio*; 10. Hector Berlioz; Mix and Match 1, i; 2, g; 3, h; 4, b; 5, c; 6, j; 7, f; 8, a; 9, d; 10, e

Quiz 192. General Knowledge

1. Nancy Astor; 2. Argentina; 3. Tourists; 4. *The Picture of Dorian Gray*; 5.(a) curling and (e) snowboarding (none of the others are actual events; one is actually a method of torture); 6. Eleven, to represent the eleven faithful disciples; 7. Morrissey and Prince; Judy Garland (Wainwright once released an entire album devoted to Judy Garland); 8. (b) a rookery was the name for an area with derelict slum housing for the poorest inhabitants; 9. Uncle Remus; 10. Badminton; 11. Frieze; 12. Stoicism; 13. Dmitri Medvedev; 14. Miserere; 15. *Philadelphia* (the song was 'Streets of Philadelphia'); 16. Woodrow Wilson (the PM is Harold Wilson); 17. Charles Darwin; 18. Linda Hamilton; 19. *The Sound of Music*; 20. Kirsty MacColl

Quiz 193. General Knowledge

Cats, Kates and C/Kathe/arines

Part 1

1   Which actress married Ned Rocknroll (her third husband), a nephew of Richard Branson, in December 2012?

2   Which three Kates married Henry VIII? (3 pts)

3   Who was Perry to Harry Enfield's Kevin?

4   Who made the headlines when she 'Kissed a Girl' in 2008?

5   Who left Tom (and the Scientologists) in 2012? Which TV show made her name? (2 pts)

6   Under what name did Katie Price first achieve fame as a glamour model?

7   The musical *Kiss Me, Kate* is an adaptation of which Shakespeare play?

8   What does Kathy Clugston do for a living? (a) she is the head of the National Union of Teachers (b) she is the deputy leader of the Scottish National Party (c) she reads the news on Radio 4

9   In which decade were Susan Coolidge's *What Katy Did* novels about a twelve-year-old American tomboy written? (a) 1870s (b) 1900s (c) 1930s

10 Who was the oldest player to appear in a Rugby World Cup final when he appeared for England (his second final appearance) in the 2007 final against South Africa?

Part 2

11   What nationality is the feminist writer and novelist Kathy Lette?

12   Which Italian noblewoman became the de facto ruler of Catholic France in 1560 through her ten-year-old son, King Charles IX?

13   The Russian Tsarina (Empress) Catherine the Great was born Sophie Frieder-erike Auguste and married Peter III of Russia, an attempt to ally Russia with her birth nation, which was: (a) Bavaria (b) Prussia (c) Sweden?

14   Terry Kath, who accidentally shot himself aged thirty-one in 1978, was lead guitarist and a founder member of which US rock band?

15   Whose reputation as a director was made by the 1966 TV play, *Cathy Come Home*, a landmark in social TV drama? (a) Ken Loach (b) Mike Leigh (c) Peter Yates

16   What were used to focus electrons and produce the images seen in earlier television sets?

17   Who was the love of Heathcliff's life in Emily Brontë's *Wuthering Heights*?

18   Prior to April 2011, by what name was the Duchess of Cambridge known?

19   Which classic late eighteenth-century comedy concerns the adventures of Kate Hardcastle and her amiable half-brother, Tony Lumpkin?

20   Who is the deputy shift leader under Gil Grissom in the early series of the original *CSI* set in Las Vegas?

Total Points: 23. Targets: Novice 12 Pro 17. Your Score:

Quiz 194. Movie Directors

Anyone else find it odd how people know the stars of movies and never the principal player, the director?

Part 1

1   Who was the first woman to win a Best Director Academy Award?

2   Which film director was born in a Quaker household, married six times and worked closely with Noël Coward in the early part of his career?

3   Which is the elder of the Coen brothers, Joel or Ethan? And which of the two used to be credited as the director? (2 pts)

4   *Fanny and Alexander* is a 1982 work, more mainstream than most of its predecessors, by which European master?

5   'The corpses of his imitators littered the world's film festivals.' Of which great European director was US critic Pauline Kael writing?

6   Who directed *West Side Story* in 1961 and the very different haunted house classic, *The Haunting*, two years later? What was his next major success, another musical, in 1965? (2 pts)

7   Who directed Oliver Reed and Vanessa Redgrave in the demented horror thriller *The Devils* (1970)?

8   Which director made eight films with James Stewart in the lead role, five of them westerns?

9   What relation is director Rob Reiner to Carl Reiner?

10   *Trees Lounge* (1996) was the directorial debut of which edgy American actor?

Part 2

11 *Mystery Train*, *Broken Flowers* and *Coffee and Cigarettes* are all films by which US independent film-maker?

12 What was the 2011 Hollywood hit directed by the in-vogue Danish director Nicolas Winding Refn?

13 What was Lisa Cholodenko's 2010 hit, a mainstream movie about two married lesbian mothers and their children's desire to know their 'natural' father?

14 What was the 1984 concert movie by Academy Award winning film director with US rock band Talking Heads? With which other major rock star has he made three documentaries in the last few years? (2 pts)

15 Whose feature film debut was the 1981 low budget horror movie *Piranha II: The Spawning*? Which action sci-fi movie made three years later properly kick-started his career? (2 pts)

16 *An Angel at My Table* and *The Piano* were indie hits for which film director of what nationality? (2 pts)

17 Who made his directorial debut with a 2011 version of Shakespeare's *Coriolanus*, in which he also took the title role?

18 Which great Italian director died on the same day as Ingmar Bergman in 2007?

19 Which two directors shot George Clooney's two 2011 movies, *The Ides of March* and *The Descendants*? (2 pts)

20 Japanese film icon Toshiro Mifune made no less than sixteen films with which influential director?

Total Points: 26. Targets: Novice 13 Pro 20. Your Score: [   ]

Quiz 195. Video Games

Give the kids a shout, if you're over forty you'll struggle . . .

Part 1

1   Which racing simulation, released in 1997, became a flagship game on Playstation for Sony and has sold over ten million copies?

2   Who is the other principal character in the Nintendo game series featuring Zelda?

3   What was the first video game to sell a million cartridges on the Atari 2600? Which were the next two releases to successively claim top spot? (Tip: name the obvious ones.) (3 pts)

4   Which game, a forerunner of many fantasy video games, was devised by Gary Gygax and Dave Arneson and launched in 1974? Who bought the rights to the game and licences in 1997, and which toy-making giant absorbed this company two years later? (3 pts)

5   In which game are Delta Squad trying to save a planet from the Locust Horde?

6   In the *Donkey Kong* games, what type of creatures are the Kongs? (Tip: they are not donkeys.)

7   *Sonic the Hedgehog* was devised for which platform?

8   *Grand Theft Auto*, *Red Dead Redemption* and *LA Noire* are all game releases by which company?

9   What are the subtitles of the first three games in the *Uncharted* series of games? (3 pts)

10 *Going Commando*, *Up Your Arsenal* and *Quest for Booty* are all games in which ongoing tongue-in-cheek adventure series?

Part 2

11 Which game has the player viewing the actions of his ancestor Altair ibn-La'Ahad? Over what is the ancestor fighting for control? Who are his opponents? (3 pts)

12 In game terms, a game with a good replay value offers the player what?

13 *Kingdom Hearts* is a spin-off from *Final Fantasy* which combines characters from that franchise with characters from which other licence?

14 Who is mentored by Aku Aku and has a sister called Coco?

15 In *Sleeping Dogs*, undercover cop Wei Shen is trying to clean up which corrupt city?

16 What terms are used to define the following types of game? (a) a game with weaponry screened from the player's point of view (b) a game where one level must be completed to access the next, often by collecting tokens of some kind (c) a game where real life experiences are replicated (d) a game where the player takes an alien character in a fantasy world and fulfils quests (e) a game where the player destroys everything in his path to reach a goal or escape a scenario? (5 pts)

Total Points: 28. Targets: Novice 11 Pro 21. Your Score:

Quiz 196. TV

An assortment of TV questions: twenty plus a bonus Muppet question

Part 1

1   How many episodes of *Heartbeat* were screened: 120, 220, or 372? Which of the show's stars sang the theme tune? (2 pts)

2   What is the name of the Prime Minister of Denmark in the acclaimed drama *Borgen*?

3   In what way did actor Dennis Haysbert beat Barack Obama in *24*?

4   Which comedy duo gave us *Fantasy Football*, the first TV football show that managed successfully to engage fans without showing any action? Which former England international made the occasional appearance doing a bit of karaoke? (3 pts)

5   Who joined the cast of *The Hour* for the second series (2012) as the BBCs Head of News?

6   What is the name of the Spanish teacher who leads the *Glee* choir?

7   What was Stephen Poliakoff's 2013 drama about a black jazz band in 1930s London? Who played the lead role of band leader Louis? (2 pts)

8   Who were Bingo, Drooper, Fleegle and Snorky?

9   Irish comedian Roy Walker is best remembered as presenter of which TV game show for fourteen years from 1986?

10 Which actor became a hot property as Detective John Kelly in the first series of *NYPD Blue* but left the series over salary negotiations? Which more recent crime series resurrected his career after he failed to 'make it big in the movies'? (2 pts)

Part 2

11 Who were Luke, Bo, Daisy and Uncle Jesse?

12 Which TV sketch show gave us the catchphrases 'Does my bum look big in this?', 'Suits you, Sir' and 'Today I have mostly been . . .'?

13 Which well-known film director appeared in *Happy Days* as Richie Cunningham?

14 How did Bill Bixby and Lou Ferrigno play the same character concurrently in a 1980s adventure series?

15 What is the profession of Keith (Rob Brydon) in *Marion and Geoff*?

16 Who was cast as Bodie in *The Professionals*, but dropped after test scenes revealed a weak dynamic between him and Doyle? (a) Anthony Andrews (b) Timothy Dalton (c) John Thaw

17 Gian Sammarco has struggled to maintain an acting career at the highest level after early success as which famous teenager?

18 Who connects Bruce Springsteen to *The Sopranos*?

19 What was Gene Roddenberry's most important contribution to our cultural universe?

20 To which cult series did the director's secretary, Julee Cruise, sing the hit theme tune? What was the name of the song? (2 pts)

21 In *The Muppet Show*, who was the main Master of Ceremonies? What was the spoof science-fiction series? Who did a cookery programme? Who played the drums? Who was Bunsen Honeydew's assistant in the Muppet Labs? (5 pts)

Total Points: 31. Targets: Novice 12 Pro 23. Your Score: [   ]

Quiz 197. US Politics

Some more recent US stuff; ten ordinary questions and a couple of trickies

Part 1

1 Which US politician was shot and fatally wounded on 4 June 1968?

2 George H. W. Bush, born in 1924, was the forty-first President of the US. Who was his gaffe-prone Vice President?

3 Republican Presidential candidate Mitt Romney was formerly Governor of which US state?

4 Who are the only two US Presidents to be impeached by a hostile House of Representatives? (2 pts)

5 What is the composition of the US Senate?

6 Who was the only Roman Catholic President of the United States?

7 What is Barack Obama's middle name?

8 What post did Franklin Roosevelt hold before he was voted as US President for the first time in 1932? (a) Attorney General (b) Senator for Massachusetts (c) Governor of New York

9 How many Presidential elections did Gerald Ford win?

10 Marion Barry was arrested and later imprisoned for possession of cocaine whilst serving which public office in 1991? To which public office did he return in 1994? (2 pts)

Part 2

11 Whose Presidency espoused the 'Square Deal' domestic policy – a notion of fairness for all? Which other President's assassination handed him the White House in 1901? With which other Republican did he fall out, splitting the party prior to the 1912 election? Which Democrat candidate reaped the benefit? (4 pts)

12 Which seven US states, by dint of their sparse population, have only one seat on the House of Representatives? (One remote, four north central, two northeast) (7 pts)

Total Points: 23. Targets: Novice 9 Pro 17. Your Score: [   ]

Quiz 198. Olympic Games

More Olympic stuff, but this time on the golden summer that was London 2012

Part 1

1   Which Great Britain swimmer followed up two Paralympic gold medals in the pool in Beijing with two more in London in 2012, both in world record times?

2   Who broke the British record for the women's 100 metres hurdles at the London Olympics in 2012?

3   Laura Trott and Dani King were two of Britain's gold medal-winning women's team pursuit trio; who was the third? Which of the trio won another gold medal? (2 pts)

4   Where were the equestrian events held at the 2012 London Olympics? How many gold medals did Team GB win? (2 pts)

5   Which Great Britain boxer won the first ever women's gold medal at the 2012 games? And who was the flag-bearer for the Ireland team who won gold in the lightweight division? (2 pts)

6   Sam Oldham, Kristian Thomas, Max Whitlock and Dan Purvis were four members of Team GB's medal-winning men's gymnastics team; who was the fifth? And in which individual discipline did he win another (silver) medal? (2 pts)

7   Which British teenager stormed through to win the Paralympic T44 100 metres in 10.90 seconds at the London 2012 Games?

8   Great Britain won twenty-nine gold medals at London 2012; but how many British athletes got a gold medal: thirty-one, forty or forty-eight?

9   Who carried the GB flag at the London 2012 closing ceremony after winning his fourth Olympic gold medal?

10 Which GB rider narrowly missed out on a 2012 Olympic showjumping medal when he clipped the third fence from the end of the Greenwich course in London?

Part 2

11 What was the venue for the archery contest at the 2012 Olympics in London?

12 In which sport were eight athletes ejected from the 2012 Olympic Games after trying to lose a match in the group stage of the competition?

13 Mo Farah won gold in the 5,000 metres and 10,000 metres; who was his training partner who won silver for the US in the 10,000 metres? In which country was Farah born before moving to the UK at the age of eight? (2 pts)

14 Which young Chinese star won both women's individual medley finals in the swimming pool? Which other teenager star took Rebecca Adlington's 800 metres freestyle title? (2 pts)

15 For all Usain Bolt's brilliance the race of the 2012 Olympics in the athletics stadium was the men's 800 metres; who won? And which British runner finished eighth and last in the final but still ran a brilliant personal best, as did seven of the eight runners? (2 pts)

16 Who directed the opening ceremony at the 2012 London Olympic Games? Who provided the soundtrack (rather than pre-released songs)? Which British actor portrayed Isambard Kingdom Brunel? Which modern inventor was given a special role? Who was escorted to the ceremony by James Bond? (5 pts)

Total Points: 27. Targets: Novice 11 Pro 20. Your Score:

Quiz 199. Reality TV

If watching unremarkable people doing nothing of interest is your thing, then knock yourself out with this one

Part 1

1   Who was the 2009 *Big Brother* entrant who attempted suicide after being ignored on the show by the woman he fancied?

2   Who was the first winner of *I'm a Celebrity, Get Me Out of Here*?

3   Where does filming for *I'm a Celebrity, Get Me Out of Here* take place?

4   Who is the only sportsperson to have won a series of *I'm a Celebrity, Get Me Out of Here*?

5   What was the popular Channel 4 series that showed ordinary people being retrained in a short time to do tasks or jobs that were out of kilter with their existing training, e.g. a Navy officer trained to be a drag artist?

6   *Frauentausch* was the German equivalent of which Channel 4 show which ran from 2003–9?

7   What was arguably TV's first reality show, created and presented by Allen Funt and launched in 1948 it used a hidden camera to highlight practical jokes?

8   Who presented *Big Brother* for its entire ten-year stint on Channel 4 and who took over for the switch to Channel 5? (2 pts)

9   After two years in Bow, east London, to where did the show move its base in 2002?

10   Which Indian actress and model was at the centre of a race row when she was criticized by other housemates in the 2007 *Celebrity Big Brother* show?

Part 2

11   Rylan Clark won *Celebrity Big Brother* in January 2013; in what way is
     Rylan a celebrity?

12   The first *Celebrity Big Brother* was timed to end on what day? Who was the
     winner? (2 pts)

13   Who won the third series of *Big Brother* and was subsequently voted fourth
     in a poll of 100 Worst Britons on Channel 4?

14   In which country is the *Big Brother* format used in a show with the title *Bigg
     Boss* (not a typo)?

15   What was the peak average viewing figures across the series of *Big
     Brother*: 5.8 million, 7.1 million or 8.3 million? And what was the figure for
     the 2012 series: 6 million, 1.8 million or 2.9 million? (2 pts)

16   Of the thirteen series of *Big Brother* to date (up to and including 2012), how
     many have been won by female contestants?

17   Which alcohol brand was the first sponsor of *Big Brother* in 2000? (a) Coors
     Lite (b) Southern Comfort (c) Magners

18   What was the name of the final series of the *Big Brother* format show to be
     aired on Channel 4 in 2010? Who won? (2 pts)

19   Who was the contestant, whose biography now lists him as a 'media
     personality', who became the first housemate-to-hate on the first series of
     Big Brother?

20   *The Only Way is Essex* is a reality show launched in 2010: who narrates the
     show and who sings the theme tune? (2 pts)

Total Points: 25. Targets: Novice 10 Pro 19. Your Score: [   ]

Quiz 200. General Knowledge

A quickie round and connection round

Part 1

1   *Twilight, New Moon, . . . , Breaking Dawn*: what is missing?

2   Which country has Luanda for a capital city? And of which former European power was it once a colony? (2 pts)

3   What gift from China arrived in the UK on 13 September 1974?

4   Owen Vister's *The Virginian* is often credited with 'inventing' the Western genre. In which year was it published: 1854, 1902 or 1939?

5   Who is Georg Hackl? (a) the designer of the famous wartime issue German handgun, the luger (b) the man credited as the first to brew authentic lager beer (c) a luger who won gold medals at five Winter Olympics from 1988 to 2002

6   Who is the only non-human to have given evidence before the US Senate, during a discussion about music in schools?

7   What rating for movies was introduced in 1982 to license non-violent pornography?

8   What physical sign is used to signify that a new Pope has been elected by the cardinals?

9   Where might you find Igglepiggle and Makka Pakka?

10 Ryan Giggs, Chris Hoy, Andrew Strauss, Jonny Wilkinson; who is the oldest and who the youngest? (2 pts)

11 Which high-profile professional footballer was jailed for six years (he served three) for causing death by dangerous driving in 2003?

12 What was the yacht with an all-female crew skippered by Tracy Edwards, which won its class in the Whitbread Round the World Race in 1989?

Part 2

A series of connected answers

13   Which singer was referenced in a Van Morrison song that later became a smash hit for Dexy's Midnight Runners?

14   Who led the resistance to the Nazis in Yugoslavia and became the country's undisputed leader after the war?

15   Who scored a hat-trick in England's opening qualifier for Euro 2012 against Bulgaria?

16   Athens 2004: Great Britain win the 4 x 100 metres gold medal. Jason Gardener, Darren Campbell, Mark Lewis-Francis and which other sprinter made up the quartet for the final?

17   Which pop star was sentenced to two months in prison for crashing his car whilst under the influence in London in 2010?

18   What's the link?

Total Points: 20. Targets: Novice 10 Pro 15. Your Score:

Answers Quizzes 193–200

Quiz 193. General Knowledge

1. Kate Winslet (Ned was born Ned Abel Smith but changed his name legally to Rocknroll; silly boy); 2. Catherine of Aragon; Catherine Howard; Catherine Parr (various spellings of Catherine allowed); 3. Kathy Burke; 4. Katy Perry (her debut single 'I Kissed a Girl' received attention disproportionate to its benign nature and a career was made); 5. Katie Holmes; *Dawson's Creek*; 6. Jordan; 7. *The Taming of the Shrew*; 8. (c) She is a newsreader; 9. The first was published in 1872 (it reads a little like a female *Tom Sawyer*); 10. Mike Catt (it was the last of his 75 caps); 11. Australian; 12. Catherine de Medici; 13. Prussia; 14. Chicago; 15. (a) Ken Loach (he made his cinema debut a year later and in 1969 made *Kes*, which cemented his position as a social commentator of note); 16. Cathode ray tubes; 17. Catherine (Cathy) Earnshaw; 18. Plain old Kate Middleton; 19. *She Stoops to Conquer* by William Goldsmith; 20. Catherine Willows

Quiz 194. Movie Directors

1. Kathryn Bigelow; 2. David Lean; 3. Joel; also Joel, although recently the brothers have taken joint credit as writers, directors and producers of their movies; 4. Ingmar Bergman; 5. Jean-Luc Godard; 6. Robert Wise; *The Sound of Music*; 7. Ken Russell; 8. Michael Mann; 9. Rob is Carl's son; 10. Steve Buscemi; 11. Jim Jarmusch; 12. *Drive*; 13. *The Kids Are All Right*; 14. *Stop Making Sense*; Neil Young; 15. James Cameron; *Terminator*; 16. Jane Campion, who is a New Zealander; 17. Ralph Fiennes; 18. Michelangelo Antonioni; 19. Clooney himself and Alexander Payne; 20. Akira Kurosawa

Quiz 195. Video Games

1. *Gran Turismo*; 2. Link; 3. *Space Invaders* (1980); *Asteroids* (1981) and *Pac-Man* (1982); 4. *Dungeons and Dragons*; Wizards of the Coast; Hasbro; 5. *Gears of War*; 6. Monkeys; 7. Sega Megadrive; 8. Rockstar Games; 9. *Drake's Fortune*, *Among Thieves* and *Drake's Deception*; 10. *Ratchet and Clank*; 11. *Assassin's Creed*; a mind-control device known as the Piece of Eden; the Knights Templar; 12. The ability to replay the game with different outcomes; 13. Disney; 14. Crash Bandicoot; 15. Hong Kong; 16. (a) first person shooter (b) platform (c) simulation (d) rpg or role playing game (e) hack and slash

Quiz 196. TV

1. 372; Nick Berry; 2. Birgitte Nyborg; 3. He was America's first African-American President, albeit a fictional one; 4. Baddiel and Skinner; Jeff Astle; 5. Peter Capaldi; 6. Mr Schuester; 7. *Dancing on the Edge*; Chiwetel Ejiofor; 8. The Banana Splits; 9. *Catchphrase*; 10. David Caruso; *CSI: Miami*; 11. *The Dukes of Hazzard*; 12. *The Fast Show*; 13. Ron

Howard; 14. The series was *The Incredible Hulk*; Bixby played Dr David Banner and Ferrigno the Hulk; 15. Taxi driver; 16. (a) Anthony Andrews (he was a good mate of Martin Shaw and there was none of the necessary friction between the two); 17. Adrian Mole; 18. Steve van Zandt, who took time off from the E-Street Band to appear as Silvio Dante in the HBO drama; 19. *Star Trek*; 20. *Twin Peaks*; 'Falling'; 21. Kermit the Frog; *Pigs in Space*; the Swedish Chef; Animal; Beaker

Quiz 197. US Politics

1. Bobby Kennedy; 2. Dan Quayle; 3. Massachusetts; 4. Andrew Johnson and Bill Clinton; 5. There are 100 Senators (two per state irrespective of size or population of that state); 6. John F. Kennedy; 7. Hussein; 8. (c) Governor of New York; 9. None (he inherited the Presidency when Nixon resigned and he was defeated by Carter in 1976); 10. Mayor of Washington; he ran for Mayor of Washington again and won; 11. Theodore Roosevelt; William McKinley; William Howard Taft; Woodrow Wilson; 12. Alaska; North and South Dakota, Montana and Wyoming; Delaware, Vermont

Quiz 198. Olympic Games

1. Ellie Simmonds; 2. Jessica Ennis in the heptathlon; 3. Joanne Rowsell; Trott also won the Omnium; 4. Greenwich Park; three (team showjumping, team dressage and Charlotte Dujardin in the individual dressage); 5. Nicola Adams; Katie Taylor; 6. Louis Smith; men's pommel horse; 7. Jonnie Peacock; 8. Forty-eight; 9. Ben Ainslie; 10. Nick Skelton; 11. Lord's Cricket Ground; 12. Badminton; 13. Galen Rupp; Somalia; 14. Ye Shiwen; Katie Ledecky of the US; 15. David Rudisha; Andrew Osagie; 16. Danny Boyle; Underworld; Kenneth Branagh; Sir Tim Berners-Lee; the Queen

Quiz 199. Reality TV

1. Sree Desari; 2. Tony Blackburn; 3. New South Wales, Australia; 4. Phil Tufnell, the former England cricketer, won the second series; 5. *Faking It*; 6. *Wife Swap*; 7. *Candid Camera*; 8. Davina McCall; Brian Dowling, the winner of the second series of the show; 9. Elstree Studios; 10. Shilpa Shetty; 11. He finished fifth in *The X Factor* in 2012 (apparently failing in one voting show qualifies you to enter another); 12. Red Nose Day; Jack Dee; 13. Jade Goody (she was also involved in the race controversy during *Celebrity Big Brother 5*, but public sympathy turned her way when she was diagnosed with cancer and subsequently died in 2009); 14. India; 15. The figures peaked at 5.8 million (and bottomed out on Channel 4 at 2.5 million for the 2009 series); 1.8 million viewers; 16. Five; 17. (b) Southern Comfort (replaced by big media brands for the next few peak years: O2, Talk Talk, Carphone Warehouse, Virgin); 18. *Ultimate Big Brother*; Brian Dowling; 19. 'Nasty Nick' Bateman; 20. Denise van Outen and Yazz ('The Only Way is Up')

Quiz 200. General Knowledge

1. *Eclipse* (they are the first four books in Stephenie Meyer's vampire series); 2. Angola; Portugal; 3. Two giant pandas; 4. 1902; 5. (c) Hankl was a great Olympian and the finest ever competitor on a luge; 6. Elmo from *Sesame Street*; 7. R-18; 8. White smoke from the chimney of the Vatican; 9. *In the Night Garden*, the bizarre children's TV pre-school programme; 10. Giggs, at thirty-nine, is the oldest, and Wilkinson the baby of the bunch at thirty-three (as of February 2013); 11. Lee Hughes; 12. *Maiden*; 13. Jackie Wilson (in 'Jackie Wilson Said (I'm in Heaven When You Smile)'); 14. Marshal Tito; 15. Jermain Defoe; 16. Marlon Devonish; 17. George Michael; 18. Jackie, Tito, Jermaine, Marlon and Michael were the five members of the Jackson 5

Quiz 201. General Knowledge

Part 1

1   Which country supplies over 90 per cent of the world's opium?

2   What type of hot climate dwellings are made from sun-dried clay bricks?

3   What is the name of Batman's butler? (Extra point for the surname)

4   *Long Way Round* and *Long Way Down* were epic motorcycle rides completed by which celebrity pair? (2 pts)

5   What was an MP's salary set at when the system was first introduced in 1911: £85, £270 or £400?

6   In which decade were the Betty Boop cartoons first drawn?

7   What took David Weir thirty-eight minutes less than Stephen Kiprotich in London in 2012?

8   What, in Japanese and Mandarin, is the unlucky number (the equivalent of our thirteen)?

9   John Edward Robinson was sentenced to death for multiple murders in 2003; he was the first convicted serial killer to have used what in his predatory habits?

10   What name is given to any other kind of freshwater fishing that does not involve fishing for gamefish (mainly salmon and trout)?

Part 2

11   Who followed Roy Plumley as host of *Desert Island Discs*?

12   What are the three different types of skiing in Olympic competition? (3 pts)

13   Approximately how many men did Napoleon's French armies lose in the Russian campaign and the disastrous retreat from Moscow in 1812: 145,000, 265,000 or 380,000?

14   The Brazilian bossa nova is a variation on which ballroom dance, also originating from Brazil?

15   Bob Dylan won an Academy Award for the song 'Things Have Changed'; for which 2000 movie soundtrack was it written?

16   Who helped found the FBI in 1935 and was the Bureau's first director, having been director of its predecessor since 1924?

17   Who was (briefly) married to Lynne Frederick after her previous husband, Peter Sellers, left her a widow?

18   Paul Hogan and Linda Koslowski became romantically involved during the making of which film?

19   Whose fictional debut was the 2010 novel, *Revenge*?

20   Lisa Gherardini is better known by what name?

Total Points: 24. Targets: Novice 12 Pro 18. Your Score: ☐

Quiz 202. War Movies

Ten straight questions and a quick-fire quiz

Part 1

1   What are the names of the two new arrivals to the Army hospital at the beginning of *M*A*S*H*, played by Donald Sutherland and Elliott Gould? (2 pts)

2   Who were the Brit/Yank combination at the heart of the success of *Where Eagles Dare* (1968), an old-fashioned throwback to wartime derring-do? (2 pts)

3   Which 1987 (Vietnam) war movie featured a real ex-marine as the hectoring Gunnery Sergeant Hartman training his new recruits?

4   Which 1964 film featured General Jack Ripper as the head of the US military?

5   Who play the three young men sent to Vietnam in Michael Cimino's *The Deer Hunter* (1978)? (3 pts)

6   Which two wartime movies earned Steven Spielberg his first two Best Director Academy Awards? (2 pts)

7   Which World War II operation was the subject of the 1977 movie *A Bridge Too Far*? The seizure of a bridge at which city was the ultimate target of the Allied paratroopers? (2 pts)

8   It was appropriate that John Wayne took the lead role in *Sands of Iwo Jima* (1949) as he had served in the Pacific during the war; true or false?

9   What was Kathryn Bigelow's 2012 follow-up to her Oscar-winning *Hurt Locker*? What was the subject matter? Who took the lead role as a driven CIA agent? (3 pts)

10   Who are the Australian troops fighting in Peter Weir's *Gallipoli* (1981)?

Part 2

We give you the film (and the year – we're generous like that); you give us the conflict in which the film was set

11 *Gone with the Wind* (1939)
12 *The Last of the Mohicans* (1992)
13 *Breaker Morant* (1980)
14 *The Duellists* (1977)
15 *Coming Home* (1978)
16 *Casablanca* (1942)
17 *Kingdom of Heaven* (2005)
18 *Cross of Iron* (1977)
19 *Jarhead* (2005)
20 *Paths of Glory* (1957)

Total Points: 28. Targets: Novice 11 Pro 21. Your Score: ☐

Quiz 203. Pets

Ten questions about man's best friend and a pet mix-up

Part 1

1   What is the most common dog breed in the UK?

2   Why were the hugely successful series of commercials by US fast food chain Taco Bell featuring a chihuahua called Gidget stopped?

3   Which TV dog was played by a Jack Russell terrier called Moose, who was succeeded in the role by his son, Enzo?

4   Cavalier King Charles Spaniel, Italian Greyhound and Shih-tzu are all eligible for which group of dog at a show?

5   Airedale, Cairn, Aberdeen and Norfolk; which of these is *not* a type of terrier?

6   A saluki, a whippet and a beagle would all come under which dog group at a show?

7   Which dog, originally bred in North America, is particularly well-adapted to water rescue due to its heavy protective coat and great size and strength?

8   Which hybrid dog was developed in the Middle Ages by poachers because it was illegal for commoners to own greyhounds?

9   What kind of dog is the cartoon legend Scooby-Doo?

10 Which Dickens character owned a bull terrier called Bulls Eye?

Part 2

Mix and Match: match the pet to the breed

1. Kingsnake; 2. Dog; 3. Gecko; 4. Newt; 5. Tortoise; 6. Cat; 7. Horse; 8. Aquarium fish; 9. Rabbit; 10. Parrot

a. African Grey; b. Dwarf Yellow Head; c. Manx; d. Lippizaner; e. Checkerboard chichlid; f. Mexican Black; g. French Angora; h. Hermans; i. Italian Crested; j. Samoyed

Your Workings:

Total Points: 20. Targets: Novice 8 Pro 15. Your Score:

Quiz 204. Business

Filthy lucre section

Part 1

1   Dame Anita Roddick, born 1942, was the founder of which high-street brand?

2   What name was given to the Irish economy during its boom years around the turn of the century?

3   What became the first telephone-only bank in 1989?

4   Which business journal was published for the first time in 1889 in the United States?

5   What famous financial institution was created by Royal Charter in 1694?

6   What was Britain's biggest export in 2009: cars, medicine or telecommunications?

7   Nine of the top ten container ports in the world are in the Far East; where is the only Western one? (Tip: it is in Europe.)

8   Where does the UK stand in the list of the top arms exporters in the world: third, fifth or seventeenth?

9   What did student Rosie Reid try to sell in her controversial contribution to eBay history in 2004? (a) her daughter (b) her virginity or (c) her peerage, as the only daughter of the Earl of Shropshire?

10 What was the biggest selling toy of 1996, inspired by a highly successful animated movie?

Part 2

11 Blockbuster, HMV, Comet, Game, Jessops; which of these retail chains did not go into administration/liquidation at the end of 2012 or beginning of 2013?

12 Which northern English city was home to both Rowntree Mackintosh and Terry's in their heyday?

13 What did Ray Kroc, a franchisee, buy from the two founder-owner brothers, Richard and Maurice, in 1955?

14 Chantiers d'Atlantique, Harland and Wolff, Blohm and Voss and Cammell Laird are all famous names in which business?

15 Which familiar high-street name was the first to offer formal dress for hire in 1860?

16 The first colour TV commercial in 1969 was for which frozen food brand?

17 Which Aussie treat was briefly rebranded as iSnack 2.0 after this awful name was deemed the best entrant to a 2009 competition?

18 In business terms (specifically used when measuring inflation) what is the RPI?

19 Which company was founded in 1901 by a gentleman whose forenames were King Camp? And which international conglomerate owns it now? (2 pts)

20 What were the five principal brands which prompted Nestlé to buy out Rowntree Mackintosh (two chocolate bars, two confectioneries and one boxed brand)? (5 pts)

Total Points: 25. Targets: Novice 10 Pro 19. Your Score:

Quiz 205. Sci-Fi Books and Comics

Part 1

1   Which character first appears in the Tintin book, *The Crab with the Golden Claws* (1941)?

2   Who wrote the *Saga of the Exiles*, a fantasy sequence involving time-travelling humans and their involvement in the feud between the Tanu and the Firvulag?

3   Which science-fantasy writer was knighted for services to literature in the 2009 New Year Honours? With what debilitating condition is he suffering? (2 pts)

4   Whose 1986 comic *Batman: The Dark Knight Returns* gave the character a new lease of life, returning to the original, darker milieu?

5   What name is given to the stylized form of Japanese comic dating back to the late nineteenth century?

6   In the series of *Batman* stories comprising 'Knightfall', who is introduced as a new nemesis? And which character covers for a recuperating Batman? (2 pts)

7   What is the name of the Egyptian wizard who allows Billy Batson to transform himself into Captain Marvel?

8   Which influential horror and sci-fi author created the Cthulhu Mythos, a shared world of old creatures and deities?

9   *The Foundation* series and *Galactic Empire* series are the work of which science-fiction writer?

10 Who created the playful fantasy world Xanth and has published over thirty works set in the world?

Part 2

11 What was the graphic novel, started in 1973, which used a cartoon strip to allegorize the Holocaust? Who created it? How were the Nazis portrayed in the work? (3 pts)

12 What is the setting for Frank Herbert's 1965 sci-fi classic, many people's pick as the out-and-out highlight of the genre?

13 Which genre within a genre comes from the title of a 1982 William Gibson short story?

14 Who created the anti-hero Thomas Covenant? From which condition, unusual in the modern age, is Covenant suffering? (2 pts)

15 *Cryptonomicon* and *Anathem* are works by which hardcore science-fiction writer?

16 As well as his Sherlock Holmes novels, Arthur Conan Doyle wrote a series of proto-sci-fi novels and stories featuring the adventurous Professor Challenger; what was the first and best-known of them, published in 1912?

17 In which year was Jules Verne's *Journey to the Centre of the Earth* published: 1864, 1895 or 1904?

18 Who wrote the seminal sci-fi works, *War of the Worlds*, *The Invisible Man* and *The Time Machine*?

19 What was the first book John Wyndham published under his own name (in 1951), now considered a classic sci-fi novel?

20 The short-story collection *The Illustrated Man* and the novel *Fahrenheit 451* were 1950s works by which writer? (a) Robert A. Heinlein (b) Brian Aldiss (c) Ray Bradbury

Total Points: 25. Targets: Novice 10 Pro 19. Your Score:

Quiz 206. Sport

A general round and a big multi-parter

Part 1

1   Who were the first sponsors of cricket's County Championship, in 1977? And who started sponsorship of one-day cricket by backing the new sixty-over matches in 1963? (2 pts)

2   Jaroslav Drobný, former Wimbledon and French Open winner, competed for Czechoslovakia in which sport at the Olympics? (a) cycling (b) ice hockey (c) field hockey (d) archery

3   Which US city was awarded the 1976 Winter Olympics only for the citizens to vote against helping to fund the event?

4   Which four English sides (up to January 2013) have won rugby union's Heineken Cup? (4 pts)

5   Which horse was declared, in 2012, formally the best ever to run? Who trained this exceptional racer? (2 pts)

6   South Africa, Qatar, Morocco, China, Australia, Barbados, Singapore; which one of these was *not* a venue for a scheduled event on the 2012 European PGA Tour?

7   Which legendary American Football star also won the Decathlon at the 1912 Olympic Games?

8   True or false: Bernie Ecclestone drove in the first Grand Prix in Monaco in 1958, finishing ninth?

9   Who was the French skiing legend who won all three Alpine events at the 1968 Winter Olympics?

10 What was the title of Lance Armstrong's 2000 autobiography detailing his fight against cancer and his route to winning multiple Tours de France?

11 Which Australian has been his country's captain for most Ashes tests?

12 Who exploded into the big-time in 1991, winning the USPGA despite entering the competition only as ninth reserve?

13 What are the five classic flat horse races in Britain? Which three courses host the races? (8 pts)

Total Points: 25. Targets: Novice 10 Pro 19. Your Score:

Quiz 207. Names

Initially, we thought . . . Oh, stop trying to be clever – all the answers are people who tend to be known by their initials and surname, e.g. J. K. Rowling

1   Crime writer; creator of Inspector Dalgleish
2   US food manufacturer with fifty-seven varieties
3   English Poet Laureate best known for *A Shropshire Lad*
4   lower case poet
5   South African PM 1978–84 and thereafter the first state President
6   Great German baroque composer, died 1750
7   Blues legend who turned eighty-seven in 2012 and is still performing
8   American-born British poet who taught Betjeman at school and became a director of publisher Faber and Faber
9   Pooh man
10   Scottish psychiatrist who wrote seminal works *The Divided Self* and *Knots*
11   England cricketer, footballer, long-jump world record holder and general sporting polymath of the Edwardian era
12   Legendary running back who may have got away with murder but still went down
13   Of Arabia
14   Playwright of the Western World?
15   Great Welsh rugby full-back
16   Creator of *Mapp and Lucia*
17   Booker-winning novelist with *Vernon God Little*
18   Comic genius, *My Little Chickadee*
19   The grandfather of cricket . . .
20   . . . and his brother

Total Points: 20. Targets: Novice 10 Pro 15. Your Score:

Quiz 208. General Knowledge

Straight up and down

Part 1

1   Who baked the cake featured on the front of the Rolling Stones album, *Let It Bleed*?

2   On 10 January 1920, the Treaty of Versailles brought what into being?

3   'Like being savaged by a dead sheep,' was Denis Healey's response to criticism by which politician, Margaret Thatcher's first Chancellor?

4   What is the name of Tintin's dog?

5   Which sprinter took the T44 100 metres, 200 metres and 400 metres titles at the 2008 Paralympics?

6   Astanga or iyengar; what are we talking about?

7   Why would a snooker player use Carvedilol?

8   What word connects a champagne glass to a vertical groove in a column?

9   What took place at Heathrow Airport on 26 November 1983?

10   Whose international rugby union team is known as the Pumas?

Part 2

11 The boy band McFly took their name from a character in which sci-fi classic?

12 'Turn on, tune in, drop out' was a famous phrase uttered during the Swinging Sixties by which US writer, born 1920?

13 When young, the Appleton sisters, Nicole and Natalie of All Saints, moved to London from which country?

14 Which Tim Burton film was turned into a Sadler's Wells ballet in 2008?

15 What connects Carly Simon, Duran Duran, Madonna, Sheryl Crow and Tom Jones?

16 Which state has the biggest number of votes in the US Electoral College, with fifty-five, and the largest number of seats in the House of Representatives with fifty-three?

17 Which footballer's early career was blighted by the management of his brothers Claude and Didier?

18 Which comedienne claims she is called 'Nana new face' by her grandson?

19 Who was the subject of a controversial new biography by Andrew Morton, published on 15 June 1992?

20 Matt Groening, born 14 February 1954, is best known as the creator of which long-running US TV series?

Total Points: 20. Targets: Novice 10 Pro 15. Your Score: [   ]

Answers Quizzes 201–208

Quiz 201. General Knowledge

1. Afghanistan; 2. Adobe; 3. Alfred Pennyforth; 4. Ewan McGregor and Charley Boorman; 5. £400 pa; 6. 1930s; 7. Winning the marathon (Weir won the Paralympic T54 marathon in 1 hour 30 minutes, Kiprotich the Olympic marathon in 2 hours 8 minutes); 8. Four; 9. He lured his victims over the internet; 10. Coarse fishing; 11. Sue Lawley; 12. Alpine, Freestyle and Cross Country (*not* slalom; slalom and downhill together make up Alpine skiing); 13. About 380,000 were lost in the campaign, with another 100,000 taken prisoner; 14. Samba; 15. *Wonder Boys*; 16. J. Edgar Hoover; 17. David Frost; 18. *Crocodile Dundee*; 19. Sharon Osbourne; 20. *La Gioconda* or the *Mona Lisa* – she was the model who sat for Leonardo

Quiz 202. War Movies

1. Hawkeye and Trapper (John); 2. Richard Burton and Clint Eastwood; 3. *Full Metal Jacket*; 4. *Dr Strangelove*; 5. Robert De Niro, John Savage and Christopher Walken; 6. *Schindler's List* (1993) and *Saving Private Ryan* (1998); 7. Operation Market Garden; Arnhem; 8. False; Wayne never served during the war, and was tormented by it (it was the studios, not the actor, who blocked his draft); 9. *Zero Dark Thirty*; the assassination of Osama Bin Laden; Jessica Chastain; 10. Turks; 11. US Civil War; 12. Anglo-French Colonial Wars; 13. Boer War; 14. Napoleonic; 15. Vietnam; 16. World War II, North African campaign; 17. The Crusades; 18. World War II, Eastern Front; 19. First Gulf War; 20. World War I, Western Front

Quiz 203. Pets

1. Labrador retriever; 2. A Hispanic lobby group protested against racial stereotyping in the ads; 3. Eddie in *Frasier*; 4. Toy dogs; 5. Aberdeen; 6. Hounds; 7. Newfoundland; 8. The lurcher; 9. Great Dane; 10. Bill Sikes in *Oliver Twist*; Mix and Match 1, f; 2, j; 3, b; 4, i; 5, h; 6, c; 7, d; 8, e; 9, g; 10, a

Quiz 204. Business

1. Body Shop; 2. Celtic Tiger; 3. First Direct; 4. *Wall Street Journal*; 5. Bank of England; 6. Medicine; 7. Rotterdam; 8. Third, behind only the US and Russia; 9. (b) she tried to sell her virginity; 10. Buzz Lightyear; 11. Game, the gaming retailer, are noticeably buoyant and seeking to occupy some of the sites deserted by these other failed businesses; 12. York; 13. McDonald's; 14. Shipbuilding; 15. Moss Bros; 16. Birds Eye peas; 17. Vegemite; 18. Retail price index; 19. Gillette; Proctor and Gamble; 20. Kit Kat, Aero, Polo, Fruit Pastilles and Quality Street

Quiz 205. Sci-Fi Books and Comics

1. Captain Haddock; 2. Julian May; 3. Terry Pratchett; early onset Alzheimer's; 4. Frank Miller; 5. Manga; 6. Bane; Azrael (Jean-Paul Valley); 7. Shazam; 8. H. P. Lovecraft; 9. Isaac Asimov; 10. Piers Anthony; 11. Maus; Art Spiegelman; as cats; 12. Dune, the sand planet; 13. Cyberpunk; 14. Stephen Donaldson; leprosy; 15. Neal Stephenson; 16. *The Lost World*; 17. 1864 (it was one of the very earliest Victorian sci-fi books – although a good argument can be made for *Frankenstein*, 1818, as the first science-fiction novel); 18. H. G. Wells; 19. *The Day of the Triffids*; 20. Ray Bradbury

Quiz 206. Sport

1. Schweppes; Gillette; 2. (b) he was part of the Czech ice hockey team at the 1948 Winter Games in St Moritz; 3. Denver, Colorado; 4. Leicester Tigers and London Wasps (twice each); Bath and Northampton Saints; 5. Frankel (there were, as always, some nay-sayers); Sir Henry Cecil; 6. Barbados; 7. Jim Thorp; 8. False. He entered as an amateur but failed to qualify; 9. Jean-Claude Killy; 10. *It's Not About the Bike* (nope, apparently it was about the drugs); 11. Alan Border (twenty-eight matches); 12. John Daly; 13. 1,000 Guineas, 2,000 Guineas (both Newmarket), Derby, Oaks (both Epsom), St Leger (Doncaster)

Quiz 207. Names

1. P. D. James; 2. H. J. Heinz; 3. A. E. Housman; 4. e. e. cummings; 5. P. W. Botha; 6. J. S. Bach; 7. B. B. King; 8. T. S. Eliot; 9. A. A. Milne; 10. R. D. Laing; 11. C. B. Fry; 12. O. J. Simpson; 13. T. E. Lawrence; 14. J. M. Synge; 15. J. P. R. Williams; 16. E. F. Benson; 17. D. B. C. Pierre; 18. W. C. Fields; 19. W. G. Grace; 20. E. F. Grace

Quiz 208. General Knowledge

1. Delia Smith; 2. The League of Nations; 3. Sir Geoffrey Howe; 4. Snowy; 5. Oscar Pistorius; 6. Yoga; 7. It is a beta blocker, used for slowing the heart rate, and would aid a steady cue arm; 8. Flute; 9. Brinks-MAT bullion robbery; 10. Argentina; 11. *Back to the Future* (the main character is Marty McFly); 12. Timothy Leary; 13. Canada; 14. *Edward Scissorhands*; 15. They have all sung Bond film songs ('Nobody Does It Better', 'View to a Kill', 'Die Another Day', 'Tomorrow Never Dies' and 'Thunderball'); 16. California; 17. Nicolas Anelka; 18. Joan Rivers; 19. Princess Diana; 20. *The Simpsons*

Quiz 209. General Knowledge

Mix and Match: I shall go and make a cuppa while you untangle this lot: match the island to the major population centre to the population of that centre

1. Colombo; 2. Nuuk; 3. Valletta; 4. Providence; 5. Havana; 6. St Helier; 7. Arrecife; 8. Port Stanley; 9. Sapporo; 10. Nassau

a. Bahamas (in 2010); b. Rhode Island (2010); c. Lanzarote (2009); d. Greenland (2010); e. Falkland Islands (2006); f. Hokkaido (2011); g. Jersey (2011); h. Sri Lanka (2011); i. Cuba (2010); j. Malta (2011)

i. 2,135,498; ii. 55,203; iii. 33,522; iv. 752,993; v. 2,115; vi. 248,948; vii. 178,042; viii. 6,966; ix. 1,921,831; x. 15,469

Total Points: 20. Targets: Novice 10 Pro 15. Your Score:

Quiz 210. Children's TV

Children's telly, both classic and recent

Part 1

1   What is the world's longest running TV programme, first broadcast in 1958 and still running today? Who was producer and (later) editor of the programme for twenty-six years from 1962? (2 pts)

2   What is the brand name adopted by the BBC for programming aimed at children from four to six years old?

3   Which cult TV animated character is helped by his friends Sam and Tucker in his efforts to save the world while keeping his supernatural state a secret?

4   What was the cult 2001 animation for young children and pre-teens about an incompetent alien's attempts to destroy the earth, with the 'help' of a malfunctioning robot called GIR?

5   Where did the Wombles live? Who was their leader? (2 pts)

6   Which drama series was axed from the BBC's schedule (as 'no longer relevant') after thirty years in 2008, around the same time as winning an online poll as the best children's TV show ever?

7   Who were the four presenters who worked on *Blue Peter* in what are nostalgically remembered as the 'golden years' from the mid-1960s to the end of the 1970s? (4 pts)

8   Who was the creative genius behind *The Muppet Show* and on which series, started in 1969, had his team already developed the puppet style that served the Muppets so well? (2 pts)

9   What were the names of the boy and girl of, respectively, the Flintstones and the Rubbles? Where did they all live? (3 pts)

10 Who is Bob the Builder's business partner and office manager? And what is his cat called? Who provides Bob's voice? (3 pts)

Part 2

11   Sportacus, Stefanie, Robbie Rotten and a host of puppets make up the cast of which odd European children's show?

12   Which programme details the adventures of Tommy Pickles, a toddler, and his friends? What is the name of his spoilt older cousin who frequently crosses the baby hero? (2 pts)

13   What type of creature is Barney? And what colour is he? (2 pts)

14   Which great dramatist read which 1928 children's classic in the last ever episode of *Jackanory* in 1996? (2 pts)

15   Who was the super-sleuth voiced by David Jason in a series which ran from 1981 to 1992 on ITV?

16   What type of creature was Professor Yaffle and in which classic stop-frame animation did he feature? (2 pts)

17   Which programme for hard-of-hearing kids ran in 1964–76 on the BBC? Who was the artist who presented a section of the show and later had his own art show on the channel? What was the name of his animated plasticine assistant? (3 pts)

18   In *He-Man and the Masters of the Universe*, what is the name of He-Man's arch-enemy? What faithful companion always fights at He-Man's side? And where does the hero live and get his power? (3 pts)

19   Who was the narrator of *Thomas the Tank Engine and Friends* when it first started as a TV show in 1984? Who took over as narrator in 1991? (2 pts)

20   What colour are 3 and 5, the main female Numberjacks in the educational children's TV series? (2 pts)

Total Points: 40. Targets: Novice 16 Pro 30. Your Score:

Quiz 211. TV Cops

More TV but this time for grown-ups – a quiz on TV sleuths

Part 1

1 What is the name of the detective in the original series of *The Killing*?
2 'Book 'em Danno' was a familiar line uttered by which policeman in which show? (2 pts)
3 'The Dead of Jericho', written by Anthony Minghella, was broadcast on 6 January 1987; which ITV programme had hit the screens?
4 Who played Gene Hunt in the US version of *Life on Mars*?
5 Which 1970s cop drama played on the man-out-of-his-environment set-up with a policeman from New Mexico on secondment, big hat and all, to New York?
6 What connects TV investigators Perry Mason and Ironside?
7 Nikki, Jack and Clarissa are the current line-up (2013) of which long-running UK crime show? Who was the original team leader and who took the role for eight series? (3 pts)
8 Who came before and after Emma Peel in *The Avengers*? (2 pts)
9 Captain Furillo, Sgt Esterhaus, Sgt Goldblume and Officer Renko are amongst the lead characters in which 1980s broad canvas TV show, regarded as a primary influence on many later shows?
10 Who is the police officer Richard Castle shadows in the police procedural comedy-drama *Castle*? What name does he give her in his novels? (2 pts)

Part 2

11 Who plays DCI John Luther and who is his lawyer friend Mark North? (2 pts)
12 What was Colin Bateman's crime drama, starting in 2003 and starring James Nesbitt in the title role?
13 What connects John Hannah and Ken Stott?
14 Who played the psychologist character created by crime writer Val McDermid for *Wire in the Blood*?
15 Who played Wallander in the UK version of the Scandinavian police show?
16 Which four actors made up the central team for the first eight series of *New Tricks*? Who joined the cast for the ninth series in 2012? (5 pts)

Total Points: 26. Targets: Novice 10 Pro 20. Your Score: ☐

Quiz 212. Rock and Pop

A normal round and a Mix and Match section

Part 1

1   *Odyssey and Oracle* was the first album recorded in Abbey Road studios after the Beatles made *Sgt. Pepper's Lonely Hearts Club Band*; who claim it as their magnum opus?

2   Who gave an incendiary live performance at Leeds University on Valentine's Day in 1970?

3   What was Mumford & Sons debut album? In which year was it released? What was the 2012 follow-up, the fastest-selling record of the year? (3 pts)

4   American band Vetiver also perform as the backing band to which singer-songwriter?

5   Which band announced the unashamedly commercial Filthy Lucre Tour in 1996?

6   Who was the sassy lead singer of 1960s hippie band Jefferson Airplane, one of rock's first wild-child women?

7   If you were listening to Matt Beringer sing live, which band would you be watching?

8   Who reached no. 1 in the UK for the first time as a guest vocalist on Professor Green's 'Read All About It'?

9   The addition of which charismatic, alcohol-fuelled singer turned struggling Glaswegian band Tear Gas into one of Scotland's most in-demand acts in the 1970s?

10 Which American singer was a journalist at the English music magazine *NME* before she launched the abrasive post-punk band Pretenders?

Part 2

Mix and Match: match the band with their place of origin

1. Editors; 2. Kaiser Chiefs; 3. Stone Roses; 4. Def Leppard; 5. Fine Young Cannibals; 6. Ian Dury; 7. Manic Street Preachers; 8. Echo and the Bunnymen; 9. Specials; 10. Massive Attack

a. Liverpool; b. Manchester; c. Birmingham; d. South Wales; e. Bristol; f. Coventry; g. Newcastle; h. Leeds; i. Sheffield; j. East London

Your Workings:

Total Points: 22. Targets: Novice 9 Pro 17. Your Score:

Quiz 213. Military History

Fifteen normal questions and a multi-parter

Part 1

1   The Luftwaffe attack that was repulsed in the Battle of Britain was the prelude to a planned invasion of Britain; what was its codename?

2   Where did the army of King Henry IV defeat the rebels and kill his principal antagonist (and former ally) Henry 'Hotspur' Percy, heir to the dukedom of Northumberland?

3   Which famous battle put an end to Napoleon's ambition to invade England in 1805?

4   William Westmoreland was a senior general and later Chief of Staff during which conflict involving the US? (a) American Civil War (b) Vietnam (c) World War II

5   Which gun was developed by Major Reginald Shepherd and Harold Turpin in Enfield in the early days of World War II?

6   From which port were the British and Allied forces evacuated from France in May–June 1940?

7   The Canadian Corps mounted a spectacular assault and took which key landmark during the 1917 Battle of Arras?

8   Huaihai was the epic battle that settled which conflict?

9   William Foster and Co. developed a prototype vehicle called Little Willie in 1915; what was it?

10   What kind of weapon was a Jezail?

Part 2

11 Which British colonial soldier drubbed the numerically superior army of the Nawab of Bengal at the 1757 Battle of Plassey?

12 Who led a raid on Harpers Ferry in 1859 that set in motion the disagreements and disaffection that would escalate into the American Civil War?

13 Matilda, Crusader, Cavalier and Cromwell were all types of what used by the British military in World War II?

14 Who was Margaret Thatcher's Secretary of State for Defence in her War Cabinet during the Falklands War? (a) John Nott (b) Admiral Lewin (c) Francis Pym

15 What name was given to the Ottoman Sultan's household troops until 1826?

16 Where did a few hundred allied Greek soldiers (including about 300 Spartans) conduct a legendary defence of a narrow pass in defiance of a vast Persian army in 480 BC? Who led this courageous last stand? Which king led the Persians? In response to which humiliating defeat (made famous by the means of communicating victory used by the Greeks) of ten years before did the invasion take place? Which naval battle later the same year saw the Persians forced into retreat? (5 pts)

Total Points: 20. Targets: Novice 8 Pro 15. Your Score: [ ]

Quiz 214. Ashes

More than a century of cricketing squabbles over the contents of a little urn and yet here we are only asking you about the last eight years or so

Part 1

1   Who was the only bowler on either side to take more than twenty wickets in the 2010–11 Ashes series in Australia?

2   Who was the last England captain to win consecutive Ashes series?

3   Who averaged 76.4 in the 2001 Ashes series in England and a mere 19.8 four years later?

4   When England made Australia follow-on in the fourth test of the 2005 Ashes series, how long was it since this had happened to Australia: 85, 146 or 191 tests?

5   Who scored a double hundred in the Adelaide test of 2006 and still finished on the losing side?

6   In 2005 England turned the tide when they scored over 400 on the first day at over five runs an over; who top scored with 90 off 102 balls? And whose seventeen overs for Australia went for 111? Who took the vital last wicket as England won by three runs and who was left stranded for Australia after a valiant rearguard 43 not out? (4 pts)

7   What was the formidable England seam quartet who gave Australia no let-up as the Ashes were won back in 2005? (4 pts)

8   Who topped the Australian wicket-taking list in 2006–7 as they white-washed a complacent and shambolic England 5–0 in the test series? Who resisted valiantly for England, scoring 490 runs at an average of over fifty? (2 pts)

9   Who came into the England side for the fifth and final test in the 2009 Ashes series and scored a hundred in the second innings as England clinched the game and the series? Whom did he replace? (2 pts)

10 Who took nine wickets each as Australia won the third test in Perth to square the series in 2010–11? How many wickets did Australian spinners take in the series at a cost of 679 runs? (3 pts)

Part 2

11   Who was the substitute fielder who ran out Australian captain Ricky
     Ponting during the crucial fourth test in the 2005 Ashes series? On which
     ground was the match played? For which county was the player registered?
     With whom did Ponting exchange words on his arrival back in the pavilion?
     Who was off the field to make way for the substitute? (5 pts)

12   Name the five England batsmen who averaged over fifty in the 2010–11
     Ashes series in Australia. (5 pts)

Total Points: 30. Targets: Novice 12 Pro 23. Your Score:

Quiz 215. World Cup

Another great sporting contest – a World Cup quiz; some straight questions and then a few thinking-cap questions

Part 1

1   Scotland have appeared eight times at the World Cup finals (a record unlikely to alter in the near future); how many times have they made it past the group stage?

2   When a dog ran on to the pitch during England's 3–1 defeat by Brazil at the 1962 World Cup, which England striker caught the runaway mutt? And why did he regret it? (2 pts)

3   Whose disgraceful play-acting saw Turkey's Hakan Ünsal dismissed in the 2002 World Cup semi-final?

4   After Brazil in 2014, which next two countries will host the 2018 and 2022 World Cup tournaments? (2 pts)

5   Which two sides have beaten England more than once in open play at the World Cup finals? (2 pts)

6   Which team have played in most World Cup finals tournaments without winning the trophy?

7   Who connects the Northern Ireland teams that performed heroically at the 1958 and 1982 World Cup tournaments?

8   Which players from each of these four countries have managed ten goals in World Cup finals: Argentina, England, Peru and Poland? (4 pts)

9   Who is the highest scorer in World Cup finals for the Netherlands, with seven goals?

10 Which two players tangled leading to a famous red card in the 2006 World Cup final? Which two players had scored the goals which made the match 1–1 at the time? Who was the only man to miss a penalty in the ensuing shoot-out? (5 pts)

Part 2

11 Which four German players have scored ten or more goals in World Cup finals matches? (4 pts)

12 Who were the four Leeds players in the Scotland team which held Brazil to a 0–0 draw in the 1974 World Cup finals? (4 pts)

13 Which Premier League player scored Jamaica's first goal in a World Cup finals match (a 3–1 defeat) against Croatia in 1998? Which club was he with? Which teenager provided the cross and which English club signed him later that summer (he stayed until 2012)? (4 pts)

14 Which side denied England a qualifying spot at the 1974 World Cup finals? Who was their goalkeeper, famously described as 'a clown' by TV pundit Brian Clough, who defied England at Wembley in a 1–1 draw? Which future manager of Wales scored for Wales at Wembley in another 1–1 draw that would eventually cost England? Who scored nine goals in six qualifying games as Italy pipped England again four years later? Who took over as England coach from Don Revie halfway through this campaign? Who was manager for the disastrous 1994 qualifying campaign? Which two sides finished ahead of an unimaginative England team in the group? (8 pts)

Total Points: 40. Targets: Novice 16 Pro 30. Your Score:

Quiz 216. General Knowledge

Part 1

1   What became known as 'Wilson's gravy' in the 1960s, due to then Prime Minister Harold Wilson's supposed enthusiasm for the product?

2   Which worldwide financial body came into being in 1945?

3   Who manufactures the game console, Xbox?

4   Which 1980s band took their name from characters in the *Tintin* books of Herge?

5   Which British sporting legend won eleven Paralympic gold medals (sixteen medals in total) between 1992 and 2004?

6   What was the UK's first HIV/AIDS charity, launched in 1982?

7   The 'legal high' mephedrone is the scientific name for which twenty-first-century street drug?

8   What term is given to the solid slab above a doorway in older buildings, supported either on columns or adjacent walls?

9   Three Rembrandt paintings and some other exhibits were stolen from the Isabella Stewart Gardner Museum in 1990 in which US city?

10 What is unusual about the Bay to Breakers 12 km run in San Francisco?

11 What connects Northampton RFC and Southampton FC?

12 Who was executed by firing squad in Utah State prison on 17 January 1977?

Part 2

13 The Rolling Stones had eight no. 1 hit singles in the UK, and eight in the US, but, rather oddly, only four topped the chart on both sides of the Atlantic, all between 1965 and 1969; what were the four songs? (4 pts)

14 Which four sides since World War II have managed to retain the FA Cup the following season? (4 pts)

Total Points: 20. Targets: Novice 10 Pro 15. Your Score: [   ]

Answers Quizzes 209–216

Quiz 209. General Knowledge

Mix and Match 1, h, iv; 2, d, x; 3, j, viii; 4, b, vii; 5, i, i; 6, g, iii; 7, c, ii; 8, e, v; 9, f, ix; 10, a, vi

Quiz 210. Children's TV

1. *Blue Peter*; Biddy Baxter; 2. CBeebies; 3. Danny Phantom; 4. *Invader Zim*; 5. Wimbledon Common; Great Uncle Bulgaria; 6. *Grange Hill*; 7. Valerie Singleton (1962–72), John Noakes (1965–78), Peter Purves (1967–78), Lesley Judd (1972–9); 8. Jim Henson; *Sesame Street*; 9. Pebbles and Bamm-Bamm; Bedrock; 10. Wendy; Pilchard; Neil Morrissey; 11. *Lazy Town*; 12. *Rugrats*; Angelica; 13. Barney is a purple dinosaur; 14. Alan Bennett read *The House at Pooh Corner* by A. A. Milne; 15. Dangermouse; 16. A woodpecker in *Bagpuss*; 17. *Vision On*; Tony Hart (*Take Hart*); Morph; 18. Skeletor; Battle Cat (accept Cringer, the cat); Castle Grayskull; 19. Ringo Starr; Michael Angelis; 20. Pink and turquoise

Quiz 211. TV Cops

1. Sarah Lund; 2. Steve McGarrett in *Hawaii Five-0*; 3. *Inspector Morse*; 4. Harvey Keitel; 5. *McCloud*; 6. They were both played by Raymond Burr; 7. *Silent Witness*; Sam Ryan (Amanda Burton); 8. Cathy Gale (played by Honor Blackman) and Tara King (played by Linda Thorson); 9. *Hill Street Blues*; 10. Kate Beckett; Nikki Heat; 11. Idris Elba; Paul McGann; 12. *Murphy's Law*; 13. Both have played Ian Rankin's Inspector Rebus on TV; 14. Robson Green; 15. Kenneth Branagh; 16. Amanda Redman, James Bolam, Alun Armstrong, Dennis Waterman; Denis Lawson

Quiz 212. Rock and Pop

1. The Zombies; 2. The Who; 3. *Sigh No More*, 2009; *Babel*; 4. Devendra Banhart; 5. It was the Sex Pistols reunion tour; 6. Grace Slick; 7. The National; 8. Emeli Sandé; 9. Alex Harvey (they became the Sensational Alex Harvey Band); 10. Chrissie Hynde; Mix and Match 1, g; 2, h; 3, b; 4, i; 5, c; 6, j; 7, d; 8, a; 9, f; 10, e

Quiz 213. Military History

1. Operation Sealion; 2. Shrewsbury; 3. Battle of Trafalgar (Napoleon had 180,000 troops massed at Boulogne in anticipation of a French naval victory); 4. (b) Vietnam (Westmoreland was in charge for the most intense period of the war in 1964–8 before his move 'upstairs'); 5. Sten gun (an acronym of their names and Enfield); 6. Dunkirk; 7. Vimy Ridge; 8. The Chinese Civil War (it confirmed the Communist Party as China's new rulers); 9. A tank (they were developed to counter the awkward terrain presented by trench warfare); 10. A long-barrelled, accurate musket (it was favoured by the Afghan tribesmen who

successfully resisted a British invasion in 1839); 11. Robert Clive or Clive of India (Clive committed suicide, his reputation spoiled by an attempted official censure for his high-handed methods on a second stint in India); 12. John Brown; 13. Tank; 14. John Nott, although the others were both part of the War Cabinet; 15. Janissaries; 16. Thermopylae; King Leonidas of Sparta; King Xerxes I; Battle of Marathon (after which, according to legend, a messenger ran to bring news of the victory to Athens); Battle of Salamis

Quiz 214. Ashes

1. James Anderson with twenty-four; 2. Andrew Strauss in 2009 and then 2010/11; 3. Damien Martyn; 4. 191 tests; 5. Paul Collingwood; 6. Marcus Trescothick; Brett Lee; Steve Harmison; Lee again; 7. Andrew Flintoff, Steve Harmison, Matthew Hoggard and Simon Jones (with Ashley Giles lending solid support they didn't have a weak link, whereas the fourth bowler was a constant issue for Australia); 8. Stuart Clark; Kevin Pietersen; 9. Jonathan Trott; Ravi Bopara (the test careers of the two are living proof that natural talent is only half the game); 10. Mitchell Johnson and Ryan Harris (they contributed zilch in the other four matches); five (three for Xavier Doherty, one each for Michael Beer and part-time bowler Marcus North; Swann took fifteen for England); 11. Gary Pratt; Trent Bridge; Durham; Duncan Fletcher, the England coach (Ponting was upset that England had used subs frequently throughout the series); Simon Jones (he didn't bowl again that summer, making a nonsense of Ponting's outburst; the Australian captain did later apologize); 12. Alistair Cook, Jonathan Trott, Ian Bell, Kevin Pietersen and Matt Prior

Quiz 215. World Cup

1. None (they have the unfortunate record of most appearances in the finals without making the knockout rounds – Wales and both Irish teams have gone further); 2. Jimmy Greaves; the dog weed on him; 3. Rivaldo of Brazil; 4. Russia in 2018, Qatar in 2022 (neither is remotely fit for purpose but when has that ever bothered FIFA?); 5. Brazil (1962, 1970 and 2002) and Germany (1970 as West Germany and 2010); 6. Mexico have appeared fourteen times (one more than England); 7. Billy Bingham, who played in 1958 and was the manager in 1982; 8. Gabriel Batistuta, Gary Lineker, Teófilo Cubillas and Grzegorz Lato (Batistuta got a few 'soft' goals, the others delivered when it mattered, Cubillas carried his side almost single-handedly and possessed one of the most explosive shots in football history); 9. No, it isn't Cruyff (or Van Basten), it's Johnny Rep; 10. Zinedine Zidane and Marco Materazzi; Zidane and Materazzi; David Trezeguet; 11. Miroslav Klose, Gerd Müller, Jürgen Klinsmann and Helmut Rahn (Rahn was a goalscoring winger and notori-ous boozer in the German side that won in 1954; bad luck if you went for Rummenigge who got nine; 12. David Harvey, Billy Bremner, Peter Lorimer and Joe Jordan; 13. Robbie Earle (Wimbledon); Ricardo Gardner (Bolton Wanderers); 14. Poland; Jan Tomaszewski; John Toshack; Roberto Bettega; Joe Mercer; Graham Taylor; Norway and Holland.

Quiz 216. General Knowledge

1. HP Sauce; 2. International Monetary Fund; 3. Microsoft; 4. The Thompson Twins, although in *Tintin* the two are called Thomson and Thompson (different spellings); 5. Wheelchair racer Tanni Grey-Thompson; 6. Terrence Higgins Trust; 7. Meow meow; 8. Lintel; 9. Boston; 10. Most competitors run naked; 11. Both are nicknamed the Saints; 12. Gary Gilmore; 13. '(I Can't Get No) Satisfaction', 'Get Off My Cloud' (both 1965), 'Paint It Black' (1966) and 'Honky Tonk Women' (1969); 14. Newcastle (1951–2), Tottenham (1961–2 and 1981–2), Arsenal (2002–3) and; Chelsea (2009–10)

Quiz 217. General Knowledge

Part 1

1 Which company opened its first fish and chip restaurant near Leeds in 1928?

2 Who did Barack Obama appoint as head of military operations in Afghanistan after sacking his predecessor?

3 Which singer successfully sued the BNP in 2009 for using one of her songs without permission on an advertising campaign? What was the song? (2 pts)

4 Who, aged twenty in 1989, became the youngest principal dancer at the Royal Ballet?

5 Which city provides the setting for Michael Mann's 1995 crime movie, *Heat*?

6 What do Hunterston and Torness in Scotland, Trawsfynydd in Wales, Oldbury on the Severn Estuary and Dungeness in Kent have in common?

7 What was first produced by Albert Hoffmann in 1938 from ergotamine, a fungus-derived chemical?

8 Sculptor Eric Gill was also one of the earlier artists working in what medium, through which his name is immortalized?

9 Who escaped from Wandsworth prison in July 1965, just over a year into a thirty-year prison sentence?

10 Which sporting event was British TV's most watched broadcast in 1998?

Part 2

11 What would be the Western equivalent of a Japanese *ikebana* enthusiast?

12 Where is the hormone melatonin produced in the brain, and what is its principal purpose? (2 pts)

13 Who was born Nicolas Coppola in 1964?

14 The melody for the hymn, 'I vow to thee, my country', was adapted by Gustav Holst from which of his own works?

15 Whose multimillion-selling greatest hits album was simply entitled *Legend*?

16 What was the prison in Iraq where US soldiers were prosecuted for torturing prisoners?

17 Who was the actress briefly married to Mike Tyson?

18 Which actor was the first male nude centrefold in *Cosmopolitan* magazine?

19 What car was launched as the saviour of British Leyland on 7 October 1980?

20 What nickname is shared by a former royal and a rapper?

Total Points: 22. Targets: Novice 11 Pro 17. Your Score: ☐

Quiz 218. Sci-Fi Movies

Strange places and aliens – another sci-fi quiz

Part 1

1 Which spaceship (also the title) in a 1974 movie has Doolittle, Pinback, Boiler and Talby?

2 Which two actors played the central character Joe in Rian Johnson's film *Looper*? (2 pts)

3 What is the period setting for Guillermo del Toro's *Pan's Labyrinth* (2006)?

4 What was the cheesy 1966 sci-fi classic that saw scientists shrunk and injected into a sick man's bloodstream? Who was along for the ride as a token female? (2 pts)

5 Who provided the narration at the beginning of each sequence of *The Princess Bride* (1987)? What is the name of the princess? (2 pts)

6 What was the 1975 film, from a story by Ira Levin, about the strangely perfect wives and mothers of a typical suburban American town?

7 Who connects Uncle Fester in *The Addams Family* movies to Doc Brown in the *Back to the Future* series?

8 What are the names of the characters played by Laurence Fishburne and Carrie-Anne Moss in *The Matrix* trilogy? (2 pts)

9 In what year is the cult sci-fi movie *Barbarella* set: 5,000, 20,000 or 40,000? And who is the character, played by Milo O'Shea, that Barbarella is sent to look for at the start of the movie? (2 pts)

10 What is the name of the computer on board the ship in *2001: A Space Odyssey*?

Part 2

11   *Contact* was a 1997 Robert Zemeckis film about intelligent alien life; who wrote the source novel and who played scientist Ellie Arroway? (2 pts)

12   What was Ron Howard's 1995 film about a real 1970 lunar mission and who played the Commander, Jim Lovell, at the centre of the story? (2 pts)

13   What is the name of Buffy's watcher in the movie of *Buffy the Vampire Slayer*? And which actress played this first prototype Slayer? (2 pts)

14   What was the 2005 movie that finished off the story started in the hastily abandoned TV series *Firefly*?

15   Who wrote the source books for *Minority Report*, *The Adjustment Bureau* and *Total Recall*?

16   Agent Smith is the nemesis of the freed humans re-entering the matrix in *The Matrix* trilogy; what other five surnames are used for agent programmes in the films? (5 pts)

Total Points: 28. Targets: Novice 11 Pro 21. Your Score: ☐

Quiz 219. Discoveries and Inventions

A quiz on the Eureka moments that changed our lives

Part 1

1 What did John Boyd Dunlop develop in 1887 to alleviate headaches induced in bicyclists by uneven roads?

2 What was John Harrison (1693–1776) famous for designing and crafting?

3 What was the principal function of the pulley system invented in the third century BC and known as Archimedes' Screw?

4 Which Mancunian scientist first developed the theory that atoms of different elements combined in specific ratios to make familiar compounds, paving the way for chemical atomic theory?

5 Who devised dynamite and gelignite as a means for blasting tunnels, mines and quarries in the nineteenth century?

6 Hahn, Strassman, Meitner, Frisch and Fermi were amongst the scientists who contributed to the discovery of what in the 1940s?

7 Velcro comes from *velours* and *crochet*, which are the French words for what?

8 In 1522 Juan Sebastián del Cano (or Elcano) completed the first circumnavigation of the world; who began the expedition as its captain but was killed en route?

9 Frozen food was pioneered by whom? (a) George Dewhurst, a butcher (b) Emrys Findus, a fishmonger (c) Clarence Birdseye, founder of Birds Eye foods

10 What name is given to the theory that, when considering various hypotheses to cover a situation, opt for the one which makes least assumptions?

Part 2

Mix and Match: match the inventor to their contribution

1. Typewriter; 2. Gramophone; 3. Hydraulic lift; 4. Spinning frame; 5. Petrol engine; 6. Windscreen wipers; 7. Bagless vacuum cleaner; 8. Laser; 9. Hovercraft; 10. Colour photography

a. Richard Arkwright, 1768; b. Mary Anderson, 1902; c. Christopher Cockerill, 1959; d. Thomas Edison, 1877; e. Gottlieb Daimler, 1885; f. James Clerk Maxwell, 1861; g. Charles Townes, 1960; h. Elisha Otis, 1854; i. James Dyson, 1991; j. William Burt, 1829

Your Workings:

Total Points: 20. Targets: Novice 8 Pro 15. Your Score:

Quiz 220. History

Ten straight and a Mix and Match section

Part 1

1   Which great ancient city fell to the Persian Empire in 539 BC?
2   What was the gift to secretaries everywhere of Marcus Tullius Tiro in the seventh century BC?
3   Which historian's *Annals* and *Histories* chronicle the years from the death of Augustus to the Year of Four Emperors in AD 70?
4   In which country did Sirimavo Bandaranaike become the modern world's first female head of government?
5   What name was given to the followers of the banned fourteenth-century preacher, John Wycliffe?
6   Russian tanks rolled into the streets of which European capital city in 1956 after an uprising led by that country's Prime Minister?
7   Which of the following did not offer support to the US during the Vietnam War: Australia, New Zealand, South Korea or the United Kingdom?
8   Simon Sudbury, the Archbishop of Canterbury, was beheaded during which uprising?
9   How many colonies (states in modern parlance) rebelled against British expansion of Quebec (formerly French Canada) into the area around the Great Lakes in the 1770s?
10 Women serving in the forces during the war could be in the WAAF, the ATS or the WRNS; what do these acronyms stand for? (3 pts)

Part 2

Mix and Match: match the date to the event

1. 490 BC; 2. 312; 3. 1564; 4. 476; 5. *c.*1600 BC; 6. 1455; 7. 1687; 8. 1088; 9. 1509; 10. 1825

a. Fall of the Western Roman Empire; b. Modern alphabet invented; c. Birth of Shakespeare; d. Invention of the watch; e. Battle of Marathon where the Greeks repelled the Persians; f. World's first university founded in Bologna; g. First steam locomotive built (the *Rocket*); h. Newton publishes his *Principia Mathematica*; i. Roman Emperor Constantine converted to Christianity; j. First book printed with moveable type

Your Workings:

Total Points: 22. Targets: Novice 9 Pro 17. Your Score:

Quiz 221. Fine Art and Architecture

Ten questions and a Mix and Match section about art and architecture

Part 1

1 Who was the French painter, linked to the Impressionists, who developed the style of painting with myriad tiny dots that became known as pointillism?

2 What was John James Audubon noted for painting?

3 Who designed the great church in Barcelona called the Sagrada Familia?

4 Art collector Peggy Guggenheim was married for a while to which important modern artist? (a) Marcel Duchamp (b) Max Ernst (c) Mark Rothko

5 The start of the Italian Renaissance is dated by some scholars as beginning with a sculptor, Donatello, a painter, Masaccio and an architect; who was the architect?

6 Where in Britain, in 1992, did a serious fire threaten one of the world's great art collections?

7 Which arts and crafts school was founded by Walter Gropius in Weimar in 1919?

8 Which of these was *not* designed, at least in part, by Sir Christopher Wren: Greenwich Observatory; Ashmolean Museum, Oxford; Brighton Pavilion; Hampton Court Palace?

9 What architectural term is used for a building with a circular plan and (usually) a domed roof?

10 British artist Anthony Caro is active in which artistic endeavour?

Part 2

Mix and Match: match the architect to their famous edifice

1. Norman Foster; 2. Charles Barry; 3. Giles Gilbert Scott; 4. Jorn Utzon; 5. John Soane; 6. Christopher Wren; 7. James Gibbs; 8. Richard Rogers; 9. Charles Rennie Mackintosh; 10. Nicholas Grimshaw

a. Sydney Opera House; b. St Paul's Cathedral, London; c. Glasgow School of Art; d. Anglican Cathedral, Liverpool; e. Houses of Parliament; f. Eden Project, Cornwall; g. Millennium Dome; h. Wembley Stadium; i. St Martin-in-the-Fields; j. Bank of England

Your Workings:

Total Points: 20. Targets: Novice 8 Pro 15. Your Score:

Quiz 222. Boxing

The noble art, which is the rather inappropriate nickname for boxing – twenty straight questions

Part 1

1   Who became WBO light-heavyweight world champion after the incumbent Jürgen Brähmer was unable to fight due to a pending court case and then claimed he had an eye injury three days before the rescheduled fight?
2   What was the venue for the 'Fight of the Century', the fight between Muhammad Ali and Joe Frazier in 1971?
3   Who beat James DeGale for the British super-middleweight title in May 2011?
4   Who wrote *The Fight*, an account of the author's experiences at the famous Ali–Foreman World Heavyweight Championship fight in 1974?
5   What is the name of Muhammad Ali's boxer daughter?
6   Who was the first fighter to beat Ricky Hatton?
7   Who gave his name to the belts awarded to British boxing title holders?
8   From which boxer did Muhammad Ali (then Cassius Clay) first win the heavyweight world title?
9   Which world title-holding boxer was known as Hands of Stone?
10 The Rumble in the Jungle, the 1974 Ali–Foreman world title fight, took place in which African city?

Part 2

11 Who retired as Middleweight World Champion in 1977 after a record four-teen successful defences?

12 Boxing fans in London caused a near-riot when Marvin Hagler beat which home favourite for the World Middleweight title?

13 Which British boxer became World Featherweight Champion in 1985?

14 Who ran a heavyweight tournament in the mid-1980s in an attempt to clarify the heavyweight supremacy? Who emerged as undisputed champion in 1987? (2 pts)

15 Which two British boxers contested the fight known as Judgement Day, a WBO/WBC Super-Middleweight unifier? (2 pts)

16 Who nearly died after a 1991 world title fight with Chris Eubank? Where did the fight take place? (2 pts)

17 Which fighter was known as the Golden Boy?

18 Who beat Evander Holyfield to become undisputed Heavyweight Champion in 1999?

19 Who won Britain's only boxing gold medal at the 2008 Olympics in Beijing?

20 What was the venue for Lennox Lewis's pummelling of Mike Tyson in 2002? Why not Las Vegas? (2 pts)

Total Points: 24. Targets: Novice 10 Pro 18. Your Score:

Quiz 223. Theatre

Things theatrical – ten straight questions and a Mix and Match section

Part 1

1 Keira Knightley made her West End stage debut in 2009 in which play by the French comedy dramatist Molière?

2 Angela Worthington is the mother of which theatrical trio? For what popular song is she remembered? (4 pts)

3 Whose first play, *Forty Years On*, opened in the West End in 1969?

4 What was the David Hare play that saw Nicole Kidman bare all on the London stage?

5 True or false: Brian Blessed was in the original production of *Cats*?

6 Who played Viola in Sir Peter Hall's 2011 production of *Twelfth Night* at the National Theatre?

7 Who performed Mark Ravenhill's one-man musical about the Great Plague of London, *Ten Plagues* (2011)?

8 By what name are musical comedy duo Laura Corcoran and Matthew Floyd Jones better known professionally?

9 What are the names of the three stages at the Royal National Theatre? (3 pts)

10 *Cloud Nine*, *Top Girls* and *Serious Money* were all plays written at the height of which modern playwright's popularity?

Part 2

Mix and Match: match the musical to the composers and lyricists

1. *Into the Woods*; 2. *West Side Story*; 3. *Annie Get Your Gun*; 4. *Jerry Springer: The Opera*; 5. *Kiss Me, Kate*; 6. *The Sound of Music*; 7. *Brigadoon*; 8. *Miss Saigon*; 9. *Jesus Christ Superstar*; 10. *Legally Blonde*

a. Richard Rodgers and Oscar Hammerstein II; b. Stephen Sondheim; c. Andrew Lloyd Webber and Tim Rice; d. Irving Berlin; e. Alan Jay Lerner and Frederick Loewe; f. Claude-Michel Schönberg and Alain Boublil; g. Nell Benjamin and Laurence O'Keefe; h. Cole Porter; i. Leonard Bernstein and Stephen Sondheim; j. Richard Thomas and Stewart Lee

Your Workings:

Total Points: 25. Targets: Novice 10 Pro 19. Your Score:

Quiz 224. General Knowledge

Well, it is if you listen to the radio . . .

Part 1

1   Who celebrated forty-five years as presenter of Radio 4's *Just a Minute* in 2012?

2   Who succeeded Chris Moyles on the Radio 1 breakfast show in 2012?

3   What was the rather morbid luxury chosen on *Desert Island Discs* by Stephen Fry and Lynn Barber?

4   Who were the team of impressionists who ran for three popular seasons on Radio 4 before transferring to TV in 2002?

5   Where would you find the Aldridges, the Woolleys and the Grundys? (2pts – detail needed for both points)

6   Who moved from Five Live to *Woman's Hour* in 2007? Which long-standing presenter did she join to anchor the show? (2 pts)

7   Along with Tim Brooke-Taylor, Barry Cryer and Graeme Garden, who was the fourth panellist on *I'm Sorry, I Haven't a Clue* from 1974 until his death in 1996? And who was the show's host from 1972 to his death in 2008? Who has replaced him as regular host after a series of guest appearances in the role? (3 pts)

8   Which 'trilogy' in five parts was originally conceived as a radio programme and transmitted in 1978? Which familiar radio voice was hired as the narrator (or The Book, as the programme billed him)? (2 pts)

9   Which radio and TV personality presented the first show on BBC 6 Music, the Beeb's new digital channel in 2002? (a) Tom Robinson (b) Stuart Maconie (c) Phil Jupitus

10   Who has hosted a weekday evening show on Radio 1 since 2003 when his contract at XFM ended?

Part 2

11 Which station was originally known as Melody FM before it was purchased by magazine empire Emap in the late 1980s?

12 Which ex-footballer, no stranger to the glare of the media, hosts a weekly post-match phone-in on Talksport on Saturday evenings (as of January 2013)?

13 *Round at Chris's* was a Saturday morning radio show which kick-started the rise to stardom of Chris Evans; on which station did it air? Who was his co-host? (2 pts)

14 What was aired on Radio 1 for the first time on 1 October 1967?

15 Which commercial radio station dominated the sector after the demise of pirate station Radio Caroline in 1967–8? On what wavelength was it transmitting? (2 pts)

16 Which Radio 4 comedy stars Julia Sawalha and is based on a comic strip from the *Guardian* newspaper?

17 Which radio comedy, transmitted for eighteen years from 1959, concerned life aboard the HMS *Troutbridge*, and starred Leslie Phillips, Ronnie Barker and Jon Pertwee, amongst others?

18 Who was the narrator for both the radio version and the later TV version of the Matt Lucas/David Walliams comedy show *Little Britain*?

19 What is the programme name for the BBC's cricket coverage which has a cult following way beyond the normal boundaries of a sports broadcast?

20 Which independent local radio station launched in 1973 with an announcement by Richard Attenborough followed by a jingle and Simon and Garfunkel's 'Bridge Over Troubled Water'? Which former Radio 1 DJ was the station's first breakfast show presenter? What was the name of the traffic-watch device launched by the station in 1976? Which TV personality ramped up the ratings in the late 1980s with a breakfast show borrowing its flavour from his anarchic TV shows? (4 pts)

Total Points: 30. Targets: Novice 15 Pro 23. Your Score:

Answers Quizzes 217–224

Quiz 217. General Knowledge

1. Harry Ramsden; 2. General David Petraeus; 3. Vera Lynn; 'The White Cliffs of Dover'; 4. Darcey Bussell; 5. Los Angeles; 6. All have nuclear reactors in the vicinity; 7. LSD (lysergic acid diethylamide); 8. Typography (he gave his name to the classic font, Gill Sans); 9. Ronald Biggs; 10. England's World Cup match against Argentina on ITV1; 11. A flower arranger (*ikebana* is flower arranging with lots of design aesthetic and feng shui principles thrown in); 12. Pineal gland; it is a hormone which forms part of the sleep-wake cycle and is a constituent of sleeping draughts; 13. Nicolas Cage (his father was August Coppola, brother of film director Francis Ford Coppola); 14. 'Jupiter Suite' from *The Planets*; 15. Bob Marley; 16. Abu Ghraib; 17. Robin Givens; 18. Burt Reynolds; 19. Mini Metro; 20. Fergie (Sarah Ferguson, former wife of Prince Andrew, and Stacy Ann Ferguson, singer with Black Eyed Peas)

Quiz 218. Sci-Fi Movies

1. *Dark Star*; 2. Both Joseph Gordon Levitt and Bruce Willis play the character at different ages; 3. Franco's Spain during World War II; 4. *Fantastic Voyage*; Raquel Welch; 5. Peter Falk as the sick boy's grandfather; Buttercup; 6. *The Stepford Wives*; 7. Christopher Lloyd, who plays both characters; 8. Morpheus and Trinity; 9. 40,000; Duran Duran; 10. HAL 9000 (HAL is fine); 11. Carl Sagan; Jodie Foster; 12. *Apollo 13*; Tom Hanks; 13. Merrick; Kristy Swanson; 14. *Serenity*; 15. Philip K Dick; 16. Jones, Brown, Johnson, Jackson, Thompson

Quiz 219. Discoveries and Inventions

1. Pneumatic tyre; 2. Clocks and watches, including maritime clocks; 3. Drawing or pumping water from a well; 4. John Dalton, who later gave his name to the city's technological college (where my mum taught); 5. Alfred Nobel (he became wealthy on the profits and bequeathed much of it to the prizes that bear his name); 6. Nuclear fission; 7. Velvet and hook; 8. Ferdinand Magellan; 9. (c) Clarence Birdseye was a living, breathing person; 10. Occam's razor; Mix and Match 1, j; 2, d; 3, h; 4, a; 5, e; 6, b; 7, i; 8, g; 9, c; 10, f

Quiz 220. History

1. Babylon; 2. He developed the first known method of shorthand; 3. Tacitus; 4. Ceylon (now Sri Lanka); 5. Lollards; 6. Budapest; 7. The UK played no formal part in the war; 8. The Peasants' Revolt; 9. Thirteen; 10. Women's Auxiliary Air Force; Auxiliary Territorial Service and Women's Royal Naval Service; Mix and Match 1, e; 2, i; 3, c; 4, a; 5, b; 6, j; 7, h; 8, f; 9, d; 10, g

Quiz 221. Fine Art and Architecture

1. Georges Seurat; 2. Birds; 3. Antoni Gaudí; 4. (b) Max Ernst; 5. Brunelleschi; 6. Windsor Castle; 7. Bauhaus; 8. Wren had nothing to do with Brighton Pavilion, which was begun in 1787, over sixty years after his death in 1723; 9. Rotunda; 10. Caro is a sculptor, a former student of Henry Moore; Mix and Match 1, h; 2, e; 3, d; 4, a; 5, j; 6, b; 7, i; 8, g; 9, c; 10, f

Quiz 222. Boxing

1. Nathan Cleverly; 2. Madison Square Garden, New York; 3. George Groves; 4. Norman Mailer; 5. Laila Ali; 6. Floyd Mayweather; 7. Earl of Lonsdale; 8. Sonny Liston; 9. Roberto Duran; 10. Kinshasha, Zaire; 11. Carlos Monzon; 12. Alan Minter; 13. Barry McGuigan; 14. Don King; Mike Tyson; 15. Chris Eubank and Nigel Benn; 16. Michael Watson; White Hart Lane; 17. Oscar de la Hoya; 18. Lennox Lewis; 19. James DeGale; 20. Memphis; Tyson was banned from the state of Nevada

Quiz 223. Theatre

1. *The Misanthrope*; 2. Edward, James and Robert Fox; Noël Coward's 'Don't Put Your Daughter on the Stage, Mrs Worthington'; 3. Alan Bennett; 4. *The Blue Room*; 5. True (Blessed played Old Deuteronomy); 6. His daughter, Rebecca Hall; 7. Marc Almond; 8. Frisky & Mannish; 9. Olivier, Lyttelton and Cottesloe; 10. Caryl Churchill; Mix and Match 1, b; 2, i; 3, d; 4, j; 5, h; 6, a; 7, e; 8, f; 9, c; 10, g

Quiz 224. General Knowledge

1. Nicholas Parsons; 2. Nick Grimshaw; 3. Poison pills; 4. *Dead Ringers*; 5. A point for *The Archers*, a second for Ambridge; 6. Jane Garvey; Jenni Murray; 7. Willie Rushton; Humphrey Lyttelton; Jack Dee; 8. *The Hitchhiker's Guide to the Galaxy*; Peter Jones; 9. (c) Phil Jupitus; 10. Zane Lowe; 11. Magic (105.4) FM; 12. Stan Collymore; 13. GLR (Greater London Radio, the BBC London channel); Carol McGiffin, his first wife; 14. The official chart rundown; 15. Radio Luxembourg; 208 medium wave; 16. *Clare in the Community*; 17. *The Navy Lark*; 18. Tom Baker; 19. *Test Match Special*; 20. Capital Radio; Kenny Everett; the Flying Eye; Chris Tarrant

Quiz 225. General Knowledge

Part 1

1   Which motor company was founded in 1914 by Lionel Martin and Robert Bamford?

2   Which central European country made a Unilateral Declaration of Independence in 2008, after eight years of UN supervision?

3   As of 2009, which country's healthcare system was regarded as the world's best by the World Health Organization? (a) Great Britain (b) New Zealand (c) France

4   Over which river does the ferryman Charon row the dead in Greek mythology?

5   What line of work have Roger Ebert, David Thomson, Philip French and Pauline Kael had in common?

6   Who had cats called Kari and Oke and another pair called Jack and Jill?

7   Apple has the iPhone; what name is given to the multimedia platform for other brands of phone?

8   The Japanese watercolourist Hokusai painted thirty-six different views of which landmark in his home country?

9   Which British TV presenter was murdered outside her London property in April 1999? Who was wrongly convicted of the murder in 2001? (2 pts)

10 In 1992, the Toronto Blue Jays became the first team from outside the US to win what sporting title?

Part 2

11 Who is the official head of state of the Central American republic of Belize? What was its former name (until 1971)? And of which civilization was it a part until *c*.AD 900? (3 pts)

12 Which British politician delivered a famous speech on 3 February 1960 about the 'wind of change' blowing through Africa?

13 What is the landmark known as Itaipu in South America?

14 *Centuries*, first published in 1555, is the main work of which French physician and astronomer?

15 Which two members of the same band were best man and bridesmaid at the 1986 wedding of Bob Geldof and Paula Yates? (2 pts)

16 Where would you find the Tycho Crater and the Sea of Fertility?

17 What is Daniel Ek's contribution to online music?

18 Welsh painter Gwen John also modelled for and became the mistress of which renowned sculptor? (a) Henry Moore (b) Auguste Rodin (c) Jacob Epstein

19 Who would preside over a magistrate's court?

20 An allergy to what threatened Jade Johnson's career as a triple-jumper?

Total Points: 24. Targets: Novice 12 Pro 18. Your Score:

Quiz 226. Name the Album

We give you three tracks and the date, you give us the artist and title of the classic album (2 pts per question)

Part 1

1 'Cracked Actor', 'Drive-in Saturday', 'Jean Genie' (1973)
2 'Breathe', 'Brain Damage', 'Money' (1973)
3 'Mr Tambourine Man', 'It's Alright Ma, I'm Only Bleeding', 'Subterranean Homesick Blues' (1965)
4 'Run for Your Life', 'Nowhere Man', 'Drive My Car' (1965)
5 'Natural Mystic', 'Three Little Birds', 'Jamming' (1977)
6 'Rat Salad', 'War Pigs', 'Iron Man' (1970)
7 'So Far Away', 'Ride Across the River', 'Money for Nothing' (1985)
8 'Rent', 'It's a Sin', 'What Have I Done to Deserve This?' (1987)
9 'Date Stamp', 'Poison Arrow', 'The Look of Love' (1982)
10 'Never Say Goodbye', 'Wanted Dead or Alive', 'You Give Love a Bad Name' (1986)

Part 2

11 'Computer Blue', 'Let's Go Crazy', 'When Doves Cry' (1984)
12 'Pretty Maids All in a Row', 'Life in the Fast Lane', 'New Kid in Town' (1976)
13 'This Night', 'Tell Her About It', 'Uptown Girl' (1983)
14 'Hello Earth', 'The Big Sky', 'Running Up that Hill' (1985)
15 'Will Anything Happen?', 'Picture This', 'Heart of Glass' (1978)
16 'You Can't Always Get What You Want', 'Midnight Rambler', 'Gimme Shelter' (1969)
17 'The Girl is Mine', 'Beat It', 'Billie Jean' (1982)
18 'Seaside Rendezvous', 'I'm in Love with My Car', 'Bohemian Rhapsody' (1975)
19 'Tales of Brave Ulysses'; 'Sunshine of Your Love'; 'Strange Brew' (1967)
20 'Black Dog', 'The Battle of Evermore'; 'Stairway to Heaven' (1971)

Total Points: 40. Targets: Novice 16 Pro 30. Your Score: [   ]

Quiz 227. Movies Awards

Twenty questions on the Academy Awards and other movie prizes

Part 1

1 How many Academy Awards did *West Side Story* win: none, two or ten?

2 Which two actresses were nominated for Academy Awards in 1966 for their work in *The Sound of Music* (neither won)? Which of them won the previous year and for which film? (4 pts)

3 What was the 2000 Michael Mann film about the tobacco industry that won him his only (thus far) Best Director nomination for an Academy Award? Which actor was also nominated for his work in the film? (2 pts)

4 Which movie earned Katharine Hepburn her final Academy Award in her seventies?

5 Which ten-year-old actress won an Academy Award for her performance in *Paper Moon* (1973)?

6 Which Oscar winner gave her acceptance speech in sign language in tribute to her parents, who were deaf?

7 Who are the youngest and oldest recipients of the Best Actor and Best Actress Academy Awards (aged twenty-nine and seventy-six for men, twenty-one and eighty for women)? (4 pts)

8 John Chambers won a special Academy Award for his work on *Planet of the Apes* (1968); in which field?

9 What connects George C. Scott (*Patton*, 1970) with Marlon Brando (*The Godfather*, 1972)?

10 Robert Downey Jr (Best Actor, 1993 ceremony) and Kenneth Branagh (Best Supporting Actor, 2012) both won Academy Award nominations for portraying previous nominees. Whom did they portray? (2 pts)

Part 2

11   Who is the only man to win the Best Actor Academy Award for a perform-
      ance in a film of a Shakespeare play? Who came close in 1990, earning a
      nomination for a film of a play which emulated a role taken by his predeces-
      sor? (2 pts)

12   Simone Signoret (*Room at the Top*, 1959) is one of three French-born
      actresses to garner an Academy Award for Best Actress. Who was the first
      (for *It Happened One Night*) and who was the most recent, for a 2007 role?
      (2 pts)

13   Who has won most nominations for Academy Awards for acting with
      seventeen? Which was the film that won them the most recent of their
      three wins – a miserly return from so many nominations? (2 pts)

14   Who, in 2013 at the Eighty-fifth Academy Awards, became the oldest and
      youngest nominees for Best Actress? Who pipped both to the award?
      (3 pts)

15   Who is the only actor to have won three Best Actor Academy Awards?

16   Sandy Powell has won three Academy Awards and been nominated on six
      other occasions; what is her job?

17   Who holds the record (with twenty-six) for the most Academy Awards?

18   Who won a 1969 Best Supporting Actress award for her appearance in a
      horror movie, *Rosemary's Baby*, the first time the genre had produced
      a winner?

19   Who received an Academy Award in 1987, thanked her hair and makeup
      stylists but failed to thank the director and scriptwriter of the film involved?

20   What rare full set at the Academy Awards is shared by *It Happened One
      Night* (1934), *One Flew Over the Cuckoo's Nest* (1975) and *The Silence of
      the Lambs* (1991)?

Total Points: 33. Targets: Novice 13 Pro 25. Your Score:

Quiz 228. Medicine

Doctor, doctor . . . Well if you have one in your team you're laughing, as here are twenty questions on medical science

Part 1

1   What is the proper medical name for the complaint commonly called German measles?

2   For what condition would you take ACE inhibitors and calcium channel blockers?

3   What is infectious mononucleosis usually known as, and which virus is a primary cause of the disease? (2 pts)

4   What name is given to a psychological test which monitors a subject's response to a series of inkblots?

5   Shingles (herpes zoster) is a painful rash, usually an adult reoccurrence of which childhood viral disease?

6   What kind of tissue is the thyroid and where is it found? (2 pts)

7   In which city was the first heart transplant performed in 1967?

8   Harald zur Hausen's work has led to the 2006 release of a vaccine against what?

9   Meningitis is a disorder of (a) the lungs (b) the brain (c) the endocrinal glands?

10 Which infectious disease is believed to have infected the most people throughout history? (a) tuberculosis (b) malaria (c) smallpox

Part 2

Identify, in plain English, the special areas of study related to these disciplines

11 Pulmonology

12 Oncology

13 Orthopaedics

14 Neurology

15 Obstetrics

16 Radiology

17 Geriatrics

18 Myology

19 Paediatrics

20 Dermatology

Total Points: 22. Targets: Novice 9 Pro 17. Your Score:

Quiz 229. Religion

Not necessarily the ones you follow, but religion in its many forms

Part 1

1   The Dome of the Rock is the oldest Islamic building in the world; in which city can it be found?

2   Which saint lived on top of a six-foot wide column in the desert?

3   24 March is Lady Day or Annunciation, which commemorates what in the Christian calendar?

4   Who made the first translation of the Bible into English?

5   According to the New Testament, what did Jesus give his disciples to encourage their remembrance of his body and his blood?

6   How many books of Moses are there in the Bible?

7   Which saint was the founder of the Jesuit order?

8   Roughly what proportion of Christian believers are adherents to the Roman Catholic Church: 38 per cent, 51 per cent or 64 per cent? (2009 stats)

9   What is proscribed for Muslims in the holy month of Ramadan?

10 What is the Hebrew term for the Day of Atonement, one of the holiest days in the Jewish calendar?

Part 2

11 The biblical tale of Cain, son of Adam and Eve, killing his brother Abel is well known, but who was the third brother?

12 Which branch of Christianity was developed by Mary Baker Eddy around 1879?

13 What is the Islamic body of law founded on the teachings of the Qur'an and adopted rigorously by hardliners?

14 If you undertook the pilgrimage of the Way of St James, where would you finish?

15 The Hieronymites are a Christian order who follow the teachings of which saint, the principal translator of the Bible into Latin?

16 Who killed 1,000 Philistines with the jawbone of a donkey or an ass?

17 Who was the son of Abraham and Sarah?

18 Which biblical figure is referred to as Dawud in the Qur'an?

19 Which old religion, based in India, preaches the non-violent path of Ahimsa to its four million plus followers? (a) Sufism (b) Asceticism (c) Jainism

20 Which Papal name has been used more often? (a) Benedict (b) Pius (c) Clement

Total Points: 20. Targets: Novice 8 Pro 15. Your Score:

Quiz 230. Premier League

Twenty questions on that altar to Mammon, the Premier League

Part 1

1 Which Premier League footballer had cause to regret dabbling with diet pills in 2010–11?

2 Who went the other way when James Milner joined Manchester City from Aston Villa in 2010?

3 Who scored the Premier League's first hat-trick in a match between Leeds and Tottenham in August 1992?

4 Who became the Premier League's oldest goalscorer playing for West Ham on Boxing Day, 2006?

5 Who were the manager, team captain and top scorer when Middlesbrough enjoyed their best Premier League finish (seventh) in 2004–5? (3 pts)

6 What do Peter Schmeichel, Brad Friedel, Paul Robinson and Tim Howard have in common?

7 Who managed Bolton to four successive top eight Premier League finishes from 2003–4?

8 Who was suspended by Manchester City after he appeared to refuse to take the field as a substitute during a Champions League match?

9 Which newly promoted side finished fifth in the Premier League in 2000–2001, only losing a Champions League spot to Liverpool on the last day of the season? Who was their manager, unceremoniously sacked the following season as the club fell from grace and were relegated? (2 pts)

10 Whose Premier League management career runs: Blackburn Rovers, Manchester City, Fulham, QPR?

Part 2

11 Which club's fourteen-year sojourn in the top flight ended in 2000? Who was their manager, an overseas coach with a known dislike of English football and an inflated sense of his own ability? (2 pts)

12 Who was substituted by Manchester City manager Roberto Mancini for 'showboating' in a 2011 pre-season friendly?

13 Which fixture has produced the most red cards in the first eighteen years of the Premier League? (2 pts)

14 Who, in 1997, scored a hat-trick of such quality against Leicester City that all three goals featured on *Match of the Day*'s goal of the month?

15 Who has scored in the Premier League for Tottenham, Middlesbrough, Everton, Liverpool, Leeds and Hull?

16 Southampton returned to the Premier League for the 2012–13 season; when did they go down last, and who was their manager when they were relegated? (2 pts)

17 Which colourful character was the manager of Blackpool during their solitary and entertaining season in the Premier League?

18 Which club were relegated from the Premier League in 2007–8, establishing a record low points total (eleven) and confirming their demotion as early as March?

19 Which four men managed Charlton Athletic in a transitional and disastrous 2006? (4 pts)

20 What is Everton's highest league finish in the first twenty years of the Premier League? And their lowest? (2 pts)

Total Points: 30. Targets: Novice 12 Pro 23. Your Score:

Quiz 231. Science

Just fifteen questions here

Part 1

1 F = ma. What is this?

2 Cochineal, extracted from beetles, is used in the making of which pigment?

3 What are found in versions called up, down, strange, charm, bottom and top? Who devised this name? (2 pts)

4 In the most commonly used periodic table of elements, how many columns are there at the widest point: eight, twelve or eighteen?

5 The invention of the Crookes Tube (*c.*1870, named after English scientist William Crookes) led to the observation of what, which in turn allowed the development of television?

6 If diamond is the hardest precious stone at 10 Mohs, which is the softest at 2.5?

7 Zenography is the study of (a) human migration patterns (b) the planet Jupiter (c) alternative religions?

8 Which German academic succeeded the Dane Tycho Brahe as the imperial mathematician in Prague in 1601?

9 Russian chemistry professor Dmitri Mendeleev is credited with devising the first of what type of chart in the late 1860s?

10 What is the planet's principal method of removing toxic carbon dioxide from the atmosphere?

11 What is the name given to the period (billions of years) which preceded any life signs on earth?

12 What length is a fathom, the imperial measurement of water depth?

13 In what way does adding hydrogen to lithium and carbon make neon?

14 In which year was the first BlackBerry smartphone released (within one year either side)?

15 Whose 1900 work on black body radiation paved the way for later breakthroughs in quantum theory?

Total Points: 16. Targets: Novice 5 Pro 12. Your Score:

Quiz 232. General Knowledge

A trivia list and a couple of multi-part questions

Part 1

1   Who's taller, Barbara Windsor or Kylie Minogue?
2   Who's taller, Madonna or Victoria Beckham?
3   Who's taller, Mick Jagger or Michael Jackson?
4   Who's taller, Chris Evans or Graham Norton?
5   Who's taller, Peter Crouch or Steven Finn?
6   Who's taller, Bono or Martin Freeman?
7   Who's taller, John Wayne or James Stewart?
8   Who's taller, Steve Redgrave or Jamie Theakston?
9   Who's taller, Nicole Kidman or Naomi Campbell?
10 Who's taller, Shane Richie or Sigourney Weaver?

Part 2

11 What are the seven countries sandwiched between Mexico to the north and Colombia to the south? (7 pts)
12 Which seven players have scored 150 Premier League goals or more? (Tip: three were still active in the 2012–13 season.) (7 pts)

Total Points: 24. Targets: Novice 12 Pro 18. Your Score: [   ]

Answers Quizzes 225–232

Quiz 225. General Knowledge

1. Aston Martin; 2. Kosovo; 3. (c) France; 4. Acheron; 5. They are/were all film critics; 6. They were *Blue Peter* pets; 7. Android; 8. Mount Fuji; 9. Jill Dando; Barry George (the verdict was quashed in 2007 and he was cleared in a 2008 re-trial); 10. Baseball's World Series; 11. Queen Elizabeth II; British Honduras; Mayan; 12. Harold Macmillan; 13. The world's largest dam, straddling Paraguay and Brazil; 14. Nostradamus (Michel de Nostradame); 15. Dave Stewart and Annie Lennox of the Eurythmics; 16. Moon; 17. He is co-founder and CEO of Spotify; 18. (b) Rodin (Gwen was the sister of the painter Augustus John); 19. Justice of the Peace; 20. Sand

Quiz 226. Name the Album

1. *Aladdin Sane*, David Bowie; 2. *The Dark Side of the Moon*, Pink Floyd; 3. *Bringing It All Back Home*, Bob Dylan; 4. *Rubber Soul*, Beatles; 5. *Exodus*, Bob Marley and the Wailers; 6. *Paranoid*, Black Sabbath; 7. *Brothers in Arms*, Dire Straits; 8. *Actually*, Pet Shop Boys; 9. *The Lexicon of Love*, ABC; 10. *Slippery When Wet*, Bon Jovi; 11. *Purple Rain*, Prince and the Revolution (deduct half a point for just Prince); 12. *Hotel California*, The Eagles; 13. *An Innocent Man*, Billy Joel; 14. *Hounds of Love*, Kate Bush; 15. *Parallel Lines*, Blondie; 16. *Let It Bleed*, Rolling Stones; 17. *Thriller*, Michael Jackson; 18. *A Night at the Opera*, Queen; 19. *Disraeli Gears*, Cream; 20. IV, *Led Zeppelin*

Quiz 227. Movie Awards

1. Ten, from eleven nominations, including Best Picture and Best Director; 2. Julie Andrews and Peggy Wood; Andrews for *Mary Poppins*; 3. Michael Mann; Russell Crowe; 4. *On Golden Pond*; 5. Tatum O'Neal; 6. Louise Fletcher (Nurse Ratched in *One Flew Over The Cuckoo's Nest*); 7. Adrien Brody (*The Pianist*); Henry Fonda (*On Golden Pond*); Marlee Matlin (*Children of a Lesser God*); Jessica Tandy (*Driving Miss Daisy*); 8. He designed and made the breathable prosthetic latex masks for the ape characters; 9. Both won the Academy Award for Best Actor but declined to receive it (Scott disliked the ceremony, dismissing it as a 'meat parade' while Brando made a gesture about Native American rights); 10. Downey played Charlie Chaplin in a biopic of the star's life, while Branagh channelled Laurence Olivier with uncanny precision in *My Week With Marilyn*; 11. Laurence Olivier (*Hamlet*, 1948); Kenneth Branagh for *Henry V*; 12. Claudette Colbert (who later became a US citizen) and Marion Cotillard; 13. Meryl Streep; she won in 2012 for her portrayal of Margaret Thatcher in *The Iron Lady*; 14. Emmanuelle Riva (for *Amour* – the ceremony was on her eighty-sixth birthday) and Quvenzhané Wallis (for *Beasts of the Southern Wild*, not yet ten at the time); Jennifer Lawrence (for *Silver Linings Playbook*); 15. Daniel Day-Lewis; 16. Costume designer; 17. Walt Disney;

18. Ruth Gordon; 19. Cher; 20. They swept the five main Academy Awards (Best Picture, Director, Actor, Actress and Screenplay)

Quiz 228. Medicine

1. Rubella; 2. Hypertension, or high blood pressure (ACE inhibitors widen the blood vessels, while calcium channel blockers relax the muscles around the heart); 3. Glandular fever; Epstein-Barr virus; 4. Rorschach test; 5. Chickenpox; 6. It is cartilage and it is in the larynx; 7. Cape Town; 8. Cervical cancer; 9. (b) The brain; 10. Malaria (meaning 'bad air' in Italian); 11. Lungs and lung disease; 12. Cancers; 13. Trauma to the skeletal system (bones and joints); 14. Study of the nervous system and its disorders; 15. Pre and post-natal care of pregnant women; 16. The use and study of X-rays and similar technologies; 17. Study of ageing and the aged; 18. Function, structure and disorders of the muscular system; 19. The general care and treatment of children; 20. Skin disease

Quiz 229. Religion

1. Jerusalem; 2. St Simeon Stylites; 3. The appearance of the angel, Gabriel, to the Virgin Mary; 4. William Tyndale; 5. Bread and wine; 6. Five (they are the first five books of the Old Testament); 7. Ignatius of Loyola; 8. Just over half, so 51 per cent; 9. Eating or drinking (or, indeed, smoking or engaging in sexual intercourse) during daylight hours; 10. Yom Kippur; 11. Seth; 12. Christian Science; 13. Sharia law; 14. Santiago de Compostela; 15. Saint Jerome (they are sometimes called the Order of Jerome); 16. Samson; 17. Isaac; 18. David, King of Israel; 19. Jainism; 20. (a) Benedict (sixteen times, compared to fourteen for Clement and twelve for Pius)

Quiz 230. Premier League

1. Manchester City's Kolo Touré, who was suspended after taking the pills that contained a proscribed substance; 2. Stephen Ireland; 3. Eric Cantona; Leeds won 5–0; 4. Teddy Sheringham; 5. Steve McLaren; Gareth Southgate; Jimmy Floyd Hasselbaink; 6. They are all goalkeepers who have scored a goal in the Premier League, all except Robinson in a lost cause; 7. Sam Allardyce; 8. Carlos Tévez; 9. Ipswich Town; George Burley; 10. Mark Hughes; 11. Wimbledon; Egil Olsen; 12. Mario Balotelli; 13. Liverpool v. Everton; 14. Dennis Bergkamp; 15. Nick Barmby; 16. 2004–5; Harry Redknapp; 17. Ian Holloway; 18. Derby County; 19. Alan Curbishley (who had been manager, jointly or solely, for fifteen years), Iain Dowie, Les Reid and Alan Pardew; 20. Fourth and seventeenth (three times)

Quiz 231. Science

1. Force equals mass times acceleration, Newton's Second Law; 2. Red; 3. Quarks; Murray Gell-Mann, the US physicist; 4. Eighteen; 5. Cathode rays; 6. Amber; 7. (b) the planet Jupiter (from Zenos, one of the many written forms of the Greek God, Zeus, Jupiter to the

Romans); 8. Johannes Kepler; 9. Table of elements, or Periodic Table; 10. Photosynthesis in plants; 11. Precambrian or cryptozoic; 12. 6 feet, or 1.829 metres; 13. The atomic numbers of hydrogen (1), lithium (3) and carbon (6) add up to the atomic number of neon (10); 14. 2003; the first BlackBerry release was a pager in 1999; 15. Max Planck

Quiz 232. General Knowledge

1. Kylie, by two inches; 2. Posh, by two inches; 3. Jacko, by two inches; 4. Chris Evans, by four inches; 5. Crouch, by one inch; 6. Bono, by an inch or two (Martin is just a wee little hobbit); 7. Stewart was six foot three but gangly and looked taller, but Wayne was a strapping six foot four; 8. Sir Steve, by one inch; 9. Kidman, by one inch; 10. Shane, by one inch; 11. Guatemala, Belize, El Salvador, Honduras, Nicaragua, Costa Rica, Panama; 12. Alan Shearer; Andrew Cole; Thierry Henry, Robbie Fowler, Frank Lampard, Wayne Rooney, Michael Owen

Quiz 233. General Knowledge

This one is a bit of a tricky Dicky (or a tricky Richard, or tricky Richardson . . .)

Part 1

1   Who was executed in York on 7 April 1739 for stealing a horse?

2   Who married Catherine Hogarth in 1836 but became separated in 1858 when he fell in love with Ellen Ternan, an actress?

3   Prominent English actress Natasha Richardson died after sustaining a head injury in a skiing accident in 2009. Who is her actress mother and who was the grieving husband she left behind? (2 pts)

4   Who is the surviving half of the duo who cooked on TV as *Two Fat Ladies*?

5   Barry Richards was a great South African batsman who played only two tests as his career coincided with the freeze out of South Africa from international sport; which English county benefited from his genius and who made a formidable opening partnership with him? (2 pts)

6   Which TV programme did Dickie Davies present on ITV from 1968 until 1985?

7   What was the 1987 film based on the life and premature death of rock 'n' roll singer Richie Valens?

8   Who, in 2009, starred in a reboot of *Minder* on Channel 5, playing a character called Archie Daley, nephew of the original wheeler and dealer?

9   With what is Captain Ahab fixated in one of the great American novels?

10 Who took the feeble penalty saved by Ricardo for Portugal in their Euro 2004 shoot-out win against England? And who then scored for Portugal to seal the victory? (2 pts)

Part 2

11 What was the name of Wendy Richard's long-running character in *East-Enders*?

12 Which Jamaican-born US sprinter added an individual gold medal in the 400 metres at the 2012 Olympics to the relay golds she won in 2004 and 2008?

13 Which Yorkshireman's fussy mannerisms made him the first 'celebrity umpire' in international cricket?

14 Which character from the TV cartoon *Wacky Races* was so popular that Hanna-Barbera gave him his own show?

15 Who was 'Livin' la Vida Loca' in 1999? Where is he from? (2 pts)

16 In which 1999 thriller does Jude Law play the charismatic playboy Dickie Greenleaf?

17 What were Cliff Richard's first and last UK no. 1 singles, forty years apart in 1959 and 1999? (2 pts)

18 Who was suspended from coaching rugby for three years in 2009 over his involvement in faking an injury to Tom Williams to expedite a substitution during a Harlequins game against Leinster?

19 Who co-writes the Rolling Stones's original material with Mick Jagger? What was the one-word title of his 2010 autobiography? (2 pts)

20 Who was the first (and thus far only) jockey to be knighted, dominating the sport in the years either side of the war and ending with nearly 5,000 winners?

Total Points: 26. Targets: Novice 13 Pro 20. Your Score:

Quiz 234. Rock and Pop

A general quiz for all ages

Part 1

1   Who were the *Village Green Preservation Society*, according to their 1968 classic album?

2   The Foxboro Hot Tubs is an alter ego (usually used for secret gigs, but also used to record an album) of which multi-platinum selling American band?

3   *The Suburbs* was the third (2010) album by which arty rock band?

4   Cerys Matthews was the lead singer in which 1990s rock band?

5   The Police's Stewart Copeland had previously played with which American psychedelic band? (a) Love (b) The Grateful Dead (c) Curved Air

6   Who financed the recording of Joy Division's first, influential album, *Unknown Pleasures*?

7   Where was the piece of reclaimed land in Alabama that became a music hotbed and saw the launch of the careers of (amongst others) Wilson Pickett and Aretha Franklin?

8   Late in 2012 Adele's album became the fourth bestselling album of all time in the UK; which 1990s album did it push back into fifth place and which three records remain above it? (One studio album and two hits packages) (4 pts)

9   Their fourth album, *Autobahn* (1973), was the definitive recording in the career of which band?

10 Who was the radical and controversial rock critic who started out at *Rolling Stone* by writing a scathing review of the MC5's album which other critics were fawning over? Who played a (generously jocular) version of him in the 2000 movie *Almost Famous*? (2 pts)

Part 2

11 Which hard rock band's finest moment was their 1978 live album, *Live and Dangerous*? What was the controversy behind the record? (2 pts)

12 Who recruited DJ Darren Emerson and produced their most successful album to date in 1996, the wittily titled *Second Toughest in the Infants*?

13 1995 was the last year (up to and including 2012) that the Christmas no. 1 was an original (and not reissued) song written entirely by the performing artist; who was that artist, enjoying his final UK no. 1?

14 Chuck D and Flavor Flav were part of which pioneering act who pushed rap into the mainstream in the late 1980s?

15 What was the production team responsible for the early chart success of Kylie Monogue and Jason Donovan, amongst others?

16 What was Jay-Z's first UK no. 1 hit single (in 2009)? Which other two stars appear on the record? From which album was it taken (also his biggest UK hit charting at no. 4)? What was the follow-up, featuring Alicia Keys on vocals? (5 pts)

Total Points: 25. Targets: Novice 10 Pro 19. Your Score: ┌──────────────┐

Quiz 235. Plants

Fifteen straight questions

1 What is the common name for the west Asian lily, *lilium candidum*? (It wasn't named after the pop star.)

2 What distinguishes angiosperms from other members of the plant kingdom? (a) flowers (b) leaves (c) roots?

3 A plant from the genum lonicera is most likely to be a (a) virginia creeper (b) lobelia (c) honeysuckle?

4 What is the alternative name of the flowering plants convolvulus; the name describes more accurately why you don't want them in your garden, despite their pretty flowers?

5 Plums, pears, peaches, apricots; which of these does not belong to the tree genus prunus?

6 The tree *Araucaria araucana* is commonly called what due to its unusual spiky design?

7 What foodstuff would you get from the tree *acer saccharum*?

8 What is the proper name for a gum tree?

9 Cardamom; ginger; clove; galangal; which of these is not a member of the zingiber genus?

10 *Sequoia sempervirens* is the proper name for which iconic protected Californian tree?

11 Azaleas are a sub-genus of which larger plant group?

12 The ilex and the hedera are commonly associated with which time of year?

13 What do aquilegia, delphiniums, horse chestnut and laburnum have in common?

14 *Chalara fraxinea* is a disease, detected in Suffolk in the UK in 2012, that is fatal to which species of tree?

15 Beans and alfalfa are amongst a group of plants that can beneficially convert which element into a useful energy source for other plants?

Total Points: 15. Targets: Novice 6 Pro 11. Your Score: [   ]

Quiz 236. British Politics

Part 1

1   How many seats did the Liberal Democrats win in the 2005 election: twenty-nine, forty-five or sixty-two?

2   Which British politician punched a spectator who threw an egg at him during the 2001 election campaign?

3   Tony Blair became Labour Party leader in 1994; whose death caused the vacancy?

4   Who became Britain's first black female MP in 1987?

5   Which scandal led directly to the resignation of Prime Minister Harold Macmillan in 1963?

6   Which new cabinet minister responded to upcoming revelations about his private life in 1997 by taking the surprising step of announcing he was leaving the wife and settling in with the mistress?

7   Who led the Labour Party in 1992–4, and who did he succeed as leader when the party failed to win the 1992 election? (2 pts)

8   Joan Ruddock, the MP for Lewisham Deptford since 1987 and a former Labour cabinet minister, was chair of which lobbying group before entering Parliament?

9   Members of which party won five seats in Westminster at the 2010 UK General Election but never attend Parliament?

10 Which officer of the government is responsible for the day-to-day management of Parliamentary affairs, a post which now goes hand in hand with the office of Lord Privy Seal and carries a cabinet position with no specific portfolio?

11 What major new political party was launched on 25 March 1981?

12 Which two former British Prime Ministers died in 2005? (2 pts)

Part 2

A succession of British Prime Ministers from World War I onwards; eight of them are missing

13 David Lloyd George (Lib); Andrew Bonar Law (Con); Stanley Baldwin (Con); Ramsay MacDonald (Lab); MISSING; Ramsay MacDonald (Lab); Stanley Baldwin (Con); MISSING; Winston Churchill (wartime coalition); Clement Attlee (Lab); MISSING; Anthony Eden (Con); Harold Macmillan (Con); MISSING; MISSING; Edward Heath (Con); Harold Wilson (Lab); MISSING; Margaret Thatcher (Con); MISSING; Tony Blair (Lab); MISSING; David Cameron (Con) (8pts)

Total Points: 22. Targets: Novice 9 Pro 17. Your Score: [   ]

Quiz 237. Classic Books

Some questions on classic literature

Part 1

1   Who created Dr Jekyll and Mr Hyde?

2   Which of these is the only novel set in the same time period it was written: *A Tale of Two Cities*; *Middlemarch*; *War and Peace*; *Jane Eyre*?

3   To what does Villette refer in Charlotte Brontë's novel of that name? (a) the heroine's family name (b) a town in France where the heroine spent her childhood (c) the city of Brussels

4   What is the house rented by Mr Lockwood at the start of *Wuthering Heights*?

5   Who wrote the 1918 novel of love in the American hinterland, *My Antonia*? (a) Edith Wharton (b) Henry James (c) Willa Cather

6   Joseph Andrews, Jonathan Wild and Tom Jones are all the subjects of novels by which eighteenth-century writer?

7   What is the profession of Emma Bovary's husband in Flaubert's *Madame Bovary*? (a) army colonel (b) country doctor (c) government minister

8   Clym Yeobright and Eustacia Vye are the ill-fated lovers in which Thomas Hardy novel? (a) *The Return of the Native* (b) *The Woodlanders* (c) *The Mayor of Casterbridge*

9   Which US city is the setting for Nathaniel Hawthorne's classic, *The Scarlet Letter*?

10   Which Henry James novel concerns Isabel Archer and the machinations of the subtle Gilbert Osmond?

Part 2

11　What novel by French artillery officer Choderlos de Laclos has been turned into both a stage play and a screenplay by Christopher Hampton?

12　The madman Kurtz is a mystery at the centre of which novel by whom? (2 pts)

13　Thomas Gradgrind, Mr Creakle and Wackford Squeers are all foul examples of what profession in novels by which writer? (2 pts)

14　Which book's alternative title was *The Modern Prometheus*?

15　Published in 1811, which was the first of Jane Austen's six major novels?

16　The St Trinian's films are set in which fictional county, originally the creation of the Victorian novelist Anthony Trollope?

17　Who rode a horse called Rocinante and tilted at windmills?

18　Which great Victorian novel revolves around the fearsome anti-heroine Becky Sharp, and who is the author? (2 pts)

19　In which classic novel do we first hear of Bertha Mason? And in which twentieth-century novel does she become the principal character? (2 pts)

20　What are the three adjectives from this list that Jane Austen uses to describe Emma Woodhouse in the opening sentence of the novel Emma: attractive, clever, handsome, intuitive, precise, pretty, rich, sensible, well-appointed? (3 pts)

Total Points: 26. Targets: Novice 10 Pro 20. Your Score:

Quiz 238. Golf

'A good walk spoiled', as Mark Twain is alleged to have dubbed the game

Part 1

1   Who, in 2010, became the second German golfer to win one of the four Major tournaments?

2   1994 was the last year no US players won a Major; which three players, one European and two from the rest of the world, carved up the four titles between them? (3 pts)

3   Who were the two players involved in an epic duel at the Open Championship at Turnberry in 1977? (2 pts)

4   Which two Scottish players have won a Major championship since World War II? (2 pts)

5   Who, in 2008, became the first European-based player to win the USPGA, and who was the first British-born player to emulate him, in 2012? (2 pts)

6   Who holds the record for European Tour wins (fifty), a record that may not be matched as the strength in depth has grown?

7   What record did Julius Boros set (it is still unbroken) when he won the 1968 USPGA Championship in 1968?

8   Which 2007 winner of the USPGA remains the only male Asian golfer to win a Major tournament?

9   Which two European players have amassed the most points in the Solheim Cup (25 and 24)? Which US player heads their list with 18.5? (3 pts)

10 As of the end of the US Masters in 2013, there was only one non-British European golfer in the world's top twenty; who was the player?

11 Where, respectively, are the Royal Birkdale and Royal St George's golf clubs, both championship links courses? (2 pts)

12 As of April 2013, how many of the top ten players on the LPGA women's professional rankings are from outside the Far East?

Part 2

13 Which four South African golfers have won more than one Major Championship (before the end of 2012)? (4 pts)

14 Which four Spanish golfers have lifted ten or more titles on the European Tour? (4 pts)

Total Points: 28. Targets: Novice 11 Pro 21. Your Score:

Quiz 239. True Crime

Some heinous murderers (and one less culpable convict) with a big multi-parter on the Krays to wrap things up

1 For what crime were American teenagers Eric Harris and Dylan Klebold responsible?
2 Where was the commune, Jonestown, base of cult leader Jim Jones and scene of a mass suicide in 1978?
3 In which year was the Gunpowder Plot to blow up Parliament?
4 Who is Anders Behring Breivik?
5 Francis Galton made a massive contribution to crime-solving in 1891; what was it?
6 Who shot and killed David Blakely outside a Hampstead pub in 1955? What was notable about her execution at Holloway prison the same year? (2 pts)
7 In January 2005 Sarah McCaffery was convicted of what act which rendered her not in control of her car? (a) eating an apple (b) talking to her passenger (c) using her satnav
8 In which year was the death penalty formally abolished in the United Kingdom: 1959, 1965 or 1969?
9 Who became known as the Moors Murderers? (2 pts)
10 Peter Sutcliffe, sentenced to life in prison in 1981, was a serial killer known by which name?
11 What was the nickname given to the criminal organization run by the Kray twins in East London in the 1960s? Who was their south London rival, and who was his henchman murdered by Ronnie Kray in a Mile End Road pub? What was the name of the pub? Which thief and occasional associate of the twins was stabbed to death by Reggie Kray in 1966? Who led the Scotland Yard investigation that led to the twins' arrest and conviction? What was their celebrity-frequented nightclub in Bow Road? What was the nickname of Frank Mitchell, of whose murder the twins were acquitted during their trial? For what reason were the twins briefly released under heavy armed guard in 1982? Who was the controversial and outspoken judge who presided over the twins' trial and handed them record sentences? (10 pts)

Total Points: 22. Targets: Novice 9 Pro 17. Your Score: [   ]

Quiz 240. General Knowledge

A warm-up followed by a ten-pointer

Part 1

1   It has a population over three million, its currency is the lek and its international dialling code is +355. Which country is it?

2   On 3 April 1949 Britain became a founder member of which international body?

3   The towns of Cowes and Ventnor are in which part of Britain?

4   Martin Schreiber made millions from a low-key photography portfolio shot in 1979. Who, or what, was the subject?

5   Which actress is the great granddaughter of former Prime Minister Herbert Asquith?

6   What song by a white New York band did Barack Obama use as his campaign anthem in 2008?

7   In 1983 Sally Ride became the first American woman to do what?

8   Which of the following is *not* true about the artist Yves Klein? (a) he painted only using blue pigments (b) he was a black belt in judo (c) he devised the French version of the driving test?

9   Which up and coming star had to try and stop *The Blob* in 1958?

10 What is the first grade of judo, just below a black belt?

11 Name the seven cities or countries that feature in the titles of Shakespeare plays, assuming all are given their full title. (Tip: three of the plays – and one duplicate – are usually known by an abbreviated name.) (7 pts)

Total Points: 17. Targets: Novice 9 Pro 13. Your Score:

Answers Quizzes 233–240

Quiz 233. General Knowledge

1. Dick Turpin; 2. Charles Dickens; 3. Vanessa Redgrave; Liam Neeson; 4. Clarissa Dickson-Wright; 5. Hampshire; Gordon Greenidge, the West Indies opener; 6. *World of Sport* (the Saturday afternoon sports show famous for its wrestling); 7. *La Bamba*; 8. Shane Richie; 9. The great white whale that bit off his leg in *Moby Dick* (Herman Melville); 10. Darius Vassell; Ricardo himself; 11. Pauline Fowler; 12. Sanya Richards-Ross; 13. Harold 'Dickie' Bird; 14. Dick Dastardly; 15. Ricky Martin; Puerto Rico; 16. *The Talented Mr Ripley*; 17. 'Living Doll' and 'Millennium Prayer'; 18. Dean Richards; 19. Keith Richards; *Life*; 20. (Sir) Gordon Richards

Quiz 234. Rock and Pop

1. The Kinks; 2. Green Day; 3. Arcade Fire; 4. Catatonia; 5. Curved Air; 6. Factory Records' Tony Wilson; 7. Muscle Shoals; 8. Oasis, *(What's the Story) Morning Glory* is now fifth; Abba's *Gold* remains third, the Beatles' *Sgt Pepper's Lonely Hearts Club Band* is second and Queen's *Greatest Hits* sits at the top of the pile; 9. Kraftwerk; 10. Lester Bangs; Philip Seymour Hoffman; 11. Thin Lizzy; it was heavily tweaked by producer Tony Visconti (one track was a studio recording with added audience noise!) but the fans didn't care; 12. Underworld; 13. Michael Jackson; 14. Public Enemy; 15. Stock, Aitken, Waterman; 16. 'Run This Town'; Kanye West and Rihanna; *Blueprint 3*; 'Empire State of Mind'

Quiz 235. Plants

1. Madonna lily; 2. Angiospermae are the division of flowering plants (also known as anthophyta, they are easily the biggest division within the plant kingdom); 3. Honeysuckle; 4. Bindweed (they eventually strangle other plants); 5. Pears; prunus are the stone fruits; 6. Monkey puzzle tree; 7. Maple syrup; 8. Eucalyptus; 9. Clove is a kind of myrtle and is the odd one out here; 10. Coast redwood (accept giant redwood or even just redwood); 11. Rhododendrons; 12. Christmas (ilex is holly and hedera is ivy); 14. The ash or *fraxinus excelsior* (the disease is called ash dieback in English); 15. Nitrogen

Quiz 236. British Politics

1. Sixty-two, their highest since World War II; 2. John Prescott; 3. John Smith; 4. Diane Abbott; 5. Profumo affair; 6. Robin Cook; 7. John Smith; Neil Kinnock; 8. CND (Campaign for Nuclear Disarmament); 9. Sinn Fein (they choose not to attend Westminster); 10. Leader of the House of Commons; the current incumbent (January 2013) is Andrew Lansley; 11. Social Democratic Party; 12. Ted Heath and James Callaghan; 13. (a) Baldwin's second term (Con); (b) Neville Chamberlain (Con); (c) Churchill's second term (Con); (d) Alec Douglas-Home (Con); (e) Wilson's first term (Lab); (f) James Callaghan (Lab); (g) John Major (Con); (h) Gordon Brown (Lab)

Quiz 237. Classic Books

1. Robert Louis Stevenson; 2. *Jane Eyre* (*Tale of Two Cities* is set in the French Revolution, seventy years earlier; *Middlemarch* goes back forty years and *War and Peace* sixty years); 3. (c) Brussels, the setting for much of the book; 4. Thrushcross Grange; 5. (c) Willa Cather; 6. Henry Fielding; 7. (b) he is a country doctor; 8. (a) *The Return of the Native*; 9. Boston; 10. *Portrait of a Lady*; 11. *Les Liaisons Dangereuses* (*Dangerous Liaisons*); 12. Joseph Conrad's *Heart of Darkness*; 13. Schoolmasters in Charles Dickens's novels; 14. *Frankenstein*; 15. *Sense and Sensibility*; 16. Barsetshire; 17. *Don Quixote*; 18. *Vanity Fair* by William Thackeray; 19. She is Rochester's first wife in *Jane Eyre* and becomes the subject of Jean Rhys's *Wide Sargasso Sea*; 20. Handsome, rich and clever

Quiz 238. Golf

1. Martin Kaymer; 2. José María Olazábal won the Masters, Ernie Els the US Open and Nick Price won the Open and the PGA; 3. Tom Watson held off Jack Nicklaus to win; 4. Sandy Lyle and Paul Lawrie; 5. Padraig Harrington, Rory McIlroy; 6. Seve Ballesteros; 7. Oldest player (forty-eight) to win a Major; 8. Yang Yong-eun of Korea (accept Yang of Korea); 9. Laura Davies has 25 career points – she overtook Annika Sörenstam in 2011, but has played in more contests (all twelve in fact); Juli Inkster heads the US list; 10. Sergio García; 11. Royal Birkdale is in Southport, Lancashire, and the St George's is in Sandwich, Kent; 12. Three (Stacy Lewis (no. 2) of the US, Suzann Pettersen (no. 6) of Norway and Karrie Webb (no. 10) of Australia; 13. Gary Player, Ernie Els, Bobby Locke and Retief Goosen; 14. Seve Ballesteros, José María Olazábal, Miguel Ángel Jiménez and Sergio García

Quiz 239. True Crime

1. The Columbine shootings; 2. Guyana; 3. 1605; 4. The gunman who murdered over 100 people in Norway in 2011; 5. Fingerprint classification (accept anything to do with fingerprints); 6. Ruth Ellis; she was the last woman to be hanged in Britain; 7. (a) eating an apple; 8. 1969 (in 1965 a trial abandonment of five years was announced but a permanent abolition came four years later); 9. Ian Brady and Myra Hindley; 10. Yorkshire Ripper; 11. The Firm; Charlie Richardson; George Cornell; The Blind Beggar; Jack 'The Hat' McVitie; Inspector Nipper Read; Double R; Mad Axeman; the funeral of Violet, their mother; Lord Justice Melford

Quiz 240. General Knowledge

1. Albania; 2. NATO; 3. The Isle of Wight; 4. Madonna (they were the nudes which made Schreiber millions when he sold them to *Playboy* in 1985); 5. Helena Bonham Carter; 6. 'Fake Empire' by the National; 7. Travel in space; 8. (c) to the best of my knowledge, he had nothing to do with the French driving test; 9. Steve McQueen; 10. Brown; 11. *The Two*

Gentlemen of VERONA; *The Merchant of VENICE* (and *Othello, the Moor of VENICE*, for a bonus point); *Timon of ATHENS*; *The Merry Wives of WINDSOR*; *Hamlet, Prince of DENMARK*; *Cymbeline, King of BRITAIN* (toughie, double points); *Pericles, Prince of TYRE* (you can have two points for that one as well, no one remembers it)

Quiz 241. General Knowledge

Part 1

1   Which is the only US state in which coffee is grown commercially?

2   Which German airship ended its first flight across the Atlantic in 1928?

3   The first Jewish ghetto was found in which European city?

4   In a 2009 newspaper article listing the '50 Greatest Mothers' of all time, who came out on top?

5   The sexy 1960s (banned) song 'Je t'Aime . . .' was recorded by Serge Gainsbourg and which English model cum actress?

6   The University of Colorado sports a grill called the Albert Packer Memorial Grill; who was Packer? (a) a cannibalistic murderer (b) the chef reputed to have made the first beefburger (c) a local chef who died after locking himself in his freezer

7   What are named officially using the Bayer designation system? (a) stars (b) the earth's strata (c) dog breeds

8   Which Victorian classical painter became the first British artist to be awarded a life peerage?

9   Which now-established heart-throb played Hugh Grant's teenage co-star in the adaptation of Nick Hornby's novel, *About a Boy*?

10 Which racing driver taught Prince Andrew to drive?

Part 2

11 In 2010, which had the greater population density: North Korea, Vietnam or Thailand?

12 In 2010, which had the greater population density: South Africa, Nigeria or Ghana?

13 In 2010, which had the greater population density: Peru, Argentina or Mexico?

14 In 2010, which had the greater population density: Canada, Australia or Sudan?

15 In 2010, which had the greater population density: Estonia, Slovakia or Croatia?

16 In 2010, which had the greater population density: Greece, Spain or Italy?

17 In 2010, which had the greater population density: United Kingdom, Germany or Belgium?

18 In 2010, which had the greater population density: France, Poland or Portugal?

19 In 2010, which had the greater population density: United States, Russia or Brazil?

20 In 2010, which had the greater population density: Pakistan, Sri Lanka or Turkey?

Total Points: 20. Targets: Novice 10 Pro 15. Your Score:

Quiz 242. Song and Dance

Some top-tappin' teasers from musicals

Part 1

1   In which musical did the song 'There Is Nothin' Like a Dame' first feature? Who wrote the music and lyrics? (3 pts)

2   Everyone remembers Judy Garland was in *A Star is Born* (1954); but who played opposite her as fading star Norman Maine? And who reprised Garland's role in a 1976 version of the film? (2 pts)

3   Which three characters accompany Dorothy on her quest to find the Wizard of Oz in the 1939 movie? (3 pts)

4   Who play the 'star-crossed lovers' in *West Side Story* (1961), and which two supporting actors won Academy Awards? (4 pts)

5   *The Gay Divorcee*, *Top Hat* and *Swing Time* all featured which famous musical film partnership? (2 pts)

6   With lyrics by Arthur Freed and a tune by Nacio Herb Brown, which song provided an iconic film moment in a movie bearing it's name in 1952, some twenty-three years after it was published?

7   *Mary Poppins*, *My Fair Lady*, *The Sound of Music* and *West Side Story* were all huge box office hits in the early 1960s; which film came first in 1961 and which was the last to be released, in 1965? (2 pts)

8   *A Little Night Music*, *Sunday in the Park with George* and *Into the Woods* are all musicals with lyrics and music by which master of the genre? (2 pts)

9   What is the name of the widowed military man at the centre of *The Sound of Music*, and where was Maria headed before she turned his life upside down and became his second wife? (2 pts)

10 Who sang in *The King and I*, *My Fair Lady* and *West Side Story*?

Part 2

11 If it was Cary Grant, Katharine Hepburn, James Stewart and Ruth Hussey in 1940, who were the same foursome in 1956? Which of these eight won an Academy Award for their work in the film? And what films are we talking about? (6 pts)

12 Who played Eliza Doolittle in a successful stage version of *My Fair Lady* in the 1950s? To whom did she lose out in her efforts to get the role in the film? What film did she make after failing to get Eliza? And how did she get her 'revenge'? Who got the lead male part in both stage and screen versions? (5 pts)

Total Points: 33. Targets: Novice 13 Pro 25. Your Score:

Quiz 243. Sci-Fi TV

More danger, dark stars and derring-do

Part 1

1 Whose role as Counsellor Deanna Troi in *Star Trek; Next Generation* made her a pin-up for the next generation of teenagers?

2 Which 1970s series, about SHADO, an organization protecting the earth from alien attack, was Gerry Anderson's first live-action series in 1970–71?

3 Who is/was Sydney Bristow? Who played the part? (2 pts)

4 Which TV hero has friends called Chloe, Pete and Lana? Who was originally his friend but became an antagonist? (2 pts)

5 Which series co-starred Welsh actor John Rhys-Davies (Gimli in *The Lord of the Rings*) as one of a group of characters encountering alternative earths as they try to get home? (a) *Eureka* (b) *Sliders* (c) *Scanners*

6 What is the town set aside by the US government for scientific geniuses to do their experiments without endangering the populace? Who is the town's sheriff? (2 pts)

7 Where does high-school student Liz Parker (played by Shiri Appleby) encounter aliens?

8 Which series follows two government agents as they monitor and assist a number of abducted people who have unexpectedly returned to earth? Who abducted them? (2 pts)

9 Which series concerns a group of genetically enhanced soldiers on the run from a sinister corporation called Manticore? Who played the lead role of Max Guevara? (2 pts)

10 Which writer/director created *Alias* and had a hand in the creation of *Lost* and *Fringe* as well as directing the resurrection of the *Star Trek* movie franchise?

Part 2

11 Who was a big fan of the series *Alias* and played a terrorist who took control of the company's offices in the two-part episode 'The Box' in season one?

12 Who heads up the *Fringe* Division of Homeland Security in the first four seasons of the hit sci-fi show?

13 For how many episodes did the cult sci-fi show *Firefly* run: eleven, sixteen or twenty-two? What was the name of the owner and captain of the space-ship *Serenity*? (2 pts)

14 In which sci-fi show are an organization called ZFT revealed to be behind 'the Pattern', a series of unusual but connected events?

15 A cheerleader, an ex-con, a cop, an art dealer, a political candidate . . . What are they?

16 Which two characters from *Star Trek: Next Generation* crossed over into the third strand of the franchise, *Deep Space Nine*? What was the name of the head of security, a shapeshifter, in *Deep Space Nine*, and what race was Quark, the bar owner? Who are the mysterious aliens who travel down the wyrmhole and attempt to conquer the universe? (5 pts)

Total Points: 26. Targets: Novice 10 Pro 20. Your Score:

Quiz 244. Around Britain

How much do you know about the place where you live (assuming you live in Britain)?

Part 1

1   Liverpool lies at the mouth of which river?
2   Which of these Irish counties is in the Republic, as opposed to Northern Ireland? (a) Fermanagh (b) Antrim (c) Clare (d) Down
3   The road from Sumburgh Head to Isbister runs the length of which island?
4   What is the area and administrative region to the south and west of Cardiff? (a) Rhondda Cynon Taff (b) Vale of Glamorgan (c) Caerphilly
5   Ironbridge Gorge is the site of the world's first iron bridge; in which county can it be found and which river does it span? (2 pts)
6   The remote Scottish island of St Kilda boasts a population of how many: none, twenty-seven or 240?
7   Who bought Warwick Castle from the Greville family (owners since 1604 when they were given the property by King James I) in 1978?
8   The towns of Boston and Spalding both lie in which English county?
9   Both Dundee and Perth lie on the inlet to which major Scottish river?
10   Kingston upon Hull lies on the mouth of which river? Which famous fishing town lies to the south on the opposite side of the estuary? (2 pts)

Part 2

11 Leave the A1 By Newark and turn northeast along the A46; where is the next big town?

12 Take the A12 north from Lowestoft; what is the next significant town up the coast?

13 Head up the M40 from London and there is a large stretch between junctions 8 and 9; which town or city to the west is being bypassed?

14 Take the A354 due south from Dorchester in Dorset and you arrive at which famous sailing town?

15 Travel south (and slightly west) from Chester on the A483; what is the first town you reach after crossing the border into Wales?

16 Take the A2 (not the A20/M20) north from Dover and which is the first major town or city you reach?

17 Leave the M6 at junction 32 to join the M55 heading west – where are you going to end up?

18 Head south and east from Middlesbrough, go through Whitby and carry on down the coast; what's the next major town?

19 Which town lies on the A77/M77 between Ayr and Glasgow?

20 The A90 links Perth with Aberdeen; which other city does it bisect en route?

Total Points: 22. Targets: Novice 9 Pro 17. Your Score:

Quiz 245. Kings and Queens

Here are twenty events in British history – just tell us which monarch was on the throne

Part 1

1   World War I
2   The Act of Union, which united the kingdoms of England and Scotland
3   The Jacobite rebellion of Bonnie Prince Charlie
4   The Babington Plot (an assassination attempt)
5   Abolition of Slavery
6   The commencement of work on Westminster Abbey
7   Signing of the Magna Carta
8   Great Fire of London
9   The Abolition of the Monasteries
10 American War of Independence

Part 2

11 The Spanish Armada
12 Great Exhibition
13 Assassination of Thomas à Becket, Archbishop of Canterbury
14 The burning of 283 'heretics' at the stake, including Bishop Latimer, Bishop Ridley and Thomas Cranmer, Archbishop of Canterbury
15 Suez Crisis
16 Compiling of the Domesday Book
17 Defeat of a numerically superior French army at the Battle of Crécy
18 Ditto at the Battle of Agincourt
19 A sound thrashing by the Scots at the Battle of Bannockburn
20 The Gunpowder Plot

Total Points: 20. Targets: Novice 8 Pro 15. Your Score:

Quiz 246. Football History

Here are the transfer paths, including loan deals (L), of ten footballers; identify the player and state which country they played for (2 pts per question)

Part 1

1   Luton Town – Arsenal – West Ham – Wimbledon – Coventry City – Celtic – West Brom – Norwich (L)

2   Crewe Alexandra – Leicester City – Birmingham City – Blackburn – Derby – Brighton (L)

3   Crewe Alexandra – Aston Villa – Bari – Juventus – Sampdoria – Arsenal – Nottingham Forest

4   Torquay United (L) – Bristol City (L) – Bristol Rovers – West Brom – Portsmouth (L) – Wigan – Blackburn – Reading

5   Lazio – Ternana (L) – Juventus – Napoli – Milan – Celtic – Sheffield Wednesday – West Ham – Charlton – Lazio – Cisco Roma

6   IBV – Crystal Palace – Brentford – Wimbledon – Ipswich Town – Charlton – Portsmouth – Coventry

7   Clyde – Chelsea – Everton – Tranmere Rovers – Kilmarnock – Motherwell

8   Southampton – Norwich City – Chelsea – Aston Villa – Middlesbrough – West Brom

9   Bayern Munich – Newcastle – Liverpool – Manchester City – MK Dons

10 Gillingham – Norwich City – Manchester United – Birmingham City – Sheffield United

Part 2

All these players enjoyed their best days with continental sides – many never played in England at all; name and country again, please

11   Cannes – Bordeaux – Juventus – Real Madrid

12   Real Madrid – Leganes (L) – Mallorca (L) – Mallorca – Barcelona – Internazionale – Anzhi Makhachkala

13   Groningen – PSV – Chelsea – Real Madrid – Bayern Munich

14   Slavia Prague – Lens – Liverpool – Bordeaux – Slavia Prague

15   Dynamo Kiev – Milan – Chelsea – Milan (L) – Dynamo Kiev

16   Cruzeiro – PSV – Barcelona – Internazionale – Real Madrid – Milan – Corinthians

17   Malmo – Ajax – Juventus – Internazionale – Barcelona – Milan – Paris St Germain

18   Vicenza – Fiorentina – Juventus – Milan – Bologna – Internazionale – Brescia

19 Independiente – Manchester United – Villareal – Atletico Madrid – Internazionale – Internacional

20 Kage – Heerenveen – Newcastle – Feyenoord – Milan – Vfb Stuttgart – Villareal – Feyenoord

Total Points: 40. Targets: Novice 16 Pro 30. Your Score: [ ]

Quiz 247. Myths and Legends

All questions relating to J. R. R. Tolkien (John Ronald Reuel, in case you ever wondered)

Part 1

1   Who is the leader of the dwarves in *The Hobbit*?
2   Gimli, the dwarf in *The Lord of the Rings*, is the son of which character from *The Hobbit*?
3   Under what name does Aragorn go when he is first encountered by the four hobbits in *The Lord of the Rings*?
4   Who is the landlord of the inn called the Prancing Pony and in which town can it be found? (2 pts)
5   Who is the husband of Galadriel and where do they live? (2 pts)
6   What is the name of the dragon who has driven the dwarves out from under the Lonely Mountain in *The Hobbit*?
7   What is the name of the horse Theoden gives to Gandalf and what is his sword called? (2 pts)
8   Apart from Gandalf, who are the other two wizards mentioned by name in *The Hobbit* and *The Lord of the Rings*? (2 pts)
9   Who collected Tolkien's unfinished stories and notes after his death and published them, first as *The Silmarillion and Unfinished Tales*, then later as a twelve-volume *History of Middle Earth*?
10 Who is the second son of Denethor, Steward of Gondor, and with whom does he fall in love while recuperating in *The Return of the King*? (2 pts)

Part 2

11   What was Gollum's name before he forgot it and became a creature of dark places?

12   What is the land to which the elves – and a chosen few others – travel when they have had enough of Middle Earth? And from where do they sail? (2 pts)

13   Who is the destroyer god and enemy of the Valar in *The Silmarillion*?

14   What is the name of the town on the River Anduin which was built by the men of Gondor to prevent the crossing of the river on to the Pelennor fields?

15   Who accompany Aragorn through the Paths of the Dead in *The Lord of the Rings*? (2 pts)

16   What terrible creature is confronted and overthrown by Gandalf in Moria? What weapon does it wield? (2 pts)

17   Which she-demon spawned the hideous giant spider Shelob, whom Frodo and Sam encounter in *The Lord of the Rings*? What is the name of the dark stairway she inhabits in that episode? (2 pts)

18   In *The Lord of the Rings*, Treebeard is the leader of which race? Where does he live? (2 pts)

19   Longbottom Leaf and Old Toby are varieties of what in Middle Earth?

20   What is the name given to the uber-Orcs bred by Saruman in the fires of his tower, Orthanc?

Total Points: 30. Targets: Novice 12 Pro 23. Your Score:

Quiz 248. General Knowledge

Part 1

1   In which US state is the Gettysburg National Military Park?

2   On New Year's Day in 1973, which other two countries became members of the EEC along with the UK? (2 pts)

3   What was the cheaper alternative to silk used to make Victorian mourning dresses?

4   Which biblical figure is the subject of an Oscar Wilde play and a Richard Strauss opera?

5   Which French city, among its other sights, has museums devoted to the works of Marc Chagall and Henri Matisse?

6   Where did Bruce Springsteen get the title for his album *The Ghost of Tom Joad*? (a) a character from a John Steinbeck novel (b) the name of a teacher who beat Springsteen as a youngster (c) a favourite uncle who never returned from the Vietnam War

7   What famous hoax, according to the Flat Earth Society, was sponsored by Walt Disney and filmed by Stanley Kubrick?

8   Which sporting event was held for the first time in the UK at Brooklands in Surrey in 1926?

9   Which TV personality, now a household name, was once part of electro-pop outfit Seona Dancing in the early 1980s? (a) Ricky Gervais (b) Russell Brand (c) Brian Cox

10 Who was the MP for the Isle of Ely in Cambridgeshire between 1973 and 1983? Which party did he represent? For which newspaper was he a regular columnist? Who was his equally famous brother? Who was their grandfather? (5 pts)

Part 2

11   What is the name of the ruling house of Monaco?

12   The diamond symbol in a pack of cards is an example of what shape belonging to the parallelogram group?

13   With which kind of TV programme is Kirstie Allsopp now associated?

14   Who composed the nineteenth-century piano suite, *Pictures at an Exhibition*? Which prog rock group recorded a play on this work in 1971? (2 pts)

15   Which musical icon was born Robert Zimmerman in Duluth in 1941?

16   Three sides helped found both the Football League (1888) and the Premier League (1992); which three? (3 pts)

17   True or false: Ulrika Jonsson, never the brightest chip, has spent so long in Britain she can't remember how to speak Swedish?

18   Which MP announced that he was dating one of the Cheeky Girls in December 2006? And who was the TV personality he ditched for Gabriela? (2 pts)

19   Which car manufacturer sports a model called the Octavia? Who are this maker's parent company? (2 pts)

20   Who married Maurice Gibb of the Bee Gees on 18 February 1969?

Total Points: 30. Targets: Novice 15 Pro 23. Your Score:

Answers Quizzes 241–248

Quiz 241. General Knowledge

1. Hawaii; 2. *Graf Zeppelin*; 3. Venice (the word ghetto comes from an Italian term for a slag heap – there was one in the Canareggio quarter of Venice where the Jewish quarter was established in the early sixteenth century); 4. The Virgin Mary; 5. Jane Birkin; *Blow Up*; 6. (a) a cannibalistic murderer (student humour, eh?); 7. (a) stars (each star is given a Greek letter followed by a styling of the constellation in which it is found, thus betelgeuse is noted α Ori to signify it is the alpha star within the constellation Orion); 8. Frederick, Lord Leighton; 9. Nicholas Hoult; 10. Graham Hill; 11. Vietnam (272) with Thailand (131) a long way third.; 12. Nigeria has a density of 165, while South Africa, with all that rolling veldt, stands at only 40; 13. None of these are high, but overcrowded Mexico City raises the Mexico average to 57; 14. Sudan, despite the large desert stretches, has a density of 19 (Canada and Australia stand at just 3 people per sq km); 15. The Slovak Republic has a density of 112, with Estonia a long way third on only 29; 16. Italy, by a distance on 193 (the other two are less than 100); 17. Belgium has a really high density at 341, slightly less than England on its own, but more than the UK; 18. Poland stands at 123, just five higher than France with Portugal two further back on 116; 19. The US is highest on 32 (Russia is only 8); 20. Sri Lanka is a massive 328 and easily the highest of these three

Quiz 242. Song and Dance

1. *South Pacific*; Rodgers and Hammerstein; 2. James Mason; Barbra Streisand; 3. The Tin Man, the Cowardly Lion and the Scarecrow; 4. Natalie Wood and Richard Beymer; Rita Moreno and George Chakiris; 5. Fred Astaire and Ginger Rogers; 6. 'Singin' in the Rain'; 7. *West Side Story* was out in 1961, with *The Sound of Music* in 1965 (both the others were released in 1964); 8. Stephen Sondheim; 9. Captain (George) von Trapp; a nunnery; 10. Marni Nixon, who provided the singing voice for Deborah Kerr, Audrey Hepburn and Natalie Wood respectively; 11. Bing Crosby, Grace Kelly, Frank Sinatra and Celeste Holm; James Stewart won the Oscar; these are the casts in the film *Philadelphia* and the later musical version, *High Society*; 12. Julie Andrews; Audrey Hepburn; *Mary Poppins*; she won an Academy Award for *Mary Poppins*, while Hepburn failed to even pick up a nomination; Rex Harrison

Quiz 243. Sci-Fi TV

1. Marina Sirtis; 2. UFO; 3. The main character in *Alias*; Jennifer Garner; 4. Clark Kent in *Smallville*; Lex Luthor; 5. (b) *Sliders*; 6. *Eureka*; (John) Carter; 7. Roswell (High); 8. *The 4400*; humans from the future looking to alter their timeline; 9. *Dark Angel*; Jessica Alba; 10. J.J. Abrams; 11. Quentin Tarantino; 12. Philip Broyles (Lance Reddick); 13. Eleven; Malcolm Reynolds; 14. *Fringe*; 15. *Heroes*; 16. Miles O'Brien and Commander Worf; Odo; he is a Ferengi; the Dominion

Quiz 244. Around Britain

1. Mersey; 2. (c) Co. Clare is in the Republic; 3. The mainland of Shetland; 4. (b) Vale of Glamorgan; 5. Shropshire; River Severn (the bridge was constructed by Abraham Darby after the original designer died, and was opened in 1781); 6. None, the last permanent resident left in 1930 (the island is home to a few thousand puffins and Europe's largest gannet colony); 7. Madame Tussauds (strictly speaking, the Tussauds Group); 8. Lincolnshire; 9. River Tay; 10. Humber; Grimsby; 11. Lincoln; 12. Great Yarmouth; 13. Oxford; 14. Weymouth; 15. Wrexham; 16. Canterbury; 17. Blackpool; 18. Scarborough; 19. Kilmarnock; 20. Dundee

Quiz 245. Kings and Queens

1. George V; 2. Anne; 3. George II; 4. Elizabeth I; 5. William IV; 6. Edward the Confessor; 7. John; 8. Charles II; 9. Henry VIII; 10. George III; 11. Elizabeth I; 12. Victoria; 13. Henry II; 14. Mary I; 15. Elizabeth II; 16. William I (William the Conqueror or William of Normandy); 17. Edward III; 18. Henry V; 19. Edward II; 20. James I

Quiz 246. Football History

1. John Hartson (Wales); 2. Robbie Savage (Wales); 3. David Platt (England); 4. Jason Roberts (Grenada); 5. Paolo di Canio (uncapped); 6. Hermann Hreidarsson (Iceland); 7. Pat Nevin (Scotland); 8. Andy Townsend (Republic of Ireland); 9. Dietmar Hamman (Germany); 10. Steve Bruce (uncapped); 11. Zinedine Zidane (France); 12. Samuel Eto'o (Cameroon); 13. Arjen Robben (Netherlands); 14. Vladimir Smicer (Czech Republic); 15. Andrei Shevchenko (Ukraine); 16. Ronaldo (Brazil); 17. Zlatan Ibrahimovic (Sweden); 18. Roberto Baggio (Italy); 19. Diego Forlán (Uruguay); 20. Jon Dahl Tomasson (Denmark)

Quiz 247. Myths and Legends

1. Thorin Oakenshield; 2. Gloin; 3. Strider; 4. Barleyman Butterbur; Bree; 5. Celeborn; Lothlorien; 6. Smaug; 7. Shadowfax; Glamdring; 8. Saruman (the White) and Radagast (the Brown); 9. His son, Christopher; 10. Faramir; Eowyn of Rohan; 11. Smeagol; 12. Valinor; The Grey Havens; 13. Melkor; 14. Osgiliath; 15. Legolas and Gimli; 16. A balrog; a whip of flame; 17. Ungoliant; Cirith Ungol; 18. Ents; Fangorn forest; 19. Pipe tobacco; 20. Uruk-Hai

Quiz 248. General Knowledge

1. Pennsylvania; 2. Ireland and Denmark; 3. Bombazine; 4. Salome; 5. Nice; 6. (a) Tom Joad is a central character in John Steinbeck's *The Grapes of Wrath*; 7. The moon landings (they are wrong, just like the creationists and the climate-change deniers); 8. Grand Prix; 9. Ricky Gervais; 10. Clement Freud; Liberal Party; *Racing Post*; Lucian Freud, the painter; Sigmund Freud, the psychoanalyst; 11. Grimaldi; 12. Rhombus, which is a type of

parallelogram; 13. Home makeovers; 14. Modest Mussorgsky; Emerson, Lake and Palmer; 15. Bob Dylan; 16. Aston Villa, Blackburn Rovers and Everton; 17. False (in fact Ulrika is pretty smart and speaks French and German to a high standard as well as English and, of course, her native Swedish); 18. Lembit Opik; weather presenter Siân Lloyd; 19. Skoda; VW; 20. Lulu

Quiz 249. General Knowledge

Fifteen normal questions and a *Simpsons* bumper

Part 1

1   Who was the original presenter of the BBC's music show, *The Old Grey Whistle Test*?

2   Dracula's castle is situated in Transylvania; in which modern country is the region of Transylvania?

3   How are David Tennant and Peter Davison connected both personally and professionally? (2 pts)

4   What connects *The Ballad of Reading Gaol* and the boxing code of conduct?

5   Which country singer married Nicole Kidman in 2006?

6   The high-class, eighteenth-century prostitute Kitty Fisher once took umbrage at being paid (by the Duke of York, allegedly) with a £50 note instead of her customary 100 guineas; what did she do with the offending note? (a) put it in her underwear as a gift for her next client (b) sent it to the Duke's wife with a note saying the Duke had left it at her apartment (c) baked it in a pie and ate it for breakfast

7   In 1862 Dr Harvey prescribed the first example of what to a patient, who had a condition increasingly common in the twenty-first century?

8   What beats an earl but is topped by a duke?

9   Which is longer, a perch, a fathom or a nail?

10 Which historical figure's work was continued by her daughters Christabel and Sylvia?

11 What connects Tin Tin, Hercules Poirot and Audrey Hepburn?

12 Which stand-up comedian held sway in the Roman era sitcom *Up Pompeii*?

13 Which programme fiddled a vote to name a cat in 2007?

14 Who was the Fresh Prince of Bel-Air in 1990–96?

15 Where would you hear the song 'Hooky Street', written and sung by John Sullivan?

Part 2

16 In *The Simpsons*, what are the names of the following? (a) the headmaster (b) the Chief of Police (c) the doctor – the regular, competent one (d) Mr Burns PA (e) the serial killer (f) the creator of Malibu Barbie dolls (g) the goody-two-shoes neighbour (h) the Reverend (i) the school bully (j) the Asian shopkeeper (10 pts)

Total Points: 26. Targets: Novice 13 Pro 20. Your Score:

Quiz 250. Westerns

A Wild West extravaganza – or a quiz, at least

Part 1

1   Which two actors starred alongside Clint Eastwood in *The Good, the Bad and the Ugly*? (2 pts)

2   *The Treasure of the Sierra Madre* (1948) was a rare western outing for which Hollywood star?

3   *Rio Bravo* (1959) starred which singer as an (appropriately) drunken deputy?

4   The 1939 John Ford western, *Stagecoach*, was the making of John Wayne, hitherto a second division player; which female co-star was given lead billing on the film's release?

5   Who took the title role in the 1953 western *Shane*, and who played the same character in a 1960s TV series? (2 pts)

6   Which western was Marlon Brando's only film as director, and on whose life was the central character, Rio (played by Brando), based? (2 pts)

7   In Robert Altman's gritty, mud-splattered 1971 western *McCabe and Mrs Miller*, who starred alongside Warren Beatty as a drug-addicted English brothel-keeper?

8   Who played against type as Frank, the hired killer for the railroad companies, in *Once Upon a Time in the West*?

9   *Shanghai Noon* was a 2000 'comedy martial arts western'; who were the two stars of this odd hybrid? (2 pts)

10 How did Jeff Bridges follow in John Wayne's footsteps in 2010, and who made the movie? (2 pts)

Part 2

Mix and Match: match the gunslinger to actor

1. Doc Holliday in *Tombstone* (1993); 2. Doc Holliday in *Gunfight at the OK Corral* (1957); 3. Doc Holliday in *Wyatt Earp* (1994); 4. Jesse James in *The Assassination of Jesse James* (2007); 5. Jesse James in *American Outlaws* (2001); 6. Billy the Kid in *Young Guns* (1988); 7. Billy the Kid in *The Left Handed Gun* (1959); 8. Wild Bill Hickok in *Wild Bill* (1995); 9. Wild Bill Hickok in *Calamity Jane* (1953); 10. Wild Bill Hickok in *The Plainsman* (1936)

a. Kirk Douglas; b. Emilio Estevez; c. Val Kilmer; d. Howard Keel; e. Gary Cooper; f. Colin Farrell; g. Dennis Quaid; h. Jeff Bridges; i. Paul Newman; j. Brad Pitt

Your Workings:

Total Points: 25. Targets: Novice 10 Pro 19. Your Score:

Quiz 251. Wildlife

The animal world

Part 1

1   What would you expect to find in a formicary?
2   If a male is a hob, a female a jill and a youngster a kit, what is the animal?
3   Echolocation describes what phenomenon of the animal world?
4   Which is bigger, a stoat or a weasel?
5   Minke, Bowhead and Sei are all breeds of which animal?
6   Are crocodiles reptiles, amphibians or mammals?
7   What is the hellbender, a species native to eastern North America?
8   An interest in orthoptera would suggest a fascination with what creatures?
9   Which is the most common group of fishes: the perch, the eel or the salmon?
10 What is the largest species of rodent?

Part 2

11 What animal can also be a benign tumour, a pier or an SI unit used to measure chemical substances?
12 What name is given to all hoofed mammals?
13 How many species of cats (*felidae*) are known: 35, 81 or 210?
14 Which is fastest through the water: a salmon, a penguin or a dolphin?
15 Which of the following is used for pain relief by the Yupik Eskimos? (a) the anal glands of a bear (b) the mammary glands of a female polar bear (c) the testicles of a beaver
16 Which insect is fastest through the air, reaching speeds of up to 45 mph?
17 A European robin, an albatross or a tawny owl; which is likely to live longest assuming a full lifespan?
18 Roughly how many known species of beetle and weevil are there: 18,000, 95,000 or 250,000?
19 What is the IUCN Red List?
20 Jackdaws, magpies, ravens and rooks are all species of which group of birds?

Total Points: 20. Targets: Novice 8 Pro 15. Your Score: [   ]

Quiz 252. Food and Drink

It's made me hungry just typing this . . .

Part 1

1 Which Hungarian wine region has UNESCO World Heritage status?

2 *Taste of the Sea* was the first TV cookery series presented by which now-familiar figure?

3 Which vitamin aids bone formation?

4 Chicory, Jerusalem artichoke and salsify are all part of which plant family?

5 Which cake was produced for the wedding of the Princess Victoria in 1884?

6 Which is the primary grape used to make the fresh, young red wines marketed as 'Beaujolais Nouveau'?

7 The Sardinian cheese *casu marzu* is banned under Italian health law because (a) it is filled with live maggots and deemed unfit (b) consumption of the rind has potent hallucinogenic qualities (c) the flavour is achieved by adding urine during the fermentation process?

8 Who, in 1669, was appointed cellar master of a Benedictine abbey in Hautvilliers, France?

9 What branded food was patented by a zealously healthy doctor from Battle Creek, Michigan, in 1884?

10 What was the Spanish restaurant, often labelled the 'best in the world', that closed down in 2011?

Part 2

11   Why is Madeira cake so called?

12   Belvedere is a famous brand of what?

13   By what name was Phyllis Primrose-Pechey known in her time as a TV personality?

14   The aristocrat John Montagu gave his name to an everyday food; what was his title?

15   What is the traditional name for a large cooking pot with an arched lid to provide extra room for roasts or other bulky dishes?

16   If you ate something *con fagioli* in Italy, with what would it be served?

17   Barbera d'Asti, Barolo and Gavi di Gavi are all native to which Italian wine-growing region? (a) Calabria (b) Sicily (c) Piedmont

18   What percentage (to the nearest round ten) of the US wine output is produced in California?

19   Limburger is a famously smelly cheese from which country?

20   A French *mirepoix* is a combination of which three vegetables finely chopped and spiced to be used as the base for a casserole or soup or stock? (3 pts)

Total Points: 22. Targets: Novice 9 Pro 17. Your Score:

Quiz 253. Harry Potter

Part 1

1   What are the names of Harry's parents? (2 pts)
2   Who is the teacher, sent from the Ministry of Magic, who punishes and tortures Harry in *Harry Potter and the Order of the Phoenix*?
3   What is the address of the Dursley family at the start of the *Harry Potter* series?
4   What is the name of Lord Voldemort's snake?
5   Who rescues Harry, Hermione, Ron and various other prisoners from Malfoy Manor in *Harry Potter and the Deathly Hallows*?
6   Who is *The Prisoner of Azkaban*?
7   What is the newspaper edited by Luna Lovegood's father, Xenophilius?
8   Who is Harry's first girlfriend at Hogwarts?
9   Who is the Minister of Magic in the earlier *Harry Potter* books, and who replaces him after he fails to give credence to reports of Voldemort's return? (2 pts)
10 What is the name of Ron's mother and younger sister respectively? (2 pts)

Part 2

11 What is the name given to the sport played at Hogwarts (a kind of airborne lacrosse)? What position does Ron play? (2 pts)
12 Which school did Fleur Delacour represent in the tri-wizard tournament, and who is the headmistress? (2 pts)
13 Who is the Charms Master and Head of Ravenclaw House?
14 With whom does Hermione attend the ball at the end of *Harry Potter and the Goblet of Fire*?
15 Where in London is the wizards' shopping centre? And what is the name of the wandmakers found there? (2 pts)
16 'It was either a very big cat or a very small tiger.' What is Harry describing?
17 Firenze, one of the teachers at Hogwarts, is of what race?
18 Who tortured Neville Longbottom's parents and sent them mad?
19 What is the name of the wizarding bank and who runs it? (2 pts)
20 Sir Nicholas de Mimsy-Porpington appears in the books; who or what is he and by what name is he more commonly known? (2 pts)

Total Points: 28. Targets: Novice 11 Pro 21. Your Score:

Quiz 254. Sport

This and that, bats and balls

Part 1

1 What is the name of the two Ukrainian brothers who have held boxing World Heavyweight titles in the twenty-first century? (2 pts)

2 Which country won seven of the first eight gold medals in ice hockey at the Winter Olympics? Who beat them in the 1936 Games? (a) Great Britain (b) Soviet Union (c) Finland (2 pts)

3 What is the difference between short track and long track speed skating?

4 What happens at Naas, Ffos Laas and Chantilly?

5 Where do London Wasps play their home games? And which Premiership rugby union club used to play at Watford's Vicarage Road ground? (2 pts)

6 Where did Dettmar Cramer follow Udo Lattek with equal success?

7 Which golf tournament is referred to as the 'fifth Major' due to the unusually strong international field it attracts?

8 Who was the first black player to play in baseball's major leagues in 1947? For which side? (2 pts)

9 With which team did Fernando Alonso win the Formula 1 Drivers' Championship in 2005 and 2006?

10 What do former tennis professionals Mark Petchey, Brad Gilbert and Ivan Lendl have in common?

Part 2

11   Where might the Balgove, the Eden, the Strathtyrum and the Jubilee be found?

12   With which sporting venue would you associate Becher's Brook and the Melling Road?

13   What title has the recipient of the Venus Rosewater Dish just won?

14   Australian squash player Ross Norman ended whose five-year (and 555 match) unbeaten run in 1986?

15   Which rugby league side were voted BBC Sports Team of the Year in 2006 after completing a clean sweep of major trophies in 2006?

16   In which male-dominated sport is Danica Patrick widely regarded as the most proficient female performer?

17   Maurice Garin won the first staging of which event in 1903?

18   In which sport did Nicola Minichiello and Gillian Cooke of Great Britain win the 2009 World Championships?

19   Who did Boston Red Sox beat to end an eighty-five-year World Series drought in 2004? What was the supposed origin of their eighty-five-year 'curse'? (2 pts)

20   Who became the youngest ever winner of the World Snooker Championship in 1990?

Total Points: 25. Targets: Novice 10 Pro 19. Your Score:

Quiz 255. Action Movies

More high octane heroics

Part 1

1   Who played slave turned bounty-hunter Django in Tarantino's *Django Unchained*?

2   The onscreen wife of which iconic all-American movie hero was played by Bonnie Bedelia?

3   *Enter the Dragon* was the breakthrough in the US for which Hong Kong action star?

4   What is the name of the fisherman who helps track the great white shark in *Jaws*, and who plays him? What is the name of his boat? (3 pts)

5   Who is action hero Bryan Mills?

6   Who plays the younger version of Tommy Lee Jones in a time-travel plot strand in *Men in Black III*?

7   Which role came first for Stallone: Rocky or Rambo?

8   Who starred in the first film featuring the character Zorro, in 1920?

9   Which rapper turned up in *Tank Girl* as a mutant, talking kangaroo?

10   What is the name of the Emperor in Ridley Scott's *Gladiator*, and who plays the role? (2 pts)

Part 2

11   Which 2000 action movie became the biggest grossing foreign language film in the US to that date?

12   Who faced off in the 1997 action thriller *Face/Off*? (2 pts)

13   Which Korean director made his Hollywood debut with *Hard Target* (1993), a US take on his established hard-boiled, noirish thrillers?

14   What is the name of Tom Cruise's character in the *Mission Impossible* movies?

15   Whose novels form the source for Tom Cruise's character Jack Reacher in the 2012 movie of that name?

16   The 2012 movie *The Avengers Assemble* teams up which four superheroes, all previously with their own movies? Who directed the 2012 caper? (5 pts)

Total Points: 24. Targets: Novice 10 Pro 18. Your Score:

Quiz 256. General Knowledge

Part 1

1 Where did Flight 103 explode in 1988?

2 Where were members of the MacDonald clan massacred for failing to pledge allegiance to the king in 1692?

3 If a Victorian protester marched under the black flag, what would his political affiliation have been?

4 Under what name did music-hall entertainer Joseph Pujol perform in the first half of the twentieth century?

5 What was the company formed especially to produce the Monty Python film, *Life of Brian*? And which musician provided the money behind the company? (2 pts)

6 Agbani Darego was the first black African to win (a) the Olympic women's marathon title (b) Miss World or (c) an Academy Award (for hair and makeup on *Bonnie and Clyde*)?

7 Which is the oldest of these periods in the earth's history: Cambrian, Silurian or Jurassic?

8 Who was the architect and planner commissioned by Napoleon III to redesign the centre of Paris around the River Seine in the mid-nineteenth century?

9 Which of these facts about Tommy Lee Jones is *not* true: he shared a room with Al Gore at Harvard; he made his screen debut in *The Waltons*; he is a seriously competitive polo player; he is part-Cherokee?

10 Which sporting trophy changed hands in 1983 for the first time since its inception in 1851? Who won and where? Who were the holders for 132 years? Which Prime Minister effectively said everyone could have a day off? (5 pts)

Part 2

11   In which country was the Caesar salad devised, in 1926, by Caesar Cardini? (a) Mexico (b) Italy (c) United States

12   What was the name of Ian Fleming's house in Jamaica, later used as a Bond movie title?

13   What is the significance of 21.28 in the evening on Sunday, 20 July 1969?

14   Who would traditionally dance a hornpipe?

15   Who, in 2000, scathingly referred to Robbie Williams as 'the fat dancer from Take That'?

16   Jean Michel Jarre had the distinction of being the first Western musician to have performed where? (a) Soviet Russia (b) North Korea (c) China

17   Whose planned marriage to Julia Roberts was broken off days before the ceremony in 1991?

18   Who (allegedly) said 'yes' to Reggie Kray and Maurice Gibb, but 'no' to Warren Beatty?

19   Richard Pryor, the comedian, died in 2005 after suffering from which condition for many years?

20   In 1897, taxi driver George Smith became the first person to be charged with which now-common offence?

Total Points: 25. Targets: Novice 13 Pro 19. Your Score:

Answers Quizzes 249–256

Quiz 249. General Knowledge

1. Bob Harris; 2. Romania; 3. They played the tenth and fifth incarnations of Doctor Who, and Tennant later married Davison's daughter, Georgia Moffett; 4. The Marquess of Queensbury devised the initial rules of boxing, which still stand in principle today; he also accused Oscar Wilde of sodomy, which led to the author's imprisonment and his composing the poem; 5. Keith Urban; 6. (c) She baked it in a pie (very flash, especially for the eighteenth century); 7. A diet (Harvey's diet was a protein-based affair not unlike the Atkins Diet); 8. A Marquess; 9. A perch (or pole) is 5.5 yards, a fathom six feet while a nail was a cloth measurement of only 2¼ inches; 10. Emmeline Pankhurst; 11. They are all Belgian; 12. Frankie Howerd; 13. *Blue Peter* (viewers had voted for the name Cookie but TV staff decided to pretend that Socks was the winning name); 14. Will Smith; 15. During the end credits of *Only Fools and Horses*; 16. (a) Seymore Skinner (b) Chief Wiggum (c) Dr Julius Hibbert (d) Waylon Smithers (e) Sideshow Bob (f) Stacey Lovell (g) Ned Flanders (h) Reverend Lovejoy (i) Nelson Muntz (j) Apu

Quiz 250. Westerns

1. Lee Van Cleef and Eli Wallach; 2. Humphrey Bogart; 3. Dean Martin; 4. Claire Trevor; 5. Alan Ladd; David Carradine; 6. *One-Eyed Jacks*; Billy the Kid; 7. Julie Christie; 8. Henry Fonda; 9. Jackie Chan and Owen Wilson; 10. He starred as Rooster Cogburn in a remake of *True Grit* by the Coen Brothers; Mix and Match 1, c; 2, a; 3, g; 4, j; 5, f; 6, b; 7, i; 8, h; 9, d; 10, e

Quiz 251. Wildlife

1. Ants; 2. A ferret; 3. The ability to navigate by sound, like bats; 4. Stoats are up to three times the size of a weasel; 5. Whale; 6. Reptiles; 7. A type of giant salamander; 8. Grasshoppers, crickets and locusts; 9. Perches (perciformes); there are about 7,000 known species; 10. Capybara, a herbivorous South American rodent resembling a giant guinea pig; 11. Mole; 12. Ungulates; 13. Thirty-five (species should not be confused with breed); 14. A dolphin can hit speeds of around 40 mph, while salmon and penguins get up to about 25 mph; 15. Beaver testicles (I'll stick with paracetamol); 16. Dragonfly; 17. The albatross (they often live to well over twenty and sometimes over thirty; a tawny owl should live to fifteen or so, and a robin could reach ten or twelve; 18. There are about 250,000; 19. The IUCN is the International Union for Conservation of Nature and the Red List is a list of endangered species of flora and fauna; 20. Corvidae, more commonly, crows

Quiz 252. Food and Drink

1. Tokay or Tokaj; 2. Rick Stein; 3. Vitamin D; 4. Daisy (asteraceae); 5. Battenburg, named for Lord Battenburg, her husband; 6. Gamay; 7. (a) maggots are introduced during fermentation and the cheese is eaten whilst the little fellers are still wriggling around inside; 8.

Dom Perignon; 9. Kellogg's Corn Flakes; 10. El Bulli; 11. It is intended to be accompanied by a glass of Madeira; 12. Vodka; 13. Fanny Craddock; 14. Earl of Sandwich; 15. Dutch oven; 16. Beans, usually borlotti beans (pale kidney beans); 17. They are all Piedmont wines (the land around Turin provides the biggest number of prestige wines of any Italian region); 18. Fractionally under 90 per cent, from 2009 statistics (Washington and New York states are the only other areas with over 1 per cent); 19. Germany; 20. Celery, onion and carrot

Quiz 253. Harry Potter

1. James and Lily Potter; 2. Dolores Umbridge; 3. 4 Privet Drive; 4. Nagini; 5. Dobby, the freed house elf; 6. Sirius Black, Harry's Godfather; 7. The Quibbler; 8. Cho Chang; 9. Cornelius Fudge; Rufus Scrimgeour; 10. Molly and Ginny (Virginia); 11. Quidditch; goal minder; 12. Beauxbatons; Mme (Olympe) Maxine; 13. (Filius) Flitwick; 14. Viktor Krum; 15. Diagon Alley; Ollivander's; 16. Crookshanks, Hermione's cat; 17. He is a centaur; 18. Beatrix Lestrange; 19. Gringott's and it is run by goblins; 20. He is the Gryffindor House ghost and is known as Nearly Headless Nick

Quiz 254. Sport

1. Vitali and Wladimir Klitschko; 2. Canada; Great Britain, with a team made up of Canadians with British antecedents; 3. Long track, referred to as simply 'speed skating' at the Olympics, is a race against the clock, while short track is a mass start race; 4. Horse racing; 5. High Wycombe (which isn't London at all); Saracens, although the club is nominally based in St Albans; 6. At Bayern Munich in the 1970s as they won three successive European Cups; 7. The Players Championship (the strong field is possibly down to the huge prize money on offer); 8. Jackie Robinson; Brooklyn Dodgers; 9. Renault; 10. All have coached Andy Murray; 11. They are four of the seven courses at St Andrews Golf Club; 12. Aintree Racecourse, home of the Grand National; 13. Wimbledon ladies' singles; 14. Jahangir Khan; 15. St Helens; 16. Motor racing; she finished fourth in the Indianapolis 500 in 2005; 17. Tour de France; 18. Bobsleigh; 19. St Louis Cardinals; the sale of Babe Ruth to the New York Yankees in 1919; 20. Stephen Hendry

Quiz 255. Action Movies

1. Jamie Foxx; 2. John McClane (*Die Hard*); 3. Bruce Lee; 4. Quint played by Robert Shaw; *Orca*; 5. He is the ex-CIA agent played by Liam Neeson in *Taken*; 6. Josh Brolin; 7. Rocky was 1976, the first Rambo film (*First Blood*) came out in 1982, the same year as *Rocky III*; 8. Douglas Fairbanks (*The Mark of Zorro*); 9. Ice-T; 10. Commodus; Joaquin Phoenix; 11. *Crouching Tiger, Hidden Dragon*; 12. John Travolta and Nicolas Cage; 13. John Woo; 14. Ethan Hunt; 15. Lee Child; 16. Iron Man, Thor, Captain America and the Hulk; Joss Whedon

Quiz 256. General Knowledge

1. Over Lockerbie; 2. Glencoe; 3. The anarchist movement; 4. Le Pétomane (his act consisted of farting well-known tunes); 5. HandMade Films; George Harrison; 6. (b) Miss World; 7. Cambrian, the first period of the Palaeozoic era; 8. (Georges-Eugène) Haussman; 9. Tommy Lee was never in *The Waltons*; 10. The America's Cup; *Australia II* off Newport, Rhode Island; New York Yacht Club; Bob Hawke said any boss who sacked anyone that day was 'a bun'; 11. (a) Mexico; 12. Goldeneye; 13. Neil Armstrong became the first man to set foot on the moon; 14. Sailors; 15. Noel Gallagher; 16. (c) China, in the autumn of 1981; 17. Kiefer Sutherland; 18. Barbara Windsor; 19. Multiple sclerosis; 20. Driving whilst drunk – he was fined £1

Quiz 257. General Knowledge

Part 1

1   Which order of distinction, also known as the Order of St George, was created by King Edward III in 1348?

2   Who was the founder of the Monster Raving Loony Party. In which election did the party first stand: 1974, 1979 or 1983? (2 pts)

3   On 17 May 1991, Helen Sharman became the first Briton to do what?

4   Approximately how many books are there in the British Library collection: eight, fourteen or twenty-six million?

5   Who was the British nurse executed by a German firing squad for spying in 1915?

6   Which film director founded the Police Memorial Trust after the death of PC Yvonne Fletcher?

7   What connects the Bible to the boundary between the earth's liquid core and viscous mantle?

8   On 19 May 1867, Queen Victoria laid the foundation stone to which building to commemorate her late husband?

9   If the founder of Fiat, Gianni Agnelli, had been born English, what would his name have been? (2 pts, 1 for each name)

10 What is the trophy at stake when England and Scotland meet in the rugby union Six Nations tournament every year?

Part 2

11   St Columba left Ireland and took up residence with his followers on which Scottish island?

12   Who was editor of the *Daily Mirror* between 1995 and 2004?

13   Which fortified French medieval city lends its name to a popular tile-laying board game?

14   In some forms of Hinduism the three main cosmic functions are creation, maintenance and destruction; which three forms, in some versions called the Trimurti, represent these functions? (3 pts)

15   Who provided the bulk of the soundtrack to the 2010 movie, *Iron Man 2*?

16   Who won the 2011 PFA Player of the Year award despite the fact that his side were relegated at the end of the season?

17   What is the Wonderland Center, in West Hollywood, California?

18   Who was wisely advised by Lenny Henry to change his performing name from Shane Skywalker?

19   Which twenty-four year-old superstar was killed when his Porsche was involved in a collision in California in 1955?

20   Who is the actress daughter of actress Joanna David?

Total Points: 24. Targets: Novice 12 Pro 18. Your Score:

Quiz 258. Movies

General titbits with a second half that's the wrong way round . . .

Part 1

1   Which British character actor, also famous for his comic monologues, played the station master in *Brief Encounter* (1945)?

2   What was Jean Renoir's 1939 film about the decline of the aristocracy, released between the invasions of Czechoslovakia and France by the Third Reich?

3   In which film is Benjamin Braddock seduced by Mrs Robinson? And whose songs adorn the soundtrack? (2 pts)

4   Which American film icon chaired the Cannes jury that awarded the Palme d'Or to *Pulp Fiction* in 1994?

5   Who played John McClane's son, Jack, fighting alongside dad in *A Good Day to Die Hard*?

6   What does Otto (Kevin Kline) use to torture Ken (Michael Palin) in *A Fish Called Wanda*?

7   There were protests from movie buffs when a concrete car park in Gateshead was knocked down in 2010; why?

8   What is the essentially unfunny subject matter of Seth Rogen's 2011 comic movie, *50/50*?

9   What was strongman Carl Dane's contribution to J. Arthur Rank's film studio in 1932–48?

10 With which major star did director John Ford make fourteen films?

Part 2

Identify these people, places or things from the movies

11   Bach; Tchaikovsky; Dukas: Stravinsky; Beethoven; Panchielli; Mussorgsky

12   Hans Gruber

13   Roger O. Thornhill

14   Leonard, Adolph (Arthur), Julius Henry, Milton and Herbert Manfred

15   LV-426

16   Voight-Kampff machine

17   Michael Myers

18   Father Karras

19   Jack Torrance

20   Joliet Jake and Elwood

Total Points: 21. Targets: Novice 11 Pro 16. Your Score:

Quiz 259. Light Entertainment

A bit like this quiz

Part 1

1 'College Boy' by Derek New is the familiar theme to which long-running quiz show?

2 Who duetted with 2010 *X Factor* winner Matt Cardle in the final of that year's show?

3 Who hosts *Saturday Night Takeaway*, ITV's flagship weekend light entertainment show?

4 Who were the three hosts of the long-running quiz show *Blankety Blank*? (3 pts)

5 Who beat One True Voice to the *Popstars: The Rivals* title in 2002? Who managed the two bands as they fought it out? (3 pts)

6 Which opera singer won the first series of *Britain's Got Talent* in 2007? What was his job before his success in the show? (2 pts)

7 Who hosted the two generations (1980s and late 1990s) of *The Price Is Right*? (2 pts)

8 Where have Nick Hancock, Paul Merton and Frank Skinner invited guests to put the things they dislike? (2 pts)

9 Betty, a former dinner lady, and muscle-man Miles O'Keeffe were sidekicks on whose early shows?

10 'Tonight, Matthew, I'm going to be . . .' was an oft-heard line in which show in 1993–2004? Who replaced Matthew for the show's death throes? (2 pts)

Part 2

Devoted entirely to *Strictly Come Dancing*

11   Who is the head judge of *Strictly Come Dancing*? Who was the first judge to be dropped from the show and who came in as a replacement? (3 pts)

12   Which professional dancer always got the tall partners in the early series of *Strictly Come Dancing*? And which two leggy ladies reached the final with him as their partner? (3 pts)

13   Who is the only celebrity over fifty to reach the final of *Strictly Come Dancing*?

14   Which two celebrity dancers (both pop stars) scored the most tens in a *Strictly* series (not including the tens awarded by Darcey Bussell as a fifth guest judge in 2009)? (2 pts)

15   As of the end of the 2012 series, which two dances have yet to have any couple score four tens for a full-house-forty? (2 pts)

16   Who was Anton du Beke's partner when they were awarded four scores of less than twenty out of forty by the judges?

17   What are the contributions to *Strictly Come Dancing* of Alan Dedicoat and Dave Arch? (2 pts)

18   2004 was the only time the final of *Strictly Come Dancing* was held somewhere other than London; where?

19   Which three professional dancers have taken part in every series of *Strictly Come Dancing* (to the end of 2012)? Who is the only one of the three to win the trophy (in the very first series) and who was their partner? (5 pts)

20   What is the name of the *Strictly Come Dancing* weekday evening chat show? Who was the show's presenter in 2004–2010? And who took over when the usual presenter was on maternity leave and stayed in the job? What role does the original presenter now have on the show? (4 pts)

Total Points: 42. Targets: Novice 17 Pro 32. Your Score: [   ]

Quiz 260. Human Body

Part 1

1. Which side of the heart serves the lungs with blood? What is the main vessel carrying blood from the heart to the lungs? (2 pts)
2. What are the conducting cells in the nervous system?
3. Where in the human body can you find the parietal and lacrimal bones?
4. What are the two bones at the vulnerable base of the spine? (2 pts)
5. What are the bones that form the jaw? (2 pts)
6. How many pairs of ribs are there in the human skeleton? How many of these are described as 'floating'? (2 pts)
7. Where in the human body would you find an aortic arch, a tricuspid valve and interventricular septum?
8. The surface area of the average pair of adult human lungs would cover (a) a couple of tennis courts (b) the football pitch at Wembley (c) the grounds of Buckingham Palace?
9. What separates the thoracic and abdominal cavities?
10. What is the largest muscle in the human body?
11. What can't you do if your cochlea malfunctions?
12. Where in the human body is the vas deferens and what does it carry? (2 pts)
13. What accounts for about 55 per cent of the volume of blood in the body?
14. Where is the plantar fascia?
15. Which contains most fat, assuming equal weight: avocado, poached salmon or chick peas?

Total Points: 20. Targets: Novice 8 Pro 15. Your Score:

Quiz 261. History

Part 1

1   Which city, in the northeast of the seceded territories, was the capital of the Confederate States during the US Civil War?

2   Which two wolf-suckled brothers founded Rome, according to legend?

3   What was the part of southern Syria seized and annexed (and still controlled) by Israel during the Six-Day War?

4   What distinctive first did Valentina Tereshkova achieve in 1963?

5   Which historic organization was officially formed in Poland in 1980?

6   Who was President of the US when they landed a man on the moon?

7   Henry VIII is buried alongside which of his wives at Windsor Castle?

8   What would one do with a denarius or sestertius in the Roman Empire?

9   Who was shot by Charles Guiteau on 2 July 1881, and died in hospital eleven weeks later?

10   In 1960 Congo (now the Democratic Republic of Congo) gained freedom from which European power?

Part 2

11   In 1809, how did George Canning and Viscount Castlereagh attempt to resolve their political differences?

12   St George is the oldest New World English town; where can it be found? (a) Bermuda (b) Newfoundland (c) The Bahamas

13   A Commonwealth and a Dominion were finally recognized by the Statute of Westminster in 1931 as having independent sovereign status from the United Kingdom; what were these two states? (2 pts)

14   Who overthrew Darius III and installed himself as King of Persia in 330 BC?

15   The Estates-General was the principal legislative body in pre-revolutionary France; which three sections of society made up the component bodies? Where did the Third Estate convene when they were excluded from the Estates-General in 1789? In which year was France officially declared a republic? (5 pts)

16   Which country was terrorized by the Tonton Macoute death squads in the 1960s and 1970s? Who was the ruler who introduced the death squads? Who was the first democratic leader of the country in 1990? Which former US President persuaded a military junta to back down after they attempted a 1994 coup? What is the name for the large island where this country lies, occupying the western third? (5 pts)

Total Points: 25. Targets: Novice 10 Pro 19. Your Score:

Quiz 262. Cricket

1　Which five cricketers (all bowlers, all finishing their test career after 2000) have been out for nought more than thirty times in test cricket (to the end of 2012)? Which two good batsmen, one a former Australia captain, one a former England captain, contemporaries of each other, got twenty-two and twenty ducks respectively? Which heavy-scoring former England captain got a pair (two noughts) on his test debut in 1975? (8 pts)

2　In which year did Gary Sobers become the first man to hit six sixes in an over of a first-class cricket match? For which county was he playing and who were their opponents? Who was the luckless bowler? And what happened on the fifth ball? (5 pts)

3　When did the County Championship split into two divisions: 1989, 1995 or 2000? Who were the first winners of the top division? Who were the only side to have won three times (to 2012)? Which team became the first, in 2012, to follow a title with relegation? (4 pts)

4　Which ten England batsmen have accumulated most runs in a test match career? (Two are still playing.) (10 pts)

5　Who, by the end of summer 2012, were the highest wicket-takers for each test-playing nation in one-day internationals? (England, Australia [there are two equal wicket-takers], West Indies, South Africa, India, Pakistan, Sri Lanka, New Zealand, Zimbabwe, Bangladesh) (11)

6　Which four batsmen have scored over 500 runs in an Ashes series in the last decade (2002–2012)? (4 pts)

Total Points: 42. Targets: Novice 17 Pro 32. Your Score: ☐

Quiz 263. Classical Arts

Part 1

1   Simon Rattle became the first British director of music with which famous orchestra in 2002? (a) New York Philharmonic (b) Berlin Philharmonic (b) Sydney Symphony Orchestra

2   Who wrote his seventh symphony during the German siege of Leningrad, his home city, in 1941–2?

3   Which famous Puccini opera premiered at Milan's La Scala on 17 February 1904?

4   Who, in 2006, became the Royal Ballet's first resident choreographer for sixteen years? What was the name of the avant-garde company he formed, aged twenty-two? (2 pts)

5   Robin Oakapple is in love with Rose in which Gilbert and Sullivan operetta? (a) *Iolanthe* (b) *The Yeomen of the Guard* (c) *Ruddigore*

6   Who wrote *L'Orfeo*, which premiered in 1607 and the earliest opera still in regular performance today?

7   Who published the *Winterreise* song cycle in 1827, aged thirty, but was dead within a year?

8   By what English name is the Mozart opera *Die Zauberflöte* known?

9   *The Dream of Gerontius*, a cantata, and *The Enigma Variations*, an orchestral work, were composed by which English maestro around the turn of the last century?

10 Which experimental composer scored a ballet, *Parade*, for typewriters, airplane propellers, ticker-tape, whistles and other worldly sounds? (a) Erik Satie (b) Arnold Schoenberg (c) Pierre Boulez

CLASSICAL ARTS

Part 2

11 Whose ballet scores included *The Firebird* and *The Rite of Spring*?

12 Whose first symphony, *The Gothic*, is a massive 1928 work claimed by the *Guinness Book of Records* as the 'largest' (though, oddly, not the longest) ever written? (a) Havergal Brian (b) Wilhelm Stenhammer (c) Paul Hindemith

13 In which opera does a clown, Canio, blur performance and reality and stab his wife, Nedda, and her lover, Silvio?

14 Which composer, best known for his piano works and studies, wrote the music for the ballet, *Les Sylphides*?

15 Which great ballet dancer was born Edris Stannus in Ireland and died in 2001 at the ripe old age of 102?

16 Wagner's *Ring Cycle* took him twenty-six years to write (1848–74); what is the proper German name for the cycle, and (in English or German) what are the four component operas called? Which German town holds an annual festival devoted entirely to Wagner's operas? (6 pts)

Total Points: 22. Targets: Novice 9 Pro 17. Your Score:

Quiz 264. General Knowledge

Part 1

1   In 1975, a gunboat from which country opened fire on British fishing vessels in the North Sea?

2   Who returned his MBE in 1969, in protest at UK and US involvement overseas?

3   Which US politician and ecological spokesman, born 1948, won the 2007 Nobel Peace Prize?

4   True or false: contrary to popular belief, Cheddar cheese accounts for only 18 per cent of the British cheese market?

5   Which long-serving and confrontational Labour MP is sometimes referred to as the Beast of Bolsover after the constituency he has represented since 1970?

6   What new post did Tony Hall take up in March 2013, and which post did he leave to do so? (2 pts)

7   What name is given to the supercontinent which formed the earth's only land mass about 240 million years ago?

8   Eva Gouel, Marie-Thérèse Walter and Françoise Gilot were all lovers and muses of which twentieth-century artist?

9   Which woman involved in a court case claimed to have had 'worst press than a paedophile or a murderer' in an interview on *GMTV*?

10 What took Ronnie O'Sullivan five minutes and twenty seconds in 1997? In which city did it take place? (2 pts)

Part 2

11 What type of high-street outlet was legalized from 1 May 1961 in a piece of legislation announced in 1960?

12 In which football stadium were eleven people killed in 1971 when a stairway collapsed inside the ground?

13 What is the sea that sits between the European and Asian portions of Turkey? And what strait connects it to the Black Sea? (2 pts)

14 How many words of a Bond novel did Ian Fleming aim to write each day during the six weeks he spent on each novel: 600, 2,000 or 6,000?

15 Which famous rugby team was formed by William Percy Carpmael in Bradford in 1890?

16 Which member of the Leeds United team of the 1970s successfully sued David Peace and his publisher for the representation of him in the novel *Damned Utd*?

17 Paul McCartney wrote 'I'm Looking Through You' (1965) after the end of his relationship with whom?

18 Which singer was dismissed as a flash in the pan by *Billboard* magazine in 1983?

19 When Sid Vicious died on 2 February 1979, he was still under investigation concerning the death of which former girlfriend?

20 Which rock star was found dead from a self-inflicted gunshot wound in his Seattle home in 1994?

Total Points: 23. Targets: Novice 12 Pro 17. Your Score:

Answers Quizzes 257–264

Quiz 257. General Knowledge

1. Order of the Garter; 2. Screaming Lord Sutch; 1983; 3. Lift off into space; 4. Fourteen million; 5. Edith Cavell; 6. Michael Winner; 7. Gutenberg; the boundary is sometimes called the Gutenberg discontinuity after the German geophysicist who established its depth, while the Gutenberg Bible was one of the earliest printed editions; 8. Royal Albert Hall; 9. Johnny Lamb; 10. Calcutta Cup; 11. Iona; 12. Piers Morgan; 13. Carcassonne; 14. Brahma, the creator, Vishnu, the stabilizer, and Shiva, the great rejuvenator; 15. AC/DC; 16. Scott Parker; 17. A rehab centre for the rich and famous; 18. Shane Richie; 19. James Dean; 20. Emilia Fox

Quiz 258. Movies

1. Stanley Holloway; 2. *La Règle du Jeu* (*The Rules of the Game*); 3. *The Graduate*; Simon and Garfunkel; 4. Clint Eastwood; 5. Jai Courtney; 6. Chips (he shoves them up Ken's nose); 7. It was the setting for an iconic chase in *Get Carter*; 8. Cancer; 9. He was the man who struck the gong; 10. John Wayne; 11. The composers to whose music the Disney corporation orchestrated the seven sections of *Fantasia*; 12. The villain played by Alan Rickman in *Die Hard*; 13. The central character, played by Cary Grant, in Hitchcock's *North by Northwest*; 14. The real names of the Marx Brothers; 15. The planet where the alien eggs are discovered in the *Alien* movies; 16. The machine used in *Blade Runner* to 'truth-test' whether an individual is a replicant; 17. The homicidal maniac in a mask in *Halloween*; 18. The priest cum psychiatrist who tries to help the possessed girl in *The Exorcist*; 19. Jack Nicholson's character in *The Shining*; 20. The Blues Brothers

Quiz 259. Light Entertainment

1. *University Challenge*; 2. Rihanna; 3. Ant and Dec; 4. Terry Wogan, Les Dawson and Paul O'Grady; 5. Girls Aloud; Louis Walsh (girls) and Pete Waterman (boys); 6. Paul Potts; he was a phone shop manager; 7. Leslie Crowther and Bruce Forsyth; 8. *Room 101*; 9. Graham Norton; 10. *Stars in Their Eyes* (the presenter was Matthew Kelly); Cat Deeley; 11. Len Goodman; Arlene Phillips was replaced by Alesha Dixon in 2009; 12. Ian Waite; Denise Lewis and Zoe Ball; 13. Pamela Stephenson; 14. Harry Judd and Rachel Stephens (twenty-five each); 15. Rumba (thirty-nine) and samba (thirty-eight); 16. Ann Widdecombe; 17. Alan is the announcer, while Dave Arch is the musical director and band leader; 18. Tower Ballroom, Blackpool; 19. Erin Boag, Brendan Cole and Anton du Beke; Brendan, with newsreader, Natasha Kaplinsky; 20. *It Takes Two*; Claudia Winkleman; Zoe Ball; she co-presents the Sunday evening results show

Quiz 260. Human Body

1. Right side (ventricle and atrium); pulmonary artery; 2. Neurons; 3. Skull; 4. Sacrum and coccyx; 5. Maxillae and mandible; 6. Twelve; two pairs (numbers eleven twelve); 7. The heart; 8. (a) a couple of tennis courts (still pretty impressive when you reflect that its tucked away neatly inside your chest); 9. Diaphragm; 10. The gluteus maximus in the buttocks; 11. Hear properly (it is the working part of the ear); 12. In the reproductive organs of the male (it is the tube which carries sperm prior to ejaculation – hence, vasectomy, the severing of this tube); 14. It is the large band of tissue on the underside of the foot; 15. Avocado, exceptionally high for a fruit, with 16 per cent fat content (salmon comes in *c*.13 per cent while chickpeas are low-fat but high in carbohydrates and proteins)

Quiz 261. History

1. Richmond, Virginia; 2. Romulus and Remus; 3. Golan Heights; 4. First woman in space; 5. Solidarity, the trade union; 6. Richard Nixon; 7. Jane Seymour (third wife); 8. Spend them, they are coins; 9. US President James Garfield; 10. Belgium; 11. By fighting a duel (they both survived and promptly resigned their positions); 12. (a) Bermuda; 13. The Commonwealth of Australia (formed 1901) and the Dominion of New Zealand (formed 1876); 14. Alexander the Great; 15. The First Estate was the clergy, the Second the nobility and the Third the commonality, including merchants and the free peasantry from the rural areas; in an indoor tennis court; 1792 (Louis XVI was executed the following year); 16. Haiti; Papa Doc Duvalier; (Jean-Bertrand) Aristide; Jimmy Carter; Hispaniola

Quiz 262. Cricket

1. Courtney Walsh (forty-three); Chris Martin (thirty-six); Glenn McGrath (thirty-five); Shane Warne (thirty-four); Muttiah Muralitharan (thirty-three) (Martin is the real bunny here, he played a lot less games and averages 2.36; Steve Waugh and Michael Atherton; Graham Gooch; 2. 1968; Nottinghamshire; Glamorgan; Malcolm Nash; he was caught by Roger Davis but the fielder fell over the ropes; 3. 2000; Surrey; Sussex; Lancashire; 4. Graham Gooch; Alec Stewart; David Gower, Geoffrey Boycott, Michael Atherton; Colin Cowdrey; Kevin Pietersen; Walter Hammond; Alistair Cook; Andrew Strauss; 5. Muttiah Muralitharan (SL); Wasim Akram (Pak); Shaun Pollock (SA); Glenn McGrath and Brett Lee (Aus); Anil Kumble (Ind); Daniel Vettori (NZ); Heath Streak (Zim); Jimmy Anderson (Eng); Courtney Walsh (WI); Abdur Razzak (Ban); 6. Michael Vaughan (2002–3); Ricky Ponting (2006–7); Michael Hussey (2010–11); Alistair Cook (2010–11, amassing the highest aggregate, with 766 runs, only bettered by Bradman and Hammond in a five-test series)

Quiz 263. Classical Arts

1. (b) Berlin Philharmonic; 2. Dmitri Shostakovich; 3. *Madama Butterfly*; 4. Wayne McGregor; Random Dance Company; 5. (c) Ruddigore; 6. (Claudio) Monteverdi; 7. Franz Peter Schubert; 8. *The Magic Flute*; 9. Edward Elgar; 10. (a) Erik Satie; 11. Igor Stravinsky; 12. (a) Havergal Brian (1876–1972; largely ignored in his lifetime, he wrote thirty-two symphonies); 13. Leoncavallo's *I Pagliacci*; 14. Frédéric Chopin; 15. Dame Ninette de Valois; 16. *Der Ring des Nibelungen*; *The Rhine Gold* (*Das Rheingold*), *The Valkyrie* (*Die Walküre*), *Siegfried* (*Siegfried*) and *Twilight of the Gods* (*Götterdämmerung*); Bayreuth

Quiz 264. General Knowledge

1. Iceland, in what became known as the Cod War; 2. John Lennon; 3. Al Gore; 4. False, it is 55 per cent according to a 2008 set of statistics; 5. Dennis Skinner; 6. Director-General of the BBC; Chief Executive of the Royal Opera House; 7. Pangea; 8. Pablo Picasso; 9. Heather Mills-McCartney; 10. Snooker's fastest professional tournament break of 147; Sheffield at the World Championships; 11. Betting shops; 12. Ibrox Park, home of Rangers FC in Glasgow; 13. Sea of Marmara; Bosphorus; 14. 2000; 15. The Barbarians; 16. Johnny Giles; 17. Jane Asher; 18. Madonna; 19. Nancy Spungen; 20. Kurt Cobain

Quiz 265. General Knowledge

All things Peter (with nary a mention of Paul or Mary)

Part 1

1   Which England cricketer was dropped from the side in 2011 after sending derogatory text messages about his team-mates to their South African opponents?

2   Who wrote a series of books about a medieval detective monk called Brother Cadfael?

3   The Peterloo Massacre of 1819, where cavalry charged a crowd demanding Parliamentary reform, took place in which English city?

4   In which old English county is the city of Peterborough?

5   Where is the church commonly known as St Peter's Basilica?

6   What connects the area across the bay from Tampa, Florida, in the US and the Soviet city of Leningrad?

7   Who scored 'the other goal' for England in 1966?

8   Which semi-humorous 1960s business book posited the theory that companies promote competent employees until they reach the point at which they become incompetent?

9   What was the name of Peter Perfect's car in the *Wacky Races* cartoons?

10 *The True History of the Kelly Gang* earned Australian novelist Peter Carey a second Booker Prize; which book won him his first?

Part 2

11 Who was the oldest and best known of the famous dynasty of Flemish Renaissance painters?

12 Which tennis player was known as 'Pistol Pete' because of his ferocious serve?

13 Singer Peter Gabriel was the lead vocalist with which famous prog-rock band in the early 1970s?

14 Who played the hapless Inspector Clouseau in the 1960s series of *Pink Panther* films?

15 What was unusual about Peter Finch's Best Actor Academy Award in 1977 for the previous year's *Network*?

16 With which role is actor Peter Falk indelibly associated?

17 Who connected *Doctor Who* to *Blue Peter* in the 1960s and 1970s?

18 What nationality was the brilliant jazz pianist Oscar Peterson?

19 Chelsea and Czech Republic goalkeeper Petr Čech wears a distinctive helmet after an accident nearly causing his death whilst playing against which club?

20 The organization PETA, based in Virginia in the United States, conducts global campaigns in what cause?

Total Points: 20. Targets: Novice 10 Pro 15. Your Score:

Quiz 266. TV Sitcoms

Part 1

1   Who played the father of the household, Sid Abbott, in the 1970s sitcom *Bless this House*? Which blonde bombshell played his daughter, Sally? (2 pts)

2   Where does Stacey come from in the TV comedy *Gavin and Stacey*?

3   Which *Thick of It* character was once described in the programme as 'a fart in a frock'?

4   Who played Ally McBeal for five years on Fox? What was the name of Ally's unconventional boss? (2 pts)

5   Who wrote the sitcom *Bread* and what was the name of the family of bene-fit scroungers around whom the programme revolved? (2 pts)

6   Who played a sparring couple, Ben and Susan Harper, in *My Family* for eleven years from 2000? What was Ben's profession? (3 pts)

7   Who links *Rising Damp* to *Porridge*?

8   Which sitcom takes place (mostly) in 23 Meteor Street, Tufnell Park, London?

9   Who starred alongside Eric Sykes (playing himself) in the sitcom *Sykes*, which ran for five years in the 1960s and returned in colour the following decade?

10 In the US sitcom *Taxi*, what is the name of the company employing the drivers?

Part 2

11   Who played Gavin and Stacey in the popular BBC sitcom? What were the names of their respective best friends and which up-and-coming star played Gavin's pal's sister? (5 pts)

12   What was the job title of Ian Fletcher (Hugh Bonneville) in the BBC comedy *2012*? Who starred as Sally, his personal assistant? What was the name of the PR guru played by Jessica Hynes? Who provided the show's narration? (4 pts)

Part 3

Some classic quotes from *Blackadder*

13   'You fiend – never before have I encountered such corrupt and foul-minded perversity. Have you ever considered a career in the Church?' Who is appalled at Blackadder's behaviour, mainly because he has just been framed and diddled out of large amounts of cash?

14   'I find his films about as funny as getting an arrow through the neck and then discovering there's a gas bill tied to it.' Who is *Blackadder* dismissing here?

15   'The most over-rated human being since Judas Iscariot won the AD 31 Best Disciple Competition.' Who is Blackadder describing in 'Nob and Nobility'?

16   Which British Prime Minister does Blackadder describe as 'about as effective as a cat flap in an elephant house'?

17   'Well, now, look Dr Johnson, I may be as thick as a whale omelette, but even I know that a book's got to have a plot.' Who is voicing his literary opinion? Who played Dr Johnson? (2 pts)

Total Points: 30. Targets: Novice 12 Pro 23. Your Score:

Quiz 267. Geography

North, south, east and west

Part 1

1 Which lies furthest north: Aberdeen, Fort William or Inverness?

2 Leeds, Hull or Bolton – which is furthest to the south?

3 Which lies furthest to the east: Baltimore, Montreal, Miami or Boston?

4 Which lies furthest to the east: Beijing, Bangkok or Shanghai?

5 Which is closest geographically to Japan: South Korea, the Philippines or Vietnam?

6 Which is closest to the line of longitude 180 degrees from the Greenwich Meridian: New Zealand, Japan or Hawaii?

7 Which is furthest away from Los Angeles: San Diego, San Francisco or Las Vegas?

8 What connects the UK, Spain, Algeria, Mali and Ghana?

9 Which lies furthest to the east along the south coast: Brighton, Chichester, Hastings or Eastbourne?

10 If London is 51/28N and 0/27W, which major cities are (a) 40/43N and 74/00W (b) 33/56S and 151/10E (c) 35/33N and 139/46E (d) 22/50S and 43/15W? (4 pts)

Part 2

11 What are the five neighbours of Mozambique? (5 pts)

12 Which five African countries have a Mediterranean coastline? (5 pts)

13 Which five US states have a border on the Gulf of Mexico? (5 pts)

Total Points: 28. Targets: Novice 11 Pro 21. Your Score:

Quiz 268. History

Part 1

1 Which courtier and favourite of Queen Elizabeth I was executed in 1618 on the signature of her successor?

2 Who was the last Viceroy of India before the former colony was granted independence in 1950?

3 Julius Caesar's nominated heir, Octavian, later ruled Rome under what name?

4 Pliny the Elder describes a Ritual of Oak and Mistletoe; to which priest-like cult does he ascribe the ritual and what is it meant to resolve?

5 Whose armies sacked the Christian city of Constantinople in 1204?

6 In 1934, Hitler ordered the murder of his opponents in the Nazi party. How has this event come to be known?

7 Who was the leader of the Spanish conquistadores whose bullets and diseases wiped out more than 90 per cent of the Inca population of South America in the first half of the sixteenth century? Who was the Inca Emperor of the time? (2 pts)

8 What did Albert Berry do from a height of 1,500 feet in 1912, the first man to do so?

9 Which city, lying at the foot of Mount Parnassus, was home to an oracle of the God, Apollo?

10 Which country, later part of Yugoslavia, but now an independent country again, was annexed by Austria (with the tacit support of Germany) in 1908?

Part 2

11   When the US Army took Texas in the nineteenth century, which other two
      states did Mexico cede to the US for about $15 million?

12   Which Muslim Caliph reconquered Jerusalem in 1187?

13   Who was the stepmother of Thutmose III, Pharaoh of Egypt, who ruled
      alongside her offspring for twenty-two years in the fifteenth century BC?

14   Which famous courtier, scholar and mistress of Louis XVI was born in 1721?

15   In which modern-day country is the city of Troy? What was the name given
      to it by the Romans under the Emperor Augustus? Which city supplanted it
      as the primary Roman stronghold in the region? (3 pts)

16   The Kazan Kremlin in Kazan (Russia) is the only surviving fortress built by
      which ethnic group, who were conquered by Ivan the Terrible? (a) Mongols
      (b) Cossacks (c) Tatars

17   Isabella of France united with which rebel to oust her incompetent husband,
      Edward II, as King of England? (a) Roger de Mortimer (b) Simon de Montfort
      (c) John of Gaunt

18   Which branch of Protestant teaching began in the city of Geneva in the
      1540s?

19   Who led the Scots to a famous victory over a larger English force at
      Bannockburn on 23 June 1314?

20   The Russian Social Democratic Labour Party split into two after a 1904
      disagreement; who led the Bolshevik faction, and what was the name of
      their erstwhile colleagues, led by Martov? (2 pts)

Total Points: 24. Targets: Novice 10 Pro 18. Your Score:

Quiz 269. Crime Fiction

Whodunnit? Ten questions about crime books followed by a mixed bag of clues

Part 1

1   What was John le Carré's second George Smiley novel, set in an English public school?

2   Who was the author of the Gothic mystery, *The Murders in the Rue Morgue*?

3   *Evil Under the Sun* and *Death on the Nile* are familiar works by which famous crime writer?

4   Which former Champion Jockey wrote a hugely successful series of mysteries about the racing world, including *Dead Cert* and *Whip Hand*?

5   Who writes about the investigations of the Ladies No. 1 Detective Agency?

6   Whose crime stories feature a heroine torn between a cop, Joe Moretti, and the mysterious Ranger?

7   Who was the gentleman-burglar creation of E. W. Hornung?

8   Which US author wrote the classic noir novel, *The Maltese Falcon*?

9   Which author, who died early in 2009, created the fictional lawyer, Rumpole of the Bailey?

10 Fictional detective Lord Peter Wimsey was the creation of which writer, born 1893?

Part 2

Mix and Match: match the solver of crime to the author

1. Father Brown; 2. Harry Bosch; 3. Inspector Wexford; 4. Lincoln Rhyme; 5. Alex Cross; 6. John Rebus; 7. Albert Campion; 8. Temperance Brennan; 9. Precious Ramotswe; 10. Paul Temple

a. Alexander McCall Smith; b. Francis Durbridge; c. Ian Rankin; d. Margery Allingham; e. Kathy Reichs; f. Ruth Rendell; g. Jeffrey Deaver; h. Michael Connelly; i. G. K. Chesterton; j. James Paterson

Your Workings:

Total Points: 20. Targets: Novice 8 Pro 15. Your Score:

Quiz 270. Olympic Games

Ten straight questions and a ten point mix 'em up

Part 1

1 Which multiple gold-medal distance runner between the two world wars was known as the Flying Finn?

2 The 1956 Games were the first Olympic Games to be held outside Europe or the United States; where were they?

3 In 1984 in Los Angeles, who sent a team to the Olympics for the first time since 1932?

4 The first London Olympics were held in 1908, but the city acted as stand-in host after (a) a newly constructed stadium in Madrid collapsed with many fatalities (b) Mount Vesuvius erupted and funds were diverted from the Rome Games to deal with the disaster, or (c) an outbreak of cholera rendered the city of Copenhagen unusable?

5 Which GB athlete won javelin medals at three consecutive Olympic Games from 1992? Who was the great Czech javelin thrower who won gold on all three occasions? (2 pts)

6 In 1980 Sebastian Coe won the 1,500 metres and Steve Ovett the 800 metres for Britain; why was this a surprise, given they were the two best middle-distance runners in the world?

7 Two of Britain's three Olympic tennis medals were won in London in 2012; which pair won a silver in the men's doubles in Atlanta in 1996? (2 pts)

8 What is the connection between the Olympic light heavyweight boxing tournament in Antwerp in 1928 and the four-man bobsleigh contest at the 1932 Winter Olympics at Lake Placid? (2 pts)

9 Why was there only a two-year gap between the Winter Olympics in Albertville (1992) and Lillehammer (1994)?

10 Bonnie Blair won five Olympic gold medals for the US in which sport?

Part 2

Mix and Match: all these athletes won medals for Britain at the 2008 Olympics in Beijing (I know, so mean, why couldn't it be 2012?); match the athlete to the sport

1. Bryony Shaw; 2. Louis Smith; 3. Cassie Patten; 4. Zac Purchase; 5. Natasha Danvers; 6. Paul Goodison; 7. David Price; 8. Sarah Stevenson; 9. Tim Brabants; 10. Heather Fell

a. Sailing; b. Taekwondo; c. Windsurfing; d. Rowing; e. Canoeing; f. Gymnastics; g. Modern Pentathlon; h. Swimming; i. Boxing; j. Hurdling

Total Points: 23. Targets: Novice 9 Pro 17. Your Score:

Quiz 271. Alter Egos

Other names, pseudonyms and nicknames

Part 1

1 Which member of the royal family has the middle names Elizabeth Alice?
2 Which public figure bears de Pfeffel as one of his middle names?
3 Which fictional character's 'real' name within her fictional universe is Selina Kyle?
4 By what names did George Logan and Patrick Fyffe go by when they dragged up for their stage act? (2 pts)
5 By what name did singer Yusuf Islam go before adopting his Muslim name?
6 Which early horror actor was born with the rather less doom-laden name of William Henry Pratt?
7 Who was born Arthur Jefferson in the Lake District in 1890 and went on to make up half of one of America's great comedy partnerships?
8 If you had seen Harry Webb as the support act to Richard Wayne Penniman at a gig in the early 1960s, who would you have been watching? (2 pts)
9 Welsh singer Michael Barrett enjoyed enormous UK chart success in the 1980s with a string of old-fashioned rock 'n' roll hits under which name?
10 Reginald Smith and his daughter Kim both enjoyed pop success; what names did they use? (2 pts)

Part 2

Mix and Match: match the real name to the rapper

1. Russell Jones; 2. Marshall Mathers; 3. Curtis Jackson; 4. Elliot Gleave; 5. Patrick Okogwu; 6. Andre Young; 7. William Drayton Jr; 8. Christopher Wallace; 9. Dylan Mills; 10. O'Shea Jackson

a. Eminem; b. Notorious BIG; c. Dizzee Rascal; d. Ol' Dirty Bastard; e. Tinie Tempah; f. Ice Cube; g. 50 Cent; h. Dr Dre; i. Flavor Flav; j. Example

Your Workings:

Total Points: 23. Targets: Novice 12 Pro 18. Your Score:

Quiz 272. General Knowledge

Part 1

1 Which famous postage stamp became available for use in 1840?

2 Christa McAuliffe and six colleagues died on 28 January 1986. How?

3 In which city are the UNESCO headquarters?

4 What does GI in 'GI diet' stand for?

5 What is the modern name for the old Roman city of Deva?

6 Mohammed bin Hamman and Jack Warner were high profile resignations from which body amidst allegations of corruption in 2011?

7 What scale is used to measure windspeed?

8 By what names are Messrs Passmore and Proesch better known in art circles?

9 Who is tallest: Tom Cruise, Brad Pitt, Hugh Grant or Clint Eastwood?

10 What was the 2003 Michael Lewis book that showed how a legendary baseball coach calculated the true value of players?

Part 2

11 What brought flights across Britain and northern Europe to a halt in April 2010?

12 What is the name given to someone who studies things dug from the ground, especially fossils?

13 Aneto, Posets and Perdido are the three highest peaks in which European mountain range?

14 A winner of a Nebula Award would have written what?

15 Who made a series of late career recordings known as the 'American Recordings', which have been released in the years either side of his death in 2003?

16 Stade de Reims, Fiorentina, Milan and Eintracht Frankfurt; what's the connection?

17 What school did David Cameron attend?

18 Which Anglo-Indian actor was born Krishna Banji?

19 Which colourful former Liverpool footballer bought the rights to the titles Lord and Lady of the Manor of Frodsham?

20 Who was the husband and colleague of actress Sheila Hancock who died in 2002?

Total Points: 20. Targets: Novice 10 Pro 15. Your Score: [ ]

Answers Quizzes 265–272

Quiz 265. General Knowledge

1. Kevin Pietersen; 2. Ellis Peters (if anyone puts Edith Pargeter, her real name, give them the point but tell them not to show off); 3. Manchester; 4. Cambridgeshire; 5. Vatican City; 6. Both are called St Petersburg (the city of St Petersburg is a quieter twin of Tampa and a popular holiday destination, while Leningrad changed its name back to the original St Petersburg in 1991 after the collapse of the Soviet regime); 7. Martin Peters scored England's other goal when they beat West Germany 4–2 in the World Cup final with a hat-trick from Geoff Hurst; 8. *The Peter Principle*; 9. The Turbo Terrific; 10. *Oscar and Lucinda*; 11. Pieter Brueghel the Elder; 12. Pete Sampras; 13. Genesis; 14. Peter Sellers; 15. It was awarded posthumously after Finch died in January of a heart attack (the only other actor to have received a posthumous Academy Award for acting was Heath Ledger, who won Best Supporting Actor in 2008); 16. Columbo, the title role in the US TV cop show; 17. Peter Purves, who was a Doctor's companion in the early years of *Doctor Who* and a *Blue Peter* presenter in 1967–78; 18. Canadian, he was born in Montreal in 1925 and died in his home country eighty-two years later; 19. Reading (he was injured in a clash with Stephen Hunt); 20. Animal rights (PETA stands for People for the Ethical Treatment of Animals)

Quiz 266. TV Sitcoms

1. Sid James; Sally Geeson; 2. Barry Island in Wales; 3. Terri Coverley; 4. Calista Flock-hart; Richard Fish; 5. Carla Lane; Boswell; 6. Robert Lindsay and Zoë Wanamaker; dentist; 7. Richard Beckinsale, who plays Alan in *Rising Damp* and Godber in *Porridge*; 8. *Spaced*; 9. Hattie Jacques; 10. Sunshine Cab Company; 11. Matt Horne and Joanna Page; Smithy and Nessa; Sheridan Smith; 12. Head of Delivery; Olivia Colman; Siobhan Sharpe; David Tennant; 13. The Baby-eating Bishop of Bath and Wells; 14. Charlie Chaplin; 15. The Scarlet Pimpernel; 16. Pitt the Elder; 17. Hugh Laurie's Prince George; Robbie Coltrane

Quiz 267. Geography

1. Inverness; 2. Bolton; 3. Boston; 4. Shanghai, on the eastern coast of China; 5. South Korea; 6. New Zealand; 7. San Francisco; 8. All lie on the Prime Meridian; 9. Hastings; 10. (a) New York (b) Sydney (c) Tokyo (d) Rio de Janeiro; 11. South Africa, Zimbabwe, Zambia, Malawi, Tanzania; 12. Algeria, Tunisia, Morocco, Libya, Egypt; 13. Texas, Louisiana, Mississippi, Alabama and Florida

Quiz 268. History

1. Sir Walter Raleigh; 2. (Louis) Mountbatten; 3. Augustus; 4. Druids; infertility issues; 5. The Christian armies of the Fourth Crusade; 6. Night of the Long Knives; 7. (Francisco) Pizarro; Atahualpa; 8. Make a parachute jump from an aeroplane; 9. Delphi; 10.

Bosnia-Herzegovina; 11. New Mexico and California; 12. Saladin; 13. Hatshepsut; 14. Madame de Pompadour; 15. Turkey; Ilium; Constantinople; 16. (c) Tatars; 17. (a) Roger de Mortimer, who in turn was ousted by Edward's son, also Edward; 18. Calvinism; 19. Robert the Bruce; 20. Lenin; Mensheviks

Quiz 269. Crime Fiction

1. *A Murder of Quality*; 2. Edgar Allan Poe; 3. Agatha Christie; 4. Dick Francis; 5. Alexander McCall Smith; 6. Janet Evanovich; 7. Raffles; 8. Dashiell Hammett; 9. John Mortimer; 10. Dorothy L. Sayers; Mix and Match 1. i; 2, h; 3, f; 4, g; 5, j; 6, c; 7, d; 8, e; 9, a; 10, b

Quiz 270. Olympic Games

1. Paavo Nurmi; 2. Melbourne; 3. China; 4. b. Vesuvius ruined large parts of Naples and funds earmarked for the Rome Games were diverted to help repair the city; 5. Steve Backley; his nemesis was Jan Zelezny of the Czech Republic; 6. They won each other's races (Coe was the better 800 metre runner; Ovett was favourite for the 1,500 metres); 7. Tim Henman and Neil Broad (Broad was South African but represented Great Britain); 8. Eddie Eagan, the light heavyweight champion, was also in the winning bobsleigh team (1 point for the answer without knowing the name); 9. The IOC decided to split the Summer and Winter Olympics so there was an event each two years; 10. Speed skating; Mix and Match 1, c; 2, f; 3, h; 4, d; 5, j; 6, a; 7, i; 8, b; 9, e; 10, g

Quiz 271. Alter Egos

1. Princess Anne; 2. Boris Johnson; 3. Catwoman in the *Batman* comics; 4. (Dr Evadne) Hinge and (Dame Hilda) Bracket; 5. Cat Stevens; 6. Boris Karloff; 7. Stan Laurel; 8. Cliff Richard and Little Richard; 9. Shakin' Stevens (the UK's biggest selling singles act of the decade); 10. Marty and Kim Wilde; Mix and Match 1, d; 2, a; 3, g; 4, j; 5, e; 6, h; 7, i; 8, b; 9, c; 10, f

Quiz 272. General Knowledge

1. Penny Black; 2. They were the astronauts aboard the *Challenger*, which exploded on take-off from Cape Canaveral; 3. Paris; 4. Glycaemic Index; 5. Chester; 6. FIFA; 7. Beaufort; 8. Gilbert and George; 9. Eastwood, at a whopping six foot four; 10. *Moneyball*; 11. A cloud of volcanic ash; 12. Palaeontologist; 13. Pyrénées; 14. Science fiction; 15. Johnny Cash; 16. They were the teams beaten (Reims twice) by Real Madrid in the first five European Cup finals from 1956 to 1960; 17. Eton; 18. Ben Kingsley; 19. Djibril Cissé; 20. John Thaw

Quiz 273. General Knowledge

Part 1

1 Which traffic measure was first used in Oklahoma City in 1935?

2 Anna Kournikova, MyDoom and Koobface are all types of what?

3 Which famous explorer, perhaps New Zealand's most famous son, died on 11 January 2008?

4 What is the name of the central wolf character in Jack London's *The Call of the Wild*?

5 The NEC is a purpose-built exhibition centre to the west of which major British city?

6 What began life as the Royal Yacht Squadron's 100 Guinea Cup in 1851?

7 What is the name of Mickey Mouse's pet dog?

8 What links a great Impressionist painter to a great French film director of the 1930s and after?

9 Who is tallest: Keira Knightley, Helen Mirren, Gillian Anderson or Kate Moss?

10 What feat was first performed (or at least recognized) by Captain Matthew Webb on 24 August 1875?

Part 2

11 Which Bob Dylan song did research reveal was the most popular tune with buskers in London and New York?

12 Who shot Harry Whittington in 2006?

13 Nantucket is a small island off the coast and within the boundaries of which US state?

14 What was the title of Jeffrey Archer's first novel after his release from prison?

15 Who was the last unmarried Prime Minister of Great Britain?

16 Why did Italian club Perugia sack Korean striker Ahn Jung-Hwan in 2002?

17 Which footballer's wife did a Bisto advert in the 1960s?

18 Which pop star has sometimes travelled under the name Mother Bernadette Marie?

19 Who was found guilty of assault after attacking Matthew Simmons on 25 January 1995?

20 In which year were front seat-belts made compulsory in the UK: 1971, 1978 or 1983?

Total Points: 20. Targets: Novice 10 Pro 15. Your Score:

Quiz 274. Name the Band

Figure out the band's name from the line-up

Part 1

All from the 1960s

1   Obie Benson, Duke Fakir, Lawrence Payton, Levi Stubbs
2   John Cale, Sterling Morrison, Lou Reed, Mo Tucker
3   Allan Clarke, Eric Haydock, Tony Hicks, Graham Nash, Don Rathbone
4   Florence Ballard, Diana Ross, Mary Wells
5   Mick Avory, John Dalton, Dave Davies, Ray Davies, John Gosling
6   Al Jardine, Bruce Johnston, Mike Love, Brian Wilson, Carl Wilson, Dennis Wilson
7   Rod Argent, Paul Atkinson, Colin Blunstone, Hugh Grundy, Chris White
8   Denny Doherty, Cass Elliot, John Phillips, Michelle Phillips
9   Roger Daltrey, John Entwistle, Keith Moon, Pete Townshend
10 Ginger Baker, Eric Clapton, Jack Bruce

Part 2

All from the 1970s

11 Lindsey Buckingham, Mick Fleetwood, John McVie, Christine McVie, Stevie Nicks
12 Dave Gilmour, Nick Mason, Roger Waters, Rick Wright
13 Sheila Ferguson, Valerie Holiday, Fayette Pinkney
14 Rick Buckler, Bruce Foxton, Paul Weller
15 Eddie Levert, William Powell, Walter Williams
16 John Bonham, John Paul Jones, Jimmy Page, Robert Plant
17 Philip Bailey, Larry Dunne, Johnny Graham, Ralph Johnson, Al McKay, Gary L. Morgan, Fred White, Maurice White, Verdine White, Andrew Woolfolk
18 Brian Robertson, Brian Downey, Scott Gorham, Phil Lynott
19 Martin Lee, Lee Sheriden, Nicky Stevens, Sandra Stevens
20 Topper Headon, Mick Jones, Paul Simonon, Joe Strummer

Total Points: 20. Targets: Novice 8 Pro 15. Your Score:

Quiz 275. Movies

Here is a brief (and occasionally tongue-in-cheek) plot of a well-known movie – just name the movie

Part 1

1   Two blokes hang together, and one escorts the boss's girl; the boys make a mess, and another feller has to clean up; meanwhile some other hardnut upsets his employers and a diner is held up at gunpoint.

2   An acrophobic chap agrees to follow another man's blonde wife around San Francisco. Things go downhill, both literally and metaphorically.

3   A spy, a card game, a golf match and a deadly bowler hat.

4   Three people go missing in the woods. We see the video.

5   A former pilot has to land a plane after the crew suffer a breakdown (although he has an inflatable co-pilot for help). How we laugh.

6   A man washes up on shore, wrongly assuming he is dead, sees a dog and says, 'I always hoped there would be dogs.'

7   It begins at a railway station with a piece of grit in the eye and a clean hankie . . .

8   The memoirs of a mass murderer who killed all eight members of a family.

9   Two cool dudes dress up as girls to escape the mob and find very different brands of love.

10 A wedding, some hunting and a war.

Part 2

11 Heroic humans battle bugs but turn out to be the bad guys. All done with maximum splatter.

12 A strange boy does hairdressing with a difference while sporting a shock wig and a bondage suit.

13 Man goes forward in time and discovers his planet is now ruled by a previously subordinate species.

14 Travel back in time in a collectible sports car and meet your mum when she was a teenybopper!

15 A nut-job kills his sister and then puts on a mask and kills a few more.

16 Whatever you do, don't watch the video.

17 Mods and rockers with music and Sting.

18 A man deliberately eats too much.

19 Reach thirty, get killed.

20 Chased by a Peterbilt gasoline truck.

Total Points: 20. Targets: Novice 10 Pro 15. Your Score: ☐

Quiz 276. Geography

Includes a Mix and Match quiz

Part 1

1 Sierra Leone, Senegal, Morocco, Mali: which of these African countries does not have an Atlantic coast?

2 What is the twin city of St Paul – between them they make up 60 per cent of the population of the US state of Minnesota?

3 Which is the only major Australian city on the western seaboard?

4 Which Asian country is bigger than France, Spain and Germany combined but has a population of little over two million?

5 Annapurna is a mountain lying within the boundaries of which country?

6 In which body of water does the Isle of Man lie?

7 Which two EU member states have a population of less than a million? (2 pts)

8 What are the two adjacent regions in the east of France which have changed hands between France and Germany many times? What is the area's major city? (3 pts)

9 Lake Baikal is the largest inland body of water in which country?

10 Which river forms part of the boundary between Mexico and the United States?

Part 2

Mix and Match: match the Asian country to the city

1. Burma; 2. Tashkent; 3. Rawalpindi; 4. Hanoi; 5. Basra; 6. Beirut; 7. Jakarta; 8. Sapporo; 9. Katmandu; 10. Manila

a. Vietnam; b. Uzbekistan; c. Philippines; d. Nepal; e. Rangoon; f. Indonesia; g. Japan; h. Lebanon; i. Iraq; j. Pakistan

Your Workings:

Total Points: 23. Targets: Novice 9 Pro 17. Your Score:

Quiz 277. Transport

Anyway, anyhow, anywhere

Part 1

1   Which aviation service was launched in Australia in 1928?

2   What was the major eastern destination of the trains that travelled by various routes under the name of the Orient Express?

3   What started running between London and Edinburgh in 1862?

4   Who crashed an Airspeed Oxford into the Thames Estuary in January 1941?

5   Where did the UK's first modern light rail system open in 1980? (a) Manchester (b) Newcastle upon Tyne (c) Docklands

6   Swedish-born Carl Wickman started a bus company when he was laid off work in Minnesota in the early twentieth century; to what did the company change its name in 1926?

7   From where might one take a Brittany Ferries passenger ship to Bilbao in northern Spain?

8   Who landed at Cape Cod, Massachusetts, in 1620? Where had they come from and aboard which vessel? (3 pts)

9   What is kept in a binnacle? (a) an aircraft's black box recorder – the binnacle is the outer casing (b) a ship's compass (c) an iridium block which provides ballast on a modern hot-air balloon?

10 What is the world's largest railway station?

Part 2

Mix and Match: connect the ship to the captain or significant passenger

1. *Bellerophon*; 2. *Fram*; 3. *Discovery*; 4. *Calypso*; 5. HMS *Sophie*; 6. *Santa Maria*; 7. *Adventure* and *Grenville*; 8. *Cinque Ports*; 9. *Nautilus*; 10. *Black Pearl*

a. Napoleon Bonaparte surrenders to the British; b. Robert Falcon Scott travels to the South Pole, with Shackleton amongst the crew; c. Captain Jack Aubrey in Patrick O'Brian's fiction; d. Christopher Columbus discovers the New World in 1492; e. Alexander Selkirk, the inspiration for *Robinson Crusoe*; f. Captain Nemo goes *20,000 Leagues Under the Sea*; g. Roald Amundsen discovers the South Pole; h. Pirate ship of Captain Jack Sparrow; i. Jacques Cousteau goes diving; j. Captain James Cook voyages to the Antarctic

Your Workings:

Total Points: 22. Targets: Novice 9 Pro 17. Your Score:

Quiz 278. Sport

Part 1

1   Who became the first undisputed Super-Middleweight Champion in 2007 when he beat Mikkel Kessler in November 2007?

2   What connects Sir Barnaby, Supreme Rock and Primmore's Pride?

3   What historic first for a British cyclist did Mark Cavendish achieve in 2011?

4   In January 2013 England beat Australia in a three match series for the first time at which sport? (a) netball (b) water polo (c) speedway

5   What are the two showpiece races of the March Cheltenham National Hunt Festival, run nowadays on the first and fourth day of the meeting? (2 pts)

6   Who plied their trade at the Polo Grounds in the 1950s?

7   Who are the three Finnish drivers to have won the Formula 1 Drivers' Championship (up to March 2013)? (3 pts)

8   Who did Stephen Hendry beat to win his record-breaking seventh world title in 1999?

9   For what is sportswoman Rhona Martin best remembered?

10 Mark Loram is the only British winner (in 2000) of which event, which started in 1995?

Part 2

11 Which five boxers beat Muhammad Ali during his career? (5 pts)

12 Tigers, Lions, Red Wings and Pistons; where are they based and what does each of them do? (5pts)

Total Points: 23. Targets: Novice 9 Pro 17. Your Score: [   ]

Quiz 279. Books

Part 1

1 For what is the Kate Greenaway Award presented?

2 Which great work of American literature is narrated by Ishmael and takes place aboard the *Pequod*?

3 *Man's Best Friend* (1984), the first of the *Wicked Willie* series by Peter Mayle and Gray Jolliffe, was a humorous runaway bestseller; who or what is Wicked Willie?

4 Which annual publication is often termed 'The Bible of Cricket'?

5 Where does Professor Lidenbrock lead his expedition in Jules Verne's 1864 novel?

6 In Edgar Rice Burroughs' *Tarzan of the Apes*, what was the title in England to which Tarzan was the heir?

7 *As I Walked Out One Midsummer's Morning* is the second part of an auto-biographical trilogy by which English poet and writer? What is the even better known first part? (2 pts)

8 What is the geographical setting of *Lorna Doone*, R. D. Blackmore's romance which takes place in the seventeenth century?

9 What was the title of Aravind Adiga's debut novel, the 2008 Booker Prize winner?

10 Who was the Irish writer best known for her comedy of manners, *Good Behaviour*, written in 1981?

Part 2

11   *The Moon's a Balloon* and *Bring on the Empty Horses* were entertaining memoirs written in the 1970s by which English film star?

12   What was the main profession of Arthur Conan Doyle, and in which city did he live and work? (2 pts)

13   What does bestselling author Lorna Byrne claim to have been seeing for most of her life? (a) the ghost of her mother (b) angels (c) the imprimata of Christ in everyday objects

14   *The Day of the Scorpion, The Towers of Silence* and *A Division of the Spoils* are the second, third and fourth books in Paul Scott's *Raj Quartet*; what is the first, also the name given to the TV dramatization of the books?

15   What was Andrew Miller's 2011 prize-winning novel about the clearance of an overcrowded graveyard in pre-revolutionary France?

16   Which perennial bestseller was conceived during a shooting party in Ireland in 1951 and first saw publication in 1955?

17   Rudolf Rassendyll is at the heart of which classic adventure story?

18   What nationality is the novelist Milan Kundera?

19   Which French novel by which twentieth-century existentialist centres on the random killing of an Arab by a man named Meursault? (2 pts)

20   By what name is the fictional figure Sir Percy Blakeney better known?

Total Points: 23. Targets: Novice 9 Pro 17. Your Score:

Quiz 280. General Knowledge

Part 1

1   Who was Emperor of Ethiopia from 1930 to 1974, having been regent from 1916? Which religion recognizes him as a god among men? (2 pts)

2   Which giant US bank went bankrupt on 15 September 2008?

3   Who became General Secretary of the Communist Party in the Soviet Union in March 1985?

4   For what are Edmund Dulac and Arthur Rackham best known?

5   The wetland area known as the Fens crosses which three English counties?

6   Which former *X Factor* winner was punched by a bitter reject from the programme at a 2009 book launch?

7   What connects Napoleon in exile to the Boer War?

8   What great work was commissioned by Pope Julius II in 1508 and who completed it four years later? (2 pts)

9   Who is tallest: Bruce Springsteen, Robbie Williams, Elton John or Prince?

10 What was first won by Charles Collier on a Matchless in 1907?

Part 2

11   According to an *Observer* interview (December 2012), who did Adam Ant most want to be when he was growing up? (a) Elvis Presley (b) Audrey Hepburn (c) George Best

12   Who was the captain of the HMS *Bounty* who was put overboard when the crew mutinied?

13   Skellig Michael is a monastery island off the southwest coast of which country?

14   Who wrote the mammoth work, *À la Recherche du Temps Perdu* (*Remembrance of Things Past*), published in seven volumes between 1913 and 1927?

15   Which teenager was listed by *Forbes* magazine as the third most influential celebrity in the world in 2012?

16   Which two sides won the European Cup on three consecutive occasions in the 1970s? (2 pts)

17   What is the born name of Pope Benedict XVI?

18   Explorer Ranulph Fiennes is related in what way to the actors Ralph and Joseph?

19   What was the name of Wayne Bridge's girlfriend, with whom then-England captain John Terry was revealed to have had an affair?

20   Once labelled Hollywood's 'Golden Couple', which two screen stars were divorced on 7 August 2001? (2 pts)

Total Points: 24. Targets: Novice 12 Pro 18. Your Score:

Answers Quizzes 273–280

Quiz 273. General Knowledge

1. Parking meters; 2. Computer virus; 3. Sir Edmund Hillary; 4. Buck; 5. Birmingham; 6. America's Cup; 7. Pluto; 8. The artist Pierre Auguste Renoir was the father of director Jean Renoir; 9. Keira Knightley at five foot seven; 10. Swimming the English Channel; 11. 'Knocking On Heaven's Door'; 12. US Vice President Dick Cheney in a hunting accident (Cheney has never offered a public apology); 13. Massachusetts; 14. *False Impression*; 15. Edward Heath; 16. His goal knocked Italy out of the 2002 World Cup (the Perugia chairman felt aggrieved); 17. Tina Moore, aka Mrs Bobby; 18. Sinead O'Connor; 19. Eric Cantona (Simmons was the Crystal Palace fan he kung-fu kicked); 20. 1983

Quiz 274. Name the Band

1. The Four Tops; 2. Velvet Underground; 3. The Hollies; 4. The Supremes; 5. The Kinks; 6. The Beach Boys; 7. The Zombies; 8. The Mamas and The Papas; 9. The Who; 10. Cream; 11. Fleetwood Mac; 12. Pink Floyd; 13. The Three Degrees; 14. The Jam; 15. The O'Jays; 16. Led Zeppelin; 17. Earth, Wind and Fire; 18. Thin Lizzy; 19. Brotherhood of Man; 20. The Clash

Quiz 275. Movies

1. *Pulp Fiction*; 2. *Vertigo*; 3. *Goldfinger*; 4. *Blair Witch Project*; 5. *Airplane!*; 6. *A Matter of Life and Death*; 7. *Brief Encounter*; 8. *Kind Hearts and Coronets*; 9. *Some Like It Hot*; 10. *The Deer Hunter*; 11. *Starship Troopers*; 12. *Edward Scissorhands*; 13. *Planet of the Apes*; 14. *Back to the Future*; 15. *Halloween*; 16. *The Ring*; 17. *Quadrophenia*; 18. *Super Size Me*; 19. *Logan's Run*; 20. *Duel*

Quiz 276. Geography

1. Mali (which is landlocked); 2. Minneapolis; 3. Perth; 4. Mongolia; 5. Nepal; 6. Irish Sea; 7. Malta and Luxembourg; 8. Alsace and Lorraine; Strasbourg; 9. Russia; 10. Rio Grande; Mix and Match 1, e; 2, b; 3, j; 4, a; 5, i; 6, h; 7, f; 8, g; 9, d; 10, c

Quiz 277. Transport

1. The Flying Doctor; 2. Istanbul (the route was discontinued in 1977 when the terminus became Vienna); 3. *The Flying Scotsman*; 4. Amy Johnson; 5. (b) Newcastle (the service uses the old railway network and is called the Tyne and Wear Metro); 6. Greyhound Lines; 7. Portsmouth; 8. The Pilgrim Fathers; Plymouth, *The Mayflower*; 9. (b) it's a ship's compass; 10. Grand Central Terminal (the correct name since 1913, although Grand Central Station is still in common use), New York; Mix and Match 1, a; 2, g; 3, b; 4, i; 5, c; 6, d; 7, j; 8, e; 9, f; 10, h

Quiz 278. Sport

1. Joe Calzaghe; 2. They are all eventing horses ridden by Pippa Funnell; 3. Winning the Green Jersey; 4. Netball; 5. Champion Hurdle and Gold Cup; 6. New York Giants baseball team; 7. Keke Rosberg (1982), Mika Hakkinen (1998, 99), Kimi Raikkonen (2007); 8. Mark Williams; 9. Captaining the British curling team to a gold medal at the Winter Olympics in Salt Lake City; 10. Speedway Grand Prix Series; 11. Joe Frazier, Ken Norton, Leon Spinks, Larry Holmes and Trevor Berbick; 12. Detroit; they play baseball, American football (NFL), ice hockey and basketball respectively

Quiz 279. Books

1. Children's book illustration; 2. *Moby Dick*; 3. A talking penis; 4. *Wisden Cricketers' Almanack*; 5. *A Journey to the Centre of the Earth*; 6. Lord Greystoke; 7. Laurie Lee; *Cider with Rosie*; 8. Exmoor; 9. *The White Tiger*; 10. Molly Keane; 11. David Niven; 12. Doctor; Edinburgh; 13. (b) Angels; 14. *The Jewel in the Crown*; 15. *Pure*; 16. *The Guinness Book of Records* (now *Guinness World Records*); 17. *The Prisoner of Zenda* (Anthony Hope); 18. Czech; 19. *L'Etranger*, Albert Camus; 20. The Scarlet Pimpernel, in the book by Baroness Orczy

Quiz 280. General Knowledge

1. Haile Selassie; Rastafarianism; 2. Lehman Brothers; 3. Mikhail Gorbachev; 4. Children's book illustration; 5. Lincolnshire, Cambridgeshire and Norfolk; 6. Leona Lewis; 7. The island of St Helena (Napoleon spent his last six years exiled on this remote South Atlantic island, which was also used to house some 6,000 Boer prisoners during the Boer War); 8. The painting of the ceiling of the Sistine Chapel; Michelangelo; 9. Robbie Williams at six foot one; 10. Isle of Man TT race; 11. (c) George Best; 12. Ivo Bligh; 13. Ireland (it lies a few miles off the Kerry coast); 14. Marcel Proust; 15. Justin Bieber; 16. Ajax Amsterdam and Bayern Munich; 17. Joseph Ratzinger; 18. He is their cousin; 19. Vanessa Perroncel; 20. Tom Cruise and Nicole Kidman

Quiz 281. General Knowledge

Part 1

1   Which gardener is associated with the gardens at Great Dixter? (a) Gertrude Jekyll (b) Christopher Lloyd (c) Vita Sackville-West

2   Who won a landslide victory in the 1990 election in Burma, only for the military rulers to refuse to hand over power?

3   Bulgarian dissident Georgi Markov died in 1978, four days after he was attacked in London; how was he killed?

4   *Knots and Crosses* was the first novel by which Scottish author to feature which modern detective? (2 pts)

5   The town of Sheerness is at the mouth of which river?

6   Film-maker Robin Whitehead died of a drug overdose whilst making a documentary on which rock star?

7   Which US state contains the National Park known as the Everglades?

8   The NRA is an old organization that has been turned into a right-wing lobby group in the US; for what is NRA an acronym?

9   Who is tallest: George W. Bush, Nicole Kidman, Tony Blair, Kate Moss?

10 From where in Spain does Rafael Nadal come?

Part 2

11 In 1930 Ellen Church was the first (a) female trade union leader (b) air hostess to take to the air or (c) woman to join a serving unit of the armed forces?

12 In which sport did Great Britain's Sarah Storey win four gold medals at the 2012 Paralympics?

13 Which famous seasonal story by Charles Dickens was published on 16 December 1843?

14 If Jackson Smith, son of Patti, is the second, who was the first?

15 If a Frenchman called Guillaume Tisserand had he been born in England, what would have been his name?

16 What particular type of sports equipment would you associate with the brand TaylorMade?

17 If a first-year student is a freshman or fresher, what term is sometimes used for a second-year student?

18 By what name is scientist Brooke Magnanti better known?

19 What new mode of marine transport was launched at Southampton in 1959?

20 Which four London stations feature on a standard Monopoly board? (4 pts)

Total Points: 24. Targets: Novice 12 Pro 18. Your Score:

Quiz 282. Video Games

Part 1

1 What was the 1989 fantasy game developed for Apple computers by Jordan Mechner and used as the basis for a 2010 Disney movie??

2 Which video game sold over one billion units in six weeks in 2010?

3 What were the huge-selling fourth and fifth instalments of the *Elder Scrolls* series of games?

4 Who is Master Chief Petty Officer John-117?

5 In the *Grand Theft Auto* series of games, Liberty City and Vice City of the fictional world equate to which real US cities? (2 pts)

6 Which company introduced the Super Mario Bros to the world in 1985? What is the name of Mario's brother? (2 pts)

7 What is, by a huge distance, the bestselling Wii game in history?

8 Objections to the violence in which arena fighting game played a major role in the development of ratings for video games?

9 Hironobu Sakaguchi launched which game in 1987, not knowing it would spawn an entire media empire?

10 Who is the hero of the PS3 game *Resistance: Fall of Man*?

Part 2

11 The series of games which go by the name of *Biohazard* in Japan, where they originate, are known by which name in the US and UK?

12 Which video game revolves around the action at the King of Iron Fist Tournament?

13 With over twenty million copies sold, what is comfortably the biggest selling game on the PC platform?

14 Which unfolding adventure game, released initially for the Mac OS system, takes place on an unfathomable island, which the player explores in the guise of a character called the Stranger?

15 *Rainbow Six* and *Ghost Recon* were military games given weight by the use of which bestselling author's name?

16 Which game series takes places on the continent of Tamriel on the world Nim?

17 Which 2005 launch by RedOctane introduced gamers to the Rock Meter and Star Power?

18 Who lent his name to a top-selling series of skateboarding games?

19 Which game series, rebooted in 2013, featured Lara Croft? Which British actress provided Lara's voice in 2006–2008? (2 pts)

20 The half-demon half-angel killer Dante is the central character in which adult games franchise?

Total Points: 23. Targets: Novice 9 Pro 17. Your Score:

Quiz 283. Gardeners' Question Time

Part 1

1 Which film director's garden is preserved at Dungeness in Kent?

2 In which year did the Chelsea Flower Show take place for the first time: 1876, 1913 or 1934?

3 What was the name given to the wartime campaign for self-sufficiency and increase of food supply amongst the population?

4 Who was the first face of gardening on the BBC (he started working for the corporation in 1959 and was the front of *Gardeners' World* from 1969 to 1976)?

5 Which triumvirate formed the team at the heart of *Ground Force*, a garden makeover programme which thrived on the success of *Gardeners' World*? (3 pts)

6 With which aspect of gardening is David Austin associated?

7 Delphiniums take their name from (a) a huge botanic garden devoted to the genus in Delft, Netherlands (b) the Latin name for a dolphin because the flowers have a similar shape or (c) the genus was adapted and hybridized by botanist Delphine Seguyard in the nineteenth century?

8 The nasturtium genus are an edible group of plants sold under what name in foodstores?

9 On 9 April 1947 the BBC broadcast a radio programme called *How Does Your Garden Grow?* The programme is still running under which name?

10 What is the garden, built for Catherine de Medici, situated between the Louvre and the Place de la Concorde?

Part 2

11   Which writer lived at and developed the gardens at Sissinghurst in Kent?

12   Bob Flowerdew is a devotee of what specific style of gardening?

13   Broom, gorse and jasmine all flower in what colour?

14   What common garden ingredient, in the US, comes in Kentucky Blue, Zoysia, Buy Buffalo and Fescue?

15   *Phytophthora infestans* is an unwelcome disease commonly known as (a) peach leaf curl (b) black spot or (c) potato blight?

16   They are a herbaceous perennial known in Japan as *giboshi*, and occasionally as plantain lilies; they enjoy shade and produce spectacular variations of foliage; what are they?

17   Westonbirt in Gloucestershire is the country's biggest garden of what specific type?

18   Exhibitors from Taiwan displayed at the Chelsea Flower Show for the first time in 2010 and wowed visitors with a stunning array of what?

19   Where might you win a Hogg Award for trees or a Knightian Award for vegetables and herbs?

20   Hyacinthoides is not a hyacinth, but a plant seen commonly in woodlands and also grown as a border flower in gardens; what is it?

Total Points: 22. Targets: Novice 9 Pro 17. Your Score: [   ]

Quiz 284. TV

Ten straight questions plus a Mix and Match section

Part 1

1   The board game Balderdash uses the same principles as which long-running TV game show?

2   Who was the scriptwriter behind the comedy drama *Coupling*, which ran from 2000 to 2004?

3   What was the first (1979) hit natural history programme narrated by David Attenborough?

4   The Rembrandts 'I'll Be There For You' was the theme tune to which popular series?

5   Which former Labour MP made his first appearance on TV in a daytime show called *Day to Day*?

6   Which TV drama had a reprehensible main character called Percy Topliss, and which actor's career got a leg-up playing the part? (2 pts)

7   Comic actor Terry Thomas was the first guest on which iconic chat show in 1971?

8   Which current affairs programme ran on ITV for thirty-five years starting in 1963?

9   Who narrated the BBC's *Walking with Dinosaurs*, the corporation's first use of heavy-duty expensive CGI for a factual programme?

10 Which of the Osbourne children refused to partake in their fly-on-the-wall TV show?

Part 2

Mix and Match: match the presenter to the TV show with which they have been associated

1. Hugh Scully; 2. Robert Robinson; 3. Antoine de Caunes; 4. Alan Titchmarsh; 5. Denis Norden; 6. Magnus Magnusson; 7. Nick Ross; 8. Richard Whiteley; 9. Phil Drabble; 10. Melvyn Bragg

a. *The South Bank Show*; b. *Crimewatch*; c. *Gardeners' World*; d. *It'll Be Alright on the Night*; e. *One Man and His Dog*; f. *Countdown*; g. *Antiques Roadshow*; h. *Mastermind*; i. *Call My Bluff*; j. *Eurotrash*

Your Workings:

Total Points: 21. Targets: Novice 8 Pro 16. Your Score:

Quiz 285. Shakespeare

The Bard of Avon (as some people insist on calling him)

Part 1

1 What famous stage direction prefaces the death of Antigonus in Shakespeare's *The Winter's Tale*?

2 In *The Comedy of Errors*, in which two cities are the two sets of twins based? (2 pts)

3 Which play is popularly believed to have been written because Queen Elizabeth I liked the character of Sir John Falstaff from the *Henry IV* plays?

4 Which of Shakespeare's plays (probably a collaboration) tells the story of Palamon and Arcite? Which even older classic of English literature featured a version of the same story? (2 pts)

5 Prospero is the rightful duke of which city in *The Tempest*? What is the name of his spirit-servant? (2 pts)

6 Who accompanies Macbeth in the opening scene of the play, and what is his role later in the play? (2 pts)

7 Which tragic Shakespearean hero strangles his own wife in a fit of jealousy? Who puts him up to it? (2 pts)

8 Who is the friend of Romeo and the house of Montague whose death sets off the tragic events of *Romeo and Juliet*? Who kills him? (2 pts)

9 What was the semi-humorous narrative poem Shakespeare wrote in 1592–3 about a Greek god and her mortal lover?

10 Of what profession are Dogberry (*Much Ado About Nothing*), Dull (*Love's Labours Lost*) and Elbow (*Measure For Measure*)?

Part 2

Some Shakespearean quotes

11   'Age cannot wither her, nor custom stale her infinite variety.' Who is describing who in which play? (2 pts)

12   'All the world's a stage, and all the men and women merely players.' Who speaks these famous lines, the beginning of a speech referred to as the 'seven ages of man'? In which play? (2 pts)

13   'Neither a borrower nor a lender be.' Who gives his son this advice in *Hamlet*?

14   'We few, we happy few, we band of brothers.' Who says this?

15   'I am no orator as Brutus is; but as you know me all, a plain blunt man.' Who is being a little disingenuous in which play? (2 pts)

16   'Out, out, brief candle! Life's but a walking shadow, a poor player that struts and frets his hour upon the stage and then is heard no more.' Who is getting a bit worked up?

17   'And thus I clothe my naked villainy, with odd ends stol'n forth of holy writ, and seem a saint, when most I play the devil.' Who is revelling in his own wickedness?

18   'Oh happy dagger, this is thy sheath! there rust, and let me die' Who is on the point of suicide?

19   'Some are born great, some achieve greatness and some have greatness thrust upon 'em.' Who is deceiving himself into believing his mistress (employer) is in love with him? Who is his mistress? (2 pts)

20   'Uneasy lies the head that bears the crown.' Which king is in contemplative mood?

Total Points: 30. Targets: Novice 9 Pro 23. Your Score:

Quiz 286. Rock and Pop

A general miscellany of modern music

Part 1

1 Which famous pop partnership started out singing together as an act called Tom and Jerry when they were teenagers in the 1950s?

2 Cheryl James and Sandra Denton performed under which tasty pseudonym in the 1980s and 1990s?

3 Who was the lead man in 1980 band Orange Juice?

4 Cee-Lo Green and Danger Mouse; what's the band?

5 Who's first solo album was her *Miseducation* (1998)?

6 What was voted by a Mojo panel in 2005 as Bob Dylan's greatest song?

7 Which folk singer, once of Fairport Convention, sang with Robert Plant on Led Zeppelin's 'The Battle of Evermore'?

8 What personal crisis sparked the anger of Marvin Gaye's album, *Here, My Dear*? (a) his divorce (b) the death of his father (c) the wrongful imprisonment of a friend by a white court

9 Which thirty-five year-old released the 'punk' album *New Boots and Panties!!* in 1977?

10 Who released the 1985 album, *Don't Stand Me Down*, which polarized critics like few others?

Part 2

11 Who was the Nice man who sang with a backing band called Cockney Rebel? What was their biggest UK hit (wording must be correct)? (2 pts)

12 Allen Toussaint was a producer and key player in the soul music coming out of which US city in the 1960s and 1970s?

13 Which experimental European band released an album entitled ( ) – not a misprint – in 2002, with no song names for the eight tracks and the entire work sung in a made-up language called Hopelandic?

14 Which bassist also has a reputation as an English cheesemaker?

15 Under what name did Tjinder Singh and his mates from Wolverhampton flirt with superstardom in the late 1990s? What was their no. 1 hit, mixed by Fatboy Slim? (2 pts)

16 Which French synth pop duo provided the heavy-selling soundtrack to the 2000 movie *The Virgin Suicides*?

17 What was Plan B's 2012 movie soundtrack which became his second UK no. 1 album?

18 Lily Allen, Paloma Faith, Florence (and the Machine) Welch, Lana Del Rey, Emeli Sandé; who is the oldest and who's the baby? (2 pts)

19 *The Healer* (1989) was a welcome return for which blues legend, who had been quiet for two decades?

20 Who comfortably heads the list of multiple Brit Award winners?

Total Points: 23. Targets: Novice 9 Pro 17. Your Score:

Quiz 287. Births, Deaths and Marriages

Ten quickies and a mix up

Part 1

1   Which entrepreneur, designer and restaurateur was married to which best-selling writer? (2 pts)

2   Which Beatle married which Bond girl? (2 pts)

3   Which singer was married for four years to rapper Nas, until a 2009 split?

4   Which major US TV star of the 1960s and early 1970s eloped with Cuban entertainer and bandleader Desi Arnaz in 1940?

5   What is the occupation of Tony Blair's wife, Cherie, and what was that of her father? (2 pts)

6   Who are the parents, now deceased, of Heavenly Hiraani Tiger Lily? (2 pts)

7   Prior to her marriage to racehorse owner, Charlie Brooks, to whom was discredited former newspaper editor Rebekah Brooks married?

8   Which model went from the arm of Michael Hutchence to Billy Corgan of Smashing Pumpkins?

9   Crystal Harris, twenty-four, got engaged in 2011 to which man, sixty years her elder?

10   Peter Phillips is eleventh in line to the throne; what is the name of his wife? Where is she from? And what is the name of their daughter, born 2010? (3 pts)

Part 2

Mix and Match: match the actor to the city of their birth

1. Sid James; 2. Keanu Reeves; 3. Kim Cattrall; 4. William Shatner; 5. Omar Sharif; 6. Michael Gambon; 7. Kenneth Branagh; 8. Arnold Schwarzenegger; 9. Juliette Binoche; 10. Peter Alliss

a. Dublin, Ireland; b. Montreal, Canada; c. Graz, Austria; d. Liverpool, England; e. Paris, France; f. Johannesburg, SA; g. Belfast, N. Ireland; h. Berlin, Germany; i. Alexandria, Egypt; j. Beirut, Lebanon

Your Workings:

Total Points: 26. Targets: Novice 13 Pro 21. Your Score:

Quiz 288. Radio

For those who prefer their entertainment purely aural

Part 1

1   Which two celebrities were on the panel of *Just a Minute* from the first programme in 1967 until their respective deaths in 1999 and 2009? (2 pts)

2   What was the short-lived (1932–3) radio show starring Groucho and Chico Marx?

3   In what capacity is James Alexander Gordon a familiar voice on BBC radio?

4   What name was given to the precursor of Radio 2, which was used by the BBC to transmit entertainment shows and easy listening music?

5   Which radio programme was originally billed as 'an everyday story of country folk'?

6   Jack de Manio, Brian Redhead and Sue MacGregor were all long-term presenters of which current affairs programme?

7   Which radio show regularly features a drama segment called 'Ladies of Letters'? Which two actresses perform this drama? (3 pts)

8   Which radio show includes games called 'Uxbridge Dictionary', 'One Song to the Tune of Another' and 'Mornington Crescent'?

9   Which two presenters, one from Radio 4 and one from Five Live, covered the death of Diana, Princess of Wales in 1997, when the BBC compressed stations 2, 3, 4 and 5 into single blanket coverage? (2 pts)

10 'Flowers in the Rain' by the Move was the first song played on which new radio station in 1967? Who was the DJ? (2 pts)

Part 2

11   What first began transmitting on 6 September 1994 on 100.7 FM?

12   Which radio station started in the 1990s as a forum for hip-hop and urban music when the major stations were largely ignoring these genres?

13   Who is the BBC's outspoken Ulster-born match commentator and former host of the weekly phone-in programme *606*?

14   In which slot on Radio 4 did Rabbi Lionel Blue acquire cult status in the 1990s?

15   Which Radio 1 DJ had a penchant for classic rock and the nickname Fluff?

16   Which radio comedy series stars its creator and writer John Finnemore alongside Stephanie Cole, Benedict Cumberbatch and which other high-profile star? (2 pts)

17   Which radio programme spent forty-six years from 1946 to 1992 touring the country and speaking to people in a variety of communities, one each week?

18   Who is the most famous of the characters created for radio (and later TV) by comedian and writer Graham Fellows?

19   Who followed his *Solution* (1992–6) on radio with his *Revolution* (1998) and his *Lectures* (1999–2002 and later on TV)?

20   What is the BBC Radio 4 consumer programme which began broadcasting in 1970?

Total Points: 26. Targets: Novice 13 Pro 20. Your Score:

Answers Quizzes 281–288

Quiz 281. General Knowledge

1. (b) Christopher Lloyd; 2. Aung San Suu Kyi; 3. Stabbed with a poison-tipped umbrella; 4. Inspector Rebus (Ian Rankin); 5. Medway; 6. Pete Doherty; 7. Florida; 8. National Rifle Association (they are regarded as one of the most wealthy and influential political lobby groups in the US – in 2008 they spent $100 million opposing Obama); 9. Tony Blair at six foot; 10. Majorca; 11. (b) She was the first air hostess; 12. Cycling; 13. *A Christmas Carol*; 14. Jack White (husbands of Meg White); 15. William Weaver; 16. Golf clubs; 17. Sophomore; 18. She is Belle du Jour, the call girl of literary and TV fame (*Diary of a Call Girl*); 19. Hovercraft; 20. Liverpool Street, Fenchurch Street, Marylebone and King's Cross

Quiz 282. Video Games

1. *Prince of Persia*; 2. *Call of Duty: Black Ops*; 3. *Oblivion* and *Skyrim*; 4. The lead character in the first *Halo* game, *Halo: Combat Evolved*; 5. New York and Miami; 6. Nintendo; Luigi; 7. *Wii Sports*; 8. *Mortal Kombat*; 9. *Final Fantasy*; 10. Sgt Nathan Hale; 11. *Resident Evil*; 12. *TEKKEN*; 13. *The Sims*; 14. *Myst*; 15. Tom Clancy; 16. The *Elder Scrolls* series; 17. *Guitar Hero*; 18. Tony Hawks; 19. *Tomb Raider*; Keeley Hawes; 20. *Devil May Cry*

Quiz 283. Gardeners' Question Time

1. Derek Jarman; 2. 1913; 3. Dig for Victory; 4. Percy Thrower; 5. Alan Titchmarsh, Charlie Dimmock and Tommy Walsh; 6. Roses; 7. (b) so named for their dolphin-shaped flowers; 8. Watercress; 9. *Gardeners' Question Time*; 10. Jardin des Tuileries; 11. Vita Sackville-West; 12. Organic gardening; 13. Yellow; 14. Grass seed; 15. It is potato blight, usually called 'late blight' to distinguish it from 'early blight' (*altermaria solani*); 16. Hostas; 17. Arboretum (a garden devoted principally to the cultivation and display of trees); 18. Orchids; 19. RHS Chelsea Flower Show; 20. Bluebell

Quiz 284. TV

1. *Call My Bluff*; 2. Steven Moffat; 3. *Life on Earth*; 4. *Friends*; 5. Robert Kilroy-Silk; 6. *The Monocled Mutineer*; Paul McGann; 7. *Parkinson*; 8. *World in Action*; 9. Kenneth Branagh; 10. Aimee Osbourne, who deserves to be held up as a beacon of good taste; Mix and Match 1, g; 2, i; 3, j; 4, c; 5, d; 6, h; 7, b; 8, f; 9, e; 10, a

Quiz 285. Shakespeare

1. 'Exit, pursued by a bear'; 2. Ephesus and Syracuse; 3. *The Merry Wives of Windsor*; 4. *The Two Noble Kinsmen*; Chaucer's 'Knight's Tale' from *The Canterbury Tales*; 5. Milan; Ariel; 6. Banquo; he is killed by Macbeth and returns as a ghost to haunt him; 7. Othello, Iago; 8. Mercutio; Tybalt, Juliet's cousin; 9. *Venus and Adonis*; 10. Constables (the law in

Shakespeare plays were usually portrayed as a bit dim and served as a comic turn); 11. Enobarbus speaking about Cleopatra in *Antony and Cleopatra*; 12. Jaques in *As You Like It*; 13. Polonius; 14. Henry V; 15. Mark Anthony in *Julius Caesar*; 16. Macbeth; 17. Richard III; 18. Juliet in *Romeo and Juliet*; 19. Malvolio is reading the letter purporting to be from his Mistress, Olivia, declaring her love for him in *Twelfth Night*; 20. King Henry IV in Part 2

Quiz 286. Rock and Pop

1. Simon and Garfunkel; 2. Salt-n-Pepa; 3. Edwyn Collins; 4. Gnarls Barkley; 5. Lauryn Hill; 6. 'Like a Rolling Stone'; 7. Sandy Denny; 8. (a) His divorce from Anna Gordy, sister of Motown's Berry Gordy (Gaye's settlement was the proceeds from the album); 9. Ian Dury (the press rather lazily lumped him in with punk although he did qualify as disaffected); 10. Dexy's Midnight Runners; 11. Steve Harley (who previously sang with the Nice); 'Make Me Smile (Come Up and See Me)'; 12. New Orleans; 13. Icelandic band, Sigur Rós; 14. Alex James of Blur; 15. Cornershop; 'Brimful of Asha'; 16. Air; 17. *Ill Manors*; 18. Paloma is positively withering away at thirty-one (as of January 2013), while Emeli is a tender twenty-five; 19. John Lee Hooker; 20. Robbie Williams, with seventeen, including five with Take That

Quiz 287. Births, Deaths and Marriages

1. Shirley Conran and Terence Conran; 2. Ringo Starr and Barbara Bach; 3. Kelis; 4. Lucille Ball; 5. Cherie is a barrister, and her father, Tony Booth, was an actor; 6. Paula Yates and Michael Hutchence; 7. Ross Kemp; 8. Helena Christensen; 9. Hugh Hefner; 10. Autumn Kelly; Canada (Quebec), Savannah; Mix and Match 1, f; 2, j; 3, d; 4, b; 5, i; 6, a; 7, g; 8, c; 9, e; 10, h

Quiz 288. Radio

1. Derek Nimmo and Clement Freud; 2. *Flywheel, Shyster, and Flywheel*; 3. He reads the classified football results on Five Live; 4. The Light Programme; 5. *The Archers*; 6. Radio 4's *Today* programme; 7. *Woman's Hour* on Radio 4; Patricia Routledge and Prunella Scales; 8. *I'm Sorry, I Haven't a Clue*; 9. James Naughtie and Peter Allen; 10. Radio 1; Tony Blackburn; 11. Heart FM; 12. Kiss FM; 13. Alan Green; 14. He became popular for his slightly off-beam observations on the 'Thought for the Day' slot on the *Today* programme; 15. Alan Freeman; 16. *Cabin Pressure*; Roger Allam; 17. *Down Your Way*; 18. John Shuttleworth; 19. Mark Steel; 20. *You and Yours*

Quiz 289. General Knowledge

Part 1

1 Why did a Saturday in February 2009 become known as Black Saturday in Australia?

2 27 October 1886 saw the dedication of which famous US landmark, a gift from France?

3 Which author went *Round Ireland with a Fridge*?

4 Which is furthest to the east: Dover, Great Yarmouth or Colchester?

5 Which rapper made the 'Yes We Can' video as part of Barack Obama's bid for the Presidency of the US?

6 For what is the Gellert Hotel in Budapest best known?

7 What was the rival to the VHS video format in the early 1980s?

8 Which visitor to Britain, in 2012, declared in July that London didn't look ready to host the Olympics, before being consigned to the dustbin of history four months later?

9 How many children did Belinda Lang and Gary Olsen have in the 1990s?

10 Who became the youngest winner of the Wimbledon men's singles title in 1985?

Part 2

11 German Chancellor, Angela Merkel, is the leader of which right of centre political party?

12 Which English city is equidistant ('near as makes no difference', as my nan might have said) from both Edinburgh and London?

13 The cathedral known as the Hagia Sophia is so named because (a) it was named for the Christian martyr Saint Sophia during the Byzantine occupation (b) Sophia was the favourite mistress of Sultan Mahmud II or (c) the words mean Holy Wisdom in classical Greek?

14 Which feminist and pacifist wrote *Testament of Youth* (1933), a memoir of her time in World War I?

15 Who, appropriately, had the 1,000th UK no. 1 hit single in 2005?

16 Which stadium has hosted the most European Cup finals (seven)?

17 By what name is Bianca Pérez Morena de Macías more frequently known?

18 Who is the famous acting nephew of Denis Lawson (*Holby City*, *Bleak House*, *New Tricks*)?

19 In which country house (a World Heritage Site) was Sir Winston Churchill born?

20 Which supermodel had a relationship with stage magician David Copperfield in the 1990s?

Total Points: 20. Targets: Novice 10 Pro 15. Your Score:

Quiz 290. Bond Movies

Part 1

1   Which other Bond movie regular was in the same drama class at RADA as Roger Moore?

2   The unofficial Bond movie *Never Say Never Again* was effectively a remake of which earlier film? And with which official Bond movie did it clash on release? (2 pts)

3   What was the first gadget Bond used during *Dr No*?

4   Which car was Bond driving in *Thunderball* and *Goldfinger*? (2 pts: 1 for the make, 1 for the model)

5   Mary Goodnight; Plenty O'Toole; Melanie Dancepole; Pussy Galore: which of these names has never been used in a Bond movie?

6   Which Bond actor has starred in the most official Bond movies?

7   Who was the oldest actor to play Bond?

8   In what does Bond chase Blofeld in *On Her Majesty's Secret Service*?

9   What does Oddball crush in his hand in *Goldfinger* to impress his strength upon the watching Bond?

10 Where does Bond land after the would-be assassin he chases down the Thames in a powerboat blows herself up in *The World Is Not Enough*?

Part 2

11 Which sports star played the bodyguard of Zukovsky (Robbie Coltrane) in *The World Is Not Enough*?

12 Who co-starred alongside Daniel Craig as James Bond in the 2012 short film *Happy and Glorious*?

13 What was Vic Flick's contribution to the James Bond movie franchise? (a) he performed all Sean Connery's stunts (b) he bred the Persian cats which always accompany Blofeld (c) he played the surf guitar lines on the theme tune

14 Which Bond movie included a fleeting role for Joanna Lumley?

15 Barbara Bach; Izabella Scorupco; Charlize Theron; Michelle Yeoh; which actress has *not* appeared in a Bond movie?

16 Which Bond movie finds 007 up against a voodoo cult including killers like Tee Hee and Baron Samedi? What is Tee Hee's distinguishing feature? (2 pts)

17 Who plays rogue agent Alex Trevelyan in *Goldeneye*, and what is his MI6 number? (2 pts)

18 Which steel-toothed villain proved so popular in *The Spy Who Loved Me* that he was brought back for a second airing? In which film did he reappear? (2 pts)

19 Dame Judi Dench became a familiar figure as M, but who took the role in the first eleven Bond movies until his death in 1981?

20 Which three actors have played gadgets expert Q in the official Bond movies? (3 pts)

Total Points: 27. Targets: Novice 11 Pro 20. Your Score:

Quiz 291. Costume Drama

More chiffon and chicanery from both big and small screens (not that TVs can really count as small these days)

Part 1

1 Whose breakthrough was her role as Mariette Larkin in *The Darling Buds of May* (1991)? Whose books provided the basis of the show? (2 pts)

2 Which historical period provides the setting for *Master and Commander*, the naval epic based on Patrick O'Brian's novels? What was the position held by Paul Bettany's character, Stephen Maturin? (2 pts)

3 Which British costume drama holds the record for the most Emmy (US TV) nominations received by a non-US drama series, with twenty-seven? Who won the Best Supporting Actress two years running for her work in the show? (2 pts)

4 If Matthew Goode and Ben Whishaw replicated Jeremy Irons and Anthony Andrews, what 2008 film are we talking about? Which other theatrical knight replicated Laurence Olivier? (2 pts)

5 Who brought Fitzgerald's *The Great Gatsby* to the screen in 2013? Who was cast as the charismatic Jay Gatsby? (2 pts)

6 What connects the TV dramas *By the Sword Divided* and *The Devil's Whore* to the films *To Kill a King* and *The Witchfinder General*?

7 How did Keira Knightley emulate Greta Garbo and Vivien Leigh in 2012?

8 In which state did most of the action in *Gone with the Wind* take place?

9 What connects Maria Doyle Kennedy, Natalie Dormer, Anita Briem, Joss Stone, Tamzin Merchant and Joely Richardson?

10 Keeley Hawes, Rachael Stirling, Anna Chancellor and Jodhi May in a ripe piece of sapphic Victoriana; what was the 2002 series?

11 Who played Harry Selfridge in the 2013 ITV dramatization of the birth of the London store? What 2012 BBC drama had stolen a march on ITV with its depiction of life in an Edwardian department store? (2 pts)

12 Robert Newton (1950), Orson Welles (1972) and Charlton Heston (1990) all played which villainous figure in adaptations of a famous children's story? (a) Captain Hook (b) Carver Doone (c) Long John Silver

13 Who played the two Boleyn sisters in *The Other Boleyn Girl* (in the version Justin Chadwick directed in 2008)? (2 pts)

14 Which decade provided the milieu for Dennis Potter's dark fantasy *Pennies from Heaven* (1978), starring Bob Hoskins and Cheryl Campbell? Who took the Hoskins role in a 1981 Hollywood remake? (2 pts)

Part 2

Make the connection

15 Which English actress won two Best Actress Academy Awards in the 1970s?

16 Which northeast-born character actress was made a dame of the British Empire in 1960?

17 Who played a scheming Southern belle in Jezebel?

18 Who is James McAvoy's long-term partner?

19 Who played the housewife-in-crisis in Woody Allen's 2013 offering, *Blue Jasmine*?

20 What's the connection?

Total Points: 28. Targets: Novice 11 Pro 21. Your Score:

Quiz 292. Tourist Attractions

Part 1

1   The tourist attractions near Luxor are found in which country?

2   What is the famous National Park found mainly within the borders of Tanzania?

3   The ancient city of Machu Picchu is in which modern-day country?

4   What is the tourist-laden coastal area at the southern end of Portugal, and what is the region's major city? (2 pts)

5   Which famous Scottish feature runs from just southwest of Inverness to Fort Augustus?

6   What are the top three tourist attractions in Paris? (3 pts)

7   The street known as The Pleasance is part of the cultural life of which city?

8   If you watched the famous Lipizzaner horses perform in their home city, where would you be?

9   In which Spanish city is the historic building known as the Alhambra?

10 The Brazilian resort state of Espírito Santo has some of the country's finest beaches, and an island capital, Vitória; how does Espírito Santo translate?

Part 2

11 Which of these is *not* an attraction in the mountainous state of Alberta, Canada? (a) Dinosaur Provincial Park (b) Head-Smashed-In Buffalo Jump (c) Look-No-Hands Glacier Slide

12 What is the only designated World Heritage Site in New York?

13 In which Chinese city is the palace known as the Forbidden City? Of which dynasty was it the imperial centre? (2 pts)

14 The Salzkammergut is a forested tourist area in which country?

15 What was the French royal palace and hunting lodge about 50 km from Paris that now has a forest used as a wildlife preserve rather than a killing ground?

16 The composers Smetana and Dvořák and the artist Alphonse Mucha all have museums devoted to them in which European capital?

17 Which religious building lies on the south side of Red Square in Moscow?

18 Which city in Italy boasts the world's oldest botanical garden still in existence, created by the Venetian Republic in 1545? (a) Bologna (b) Padua (c) Treviso

19 The church of San Lorenzo in Florence contains the mausoleum of which famous political family?

20 Which Italian city boasts a famously un-vertical free-standing belltower alongside its cathedral in the city's main square?

Total Points: 24. Targets: Novice 10 Pro 18. Your Score:

Quiz 293. TV Soaps

Part 1

1   Which soap opera was originally conceived as a show called *The Midland Road* for chat-show presenter Noele Gordon?

2   Rebecca Michael, Alexia Demetriou are two; who is the third and what is the *EastEnders* link? (2 pts)

3   What was Phil Redmond's youth-oriented follow-up to *Brookside*, which started on Channel 4 in 1995?

4   Who did Katy Harris kill next after killing her own father, Tommy, in *Coronation Street* in 2005?

5   Which TV series gave acting opportunities to a series of busty *Playboy* models including Erika Eleniak, Carmen Electra and Donna D'Errico?

6   Which *Brookside* character was UK TV soap's first openly gay character?

7   What was the companion show to *Casualty*, started thirteen years later in 1999?

8   Which twenty-three year-old jobbing writer pitched *Coronation Street* to Granada TV in 1960, and was given a sixteen-week run to make the show popular?

9   Where and how did the dangerous businessman Alan Bradley meet his end in *Coronation Street* in 1989? (2 pts)

10 Which *Dallas* character (and actress, please) was nicknamed the Poison Dwarf by Terry Wogan, a huge fan of the show? (2 pts)

Part 2

11 Which former master of ceremonies played the angel/demon who forces JR to reflect on his life in the final episode of the original *Dallas*?

12 Which two weekday nights were chosen by the BBC to showcase their new flagship soap, *EastEnders*, in 1985? (2 pts)

13 Who was the waiter who married Deirdre Barlow in *Coronation Street* in 1995? And whose life did his kidney save after his death in the same year? (2 pts)

14 Who took over the garage in the Arches in *EastEnders* in 1991?

15 Who buried Max Branning alive in a coffin but later freed him? And who tried to deliberately run him over? (2 pts)

16 What is the name of the *Emmerdale* pub, and which double act ran it for twenty years before the death of actor Arthur Pentelow? (3 pts)

17 Which medical drama gave George Clooney his big break?

18 What did Ena Sharples actually steal when she was caught shoplifting in *Coronation Street* in 1966?

19 What is the name of the town (Southampton, loosely disguised) where the action of 1980s soap *Howards' Way* takes place?

20 Erinsborough is a fictitious suburb that provides the setting for *Neighbours*; in which city is Erinsborough and on what street do most of the characters live? (2 pts)

Total Points: 29. Targets: Novice 12 Pro 22. Your Score:

Quiz 294. European Football

Part 1

A few long-winded questions about a long-winded competition, the Champions League, charting the history of the epic confrontations between Barcelona and Chelsea in recent years

1   Who scored three goals in the tie as Chelsea were beaten 6–4 on aggregate in 2000 despite winning 3–1 at Stanford Bridge? Who was Chelsea coach at the time? And who was sent off for a professional foul in the second leg? (3 pts)

2   In 2005 which future Chelsea player scored an own goal at the Nou Camp to give Mourinho's side a vital away goal? Who scored Chelsea's opener after eight minutes of the return leg as they ran up a three-goal lead inside twenty minutes? Who pegged them back with two first half goals before John Terry's winner clinched the tie? (3 pts)

3   Which Spanish international was sent off at Stamford Bridge in 2006 as Barca won 2–1 away from home, sparking furious protests from the Chelsea camp? Who scored in both group games the following year as Chelsea managed to keep all their players on the pitch and picked up four points? Which former Chelsea player scored for Barca in the 2–2 draw at the Nou Camp? (3 pts)

4   Who was in charge at Stamford Bridge when the two clubs next met in 2009 in the semi-finals? Who scored a late goal to level the scores and seal the tie for Barca on away goals after Chelsea were denied a couple of decent penalty appeals? Who was 'sent off' after the final whistle for a complete loss of self control as he conducted a tirade against an admittedly very poor referee? (3 pts)

5   Who scored the only goal of the first leg of the semi-final in 2012? Who was sent off after thirty-seven minutes of the second leg, shortly after Barca levelled the scores on aggregate? Who scored Chelsea's crucial first goal just before half time which put them back in front on away goals and set the scene for an inspired defensive display in the second half? (3 pts)

Part 2

This section examines life beyond the Champions League

6   Immediately before it became the Europa League, what was the name of this tournament? And under what name did it start in 1971–2? Which two English sides contested the first final? (4 pts)

7   Which two English clubs did Celtic beat en route to the final of the predecessor of the Europa League in 2003? Who beat them 3–2 in the final? Who scored both Celtic goals and who was their manager? (Neither is Scottish.) (5 pts)

8   The European Cup Winners' Cup was the first European trophy won by a British side; who claimed it in 1963 and who emulated them two years later? Which two Scottish sides have lifted this trophy? (4 pts)

9   Which three British sides have reached only one European final and lost it? (In each case it was the Europa League or one of its predecessors.) And which three English clubs won the only European final they reached? (In two cases it was the Cup Winners' Cup.) (6 pts)

10   Liverpool won a European trophy in each year from 1976 to 1979; which two sides made up the numbers in those four finals? And who were Liverpool's opponents when they won what is now the Europa League in 2001? What was the score in this rather silly game? (4 pts)

Total Points: 38. Targets: Novice 15 Pro 29. Your Score:

Quiz 295. Theatre

Part 1

1 Who is the daughter of Lady Bracknell in Oscar Wilde's *The Importance of Being Earnest*?

2 Which familiar British TV face won a Tony Award (Broadway theatre's awards) in 2012 for his performance in a transfer from London?

3 *The Room* (1957) was the first work by which modern British playwright?

4 What parts did the Redgraves play in London in 1991 that the Cusacks played in Dublin the previous year?

5 Who played Arnold, the drag queen at the centre of *Torch Song Trilogy*, when it first ran in London in 1985? Who wrote the play? What other performance helped earned the star an Olivier Award that year? (3 pts)

6 The Bridge Project was a three-year collaboration between the Old Vic and which high-profile director?

7 Dominic West and Clarke Peters both appeared in *The Wire* and were reunited in a 2011 production of which Shakespeare play?

8 Who played Benedick and Beatrice in a 'celebrity' production of *Much Ado About Nothing* at the Wyndham's Theatre in 2011? (2 pts)

9 Who was the first artistic director of Shakespeare's Globe when it opened in 1995? Who replaced him in 2005? (2 pts)

10 *The Mousetrap* is comfortably the longest running show in the West End; which three other shows opened in the 1980s and remain open (two musicals and a thriller playing at the Fortune Theatre)? (3 pts)

Part 2

Name the theatres that are found at each address
11 10 Cambridge Street, Edinburgh
12 53 Southwark Street, London
13 24–25 High Street, Kingston upon Thames
14 St Ann's Square, Manchester
15 Beaumont Street, Oxford
16 Howell Croft South, Bolton
17 Sloane Square, London
18 Corporation Street, Coventry
19 269 Kilburn High Road, London
20 2 Charing Cross Road, London

Total Points: 26. Targets: Novice 10 Pro 20. Your Score:

Quiz 296. General Knowledge

Part 1

1   The conflict-ridden city of Sarajevo now lies in which Balkan state?
2   Moctezuma was a famous ruler in which civilization?
3   A mutiny, later the subject of a Sergei Eisenstein film, took place on which Russian ship in Odessa harbour in 1905?
4   What are the first names of the fictional police duo Dalziel and Pascoe?
5   Which independent state lies at the southern tip of the Malay Peninsula?
6   What is the Palio?
7   What term is applied to the management of the space between text characters in graphic design?
8   Which politician was booed by 80,000 people in 2012?
9   What did Lady Gaga wear to the 2010 MTV Music Awards?
10 Which two skaters won successive gold medals for Great Britain in the men's individual figure skating at the 1976 and 1980 Winter Olympics? (2 pts)

Part 2

11 In 2000, Hillary Clinton was elected to the US Senate; how was this unique?
12 Which term, meaning misuse of a word or phrase, comes from a character in a play by Richard Brinsley Sheridan?
13 Spain is divided into regional provinces, of which there are how many: twenty-eight, forty-one or fifty?
14 What does the annual Pink List celebrate?
15 Who was the youngest artist to get their debut single to the top of the UK charts when 'Because We Want To' hit no. 1 in 1998?
16 Who was appointed head of elite development at the FA in 2011 despite an unremarkable track record in football management?
17 Who is singer Diana Krall's husband?
18 Failure to take which capital city in 1529 stemmed the spread of Suleiman the Magnificent's forces across Europe?
19 Who caused a stir when they landed in the US for the first time on 6 February 1964?
20 Which TV celebrity was born on 26 October 1984 to father John and mother Sharon?

Total Points: 21. Targets: Novice 11 Pro 16. Your Score:

Answers Quizzes 289–296

Quiz 289. General Knowledge

1. Bush fires killed 173 people; 2. The Statue of Liberty; 3. Tony Hawks; 4. Great Yarmouth; 5. Will.i.am from Black Eyed Peas; 6. Spa baths; 7. Betamax; 8. Mitt Romney; 9. *2point4 Children*; 10. Boris Becker; 11. Christian Democrats; 12. York; 13. (c) it means Holy Wisdom (claims of links to Saint Sophia are almost certainly untrue); 14. Vera Brittain; 15. Elvis Presley ('One Night'); 16. Wembley Stadium, in both its incarnations; 17. Bianca Jagger; 18. Ewan McGregor; 19. Blenheim Palace; 20. Claudia Schiffer

Quiz 290. Bond Movies

1. Lois Maxwell (Miss Moneypenny); 2. *Thunderball*; *Octopussy*; 3. A Geiger counter; 4. Aston M DB5; 5. Melanie Dancepole; 6. Roger Moore (seven) pips Sean Connery by one; 7. Roger Moore, who was fifty-eight when *A View to a Kill* finished shooting; 8. A bobsleigh; 9. A golf ball; 10. Into the Millennium Dome; 11. Jonah Lomu; 12. Queen Elizabeth II (it was the short film produced specially for the 2012 London Olympics); 13. (c) he was the guitarist on the theme tune; 14. *On Her Majesty's Secret Service*; 15. Charlize Theron; 16. *Live and Let Die*; Tee Hee has a hook instead of one hand; 17. Sean Bean, 006; 18. Jaws (played by Richard Kiel); *Moonraker*; 19. Bernard Lee; 20. Desmond Llewellyn (1963–99); John Cleese (two films); Ben Whishaw (from 2012; also accept Peter Burton who played Major Boothroyd, referred to as Q in later films, in *Dr No*)

Quiz 291. Costume Drama

1. Catherine Zeta-Jones; H. E. Bates; 2. Napoleonic Wars; Maturin is the ship's doctor and the books develop his relationship with Captain Jack Aubrey (Russell Crowe in the film); 3. *Downton Abbey*; Maggie Smith; 4. *Brideshead Revisited*; Michael Gambon; 5. Baz Luhrmann; Leonardo DiCaprio; 6. All are set during the English Civil War; 7. She played Anna Karenina in a movie; 8. Georgia; 9. They played Henry VIII's six wives in *The Tudors*; 10. *Tipping the Velvet*; 11. Jeremy Piven; *The Paradise*; 12. They all played Long John Silver; 13. Natalie Portman (Anne Boleyn) and Scarlett Johansson (Mary Boleyn); 14. *Pennies from Heaven*; Steve Martin; 15. Glenda Jackson; 16. Flora Robson; 17. Bette Davis; 18. Anne-Marie Duff; 19. Cate Blanchett; 20. All played Queen Elizabeth I in major movies or TV series

Quiz 292. Tourist Attractions

1. Egypt; 2. Serengeti; 3. Peru; 4. Algarve; Faro; 5. Loch Ness; 6. Eiffel Tower; Louvre; Pompidou Centre; 7. Edinburgh; 8. Vienna; 9. Granada; 10. Holy Spirit; 11. (c) Look-No-Hands Slide is made up; 12. The Statue of Liberty; 13. Beijing; Ming; 14. Austria, stretching east across the Alps from Salzburg; 15. Fontainebleu; 16. Prague; 17. St Basil's Cathedral; 18. (b) Padua; 19. The house of Medici; 20. Pisa

Quiz 293. TV Soaps

1. *Crossroads*; 2. Charlie Brooks – they have all played Janine Butcher; 3. *Hollyoaks*; 4. Herself; 5. *Baywatch*; 6. Gordon Collins; 7. *Holby City*; 8. Tony Warren; 9. Run down by a tram in Blackpool; 10. Lucy, played by Charlene Tilton; 11. Joel Grey, who played the MC in *Cabaret*, brings similar sinister relish to the part; 12. Tuesday and Thursday; 13. Samir Rachid; Tracy, Deirdre's daughter; 14. Phil and Grant Mitchell; 15. Tanya (Cross), his ex-wife (with help from Sean Slater); Tanya confesses to it but the driver was really Lauren, their daughter; 16. The Woolpack; Henry Wilks and Amos Brierley; 17. *ER*; 18. Two tins of salmon; 19. Tarrant; 20. Melbourne; Ramsay Street

Quiz 294. European Football

1. Tore André Flo; Gianluca Vialli; Celestine Babayaro; 2. Juliano Belletti; Eidur Gudjohnsen; Ronaldinho; 3. Asier del Horno; Didier Drogba; Eidur Gudjohnsen; 4. Guus Hiddink; Andres Iniesta; Didier Drogba; 5. Didier Drogba; John Terry; Ramires; 6. UEFA Cup; Inter-Cities Fairs Cup; Tottenham and Wolves; 7. Blackburn Rovers (second round) and Liverpool (quarter-final); Porto; Henrik Larsson and Martin O'Neill; 8. Tottenham; West Ham; Rangers and Aberdeen; 9. Wolves in 1972; Middlesbrough in 2006; Fulham in 2010; Manchester City (CWC in 1970), Ipswich Town (UEFA Cup in 1981) and Everton (CWC in 1985); 10. Borussia Mönchengladbach (European Cup 1977 and UEFA Cup 1979) and Club Bruges ((UEFA Cup 1976 and European Cup 1978); Alaves 5–4 (it was like watching an under-sevens match – everyone attacking and forgetting to get back and defend)

Quiz 295. Theatre

1. Gwendolen Fairfax; 2. James Corden in *One Man, Two Guvnors*; 3. Harold Pinter; 4. Chekhov's *Three Sisters*; 5. Antony Sher; Harvey Fierstein; *Richard III*; 6. Sam Mendes; 7. *Othello*; 8. David Tennant and Catherine Tate; 9. Mark Rylance; Dominic Dromgoole; 10. *The Woman in Black* and the musicals *The Phantom of the Opera* and *Les Misérables*; 11. Traverse Theatre; 12. Menier Chocolate Factory; 13. Rose Theatre; 14. Royal Exchange; 15. Oxford Playhouse; 16. Octagon Theatre; 17. Royal Court Theatre; 18. Belgrade Theatre; 19. Tricycle Theatre; 20. Garrick Theatre

Quiz 296. General Knowledge

1. Bosnia-Herzegovina; 2. Aztec; 3. *Battleship Potemkin*; 4. Andy and Colin; 5. Singapore; 6. An annual horse race around the streets of Siena; 7. Kerning; 8. Chancellor George Osborne, when his entry into the Olympic Stadium was announced during the London Games; 9. A dress made of meat; 10. John Curry and Robin Cousins; 11. She was still First Lady to the President; 12. Malapropism; 13. Fifty exactly, most named after their principal city or town, e.g. Cadiz, Sevilla, Valencia; 14. The most influential gay and lesbian contributors in the UK; 15. Billie Piper; 16. Gareth Southgate; 17. Elvis Costello; 18. Vienna; 19. The Beatles; 20. Kelly Osbourne

Quiz 297. General Knowledge

Name the year using the given events; half a point for one year either way

Part 1

These are the years of the 1970s; just identify which is which

1   First test-tube baby is born; John Travolta has his big year with *Grease* and *Saturday Night Fever*; a Polish Cardinal is elected Pope; Argentina win the World Cup

2   Idi Amin seizes power in Uganda; Charles Manson is sentenced to death in California; George Harrison's Concert for Bangladesh in New York; Ian Paisley and others form the DUP in Northern Ireland; sixty-six die in Ibrox stadium disaster

3   Work on the World Trade Center is completed; the Queen opens the Sydney Opera House; Jackie Stewart wins his third F1 Driver's Championship then retires; the Yom Kippur War breaks out between Israel and its Arab neighbours

4   Nottingham Forest win the European Cup; Airey Neave is killed in a car-bomb attack; Ayatollah Khomeini returns to Iran; Sony Walkman cassette-player is launched

5   The Beatles disband; the 'dirtiest Cup final ever' between Chelsea and Leeds; four people are shot by state national guard at Kent State University, Ohio; Jimi Hendrix and Janis Joplin are both found dead from drug overdoses

6   China's Terracotta Army is discovered; BBC launches Ceefax; ABBA win the Eurovision Song Contest with 'Waterloo'; Harold Wilson wins two General Elections

7   Liverpool win the league; Bjorn Borg wins Wimbledon for the first time; George W. Bush is fined for drunk-driving; inflation hits 17 per cent; Israeli commandos storm Entebbe airport and rescue hostages

8   Bloody Sunday in Derry where fourteen protesters are shot; the SALT 1 accord between the US and the Soviet Union; *The Joy of Sex* by Alan Comfort is published; Gough Whitlam is Australia's first Labour Prime Minister for twenty-three years

9   Red Rum wins a third Grand National; *Star Wars* is the year's top-grossing movie; Heathrow Underground link opens; Virginia Wade wins Wimbledon

10 Microsoft is founded; Saigon falls as the US lose the Vietnam War; Boston Red Sox beat Cincinnati Reds in the World Series's 'greatest game'; Angola declares independence from Portugal – cue civil war

Part 2

Less easy, but the questions are in a logical order – you just need to work out what

11 British Coal is nationalized; Jackie Robinson becomes the first African American to play major league baseball; Princess Elizabeth marries Philip; the Muslim part of the newly independent Indian subcontinent adopts the name Pakistan

12 Claudette Colvin and later Rosa Parks are arrested after refusing to give up a seat to a white woman in Alabama; elevated trains are shut down in Manhattan; eighty-three people are killed after a collision at Le Mans; James Dean is killed in a car crash

13 War criminal Adolf Eichmann becomes the only man to be hanged in Israel after a civil conviction; *West Side Story* wins ten Academy Awards; Algeria gains independence from France; Ipswich Town win their first (and thus far only) league title

14 Elvis marries Priscilla; Sandy Shaw sings 'Puppet on a String' at Eurovision; homosexuality is decriminalized; *Bonnie and Clyde* is released.

15 The SAS storm the Iranian embassy in London; John Lennon is murdered; West Ham win the FA Cup; Borg beats McEnroe in an epic Wimbledon final; Ian Curtis hangs himself

16 WPC Yvonne Fletcher is shot outside the Libyan embassy in London; the IRA bomb the Grand Hotel in Brighton during the Conservative Party Conference; Tommy Cooper collapses and dies of a heart attack during a live TV show; British Telecom is privatized

17 Mikhail Gorbachev wins Nobel Peace Prize; the Community Charge is introduced in England; *Mr Bean* makes his TV debut; the Valdez tanker spill leads to prosecution of Exxon executives

18 Grand National called off after a starting cock-up; Suede's debut album wins the Mercury Music Prize; Arsenal and Sheffield Wednesday contest both domestic Cup finals; the film of *Jurassic Park* breaks box office records

19 Jill Dando is shot and killed outside her front door by an as yet unknown assailant; the Scottish Parliament convenes for the first time in 292 years; the Columbine shootings take place in Colorado; Hicham El Guerrouj sets a new mile record, which remains unbroken (as of January 2013)

20 Appalling casualties result when Russian forces storm Beslan School where Chechen rebels are holding hostages; Facebook is launched; a tsunami devastates the coastlines of the Indian Ocean; ten new members, including eight from Eastern Europe, join the European Union

Total Points: 20. Targets: Novice 10 Pro 15. Your Score:

Quiz 298. Movie Quotes

Part 1

1   Which great director once said: 'If I made Cinderella people would be look-ing for the body in the coach'?

2   'My mama always said, life is like . . .' what? And in which film was it said? (2 pts)

3   'The toilet seat's up, man!' Which character in which Coen brothers movie believes this to be a sure-fire indication that he isn't sharing his living accommodation with a wife or partner? (2 pts)

4   'No dinosaurs were harmed in the making of this motion picture': this line appears as the credits roll during which movie?

5   'Have you ever done it in an elevator?' Which actor probably wished he had never been asked the question by the end of which 1987 movie? (2 pts)

6   'We want the finest wines available to humanity. We want them here, and we want them now!' Which booze-fuelled movie and what is the setting? (2 pts)

7   Which pop star does Hugh Grant quote when he first admits he loves Andie MacDowell in *Four Weddings and a Funeral*?

8   'Oh no, it wasn't the airplanes, it was beauty killed the beast.' A sad end to which movie?

9   'To err is human, but it feels divine', and 'When women go wrong, men go right after them' are quips from which female wit and actress?

10 'I love the smell of napalm in the morning . . . It smells like . . .'; what did it smell like to a near psychotic Robert Duvall? What's the movie? (2 pts)

Part 2

11 'This girl, single-handed, may make bosoms a thing of the past.' Which new star was Billy Wilder talking about?

12 'As far back as I can remember, I always wanted to be a gangster. To me, being a gangster was better than being President of the United States.' Which actor playing which part at the beginning of which movie directed by which movie-maker? (4 pts)

13 Who declared, in which movie: 'My name is Maximus Decimus Meridius, Commander of the Armies of the North, General of the Felix Legions, loyal servant to the true emperor, Marcus Aurelius. Father to a murdered son, husband to a murdered wife. And I will have my vengeance, in this life or the next'? (2 pts)

14 'I always get the fuzzy end of the lollipop'; which actress bemoaning her ill luck in which movie? (2 pts)

15 Which movie opens with Charles Gray saying, 'I would like, if I may, to take you on a strange journey'?

16 'Fasten your seat belts, it's gonna be a bumpy night.' Which screen icon in *All About Eve*?

17 'When nine hundred years old you will reach, look as good you will not, hmm?' Who is suggesting that looks may be deceptive in which film? (2 pts)

18 'That's a real badge. I'm a real cop. And this is a real, firing gun.' Which actor in the first of which series of buddy-cop movies? (2 pts)

19 'All right, Mr DeMille, I'm ready for my close-up.' Which star at the end of Billy Wilder's *Sunset Boulevard*?

20 'Round up the usual suspects' is the famous last line to which classic movie?

Total Points: 32. Targets: Novice 13 Pro 24. Your Score: ☐

Quiz 299. Computer Science

Technology: gizmos, gadgets and geeks

Part 1

1 Pong (released 1972) was a signature game in the armoury of which pioneering arcade game company?

2 What was the 2011 revenue figure for Apple Inc: $65 billion, $90 billion or $108 billion?

3 In which year did Apple launch the iMac?

4 What was the name of the precursor to the Macintosh, launched unsuccessfully by Apple a year before the Mac?

5 Which company first introduced mass-produced printers to accompany the sale of home computers?

6 Which is the world's largest manufacturer of microchips and semiconductors and other computer processing paraphernalia?

7 What was Microsoft's biggest acquisition to date, made in 2011 and costing over $8 billion? Where does the acquired company have its base? (2 pts)

8 What was the portable computer programming language devised by James Gosling and released in 1991?

9 If the T and L in HTML are Text and Language, what are the H and M? (2 pts)

10 In which country did the music streaming site Spotify originate?

Part 2

11 What percentage of Facebook users declare themselves to be over fifty-five: 9 per cent, 5 per cent or less than 1 per cent?

12 What was the most recent (October 2012) release of Windows, developed with the increasing use of tablets in mind?

13 What does the acronymic family of computer languages BASIC stand for? (2 pts)

14 What was the mini tablet launched by Amazon worldwide in 2012?

15 What is the name given to the component in a computer's hard drive that performs the mathematical or real number functions?

16 In which year did Charles Babbage complete the prototype of his Difference Engine, the world's first automated calculating machine? (a) 1822 (b) 1849 (c) 1902

17 Which four products make up the 2010 version of Microsoft Office for home use? (4 pts)

Total Points: 23. Targets: Novice 7 Pro 17. Your Score:

Quiz 300. Business

Another chance for the capitalists to shine

Part 1

1   Michael O'Leary is the outspoken head of which corporation?
2   Which retail chain was started in Maldon, Essex, by Jack Cohen in 1956?
3   Which legendary brand was registered as a trademark with the US Patent Office on 15 June 1903?
4   Which company released their first personal computer on 11 August 1981?
5   Who was triumphant in court when BA admitted they had pursued a 'dirty tricks' campaign in 1993?
6   In 1990 the Logitech Fotoman was the first commercially available what?
7   What is Africa's busiest airport?
8   Who were finally cleared to buy rival music company EMI in 2012?
9   Who had a great business idea whilst travelling from Leicester to Loughborough for a temperance meeting in 1841?
10 In which decade was the Weight Watchers organization founded in Brooklyn by housewife Jean Nidetch?

Part 2

Mix and Match: match the brand to the traditional proprietor of these confectionery items

1. Kit Kat; 2. Milky Bar; 3. Turkish Delight; 4. Chocolate Orange; 5. Roses; 6. Toblerone; 7. Maltesers; 8. Reese's Peanut Butter Cup; 9. Juicy Fruit; 10. Liquorice Allsorts

a. Bassetts; b. Rowntree; c. Fry's; d. Wrigley Company; e. Suchard; f. Mars Inc; g. Hershey Company; h. Nestlé; i. Cadbury; j. Terry's

Your Workings:

Total Points: 20. Targets: Novice 8 Pro 15. Your Score:

Quiz 301. Fine Art and Architecture

Part 1

1 Who painted *Diana and Actaeon*, on display at the National Gallery of Scotland and regarded as one of the finest nude studies in art history?

2 Which performer was the subject of a one-off screenprint by Andy Warhol which sold for $100 million in 2009?

3 *Dirty Words Pictures* and *Naked Shit Pictures* are works by which modern artists?

4 Who was the model who posed for many Pre-Raphaelite paintings, most famously Millais' *The Death of Ophelia*?

5 The sixteenth-century painters Tintoretto and Titian, and Giambattista Tiepolo, active the following century, were all native to which Italian city?

6 What did van Gogh do in 1787 in remorse at issuing threats to his friend, Gauguin?

7 Which of these painters is *not* associated with the Fauvist movement: Henri Matisse; Raoul Dufy; Maurice de Vlaminck; Piet Mondrian?

8 Which French painter, with Picasso, was the principal pioneer of Cubism?

9 Which artist collaborated with film director Luis Buñuel on a number of Surrealist movies in the 1920s and 1930s?

10 Spencer Frederick Gore was the first President of which artistic group, founded in 1911 in London?

11 What was the art movement founded before World War I by Wassily Kandinsky and Franz Marc and others sharing their inclination?

12 Which Pre-Raphaelite prodigy was the youngest ever student at the Royal Academy, aged eleven, in 1840 (he was made President of the Academy in 1896, but died later that year)?

13 Which Impressionist master was the subject of a 2013 Royal Academy exhibition entitled *Portraying Life*?

14 Who was the subject of James McNeill Whistler's *Arrangement in Grey and Black No. 1*?

Part 2

Make the connection

15   What replaced Tŷ Hywel in 2006?
16   Which £59 million cultural edifice opened in Paris in 1977?
17   Which major media company relocated to a purpose-built site in Horseferry Road in 1994?
18   Which major city is served by Barajas International Airport?
19   Bon Jovi was the first band to play a public gig at which London venue in summer 2007?
20   What's the link?

Total Points: 20. Targets: Novice 8 Pro 15. Your Score:

Quiz 302. Motorsport

Four wheels, two wheels, anything fast

Part 1

1   Since the Speedway World Cup started in 2001, only four teams have won; Australia won the first two, Sweden won in 2003 and 2004; which two teams have won every event since? (2 pts)

2   What was the US-built car designed to compete with Ferrari in GT Sports Car racing in the 1960s?

3   The 1959 DBR1 was the only Aston Martin model ever to win which prestigious race?

4   Where could you watch the Sussex Trophy, the Glover Trophy and the Whitsun Trophy?

5   Who manufactures the GT40 range of sports cars?

6   Which British racer won nine 500 cc motorbike championships in the 1950s and 1960s?

7   What reached 174.88 mph on 3 February 1928?

8   Who, in 2009, became the sole tyre supplier to Moto GP after Michelin opted out?

9   What are the three classes of Grand Prix Motorcycle Racing?

10 Which great Italian rider of the 1960s and 1970s won eight Moto GP (or old style 500 cc) world titles and seven 350 cc titles? Which more recent Italian won the last of his seven Moto GP titles in 2009? (2 pts)

Part 2

11   Which two Spanish riders pushed defending champion Casey Stoner into third place in the 2012 Moto GP drivers' championship? (2 pts)

12   Which British rider recovered from an appalling crash to win the 500 cc world championship in 1976 and again in 1977?

13   Who won five consecutive TT Formula One titles in the 1980s and also holds the record (twenty-six) for most wins in the Isle of Man TT race schedule?

14   Who was the first British winner of the Indianapolis 500 (he won the Formula 1 championship in the same year, another first)?

15   Which manufacturer has dominated the Le Mans twenty-four-hour race in recent years, winning six out of seven races between 2006 and 2012?

16   Where is the British leg of the Speedway Grand Prix series held each year?

17   Which British driver, who drove F1 as well as sports cars, was a five-time winner of the Le Mans twenty-four-hour race? Which Belgian was the only man to have bettered that tally until Tom Kristensen racked up eight wins in recent years? (2 pts)

18   Which New Zealander won six Speedway world championship including a hat-trick between 1968 and 1970? Which Swede matched him with a sixth title in 2005? (2 pts)

19   Which team have won UK speedway Elite League most times since the modern league was established in 1997?

20   In February 2013 Danica Patrick made history by becoming the first woman to start in pole position in which race?

Total Points: 25. Targets: Novice 10 Pro 19. Your Score:

Quiz 303. Medicine

For the wannabe doctors (or, indeed, the real ones)

1   Someone who is anaemic is probably deficient in what mineral?

2   What is the main use for nootropic drugs?

3   What is the name of the UK's premier (and the world's oldest) eye hospital, on the Mile End Road, east London? In which decade was the hospital established: the 1770s, the 1800s or the 1850s? (2 pts)

4   What is the level of a hospital medical practitioner immediately below that of a consultant?

5   What is the common term for the commonly misused drug group, benzodiazepines?

6   What would you probably be prescribed to combat excessive fluid retention in the body?

7   Carl Djerassi was the principal mover in the development of which medical discovery in the 1950s?

8   What is the difference between optometry and ophthalmology?

9   What were the four 'humours', which provided the basis for most medicinal study prior to the Renaissance? (4 pts)

10   What was William Röntgen's major medical contribution in 1895?

11   Emphysema; tuberculosis; pleurisy; encephalomyelitis; which of these is *not* a disease of the lungs?

12   Paul Ehrlich's research led him to test various arsenic compounds and find a cure for which hitherto untreatable (and eventually fatal) sexually transmitted disease?

13   The discovery and preparation of which substance earned Alexander Fleming, Ernst Chain and Howard Florey the 1945 Nobel Prize for Medicine?

14   Norethynodrel was licensed by the US drug authority in 1960; what was it for?

15   What is the gas used as a natural relaxant by the body, deficiency of which can cause heart disease?

Total Points: 19. Targets: Novice 8 Pro 14. Your Score:

Quiz 304. Movies

A quick quiz plus a couple of long questions

Part 1

Identify these people or places or things
1   'Fast Eddie' Felson (2 pts)
2   Bedford Falls
3   Michael Hfuhruhurr (2 pts)
4   David St Hubbins, Nigel Tufnell and Derek Smalls
5   Bane
6   Gordon Gekko (2 pts)
7   Colonel Trautman
8   Mr Bridger (2 pts)
9   *After . . .*, *Another . . .*, *Shadow of . . .*, *. . . Goes Home* and *Song of . . .*
10 Gareth Mallory (2 pts)

Part 2

11 Which two directors collaborated on the 1983 version of *Scarface*, starring Al Pacino? What was the name of Pacino's character? Where did the character supposedly hail from? Who played the same gangster in a 1932 version of the movie? (5 pts)

12 In 2010 the *Guardian* listed its top twenty-five films in seven categories: Romance, Crime, Comedy, Action and War, Arthouse, Sci-Fi and Fantasy and Horror. Try and guess the seven no. 1 films. The dates of release were (not in category order): 1945, 1960, 1966, 1968, 1974, 1977, 1979. (7 pts)

Total Points: 27. Targets: Novice 14 Pro 20. Your Score: [   ]

Answers Quizzes 297–304

Quiz 297. General Knowledge

1. 1978; 2. 1971; 3. 1973; 4. 1979; 5. 1970; 6. 1974; 7. 1976; 8. 1972; 9. 1977; 10. 1975; 11. 1955; 12. 1962; 13. 1947; 14. 1967; 15. 1980; 16. 1984; 17. 1988; 18. 1993; 19. 1999; 20. 2003

Quiz 298. Movie Quotes

1. Alfred Hitchcock; 2. '. . . a box of chocolates'; *Forrest Gump*; 3. The Dude (Jeff Bridges) in *The Big Lebowski*; 4. *The Flintstones*; 5. Michael Douglas, after Glenn Close makes advances then stalks him in *Fatal Attraction*; 6. *Withnail and I*; they are in an old-fashioned tea shop; 7. David Cassidy (while he was still with the Partridge Family) who had a hit with the song 'I Think I Love You'; 8. *King Kong*; 9. Mae West; 10. '. . . victory'; *Apocalypse Now*; 11. Audrey Hepburn; 12. Ray Liotta as Henry Hill in *Goodfellas* directed by Martin Scorsese; 13. Russell Crowe in *Gladiator*; 14. Marilyn Monroe (as Sugar Kane) in *Some Like It Hot* (2 pts); 15. *The Rocky Horror Picture Show*; 16. Bette Davis; 17. Jedi master Yoda in *Return of the Jedi*; 18. Mel Gibson in *Lethal Weapon*; 19. Gloria Swanson; 20. *Casablanca*

Quiz 299. Computer Science

1. Atari; 2. $108 billion; 3. 1998; 4. Lisa; 5. Hewlett Packard; 6. Intel (Integrated Electronics); 7. Skype; Luxembourg; 8. Java; 9. Hyper and Markup; 10. Sweden; 11. 0.05; 12. Windows 8; 13. Beginner's All-Purpose Symbolic Instruction Code; 14. Kindle Fire; 15. FPU (floating point unit); 16. 1822 (Babbage developed a second version in the 1840s); 17. Excel, Word, PowerPoint and OneNote

Quiz 300. Business

1. Ryanair; 2. Tesco; 3. Pepsi-Cola; 4. IBM; 5. Richard Branson's Virgin Atlantic; 6. Digital camera; 7. Johannesburg; 8. Universal Music; 9. Thomas Cook; 10. 1960s; Mix and Match 1, b; 2, h; 3, c; 4, j; 5, i; 6, e; 7, f; 8, g; 9, d; 10, a

Quiz 301. Fine Art and Architecture

1. Titian; 2. Elvis Presley; 3. Gilbert and George; 4. Elizabeth Siddal (Millais made her lie in a bath of water; she caught a chill and the artist was forced to pay her medical fees); 5. Venice; 6. Cut off part of his ear; 7. Mondrian was part of the De Stijl movement; 8. Georges Braque; 9. Salvador Dalí; 10. The Camden Town Group (the group included Augustus John, Wyndham Lewis and Walter Sickert); 11. Der Blaue Reiter (The Blue Rider); 12. John Millais; 13. Edouard Manet; 14. The second part of the official title of the painting is *The Artist's Mother*; 15. The Senedd, seat of the National Assembly for Wales

in Cardiff Bay; 16. Pompidou Centre; 17. Channel 4; 18. Madrid; 19. O2 Arena; 20. All were designed by Richard Rogers

Quiz 302. Motorsport

1. Poland and Denmark; 2. Shelby Daytona (Cobra) Coupe; 3. Le Mans; 4. Goodwood (the Goodwood Revival motor racing meeting); 5. Ford; 6. Mike Hailwood; 7. Malcolm Campbell's *Bluebird*; 8. Bridgestone; 9. Moto GP, 250 cc and 125 cc; 10. Giacomo Agostini; Valentino Rossi; 11. Jorge Lorenzo (winner) and Dani Pedrosa (second); 12. Barry Sheene; 13. Joey Dunlop; 14. Jim Clark; 15. Audi; 16. Cardiff's Millennium Stadium; 17. Derek Bell; Jacky Ickx; 18. Ivan Mauger; Tony Rickardsson; 19. Poole Pirates; 20. Daytona 500

Quiz 303. Medicine

1. Iron; 2. They are smart drugs, most commonly used as memory enhancers; 3. Moorfield (founded by John Cunningham Saunders in 1805); 4. (Specialty) Registrar; 5. Tranquilizers (including temazepam and diazepam); 6. Diuretics; 7. The pill (or oral contraception); 8. Optometry is the examination of eyesight, ophthalmology the study of ocular disease; 9. Yellow bile, blood, phlegm, black bile; 10. Pioneering work on the X-ray; 11. Encephalomyelitis (often referred to with the prefix myalgic and shortened to ME, this is a brain condition symptomized by extreme fatigue); 12. Syphilis; 13. Penicillin; 14. It was the first widely available contraceptive pill; 15. Nitric oxide (the gas is a by-product of nitroglycerine, which was used as a treatment for angina as early as 1870)

Quiz 304. Movies

1. Paul Newman's character in *The Hustler* and *The Color of Money*; 2. The town where *It's a Wonderful Life* is set; 3. Steve Martin's character in *The Man with Two Brains*; 4. Spinal Tap, the fictional band in *This Is Spinal Tap*; 5. The vengeful masked warrior in *The Dark Knight Rises*; 6. Michael Douglas's 'greed-is-good' character in *Wall Street*; 7. Rambo's mentor in the series of movies starring Sylvester Stallone; 8. The criminal mastermind (played by Noël Coward) who engineers *The Italian Job* from his prison cell; 9. The various sequels to *The Thin Man*, also starring William Powell and Myrna Loy; 10. The Ralph Fiennes character who becomes Bond's new boss at the end of *Skyfall*; 11. Brian de Palma directed the film from an Oliver Stone screenplay; Tony Montana; Cuba; Paul Muni; 12. *Brief Encounter* (1945); *Chinatown* (1974); *Annie Hall* (1977); *Apocalypse Now* (1979); *Andrei Rublev* (1966); *2001: A Space Odyssey* (1968); *Psycho* (1960)

Quiz 305. General Knowledge

Part 1

1   In motorcycle terms, what does BSA stand for?

2   When Belgium became independent from the Netherlands in 1830, it was divided into two parts; Flemish-speaking Flanders was one; what was the French-speaking part?

3   Which ill-fated ship, subject of many a ghost story and rumour, set sail from New York in 1872?

4   What was the occupation of Patricia Cornwell that prepared her for success as a crime writer?

5   Which city in India gives its name to a form of sporting legwear?

6   'Family man' Eliot Spitzer resigned as Governor of New York after it was revealed that he had (a) beaten his wife (b) abused his children or (c) visited a high-class call-girl?

7   How many bones are there in the skull? (2 pts; 1 pt for two either way)

8   In 2012 a soft drinks company invited readers online to think up a new name for Mountain Dew; the idea was abandoned when the poll winner turned out to be what? (a) Raccoon Spit (b) Sarah Palin's Favourite Tipple (c) Hitler Did Nothing Wrong

9   What relation is film director Guillermo del Toro to actor Benicio del Toro?

10 Which ski event is to be introduced for women for the first time at the 2014 Winter Olympics?

Part 2

11   What is Superman's Achilles heel in the traditional versions of the tale?

12   What is the London theatre on Argyll Street (off Oxford Street) opened by Walter Gibbons in 1910 and synonymous with the heyday of music hall?

13   What are the names of the Fox and the Hound in both the original story and the Disney movie? (2 pts)

14   What is the other name for Hades, ruler of the Underworld in Greek mythology?

15   Sell a million copies of an album in the US and what do you get? What is the equivalent sales target in the UK? (2 pts)

16   Norrin Radd from Zenn-la made a deal and became which Marvel super-hero?

17   What was the black comedy about two old dears bumping people off, written for the stage by Joseph Kesselring in 1939 and turned into a Cary Grant movie five years later?

18   Who was punished by Zeus for giving fire to mortal men? What kind of creature was he? (2 pts)

19   What philosophical term is given to Kant's musings about the real or apparent incompatibility of accepted facts?

20   What's the Part 2 connection?

Total Points: 24. Targets: Novice 12 Pro 18. Your Score: _____

Quiz 306. TV Soaps

Part 1

1   Stan and Eddie brewed beer in the bath in *Coronation Street* in 1977 prompted by a strike by the brewery draymen; what was the name of the brewery?

2   Who were the first landlord and landlady of the Queen Vic in *EastEnders*? (2 pts)

3   Who were the two feuding families at the centre of *Dallas*? (2 pts)

4   Why did seventeen million viewers watch episode 523 of *Neighbours*?

5   What number comes after Beverly Hills in the teen soap about the Walsh family and the kids' new school that ran throughout the 1990s?

6   Collins, Grant and Corkhill were three of the central families in which British soap opera?

7   What is the name of Derek Thompson's character in *Casualty*, the only original member of the cast still in the show?

8   Who were the parents of David and Ken Barlow? (2 pts)

9   Who tried to murder the entire Platt family by driving them into the canal in *Coronation Street* in 2003?

10   What was the spin-off from *Dallas*, featuring Gary, another brother, and in which state was it set? (2 pts)

Part 2

11   *Dynasty* was the ABC network's response to the success of which CBS show?

12   What revelation made Roy Cropper revise his initial feelings for Hayley Patterson in *Coronation Street* in 1998?

13   What was Uncle Harry Slater's crime against his brother's family that was eventually revealed in *EastEnders*?

14   Which *EastEnders* character's battle with HIV did much to break down prejudice against those with the disease in the 1990s?

15   What is the fictional village that provided the setting for *Emmerdale Farm*, as the soap was called when it launched in 1972? Which family owned the titular farm? (2 pts)

16   What drastic plot device did script consultant Phil Redmond come up with to shake up *Emmerdale* in December 1993?

17   Who was Carol Hathaway and who played her? (2 pts)

18   Which two *Hollyoaks* stars transferred to the comedy series *Two Pints of Lager and a Packet of Crisps, Please* in 2001 and stayed to the final episode in 2011? (2 pts)

19   Why did Ken Barlow's Uncle Albert refuse to ride in his new car in *Coronation Street* in 1980?

20   Which early soap revolved around the lives and loves of the Harrington family in America in the 1960s?

Total Points: 27. Targets: Novice 11 Pro 20. Your Score:

Quiz 307. TV Vampires

Some of you may be a bit long in the tooth for this one

Part 1

1 Which TV vampire show is based on characters created by Charlaine Harris in *The Southern Vampire Mysteries*? Who is the principal character and which well-known film actress took the role? (3 pts)

2 What is the nature of Misha Collins's character, Castiel, in *Supernatural*?

3 Which undead series was set in Toronto and revolved around the relationship between an ex-cop PI and a vampire son of Henry VIII?

4 What connects Elena Gilbert and Katherine Pierce in *The Vampire Diaries*? (2 pts for full details)

5 Which 1998 vampire series starred Jack Davenport as a policeman investigating the disappearance of his best friend?

6 In 1977 Louis Jourdan, a French actor, made a splendid Dracula in a two-part BBC TV film; which stalwart English actor played Van Helsing? (a) Albert Finney (b) Frank Finlay (c) Corin Redgrave

7 Who is the Sheriff of Vampire Area 5 in *True Blood*? And who is the Vampire King of Mississippi who becomes a principal antagonist in season three? (2 pts)

8 Who played the main love interest, Beth Turner, in the cult vampire series, *Moonlight*, cancelled after the first series was hampered by the writer's strike in the US?

9 What is the true nature of the 'social worker' Mary Ann Forrester in *True Blood* (mainly in season two)? Who is her assistant? (2 pts)

10 What are the names of the two sibling demon-hunters at the centre of *Supernatural*? (2 pts)

Part 2

Buffy the Vampire Slayer – the pioneer vamp show

11   Who is Spike's nut-job girlfriend?

12   What is the name of the nightclub frequented by the students? What is the name of Oz's band, who make regular appearances? (2 pts)

13   Who is the second Slayer brought into being when Buffy 'dies' at the end of the first season? Who is her rather incompetent Watcher? (2 pts)

14   Who is the Wiccan at the school who Willow turns into a rat?

15   With whom does Cordelia fall in love in *Angel*, until he returns to his own world, having realized it is Angel with whom she is really in love?

16   Which series four episode of *Buffy* contained no dialogue for thirty minutes and won an Emmy nomination for its screenplay, a near-unprecedented accolade for a sci-fi show?

17   What is the name of Angel's son? Who is his mother? And who kidnaps him and raises him as a warrior in a hellish alternative dimension? (3 pts)

18   Who takes over as Principal of Sunnydale High when Principal Flutie is eaten by the hyena-students? And who is head of the school when it reopens in season seven of *Buffy*? (2 pts)

19   What is the name of Giles's girlfriend in series two of *Buffy* and who kills her? (2 pts)

20   What are the names of the seven 'Big Bads', the fearsome opponents Buffy must defeat at the climax to each series of the show (one per series)? (7 pts)

Total Points: 38. Targets: Novice 15 Pro 29. Your Score: ⌐‾‾‾‾‾‾‾‾‾‾‾⌐

Quiz 308. London

Part 1

1 What was approved in 2003 and completed close to London Bridge in 2012?

2 Which three London boroughs have been conferred the 'Royal' prefix? (3 pts)

3 By what name is the London building officially called Westminster Palace known?

4 What started in Pudding Lane, London, in 1666?

5 What was the name of the party boat sunk in the River Thames with loss of fifty-one lives in 1989?

6 Where in London were a number of people injured as shoppers grew frantic at an IKEA store opening in 2005?

7 What took place on the streets of London for the first time on 28 March 1981?

8 What opened in Regent's Park in 1828?

9 What was the venue for the annual Bartholomew Fair, held in London from 1133 to 1752?

10 Which former London street is synonymous with low-quality writing?

Part 2

11 Where did thirty-one people lose their lives in a rail crash in London in 1999?

12 Shakespeare is buried at Holy Trinity Church, Stratford-upon-Avon; but which London church houses a tomb devoted to the playwright?

13 What are current estimates for the number of unexploded World War II bombs in London? (a) between 100 and 200 (b) somewhere between 1,000 and 1,500 (c) around 5,000

14 Why were no true cockneys born between 1941 and 1961?

15 If you had a wedding reception in the largest public building in the only park in the borough of Kensington and Chelsea, where would your guests head for? (2 pts)

16 Which was the first London football club to play in the top flight of English football? (2 pts)

17 Islington shares a border with which four London boroughs? (4 pts)

Total Points: 24. Targets: Novice 10 Pro 18. Your Score:

Quiz 309. History

A general section

Part 1

1 By what name is King Nebuchadnezzar's seventh-century BC garden better known?

2 Who united the various Mongol tribes in the twelfth and thirteenth centuries and conquered most of what is now China, eastern Russia and central Asia?

3 What happened at Fotheringay Castle on 7 February 1587?

4 Prime Minister Ian Smith declared which country a republic in 1970?

5 Which country, in 1809, ceased being part of Sweden? Of which country did it become a principality for just over 100 years? (2 pts)

6 What was the cost of the first TV licence in 1946? (a) sixpence (b) two shillings (c) five shillings

7 Queen Boudicca was the ruler of which rebel tribe in Roman Britain? In which century was she killed? And on the site of which modern railway station was she (probably) killed? (3 pts)

8 With whom had the Japanese been at war for two years before the outbreak of World War II and their alliance with Germany?

9 Which three Roman statesmen formed the First Triumvirate in 60 BC? (3 pts)

10 How were the (modern) states of Laos, Thailand, Vietnam and Cambodia known to the great Western powers in the nineteenth century? Who held sway over these territories from 1884–5? (2 pts)

Part 2

11 Which eleven American states seceded from the Union at the outbreak of Civil War in 1860–61? (11 pts)

Total Points: 27. Targets: Novice 11 Pro 20. Your Score:

Quiz 310. Rock and Pop

A quick quiz followed by a big question which may involve complete guesswork

Part 1

1   Which Who album, now regarded as a classic, was initially intended as a rock opera follow-up to *Tommy* called *Lifehouse*?

2   Who was the biggest selling solo female artist of the 1960s in the UK?

3   Who were the three judges for the first three series of *X Factor* in the UK? (3 pts)

4   Which country giant first appeared on Gram Parsons' album *Grievous Angel*?

5   Who played at St Martins College of Art on 6 November 1975?

6   Which 1960s band featured Rod Argent on keyboards and the vocals of Colin Blunstone?

7   Which song provided Paul Simon with his first US no. 1 hit single after the demise of his partnership with Art Garfunkel?

8   Which classic Beach Boys song was released as the B-side to 'Wouldn't It Be Nice'?

9   What, in 1973, connected actors Kenny Lynch, James Coburn and Christopher Lee, writer and MP Clement Freud, boxer John Conteh and chat-show host Michael Parkinson?

10 What was the 1980 album by the Cure that was thirty-five minutes and twenty-four seconds longer than its title suggested?

Part 2

11 Eight polls of the greatest electric guitarists of all time have been combined to create a supposedly 'definitive' list; can you name the top ten? (Five are predominantly blues players, one is rock 'n' roll, two are out-and-out rockers and two are more esoteric and varied.) (10 pts)

Total Points: 22. Targets: Novice 9 Pro 17. Your Score:

Quiz 311. Football

Some convoluted stuff

Part 1

1   Which two unfancied sides contested the 2013 League Cup final? What was the score in a rather one-sided affair? (3 pts)

2   Which English manager has managed in Sweden, Switzerland, Denmark, Norway, Finland, the United Arab Emirates and Italy? Which three of these were posts in charge of the national team? (4 pts)

3   Who missed the final, crucial penalty as England exited the 2011 Women's World Cup on penalties? Which side beat them? (2 pts)

4   For which club did Martin Chivers, Mark Lawrenson and John Gregory all play at the same time?

5   Here's one for the mid-term memory: which unlucky player was Leeds United top scorer with nineteen goals in 1999–2000?

6   Who scored four goals in twelve minutes after coming on as a substitute against Nottingham Forest in an 8–1 rout in 1999?

7   When Liverpool sold Fernando Torres to Chelsea for c.£50 million, which two strikers did they buy with the money, and who from? (4 pts)

8   The British transfer record was broken four times in the 1960s, twice each by which two players? In each case, there were three teams involved; name the two clubs in the middle who bought, then sold, each player? (4 pts)

9   The early 1980s was the last time a club other than Celtic or Rangers won the Scottish League; which two clubs won in 1983, 1984 and 1985, and who were the two managers at the helm? (4 pts)

10 If Raith Rovers played St Johnstone over two legs, which two Scottish towns would host the games? (2 pts)

Part 2

11 Of the nineteen players who took the field for France in the 1998 World Cup final and the Euro 2000 final, which five never played in England? (Hint: they won 444 caps between them – four really serious players and one good one.) (5 pts)

12 In which year was *Match of the Day* first broadcast? Which northern stadium played host? Which Beatles song was playing over the tannoy at the start of the game? Who was the BBC's presenter and commentator? (4 pts)

13 Who were relegated from the Premier League in 2001, after thirty-four years in English football's top flight? Who was their manager that

season? Which three clubs boasted a longer tenure at the top table (and still do)? (5 pts)

Total Points: 40. Targets: Novice 16 Pro 30. Your Score: ☐

Quiz 312. General Knowledge

Part 1

1 Which President of which South American country offered to send aid to the US in the aftermath of Hurricane Katrina? (2 pts)

2 What attaches muscle to the skeleton in humans?

3 Roughly what percentage of the population of Israel is Muslim: 5 per cent, 15 per cent or 25 per cent?

4 An adaptation of which children's book (by which author) provided young Aled Jones with the hit song, 'Walking in the Air'? (2 pts)

5 Apart from the ones in Europe, where are the other Southern Alps?

6 Between 1926 and 1972 the Golden Arrow train service linked London to which other city?

7 'Blimey, I drank 5.68 litres last night and I don't even have a hangover!' How much?

8 What was the name of the cruise ship that sank off the Italian coast in January 2012? (a) *Regatta Magnifica* (b) *Francesco Schettino* (c) *Costa Concordia*

9 Singer Martha Wainwright's father was Loudon Wainwright III, but which other singer, one of a North American duo, was her mother?

10 What sport, similar to bowls or petanque, featured in the Paralympic programme?

Part 2

11 A failure in which form of transportation caused the death of forty-two people in the Dolomites in Italy on 8 March 1976?

12 In 1953 Tom Bourdillon and Charles Evans got within 100 metres of what, two days before a more famous pairing?

13 Who disappeared in Beirut in 1987 and was held hostage for the next five years?

14 Who presented her Best Supporting Actress Oscar statuette for *The Diary of Anne Frank* (1959) to the Anne Frank Museum in Amsterdam?

15 Which famous photographer has been married to both the actress Catherine Deneuve and former Miss World, Marie Helvin?

16 Who attempted the role of Holly Golightly on the London stage in autumn 2009? Who made the role her own in an iconic film performance in the 1960s? (2 pts)

17 Which two rulers signed the 1979 peace treaty between Israel and Egypt? Where? What were secret the meetings held the previous year that paved the way for the treaty? Which US President expedited the agreement? (5 pts)

Total Points: 24. Targets: Novice 13 Pro 19. Your Score:

Answers Quizzes 305–312

Quiz 305. General Knowledge

1. Birmingham Small Arms (Company); 2. Wallonia; 3. *Mary Celeste*; 4. Pathologist; 5. Jodhpur; 6. (c) He visited a call-girl (better than the other two options, at least!); 7. Twenty-two; 8. (c) Unsurprisingly the company declined to offer this message to the great American public; 9. None (Guillermo is Mexican while Benicio is from Puerto Rico); 10. Ski Jump; 11. Kryptonite; 12. London Palladium; 13. Tod and Copper; 14. Pluto; 15. Platinum disc; 300,000; 16. Silver Surfer; 17. *Arsenic and Old Lace*; 18. Prometheus; a Titan; 19. Antimony; 20. All the answers are based on elements in the periodic table: krypton, palladium, copper, plutonium, platinum, silver, arsenic, promethium, antimony

Quiz 306. TV Soaps

1. Newton and Ridley; 2. Den and Angie Watts; 3. Ewing and Barnes; 4. It was the wedding of Charlene and Scott, aka Kylie Minogue and Jason Donovan; 5. 90210; 6. *Brookside*; 7. Charlie Fairhead; 8. Frank and Ida; 9. Richard Hillman; 10. *Knots Landing*; California; 11. *Dallas*; 12. Hayley was actually Harold, a man living as a woman; 13. He fostered a child (Zoe) on his niece Kat; 14. Mark Fowler; 15. Beckindale; the Sugdens; 16. The plane crash; 17. The head nurse in *ER*, played by Julianna Margulies; 18. Will Mellor and Natalie Casey; 19. Because it was made in Germany; 20. *Peyton Place*

Quiz 307. TV Vampires

1. *True Blood*; Sooki Stackhouse, Anna Paquin; 2. An angel; 3. *Blood Ties*; 4. Katherine is Elena's doppelganger and both parts are played by the same actress, Nina Dobrev; 5. *Ultraviolet* (it was fab, but inexplicably Channel 4 only made one series); 6. Frank Finlay; 7. Eric (Northman); Russell Edington; 8. Sophie Myles; 9. She is a maenad; Benedict 'Eggs' Talley (Eggs is fine); 10. Dean and Sam Winchester; 11. Drusilla; 12. The Bronze; Dingoes Ate My Baby; 13. Faith; Wesley Wyndham-Price; 14. Amy; 15. The Grusalugg; 16. Hush; 17. Connor; Darla; Holtz; 18. Snyder; Robin Wood; 19. Jenny Calendar; Angelus; 20. (Series 1) The Master, (S2) Angelus (Angel is incorrect), (S3) Mayor Wilkins, (S4) Adam (but accept the Initiative, as Adam is their creation), (S5) the goddess Glory, (S6) Dark Willow, (S7) The First (Evil)

Quiz 308. London

1. The Shard; 2. Kensington and Chelsea and Kingston upon Thames were the first two, in 1965, and Greenwich was added in 2012; 3. Houses of Parliament; 4. The Great Fire of London; 5. The Marchioness; 6. Edmonton; 7. London Marathon; 8. The zoo; 9. Smithfield; 10. Grub Street; 11. Ladbroke Grove; 12. Southwark Cathedral; 13. (c) There are believed to be about 5,000, mainly in the river; 14. A cockney must be born within earshot of Bow Bells (the bells of St Mary-le-Bow church), and the bells were destroyed in the Blitz and

not rebuilt until 1961; 15. The Orangery in Holland Park; 16. Woolwich Arsenal won promotion to the top flight in 1903–4, sixteen years after the league was formed (it was twenty-six years before they became the first London winners of the title, by then playing simply as Arsenal); 17. Camden, Haringey, Hackney and City of London

Quiz 309. History

1. The Hanging Gardens of Babylon; 2. Genghis Khan (also known as Temujin); 3. Execution of Mary, Queen of Scots; 4. Rhodesia, now Zimbabwe; 5. Finland; Russia; 6. (b) Two shillings; 7. Iceni; first century AD; King's Cross; 8. China; 9. Julius Caesar, Crassus and Pompey; 10. Indo-China; France; 11. South Carolina; Mississippi; Florida; Alabama; Georgia; Louisiana; Texas; Virginia; Arkansas; North Carolina; Tennessee

Quiz 310. Rock and Pop

1. *Who's Next*; 2. Cilla Black; 3. Simon Cowell, Louis Walsh and Sharon Osbourne; 4. Emmylou Harris; 5. Sex Pistols, it was their first gig; 6. The Zombies; 7. '50 Ways To Leave Your Lover'; 8. 'God Only Knows'; 9. They all appeared dressed as convicts (along with Paul and Linda McCartney) on the cover of Wings' *Band on the Run*; 10. *Seventeen Seconds*; 11. 10. Eric Clapton 9. Ry Cooder 8. Stevie Ray Vaughan 7. Eddie van Halen (don't laugh, so influential) 6. Mark Knopfler 5. Chuck Berry 4. Keith Richards 3. Robert Johnson 2. B. B. King 1. Jimi Hendrix (Personally I would have included Jeff Beck and Richard Thompson instead of Clapton and Vaughan)

Quiz 311. Football

1. Swansea City and Bradford City; Swansea won 5–0; 2. Roy Hodgson; Switzerland, UAE and Finland; 3. Faye White; France; 4. Brighton and Hove Albion; 5. Michael Bridges (his promising career was effectively ended by an injury the following year); 6. Ole Gunnar Solskjaer; 7. Andy Carroll and Luis Suarez from Newcastle United and Ajax; 8. Denis Law (Man City; TORINO; Man Utd) and Alan Clarke (Fulham; LEICESTER CITY; Leeds); 9. Dundee United in 1982–3 under Jim McLean and Aberdeen the following two years under Alex Ferguson; 10. Kirkcaldy (Raith) and Perth (St Johnstone); 11. Alain Boghossian, Bixente Lizarazu, Lilian Thuram, David Trezeguet and Zinedine Zidane; 12. 1964; Anfield (Liverpool v Arsenal); 'She Loves You'; Kenneth Wolstenholme; 13. Coventry City; Gordon Strachan; Arsenal, Everton and Liverpool

Quiz 312. General Knowledge

1. Hugo Chavez of Venezuela; 2. Tendons; 3. 15 per cent; 4. *The Snowman* (Raymond Briggs); 5. On the South Island of New Zealand; 6. Paris; 7. Ten pints; 8. *Costa Concordia* (Schettino was the name of the errant captain); 9. Kate McGarrigle, who recorded with her sister Anna up to her death in 2010; 10. Boccia; 11. Cable car; 12. Mount Everest (they

charted the way up for Hillary and Tensing Norgay, but oxygen problems forced them to retreat before they reached the top); 13. Terry Waite; 14. Shelley Winters; 15. David Bailey; 16. Anna Friel; Audrey Hepburn; 17. Menachem Begin and Anwar Sadat; Washington, DC; Camp David summits; Jimmy Carter

Quiz 313. General Knowledge

Part 1

1　In which US city is the Smithsonian Institute?

2　Which city's historic docks house the HMS *Victory*?

3　Geocentric means (a) based on geometrical theory (b) revolving around the earth (c) rooted in the soil?

4　'Stately as a Galleon' and 'George, Don't Do That' were works by which great humorist?

5　Which two US states have no border with any other?

6　Where is the canyon known as the Valles Marineris?

7　What common item is a 210 x 297 mm (8¼ x 11¾ in) rectangle?

8　Who got a standing ovation from the assembled Members of Parliament in Westminster Hall when she arrived to address them on 21 June 2012?

9　Which name is shared by the actress who co-starred with Bogart in *The Maltese Falcon* and the first woman MP to sit in the House of Commons?

10　Which three Great Britain athletes have won gold medals in the women's multi-discipline track and field events (pentathlon and heptathlon) at the Olympic Games? (3 pts)

Part 2

11   Which poet died of a fever supporting insurgents in Greece in 1824, aged only thirty-six?

12   Who is the First Lord of the Treasury in the United Kingdom?

13   What name did the Romans give to the territory which incorporated the southern section of modern Portugal and parts of eastern Spain? (a) Iberia (b) Andalusia (c) Lusitania

14   Batman has made numerous appearances as part of which multi-hero crime-fighting team?

15   'The Liberty Bell' by John Philip Sousa is a piece of music best known as (a) the opening credits of *ITV News* bulletins (b) the *Monty Python* theme tune or (c) the tune which, when speeded up, became *The Benny Hill Show* tune?

16   For the 500th edition of *Match of the Day*, 1,600 children turned over cards in the opening sequence to reveal a picture of what?

17   Who is the father of Moscow gallery-owner Darya Zhukova's first child?

18   Which TV presenter represented Wales at gymnastics in the 1990 Commonwealth Games?

19   Which celebrity, born in 1932, doubled a career as an actor with that of a world-class bridge player?

20   Which actress has been in a relationship with Hollywood colleague Kurt Russell since 1983?

Total Points: 22. Targets: Novice 11 Pro 17. Your Score: [   ]

Quiz 314. Movies

A giant Mix and Match; match up the actor with the actress, film and director (3 pts per question)

1. Trevor Howard; 2. Clark Gable; 3. Richard Gere; 4. Robert Redford; 5. Christian Slater; 6. Rock Hudson; 7. John Cusack; 8. Bradley Cooper; 9. Michael Cera; 10. Jack Nicholson

a. Jane Wyman; b. Jennifer Lawrence; c. Claudette Colbert; d. Barbra Streisand; e. Ellen Page; f. Ione Skye; g. Celia Johnson; h. Patricia Arquette; i. Helen Hunt; j. Debra Winger

i. *Juno* (2007); ii. *It Happened One Night* (1934); iii. *True Romance* (1993); iv. *Silver Linings Playbook* (2012); v. *An Officer and a Gentleman* (1982); vi. *Say Anything* (1989); vii. *As Good As It Gets* (1997); viii. *Brief Encounter* (1945); ix. *All That Heaven Allows* (1955); x. *The Way We Were* (1973)

Q. Cameron Crowe; R. Taylor Hackford; S. Jason Reitman; T. David Lean; U. Sydney Pollack; V. James L. Brooks; W. Tony Scott; X. Douglas Sirk; Y. David O. Russell; Z. Frank Capra

Total Points: 30. Targets: Novice 12 Pro 23. Your Score:

Quiz 315. Science

Part 1

1   What name is given to the science of trying to improve a species by selective breeding?

2   What is the common name for iron pyrites?

3   What is the term given to the square root of the arithmetic mean of the individual squares of all the numbers in a set?

4   Which pre-calculator aid for mathematicians was first devised in a crude form by Englishman John Napier in the early seventeenth century?

5   William Smith's day job allowed him the time to examine the strata and types of rock just below the earth's surface (and develop some groundbreaking studies) as it was vital to the construction and safety of his industry; what was he? (a) a canal engineer (b) a mine architect (c) a Captain in the Royal Engineers

6   If beta rays are high-energy electrons, then what are gamma rays?

7   As well as a Latin acronym indicating something is proven, for what, scientifically, do the initials QED also stand?

8   What two names are given to the different forms of microbe, some of which photosynthesize, some of which exhibit animal behaviour patterns? (2 pts)

9   What was finally 'proved' by mathematician Andrew Wiles in 1995, having been a scientific enigma since the mid-seventeenth century?

10 What is the cube root of 125?

Part 2

Identify the following from the clue

11 $A \equiv B$

12 Eniwetok, Marshall Islands

13 Trepanning

14 πr^2

15 Maria Sklodowska

16 $X \cap Y$

17 Medulla Oblongata

18 HMS *Beagle*

19 Formula: $- 32, \times 5, \div 9$

20 RADAR

Total Points: 21. Targets: Novice 6 Pro 16. Your Score:

Quiz 316. World War II

A section on military history

Part 1

1 Which crucial battle for supremacy in North Africa began on 22 October 1942 and would result in a victory for the Allied forces?

2 Which city was the target for the second atomic bomb to be dropped in World War II, in 1945?

3 Which future President served as Supreme Commander of the Allied forces in Europe?

4 Who was appointed Commander of the Eighth Army in North Africa in 1942?

5 Who, along with his entourage, was arrested and shot near Lake Como in April 1945?

6 What post was held by Cosmo Gordon Lang at the outbreak of World War II? (a) Archbishop of Canterbury (b) Speaker of the House of Commons (c) Ambassador to the United States

7 Which city rose up against the occupying Nazis on 1 August, 1944, but was let down by the failure of the approaching Soviets to advance?

8 What was the codename given to the Normandy landings of 6 June 1944?

9 Which British battlecruiser was sunk by the *Bismarck* in May 1941, after which the RAF and Navy pursued and sunk the German battleship?

10 What position did Winston Churchill hold in Chamberlain's first War Cabinet? Who was the Leader of the Opposition appointed by Churchill as Deputy Prime Minister in 1942? (2 pts)

Part 2

11   Which naval battle in June 1942 effectively gave the US Navy dominance of the Pacific?

12   Who oversaw the military defeat of Japan in the Pacific and accepted its surrender?

13   Major-General Thomas Blamey was the commander of which segment of the Allied forces in World War II? (a) the Allied forces in the Pacific (b) the RAF (b) the Australian Army in all theatres

14   Which two nations declared war on Japan in 1941, following the attack on Pearl Harbor the previous day? (2 pts)

15   Which US President ordered the dropping of atomic bombs on Japanese targets?

16   Where did a major German counter-offensive sometimes known as the Battle of the Bulge take place from December 1944 in northwest Europe?

17   An officer of which branch of the Army would not draw a ceremonial sword to salute when on parade?

18   What was the German equivalent of the Victoria Cross during World War II? What was the medieval military order that first used the symbol? (2 pts)

19   What distinction does the New Zealander Charles Hazlitt Upham hold? (a) he was head of the Anzac forces in World War II (b) he was Second-in-Command of the Allied Navy during World War II (c) he was the only recipient of a double Victoria Cross during World War II

20   The famous raid which became known as the Dambusters raid was part of which 1943 airborne operation? Which river valley was flooded as a consequence? Who designed the special bouncing bombs used on the raid? Which RAF squadron carried out the attacks? (4 pts)

Total Points: 26. Targets: Novice 10 Pro 20. Your Score: [   ]

Quiz 317. Fashion and Photography

Part 1

1 Which musician launched a Sean John fashion line in 1998?

2 What would a dressmaker use to make a serrated edge?

3 Who simultaneously lost Chanel, Burberry and H&M modelling contracts in 2005 after she was pictured snorting drugs with boyfriend Pete Doherty?

4 For what aspect of fashion are Rigby & Peller best known?

5 Where might one wear a pair of Vans?

6 What are the clothing company Ben Sherman (founded 1963) best known for?

7 What is the head-to-toe covering worn (by law or choice) by women in many Muslim countries and cultures?

8 Who published a work called *Box of Pin-Ups* in 1965, one of the first famous collections of celebrity photographs outside Hollywood?

9 Who was the aristocratic photographer, born 1939 and known for his royal portraits (unsurprisingly, given his background of being a distant relative) and his nudes (not of the royal family!)?

10 Which American photographer is remembered chiefly for his black-and-white landscapes, especially those taken in Yosemite National Park?

Part 2

11 What was the subject matter of *Private* (2004) and *Confidential* (2007), two books by photographer Alison Jackson?

12 Who designed the cone-shaped bra for Madonna's Blonde Ambition tour in 1990? (a) Alexander McQueen (b) Jean-Paul Gaultier (c) Gianni Versace

13 The Gucci label was started in Florence in the 1920s manufacturing goods mainly from which material?

14 Which designer, born in New York in 1939, started up his Polo label in 1967?

15 What is the type of napped flannelette mainly used for nightwear?

16 What was the 'do-what-it-says-on-the-tin' name given to the BBC's first fashion show, launched in 1986? Which TV news figure presented the programme along with designer Jeff Banks? Which retail chain did Banks found in the 1970s? Who was his first wife, a 1960s pop star? Which band provided the theme tune for the show? (5 pts)

Total Points: 20. Targets: Novice 8 Pro 15. Your Score:

Quiz 318. Name the Team

Football teams from all competitions and eras (5 pts each)

1   The Manchester City side that started the 2011 FA Cup final against Stoke City: Hart; MISSING; Kompany; MISSING; Kolarov; De Jong; MISSING; Touré; MISSING; MISSING; Tévez

2   The Chelsea team that won the Champions League in 2012: Čech; Bosingwa; MISSING; MISSING; Cole; Kalou (sub: Torres 84); MISSING; Lampard; MISSING (sub: Malouda 73); MISSING; Drogba

3   The Celtic team that won the European Cup against Inter Milan in 1967: Simpson; Craig; MISSING; Clark; MISSING; MISSING; Murdoch; Auld; MISSING; Wallace; MISSING

4   The Tottenham side that started the 2008 League Cup final against Chelsea: MISSING; Hutton; Woodgate; MISSING; Chimbonda; MISSING; Jenas; Zokora; MISSING; Keane; MISSING

5   The Nottingham Forest team that won the 1979 European Cup final against Malmo: MISSING; Anderson; Lloyd; MISSING; Clark; Francis; MISSING; Bowyer; MISSING; MISSING; Birtles

6   The England team that destroyed the Netherlands 4–1 at Euro 96: Seaman; MISSING; Adams; Southgate; MISSING; Anderton; MISSING; Gascoigne; MISSING; Shearer; MISSING

7   The Wimbledon side that won the 1988 FA Cup final against Liverpool: MISSING; Goodyear; Young; MISSING; Phelan; MISSING; Sanchez; Gibson; MISSING; Fashanu; MISSING

8   The Manchester United team (inc. subs) who clinched the treble in 1999: Schmeichel; MISSING; Johnsen; MISSING; Irwin; Giggs; Beckham; MISSING; Blomqvist (sub: MISSING, 67); MISSING; Cole (sub: Solskjaer 81)

9   The Barcelona side that won the 2009 Champions League so effortlessly against Manchester United: Victor Valdes; MISSING; Touré; MISSING; Sylvinho; Busquets; Xavi; MISSING; Messi; MISSING; MISSING

10   The Liverpool team that won the extraordinary 2005 Champions League final against Milan: MISSING; Finnan (sub: Hamann 46); Carragher; MISSING; Traore; Garcia; MISSING; Gerrard; Riise; MISSING (sub: Smicer 23); MISSING (sub: Cissé 85)

Total Points: 50. Targets: Novice 20 Pro 38. Your Score: ☐

Quiz 319. Wildlife

The animal kingdom

Part 1

1 What would an oologist collect?

2 Dian Fossey (1932–85) is best remembered for her work with which animals?

3 What are the only two other species that pose a predatory threat to a wolf pack? (2 pts)

4 *Zoo Quest* in 1954 was the first TV natural history programme to feature which well-known face?

5 What appeared in the Triassic period, dominated in the Jurassic and were gone by the end of the Cretaceous?

6 Komodo Island, home to the largest reptile on earth, the Komodo dragon, is part of which state?

7 There is only one species in the mammalian order Monotremes, which makes it the only egg-laying mammal; what is it?

8 What creature comes in Brazilian, Malayan, mountain and Baird's?

9 The family of mammals labelled as Cetacea mainly consists of what creatures?

10 How many different species of ostrich exist: one, three or fourteen?

Part 2

11   Which of these mammals is not in the Perissodactyla order, along with horses and donkeys? (a) rhinoceros (b) tapir (c) hippopotamus (d) zebra

12   What more common name is given to the order of birds Falconiformes? Which other types of bird could come under this heading but are not falcons? (2 pts)

13   Which can reach the highest land speeds: a human, an elephant or a mountain goat?

14   What are the three types of great ape? (There are four species, as one type has two species) (3 pts)

15   Tree sloths and armadillos are two of three families of the order Edentata (mammals with long, sticky tongues and clawed feet); what is the other family, with three known species?

16   What is the largest recorded freshwater fish, clocking in at an impressive 5 metres long?

17   Goat; lion; camel: which of these has a gestation period longer than a human?

18   The puffin is a small variety of which bird?

19   Leatherback, big-headed and snapping are all types of what creature?

20   The order Chiroptera is made up of hundreds of species of what?

Total Points: 24. Targets: Novice 10 Pro 18. Your Score:

Quiz 320. General Knowledge

Part 1

1 For what internet phenomenon are Larry Page and Sergey Brin largely responsible?

2 Where was the first drive-through safari outside Africa opened in 1966?

3 In 1337 a chap named Edward became England's first Duke; what was his title? (a) Duke of Northumberland (b) Duke of Westminster (c) Duke of Cornwall

4 What was awarded to Bertrand Russell in 1950, Churchill in 1953 and Alexander Solzhenitsyn in 1970?

5 The city of Toronto lies on the shore of which of the Great Lakes?

6 Which state had to abandon a policy of state-endorsed polygamy in the late nineteenth century in order to be allowed to join the USA?

7 How does combining two lots of selenium with one of nitrogen make sense?

8 Who is the UK's best-known pub landlord?

9 Lucy Davis, best known as Dawn in *The Office*, is the daughter of which well-known TV comedian?

10 What are the three events that make up the snowboarding programme at the Winter Olympics? (3 pts)

Part 2

11 What did Marcus Barnett of *The Times* describe as the gardener's world cup?

12 Who was the former business partner of Ebenezer Scrooge?

13 Barcelona is the centre of which semi-autonomous region of Spain?

14 What connects authors William Blake, Daniel Defoe, Fydor Dostoevsky and Oscar Wilde?

15 Who did the Conservative Party recruit in 1978 to help win the election the following year?

16 While Manchester United have had one manager for all twenty seasons of the Premier League (1992–3 to 2012–13), how many have Chelsea had (including Rafa Benítez, but not Graham Rix or Ray Wilkins, who managed for two games and one game respectively)? (2 pts)

17 Who is the tallest out of rugby star Martin Johnson, footballer Peter Crouch, Croatian tennis star Maran Čilić and basketball superstar Kobe Bryant?

18 Shane Warne was once caught smoking on camera whilst under contract to advertise what?

19 What is the name of Emma Thompson and Greg Wise's daughter, born in 1999?

20 Which two royal married couples announced their separation on 19 March in 1976 and 1992 respectively? (4 pts)

Total Points: 26. Targets: Novice 13 Pro 20. Your Score:

Answers Quizzes 313–320

Quiz 313. General Knowledge

1. Washington, DC; 2. Portsmouth; 3. (b) revolving around the earth, from the days when astronomers thought earth the centre of the universe; 4. Joyce Grenfell; 5. Alaska and Hawaii; 6. Mars; 7. A sheet of A4 paper; 8. Aung San Suu Kyi, the recently freed Burmese opposition leader; 9. Astor (Mary and Nancy); 10. Mary Peters (1972); Denise Lewis (2000); Jessica Ennis (2012); 11. Lord Byron; 12. Prime Minister; 13. (c) Lusitania; 14. Justice League of America; 15. (b) it is the Python theme; 16. Jimmy Hill; 17. Roman Abramovich; 18. Gabby Logan; 19. Omar Sharif; 20. Goldie Hawn

Quiz 314. Movies

Mix and Match 1, g, viii, T; 2, c, ii, Z; 3, j, v, R; 4, d, x, U; 5, h, iii, W; 6, a, ix, X; 7, f, vi, Q; 8, b, iv, Y; 9, e, i, S; 10, i, vii, V

Quiz 315. Science

1. Eugenics; 2. Fool's Gold; 3. Root Mean Square (RMS); 4. Logarithm tables; 5. Smith was a canal engineer; 6. High-energy electromagnetic waves; 7. Quantum electrodynamics; 8. Algae and protozoa; 9. Fermat's Last Theorem; 10. Five; 11. A is identical to B; 12. Scene of the detonation of the first hydrogen bomb by the US in 1952; 13. Reactive surgery involving drilling a hole through the cranium in order to expose and treat the outer layer of menenges; 14. The area of a circle, where r = the radius of that circle; 15. Birth name of Marie Curie; 16. X intersects with Y; 17. The part of the brain that governs the body's voluntary impulses like swallowing and breathing; 18. The ship in which Charles Darwin undertook his voyage of scientific discovery; 19. Conversion of Fahrenheit to Celsius; 20. Radio Detection and Ranging (the use of sound waves to detect airborne threat and other subsequent uses)

Quiz 316. World War II

1. El Alamein; 2. Nagasaki; 3. Dwight D. Eisenhower; 4. Bernard Montgomery; 5. Benito Mussolini; 6. (a) He was the Archbishop of Canterbury from 1928 to 1942, when he was succeeded by William Temple; 7. Warsaw; 8. Operation Overlord; 9. HMS *Hood*; 10. First Lord of the Admiralty; Clement Attlee; 11. The Battle of Midway; 12. General Douglas MacArthur; 13. Blamey was appointed overall head of the Australian Army in 1942, having led the expeditionary force sent to assist in Europe; 14. USA and Britain; 15. Harry S. Truman; 16. The Ardennes (forest); 17. The medical corps (as non-combatants they keep the hand on the scabbard whilst saluting); 18. Iron Cross; Teutonic Order or Teutonic Knights or (for a bonus point) the Order of Brothers of the German House of Saint Mary in Jerusalem; 19. (c) Hazlitt was an inspirational soldier and joined two World War I Army

Corps officers in the distinction of receiving a bar on his Victoria Cross; 20. Operation Chastise; Ruhr; Barnes Wallis; 617 Squadron

Quiz 317. Fashion and Photography

1. P Diddy; 2. Pinking shears; 3. Kate Moss; 4. Lingerie; 5. On your feet (they are a brand of casual shoes popularized by the surfer look); 6. Shirts (adopted by first the mods and then the skinhead movement); 7. Burkha; 8. David Bailey; 9. Lord (Patrick) Lichfield; 10. Ansel Adams; 11. Jackson specializes in faking celebrity photos using look-a-like models; 12. Jean-Paul Gaultier; 13. Leather; 14. Ralph Lauren; 15. Winceyette; 16. *The Clothes Show*; Selina Scott; Warehouse; Sandie Shaw; Pet Shop Boys

Quiz 318. Name the Team

1. Richards, Lescott, Barry, Silva, Balotelli; 2. Luiz, Cahill, Mikel, Bertrand, Mata; 3. McNeill, Gemmell, Johnstone, Lennox, Chalmers; 4. Robinson, King, Lennon, Malbranque, Berbatov; 5. Shilton, Burns, McGovern, Robertson, Woodcock; 6. Neville, Pearce, Ince, McManaman, Sheringham; 7. Beasant, Thorn, Jones (Vinnie), Wise, Cork; 8. Neville, Stam, Butt, Shering- ham, Yorke; 9. Puyol, Piqué, Iniesta, Eto'o, Henry; 10. Dudek, Hyppia, Alonso, Kewell, Baros

Quiz 319. Wildlife

1. Birds' eggs; 2. Gorillas; 3. Humans and tigers; 4. David Attenborough; 5. Dinosaurs; 6. Republic of Indonesia; 7. Platypus; 8. Tapir; 9. Whales, dolphins, porpoises and similar; 10. One, the ostrich is unique within the Struthionidae family; 11. Hippopotamus (this is grouped with deer, cattle, goats, camels, etc. in Artiodactyla); 12. Birds of prey (or raptors); owls; 13. Elephant; 14. Gorillas (two species); chimpanzees and orang-utans; 15. Anteater; 16. Sturgeon; 17. Camel, at just over 400 days (lions gestate for 108 days on average, goats for 151); 18. Auk; 19. Turtles, the order Chelonia; 20. Bats

Quiz 320. General Knowledge

1. Google; 2. Longleat in Wiltshire; 3. (c) Cornwall is the country's oldest duchy, hence its use for the heir to the throne; 4. Nobel Prize for Literature; 5. Lake Ontario; 6. Utah; 7. Selenium is abbreviated to Se, nitrogen to N; put one Se before N and one after – Sense (I know, silly, but it made me chuckle); 8. It is Al Murray's comic alter-ego; 9. Jasper Carrott, whose given name is Robert Davis; 10. Halfpipe, snowboard cross (sometimes known as Boarder X) and giant slalom; 11. Chelsea Flower Show; 12. Jacob Marley; 13. Catalunya; 14. All served time in prison (Blake for fighting, Defoe for religious dissent, Dostoevsky for revolutionary activities and Wilde for homosexuality); 15. Saatchi and Saatchi; 16. Fourteen (1pt for one either way); 17. Johnson shades it at 2.01 metres; 18. Nicorette chewing gum (accept patches); 19. Gaia; 20. Princess Margaret and Lord Snowdon; Prince Andrew and Sarah Ferguson

Quiz 321. General Knowledge

Some Gorgeous Georges (or equally Gorgeous Georginas)

Part 1

1   Which famous 1960s footballer was once described by the press as 'The Fifth Beatle', a reference to his popstar lifestyle?

2   *Confessions of a Dangerous Mind* (2002) was the directorial debut of which high-profile actor?

3   If you watched test match cricket in Georgetown, who would be the home side?

4   Who had a UK no. 1 hit with 'The Ballad of Bonnie and Clyde' in January 1968?

5   Who created the aristocratic detective Thomas Linley, Lord Asherton? What is the name of his working-class sergeant? (2 pts)

6   What are the only British vessels, other than those commanded by the Admiral of the Fleet, permitted to fly the St George's Cross as their jack (standard or emblem)? (a) ships carrying aid from the Red Cross (b) ships and boats that participated in the Dunkirk evacuations (c) combatant vessels in wartime

7   Which US painter, famous for her huge canvasses of flowers, shocked the arts world when an exhibition of Alfred Stieglitz's photos of her, many unclothed, was shown in 1921?

8   Who scored Arsenal's winning goal in the 1971 FA Cup final against Liverpool? Which member of the team would win the FA Cup again as manager of the club? (2 pts)

9   Who was France's longest-serving Prime Minister (1962–8)?

10 What is the more commonly used name for the sect founded in 1650 by George Fox as the Society of Friends?

Part 2

11   Which famous old jazz tune became the theme tune of the popular Harlem Globetrotters basketball team?

12   *Georgy Girl* was a 1966 film starring which member of a famous acting family in the title role? Which Australian band had a hit with the title song? Who wrote the source novel? (3 pts)

13   What is the subject of George Stubbs's famous painting *Whistlejacket* (1762)?

14   In which popular TV programme did Jason Alexander play George Costanza?

15   In which city, taking its name from a European capital, is the University of Georgia (US) located?

16   What was George Lucas's coming-of-age film set in the rock 'n' roll era, released in 1973, four years before the first *Star Wars* movie made him a household name?

17   Which Romanian international with a divine left foot led the national team to the quarter-finals of the 1994 World Cup?

18   Who commanded the Virginia Regiment, the first military unit made up exclusively of Americans, on behalf of the British colonies against France in the 1754–8 Franco-Indian Wars?

19   Lowell George was the main man in which American country-rock band? (a) Lynyrd Skynyrd (b) Steely Dan (c) Little Feat

20   Who was born George Alan O'Dowd in Bexley, Kent, in June 1961?

Total Points: 24. Targets: Novice 12 Pro 18. Your Score: [   ]

Quiz 322. Movies

Part 1

Each list contains four films; state which actress starred in three of the films; state which is the odd film out; state who is the star of the odd film out – that actress will also appear as one of the first answers to one of the other questions (3 pts per question)

1 *A Cry in the Dark, Mamma Mia!, Burn After Reading, The Bridges of Madison County*

2 *The Duchess, Never Let Me Go, The Wings of the Dove, Anna Karenina*

3 *Nurse Betty, Miss Potter, Quills, Cinderella Man*

4 *To Die For, Eyes Wide Shut, Dead Calm, Chicago*

5 *The Edge of Love, Fight Club, Sweeney Todd, Mighty Aphrodite*

6 *The Fighter, Sherrybaby, Enchanted, Junebug*

7 *Notes on a Scandal, Charlotte Gray, Out of Africa, Veronica Guerin*

8 *Sense and Sensibility, Hideous Kinky, The Missing, Revolutionary Road*

9 *Vanilla Sky, Trouble with the Curve, Orlando, Michael Clayton*

10 *The Dark Knight, Secretary, Crazy Heart, Dogville*

Part 2

All four films here have the same actor or actress, but you must also identify which of the four was released first and which earned the star an Academy Award (3 pts per question)

11 *Vertigo, Mr Smith Goes to Washington, Philadelphia Story, Harvey*

12 *Cat on a Hot Tin Roof, Father of the Bride, Who's Afraid of Virginia Woolf?, Ivanhoe*

13 *The Lady from Shanghai, Notorious, Gaslight, Dr Jekyll and Mr Hyde*

14 *To Kill a Mockingbird, Cape Fear, Roman Holiday, The Gunfighter*

15 *Woman of the Year, Guess Who's Coming to Dinner?, Bringing Up Baby, Adam's Rib*

16 *Now Voyager, All About Eve, Jezebel, Mr Skeffington*

17 *Key Largo, The African Queen, The Barefoot Contessa, The Big Sleep*

18 *The Bride Wore Red, Mildred Pierce, Grand Hotel, Johnny Guitar*

19 *The Man with the Golden Arm, The Manchurian Candidate, From Here to Eternity, Von Ryan's Express*

20 *The Bishop's Wife, A Matter of Life and Death, Separate Tables, Casino Royale*

Total Points: 60. Targets: Novice 30 Pro 45. Your Score: [   ]

Quiz 323. Golf

Pitch and putt your way through this lot

Part 1

1. Who was the US golfer who broke a sequence of six Major championships without a US winner when he won the USPGA in 2011?

2. Who won the US Open in 1999 but was dead within a few months?

3. Which great amateur player of the 1920s won all the three Open championships his business commitments allowed him to enter?

4. Which English player, no more than a good journeyman pro on the European tour, won two of the five Senior Majors in 2012? (a) Simon Dyson (b) Roger Chapman (c) Mark James

5. Who was the first British player to win the US Open in forty years when he lifted the trophy in 2010? Who was the last to win it, in 1970? (2 pts)

6. How old was Seve Ballesteros when he won his first Open championship at Royal Lytham in 1979? (2 pts – 1 point for one either way)

7. Which three left-handed players have won a Major championship in the twenty-first century (to the end of 2012)? (3 pts)

8. Who was the last British player to win a ladies Major?

9. Who are the sole arbiters of the Rules of Golf everywhere in the world except the United States? (2 pts)

10. What is the name of the series which includes four tournaments, including the World Matchplay Championship (the series is recognized by all the major tours and so attracts strong fields and carries large numbers of ranking points towards all tour lists)?

Part 2

11 Which two father and son combinations won the Open Championship before the end of the nineteenth century (in both instances the father and son had the same Christian name)? (2 pts)

12 What is the Secondary Tour in European golf called, which can earn its leading players a card for the next year's full tour?

13 Which US golfer bucked the trend and played the Open at St Andrews in 1960 (finishing second) then won it at Birkdale the following year)?

14 Who has won the most European Orders of Merit (now the Race to Dubai), the prize for the highest earner on the European tour?

15 Who in 2011 headed the prize money list for both the USPGA tour and the European tour? Who matched this feat the following year? Which other British player finished in the USPGA tour top-ten earners in 2012, as well as placing second on the European list? (3 pts)

16 Which big-hitting and charismatic (if troubled) star espoused an unsubtle golfing philosophy that went 'just grip it – and rip it'?

17 Which multiple Major winner before and after World War II was the first woman golfer to compete against the male professionals?

18 Who put back the clock to win the Masters at Augusta in 1986 when he was forty-six years old? Who was his caddy that day? (2 pts)

19 How did Ian Woosnam's caddy cost him a chance of winning the 2001 Open Championship?

20 What is the equivalent (and older) contest to the Ryder Cup for exclusively amateur players?

Total Points: 29. Targets: Novice 12 Pro 22. Your Score:

Quiz 324. Geography

A Mix and Match section and a couple of thinking-cappers

Part 1

Mix and Match: match the Italian region to its capital city

1. Piedmont; 2. Lombardy; 3. Sardinia; 4. Sicily; 5. Tuscany; 6. Veneto; 7. Emilia Romagna; 8. Lazio; 9. Umbria; 10. Apulia (or Puglia)

a. Florence; b. Milan; c. Bologna; d. Perugia; e. Venice; f. Bari; g. Rome; h. Cagliari; i. Turin; j. Palermo

Your Workings:

Part 2

11   Which five countries control the Adriatic coastline? (5 pts)
12   Which six countries have a coast on the Black Sea? (6 pts)

Total Points: 21. Targets: Novice 8 Pro 16. Your Score:

Quiz 325. Cars

Marks for marques

Part 1

1 Which legendary designer and founder of a famous motor company also designed the first Beetle for Volkswagen?

2 Which British luxury sports car did Enzo Ferrari describe as the most beautiful car ever made? (a) E-Type Jaguar (b) Aston Martin DB5 (c) Lotus Elan

3 The Defender, Discovery and Freelander are all models made by which four-wheel-drive manufacturer?

4 The Dodge Viper is made by a subsidiary of which motor company?

5 How old does a car have to be before it has to undergo a compulsory MOT test? And what do the initials MOT stand for? (2 pts)

6 Which motoring organizations were founded in 1897 and 1905 respectively? (2 pts, plus an extra one for getting them in the right order)

7 The R8 Spyder is a 2011 release by which car manufacturer?

8 The Impreza and Evo were rival rallying and commercial brands from which two Japanese manufacturers? (2 pts)

9 Which European car, launched in 1976, showed that hatchbacks need not be clumsy and sluggish?

10 Daihatsu; Toyota; Mitsubishi; Hyundai; Honda. Which of these is not Japanese?

Part 2

Mix and Match: match the model to the car manufacturer

1. Almira; 2. Berlingo; 3. Cougar; 4. Carlton; 5. Applause; 6. Cinquecento; 7. Felicia; 8. Metro; 9. Scirocco; 10. Prelude

a. Honda; b. Skoda; c. Volkswagen; d. Austin; e. Nissan; f. Ford; g. Fiat; h. Daihatsu; i. Vauxhall; j. Citroën

Your Workings:

Total Points: 24. Targets: Novice 10 Pro 18. Your Score:

LYRICS

Quiz 326. Lyrics

Band and song please (2 pts per question)

Part 1

1 'With the lights out, it's less dangerous. Here we are now, entertain us.'
2 'Love forever, love is free, let's turn forever you and me. Windmill, windmill for the land. Is everybody in?'
3 'You must understand though, the touch of your hand makes my pulse react.'
4 'So if you're lonely, you know I'm here waiting for you, I'm just a crosshair, I'm just a shot away from you.'
5 'Rent a flat above a shop, cut your hair and get a job. Smoke some fags and play some pool, pretend you never went to school.'
6 'Russian roulette is not the same without a gun, and baby when it's love, if it's not rough it isn't fun.'
7 'When I find myself in times of trouble Mother Mary comes to me.'
8 'Poor old Johnny Ray sounded sad upon the radio'
9 'The highway's jammed with broken heroes on a last chance power drive.'
10 'No clouds in my storms, let it rain, I hydroplane into fame'

Part 2

11 'And I'll take my clothes off and it will be shameless, cos everyone knows that's how you get famous.'

12 'Mutual misunderstanding after the fact. Sensitivity builds a prison in the final act.'

13 'I like smoke and lightning, heavy metal thunder, racin' with the wind and the feelin' that I'm under'

14 'Some of those that wear forces are the same that burn crosses.'

15 'Zephyr in the sky at night; I wonder do my tears of mourning sink beneath the sun.'

16 'Living easy, living free, season ticket on a one-way ride.'

17 'Don't want to hear about it, every single one's got a story to tell. Everyone knows about it from the Queen of England to the hounds of hell.'

18 'Your name isn't Rio but I don't care for sand. Lighting the fuse might result in a Bang.'

19 'Every time you kiss me I'm still not certain that you love me. Every time you hold me, I'm still not certain that you care.'

20 'You've carried on so long you couldn't stop if you tried it. You've built your wall so high that no one can climb it.'

Total Points: 40. Targets: Novice 16 Pro 30. Your Score:

Quiz 327. Myths and Legends

Part 1

1 Who was the paladin of Charlemagne, whose defence of the Ronceveaux Pass, although unsuccessful, has passed into legend through various poetic accounts? Who provided the opposition to Charlemagne at Ronceveaux? (2 pts)

2 Who is the Norse god of love, with her cloak of falcon feathers and chariot pulled by cats?

3 What was Anubis's principal role in Egyptian mythology and how is he usually depicted? (2 pts)

4 The *Mabinogion* is a series of stories charting the mythological heritage of which people?

5 Who was the leader of the Fianna, a warrior band who are the subject of one of the four main strands of Irish mythology?

6 Who was, tragically, beloved of the Sons of Uisna in Irish mythology?

7 Paris wasn't the first to abduct Helen; which Greek hero had already kidnapped her many years earlier?

8 Who rows the dead across the River Acheron to the Underworld, and what is the name of the three-headed dog who guards the realm? (2 pts)

9 The god Apollo was proficient on which instrument?

10 Who was the minstrel associated with the outlaw band commanded by Robin Hood?

Part 2

11 Which Roman hero defended the Pons Sublicius against a numerically superior Etruscan army?

12 Who was the wife of Jason, leader of the Argonauts, whom he left for Glauce, daughter of Cleon of Corinth?

13 Which story book consists of tales told to King Shahryar by his wife Scheherezade?

14 Who killed the monster Grendel and his mother in the Anglo-Saxon epic poem?

15 If Helios represented the sun and his sister, Selene, the moon, what did their other sibling, Eos, represent?

16 Cinderella, Rapunzel and Snow White; all these tales were popularized by whose fairy tales, published in seven volumes between 1812 and 1857?

17 Who went to rescue Eurydice from the Underworld but looked back before he crossed the river and lost her again?

18 Who killed the gorgon, Medusa, and who did he take as his wife after rescuing her from a sea-monster? (2 pts)

19 What is the great monster lurking under the waves according to a description in the Bible (Book of Job)?

20 Where was the site of the primary oracle in classical Greece, and to which god was it dedicated? (2 pts)

Total Points: 25. Targets: Novice 10 Pro 19. Your Score:

Quiz 328. General Knowledge

Ten quickies and a head-scratcher

Part 1

1   Islam Karimov is the hardline President of which former Soviet Republic? (a) Uzbekistan (b) Georgia (c) Armenia

2   The oldest example of what in England is found at Bevis Marks in London? (a) coffee shop (b) synagogue (c) barber's shop

3   Who is Samuel Joseph Wurzelbacher, briefly influential in politics in 2008?

4   For which type of book is the Carnegie Medal given?

5   Which actress, who came to prominence in *Pandora's Box* (1929), pioneered the craze for bob haircuts?

6   Singer Morrissey was lead vocalist with which band before embarking on a solo career?

7   If you went to the Middle East and visited a hamam (or hammam), what would be your most likely intention? (a) praying (b) taking a bath (c) voting

8   For what is Alexandre Desplat best known? (a) he is a member of art-rock band Air (b) he is the head of the country's opposition party (c) he is an award-winning film composer

9   In which year did the sovereign of Great Britain first give a speech at Christmas? (a) 1940 (b) 1957 (c) 1965

10   Which Scottish University is Britain's third oldest after Oxford and Cambridge?

11   What are the ten most populous cities of the United States? (Clue: only six states are involved.) (10 pts)

Total Points: 20. Targets: Novice 10 Pro 15. Your Score: [   ]

Answers Quizzes 321–328

Quiz 321. General Knowledge

1. George Best; 2. George Clooney; 3. West Indies (Georgetown is the capital of Guyana); 4. Georgie Fame (he wrote the song after seeing the 1967 movie); 5. Elizabeth George; Barbara Havers; 6. (b) it was granted as a badge of honour for those civilian ships who assisted in the evacuation of Allied troops from Dunkirk; 7. Georgia O'Keeffe; 8. Charlie George; George Graham; 9. Georges Pompidou; 10. Quakers; 11. 'Sweet Georgia Brown'; 12. Lynn Redgrave; the Seekers; Margaret Forster; 13. Whistlejacket is a horse; 14. *Seinfeld*; 15. Athens; 16. *American Graffiti*; 17. Gheorghe Hagi (he was sometimes called the 'Maradona of the Carpathians'; 18. George Washington; 19. (c) Little Feat (they had a huge US following but were more of a cult attraction in Britain); 20. Boy George

Quiz 322. Movies

1. Meryl Streep; Tilda Swinton was in *Burn After Reading*; 2. Keira Knightley; *The Wings of the Dove* starred Helena Bonham Carter; 3. Renée Zellweger; *Quills* was Kate Winslet; 4. Nicole Kidman; *Chicago* was Renée Zellweger; 5. Helena Bonham Carter; *The Edge of Love* was Keira Knightley; 6. Amy Adams; *Sherrybaby* was Maggie Gyllenhaal; 7. Cate Blanchett; Meryl Streep was in *Out of Africa*; 8. Kate Winslet; *The Missing* starred Cate Blanchett; 9. Tilda Swinton; Amy Adams was in *Trouble with the Curve*; 10. Maggie Gyllenhaal; *Dogville* was Nicole Kidman; 11. James Stewart; *Mr Smith Goes to Washington* (1939) came first, but *Philadelphia Story* won him his solitary Academy Award; 12. Elizabeth Taylor; she made *Father of the Bride* in 1950, aged eighteen, and won an Academy Award for *Who's Afraid of Virginian Woolf?*; 13. Ingrid Bergman; she won one of her three Academy Awards as Best Leading Actress for *Gaslight* (1944), which came out three years after *Dr Jekyll and Mr Hyde*; 14. Gregory Peck; *The Gunfighter* (1944) was the earliest of these, and Peck won his Oscar for *To Kill a Mockingbird*; 15. Katharine Hepburn; she won one of her four Oscars for *Guess Who's Coming to Dinner?*, nearly thirty years after *Bringing Up Baby* (1938); 16. Bette Davis, who won her second Academy Award for the earliest of these four, *Jezebel* (1938); 17. Humphrey Bogart; *The Big Sleep* (1946) was the first of these, but *African Queen* won him his Oscar; 18. Joan Crawford; *Grand Hotel* (1932) was much the earliest, and *Mildred Pierce* won Crawford her solitary Oscar; 19. Frank Sinatra; *From Here to Eternity* was the earliest and also won Sinatra an Oscar; 20. David Niven; *A Matter of Life and Death* (1946) was first and *Separate Tables* won the Academy Award

Quiz 323. Golf

1. Keegan Bradley; 2. Payne Stewart, who was killed in a plane crash later that year; 3. Bobby Jones; 4. Roger Chapman; 5. Graeme McDowell; Tony Jacklin; 6. Twenty-two; 7. Phil Mickelson (four titles), Mike Weir of Canada (2003 Masters) and Bubba Watson (2012

Masters); 8. Catriona Matthew of Scotland won the Ladies Open in 2009; 9. The Royal and Ancient Golf Club at St Andrews (bonus point for the full and correct title); 10. World Golf Championships (currently the four are the World Matchplay, the Bridgestone Invitational, the HSBC Champions and the Cadillac); 11. Willie Park Sr and Willie Park Jr; Old Tom Morris and Young Tom Morris; 12. Challenge Tour (formerly the Satellite Tour); 13. Arnold Palmer (in doing so Palmer changed for good the best American players' attitude to the famous trophy); 14. Colin Montgomerie (eight times); 15. Luke Donald; Rory McIlroy; Justin Rose; 16. John Daly; 17. Babe Zaharias (before her marriage she won Olympic Gold medals in 1932 in hurdles and javelin as Babe Didrikson); 18. Jack Nicklaus; his son, Jack Jr; 19. Woosnam had fifteen clubs in his bag for the last round (fourteen is the mandatory maximum; a two-shot penalty unnerved him and a promising position was lost); 20. Walker Cup (unlike the Ryder Cup it is still contested between GB and Ireland and United States)

Quiz 324. Geography

Mix and Match 1, i; 2, b; 3, h; 4, j; 5, a; 6, e; 7, c; 8, g; 9, d; 10, f; 11. Italy, Slovenia, Croatia, Montenegro and Albania; 12. Ukraine, Russia, Georgia, Turkey, Bulgaria and Romania

Quiz 325. Cars

1. (Ferdinand) Porsche; 2. (a) E-Type Jaguar; 3. Land Rover; 4. Chrysler; 5. Three years; Ministry of Transport; 6. RAC first, then the AA; 7. Audi; 8. Subaru and Mitsubishi; 9. Volkswagen Gti (the car is still in production, and has had few rivals in its class over the years); 10. Hyundai are based in South Korea; Mix and Match 1, e; 2, j; 3, f; 4, i; 5, h; 6, g; 7, b; 8, d; 9, c; 10, a

Quiz 326. Lyrics

1. Nirvana – 'Smells Like Teen Spirit'; 2. Gorillaz – 'Feel Good Inc'; 3. Tina Turner – 'What's Love Got to Do with It'; 4. Franz Ferdinand – 'Take Me Out'; 5. Pulp – 'Common People'; 6. Lady Gaga – 'Poker Face'; 7. The Beatles – 'Let It Be'; 8. Dexy's Midnight Runners – 'Come On Eileen'; 9. Bruce Springsteen – 'Born to Run'; 10. Rihanna – 'Umbrella'; 11. Lily Allen – 'The Fear'; 12. Elton John – 'Sacrifice'; 13. Steppenwolf – 'Born to Be Wild'; 14. Rage Against the Machine – 'Killing in the Name'; 15. Madonna – 'Ray of Light'; 16. AC/DC – 'Highway to Hell'; 17. White Stripes – 'Seven Nation Army'; 18. Arctic Monkeys – 'I Bet You Look Good on the Dancefloor'; 19. Elvis Presley – 'Suspicion'; 20. Labrinth – 'Beneath Your Beautiful'

Quiz 327. Myths and Legends

1. Roland (as in 'Song of Roland' and 'Orlando Furioso'); a Basque army (not a Muslim army as many versions attest); 2. Freya; 3. God of the Afterlife; with a jackal's head; 4. The Welsh; 5. Finn MacCool (various spellings; the nearest Gaelic is Fionn mac Cumhaill); 6.

Deirdre of the Sorrows; 7. Theseus of Athens (she was rescued by her brothers, Castor and Pollux); 8. Charon, the Ferryman; Cerberus; 9. The lyre, a small portable harp; 10. Alan A'Dale; 11. Horatius (Publius); 12. Medea; 13. *One Thousand and One Nights* (half a point for the misleading Western title, *Arabian Nights*); 14. Beowulf; 15. The dawn; 16. Brothers Grimm; 17. Orpheus; 18. Perseus, Andromeda; 19. Leviathan; 20. Delphi; Apollo

Quiz 328. General Knowledge

1. (a) Uzbekistan; 2. (b) Synagogue; 3. He was 'Joe The Plumber', cited by the Republicans as symptomatic of the suspicion with which people viewed Barack Obama; 4. Children's fiction; 5. Louise Brooks; 6. The Smiths; 7. (b) Taking a bath (it is the Arabic word for a Turkish baths); 8. (c) film scores (*Girl with a Pearl Earring*, *Julie and Julia*; *The King's Speech*; *Argo*); 9. 1957, five years after Queen Elizabeth II came to the throne; 10. St Andrews; 11. New York, Los Angeles, Chicago, Houston, Philadelphia, Phoenix, San Antonio, San Diego, Dallas, San Jose

Quiz 329. General Knowledge

Part 1

1   What chronological scale began in AD 622?

2   Mozart, Schubert and Beethoven all died in which city?

3   Who was the first Republic of Ireland international to win 100 caps? What is his nickname? (2 pts)

4   Which rock star was arrested for urinating in the Alamo fort whilst wearing a dress?

5   Storms battered southern England in 1987; who had told us the previous evening they wouldn't happen?

6   What is the difference between a scalar and a vector?

7   If a Roman soldier missed you with his *pilum*, but then got you with his *gladius*, what would have happened? (And no, it isn't that, don't be dirty . . .) (2 pts)

8   In which stadium did the unrest amongst Liverpool fans take place which saw the death of thirty-nine Juventus fans, earning English clubs a lengthy ban from European competition?

9   What do Jennifer Aniston, Bryan Ferry and Vic Reeves have in common? (a) all have exhibited their paintings (b) all were fostered as children (c) all were born on 29 February

10   Comedian and TV presenter Clive Anderson originally trained and practised in which profession?

Part 2

11 Where is the UK's smallest cathedral found? (a) St Asaph (b) St David's (c) Truro

12 What is Europe's busiest motorway?

13 Who took the title Lord of Foy and Hartlepool in 2008?

14 In which year did Batman first feature in a DC comic book: 1919, 1939 or 1959?

15 What name is given to the calm point at the centre of the fierce winds that blow during a hurricane?

16 Waldemar Januszczak presents TV programmes on which topic?

17 What name is given to the walled citadel at the heart of many North African cities and towns?

18 Which British designer gave us first the mini-skirt and later the hot pants?

19 For what crime did former champion jockey Lester Piggott serve a year of a three-year sentence in 1987?

20 Which TV series saw Hollywood star Bradley Cooper make his name as a journalist called Will?

Total Points: 22. Targets: Novice 11 Pro 17. Your Score:

Quiz 330. Rock and Pop

Part 1

1 Who released the critically acclaimed 2006 rap album, *The Dusty Foot Philosopher*?

2 Who, in 1992, broke a longstanding record by topping the US Billboard chart for thirteen weeks with their first no. 1 single, 'End of the Road'?

3 Which country singer served three years for armed robbery from 1957, and was turned on to country and western by Johnny Cash's famous prison concert? Which Governor of California sanctioned his pardon? (2 pts)

4 Sam Duckworth is a one-man-band who performs under what name?

5 Who was the musician/producer at the core of Funkadelic?

6 What was the name of singer-songwriter Lloyd Cole's band in the 1980s?

7 Which Scottish singer, in 1971, was the first artist to top both the UK and US main singles and albums chart simultaneously, a feat even the Beatles never managed? What was the album and the single taken from it that hit no. 1? (3 pts)

8 On which album cover would you see Suze Rotolo, and which track by that artist was written about her? (2 pts)

9 Who supplied the distinctive artwork for the Sex Pistols' debut album, *Never Mind the Bollocks, Here's the Sex Pistols*?

10 Whose career was launched by the success of the Sugarcubes, the first Icelandic band to achieve international recognition?

Part 2

11 Which two albums, ten years apart, won the Mercury Music Prize for P. J. Harvey? (2 pts)

12 Bono, Bruce (Iron Maiden) Dickinson, Phil (Human League) Oakey, Prince, Paul Weller; who is the old boy and who is then new kid on the block? (2 pts)

13 Who announced on the US version of the Live Aid concert that 'I ain't taking s**t off today' and to what was it a reference? (2 pts)

14 *Watch the Throne* was a 2011 collaboration between which two huge-selling rap artists? (2 pts)

15 What connects Nickelback, Arcade Fire, Black Mountain and Cowboy Junkies?

16 Which left-hander was voted Best British Male Artist as well as Best British Breakthrough act at the 2013 Brit Awards?

17 What connects singer Orville Burrell to *Scooby-Doo*?

18 What was the 2011 hit for Gotye, the biggest selling single ever by an Australian artist?

19 How many studio albums (not compilations or bootlegs or remasters, just original studio albums) has Bob Dylan released in a career spanning over fifty years: twenty-six, thirty-five or forty-nine? What was the title of the most recent (2012)? (2 pts)

20 How many albums has Leonard Cohen managed in a similar timespan: seven, twelve or twenty-two? And again, what was his 2012 release? (2 pts)

Total Points: 30. Targets: Novice 12 Pro 23. Your Score:

Quiz 331. Astronomy

Part 1

1   In which UK scientific establishment was the Lovell telescope housed in the 1950s?

2   Ursa Major, the Great Bear, has which alternative name to Western astronomers?

3   Johannes Kepler studied under which other notable scientist and astronomer in Prague in the late sixteenth century?

4   Which seventy-seven year-old flew on a space shuttle (*Discovery*) in 1998?

5   Is earth twice the size of Mars or vice versa?

6   What, in simple terms, is the astronomical phenomenon known as a Black Dwarf?

7   In which (modern) country was the influential thirteenth-century observatory, Maragheh?

8   Who first discovered that there were mountains on the moon and that the Milky Way was made of up of myriad stars?

9   After *Pioneer 10* and *Voyagers I* and *II* came *Galileo*; which planet were they sent to study?

10 Which of these in *not* a known constellation? (a) Cygnus (the swan) (b) Hippocratus (the horse) (c) Lyra (the harp) (d) Phoenix

11 Which two gases are the principal components of the atmosphere of the planet Saturn? (2 pts)

12 Which satellite, named after Jove's page boy, is the biggest of those orbiting Jupiter? In which century was it discovered? (2 pts)

13 What are the two main stars in the constellation Gemini? (2 pts)

14 Bill Kaysing was the first to publish a book (in 1974) claiming what? (a) that he was abducted by aliens in the 1950s (b) that the Chinese landed on the moon a decade before the US (c) that the moon landings were a hoax

15 What was the name of the new spacecraft designed by Sergei Korolev and his team in the 1960s to replace the old *Voskhod* models?

Total Points: 18. Targets: Novice 7 Pro 14. Your Score: [   ]

Quiz 332. Light Entertainment

Part 1

1   What aired for the first time in October 1992, with the Neville Brothers and the Christians amongst the guests?

2   Which *X Factor* judge was reported to have been booed by the studio audience (off air) for humiliating the hapless Ceri Rees in 2011?

3   Boots Randolph's 'Yakety Sax!' was the famous theme to which ribald one-man comedy show?

4   What is the highest-rated light entertainment show in the history of British TV?

5   Which programme did the *X Factor* replace in 2004?

6   How did the bookies make a bundle on the 2009 series of *Britain's Got Talent*?

7   Fill in the gaps in the sequence: G4; Andy Abraham; Ray Quinn; Rhydian Roberts; MISSING; MISSING; Rebecca Ferguson; Marcus Collins; MISSING (3 pts)

8   What was the TV show that made stars out of Trinny Woodall and Susannah Constantine?

9   An episode of *Sale of the Century* from 1978 attracted twenty-one million viewers, a record for an ITV game show; what occurrence spiked the figure to well above its usual average?

10 Who compered *Saturday Live* (later *Friday Night Live*), launched in 1985 and the first TV show to give exposure to cutting-edge stand-up comics?

Part 2

11 Who were the original (2006) two presenters of ITV's *Dancing on Ice*? (2 pts)

12 Which anarchic late night show had the host enter along a gantry to Ocean Colour Scene's 'Riverboat Song'?

13 Who was the main host of the consumer programme *That's Life*, which ran for twenty-one years from 1973?

14 What was Channel 4's live performance response to *Top of the Pops*, first broadcast late on a Friday night in 1982? Which former keyboard player with Squeeze co-hosted with Paula Yates? (2 pts)

15 Which popular show saw Kevin Keegan fall off a bike, Malcolm Macdonald run a 100 metres that wouldn't have been out of place in the Olympics and a judoka called Terry Jacks show extraordinary reserves of muscle strength and fitness?

16 Who was the love-him-or-hate-him host of *You've Been Framed* for the first eight years? Who provided the voiceover once the show dropped the host altogether? (2 pts)

17 Where did Jeremy Paxman supplant Bamber Gascoigne?

18 Who were the first two presenters of TV's *Gladiators*? (2 pts)

19 Whose language on *TFI Friday* caused a rethink on the show's policy of live transmission, effectively neutering it as a creative and energetic force?

20 Who have been the three presenters of BBC's *Question of Sport* throughout its thirty-five-year history? Which boxer and rugby union player were the first team captains? (5 pts)

Total Points: 30. Targets: Novice 12 Pro 23. Your Score:

Quiz 333. Arts and Culture

A general cultural potpourri

Part 1

1 A museum dedicated to which famous Belgian artist was opened in Brussels in June 2009?

2 What was the dance pioneered in Harlem in the 1930s that became synonymous with the Jazz Age in New York?

3 Where can the famous bookshop, Shakespeare and Company, be found?

4 Where was a sculpture by Marc Quinn of Alison Lapper, pregnant and disabled, on display from 2005–2007?

5 Which collector and gallery owner launched a 2010 collection called *Newspeak*, a review of hot British artists?

6 What happened to a sculpture by Gustav Metzger at the Tate Britain in 2004?

7 Mikhail Baryshnikov, the dancer, was born in which country? And where did he claim asylum in 1974 whilst on tour with the Bolshoi Ballet? (2 pts)

8 With which artistic discipline would you associate Simone Messmer?

9 Who played poet Sylvia Plath in the 2003 biopic *Sylvia*?

10 Which composer has a steak dish named after him?

Part 2

11   Most lead female roles in opera are written for which type of singing voice?

12   What is the national dance of Poland, written in triple time?

13   Who was the theatrical impresario who ran the Old Vic in the early part of the twentieth century, and was also instrumental in the setting up of the Royal Ballet and the English National Opera?

14   What phrase indicates that a piece is to be sung unaccompanied by instruments?

15   Which contributor to the nation's culture was launched on 7 September 1992 after a few weeks of birdsong?

16   Paul Mealor's composition 'Wherever You Are' carried him to national popularity on a wave of sentiment; what is the subject matter and who first performed the piece? (2 pts)

17   What is the oldest symphony orchestra in the United States, founded in 1842?

18   The Hallé Orchestra, founded in 1857, is based in which English city?

19   Who founded the London Philharmonic Orchestra in 1932? (a) Benjamin Britten (b) Lilian Baylis (c) Thomas Beecham. What has been the orchestra's home since 1951?

20   In 2007 Roger Wright replaced Nicholas Kenyon as director of which annual musical festival?

Total Points: 22. Targets: Novice 9 Pro 17. Your Score: _____

Quiz 334. Cricket

Some questions on stars of the game past and present

Part 1

1   Who came in as a nightwatchman for Australia against Bangladesh in 2006 and ended up with 201 not out?

2   Who holds the record for the highest score in the County Championship (501 not out), playing for Warwickshire in 1994? Which unfortunate bowling attack was on the receiving end? (2 pts)

3   Which former Indian batsman and captain was known as 'The Wall' for his obduracy and defensive technique?

4   Who scored most test double centuries: Don Bradman, Brian Lara or Sachin Tendulkar?

5   Who scored 69 not out and took 4–42 as Zimbabwe pulled off a shock win against Australia in the 1983 Cricket World Cup?

6   Who scored the fastest ever test century (balls faced) against England in 1986? Who took one ball more against the same opposition twenty years later? (2 pts)

7   Who was the first black captain of the West Indies cricket team?

8   Under what name did Mohammad Yousuf start his test career before converting to Islam?

9   Who was the Pakistani umpire who had an altercation with England captain, Mike Gatting, in 1987?

10 Which England coach (assistant manager) died during a test match on the 1981 tour to the West Indies? Who scored a heroic hundred in England's second innings and dedicated it to his mentor? (2 pts)

Part 2

11 Who, in 1998, hit Surrey's Alex Tudor for thirty-four off an over and made his England debut the same summer?

12 Who chased a target of 418 (the highest winning fourth innings total in test history) to defeat Australia in May 2003? What was the venue for this extraordinary game? Which two players scored hundreds in the chase? (4 pts)

13 Who became the first cricketer to score 100 and take eight wickets in an innings in a test match in 1978?

14 Who has played cricket and football for England in a World Cup finals tournament?

15 Who is the only man to score a triple hundred at Lord's?

16 Who was captain of the England women's cricket team from 1966 to 1978?

17 Which batsman earned a ban for charging into the crowd in pursuit of an abusive fan (who called him a potato) in a match in 1997?

18 Who held the record for the highest score in test cricket for barely a year in 2003–2004?

19 Who was voted Player of the Tournament as England won the T20 World Cup in 2010?

20 Which five Australian batsmen have scored twenty-five test centuries, more than any English player (although Cook and Pietersen will almost certainly reach that target)? (5 pts)

Total Points: 30. Targets: Novice 12 Pro 23. Your Score:

Quiz 335. Scandals

Try to remember what these naughty boys and girls were up to

Part 1

1   Long before the Jimmy Savile case blew open, which 1970s pop star, born Paul Gadd, was arrested in 1997 for owning child pornography?

2   Which TV show started the week *Star Wars* opened at UK cinemas in January 1978 and ended in a nihilistic blaze of gunfire in December 1981?

3   Which cabinet minister tried (unsuccessfully) to sue the *Guardian* and *World in Action* for libel in 1995, and was later sent to prison for perjury?

4   Who was the former much-decorated Marine officer at the heart of the Iran–Contra Scandal in 1986–7? What, in a nutshell, did the scheme involve? (2 pts)

5   Who was the businessman who was imprisoned for bribery in the 1970s in a scandal which indirectly involved Home Secretary Reginald Maudling, who was forced to resign?

6   Which 1980s Conservative minister had an affair with, and a child by, his secretary, Sarah Keays?

7   David Mellor resigned as a minister in 1992; with whom was he having an affair, and what was actually the more serious but less widely covered accusation he faced? (2 pts)

8   Who was the ex-Army officer with whom Diana, Princess of Wales, had an affair whilst married to Prince Charles?

9   A tape called 'One Night in Paris', released when she was nineteen, shows which heiress and celebrity in a graphic sexual act? Which other socialite 'enjoyed' a similar career path after the release of a tape in 2007? (2 pts)

10 Which 1920s silent comedy star was accused (but later exonerated, although it finished his career) of killing Virginia Rappe after a wild Hollywood party?

Part 2

11 Which Conservative grandee was jailed for perjury and perverting the course of justice in 2001? Who was the prostitute he had been accused of paying for sex in 1986, and which newspaper had printed the story? For what position did he stand in 1999, prompting two witnesses to his perjury to come forward and reveal the truth? What unusual word did the trial judge use to describe the accused's wife in his instructions to the jury? (5 pts)

12 What name was given to the scandal that rocked the American political world in 1972 following a break-in at the White House? Who was the US President at the time? Which newspaper blew the story open, as shown in the movie *All the President's Men*? What was the codename of their FBI informant? Who was the Vice President who resigned amidst all these revelations after a separate corruption charge was brought? (5 pts)

Total Points: 23. Targets: Novice 9 Pro 17. Your Score:

Quiz 336. General Knowledge

Spelling bee; which one is spelt correctly

Part 1

1   Opaque – Opache – Oupaque
2   Minuscule – Miniscule – Minniscule
3   Definitely – Definately – Defanitely
4   Innoculate – Inoculate – Inocculate
5   Arythmic – Arrythmic – Arytyhmic
6   Liason – Liaisen – Liaison
7   Legionnaire – Legionnair – Legionaire
8   Cartillage – Cartilage – Cartilege
9   Sillouette – Silhouet – Silhouette
10 Lisentious – Licencious – Licentious

Part 2

11 Consensual – Concensual – Concencual
12 Sacreligious – Sacrilegious – Sacriligious
13 Connoiseur – Conoisseur – Connoisseur
14 Kleptomania – Cleptomania – Cleptamania
15 Diarhoea – Diarrhea – Diarrhoea
16 Psyciatric – Psychiactric – Psychiatric
17 Accomodation – Acommodation – Accommodation
18 Extasty – Exstasy – Ecstasy
19 Chihuawa – Chihuahua – Chihauhau
20 Mispelt – Misspelled – Mispelled

Total Points: 20. Targets: Novice 10 Pro 15. Your Score:

Answers Quizzes 329–336

Quiz 329. General Knowledge

1. The Islamic calendar; 2. Vienna; 3. Steve Staunton; Stan; 4. Ozzie Osbourne; 5. BBC weatherman Michael Fish; 6. A scalar has magnitude, but no direction, a vector has both; 7. He missed with his spear but got you with his sword; 8. Heysel Stadium, Brussels; 9. (a) they have all shown their paintings in public; 10. Law, as a barrister; 11. (a) St Asaph; 12. M25; 13. Peter Mandelson; 14. 1939; 15. The eye (of the storm); 16. Art; 17. Kasbah; 18. Mary Quant; 19. Tax evasion; 20. *Alias*

Quiz 330. Rock and Pop

1. K'naan; 2. Boyz II Men; 3. Merle Haggard; Ronald Reagan; 4. Get Cape Wear Cape Fly; 5. George Clinton; 6. The Commotions; 7. Rod Stewart; *Every Picture Tells a Story* and 'Maggie May'; 8. *Freewheelin' Bob Dylan*; 'Don't Think Twice It's All Right'; 9. Jamie Reid; 10. Bjork; 11. *Stories from the City, Stories from the Sea* (2001); *Let England Shake* (2011); 12. Phil Oakey is fifty-seven (as of January 2013), Bono is a mere fifty-two (all the others were born in 1958); 13. Madonna; nude photos of her taken when younger had recently appeared in *Playboy*; 14. Jay-Z and Kanye West; 15. All are Canadian; 16. Ben Howard; 17. Burrell's stage name is Shaggy, who is Scooby's minder in the cartoon series; 18. 'Somebody that I Used to Know'; 19. Thirty-five; *Tempest*; 20. Twelve; *Old Ideas*

Quiz 331. Astronomy

1. Jodrell Bank; 2. The Plough; 3. Tycho Brahe; 4. John Glenn; 5. Earth has a diameter of 12,756 km, Mars only 6,794 km.; 6. A dead star; 7. Iran; 8. Galileo; 9. Jupiter; 10. (b) Hippocratus (there is a unicorn and a winged horse but no horse); 11. Hydrogen and helium; 12. Ganymede; seventeenth century (1610); 13. Castor and Pollux; 14. (c) that the moon landings were a hoax (conspiracy theories abound, none of them with a shred of scientific evidence); 15. *Soyuz*

Quiz 332. Light Entertainment

1. *Later . . . with Jools Holland*; 2. Gary Barlow; 3. *The Benny Hill Show* (try and catch a re-run, it beggars belief that this ran for nearly twenty years); 4. *The Generation Game*; 5. *Pop Idol*; 6. Scottish singer Susan Boyle was regarded as a shoo-in for the title and a ton of punters' money was lost when she only finished second to dance troupe Diversity; 7. JLS, Olly Murs and Jahmene Douglas (they are all *X Factor* runners-up); 8. *What Not to Wear*; 9. A BBC strike meant there was little alternative; 10. Ben Elton; 11. Phillip Schofield and Holly Willoughby; 12. *TFI Friday* (Chris Evans); 13. Esther Rantzen; 14. *The Tube*; Jools Holland; 15. *Superstars*; 16. Jeremy Beadle (sales of his autobiography suggested the love-hims were in a minority); Harry Hill; 17. As presenter of *University Challenge*; 18. Ulrika Jonsson and John Fashanu; 19. Shaun Ryder (one man's maverick

genius is another man's drug-addled buffoon); 20. David Vine, David Coleman and Sue Barker; Henry Cooper and Cliff Morgan

Quiz 333. Arts and Culture

1. René Magritte; 2. Lindy hop; 3. Paris, near Notre Dame; 4. On a plinth in Trafalgar Square; 5. Charles Saatchi; 6. It was mistaken for a bag of rubbish and thrown out by a cleaner; 7. Latvia (then part of the Soviet Union); Canada; 8. Ballet; 9. Gwyneth Paltrow; 10. Gioachino Rossini was a foodie and the dish Tournedos Rossini is named in his honour; 11. Soprano; 12. Mazurka (Chopin wrote over fifty mazurkas); 13. Lilian Baylis; 14. A cappella (it means 'in chapel style'); 15. Classic FM (the birdsong tests transmissions became something of a cult at the time); 16. Letters to and from soldiers serving in Afghanistan; it was performed by the Military Wives Choir; 17. New York Symphony Orchestra; 18. Manchester; 19. (c) Beecham; Royal Festival Hall; 20. BBC Proms

Quiz 334. Cricket

1. Jason Gillespie; 2. Brian Lara; Durham; 3. Rahul Dravid; 4. Bradman, twelve times, including two 300s (Lara has nine, including two 300s; Tendulkar has six); 5. Duncan Fletcher; 6. Viv Richards; Adam Gilchrist; 7. Frank Worrell; 8. Yousuf Youhana; 9. Shakoor Rana; 10. Ken Barrington; Graham Gooch; 11. Andrew Flintoff; 12. West Indies; Antigua; Ramnaresh Sarwan and Shivnarine Chanderpaul; 13. Sir Ian Botham; 14. Clare Taylor played at the 1995 football Women's World Cup and in six cricket World Cups; 15. Graham Gooch, against India in 1990; 16. Rachel Heyhoe-Flint; 17. Inzamam-ul-Haq; 18. Matthew Hayden (some justice here because Hayden's runs were against Bangladesh, not the most intimidating of opponents); 19. Kevin Pietersen; 20. Ricky Ponting, Steve Waugh, Matthew Hayden, Don Bradman, Alan Border

Quiz 335. Scandals

1. Gary Glitter; 2. *Blake's 7*; 3. Jonathan Aitken; 4. Oliver North; selling arms to Iran and channelling the profits to help the Contra rebels in Nicaragua; 5. John Poulson; 6. Cecil Parkinson; 7. Antonia de Sancha; accepting a free holiday from an individual with links to the Palestine Liberation Organization; 8. James Hewitt; 9. Paris Hilton; Kim Kardashian (despite their protests, both stars enjoyed a higher profile after the release of the tapes); 10. Roscoe 'Fatty' Arbuckle; 11. Jeffrey Archer; Monica Coughlin, *Daily Star*; Mayor of London; 'fragrant'; 12. Watergate; Richard Nixon; *Washington Post*; Deep Throat; Spiro Agnew

Quiz 336. General Knowledge

1. Opaque; 2. Minuscule; 3. Definitely; 4. Inoculate; 5. Arrythmic; 6. Liaison; 7. Legionnaire; 8. Cartilage; 9. Silhouette; 10. Licentious; 11. Consensual; 12. Sacrilegious; 13. Connoisseur; 14. Kleptomania; 15. Diarrhoea; 16. Psychiatric; 17. Accommodation; 18. Ecstasy; 19. Chihuahua; 20. Misspelt

Quiz 337. General Knowledge

Part 1

1   Angela Berners-Wilson in 1994 was the first woman to do what in Britain?
    (a) be ordained as a Church of England priest (b) serve in the front-line as a
    member of the armed forces (c) ride in the Grand National

2   In a referendum on 8 January 1961, the people of France voted for inde-
    pendence for which country?

3   Which British historian was sentenced to three years in an Austrian jail for
    claiming there were no gas chambers at Auschwitz?

4   'Is this the kind of book you would wish your wife or servants to read?'
    asked the prosecuting counsel about which controversial work?

5   Where is Cape Horn?

6   Which poet added words in 1789 to the old folk song 'Auld Lang Syne' to
    give us the current version?

7   Which volcanic peak is Africa's highest, and in which country is it found?
    (2 pts)

8   One of the first famous people to die in 2012 was a ninety-nine year-old
    photographer; who was she, with which agency is she most closely associ-
    ated, and which actress did she famously snap during filming of the star's
    last movie? (3 pts)

9   How did Ramón Estévez become President of the United States?

10 Which Channel 4 commentator threatened to sue Channel 4 for ageism
    when they cut him from their racing broadcasting team in 2012?

Part 2

11 What is the narrow area of land to the southwest of Israel that is part of the disputed Palestinian territories? Which political group controls this area (as of March 2013)? (2 pts)

12 In which year did US forces invade Iraq as part of the response to 9/11?

13 Which city was the subject of a bestselling 'biography' by Simon Sebag Montefiore in 2011?

14 Donizetti's opera, *Lucia di Lammermoor* is based on a novel by which British author?

15 What term is used to describe the opposition front bench?

16 El Clásico predominantly refers to a match between which two sides, a much hyped feature of British TV channels in recent years?

17 Which former Miss GB is also a former paramour of Jermain Defoe, Marcus Bent and Teddy Sheringham?

18 What connects Kiefer Sutherland, Jerry Hall and Will Young?

19 Which popular entertainer stopped 'cleanin' windows' when he died aged fifty-six on 5 March 1961?

20 Who, in 1921, was born into the house of Schleswig-Holstein-Sonderburg-Glücksburg?

Total Points: 24. Targets: Novice 12 Pro 18. Your Score:

Quiz 338. Crime Movies

Heists and hold-ups

Part 1

1   Which two big names were paired up in Michael Mann's blockbuster heist movie *Heat* in 1995? (2 pts)

2   In *The Long Good Friday* (1980) Harold Shand (Bob Hoskins) is undermined by what criminal organization? Who plays his disaffected wife in the movie? (2 pts)

3   Who plays Walker, the unstoppable killer in John Boorman's *Point Blank* (1967)?

4   What was Francis Ford Coppola's first film post-*Godfather*, a low-key conspiracy thriller, starring Gene Hackman?

5   Who plays Michael Caine's telephone lover in *Get Carter* (1971)? And which TV policeman plays her husband? (2 pts)

6   Who plays the psychopath femme fatale Phyllis Dietrichson in *Double Indemnity* (1944)? And who was the film's director who persuaded her to take the part against her initial instincts? (2 pts)

7   Who starred across from Bogart in the 1941 film, *The Maltese Falcon*?

8   What is the name of the ex-con who hires Marlowe in *Farewell, My Lovely* (1944) to search for his girlfriend, Velma? Which regular femme fatale played Velma? (2 pts)

9   Who played Philip Marlowe in the 1973 movie *The Long Goodbye*?

10 Which of the Dirty Harry movies was directed by Clint Eastwood himself? (a) *The Enforcer* (b) *Sudden Impact* (c) *The Dead Pool*

Part 2

11   Who made an impressive big-movie debut as hacker cum investigator Lisbeth Salander in the original *Girl with the Dragon Tattoo* (2009)? Who took the role in the 2011 Hollywood remake? (2 pts)

12   What is the Pink Panther, in the comedy crime caper of that name? What is the name of the policeman investigating the crime and who took the role? (3 pts)

13   Who play the two FBI agents investigating racial murders in Mississippi in the 1960s in Alan Parker's *Mississippi Burning* (1988)? (2 pts)

14   Which film stars John Huston and Faye Dunaway as a duplicitous (and possibly incestuous) father and daughter? What is the name of the PI who is on their case, and who portrayed him? (3 pts)

15   Peter Yates's first movie made in Hollywood (in 1968) featured a memorable San Francisco car chase. What was the film? Who played the title role? (2 pts)

16   The Italian film *Ossessione* (1944) used the same noir plot as which later (1946) Hollywood classic directed by Tay Garnett? Who played the two leads in the Hollywood film and what was the occupation of the lead female character? Who co-starred in a less impressive 1980s remake? (6 pts)

Total Points: 33. Targets: Novice 13 Pro 25. Your Score:

Quiz 339. Media

Another section on the abusive and intrusive

Part 1

1   William Shatner was a key figure in the marketing campaigns for which home computer in the early 1980s?

2   IPC are the biggest magazine publisher in the UK; the acronym IPC originally stood for what?

3   Who was appointed to head up the *News of the World* in 2000? Who succeeded her in 2003? (2 pts)

4   Who was the *News of the World*'s new editor in 1994, the youngest to put in charge of a major newspaper for well over a hundred years? Which rival did he join the following year? (2 pts)

5   Alan Rusbridger was appointed editor of which newspaper in 1995, and remains in the role (April 2013)?

6   Which newspaper, launched in 2010, has been the fastest growing daily on the UK market over the last two years?

7   What ordeal did Alan Johnston of the BBC suffer in 2007?

8   With which modern media phenomenon is Jack Dorsey associated?

9   What is the name of the parent company of the *Daily Mail* and *Mail on Sunday*?

10 Who was Chairman of News Corp when the 2011 phone-hacking scandal broke?

Part 2

11 What are regarded as the two primary serious newspapers of record in France? (2 pts)

12 Who resigned as Director General of the BBC in 2012 after unsubstantiated claims were made on *Newsnight*? Which Conservative peer was the victim of wrongful suggestions on the programme? (2 pts)

13 What role does the ASA play in advertising?

14 Which magazine, launched in 1841 and one of the earliest to publish cartoons, was closed in 1992 after 150 years of satirical humour?

15 In which decade was *Time* magazine first published in the US?

16 Which year saw the launch of *Private Eye*: 1953, 1961 or 1970? Who have been the magazines only two editors throughout its history? Who used his publishing empire to print a mocking magazine *Not Private Eye* after winning a libel case against the magazine? Which incident caused retailer WHSmith to refuse to stock the magazine in the late 1990s? (5 pts)

Total Points: 24. Targets: Novice 10 Pro 18. Your Score: [   ]

Quiz 340. Around Britain

More sights and cities

Part 1

1   Eas a' Chual Aluinn is the biggest of its kind in Britain; what is it?

2   Snaefell is the highest peak on which land mass within the British Isles?

3   Where is the largest Neolithic stone circle in Britain?

4   Which old Roman road connected Lincoln to Exeter?

5   Which three towns, one in Berkshire, one in Kent and one in Warwickshire, have been accorded the 'Royal' prefix? And which small Wiltshire town was so honoured in 2011 for its role in honouring repatriated military dead? (4 pts)

6   A visit to which Hampshire country home might take in the National Motor Museum, the James Bond Experience and the World of Top Gear?

7   Which is the longest river in the British Isles (Britain and Ireland)?

8   Corn Du, Pen y Fan, Cribyn and Waun Rydd are amongst the highest peaks in which mountain range in the United Kingdom?

9   Wallsend, Jarrow and Hebburn are all areas within which British city?

10 In which county in England is Cheddar Gorge found?

11 What are the ten biggest cities or towns (population) in the UK that are *not* in England? (10 pts)

Total Points: 23. Targets: Novice 9 Pro 17. Your Score:

Quiz 341. History

Twenty straight questions

Part 1

1 The Egyptian Pharaoh referred to simply as Cleopatra was not the first of that name; what was her official number?

2 Where was Hitler reputed to be planning to make the capital city of occupied Britain?

3 Which famous Marxist revolutionary was reported killed in Bolivia in 1967?

4 European settlers founded a colony at Port Jackson on 26 January 1788. By what name is Port Jackson now known?

5 The Pilgrim Fathers landed in Massachusetts in 1620 aboard which vessel?

6 What was the name of the commission established in 1963 to investigate the death of John F. Kennedy?

7 Which force, under Alaric I, sacked the city of Rome in 410 AD?

8 In an 1894–5 war China got a complete whupping at the hands of which other power?

9 The *Theatrum Orbis Terrarum* (*Theatre of the World*), created by Abraham Ortels and printed in 1570, is regarded as the first instance of what type of publication?

10 What was discovered at Ballarat, Victoria, Australia, in 1851?

Part 2

11   The Zimbabwean capital city changed its name from what to Harare in 1980?

12   Which former British colony officially became a republic on 24 January 1950?

13   Construction of which modern edifice began in Egypt in 1859?

14   What was brought into effect in the US by the Volstead Act?

15   The period of the Reconquista in European history covers what recurring struggle?

16   What was the second wall built by the Romans in Scotland, some twenty years after Hadrian's Wall and north of that edifice, between the Firth of Forth and the Firth of Clyde?

17   What was the name given to the body of secular and ecclesiastical dignitaries and nobles who advised the monarchs of Anglo-Saxon England?

18   Which philosopher, lawyer and writer was murdered in 43 BC after speaking out against Mark Antony and advocating a return to the Republic?

19   Publish something naughty in the seventeenth century and you were liable to have the letters S and L branded on your cheeks; for what did the letters stand? (a) scurrilous and licentious (b) seditious and libellous (c) sordid and lewd?

20   The Thin Red Line was first used to describe the heroism of (a) Wellington's troops at the Battle of Waterloo (b) the staunch resistance of the Scots Ninety-Third Highlanders at the Battle of Balaclava (c) the defence of the Bridge at Arnhem by the red berets (paratroop regiment) during Operation Market Garden in World War II?

Total Points: 20. Targets: Novice 8 Pro 15. Your Score:

Quiz 342. Olympic Games

Part 1

1 Which two track and field disciplines were added to the former women's pentathlon to turn it into the current heptathlon? (2 pts)

2 Whose record did Michael Phelps beat when he won his eighth Olympic gold medal at a single games? How long had that record stood? (2 pts)

3 Which GB rider won a gold medal in the equestrian eventing at the 2004 Olympics after the original winner, Germany's Bettina Hoy, incurred a post-event penalty?

4 Which were the last Olympic Games to be associated with a terrorist attack?

5 What unfortunate distinction do Portuguese marathon runner Francisco Lazaro (Stockholm, 1912) and Danish cyclist Knud Jensen (Tokyo, 1964) have in common?

6 Maria Gorokhovskaya won a record seven medals at the 1952 Olympics; in which sport? (a) swimming (b) skiing (c) gymnastics

7 'Tell me I'm not dreaming . . . That's not possible . . . I think I'm going to be sick.' Who was astonished at his own huge Olympic and world record in 1968? In which discipline? (2 pts)

8 Who was the US athlete, one of the pre-race favourites, who tripped over Zola Budd in the women's 1,500 metre race at the 1984 Olympics, effectively ending the chances of both?

9 Who provided a memorable opening to a generally poor Olympics in Atlanta in 1996 when he lit the Olympic cauldron?

10 Jeannette Altwegg was the last British woman to win an individual gold medal in which sport, at the 1952 Winter Olympics?

Part 2

11   Which was the last US city to host the Winter Olympics in 2002?

12   Janica Kostelić and her older brother Ivica won nine Olympic medals between 2002 and 2010 in the skiing events; which country's first skiing medals were they?

13   Which German skater won the most Olympic medals of any female skater (nine) including medals in the 5,000 metres at five successive games (1992–2006), but was later banned for an alleged doping offence?

14   Who won Great Britain's first ever skiing medal in 2002 only to have it taken away after a positive drug test? What popular medication was proved to have contained the banned substance? (2 pts)

15   Trischa Zorn is the most decorated Paralympian in the history of the Games; what is her disability and in which sport did she compete? (2 pts)

16   Great Britain has won the coxless fours at the Olympic Games on every occasion since 2000; can you name the ten rowers who have won sixteen gold medals between them in the event? (10 pts)

Total Points: 30. Targets: Novice 12 Pro 23. Your Score: ⬚

Quiz 343. Classical Arts

Part 1

1   Mark-Anthony Turnage and Richard Thomas collaborated on an opera, performed in 2011 at the Royal Opera House, about the life of which tragic celebrity?

2   Who composed a symphony for piano, jazz band and orchestra called *Rhapsody in Blue* in 1924?

3   Which contemporary composer (born London, 1944) shares his name with a medieval English composer who died in 1545?

4   Which theatre on St Martin's Lane in London has been the home of the English National Opera since 1968?

5   Under what pseudonym did the composer Philip Heseltine work?

6   Which great opera singer gave her valedictory performance in Covent Garden on 4 July 1965?

7   A new ballet, *Eternal Damnation to Sancho and Sanchez*, was booed at Sadler's Wells in 2009. What was the subject matter? (a) incest within the royal family set to Vaughan Williams, (b) Popes raping and murdering nuns set to Ravel waltzes (c) an interpretation of the Spanish invasion of Mexico set to Erik Satie?

8   Which famous Tchaikovsky ballet was premiered at the Bolshoi Theatre, Moscow, on 3 March 1877?

9   Whose *Missa Papae Marcelli* is regarded as one of the finest examples of medieval polyphonic choral music?

10 The Royal Ballet version of *La Fille Mal Gardée* is a modern pastoral ballet by which choreographer?

Part 2

11   Which composer's best-known works include his *Music for Royal Fireworks* and *Messiah*, both written in the 1740s?

12   The plot of *The Marriage of Figaro* by Mozart is a continuation of which story, also an opera (although the famous version is later than *The Marriage of Figaro*)? Which playwright wrote the stage plays on which both are based? Who wrote the later opera of the first part of the story? (3 pts)

13   Which Polish composer (1933–2010) found belated stardom in the early 1990s when sales of his 1977 third symphony (*Symphony of Sorrowful Songs*) rocketed when it was re-released?

14   What was founded in Paris in 1909 by Russian ex-pat Sergei Diaghilev and choreographer Mikhail Fokine?

15   'The Dance of the Seven Veils' is an interlude during which opera by Richard Strauss?

16   *Thespis* was the first of fourteen comic operas written by which famous collaboration (first and second names, please)? Which of their works, with an Eastern flavour, ran for longest on its initial run? Which of the pair wrote the libretto rather than the music? What was the name of the impresario who opened a theatre in London to showcase their work and what was the theatre? (6 pts)

Total Points: 23. Targets: Novice 9 Pro 17. Your Score:

Quiz 344. General Knowledge

Part 1

1   Who was assassinated outside the Audubon Ballroom in New York on 21 February 1965?

2   Which writer and economist was a co-founder of the International Monetary Fund as well as being a primary mover in the formation of the Arts Council?

3   The Christian sect, the Valesii, active in Rome in the third century, indulged in which ritual? (a) self-castration (b) sacrifice of all female children (c) self immolation (setting themselves on fire)

4   Who wrote a great poetic account of 'The Charge of the Light Brigade'?

5   Add together the time difference between London and New York, London and Paris and London and Moscow; what number do you have?

6   What was the name of the Grasmere home of William Wordsworth and his sister Dorothy from 1799 to 1808?

7   Where was the world's oldest university founded in 859? (a) Bologna, Italy (b) Fes, Morocco (c) Tashkent, Uzbekistan

8   Which organization launched its magazine in 1888, and has seen it feature some of the most outstanding nature photography of the last 125 years?

9   Which iPhone app, released in December 2009, has sold over twelve million units in the first twelve years?

10 Where did two bombs disrupt a major US sporting event in April 2013, immediately killing three people and injuring over 170?

Part 2

11 Why would a Muslim perform *wudu* and use a *musallah*?

12 What is the sweet, sparkling white wine from Piedmont?

13 What is the medieval language spoken in parts of southern France and small enclaves of Spain and Italy which also gives its name to a modern region of France?

14 Where did the first WHSmith bookstore open in 1848? In which town are the company's headquarters now? (2 pts)

15 'Come On You Reds' was a 1994 no. 1 hit for Manchester United FC and was recorded with which enduring rock band?

16 Which three clubs shared the trophy as England dominated the European Cup from 1977 to 1982? (3 pts)

17 Which famous divorcee was the first woman to feature on the cover of *Time* magazine (1936)?

18 Who is Drew Barrymore's celebrity godfather?

19 Which sportsman was voted Ireland's sexiest man in 2004?

20 Which famous film star couple were married in Montreal in 1964?

Total Points: 23. Targets: Novice 12 Pro 17. Your Score: ☐

Answers Quizzes 337–344

Quiz 337. General Knowledge

1. Be ordained as a Church of England priest; 2. Algeria; 3. David Irving; 4. D. H. Lawrence's *Lady Chatterley's Lover*; 5. At the southern tip of the continent of South America; 6. Robert Burns; 7. Kilimanjaro; Tanzania; 8. Eve Arnold; Magnum; Marilyn Monroe; 9. Ramón Estévez is the birth name of actor Martin Sheen who played the President in *The West Wing*; 10. John McCrirrick; 11. Gaza Strip; Hammas; 12. 2003; 13. Jerusalem; 14. Walter Scott (*The Bride of Lammermoor*); 15. Shadow Cabinet; 16. Real Madrid v. Barcelona; 17. Danielle Lloyd; 18. They all have twin siblings; 19. George Formby; 20. Prince Philip, Duke of Edinburgh

Quiz 338. Crime Movies

1. Robert De Niro and Al Pacino; 2. The IRA; Helen Mirren; 3. Lee Marvin; 4. *The Conversation*; 5. Britt Ekland; Terence Rigby (from *Softly, Softly*); 6. Barbara Stanwyck; Billy Wilder; 7. Mary Astor; 8. Moose; Claire Trevor; 9. Elliott Gould; 10. (b) *Sudden Impact* in 1983; 11. Noomi Rapace; Rooney Mara; 12. A large diamond; Inspector Clouseau (Peter Sellers); 13. Gene Hackman and Willem Dafoe; 14. *Chinatown*; Jake Gittes (played by Jack Nicholson); 15. *Bullitt*; Steve McQueen; 16. *The Postman Always Rings Twice*; John Garfield and Lana Turner; Turner's character, Cora, was a waitress; Jack Nicholson and Jessica Lange

Quiz 339. Media

1. Commodore 64; 2. International Publishing Corporation; 3. Rebekah Brooks; Andy Coulson; 4. Piers Morgan; *Daily Mirror*; 5. *Guardian*; 6. The *i*, the mini version of the *Independent*; 7. He was imprisoned by militants in Gaza for 114 days; 8. Founder of Twitter; 9. Associated Newspapers; 10. James Murdoch; 11. *Le Monde* and *Le Figaro*; 12. George Entwistle; Lord McAlpine; 13. The Advertising Standards Authority tries to ensure the public is not misled by advertisers and investigates any significant complaints; 14. *Punch*; 15. 1920s; 16. *Private Eye* was launched in 1961; Richard Ingrams and Ian Hislop; Robert Maxwell, who had frequent run-ins with *Private Eye*; the controversial cover following the death of Princess Diana (WHSmith had taken well over ten years to stock the magazine in the first place)

Quiz 340. Around Britain

1. A waterfall in the remote Highlands of Scotland; 2. Isle of Man; 3. Avebury, Wiltshire, about thirty miles from the site at Stonehenge; 4. Fosse Way; 5. Windsor (actually Windsor and Maidenhead, but the status is bestowed because of Windsor); Tunbridge Wells; Leamington Spa; Wootton Bassett; 6. Beaulieu (Palace House); 7. River Shannon; 8. Brecon Beacons; 9. Newcastle upon Tyne; 10. Somerset; 11. Glasgow; Belfast; Edinburgh; Cardiff; Swansea; Aberdeen; Dundee; Newport; Derry (Londonderry); Falkirk

Quiz 341. History

1. Cleopatra VII (seventh); 2. Oxford; 3. Che Guevara; 4. Sydney; 5. *Mayflower*; 6. Warren Commission; 7. Visigoths; 8. Japan (the First Sino-Japanese War); 9. Atlas; 10. Gold (discoveries of gold deposits in Victoria and New South Wales set off the Australian gold rush); 11. Salisbury; 12. India; 13. Suez Canal; 14. Prohibition; 15. The reconquest of the Iberian peninsula (Spain and Portugal) by the Catholic allies from the Moorish rulers; 16. Antonine Wall; 17. Witanegamot or Witan; 18. (Marcus Tullius) Cicero; 19. (b) seditious and libellous; 20. (b) the red-coated Ninety-Third held fast against massive odds despite having only enough men to form a double line of riflemen

Quiz 342. Olympic Games

1. Javelin and 800 metres track race; 2. Mark Spitz; thirty-six years (1972–2008); 3. Leslie Law; 4. Atlanta, 1996, when a bomb caused over a hundred injuries and killed one person at a pre-Games concert; 5. They are the only two athletes who have died during competition at the Olympic Games (there have been other instances where athletes have died in practice); 6. (c) Gymnastics; 7. Bob Beamon in the long jump in Mexico in 1968; 8. Mary Decker; 9. Muhammad Ali; 10. Figure skating; since then the British have failed to win a medal of any colour in the event; 11. Salt Lake City; 12. Croatia (Janica won four gold and two silver in 2002 and 2006; Ivica won three silver across 2006 and 2010); 13. Claudia Pechstein (the ban was based on circumstantial evidence rather than a positive test so remains a debatable conviction); 14. Alain Baxter; an inhaler (Vicks) bought in the US; 15. Trischa is blind and won fifty-five medals (yep, fifty-five), forty-one of them gold, between 1980 and 1996; swimming; 16. James Cracknell (2000, 2004); Steve Redgrave (2000); Tim Foster (2000); Matthew Pinsent (2000, 2004); Steve Williams (2004, 2008); Ed Coode (2004); Tom James (2008, 2012); Pete Reed (2008, 2012); Andrew Triggs-Hodge (2008, 2012); Alex Gregory (2012)

Quiz 343. Classical Arts

1. Anna Nicole Smith; 2. George Gershwin; 3. John Tavener; 4. Coliseum; 5. Peter Warlock; 6. Maria Callas; 7. (b) Javier de Frutos's work was mocked by critics and audiences alike; 8. *Swan Lake*; 9. Palestrina; 10. Sir Frederick Ashton; 11. (George Frederick) Handel; 12. *The Barber of Seville*; Beaumarchais; Rossini; 13. Henryk Gorecki; 14. Ballets Russes; 15. *Salomé*; 16. William S. Gilbert and Sir Arthur Sullivan; *The Mikado*; Gilbert; (Richard) D'Oyly Carte, the Savoy Theatre

Quiz 344. General Knowledge

1. Malcolm X; 2. John Maynard Keynes; 3. (a) Worse, they believed that any visitors to their monastery should be treated in the same manner; 4. Alfred, Lord Tennyson; 5. Ten (hours); 6. Dove Cottage; 7. (b) the University of al-Karaouine was founded in Fes; 8. *National Geographic*; 9. Angry Birds; 10. Boston; 11. To pray (*wudu* is the ritual cleaning

before prayer and a *musallah* is a prayer mat); 12. Moscato; 13. Occitan, also referred to as Langue d'Oc; 14. Euston Station, London; Swindon (2 pts); 15. Status Quo; 16. Liverpool (1977, 1978 and 1982); Nottingham Forest (1979, 1980); Aston Villa (1981); 17. Wallis Simpson; 18. Steven Spielberg; 19. Brian O'Driscoll; 20. Richard Burton and Elizabeth Taylor (2 pts)

Quiz 345. General Knowledge

Part 1

1 Where was the West German government based when the country was divided between East and West?

2 What is the third most common Russian surname, the equivalent of the English name Smith? (a) Kuznetsov (b) Grishenko (c) Vasilyev?

3 Who is the creative director of Smythson, the exclusive Bond Street purveyor of leather goods and personal stationery?

4 For what role was actress Elisabeth Sladen, who succumbed to cancer in 2011, best known?

5 Who created the monocle wearing old Etonian character Psmith?

6 Which Ali Smith novel won the 2005 Whitbread Book of the Year?

7 Hannibal Smith was a member of which crime-fighting team?

8 Which TV comedy actress won a Laurence Olivier Award (Best Actress in a Musical) for her performance as Elle in *Legally Blonde* in 2011?

9 Smith and Wesson was founded in 1852 for the commercial production of what?

10 What was Adam Smith's major work, arguably the first important economic treatise, published in 1776?

Part 2

11 What was Kevin Smith's self-financed 1994 directorial feature film debut?

12 Which 1980s band (still active) has Robert Smith as singer, guitarist and principal songwriter?

13 Who was the celebrated New York photographer who had an intense relationship with singer Patti Smith and shot her album cover portraits?

14 Who is credited with saving the life of New England colonist John Smith in the early seventeenth century?

15 Edward Smith is remembered as the captain of which sailing vessel?

16 What post was held by Helmut Schmidt between 1974 and 1982?

17 Which TV character is served loyally by an aide called Waylon Smithers?

18 Which celebrity couple met whilst shooting the film *Mr and Mrs Smith*?

19 Where in London has a famous meat market been located for over 800 years?

20 Why would a film director choose to have his name on a film he had made changed to Alan Smithee?

Total Points: 20. Targets: Novice 10 Pro 15. Your Score:

Quiz 346. TV

Another twenty on the box of delights, plus a little five-point bonus

Part 1

1 The well-received first series of *The Hour* in 2011 was about the making of a TV news programme during which political crisis? Who played the show's producer, a pioneering woman in the industry? (2 pts)

2 What is the in-joke name of Michael Gambon's author-character in Dennis Potter's *The Singing Detective*? Who played Nurse Mills, the angel who pervades his waking dreams? (2 pts)

3 Who presented BBC programmes on *The Victorians* and *Empire* in 2009 and 2012 respectively?

4 Which make of car was Gene Hunt's pride and joy in the TV series *Life on Mars*?

5 How are Si King and Dave Myers better known on the TV?

6 Andy Hamilton, Richard Curtis and Clive Anderson all cut their teeth in TV in the early 1980s writing for which comedy sketch show?

7 Which TV character wore a blue candy-striped romper suit?

8 Who was Captain Scarlet's boss, and what was the alien force threatening the planet? (2 pts)

9 Which other TV programme introduced the character of Frasier, played by Kelsey Grammer?

10 What event at the end of an episode called 'A House Divided' in 1981 was the biggest TV sensation of the day and had both the US and UK guessing for six months before the revelation in the next series?

Part 2

11 Which TV character had the unusual middle name Iolanthe?

12 Who were the three Goodies? (3 pts)

13 *I'm Alan Partridge* finds the DJ down on his luck after the heights of which previous show? Who created this monster? (2 pts)

14 Vicki Pollard, Harvey Pincher and Bubbles deVere are all characters in which comedy series?

15 Where did Gobo, Mokey, Wembley, Boober and Red live?

16 What part in two versions of a classic adventure story was played by Nickolas Grace in the 1980s and Keith Allen in the 2000s?

17 What kind of creature is Sooty's girlfriend, Soo?

18 What connects the support roles played by Robert Glenister, Tobias Menzies and Simon Russell Beale in *Spooks*?

19 Which English city provided the location for Summerdown School, where the 2001–2004 drama *Teachers* was set?

20 Which adventure programme impinged the image of Lucy Lawless in a skimpy costume on the consciousness of a generation of teenagers?

21 Who co-wrote *The Office* with Ricky Gervais? What is the name of the 'legendary' sales rep played by Ralph Ineson and idolized by David Brent? With which other office does Brent's team merge at the start of the second series? What is the name of Dawn's boyfriend? An instrumental version of which song provides the show's theme tune? (5 pts)

Total Points: 31. Targets: Novice 12 Pro 23. Your Score:

Quiz 347. TV Cops

A section on TV DIs and PIs

Part 1

1   Which series was set in Bristol and featured a DJ cum detective? Who played the detective? (2 pts)

2   What was the name given to the crime-fighting team made up of Lewis Collins and Martin Shaw as Bodie and Doyle? Who played their boss? (2 pts)

3   Which long-running show started with a successful one-off drama called *Woodentop* (1983), growing into a show which ran until 2010?

4   What is the central premise of the US show *Dexter*? And who plays the lead character? (2 pts)

5   Who won three consecutive Best Actress in a TV Drama Emmy awards in 1983–5 and again in 1988? Which actress won in the two intervening years? (2 pts)

6   What was the name of the main character in *The Saint*, the 1960s adventure series starring Roger Moore? Who reprised the role in the late 1970s? (2 pts)

7   Which half of a comedy writing duo wrote the northeast-set *Spender* along with its star, Jimmy Nail? What was the name of Spender's informant/ sidekick? (2 pts)

8   What was the 1970s police drama starring Karl Malden and Michael Douglas?

9   What was the name of David Janssen's character in *The Fugitive* (1963–7)? Who played the role in a 1993 movie version? (2 pts)

10   Where was Special Agent Dale Cooper assigned in 1990, and whose murder was he investigating? (2 pts)

Part 2

11   Who played Gene Hunt in the TV police drama *Life on Mars*? What was the name of the policeman from the future who arrives to work with Hunt? And who arrived for the follow-up *Ashes to Ashes*? On whose songs are the titles of both series based? (4 pts)

12   Who played Carter and Regan in the original TV series of *The Sweeney*? How did Carter address Regan in the programme? Who reprised the roles in the 2012 movie of the same name? (5 pts)

13   What particular type of case do the team investigate in *Waking the Dead*? What is the name of the lead detective, played by Trevor Eve, and who plays Grace, his psychoanalyst partner? Who played the forensic pathologist, Eve Lockart, in the later series, and what was the name of her spin-off series? (5 pts)

Total Points: 32. Targets: Novice 13 Pro 24. Your Score: ☐

Quiz 348. Movies

A couple of themed movie quizzes

Part 1

A short section on the settings for various movies

1   What was the setting for the bulk of *Don't Look Now*, the eerie chiller starring Donald Sutherland and Julie Christie from 1974?

2   Tony Curtis and Jack Lemmon are on their way to which American city when they board the train near the beginning of *Some Like It Hot*?

3   What was the setting for John Boorman's 1972 thriller, *Deliverance*?

4   Which city is celebrated in Fellini's *La Dolce Vita*?

5   Terence Davies's 1988 film *Distant Voices, Still Lives* is a record of working-class life in which city in the post-war years?

6   Which Yorkshire town provides the setting for the gritty urban drama *Kes* (1969)?

7   Which town in upstate New York provides the repetitive setting for *Groundhog Day*?

8   What is the name given to the Louisiana community that provides the setting for the 2012 film *Beasts of the Southern Wild*?

9   Which city connects *Vertigo*, *Dirty Harry* and *Milk*?

10 What is the setting for Spielberg's 1987 adaptation, *Empire of the Sun*?

Part 2

Here is a list of films whose titles are made up of two names (like *Tom & Jerry*); we give you one name and one star, you give us the other name and star – *comprende*? (2 pts per question)

11 Frankie (Michelle Pfeiffer) and who (1991)?
12 Thunderbolt (Clint Eastwood) and who (1974)?
13 Sid (Gary Oldman) and who (1986)?
14 Butch Cassidy (Paul Newman) and who (1969)?
15 Romeo (Leonardo DiCaprio) and who (1996)?
16 Samson (Victor Mature) and who (1949)?
17 Thelma (Geena Davis) and who (1991)?
18 Bonnie (Faye Dunaway) and who (1967)?
19 Harold (Bud Coert) and who (1971)?
20 Pat Garrett (James Coburn) and who (1973)?

Total Points: 30. Targets: Novice 15 Pro 24. Your Score: [   ]

Quiz 349. Non-fiction Books

For those who like their reading a bit more real

Part 1

1 Thomas Carlyle's three-volume account of which historic period made his reputation as an author?

2 Whose mantra of self love, *You Can Heal Your Life*, hit the top of the best-seller lists in 1984?

3 From what angle did Neil MacGregor publish a history of the world in 2010?

4 Which part of England provided the setting for the books by James Herriot about a country veterinary practice?

5 What is the subtitle of Joshua Foer's 2007 book, *Moonwalking with Einstein*? (a) *The Art and Science of Remembering Everything* (b) *Inside the Mind of a Genius* (c) *Explorations of the Varietal Experience of the Unconscious Mind*?

6 Who went from soldier to author with *Bravo Two Zero*, his 1993 account of an SAS operation during the First Gulf War?

7 What was the full title of Lynne Truss's book about punctuation which became a surprise bestseller in 2003? (2 pts)

8 What was Monty Roberts's 1996 bestseller about his life with animals (it sold five million copies worldwide and became a Hollywood film)? (2 pts for the proper title)

9 What connects Cardinal Manning (who converted to Catholicism and became Archbishop of Westminster), General Gordon (he of China and Khartoum fame), Thomas Arnold (reformist headmaster of Rugby School and campaigner) and Florence Nightingale (nursing pioneer)?

10 What was the 1987 memoir by former MI5 officer Peter Wright which the UK government tried to ban, thereby assuring it of wide readership and success? Which film director – working as a journalist at the time – co-wrote the book? (2 pts)

Part 2

Mix and Match: whose autobiography?

1. Alec Guinness; 2. Roald Dahl; 3. Mae West; 4. Maya Angelou; 5. Clive James;
6. Anne Robinson; 7. Errol Flynn; 8. Dirk Bogarde; 9. Miranda Hart; 10. Tony Blair

a. *An Ordinary Man*; b. *Unreliable Memoirs*; c. *Is It Just Me?*; d. *Goodness Had Nothing to Do with It*; e. *A Journey*; f. *Boy*; g. *My Wicked Wicked Ways*; h. *Memoirs of an Unfit Mother*; i. *Blessings in Disguise*; j. *I Know Why the Caged Birds Sing*

Your Workings:

Total Points: 23. Targets: Novice 9 Pro 17. Your Score:

Quiz 350. Rugby Union

The oval ball, posh version

Part 1

1   Who is the only England rugby union captain to have led his side to three Grand Slams in the years since World War II?

2   Who scored all but three of Leinster's points in their 33–22 win over Northampton in the 2011 Heineken Cup final?

3   Who scored six tries in the 2011 Rugby World Cup without him or his team making a significant impact on the tournament?

4   The first international match took place in which city in which decade? (2 pts)

5   In which year were Australia, New Zealand and South Africa invited to join the International Rugby Board: 1929, 1948 or 1960?

6   What was the venue for the 1995 Rugby World Cup final and who presented the trophy to the winning South African team? (2 pts)

7   Why did England get a standing ovation from the Irish crowd before Ireland's opening match of the 1973 Five Nations at Lansdowne Road?

8   Who scored 'the greatest try of all time' when the Barbarians beat the 1973 All Blacks in a scintillating game of rugby? Who was the captain of the Baa Baas that day? (2 pts)

9   Which two members of the 1970s and early 1980s England team set up a successful business selling sportswear which remains a strong brand today? (2 pts)

10 Which Welshman converted an injury-time try to deny England a Grand Slam in 1999?

Part 2

11   Toulouse have won the Heineken Cup a record four times; who are the only other French side to have won (up to January 2013), in 1997 when they beat Leicester in the final?

12   Which was the first season of professional club rugby union in England? (2 pts; 1 pt for one year out)

13   Which team contested every Premiership final in English rugby union from 2005 to 2012, winning three?

14   Who did Australia beat 142–0 in the 2003 Rugby World Cup, a record margin of victory for the tournament? Against which team did England score over 100 points in the same tournament, and who scored five tries from full-back? (3 pts)

15   Who is the only player (up to January 2013) to win 100 caps at rugby union for England, including twenty-two at World Cup tournaments, a record for any country?

16   Other than the teams competing in the Six Nations tournament, which five European sides have played in the group stages of the Rugby World Cup? (5 pts)

17   Why did the Tri-Nations tournament change its name to the Rugby Championship in 2012? Who won the 2012 tournament? Who are the record points scorer and try scorer in the history of the tournament? (Tip: both are from New Zealand.) (4 pts)

Total Points: 31. Targets: Novice 12 Pro 23. Your Score: [   ]

Quiz 351. Births, Deaths and Marriages

Part 1

1   Bo Derek was actor John Derek's fourth wife; before that he was married to Pati Behrs, a ballerina, and which other two actresses, one a Bond girl, one a US soap star? (2 pts)

2   Ali MacGraw, star of *Love Story*, met her future husband on the set of another film, *The Getaway*; who was he?

3   Which member of New Order married which TV comedienne and chat-show host? (2 pts)

4   Alison Steadman was married to which director, with whom she worked closely in the developing years of her career?

5   Who famously died in the Hotel d'Alsace on the Rue des Beaux-Arts in Paris in 1900?

6   Which stage and screen star was film director Blake Edwards's second wife, from 1969 until his death in 2010?

7   Which Hollywood star was born Anna Italiano in the Bronx in 1931, and was married to director Mel Brooks from 1964 until her death in 2005?

8   Which singer and supposed muse had a six-year marriage to Andrew Lloyd Webber which ended in divorce in 1990?

9   If Brooklyn and Cruz are first and third, who are second and fourth? (2 pts)

10 From whom was Paul McCartney's divorce confirmed in 2008, after a long and unseemly court case?

Part 2

11 Which rock star called off a planned wedding to Naomi Campbell in 1993?

12 Who is the mother of actor Ryan Phillippe's children?

13 Which 1960s singer and Eurovision contestant was born Kathleen O'Rourke in Ilford in 1938?

14 What connects the births of Paddy Ashdown, Lib-Dem peer, Colin Cowdrey, former England cricket captain, Spike Milligan, comedian and writer, and George Orwell, novelist and socialist?

15 If Brad Pitt is effectively no. 3 for Angelina Jolie, which two actors were nos 1 and 2? (2 pts)

16 Identify the following people who all died in 2007? (a) Cricklewood comedy writer (b) World Cup redhead (c) I to Yul (d) *Mastermind* mastermind (e) One of the a singing threesome (5 pts)

Total Points: 24. Targets: Novice 12 Pro 19. Your Score:

Quiz 352. General Knowledge

Part 1

1 Who received a diary for her thirteenth birthday on 11 June 1942?
2 What connects Winston Churchill, Adolf Hitler, Prince Charles and D. H. Lawrence?
3 What is the common name for the sternum?
4 What are Burnt Norton, East Coker, The Dry Salvages and Little Gidding?
5 Which American airport is the world's busiest?
6 How did Nancy Shevell hit the headlines in 2011?
7 What is the name of the prison island in Table Bay, off the coast of Cape Town, South Africa, now a designated World Heritage Site?
8 What Hindi word describes a coarse fabric used for labourers' clothes, but has a more specific fashion meaning in the West?
9 Who was the former head of the *Daily Telegraph* group of newspapers convicted of fraud in 2007?
10 How did Elin Nordegren hit the headlines late in 2009?

Part 2

11 The box office take on the three *Lord of the Rings* films was about $3 billion; what was the rough combined production budget: $282 million, $425 million or $600 million?
12 That Moscow and then St Petersburg are the first and second largest cities in Russia is known to most people but which city is third? (a) Kazan (b) Nizhny Novgorod (c) Novosibirsk
13 If you sailed to France from Newhaven, where would you disembark?
14 Who is reported to have sent the poet Byron snippings of her pubic hair?
15 In 1991, aged fifteen, Judit Polgar, a Hungarian teenager, became the youngest person to achieve what?
16 Who captained the victorious Spanish team at the 2010 football World Cup?
17 Whose long-suffering wife, Veronica Lario, left him in 2009?
18 Who owned what is believed to be the last autograph signed by John Lennon?
19 Who was cleared of killing her two sons on 29 January 2003, but had already served three years in prison?
20 Which American soul singer was shot and killed by his own father in 1984?

Total Points: 20. Targets: Novice 10 Pro 15. Your Score:

Answers Quizzes 345–352

Quiz 345. General Knowledge

1. Bonn; 2. (a) Kuznetsov; 3. Samantha Cameron, wife of the British Prime Minister; 4. Sarah Jane Smith, companion to Doctor Who and star of her own spin-off show; 5. P. G. Wodehouse (the P is silent and was added by the character to make his name more distinctive); 6. *The Accidental*; 7. Colonel John Hannibal Smith was the leader of the A-Team; 8. Sheridan Smith; 9. Handguns; 10. *An Inquiry into the Nature and Causes of the Wealth of Nations* (accept *The Wealth of Nations*, which is a common abbreviation); 11. *Clerks*; 12. The Cure; 13. Robert Mapplethorpe; 14. Pocahontas; 15. *Titanic*; 16. Chancellor of West Germany (accept Germany reluctantly); 17. Mr Burns in *The Simpsons*; 18. Brad Pitt and Angelina Jolie; 19. Smithfield; 20. It is industry code for disowning a movie, usually in protest at excessive studio interference

Quiz 346. TV

1. Suez; Romola Garai; 2. Philip (E.) Marlow; Joanne Whalley; 3. Jeremy Paxman; 4. Audi Quattro; 5. Two Hairy Bikers; 6. *Not the Nine O'Clock News*; 7. Andy Pandy; 8. Colonel White; the Mysterons; 9. *Cheers*; 10. The shooting of J. R. Ewing in *Dallas*; 11. Reggie Perrin; 12. Tim Brooke-Taylor, Graeme Garden and Bill Oddie; 13. *Knowing Me, Knowing You . . .*; Steve Coogan; 14. *Little Britain*; 15. Fraggle Rock; 16. Both played the Sheriff of Nottingham in Robin Hood stories; 17. She was a panda (no, you can't have a point for 'glove puppet'); 18. They play different Home Secretaries; 19. Bristol; 20. *Xena: Warrior Princess*; 21. Stephen Merchant; Finchy (Chris Finch); Swindon; Lee; 'Handbags and Gladrags'

Quiz 347. TV Cops

1. *Shoestring*; Trevor Eve; 2. *The Professionals*; Gordon Jackson; 3. *The Bill*; 4. He is a serial killer, but only preys on other serial killers; Michael C. Hall; 5. Tyne Daly (Lacey); Sharon Gless (Cagney); 6. Simon Templar; Ian Ogilvy; 7. Ian La Frenais; Stick; 8. *The Streets of San Francisco*; 9. Dr Richard Kimble; Harrison Ford; 10. *Twin Peaks*; Laura Palmer; 11. Philip Glenister; Sam Tyler; Alex Drake (Keeley Hawes); David Bowie; 12. Dennis Waterman and John Thaw; Guv'nor; Ray Winstone and Ben Drew; 13. Cold cases (old, unsolved crimes); Peter Boyd; Sue Johnston; Tara Fitzgerald; *The Body Farm*

Quiz 348. Movies

1. Venice; 2. Miami; 3. The Appalachian Mountains; the region still resents the stereotypical view of its inhabitants; 4. Rome; 5. Liverpool; 6. Barnsley; 7. Punxsutawney; 8. The Bathtub; 9. All set in San Francisco; 10. Shanghai; 11. Johnny (Al Pacino); 12. Lightfoot (Jeff Bridges); 13. Nancy (Chloe Webb); 14. The Sundance Kid (Robert Redford); 15. Juliet

(Claire Danes); 16. Delilah (Hedy Lamarr); 17. Louise (Susan Sarandon); 18. Clyde (Warren Beatty); 19. Maude (Ruth Gordon); 20. Billy the Kid (Kris Kristofferson)

Quiz 349. Non-fiction Books

1. *The French Revolution: A History*; 2. Louise L. Hay; 3. By expressing it through *100 Objects*; 4. Yorkshire Dales; 5. (a) The book was about memory (whilst conducting the research Foer became the US memory champion); 6. Andy McNab; 7. *Eats, Shoots and Leaves: The Zero Tolerance Approach to Punctuation* (bonus point for full title); 8. *The Man Who Listened to Horses* (only 1 point for *The Horse Whisperer*); 9. They were the four subjects of Lytton Strachey's 1919 book, *Eminent Victorians*, regarded as a great early example of that literary form; 10. *Spycatcher*; Paul Greengrass; Mix and Match 1, i; 2, f; 3, d; 4, j; 5, b; 6, h; 7, g; 8, a; 9, c; 10, e

Quiz 350. Rugby Union

1. Will Carling; 2. Jonathan Sexton; 3. Chris Ashton (England); 4. Edinburgh in the 1870s (1871) when Scotland hosted England; 5. 1948 (the same year the right-wing National Party took control in South Africa); 6. Ellis Park, Nelson Mandela; 7. The previous year Wales and Scotland had declined to visit (it was the height of the Troubles in Ulster); 8. Gareth Edwards; John Dawes; 9. Fran Cotton and Steve Smith (the company is Cotton Traders); 10. Neil Jenkins; 11. Brive; 12. 1996–7; 13. Leicester Tigers; 14. Namibia; Uruguay; Josh Lewsey; 15. Jason Leonard; 16. Romania (all seven tournaments); Georgia (played in the last three); Spain (1999); Portugal (2003); Russia (2007); 17. Because Argentina joined to make four teams; New Zealand (with a clean sweep, winning all six games); Dan Carter and Christian Cullen

Quiz 351. Births, Deaths and Marriages

1. Ursula Andress and Linda Evans; 2. Steve McQueen; 3. Peter Hook and Caroline Aherne; 4. Mike Leigh; 5. Oscar Wilde; 6. Julie Andrews; 7. Anne Bancroft; 8. Sarah Brightman; 9. Romeo and Harper (they are the children of David and Victoria Beckham); 10. Heather Mills; 11. Adam Clayton of U2; 12. Reese Witherspoon; 13. Kathy Kirby; 14. They were all born in India; 15. Johnny Lee Miller and Billy Bob Thornton; 16. (a) Alan Coren (b) Alan Ball (c) Deborah Kerr (d) Magnus Magnusson (e) Luciano Pavarotti

Quiz 352. General Knowledge

1. Anne Frank; 2. All exhibited and sold their paintings; 3. Breastbone; 4. T. S. Eliot's *Four Quartets*; 5. Atlanta, Hartsfield; 6. She married Sir Paul McCartney; 7. Robben Island; 8. Dungaree; 9. Conrad Black; 10. She was the victim of Tiger Woods's infidelity, revealed after a major row and motor accident; 11. A mere $282 million, not a bad return on investment; 12. (c) Novosibirsk; 13. Dieppe; 14. Lady Caroline Lamb; 15. She became a chess grandmaster; 16. Iker Casillas; 17. Silvio Berlusconi; 18. Mark David Chapman, the man who shot him; 19. Sally Clark; 20. Marvin Gaye

Quiz 353. General Knowledge

Part 1

1   Which European country has a capital city named after a Grand Master of the Knights of St John?

2   Then known as the Office of the Chief Examiner, what American institution was established in 1908?

3   What does a herpatologist study? (a) amphibians (b) sexual diseases (c) forensic science

4   Where was New York's immigration depot situated between 1892 and 1954?

5   Which of these facts about journalist and campaigner Ludovic Kennedy (1909–2009) is *not* true? (a) his knighthood was vetoed by Margaret Thatcher but approved by John Major (b) as a Roman Catholic he was a fierce opponent of the notion of voluntary euthanasia (c) he once stood as the Liberal candidate for Rochdale

6   What is the name of Edwin Lutyens granite castle built on the edge of Dartmoor in Devon? (a) Castle Bongo (b) Castle Drogo (c) Castle Drongo

7   Whose *Tales of the Unexpected* were successfully adapted for television?

8   Which music-hall singer, who died in 1922, drew 100,000 people to her London funeral?

9   Which Academy Award-winning actor was born Eric Marlon Bishop in Texas in December 1967?

10 The Alto Douro is an attractive hilly wine region in which country?

Part 2

11 Which has the highest average July temperature: Addis Ababa, London or Moscow?

12 Which has the lowest average January temperature: Anchorage in Alaska, Reykjavik in Iceland or Ulan Bator in Mongolia?

13 Which country leads the world on spending on research and development as a percentage of GDP: Israel, Sweden or the UK? (Latest statistics, 2008)

14 Which sector provides the most Americans with employment: Services and Education (what we call the civil service), Finance or Retail and Leisure?

15 Which country employs the biggest percentage of its workforce in agriculture and fishing: China, Japan or Mexico?

16 After the US, which country gets the most income from overseas visitors?

17 Which African country has the world's lowest Human Development Index (HDI), based on life expectancy, education and standard of living? (a) Egypt (b) Nigeria (c) Zimbabwe

18 Which country has the lowest illiteracy rate: United Kingdom, Australia or Norway?

19 Which three countries have the largest amount of forest or jungle area? And which removed the biggest percentage of its forest in the years from 1990 to 2010? (4 pts)

20 Which five countries' tourists spent the most money abroad in 2009? (5 pts)

Total Points: 27. Targets: Novice 14 Pro 20. Your Score: [   ]

Quiz 354. Rock and Pop

Some poptastic teasers for you

Part 1

1   What was the name of the Comic Relief single by One Direction that reached no. 1 in March 2013?

2   Which singer changed his name from David Jones in the late 1960s to avoid confusion with the lead singer of the Monkees?

3   Who prompted thousands of complaints to the BBC by wearing a terrorist-style balaclava on *Top of the Pops* in 1994?

4   Martie Maguire, Natalie Maines and Emily Robison are the members of which country band, who were pilloried and banned from many southern states of the US for voicing opposition to the Iraq War?

5   Which band also doubled as the house band for the 1960s soul label Stax?

6   Which British guitarist featured on Modest Mouse's Billboard no. 1 album, *We Were Dead Before the Ship Even Sank*? (a) Graham Coxon (Blur) (b) Johnny Marr (The Smiths) (c) Eric Clapton?

7   On whose TV show did the Beatles make a huge impact in the US in 1964?

8   Who was the legendary producer who asked the Neville Brothers 'how slow can you go?' before cutting their slow groove album *Yellow Moon*?

9   Which US band, ushered in with the punk and new wave bands active in New York in the late 1970s, recorded the startling debut *Marquee Moon* in 1977?

10 What connects the Proclaimers to the Jesus and Mary Chain, apart from both of them being Scottish?

Part 2

11 From which three bands had the members of Crosby, Stills and Nash come before recording together in 1969? Who joined them for their second release the following year and what was the album called? (5 pts)

12 Whose two versions of the same song were at nos 1 and 2 in the charts for Christmas 2008? Who wrote the song? Which other cover version was at no. 3, and who recorded the original? (5 pts)

Total Points: 20. Targets: Novice 8 Pro 15. Your Score: [   ]

Quiz 355. Movies

Answer the questions based on the cast information given

Part 1

1 The support cast is Tony Roberts, Carol Kane, Paul Simon, Janet Margolin, Shelley Duvall, Christopher Walken, Colleen Dewhurst; what is the Woody Allen movie?

2 Martin Sheen, Marlon Brando, Robert Duvall, Frederic Forrest, with Laurence Fishburne, Harrison Ford and Dennis Hopper in smaller roles; what's the movie?

3 Henry Thomas, Drew Barrymore and Robert MacNaughton play three siblings in which classic family adventure?

4 Jesse Eisenberg, Andrew Garfield and Justin Timberlake had the juicy parts; what was the film and what was it about? (2 pts)

5 The cast is Sissy Spacek, Piper Laurie, Amy Irving, William Katt, John Travolta and Nancy Allen; what is the 1976 film?

6 Tom Cruise, Philip Seymour Hoffman, William H. Macy, Julianne Moore, John C. Reilly and Felicity Huffman were part of a huge ensemble cast in which 1999 film?

7 The film poster has Paul Henreid on the top line with two others, plus Claude Rains, Conrad Veidt, Sydney Greenstreet and Peter Lorre in support; what's the classic 1940s film and which two cast members are missing? (3 pts)

8 It co-starred Michael Caine, Liam Neeson, Katie Holmes, Gary Oldman, Cillian Murphy, Tom Wilkinson and Morgan Freeman and re-energized a major franchise; what was the film and who took the title role? (2 pts)

9 Nicolas Cage, Meryl Streep, Chris Cooper, Brian Cox, Maggie Gyllenhaal and Tilda Swinton were in this 2002 film; what was it and who wrote it largely about himself (he is played by Cage)? (2 pts)

10 Nicole Kidman, Miranda Richardson, Meryl Streep, Julianne Moore, Toni Collette, Allison Janney, Claire Danes; what's the movie from 2002? Who was Kidman playing? (2 pts)

Part 2

11   The voice list had Jack Black, Dustin Hoffman, Angelina Jolie, Ian McShane, Jackie Chan, Seth Rogen and Lucy Liu; what was the 2008 DreamWorks hit?

12   Cher, Susan Sarandon and Michelle Pfeiffer are referred to in the film's title; what is it and who was the other major player in the cast? (2 pts)

13   John Cho, Kal Penn and Neil Patrick Harris appear in all three movies in which twenty-first-century comedy series?

14   The cast is Leonardo DiCaprio, Tom Hanks, Christopher Walken, Amy Adams, Nathalie Baye, Martin Sheen, Nancy Lenehan and James Brolin; what is the film?

15   The cast list for which 1989 movie includes actors playing Billy the Kid, Napoleon, Genghis Khan, Joan of Arc and Abraham Lincoln? What was the follow-up? (2 pts)

16   The support includes Aretha Franklin, Cab Calloway, Ray Charles, Carrie Fisher and James Brown; what's the film?

17   Which weird and wonderful 1976 movie had a cast list that included Beautiful Girl Across the Hall, Lady in the Radiator, Pencil Machine Operator and People Digging in the Alley?

18   Support includes turns from John Le Mesurier, Maggie Blye, Raf Vallone, Noël Coward and Benny Hill; what's the film?

19   The support cast is Alec Guinness, Omar Sharif, Anthony Quinn, Jack Hawkins, José Ferrer and Claude Rains; what is the film and who portrayed the title character? (2 pts)

20   If the support cast includes Alan Hale, Basil Rathbone, Claude Rains and Eugene Pallette, who are the romantic leads? (2 pts)

Total Points: 30. Targets: Novice 15 Pro 23. Your Score: [   ]

Quiz 356. Discoveries and Inventions

The ingenuity of man and his opposable thumbs

1 Who invented the waterproof overcoat material gabardine in the nineteenth century? (a) Charles Macintosh (b) Thomas Burberry (c) Harry Gordon Selfridge

2 What did Marconi demonstrate in public for the first time in London in 1896?

3 What invention of George Stephenson was showcased at the opening of the Liverpool to Manchester railway in 1830?

4 Who made a diary note in 1822 to 'convert magnetism into electricity' and got around to doing so nine years later?

5 With the creation of which polyamide did Wallace Carothers revolutionize the fashion industry in 1934?

6 Alessandro di Spina and Salvino degli Armatti created and sold the first example of which artificial aid to man in Florence in 1301?

7 In which year was the ringpull can launched: 1952, 1962 or 1972?

8 What was James Ritty's contribution to the world of retail in 1879? (a) the combination safe (b) the tape measure (c) the cash register

9 Jack Kilby and Robert Noyce are credited with inventing or developing what massive contribution to modern technological advancement?

10 In which field did Henri Becquerel help a distinguished couple make significant breakthroughs?

11 Which company challenged a team headed by Jack Kilby, and including Jerry Merryman and James van Tassel, to come up with a calculating machine that could fit in a coat pocket? In which decade was it finally patented? (2 pts)

12 Which everyday office accoutrement made from wire did Johan Vaaler patent in Germany in 1899 and the US two years later?

13 What traffic control measure was installed under the supervision of Alfred Benesch in Cleveland, Ohio, in 1914?

14 What did Thomas Newcomen develop at the beginning of the eighteenth century to make drawing water more efficient? Who massively improved the efficiency of these machines fifty years later by adding a vital ingredient? (2 pts)

15 What was the Rickenbacker Company the first to produce commercially in the 1930s?

Total Points: 17. Targets: Novice 7 Pro 13. Your Score: ☐

Quiz 357. Kings and Queens

Crowned heads, not Roundheads – a quick-fire round and a teaser

1 Which future king was the subject of the 2010 movie, *The King's Speech*?
   What was the name by which his wife and family addressed him? (2 pts)

2 Which English king had the inscription *Malleus Scotorum* (Hammer of the
   Scots) on his tombstone?

3 Who became the first monarch of both England and Scotland?

4 Henry II was the first King of England of the house of Plantagenet; who was
   his mother, from whom his claim to the throne came?

5 What name was given to the head of state of the Venetian Republic?

6 In 1371 Robert II, King of Scotland, started which dynasty, which would last
   as Scottish monarchs until the Act of Union with the English crown?

7 Who was Queen Victoria's youngest daughter, who stayed with her mother
   as her private secretary, and lived until 1944, long after her siblings and
   most of her children?

8 The great warrior King Gustavus Adolphus turned which hitherto minor
   league nation into a major European power at the beginning of the seventeenth century?

9 Where does the Queen usually spend Christmas? And what is the name of
   her Scottish residence? (2 pts)

10 In which country did the crown prince kill his parents and seven other family
   members before committing suicide in 2001?

11 What are the ten European constitutional monarchies? (10 pts)

Total Points: 22. Targets: Novice 9 Pro 17. Your Score:

Quiz 358. Premier League

Part 1

1   Who were the two wingers who played nearly every game as Blackburn won the Premier League in 1994? (2 pts)

2   Which two players have received 100 yellow cards in the Premier League? (2 pts)

3   The last Premier League hat-trick of the 2009–2010 season and the first of the following season were both scored by which Chelsea player?

4   Who has scored in the Premier League for Coventry, Leeds, Tottenham, Liverpool, West Ham and Aston Villa?

5   Which three clubs were promoted to the Premier League in 2001 and all managed to stay up in their first season, the first time this had happened? (3 pts)

6   Which Manchester United quartet made up the entire midfield when the Premier League 'Team of the First 20 Years' was announced? (4 pts)

7   Whose Premier League finishes since their promotion in 2005 read 10th, 17th, 14th, 11th, 16th, 16th, 15th, despite beginning every season amongst the favourites for relegation?

8   Which Premier League side have twice been relegated whilst accumulating less than twenty points along the way?

9   Who led the consortium that saved Middlesbrough from financial ruin in 1996?

10 Steven Gerrard is the only player to have scored a goal in a Champions League final, a UEFA Cup final, an FA Cup final and a League Cup final; who were the opposition on each occasion? (4 pts)

Part 2

Who were the managers of these clubs when they won promotion to the Premier League in the years indicated?

11   Newcastle United (2009–10)
12   Wigan Athletic (2004–5)
13   Leicester City (1995–6)
14   Sunderland (1998–9)
15   Reading (2005–6)
16   Bolton Wanderers (1996–7)
17   West Bromwich Albion (2001–2 and 2003–4)
18   Crystal Palace (1996–7)
19   Wolverhampton Wanderers (2008–9)
20   Fulham (2000–2001)

Total Points: 30. Targets: Novice 12 Pro 23. Your Score: [   ]

Quiz 359. Books

Some old, some new

Part 1

1 Lilliput is the land of the tiny people in Jonathan Swift's *Gulliver's Travels*; what name does Swift give to the land of the giants?

2 Spawning 1,001 imitations, what did Simon Bond find a 101 uses for in a 1981 bestselling humour book?

3 How did *Fly Fishing* by J. R. Hartley become a household name without selling a copy?

4 Which recurring character is the hero of H. Rider Haggard's *King Solomon's Mines*?

5 What narrative device connects *David Copperfield* (Charles Dickens), *A Dance to the Music of Time* (Anthony Powell) and *Unless* (Carol Shields)?

6 What was Richard Ford's 1986 novel about journalist Frank Bascombe?

7 What was Robert Harris's successful 1992 debut, a 'what if . . .' account of post-war England under Nazi rule? Who wrote *Dominion*, a 2012 thriller with a similar theoretical historical setting? (2 pts)

8 Which ubiquitous TV presence wrote an autobiography called *Moab Is My Washpot*?

9 Which book by Mark Haddon, originally published as a children's book, won the 2003 Whitbread Award for best adult novel?

10 What was the nationality of James Bond's parents, according to Ian Fleming? (2 pts)

Part 2

11 *Summoned By Bells* was the autobiography of Poet Laureate John Betjeman; how did it differ from most memoirs?

12 In which city does the story of Wazir Akbar Khan begin in Khaled Hosseini's *The Kite Runner* (2003)?

13 Which 2002 bestseller, narrated by a character who is dead, takes its title from the last paragraph of the book? (Title and author, please) (2 pts)

14 Which poet's only published novel was *The Bell Jar*, issued under a pseudonym in 1963?

15 W. E. Johns is chiefly remembered for creating which fictional character?

16 What are the seven full-length novels written by George Eliot? (7 pts)

Total Points: 25. Targets: Novice 10 Pro 19. Your Score: [   ]

Quiz 360. General Knowledge

Part 1

1   Which familiar figure in advertising is also known as Bibendum?

2   How did Lin Miaoke become famous for not singing in 2008?

3   Which muscles enable us to extend the forearm?

4   The deltoid muscles provide movement in which part of the body?

5   How is *Die Mauer* known in English?

6   Which UK children's comic first featured the Numskulls, little people operating the various bits of the brain?

7   Which poet, author of the famous verse drama *Under Milk Wood*, was born in Swansea, Wales, in 1914?

8   How many players make up a curling team?

9   It is called the Wadi Abwab al Muluk in Egypt; what is it called in the West?

10 What did the MP for Mid Bedfordshire do that had the House of Commons (and the media) in a bit of a lather in 2012?

Part 2

11 Which former pop singer won a Gold Award at the 2005 Chelsea Flower Show?

12 What did Switzerland in 1998, Finland in 1982, Norway in 1978 and 1997, and Turkey in 1987 all achieve in a musical context?

13 Cartagena is a city on the Caribbean coastline of which South American country?

14 Classic FM has broadcast its 'Hall of Fame' – the nation's favourite 300 pieces of classical music – since 1996; only four pieces have topped the list; choose which four from the following list: Bruch's *Violin Concerto No. 1*; Grieg's *Peer Gynt Suite*; Fauré's *Requiem*; Beethoven's *Symphony No. 6 – Pastoral*; Rachmaninov's *Piano Concerto No. 2*; Mozart's *Clarinet Concerto*; Vivaldi's *Four Seasons*; Vaughan Williams's *The Lark Ascending*; Holst's *Planets Suite*; Elgar's *Enigma Variations* (4 pts)

15 What does PSP stand for, and in which year was it released in the UK? (2 pts)

16 Who connects Depeche Mode to Yazoo to Erasure? Who were the three singers with these bands? An EP covering which band's songs gave Erasure their only UK no. 1 hit? (5 pts)

Total Points: 24. Targets: Novice 12 Pro 18. Your Score:

Answers Quizzes 353–360

Quiz 353. General Knowledge

1. Malta (Valletta is named after Jean Parisot de la Vallette); 2. FBI; 3. (a) amphibians; 4. Ellis Island; 5. (b) Kennedy was an advocate of voluntary euthanasia and once stood for Parliament (separately from Rochdale) on that ticket; 6. (b) Castle Drogo; 7. Roald Dahl; 8. Marie Lloyd; 9. Jamie Foxx; 10. Portugal; 11. Moscow at 24 °C (London is 22 °C, Addis Ababa 20 °C (although it has a consistent year-round temperature of between 20–25 °C); 12. Ulan Bator (it is a long way above sea level); 13. Israel is top of the list with 4.9 (if you answered UK you were probably asleep for most of the last twenty years); 14. Services and Education account for 26.3 per cent of employees ; 15. Mexico at around 13 per cent (China and Japan are less than 5 per cent); 16. Spain; 17. Zimbabwe, unsurprisingly, given its leadership; 18. UK has 1 per cent, while both the others have no recorded adult illiteracy; 19. Brazil, Australia and Indonesia; Indonesia (it deforested by over 20 per cent in that period); 20. Germany, US, UK, China, France

Quiz 354. Rock and Pop

1. 'One Way or Another (Teenage Kicks)'; 2. David Bowie; 3. James Dean Bradfield of the Manic Street Preachers; 4. Dixie Chicks; 5. Booker T and the MGs; 6. (b) Johnny Marr; 7. Ed Sullivan; 8. Daniel Lanois; 9. Television (the album was moderately successful but crops up on Best of the Best lists nearly forty years later); 10. Both bands have brothers called Reid at their core; 11. David Crosby was ex-Byrds, Stephen Stills was from Buffalo Springfield and Graham Nash was with the Hollies; Neil Young, *Déjà Vu*; 12. 'Hallelujah' by Alexandra Burke and Jeff Buckley; Leonard Cohen; 'Run' by Leona Lewis, Snow Patrol (5 pts)

Quiz 355. Movies

1. *Annie Hall*; 2. *Apocalypse Now*; 3. *ET*; 4. *The Social Network*, about the rise of Facebook; 5. *Carrie*; 6. *Magnolia*; 7. *Casablanca*; Humphrey Bogart and Ingrid Bergman; 8. *Batman Begins*; Christian Bale; 9. *Adaptation* by Charlie Kaufman; 10. *The Hours*; Virginia Woolf; 11. *Kung Fu Panda*; 12. *The Witches of Eastwick*; Jack Nicholson; 13. *Harold and Kumar*; 14. *Catch Me If You Can*; 15. *Bill and Ted's Excellent Adventure*; *Bill and Ted's Bogus Journey*; 16. *The Blues Brothers*; 17. *Eraserhead*; 18. *The Italian Job*; 19. *Lawrence of Arabia*; Peter O'Toole; 20. Errol Flynn and Olivia de Havilland (*The Adventures of Robin Hood*)

Quiz 356. Discoveries and Inventions

1. (b) Thomas Burberry; 2. Wireless or radio; 3. *The Rocket*; 4. Michael Faraday; 5. Nylon (or Nylon 66 as it was first known; Carothers was a researcher at the DuPont plant but committed suicide two years before the 1939 launch); 6. Spectacles; 7. 1962; 8. He developed the cash register; 9. The microchip; 10. Radioactivity (the couple were Marie and Pierre Curie); 11. Texas Instruments; 1970s (1972); 12. Paper clip; 13. First electric traffic

light signal installed; 14. Steam engine (piston driven); James Watt, who added a condenser; 15. Electric guitars

Quiz 357. Kings and Queens

1. George VI; Bertie; 2. Edward I; 3. King James, who succeeded Elizabeth I in 1603, was James I of England and James VI of Scotland; 4. Empress Matilda, cousin of Henry's predecessor, King Stephen; 5. Doge (the closest equivalent in English is Duke); 6. House of Stewart (later Stuart); 7. Princess Beatrice; 8. Sweden; 9. Sandringham House; Balmoral Castle; 10. Nepal (his brother took the throne but has since ceded power to the people); 11. Belgium, Denmark, Liechtenstein, Luxembourg, Monaco, Netherlands, Norway, Spain, Sweden, United Kingdom

Quiz 358. Premier League

1. Stuart Ripley and Jason Wilcox; 2. Kevin Davies and Lee Bowyer; 3. Didier Drogba; 4. Robbie Keane; 5. Blackburn, Bolton and Fulham; 6. Cristiano Ronaldo, Roy Keane, Paul Scholes and Ryan Giggs; 7. Wigan Athletic; 8. Sunderland, in 2002–3 and 2005–6; 9. Steve Gibson; 10. Milan (Champions League, 2005); Alaves (UEFA Cup, 2001); West Ham (FA Cup, 2006); Man United (League Cup, 2003); 11. Chris Hughton; 12. Paul Jewell; 13. Martin O'Neill; 14. Peter Reid; 15. Steve Coppell; 16. Colin Todd; 17. Gary Megson; 18. Steve Coppell; 19. Mick McCarthy; 20. Jean Tigana

Quiz 359. Books

1. Brobdingnag; 2. A dead cat; 3. It was the fictional book asked for by an elderly gentleman in a famous advert for *Yellow Pages*, by which means he finally located a copy of the book; 4. Allan Quatermain; 5. All are narrated by novelists; 6. *The Sportswriter*; 7. *Fatherland*; C. J. Sansom; 8. Stephen Fry; 9. *The Curious Incident of the Dog in the Night-time*; 10. Scottish father and French mother; 11. It was written in (blank) verse; 12. Kabul, Afghanistan; 13. *The Lovely Bones* (Alice Sebold); 14. Sylvia Plath; 15. Biggles (James Bigglesworth), the flying ace; 16. *Adam Bede*; *The Mill on the Floss*; *Silas Marner*, *Romola*; *Felix Holt*, *Middlemarch*; *Daniel Deronda*

Quiz 360. General Knowledge

1. The Michelin Man; 2. She lip-synced at the opening ceremony to the Beijing Olympics; 3. Triceps (brachii); 4. Shoulders; 5. Berlin Wall; 6. The *Beezer* (it later appeared in the *Beano*); 7. Dylan Thomas; 8. Four; 9. Valley of the Kings; 10. Took a month off from her Parliamentary duties to appear on *I'm a Celebrity, Get Me Out of Here*; 11. Kim Wilde; 12. All scored nul points in Eurovision; 13. Colombia; 14. Max Bruch: *Violin Concerto No. 1* (1996–2001); Rachmaninov's *Piano Concerto No. 2* (2002–5 and 2011–12); Mozart's *Clarinet Concerto* (2006); Vaughan Williams's *The Lark Ascending* (2007–10); 15. Play Station Portable; 2005; 16. Vince Clarke; Dave Gahan, Alison Moyet and Andy Bell; the EP was 'Abbaesque'

Quiz 361. General Knowledge

Part 1

1   On 26 February 1987, the Church of England General Synod voted 'aye' to what?

2   Groceries; medical supplies; personal computers; books: which is the only one of these subject to value added tax?

3   Greenway on the River Dart is the old holiday home of which famous author?

4   The Italian city of Trieste is on the coastline of which body of water?

5   In 2005 David Cameron became leader of the Conservative Party; who was his main rival for the post?

6   Ben Nevis is Scotland's (and Britain's) highest peak; what is the second highest?

7   In which year was the Booker Prize first awarded: 1969, 1979 or 1989?

8   By what name is the sportswoman Philippa Nolan better known?

9   Where would you be most likely to find a stevedore?

10 Actresses Anna Chancellor and Helena Bonham Carter are both direct descendants of which British Prime Minister?

11 What is the remarkable feature of the refectory of the Santa Maria delle Grazie, a convent in Milan?

12 Which TV programme introduced the term 'omnishambles' into the political lexicon?

13 Which 1993 rap album was the fastest-selling debut album in the history of the Billboard chart and the first to go straight to no. 1?

14 What, in deference to the players' age, are allowed at many Seniors golf tournaments (but not the Senior Majors) that would not be permitted on the main tour?

Part 2

15 Who was the Hartlepool MP who was a major player in the rebranding of the Labour Party in the 1990s?

16 Which well-known publicist was behind a series of stories linking call-girl Pamella Bordes with various influential and high-ranking figures in 1989?

17 Which writer was once dubbed 'the queen of food porn'?

18 Which Bermondsey MP shares his name with a cricket TV analyst and writer?

19 Which former Bolton and Birmingham football player went on to become the world's highest paid trade union leader (reportedly)?

20 What's the link between the answers for Part 2?

Total Points: 20. Targets: Novice 10 Pro 15. Your Score:

Quiz 362. Monty Python

Here's something completely different . . .

Part 1

1   Which two of the Python team met at Cambridge University and worked on the *Footlights Revue* together? (2 pts)

2   Which 1966–7 TV show gave five of the six Pythons an opportunity to write or perform or both?

3   Who directed both *Life of Brian* and *The Meaning of Life*?

4   Which of the Monty Python team didn't appear live very often but was responsible for most of the design and animation?

5   Who provided much of the music for the Pythons, and appears as a minstrel in *Monty Python and the Holy Grail*?

6   How many episodes of the original Python TV series were made: twenty-four, thirty-two or forty-five?

7   Fear, surprise, ruthless efficiency and . . . What was the fourth main weapon of the Spanish Inquisition?

8   What was the team's first movie, essentially a longer version of the TV sketch show?

9   Which of the Python team wrote a fictional memoir called *A Liar's Autobiography*?

10 In *Life of Brian*, what do the people at the back during the sermon on the mount mistakenly hear as being blessed by the Lord?

Part 2

11 *Brazil* (1985) is acknowledged as Terry Gilliam's masterwork; which two equally odd films of his came out immediately before and after it? (2 pts)

12 In *Life of Brian*, who is Pontius Pilate's friend, who he introduces as a 'high wanking woman'?

13 Which two Pythons performed the famous 'Cheese Shop' sketch? (2 pts)

14 Gervaise Brook-Hampster is the winner of which contest in *Monty Python's Flying Circus*?

15 Who liked to wear 'silk stockings, suspendies and a bra'?

16 What is Brian's surname in *Life of Brian*? And what is the name of his girl-friend? What was the hummable theme tune which the crucified prisoners sing as an endpiece? Who wrote the song? (4 pts)

Total Points: 22. Targets: Novice 9 Pro 17. Your Score: [   ]

Quiz 363. Horror Movies

You might want to do this one behind the sofa

Part 1

1   What are the names of the three recurring characters in the *Scream* series directed by Wes Craven, played by Neve Campbell, Courteney Cox and David Arquette respectively? (3 pts)

2   What was the first (1988) film to feature the Lakeshore Strangler, usually just called Chucky?

3   What is the name of the deranged killer in the *Friday the 13th* series of movies? *Friday the 13th: The Final Chapter* wasn't – what number was it? (2 pts)

4   What was the 2009 return to the horror genre (starring Alison Lohman) for Sam Raimi after spending most of the previous decade making *Spider-Man* films?

5   'All work and no play makes Jack a dull boy'. What's the film?

6   *The Bird with Crystal Plumage*, *Suspiria* and *Tenebrae* are all films by which Italian horror master?

7   What was the name given to the film's masked killer in *The Texas Chainsaw Massacre*? What is the name of the only survivor of his rampage? (2 pts)

8   What was the independent horror studio founded in 1974 that lists cult classic *The Toxic Avenger* among its catalogue?

9   What was the English language name for the 1988 Dutch psycho-chiller *Spoorloos*?

10 Which film, banned for many years, was the 1972 directorial debut of Wes Craven?

Part 2

11 What was the first film in a new horror franchise (now numbering seven as of end of 2012) created by James Wan and Leigh Wannell, and starring Wannell, Cary Elwes and Danny Glover? (2 pts)

12 Which serial killer made his feature debut in *A Nightmare on Elm Street* (1984)?

13 Which British director made a foray into horror with *28 Days Later* (2002)? Which popular novelist, whose debut novel he directed two years before, wrote the screenplay? (2 pts)

14 Which 2007 cult horror hit was apparently shot on a home movie camera by two people experiencing domestic disturbances?

15 Which two killers faced off in a 2003 horror movie directed by Ronny Yu? (2 pts)

16 Which two actors met for the first time (they married four years later) on the set of the teen stalker movie *I Know What You Did Last Summer*? (2 pts)

17 Who made his first appearance in a 'grown-up' movie in 2012 in the creepy ghost story *The Woman in Black*? Who wrote the original book? (2 pts)

18 What is the full name of the boy who represents the Antichrist in *The Omen* (1976) and subsequent films in the series? Which Australian actor played the grown-up boy in *Omen III: The Final Conflict*? (2 pts)

19 After the release of F. W. Murnau's *Nosferatu* (1922), whose estate sued the studio for misappropriation of characters and story?

20 The opening of *Edward Scissorhands* is an homage to Hammer Horror and traditional *Frankenstein* movies; how was this reflected in the casting?

Total Points: 30. Targets: Novice 12 Pro 22. Your Score:

Quiz 364. British Politics

A section on the good men and true who run the country (except a lot of them are women and many of them are neither good nor true . . .)

Part 1

1   On 27 April 1992, who was elected by her fellow MPs as the first woman speaker of the House of Commons?

2   Which environmental campaigner was elected as Conservative MP for Richmond Park in the 2010 election?

3   Which new cabinet post created in 2005 took a significant chunk of responsibility away from the Home Secretary?

4   Who was the TV war correspondent who stood as an independent Parliamentary candidate in the 1997 election?

5   Which party provided the opposition to the Tories from the 1680s to the 1850s? Which party succeeded them as the other major party? (2 pts)

6   What post did Margaret Thatcher hold in Ted Heath's government before ousting him in a leadership contest?

7   What was unique about Mohammad Sarwar's election as MP for Glasgow Govan at the 1997 General Election?

8   What role did Nick Clegg adopt when the coalition government was formed after the 2010 General Election?

9   Which three leaders of the Conservative Party came and went while New Labour was in office between 1997 and 2010? (3 pts)

10 What was historic about Caroline Lucas's election as the MP for Brighton Pavilions at the 2010 election?

Part 2

11 Whose resignation as the local MP left the seat of Eastleigh, near South-ampton, vacant in 2013?

12 What was the name of the political party formed by Robert Kilroy-Silk in February 2005?

13 Cheltenham in 1966; Guildford in 1974 (twice); Torbay in 1987 and part of Sunderland ever since. What?

14 Which party went against political convention and put up a high-profile candidate against John Bercow, the current Speaker of the House at the 2010 election?

15 What benefit was introduced on 15 June 1945 and set at five shillings per child?

16 What title was held by Robert Gascoyne-Cecil, who served three terms as Conservative Prime Minister in the nineteenth century?

17 The four great offices of state in Britain are the posts of Prime Minister, Chancellor of the Exchequer, Home Secretary and Foreign Secretary; who are the only four women to have held any of these offices? (4 pts)

18 After his expulsion from the Labour Party, what London seat did George Galloway contest at the 2005 General Election? What is the common name for the loose association of socialists that he represents? Where did he pop up in 2012, winning a by-election by a landslide after resigning his seat in London in 2010? (3 pts)

19 Who (in January 2013) is the longest continuously serving female MP in Westminster, having served in Camberwell and Peckham since 1982?

20 The Scottish National Party holds a majority of the seats in the Scottish Assembly; how many seats did it win in the 2010 UK General Election?

Total Points: 28. Targets: Novice 11 Pro 21. Your Score: ▢

Quiz 365. Fine Art and Architecture

Another one for the culture vultures

Part 1

1   Which artist spent nine weeks living and working with van Gogh in Arles in 1888?

2   Who, late in life, painted a study of Isaac and Rebecca called *The Jewish Bride*?

3   Which sculptor's hit exhibition rocked the normally staid galleries of the Royal Academy in the latter part of 2009?

4   Which major twentieth-century figure, an official war artist in World War II, painted a portrait of Winston Churchill that was so detested by Churchill's wife that she destroyed it?

5   Rembrandt's *The Night Watch* is found in which famous Amsterdam museum?

6   Leon Battista Alberti, a fifteenth-century art scholar, is credited with writing the first Western book on which artistic discipline, which would distinguish Renaissance art from much of what had gone before?

7   Who was the sixteenth-century architect from Padua whose style became the presiding post-Renaissance form in Venetian architecture and spread its influence across the rest of Western Europe?

8   What term is given to a rounded vault or the ceiling of a dome?

9   The artist Giovanni Antonio Canaletto is most closely associated with scenes of Venice, his place of birth, and which other European city?

10 Which Impressionist painter had a penchant for painting dancers in an assortment of poses?

Part 2

Mix and Match: match the Turner Prize winner to their work – not necessarily the one that won the prize

1. Howard Hodgkin (1985), painting; 2. Martin Boyce (2011), installations; 3. Chris Ofili (1998), painting; 4. Damien Hirst (1995), installations; 5. Tomma Abts (2006), painting; 6. Anish Kapoor (1991), scuplture; 7. Rachel Whiteread (1993), sculpture; 8. Gilbert and George (1986), montage and performance; 9. Anthony Gormley (1994), sculpture; 10. Wolfgang Tillmans (2000), photography

a. *The Concorde Grid*; b. *Do Words Have Voices?*; c. *Snow Show*; d. *Angel of the North*; e. *Goodbye to the Bay of Naples*; f. *Jack Freak Pictures*; g. *ArcelorMittal Orbit*, London Olympic Park; h. *Lullaby Spring*; i. *The Holy Virgin Mary*; j. *Ert, Folme, Sebo* and *Ebe*

Your Workings:

Total Points: 20. Targets: Novice 8 Pro 15. Your Score:

Quiz 366. Horse Racing

If you don't know your nags, the odds are against you

Part 1

1   If you place a Yankee, how many races are you betting on, and how many bets have effectively been placed? (2 pts)

2   Who was the first jockey to ride a French horse to victory in the Derby for thirty-five years in 2011? What horse was he riding? (2 pts)

3   Who, in 1996, matched Lester Piggott's modern era record of eleven Champion Jockey titles?

4   Who was the 'voice of racing' on the BBC for fifty years from 1947 until his retirement?

5   What name is given to a race that is better quality than a handicap race but not good enough for a Group 3, the status accorded to a top domestic race (Group 2 being international and Group 1 being a classic)?

6   Which poetic horse trained by Aidan O'Brien won a unique fourth successive Ascot Gold Cup in 2009?

7   Which was the last horse (in 1970) to win the coveted Triple Crown of the 2,000 Guineas, the Derby and the St Leger? Which horse fell at the final hurdle (not literally, this is flat racing), finishing second to Encke in the St Leger in 2012? (2 pts)

8   The Sussex Stakes is always run at the end of July (occasionally very early August) as part of which summer racing festival?

9   Since the 1980–81 season, only four men have won the National Hunt Jockey's Championship for riding most winners in the season: who are those four men, and who has won the most titles? (5 pts)

10   What is the racing stable near Newmarket owned by Sheikh Mohammed? Who is the stable trainer there, recently banned for eight years for doping offences? Of which country is the Sheikh Prime Minister and Vice President? (3 pts)

Part 2

11   Which unbeaten Australian horse entered the Diamond Jubilee Stakes at Ascot in 2012, but nearly came a cropper when his complacent jockey eased up and was almost pipped on the line?

12   Which horse trained by Henrietta Knight won three successive Cheltenham Gold Cups between 2002 and 2004?

13   Which legendary grey won the 1989 Cheltenham Gold Cup, one of the all-time great National Hunt races, in conditions that worked against his front-running, clean jumping style?

14   If Crepello in 1957 was the first, and Teenoso in 1981 was the last, and there were seven others in between, what are we talking about?

15   Who was the last horse (1998–2000) to win three consecutive Champion Hurdles at Cheltenham?

16   Which was the last horse to win back-to-back Grand Nationals?

17   In 1981 a horse who had recovered from chronic leg soreness teamed up with a jockey who had recovered from testicular cancer to win the Grand National; who were the horse and rider? (2 pts)

18   Who are the only two horses to beat Red Rum in the Grand National? (2 pts)

19   What is the annual two-day (used to be one) festival of Grade 1 races in the US, held in the autumn at a prestigious track chosen by the committee?

20   Shergar; Shahrastani; Kris Kin; North Light; Workforce: what connects all these Derby winners?

Total Points: 31. Targets: Novice 12 Pro 23. Your Score:

Quiz 367. Science

More quarks, strangeness and charm

Part 1

1 If a rugby match finished 10010–1101 in binary, what would the score have been in conventional numerology?

2 A radioactive particle containing two neutrons and two protons is known as what?

3 Which German scientist gives his name to the way sound changes pitch in relation to the hearer according to direction and velocity?

4 What causes REM (rapid eye movements) during sleep in all animals and birds?

5 Whose Gaia hypothesis (1972), which stated that our biosystem is in fragile equilibrium, forms the basis for much environmental theory?

6 Which is the only type of rock that doesn't have silicon as its main component?

7 A parabola, an ellipse and a hyperbola are all types of what?

8 What was the subject matter of Rachel Carson's hugely influential 1962 book, *Silent Spring*?

9 *The Selfish Gene* and *The Blind Watchmaker* are books by which exponent of Darwinism?

10 What was the subject matter of Charles Messier's 1771 catalogue? (a) aquatic life (b) astronomical objects (c) known diseases and afflictions

Part 2

Mix and Match: match the scientific work to its author

1. *The Voyage of the Beagle*, 1845; 2. *Philosophiae Naturalis Principia Mathematica*, 1687; 3. *Dialogue Concerning the Two Chief World Systems*, 1632; 4. *De Humanis Corpora Fabrica* (*On the Fabric of the Human Body*), 1543; 5. *Ideas and Opinions*, 1954; 6. *The Interpretation of Dreams*, 1900; 7. *The Animal Kingdom, Distributed According to its Organisation*, 1817; 8. *Principles of Geology*, 1830–33; 9. *The Universe Around Us*, 1929; 10. *Species Plantarum*, 1753

a. Sir James Jeans; b. Albert Einstein; c. Sir Isaac Newton; d. Sigmund Freud; e. Georges, Baron Cuvier; f. Sir Charles Lyell; g. Charles Darwin; h. Galileo Galilei; i. Charles Linnaeus; j. Andreas Vesalius

Your Workings:

Total Points: 20. Targets: Novice 6 Pro 15. Your Score:

Quiz 368. General Knowledge

All about Billy, Willy and Williams

Part 1

1   What post did Bill Clinton hold from 1983 to 1992? (a) Mayor of Boston (b) Governor of Arkansas (c) Secretary of State

2   What was the surname of the Wild West sharpshooter known as Wild Bill?

3   Who is the highest earning female athlete of all time?

4   What was the irreverent 2003 Christmas comedy starring Billy Bob Thornton that became an instant cult hit?

5   What relation was Kaiser Wilhelm II, the last Emperor of Germany and King of Prussia, to the British Queen Victoria?

6   Which King of England and Scotland did William III (William of Orange) usurp in the Glorious Revolution of 1689?

7   Who was the owner of the chocolate factory in Roald Dahl's book, *Charlie and the Chocolate Factory*?

8   Who captained what was regarded as a poor England rugby union side to an unexpected Five Nations Grand Slam in 1980?

9   In which movie did Robin Williams earn a first Academy Award nomination playing a wartime DJ?

10 Hank Williams, born in 1923, is arguably country music's most influential early star; when did he die? (a) 1953 (b) 1973 (c) 2010

Part 2

11   Who wrote the screenplays for the movie versions of Tennessee Williams's plays *A Streetcar Named Desire* (1951) and *Cat on a Hot Tin Roof* (1958)?

12   What was will.i.am's first UK no. 1 hit single from 2012, and who featured on guest vocals on the no. 1 follow-up, 'Scream & Shout'? (2 pts)

13   Who had a lovely day in 1977 when he reached the top ten on both sides of the Atlantic?

14   Which Wolverhampton-born defender made over 160 appearances for Stockport County and has since captained a Premier League side and his country?

15   Who or what is Willy in the 1993 family film *Free Willy*?

16   What connects the first ten amendments to the US constitution to England's first football century-maker?

17   What two criteria do you have to fulfil to draw up your own Will and Testament? (2 pts)

18   In 2010, who played the Prime Minister's wife in *Ghost* and Ian Dury's wife in *Sex and Drugs and Rock and Roll*?

19   Which punk pop star and pin-up was born William Broad in 1955?

20   Which two movies earned Michelle Williams Academy Award nominations in 2010 and 2011? (2 pts)

Total Points: 23. Targets: Novice 12 Pro 17. Your Score:

Answers Quizzes 361–368

Quiz 361. General Knowledge

1. Ordination of women; 2. Personal computers; 3. Agatha Christie; 4. Adriatic Sea; 5. David Davis; 6. Ben Macdui; 7. 1969; 8. Pippa Funnell; 9. On the docks (it is the name for a dock worker); 10. Herbert Asquith; 11. Leonardo da Vinci's mural *The Last Supper*; 12. *The Thick of It*; 13. Snoop Doggy Dogg's *Doggystyle*; 14. Golf carts; 15. Peter Mandelson; 16. Max Clifford; 17. Nigella Lawson; 18. Simon Hughes; 19. Gordon Taylor, Chairman of the PFA; 20. All five were victims of illegal phone taps organized by journalists, as revealed during the 2010 story revolving around government spin doctor, Andy Coulson

Quiz 362. Monty Python

1. John Cleese and Graham Chapman (Idle was a year below them, Jones and Palin were at Oxford together); 2. *The Frost Report*; 3. Terry Jones (he and Terry Gilliam had co-directed *Holy Grail*); 4. Terry Gilliam; 5. Neil Innes; 6. Forty-five, over four series; 7. An (almost) fanatical devotion to the Pope; 8. *And Now for Something Completely Different*; 9. Graham Chapman; 10. Cheesemakers; 11. *Time Bandits* and *The Adventures of Baron Munchausen*; 12. Biggus Dickus; 13. Michael Palin as the shopkeeper and John Cleese as the customer; 14. The Upper-Class Twit of the Year; 15. Michael Palin's lumberjack in 'The Lumberjack Song' sketch?; 16. Cohen; Judith; 'Always Look on the Bright Side of Life'; Eric Idle

Quiz 363. Horror Movies

1. Sidney (Prescott), Gale (Weathers) and Dewey (Riley); 2. *Child's Play*; 3. Jason; it was the fourth film (there have been six more plus a spin-off and remake); 4. *Drag Me to Hell*; 5. *The Shining* (these are the words Jack Nicholson's mentally disintegrating character types out ad nauseam instead of writing his book); 6. Dario Argento; 7. Leatherface; Sally (Hardesty); 8. Troma Productions; 9. *The Vanishing*; 10. *The Last House on the Left*; 11. *Saw*; 12. Freddy Kruger; 13. Danny Boyle; Alex Garland; 14. *Paranormal Activity*; 15. Freddy (*Nightmare on Elm Street*) v. Jason (*Friday the 13th*); 16. Freddie Prinze and Sarah Michelle Gellar; 17. Daniel Radcliffe (Harry Potter); Susan Hill; 18. Damien Thorn; Sam Neill; 19. Bram Stoker (the film was a version of the *Dracula* story with names changed); 20. Vincent Price plays Edward's creator who perishes in the opening reel

Quiz 364. British Politics

1. Betty Boothroyd; 2. Zac Goldsmith; 3. Minister for Justice; 4. Martin Bell; 5. Whigs; Liberal Party; 6. Secretary of State for Education and Schools; 7. He became Britain's first Muslim MP, swearing the Oath of Allegiance on the Qur'an; 8. Deputy Prime Minister; 9. William Hague, Iain Duncan Smith and Michael Howard; 10. She was the first Green MP elected to the UK Parliament; 11. Chris Huhne; 12. Veritas; 13. First constituency to

declare in a general election; 14. The UK Independence Party; 15. Family allowance; 16. (3rd) Marquess of Salisbury (accept Lord Salisbury); 17. Margaret Thatcher (PM); Margaret Beckett (FS); Jacqui Smith (HS); Theresa May (HS); 18. Bethnal Green and Bow; Respect; Bradford West (accept Bradford); 19. Harriet Harman; 20. Six.

Quiz 365. Fine Art and Architecture

1. Paul Gauguin; 2. Rembrandt van Rijn; 3. Anish Kapoor; 4. Graham Sutherland; 5. Rijksmuseum; 6. Perspective; 7. (Andrea) Palladio; 8. Cupola; 9. London; 10. Edgar Degas; Mix and Match 1, e; 2, b; 3, i; 4, h; 5, j; 6, g; 7, c; 8, f; 9, d; 10, a

Quiz 366. Horse Racing

1. A Yankee is a multiplier bet; eleven bets in all, staked on 4 races (comprising six doubles, four trebles and an accumulator); 2. Mikael Barzalona; Pour Moi; 3. Pat Eddery; 4. Peter O'Sullevan; 5. A listed race; 6. Yeats; 7. Nijinsky; Camelot; 8. Glorious Goodwood; 9. John Francome, Peter Scudamore, Richard Dunwoody and A. P. McCoy; McCoy, who has won every title between 1996–7 and 2011–12, seventeen consecutive titles; 10. Godolphin; Mahmood al-Zarooni; United Arab Emirates; 11. Black Caviar; 12. Best Mate (never fell, never out of the first two in a race; 13. Desert Orchid; 14. Derby winners ridden by Lester Piggott; 15. Istabraq; 16. Red Rum in 1973 and 1974; 17. Aldaniti and Bob Champion; 18. L'Escargot and Rag Trade, who won in 1975 and 1976 respectively; 19. The Breeders' Cup (a series of classic races over varying distances culminating in the Breeders' Cup Classic); 20. All trained by Michael Stoute

Quiz 367. Science

1. 18–13; 2. An alpha particle; 3. Doppler; 4. Brain activity, or, more commonly, dreaming; 5. James Lovelock; 6. Limestone, where calcium is dominant; 7. Curve; 8. The environment; 9. Richard Dawkins; 10. Messier's *Objects* was a catalogue of all the astronomical bodies visible and identified at the time; Mix and Match 1, g; 2, c; 3, h; 4, j; 5, b; 6, d; 7, e; 8, f; 9, a; 10, i

Quiz 368. General Knowledge

1. (a) Governor of Arkansas, his home state; 2. Hickok; 3. Tennis star Serena Williams; 4. *Bad Santa*; 5. He was her grandson; 6. King James II; 7. Willy Wonka; 8. Bill Beaumont; 9. *Good Morning Vietnam*; 10. Williams died in 1953 before he was thirty, of a heart attack brought on by persistent substance and alcohol abuse; 11. Williams himself; 12. 'This Is Love'; Britney Spears; 13. Bill Withers; 14. Ashley Williams of Swansea City has also captained Wales, for whom he qualified by a familiar labyrinthine route; 15. An orca or killer whale; 16. The Bill of Rights is the name for those amendments and Billy Wright was the first England player to win 100 caps for England; 17. Being over the age of majority (legally an adult) and of sound mind (having all your marbles); 18. Olivia Williams; 19. Billy Idol; 20. *Blue Valentine* and *My Week with Marilyn*

Quiz 369. General Knowledge

Part 1

1   In which country did Hasselblad cameras originate?

2   The famous Oktoberfest takes place in which German city?

3   F, U and Th are the first three letters in which alphabet?

4   Who was the Deputy Chief Constable of Greater Manchester police who was finally cleared of corruption charges in 1986?

5   Who is the Hindi goddess of death and destruction, worshipped by the Thuggee sect, amongst others?

6   What form of currency was first used in a German hotel by an American Express customer in 1891?

7   A 96 metre statute to which leader was erected in Moscow in 1997?

8   Which British Museum artefact was smashed by dissident Irishman William Mulcahy in 1845?

9   What comes next in the sequence: London, Helsinki, Melbourne, Rome . . .?

10 Apart from Chicago, which other major US city lies on the shore of Lake Michigan, on the west side?

Part 2

11 Maimiti was the Tahitian wife of (a) mutineer Fletcher Christian (b) artist Paul Gauguin (c) cricketer Ricky Ponting?

12 Which word, suggestive of carefree and liberal living, comes from a historic kingdom which lay mainly in the western chunk of the Czech Republic?

13 Where can the islands of Guadeloupe, Montserrat and St Lucia be found?

14 What is the more common name for the prelate who holds the title of Bishop of Rome?

15 Anthony Blunt, denounced as a Soviet spy in 1979, held which role in the royal household in 1940–1972?

16 Paul Hardcastle went to no. 1 with '19' in 1985, one of the first major hits to be accredited to the song's producer; what was the subject matter?

17 Which is the oldest of these chocolate bars: Fry's Turkish Delight, Cadbury's Dairy Milk and Fry's Chocolate Cream? To within five years, when was Dairy Milk launched? What was Cadbury's second release, three years later, and why was it thus named? (4 pts)

Total Points: 20. Targets: Novice 10 Pro 15. Your Score:

Quiz 370. Rock and Pop Singles

Some top-forty flim-flam with a big head-scratcher to finish

1   Whose debut single 'Tik Tok' topped the US charts for nine weeks in 2010?
2   What was the 1976 single for which 1970s rock band Boston will always be remembered?
3   Which 1995 single gave Simply Red their only UK no. 1 hit?
4   'Spectrum (Say My Name)' was a 2012 no. 1 single in the UK, the first for which band?
5   What were Bruno Mars's first three UK solo singles, all of which went to no. 1? (3 pts)
6   Graham Nash and Elton John both sang backing vocals on which novelty hit, a huge Christmas no. 1 in 1968?
7   What was the Manchester label started by local TV personality in the late 1970s which released the debut album by Joy Division? What was the film about the label's rise and fall? (2 pts)
8   What was the first footballing no. 1, which topped the charts for the England World Cup Squad in the run-up to the 1970 tournament? And what was the much-loved song which matched it on its release for Euro 96? (2 pts)
9   What do million-sellers 'Last Christmas' (Wham), 'Moves Like Jagger' (Maroon 5 with Christina Aguilera) and 'Torn' (Natalie Imbruglia) have in common? (2 pts)
10   Which 2006 song entered the charts at no. 1 and became the first to do so on download sales only?
11   Name the ten artists who have had eight or more UK no. 1 hit singles to the end of 2012? (Note: there are four acts on seven who may have joined them by time of publication so here they are, just to avoid controversy: Eminem, Kylie Minogue, McFly and Rihanna; also, we have not included artists who had no. 1s as backing bands, such as the Shadows.) (10 pts)

Total Points: 25. Targets: Novice 10 Pro 19. Your Score: [   ]

Quiz 371. Sci-Fi Movies

Three sections on three classics

Part 1

Alien

1   What was Ridley Scott's 2012 'prequel' to the *Alien* movies?

2   What connects Lance Henriksen, Winona Ryder and Michael Fassbender in the *Alien* movies?

3   Apart from Ripley (Sigourney Weaver), who are the only two human survivors at the end of *Aliens* (1986)? (2 pts)

4   What is different about Ripley in the fourth film in the *Alien* franchise, *Alien Resurrection*?

5   Who played the prison doctor in *Alien 3*, and what was the name of the only prisoner to survive, played by Danny Webb? (2 pts)

Part 2

Blade Runner

6   The setting for *Blade Runner* is in which not-so-distant futuristic city? In which year is it set: 2019, 2035 or 2101? (2 pts)

7   What is the name of the manufacturer of the replicants in *Blade Runner*?

8   'I've seen things you people wouldn't believe. Attack ships on fire off the shoulder of Orion. I watched c-beams glitter in the dark near the Tannhäuser Gate. All those moments will be lost in time, like tears in rain.' So says Batty (Rutger Hauer) at the climax of *Blade Runner* – what does he say next?

9   Whose first important film role was as the replicant Pris in *Blade Runner*?

10   Who plays Gaff, the mysterious cop with a limp who rounds up Harrison Ford near the beginning of *Blade Runner*? What little quirk is he given to flesh out the character? (2 pts)

Part 3

Terminator

11 What is the name of the boy hunted by robots in *Terminator* and *Terminator 2: Judgment Day*? Who plays his mother in those two movies? Who plays his mother in the spin-off TV series? Which actors play the grown-up boy in the third and fourth instalments of the movie franchise? What model is the female Terminator in *T3: Rise of the Machines*? Who plays the protector-robot assigned to the boy and his mother and the TV series? What is the name of the boy's father, also a friend of his in the future, and who played him in the original movie? How many years elapsed between the release of the first and fourth movies? (10 pts, including 2 pts for the last question or 1 pt for being one year out)

Total Points: 24. Targets: Novice 10 Pro 18. Your Score: [   ]

Quiz 372. Science

No fiction, just the science

Part 1

1   What word is given to the part of a fraction above the line?

2   It used to be called quicksilver – by what name is this element now known?

3   What name is given to a positively charged electron?

4   What is defined as mass divided by density?

5   Jonas Salk's 1952 vaccine helped to reduce the suffering caused by which disease? (a) chickenpox (b) rubella (c) polio

6   What was first demonstrated in a Surrey quarry by scientist Arthur Nobel in 1867?

7   Galactose is one of the three main monosaccharides (simple sugars); what are the other two? (2 pts)

8   How many faces does a dodecahedron possess? And what 2D shape is each face? (2 pts)

9   What anomaly connects bromine and mercury?

10 In which direction would Foucault's pendulum turn if it were erected in Sydney, Australia?

Part 2

11 'Nitrogen fixing' converts nitrogen into which gas (chemical symbol NH3), useful for soil nutrition and food production?

12 Crick and Watson discovered that the DNA molecule was what particular shape?

13 If the ozone layer were to lie upon the surface of the earth, approximately how thick would it be: 3 mm, 3 cm or 3 m?

14 Where, specifically, did the first moon landing take place?

15 What is measured in Pascals?

16 The British overseas territory Gough Island, part of the Tristan da Cunha group, is a World Heritage wildlife site – in which ocean is it located?

17 How many human chromosomes are there: twelve, twenty-two or forty-six?

18 Under the same temperature and pressure all gases contain the same number of molecules; whose law? In which century did he postulate this? (2 pts)

19 In the system defined by Henry Moseley, what does the symbol Z signify in chemistry and physics?

20 Who developed the first commercial process for smelting pig iron to manufacture steel?

Total Points: 23. Targets: Novice 7 Pro 17. Your Score: ☐

Quiz 373. Food and Drink

A quick snack of ten questions followed by a mixed platter

Part 1

1   Disaronno is a brand synonymous with which liqueur?
2   Raisins are a dried variety of what fruit?
3   Seahorse won the prestigious OFM (*Observer Food Monthly*) award for best restaurant in 2012; in which seaside town is it situated?
4   What is the main ingredient in gnocchi, a type of Italian pasta?
5   Wines made by the producer Cono Sur come from which country?
6   What are Albariño, Verdejo and Grüner Veltliner?
7   Which confectionery brand is named after a play by J. M. Barrie?
8   In which northern town is Betty's original tea shop located?
9   Chiffonade is (a) cutting leafy vegetables into thin strips (b) a decorative edge to a sweet or savoury pie (c) cream or egg white beaten to a point just before it starts to form peaks?
10 What began as a magazine started by Marthe Distel but became a cookery school in 1895?

Part 2

Mix and Match: match the cookery book to its author

1. Yotam Ottolenghi; 2. Elizabeth David; 3. Eliza Acton; 4. Nigella Lawson; 5. Hugh Fearnley-Whittingstall; 6. Jamie Oliver; 7. Simon Hopkinson; 8. Madhur Jaffrey; 9. Nigel Slater; 10. Lorraine Pascal

a. *The Naked Chef*; b. *Modern Cookery for Private Families*; c. *River Cottage Cookbook*; d. *Plenty*; e. *The Kitchen Diaries*; f. *Baking Made Easy*; g. *How to Be a Domestic Goddess*; h. *Roast Chicken and Other Stories*; i. *French Provincial Cooking*; j. *Curry Nation*

Your Workings:

Total Points: 20. Targets: Novice 8 Pro 15. Your Score:

Quiz 374. Sport

All kinds of everything energetic

Part 1

1 What is the lightest boxing weight, initiated in 1987?

2 What name connects an unlucky Olympic equestrian from 2004 and a much-decorated British Olympian rider of a different sort?

3 What title is missing from the CV of tennis players John Newcombe, Jimmy Connors, Arthur Ashe, Pete Sampras, Boris Becker and Stefan Edberg?

4 Who did Amir Khan beat in 2011 to unify the WBA and IBF light welter-weight titles?

5 What took place for the first time at the Worcester Country Club, Massachusetts, in 1927?

6 Which racehorse retired in 2012 with well over £1 million in prize money and a record five wins in the King George VI Chase under his belt, as well as two Gold Cups?

7 Who was the inspirational quarterback when the San Francisco 49ers became the first team (in 1984) to win fifteen games in a modern NFL season?

8 Who was the McLaren designer at the heart of the Formula 1 spying scandal in 2006?

9 The Lakers took up residence in Los Angeles in 1960; where had they previously been based? (a) Minnesota (b) Portland (c) Charlotte

10 Anna Hemmings won five world titles in which sport? (a) canoeing (b) pistol shooting (c) showjumping

Part 2

11 Who broke the rugby league transfer record when he moved to Wigan in 1985? Which club banked the cash? (2 pts)

12 Who, in 1995, was both the British driver and the youngest ever driver to win the World Rally Driver's Championship? What make of car was he driving? Which driver has rendered the sport a little boring in recent years winning nine consecutive titles to 2012 in his Citroën? (3 pts)

13 Which four Irish or Northern Irish golfers have won Major tournaments in the twenty-first century (to the end of 2012)? (4 pts)

14 Which four players (men and women) have won all four Major tennis titles and an Olympic Gold medal in their career? Which of them did so in the same year? (5 pts)

Total Points: 24. Targets: Novice 10 Pro 18. Your Score:

Quiz 375. TV Drama

Straight questions followed by a couple of multi-parters

Part 1

1 What was the name of Bartlett's head of communications in *The West Wing* and who played his protégé Sam Seaborn? (2 pts)

2 Who is Major Richard D. Winters and who played him in an HBO series? (2 pts)

3 Which old TV face made a splendid return to form as the flaky businessman Jimmy Blake in Chancer (1990–91)? Who took a big leap up the acting pecking order after his lead part in the drama? (2 pts)

4 What was Jack Warner's job for twenty-six years from 1950?

5 *Wives and Daughters*, an adaptation of a Mary Gaskell novel, *Longitude*, the TV version of the Dava Sobel bestseller, and *Perfect Strangers*, a Steven Poliakoff drama, all won Best Actor BAFTAs for which actor in three consecutive years?

6 What was the profession of TV's Lovejoy and who played the part? Who was his aristocratic 'friend' who gets him out of a few scrapes? (3 pts)

7 Which TV cop star upped the ratings of a 1979 adaptation of Stephen King's *Salem's Lot*? Which horror director made sure it had the audience on the edge of their seats? (2 pts)

8 'Family' is a big thing for Tony Soprano; what are the names of his mother, wife and daughter? (3 pts)

9 Who is Jack Bauer?

10 Which influential drama was originally conceived as a comedy of class and manners by its creators, actresses Eileen Atkins and Jean Marsh?

Part 2

11 Which 2003 BBC drama starred John Simm as an investigative reporter called Cal McCaffrey? Who played his newspaper editor? And who was the compromised MP and personal friend whose life unravels during the series? Who starred in a competent but unnecessary American film version in 2009? (4 pts)

12 Who created *Cracker* and who played the lead role? In which city was it set? What was the main character's job? What was the subject matter of the programme's most memorable episode, 'To Be a Somebody', and for which actor did it provide a breakthrough role? (6 pts)

Total Points: 28. Targets: Novice 11 Pro 21. Your Score:

Quiz 376. General Knowledge

Part 1

1   Norwegian Roald Amundsen became the first man to reach which landmark in 1911?

2   Who removed former President Thabo Mbeki from office in a power struggle within the ANC?

3   In which European city would you find the Parthenon?

4   Which great poet became MP for Brackley in Northamptonshire in 1601?

5   France, Japan, Netherlands, Russia; which of these is not a member of the G8 group?

6   What do Fiona Volpe, Vesper Lynd and Miranda Frost have in common?

7   The modern state of Tanzania is a composite of which two older states, one an island the other on the mainland? (The modern name reflects the union.) (2 pts)

8   Which famous tune appeared in a work called *The Masque of Alfred* by eighteenth-century composer Thomas Arne?

9   What is the name of the rock band featuring actor Jack Black and Kyle Gass?

10 Everyone remembers Janet Jackson's 'wardrobe malfunction' during a 2004 televised performance; but at what event was she singing?

Part 2

11 Buddy Holly's song 'That'll be the Day' takes its title from an oft-repeated line in which classic western?

12 What did Jacob Golomb design in the 1920s to ease the discomfort caused by leather-belted shorts in the boxing ring?

13 Who was ordered to pay damages of $35 million after being found liable for murder in a much-covered civil court trial in 1997?

14 The Don (or Dnieper), the Kama and the Oka are all tributaries of which river, the longest that runs all or partly through Europe?

15 Which popular Scottish actor takes his stage name from a jazz saxophonist?

16 What did O and A levels replace in 1950? And what succeeded them in 1988? What does this acronym stand for? And what did Education Secretary Michael Gove propose introducing in 2012, before backing down when he realized no one supported him? (4 pts)

Total Points: 20. Targets: Novice 10 Pro 15. Your Score:

Answers Quizzes 369–376

Quiz 369. General Knowledge

1. Sweden (Gothenburg); 2. Munich; 3. Runic; 4. John Stalker; 5. Kali (the Thugs were a violent bandit-sect given to throttling their victims); 6. A traveller's cheque; 7. Peter the Great; 8. Portland Vase; 9. Tokyo (they are the venues for the Olympic Games after World War II); 10. Milwaukee; 11. Fletcher Christian, who settled on the island after mutinying aboard the *Bounty*; 12. Bohemian; 13. In the Caribbean; 14. The Pope; 15. Surveyor of the King's (and later Queen's) Pictures; 16. The average age of the combatants in the Vietnam War; 17. Fry's Chocolate Cream; 1905; Bournville; it was the part of Birmingham in which Cadbury's were based

Quiz 370. Rock and Pop Singles

1. Ke$ha; 2. 'More Than a Feeling'; 3. 'Fairground'; 4. Florence and the Machine; 5. 'Just the Way You Are', 'Grenade' and 'The Lazy Song'; 6. 'Lily the Pink' by the Scaffold (it was a reworking of a ballad about Lydia Pinkham, who marketed a tonic to relieve menstrual cramps in the nineteenth century); 7. Factory; *24-Hour Party People*; 8. 'Back Home'; 'Three Lions'; 9. All sold over a million copies but never made it to no. 1 in the UK (Wham were particularly unlucky, denied by the phenomenon of Band Aid); 10. 'Crazy' by Gnarls Barkley; 11. Elvis (twenty-one); the Beatles (seventeen); Cliff Richard (fourteen); Westlife (fourteen); Madonna (thirteen); Take That (eleven); Abba (nine); Spice Girls (nine); Rolling Stones (eight); Oasis (eight)

Quiz 371. Sci-Fi Movies

1. *Prometheus* (Scott disliked the film being referred to as a prequel. But it is. So there); 2. Their characters (Bishop, Call and David) are all androids; 3. Newt, the traumatized young girl found on the alien planet, and Corporal Hicks (Bishop also escapes but he is an android); 4. She is a clone of the original character with added alien DNA; 5. Charles Dance; Morse; 6. Los Angeles in 2019; 7. The Tyrell Corporation; 8. 'Time to die'; 9. Darryl Hannah; 10. Edward James Olmos; he makes tiny origami figures; 11. John Connor; Linda Hamilton; Lena Headey; Nick Stahl and Christian Bale; T-X; Summer Glau; Kyle Reese (Michael Biehn); twenty-five years (1984–2009)

Quiz 372. Science

1. Numerator; 2. Mercury; 3. Positron; 4. Volume; 5. (c) Salk was the man who formulated the polio vaccine; 6. Dynamite; 7. Glucose and fructose; 8. Twelve; pentagonal; 9. They are the only elements to take liquid form at ambient temperature; 10. Anti-clockwise; 11. Ammonia; 12. Double helix (a bit like a 3D figure of eight); 13. Only 3 mm, which is why it is so important that it is maintained and nurtured; 14. The Sea of Tranquility; 15. Pressure,

defined as Newtons per metre squared; 16. South Atlantic; 17. Forty-six (labelled A–G and then X and Y); 18. Avogadro; nineteenth century (1811); 19. Atomic number of an element; 20. (Henry) Bessemer

Quiz 373. Food and Drink

1. Amaretto; 2. Grapes; 3. Dartmouth in Devon; 4. Potato; 5. Chile; 6. White wine grapes; 7. Quality Street; 8. Harrogate; 9. (a) chiffonade is similar to julienne, but applied to leafy veg or herbs rather than firm matchsticks; 10. Cordon Bleu; Mix and Match 1, d; 2, i; 3, b; 4, g; 5, c; 6, a; 7, h; 8, j; 9, e; 10, f

Quiz 374. Sport

1. Straw-weight; 2. Hoy (Bettina, of Germany, lost the gold medal after an infringement was picked up on video after the event was over; and Chris, the great cyclist); 3. They all failed to win the French Open; 4. Zab Judah; 5. The Ryder Cup (golf); 6. Kauto Star; 7. Joe Montana; 8. Mike Coughlan; 9. (a) Minnesota; 10. Canoeing; 11. Ellery Hanley; Bradford; 12. Colin McRae; Subaru; Sebastien Loeb; 13. Padraig Harrington, Graeme McDowell, Rory McIlroy, Darren Clarke; 14. Andre Agassi, Steffi Graf, Rafael Nadal, Serena Williams; Graf won all five in 1988

Quiz 375. TV Drama

1. Toby Ziegler; Rob Lowe; 2. He is the head of Easy Company in *Band of Brothers*, and is played by British actor Damien Lewis; 3. Leslie Phillips; Clive Owen; 4. Playing *Dixon of Dock Green* on TV; 5. Michael Gambon; 6. Antiques dealer; Ian McShane; Lady Jane (Felsham); 7. David Soul; it was directed by Tobe Hooper (*The Texas Chainsaw Massacre*) and was genuinely scary; 8. Livia (a clear reference to the Machiavellian schemer in *I, Claudius*), Carmela and Meadow; 9. The main character in *24*, played by Kiefer Sutherland; 10. *Upstairs, Downstairs*; 11. *State of Play*; Bill Nighy; David Morrissey; Russell Crowe; 12. Jimmy McGovern; Robbie Coltrane; Manchester; criminal psychologist (accept profiler); the after effects of the Hillsborough disaster; Robert Carlyle

Quiz 376. General Knowledge

1. South Pole; 2. Jacob Zuma; 3. Athens; 4. John Donne; 5. Netherlands (the other five are Canada, Germany, Italy, US and UK); 6. They are all Bond girls who prove to be treacherous; 7. Zanzibar and Tanganyika; 8. 'Rule Britannia'; 9. Tenacious D; 10. The Super Bowl; 11. *The Searchers* (John Ford, 1956); it is the 'catchphrase' of John Wayne's character; 12. Elasticated waist shorts – boxer shorts; 13. O. J. Simpson; 14. River Volga; 15. Robbie Coltrane; 16. School Certificate; GCSEs; General Certificate of Secondary Education; English Baccalaureate Certificate

Quiz 377. General Knowledge

Part 1

1 What is the original Dutch meaning of the word 'Boer'?

2 Who resigned as President of Yugoslavia in 2000, after intense pressure from the electorate?

3 Which country has Angola, Zambia, Botswana and South Africa as its neighbours?

4 Which famous Elizabethan playwright was killed in a tavern brawl in Deptford before the age of thirty?

5 Which country has taken in the most refugees from Somalia since the civil wars started in the country? (a) UK (b) Ethiopia (c) Kenya (d) US

6 By what name is *Forbrydelsen* better known in the UK?

7 Which US President designed and lived in the plantation Monticello, and designed the University of Virginia, in Charlottesville, VA, near his birth town of Shadwell?

8 Which nineteenth-century composer is best remembered for his waltzes, which numbered well over 300 and included the famous 'Blue Danube Waltz'?

9 Who were *Back in Black* in 1980 and who had replaced Bon? (2 pts)

10 Which Olympic rower partnered Ben Fogle in rowing across the Atlantic – naked?

Part 2

11 Which two media personalities founded Comic Relief in 1985, working from an idea by Jane Tewson? (2 pts)

12 Whose value fell from $20 billion to $9 billion in the space of six months in 2012?

13 The French call it La Manche; what is it to the English?

14 Monica Ali's *Brick Lane* is set amongst the Muslim community in Tower Hamlets. Where was Monica Ali actually brought up? (a) Kensington Gardens (b) Peshawar (c) Bolton

15 In 2011 Adele had the bestselling single of the year in both the UK and the US, but the songs were different; which two songs and which way round? (2 pts)

16 Who was the first English manager to lift the European Cup?

17 In which city was actor John Barrowman (*Torchwood*) born: Chicago, Mumbai or Glasgow?

18 During the 2005 series of *Strictly Come Dancing*, which soap actress was heard being called Julie by her dance partner?

19 Who was the heaviest: Sylvester Stallone playing Rocky, John Prescott or Elvis Presley at the time of his death?

20 Which film director is Gwyneth Paltrow's godfather?

Total Points: 23. Targets: Novice 12 Pro 17. Your Score:

Quiz 378. TV Cops

More superior sleuths and their sidekicks

Part 1

1   Who played DI Jack Frost on TV in 1992–2010?

2   What was the fictional police station around which the stories of *The Bill* revolved?

3   Who teamed up as a hapless crime-solving duo in *The Detectives* (1993–7)? (2 pts)

4   Who played the lead role in the mellow whodunnit series *Hetty Wainthropp Investigates*?

5   Which three actresses have appeared as Jonathan Creek's sidekick? Who was Creek's boss, illusionist Adam Kraus, in the first series in 1997? (4 pts)

6   Which two actors played Dorothy L. Sayers's aristocratic sleuth Lord Peter Wimsey in the 1970s and 1980s respectively? What was the name of the complex female character played by Harriet Walter in the later series? (3 pts)

7   Who replaced John Nettles as the main policeman in *Midsomer Murders* in 2011? What relation is he to the original Tom Barnaby? (2 pts)

8   What is the name of the policewoman played by Helen Mirren in the *Prime Suspect* series? Who created the series? (2 pts)

9   Who played the head of Whitechapel's H Division, Inspector Reid, in the 2013 BBC drama *Ripper Street*? What is the name of the former Pinkerton agent who assists as his police surgeon? (2 pts)

10 Who created the dramas *The Sweeney*, *Juliet Bravo* and *The Chinese Detective*? Which long-running police show was created by his brother, Troy? (2 pts)

Part 2

CSI

11 Who was head of the *CSI* team at the start of the first series? Who eventually replaces him as shift leader? Who is the only original member of the team who has remained part of the team throughout the series? (3 pts)

12 Who has been the *CSI* team's main point of contact in the Las Vegas Police Department for the show's entire run (to the end of 2012)?

13 What is the name of the shift supervisor in the Miami strand of *CSI*? And what is the specialist skill of his deputy, Calleigh Duquesne? (2 pts)

14 Who plays Mac Taylor, head of the *CSI: NY* team? Which two of his subordinates got married during the show's run? (3 pts)

15 Which three songs by the Who provide the theme tunes to the three *CSI* strands? (3 pts)

Total Points: 32. Targets: Novice 13 Pro 24. Your Score: ☐

Quiz 379. Around Britain

Another cerebral road trip

Part 1

1 What stretch of water runs between the Pembrokeshire coast in Wales and the southeastern tip of Ireland?

2 What name is given to the spur of land between the Mersey estuary to the north and the mouth of the River Dee to the south? Which city lies further inland on the Dee? (2 pts)

3 The 170 metre Spinnaker Tower is at the centre of the rejuvenation of which city's harbour?

4 The enlightened industrialist Sir Titus Salt built good-quality accommodation for his workforce in the mid nineteenth century, creating a model village called Saltaire, now a tourist attraction; in which city can it be found?

5 Which major trunk road runs from Mansfield in Nottinghamshire to Bodmin in Cornwall (via Bristol)?

6 What is the Derbyshire home of the Duke of Devonshire, owned by the Cavendish family since 1549?

7 Which two rivers join to form the Humber estuary just south of Kingston upon Hull? (2 pts)

8 Moreton-in-Marsh, Stow-on-the-Wold and Chipping Campden are all market towns in which English National Park?

9 The city of Newcastle is often referred to as Newcastle upon Tyne to distinguish it from which other English town called Newcastle?

10 The town of Troon, with its famous golf course, looks out across the Firth of Clyde to which Hebridean island?

Part 2

We give the name of a county town and a county; you give us the name of the
county's biggest town

11 Trowbridge, Wiltshire
12 Northallerton, North Yorkshire
13 Bedford, Bedfordshire
14 Hertford, Hertfordshire
15 Chichester, West Sussex
16 Shrewsbury, Shropshire
17 Aberaeron, Ceredigion
18 Renfrew, Renfrewshire
19 Glenrothes, Fife
20 Coleraine, Londonderry

Total Points: 22. Targets: Novice 9 Pro 17. Your Score:

Quiz 380. History

Twelve quick-fire and a mull-it-over mammoth

Part 1

1   Who delivered the famous Gettysburg Address in 1863?

2   What did the recently formed United States buy from France in 1803?

3   The ancient civilizations of Babylon, Sumeria and Assyria all equate principally to which modern state? What was the old Greek name given to the lands they occupied? (2 pts)

4   Who, in 1930, landed *Gypsy Moth* in Darwin, Australia, to complete a solo flight across the world?

5   In 1822, Brazil announced its independence from which European country?

6   Who was proclaimed Lord Protector of England in 1653?

7   Edward of Lancaster (or Westminster) was the only heir to the English throne to die in battle when he was executed after the Battle of Tewkesbury in 1471; whose son was he, and who cemented his position on the throne with this victory? (2 pts)

8   Kullmann (1874) and Cohen-Blind (1866) both attempted to assassinate which nineteenth-century statesman?

9   Which war-leader made his final surrender to the US Army in 1886, effectively ending Apache resistance?

10 The Phoenician ports of Tyre and Sidon were located in which modern country? (a) Spain (b) Greece (c) Lebanon

11 Which Roman ruler and general continued the work of Paulinus and extended Roman rule in Britain into Wales, northern England and the lowlands of Scotland? (a) Hadrian (b) Agricola (c) Arcturus?

12 The old European region of Silesia is part of which modern country?

Part 2

13 For a few months between 1683 and 1685, eight previous or future English heads of state were alive simultaneously; who were they? (8 pts)

Total Points: 22. Targets: Novice 9 Pro 17. Your Score:

Quiz 381. Children's Books

Some you read yourself, some you might read to the kids

Part 1

1   What are the names of the two wicked aunties in Roald Dahl's *James and the Giant Peach*? (2 pts)

2   What is the name of the headmistress in Roald Dahl's *Matilda*?

3   What is the inn where Jim Hawkins is living at the start of *Treasure Island*?

4   *Peacock Pie* and *Bells and Grass* were poetry collections for children by which author?

5   Which author numbers *The Snow Queen* and *The Emperor's New Clothes* amongst his many folk tales?

6   What is the surname of the four children in C. S. Lewis's *The Lion, the Witch and the Wardrobe*?

7   Which children's book features three foundling sisters called Pauline, Petrova and Posy Fossil? Who is the author? (2 pts)

8   What was equally bonkers follow-up to *Alice's Adventures in Wonderland*?

9   Peter, Jack, Barbara, George, Pam, Colin and one other; who are they and who is missing? (2 pts)

10 Darrell Rivers is the main character in which series by Enid Blyton set in a Cornish boarding school?

Part 2

11 *Gangsta Granny* and *Ratburger* are bestselling kids books by which popular TV celebrity?

12 Which children's writer concerns himself with Percy Jackson and the modern-day antics of the Greek gods?

13 Theodor Geisel (1904–91) has sold millions of books for children under what name? (It is actually his middle name.)

14 What does Father Christmas need in Nicholas Allan's 2009 take on the Christmas tale, and where does he end up (alongside Sam and Captain Buckleboots) in Mark Sperring's 2012 story? (2 pts)

15 Starting with *Welcome to Dead House* in 1992, which series by R. L. Stine has become a standalone industry, with sixty-two books in the main series and countless spin-offs?

16 Who is the heroine of Philip Pullman's *His Dark Materials* trilogy? Where is she living at the start of the first book? Of what nature is her friend Iorek Byrnison? Who is her nemesis throughout the sequence? What is the title of the third and final instalment of the trilogy? (5 pts)

Total Points: 24. Targets: Novice 10 Pro 18. Your Score: [   ]

Quiz 382. Tennis

Test your all-court game

First Serve

Ten questions on Wimbledon

1   Who reached the 1974 Wimbledon final close to his fortieth birthday? Who ruined the dream by thrashing him in the final? (2 pts)

2   Apart from each other, who is the only player to beat one of the Williams sisters in a Wimbledon final?

3   Who won the 2007 Australian Open women's singles from a world-ranking position of 95?

4   Which former champion lost two Wimbledon men's singles finals to Bjorn Borg?

5   From whom did Gottfried von Cramm receive a phone call before the 1937 Wimbledon men's singles final? Which US player beat him in that match? (2 pts)

6   Which Wimbledon winner (1925 and 1928) is best-known nowadays as a clothing brand?

7   Which player was at the centre of the controversy that resulted in the Wimbledon players' strike of 1973?

8   Who was the stylish Brazilian who won three Wimbledon ladies' singles titles between 1959 and 1964?

9   Who, in 1997, became the youngest winner of the Wimbledon ladies' singles title in the professional era? Which veteran did she beat in the final? (2 pts)

10   Which tennis player, born 1981, was the last Australian to win the Wimbledon men's singles title?

Second Serve

11   Who, in 2011, became the first Chinese player to win a Grand Slam tennis
      title? Which title did she win? And who was the reigning champion whom
      she beat in the final? (3 pts)

12   Who were the two singles players when Great Britain last reached the
      Davis Cup final in 1978? (2 pts)

13   In 1992, eight years after his last singles title, John McEnroe came back
      and won the Wimbledon men's doubles with the 1991 singles champion;
      who was his partner? And with whom did he win seven Grand Slam doubles
      titles? (2 pts)

14   Which specialist doubles player has performed the remarkable feat of
      winning all four Grand Slam titles with different partners between 1999
      and 2012?

15   Whose four Grand Slam titles between 2004 and 2012 comprised, unusu-
      ally, one of each title, a career Grand Slam?

16   Who was the first woman tennis player to win all four major titles in one
      year?

17   What are the four venues for the Grand Slam tournaments in professional
      tennis? (4 pts)

Total Points: 27. Targets: Novice 11 Pro 20. Your Score: ☐

Quiz 383. True Crime

Part 1

1   Of whose murder in London, six years earlier, were Danny and Rickie Preddie convicted in August 2006?

2   Thomas Jennings was found guilty of murder in Illinois in 1911; he was the first man convicted using what type of evidence?

3   Why was Vicky Pryce on trial in 2013, and why did the trial have to start again at the end of February? (2 pts)

4   What nickname was attached by the tabloids to the serial killer Stephen Griffiths? (a) the motel murderer (b) the crossbow cannibal (c) the Strathclyde strangler

5   Which US citizen won an appeal against a 2007 murder conviction in Perugia, Italy, in 2011?

6   Who notoriously supplied corpses to Dr Knox's laboratory in Edinburgh in the late 1820s?

7   Michael Gordon Peterson was jailed for seven years in 1974 but has since been free for only sixty-nine days after a series of confrontations and violent protests in prison; to what did he change his name whilst trying to take up a career as a bare-knuckle boxer during his brief freedom?

8   William Calcraft, John Ellis and Albert Pierrepoint all killed people by which method?

9   Who were Mary Ann Nichols, Annie Chapman, Liz Stride, Kate Eddowes and Mary Jane Kelly?

10   If a victim exsanguinates, how do they die?

Part 2

11   Where were the McCann family taking their holiday when their daughter Madeleine disappeared in 2007?

12   Clifford Olson was convicted of the serial murder of eleven children in the 1980s in which country?

13   For what was Victor Conte, head of BALCO, jailed in 2005? (a) fixing NBA basketball matches (b) bribing officials during the lobbying process for hosting the Olympic Games (c) distributing illegal steroids to a number of high profile athletes

14   Often misinterpreted to be a name for any Italian crime syndicate, the Mafia are specific to which locality?

15   Who was guilty of the murder of fifteen young men in north London between 1978 and 1983?

16   Who was executed in 1989 for the rape and murder of (at least) thirty women across several US states over a period of about twenty years?

17   Folsom State Prison, made famous by the Johnny Cash song, is in which US state? In which other prison in the same state did Cash give an equally famous 1969 concert? (2 pts)

18   Which serial killer and cannibal was beaten to death by a fellow prisoner in 1994, two years into a multiple life sentence?

19   John Wayne Gacy raped and murdered over thirty teenage boys and hid the bodies in the crawl space of his home in which US city?

20   Which court's decisions are binding on all other courts within English law, apart from the ultimate arbiter, the Supreme Court?

Total Points: 22. Targets: Novice 9 Pro 17. Your Score: [   ]

Quiz 384. General Knowledge

Clues to twenty people who died in 2010 and 2011

Part 1

1   Designer who started as a trainee tailor at Anderson and Sheppard and became the shockmeister of British fashion
2   Opposition leader who had a rough time at the 1983 General Election
3   She had an *Awfully Big Adventure* in 1989
4   He wasn't Spartacus and he liked his Sugar Cane
5   The man who made his mark with Pistols
6   Racy writer?
7   A small funny man who was big in Albania
8   Brother and sister of acting dynasty
9   Master of French naturalist cinema
10 The voice of boxing

Part 2

11 The alternative Mrs Thatcher (aged eighty-seven)
12 Dishevelled TV cop (aged eighty-three)
13 Boxing knight (aged seventy-six)
14 Clinical founder (aged ninety-three)
15 Doctor's assistant (aged sixty-five)
16 Famously buttered actress (aged fifty-eight)
17 Toeless spinner (aged seventy-eight)
18 Bond scorer (aged seventy-seven)
19 Fast footballer? (aged forty-two)
20 The Big Apple (aged fifty-six)

Total Points: 20. Targets: Novice 10 Pro 15. Your Score:

Answers Quizzes 377–384

Quiz 377. General Knowledge

1. Farmer; 2. Slobodan Milošević; 3. Namibia; 4. Christopher Marlowe; 5. Kenya has absorbed over 45 per cent of the 678,000 Somalian refugees (Britain has taken just under 5 per cent); 6. *The Killing* (*Forbrydelsen* is the original Danish title, and actually means crime); 7. Thomas Jefferson; 8. Johann Strauss the Younger; 9. AC/DC; Brian Johnson; 10. James Cracknell; 11. Richard Curtis and Lenny Henry; 12. Mark Zuckerberg, after the disastrous Facebook flotation; 13. The English Channel; 14. (c) Bolton; 15. 'Someone Like You' (UK) and 'Rolling in the Deep' (US); 16. Bob Paisley with Liverpool in 1977; 17. Glasgow (his family emigrated to Illinois when he was nine); 18. Patsy Palmer (her real name is Julie Harris); 19. Presley at 16 st 8 lb; 20. Steven Spielberg

Quiz 378. TV Cops

1. David Jason; 2. Sun Hill; 3. Jasper Carrott and Robert Powell; 4. Patricia Routledge; 5. Caroline Quentin; Julie Sawalha; Sheridan Smith; Anthony Head; 6. Ian Carmichael (1970s) and Edward Petherbridge; Harriet Vane; 7. Neil Dudgeon; he is a younger cousin; 8. DCI (later DCS) Jane Tennison; Lynda La Plante; 9. Matthew Macfadyen; Homer Jackson (accept Matthew Judge, his real name); 10. Ian Kennedy Martin; *Z-Cars*; 11. Gil Grissom; Katherine Willows; Nick Stokes; 12. Captain Jim Brass; 13. Horatio Caine; ballistics; 14. Gary Sinise; Danny (Messer) and Lindsay (Monroe); 15. 'Who Are You', 'Won't Get Fooled Again' and 'Baba O'Riley'

Quiz 379. Around Britain

1. St George's Channel; 2. The Wirral; Chester; 3. Portsmouth; 4. Bradford; 5. A38; 6. Chatsworth; 7. River Trent and River Ouse; 8. Cotswolds; 9. Newcastle under Lyme; 10. Arran Isle; 11. Swindon; 12. Harrogate; 13. Luton; 14. Hemel Hempstead; 15. Crawley; 16. Telford; 17. Aberystwyth; 18. Paisley; 19. Kirkcaldy; 20. Londonderry

Quiz 380. History

1. Abraham Lincoln; 2. The state of Louisiana; 3. Iraq; Mesopotamia; 4. Amy Johnson; 5. Portugal; 6. Oliver Cromwell; 7. Henry VI; Edward IV (of York); 8. Otto von Bismarck; 9. Geronimo; 10. (c) Lebanon; 11. (b) Agricola; 12. Poland; 13. Charles II was King and James II was his heir apparent; William and Mary were waiting in the wings, as was Mary's sister, Anne; George I had just had a son, who would become George II. Richard Cromwell, nominated by his father as Lord Protector and briefly in office, was also alive, having been spared on the restoration of the monarchy as he was not signatory to Charles I's death warrant

Quiz 381. Children's Books

1. Spiker and Sponge; 2. Miss Trunchbull; 3. Admiral Benbow; 4. Walter de la Mare; 5. Hans Christian Andersen; 6. Pevensey; 7. *Ballet Shoes* by Noel Streatfeild; 8. *Through the Looking Glass*; 9. Enid Blyton's Secret Seven; the missing one is Janet, Peter's sister; 10. *Malory Towers*; 11. David Walliams; 12. Rick Riordan; 13. Dr Seuss; 14. In 2009 Santa needed a wee, and he was on the naughty step in 2012; 15. *Goosebumps*; 16. Lyra Belacqua; Jordan College, Oxford; an armoured bear (Panzerbjorn); Mrs Coulter; *The Amber Spyglass*

Quiz 382. Tennis

1. Ken Rosewall; Jimmy Connors; 2. Maria Sharapova beat Serena in 2004; 3. Serena Williams (her ranking had plummeted after a lengthy injury break); 4. Jimmy Connors; 5. Adolf Hitler; Donald Budge; 6. (René) Lacoste; 7. Niki Pilić; 8. Maria Bueno; 9. Martina Hingis; Jana Novotna; 10. Lleyton Hewitt; 11. Li Na; French Open; Francesca Schiavone; 12. John Lloyd and Chris 'Buster' Mottram; 13. Michael Stich; Peter Fleming (poor man's ears are still echoing to McEnroe's tirades); 14. Leander Paes (with Mahesh Bhupathi, Martin Damm, Lukas Dlouhy and Radek Stepanek; 15. Maria Sharapova; 16. Maureen 'Mo' Connolly; 17. Wimbledon; Roland Garros (French Open); Flushing Meadow (US Open); Melbourne Park (Australian Open)

Quiz 383. True Crime

1. Damilola Taylor; 2. Fingerprints; 3. She is Chris Huhne's ex-wife, on trial for perjury after taking a speeding fine meant for the former minister; the judge was forced to disband the initial jury after they showed no grasp of what was required of them; 4. (b) Crossbow Cannibal; 5. Amanda Knox; 6. Burke and Hare; 7. Charles Bronson, supposedly the most violent prisoner in Britain; 8. Hanging (they were all official government hangmen in the UK); 9. The victims of the unidentified killer, Jack the Ripper; 10. They bleed to death, or bleed out as the TV shows like to call it; 11. Portugal; 12. Canada (British Columbia); 13. (c) he was the man at the centre of the controversy that saw Marion Jones returning her Olympic medals won under the influence of his products; 14. Sicily; 15. Dennis Nilsen; 16. Ted Bundy; 17. California; San Quentin; 18. Jeffrey Dahmer; 19. Chicago; 20. Court of Appeal

Quiz 384. General Knowledge

1. Alexander McQueen; 2. Michael Foot; 3. Beryl Bainbridge; 4. Tony Curtis; 5. Malcolm McLaren; 6. Dick Francis; 7. Norman Wisdom; 8. Corin and Lynn Redgrave; 9. Eric Rohmer; 10. Harry Carpenter; 11. Janet Brown, impressionist; 12. Peter Falk, who played Columbo; 13. Henry Cooper; 14. Betty Ford; 15. Elisabeth Sladen who played Sarah Jane in *Doctor Who*; 16. Maria Schneider, Brando's co-star in *Last Tango in Paris*; 17. Fred Titmus, Middlesex and England spinner; 18. John Barry, film composer; 19. Gary Speed, manager of Wales; 20. Steve Jobs

Quiz 385. General Knowledge

Quotes from the learned and not so learned

1   'The art of medicine consists in amusing the patient while nature effects the cure.' Which great French thinker is not impressed by the medical profession?

2   'I haven't played to my full potential yet. And when that happens it will just be me and Tiger.' Whose extravagant and tongue-in-cheek claim?

3   'But I'll tell you – you can tell him now if you're watching it – we're still fighting for this title, and he's got to go to Middlesbrough and get some-thing, and . . . And I tell you honestly, I will love it if we beat them – love it.' Who is losing it in front of the cameras and what happened next? (2 pts)

4   'It is a truth universally acknowledged, that a single man in possession of a good fortune, must be in want of a wife.' From which famous work of liter-ature (title and author, please)? (2 pts)

5   'Let the women footballers play in more feminine clothes like they do in volleyball. They could, for example, have tighter shorts.' Which figure of authority?

6   'I love wearing them to Elton John's annual bash because mine are nicer than his. I'm a Chevalier, a knight, a sheikh and a Prince Tuareg in Western Sudan. I look like Idi Amin when I've got them all on.' Who's the medallion man?

7   'You can throw all those medals in the bin, because you won them all by cheating.' Who's the anti-medallion man and to whom is he talking? (2 pts)

8   'I didn't fight to get women out from behind the vacuum cleaner to get them on to the board of Hoover.' Which early feminist bemoans the misdirection of the movement?

9   'Our performance today would not have been the best-looking bird but at least we got her in the taxi. She weren't the best-looking lady we ended up taking home but she was pleasant and very nice, so thanks very much and let's have a coffee.' Which quixotic football manager?

10 'He moves like a parody between a majorette girl and Fred Astaire.' Truman Capote on which iconic rock star?

11 'I never forget a face, but in your case I'll be glad to make an exception.' An apocryphal quote from which movie humorist?

12 'What was it that first attracted you to millionaire Paul Daniels?' Ouch! Who is Mrs Merton winding up this time?

13 'Her manner has been described as that of a dominatrix, but with her prac-tical cropped hair and glasses, she is more like a school librarian in a black leather coat. Her insults are innocuous.' Which British TV presenter doesn't intimidate the *New York Times*?

14 What did Oscar Wilde describe as 'the unspeakable in pursuit of the inedible'?

15 'Any American who is prepared to . . . should automatically, by definition, be disqualified from ever doing so.' What heinous act was Gore Vidal talking about?

Total Points: 18. Targets: Novice 9 Pro 14. Your Score:

Quiz 386. Movies

Straightforward all-round quiz

Part 1

1 In Brian De Palma's *Blow Out*, what is the profession of John Travolta's lead character?

2 What was the cult 1971 animation about the antics of a sex-hungry cat?

3 *The Delinquents* (1989) was the much derided feature film debut of which actress cum pop star?

4 *Ma Nuit avec Maude* (*My Night with Maud*, 1969) was the third of six 'moral tales', a series of linked-but-unconnected films by which French master?

5 Which movie was the first to show a woman in her bra and slip, and also the first to show someone flushing a toilet?

6 In a purple patch in the early 1970s director William Friedkin followed up an Oscar-winning crime movie with a box office record-breaking horror movie; what were the two films? (2 pts)

7 German-born Carl Laemmle was one of the founders and then the premier producer for which of the major US film studios?

8 If Frank Sinatra and Laurence Harvey in 1962 become Denzel Washington and Liev Schreiber in 2004, what is the movie and who does Angela Lansbury become? (2 pts)

9 Which pre-war Hollywood icon was taken to the US by German director Josef von Sternberg?

10 Which chef made a cameo appearance in the woeful 2011 movie, *Love's Kitchen*?

Part 2

11 On what day of the year is *Picnic at Hanging Rock* set?

12 What song plays in contradictory fashion at the beginning of *Apocalypse Now*?

13 Who provides the voice for the reptilian Rango in the 2011 film of that name?

14 Who directed and starred in the cult biker movie from 1969, *Easy Rider*?

15 *Faster Pussycat Kill! Kill!* was a 1965 B-movie typical of the works of which cult director?

16 Which two actors were nominated for Academy Awards in the 1972 movie, *Sleuth*, playing virtually the only roles? Who starred in a 2007 remake? Which film from three years previously did this casting echo? (5 pts)

Total Points: 22. Targets: Novice 11 Pro 17. Your Score:

Quiz 387. Arts and Culture

Ten quickies and a Mix and Match section

Part 1

1 Which male singing voice comes between the high tenor range and the deep bass?

2 L. S. Lowry lived in which industrial city?

3 Which successful art fair, with a different curator each year, was first held in Regent's Park in 2003?

4 Who made a sculpture of the writer Voltaire in 1777 and lends her name to a permanent exhibition of sculptures?

5 Who drew the swallows tattooed on Kate Moss's back? (a) Pete Doherty (b) Banksy (c) Lucian Freud

6 In 2009, Albert Uderzo celebrated the fiftieth anniversary of which character, his most famous creation?

7 If you were dancing to music by Ástor Piazzolla, what dance would you most likely to be performing?

8 What would be the difference between a production of *La Traviata* by the Royal Opera and the English National Opera?

9 What is the difference between crescendo and fortissimo in classical music instruction?

10 Whose symphonies have nicknames that include *Winter Daydreams*, *Polish* and *Pathétique*?

Part 2

Mix and Match: match the artist to their speciality

1. Nicholas Hytner; 2. Vladimir Horowitz; 3. Julian Bream; 4. Cleo Laine; 5. Vaclav Nijinsky; 6. Colin Davis; 7. Elisabeth Schwarzkopf; 8. Itzhak Perlman; 9. Jean Sibelius; 10. Joan Plowright

a. Ballet dancer; b. Violinist; c. Conductor; d. Pianist; e. Opera singer; f. Composer; g. Jazz singer; h. Director; i. Classical guitarist; j. Actress

Your Workings:

Total Points: 20. Targets: Novice 8 Pro 15. Your Score:

Quiz 388. Pets

It's raining cats and dogs in this one

1   Cornish Rex, Egyptian Mau and Russian Blue are all types of what?

2   What type of creature was the king's advisor Zazu in Disney's *The Lion King*?

3   What was the name of the pet monkey owned by Michael Jackson?

4   What was the name of the White House cat adopted by the Clinton family during Bill's time in office?

5   Shubunkin, Lionhead, Dowager Princess, Fantail; three of these are popular aquarium goldfish species – which is the odd one out?

6   What was set up in Holloway in 1860 by Mary Tealby and relocated to its current site south of the river in 1871?

7   Where has Crufts Dog Show been held since 1991? And in which decade was the show first held (at the Royal Agricultural Hall, Islington, London): the 1840s, 1890s or 1940s?

8   In which classic Disney animation are the principal characters aided by a cat called Sergeant Tibbs?

9   What cat breed comes in red point, brown point and seal point?

10 Which animated movie franchise features a zebra called Marty and a hippopotamus called Gloria?

11 What absurdly misnamed household pet is a rodent of the Caviidae family originally native to the Andes in South America?

12 A tortoise belonging to the royal family of Tonga lived to what ripe old age? (a) 114 (b) 155 (c) 188

13 What is the PDSA?

14 In which year was the RSPCA founded: 1824, 1875 or 1902?

15 What was the pet owned by the Courtauld family who was given the run of their house, Eltham Palace, during the 1930s? (a) a leopard (b) a boa constrictor (c) a lemur

Total Points: 15. Targets: Novice 6 Pro 11. Your Score:

Quiz 389. Military History

Some military engagements – a quick quiz and a couple of multi-parters

Part 1

1   The great general Hannibal, scourge of the Romans for almost twenty years, was a commander in the armies of which North African city-state?

2   Who invaded Cyprus in 1974?

3   Which famous naval battle took place to the east of Cadiz in 1805?

4   Which city was the focal point of a twelve-month siege between September 1854 and 1855 during the Crimean War?

5   Which country did the United Kingdom attack in 1807 in an effort to stop its large fleet allying with Napoleon Bonaparte? (a) Portugal (b) Denmark (c) Greece

6   Which major French duchy was allied to England for much of the Hundred Years War?

7   What is the honorific often applied to the 1st Infantry Division of the US Army, its oldest fighting division invariably made up of seasoned veterans?

8   Who joined World War I on the Allied side in 1916 after the Allies offered them Transylvania and other Hungarian territories in exchange for renouncing neutrality?

9   Where were the German armoured cruisers *Scharnhorst* and *Gneisenau* tracked and sunk during World War I? (a) Falkland Islands (b) Mediterranean (c) Baltic Sea

10 After Wellington's lines failed to break as anticipated, the late arrival of the Prussian forces under which general sealed the fate of Napoleon's army at the Battle of Waterloo?

Part 2

11 Where in Northamptonshire did the battle that finally decided the English Civil War take place in 1645? Who was the Lord General of the Parliamentarian forces, and what was the name of his well-trained army? Who led the King's Royalist army? What relation was he to King Charles? (5 pts)

12 What was the battle that saw the death of US Civil War hero, General George Custer? In which state does the site of the battle lie? What was the fighting unit commanded by Custer? Which Indian tribe were allied with the Sioux in the battle? Who was the major whose attack on the Indian camp precipitated the battle? (5 pts)

Total Points: 20. Targets: Novice 8 Pro 15. Your Score:

Quiz 390. Football

A general quiz

Part 1

1　What do Abercorn, Cambuslang, Cowlairs, Third Lanark and Vale of Leven have in common?

2　Who played as an emergency centre-half for Barcelona in the 2011 Champions League final against Manchester United?

3　Who was the first female managing director of a Premier League club?

4　Which England international played in four divisions of the English league for Watford?

5　Which manager, later famous for an even more impressive achievement, led Ipswich Town to their first and only league title in 1962?

6　Who were Manchester United's opponents when David Beckham lobbed the keeper from the halfway line in 1996, and who was the embarrassed goalkeeper? (2 pts)

7　26–12–0 in 2003–4. Explain.

8　In 1982 Bristol City sold their centre forward to Newcastle for £100,000; Newcastle stumped up the cash so City avoided a winding-up order, and promptly sold the player to Birmingham the next day. Who was the future England centre forward?

9　In 1995 Arsenal spent £7.5 million on a player, and Liverpool spent £8.5 million. One was a triumph, one a disaster. Who were the players and the clubs they moved from? (4 pts)

10　Which three English clubs have been managed by former England manager Sven-Göran Eriksson? (3 pts)

Part 2

11　Which member of the Southampton side that won the 1976 FA Cup final collected his second winner's medal?

12　Why did over 4,000 English football fans attend the French Cup final in 2000?

13　Which three managers (2000–2001, 2009–10 and 2011–12) have won the Manager of the Season trophy for the Premier League without actually winning the title? (3 pts)

14　In 2000, 2001 and 2002 Manchester City were promoted, relegated and promoted again: which two managers oversaw this ding-dong era? (2 pts)

15　Which early Premier League import was a hit at Spurs, scoring twenty-one goals in his first season in 1994–5?

16　When South Africa made their debut in the World Cup in 1998, their centre-back pairing both had Premiership experience: who were they and with which clubs were they registered? (4 pts)

17　Who was Swansea City's top scorer in their first season in the Premier League in 2011–12? Whose arrival the following summer saw him resigned to a role mainly as a substitute? (2 pts)

18　Who was the first Italian player to win a Premier League title?

19　Which three Norwegian players are the only ones from their country to win the Premier League title? (They won twelve titles between them.) (3 pts)

20　The 2012 Scottish Cup final was only the second (and first since 1896) contested between which two rivals? (2 pts)

Total Points: 36. Targets: Novice 14 Pro 27. Your Score: [　　　　　　]

Quiz 391. Trivia

Part 1

1   Under what modelling name was Leslie Hornby very much the It-girl of the Swinging Sixties?

2   Socialite – actor – producer – singer – actor (twice) – politician – construction worker. Explain this sequence.

3   Where was Prince Harry on holiday when the infamous pictures of him naked appeared in the press? What game had he and his friends been playing? (2 pts)

4   What are the names of Liam Gallagher's ex-wives, both familiar figures in the entertainment world? (2 pts)

5   Berengaria, the Princess of Navarre, was the wife of which English king, but never visited England as queen?

6   Mariah Carey married the president of which record label, her later divorce leading to strained relationships with the label?

7   Actress Pauline Collins has been married since 1969 to her fellow actor from the original *Upstairs Downstairs*; what is his name?

8   Which model has dated both Anthony Kiedis of Red Hot Chili Peppers and Seal?

9   Tracey Thorn was the singer in Everything but the Girl, but who was both her life and musical partner?

10 Which TV presenter has given birth to two children by fellow presenter Vernon Kay?

Part 2

11 In which city was the Mayor of London, Boris Johnson, born?

12 Who married and adored the woman known as Betty Joan Perske in 1945 until death parted them in 1957? (a) Clark Gable (b) David Niven (c) Humphrey Bogart. By what name was Betty Joan Perske better known? (2 pts)

13 Which two men who died in 2012 had a name in common (one was a British hairdresser, the other a US writer, screenwriter and lifelong Democrat)? (2 pts)

14 Warren Beatty, such a Lothario in his youth, has been married to which actress since 1992?

15 June Carter was the wife of which country singer?

16 With which other rock star did Jerry Hall have a relationship before her longer one with Mick Jagger?

17 Of the classic Ramones line-up of Johnny, Joey, Dee Dee and Tommy, which of the four is still alive, as of January 2012?

18 At which educational establishment was Jeremy Clarkson receiving an honorary degree when he got a custard pie in the face in September 2005?

19 True or false: Andrew Lloyd Webber only accepted his peerage so he could support changes to the House of Lords as a member of the Liberal Democrats in the Upper House?

20 Who, as of November 2012, are third, fifth and tenth in line to the British throne occupied by Queen Elizabeth II? (3 pts)

Total Points: 26. Targets: Novice 13 Pro 20. Your Score:

Quiz 392. General Knowledge

Part 1

1 If Barack Obama is no. 44, who was no. 40?

2 Olof Palme, assassinated on 28 February 1986, was the serving Prime Minister of which country?

3 Which theatrical and TV stalwart came to the end of his *Good Life* in February 2013?

4 What is the highly illustrated manuscript of the Four Gospels gifted resident at Trinity College Dublin?

5 Which continent occupies the biggest percentage of the earth's total land: Antarctica, Europe or South America?

6 To what were protesters at Stokes Croft, Bristol, objecting – occasionally violently – in 2010? (a) a new by-pass (b) a new wind farm (c) a new Tesco

7 What is the portion of Egypt that lies in Asia rather than Africa, and also serves as a buffer between Egypt and Israel?

8 Which famous eighteenth-century actor-manager wrote the words to the patriotic song 'Heart of Oak' (music by William Boyce)?

9 Which notable modern artist directed his old college associates in the band Blur to make the video for their hit 'Country House'?

10 Which Caribbean author wrote the 1963 cricket classic, *Beyond a Boundary*?

Part 2

11   What was launched in 1964 as a replacement for the *Daily Herald*?

12   In an interview for a magazine, TV presenter Lorraine Kelly confessed to holding a torch for whom? (a) Andrew Marr (b) Sebastian Coe (c) Mr Spock

13   What and where is Hokkaido?

14   How many British novelists have won the Pulitzer Prize for fiction?

15   If an individual dies intestate, what does that mean in legal terms?

16   Which World Cup winner was the first player to notch up 100 appearances for four different clubs?

17   Who was John McEnroe's first wife?

18   Which famous comedian starred alongside Jerry Rafferty in the folk band, the Humblebums?

19   Who was the youngster who went missing from a shopping centre in Merseyside on 12 February 1993?

20   What was unusual about the 180 Swedish tourists who arrived at Felixstowe for a shopping trip in 1977?

Total Points: 20. Targets: Novice 10 Pro 15. Your Score:

Answers Quizzes 385–392

Quiz 385. General Knowledge

1. Voltaire; 2. Ian Poulter's oft-quoted remark in 2008 (he was world no. 26 at the time); 3. Kevin Keegan's legendary rant at Alex Ferguson as his talented but brittle Newcastle side let a twelve-point lead in the title race slip; 4. Jane Austen, *Pride and Prejudice*; 5. Sepp Blatter, President of FIFA (what an utter buffoon); 6. Bob Geldof makes light of his medal collection, 2001; 7. Brian Clough addressing the Leeds United squad on his arrival at Elland Road as the club's new manager; 8. Germaine Greer, in the *Guardian*, 27 October 1986; 9. QPR boss Ian Holloway on his side's 3–0 victory over Chesterfield.; 10. Mick Jagger; 11. Groucho Marx; 12. Debbie McGhee, who married a much older, unattractive but wealthy man; 13. Anne Robinson (it was a review of the US transfer of *The Weakest Link*); 14. Foxhunting; 15. The missing words are 'run for President'

Quiz 386. Movies

1. Movie sound engineer; 2. Fritz the Cat; 3. Kylie Minogue; 4. Eric Rohmer; 5. *Psycho*; 6. *The French Connection* and *The Exorcist*; 7. Universal; 8. *The Manchurian Candidate*; Meryl Streep; 9. Marlene Dietrich; 10. Gordon Ramsay; 11. St Valentine's Day, 14 February (1900); 12. 'The End' by the Doors; 13. Johnny Depp; 14. Dennis Hopper; 15. Russ Meyer; 16. Michael Caine and Laurence Olivier; Caine again, this time in the older role previously take by Olivier, and with Jude Law as his younger self, echoing Alfie (2004) where Law also took on an iconic Caine role

Quiz 387. Arts and Culture

1. Baritone; 2. Salford (Manchester is incorrect); 3. Frieze; 4. Madame Tussaud; 5. (c) Lucian Freud; 6. *Asterix*; 7. Tango, (bonus point for the Argentine tango); 8. The Royal Opera usually sing in the original language, the ENO usually in English; 9. Crescendo is playing with increasing volume, fortissimo is playing flat-out loud; 10. Tchaikovsky; Mix and Match 1, h; 2, d; 3, i; 4, g; 5, a; 6, c; 7, e; 8, b; 9, f; 10, j

Quiz 388. Pets

1. Cat; 2. A hornbill (half mark for 'bird'); 3. Bubbles; 4. Socks; 5. Dowager Princess; 6. Battersea Dogs and Cats Home; 7. NEC, Birmingham; it was first held in 1891, with around 2,000 dogs entered; 8. *101 Dalmatians*; 9. Siamese; 10. *Madagascar*; 11. Guinea pig; 12. 188 (the average age is reckoned to be well over 100); 13. The People's Dispensary for Sick Animals, a charitable organization offering veterinary services to the poor; 14. 1824, by a group of reformers including William Wilberforce, he of the abolition of slavery movement; 15. He was a lemur

Quiz 389. Military History

1. Carthage; 2. Turkey; 3. Trafalgar; 4. Sebastopol; 5. Denmark; 6. Burgundy; 7. The Big Red One; 8. Romania; 9. (a) Falkland Islands; 10. Blücher; 11. Naseby; Sir Thomas Fairfax, the New Model Army; Prince Rupert of the Rhine, the King's nephew; 12. Little Bighorn; Montana; Seventh Cavalry; Cheyenne; Marcus Reno

Quiz 390. Football

1. They were all founder members of the Scottish Football League; 2. Javier Mascherano; 3. Karren Brady; 4. Luther Blissett; 5. Alf Ramsey; 6. Wimbledon; Neil Sullivan; 7. It is Arsenal's win–draw–loss column in that season, when they went a whole Premier League season undefeated; 8. Mick Harford; 9. Denis Bergkamp from Inter Milan and Stan Collymore from Nottingham Forest; 10. Manchester City; Notts County; Leicester City; 11. Peter Osgood, who was in the Chelsea side that won in 1970; 12. To support Calais, regarded as 'honorary Englishmen' (the French side pulled off one of the great giant-killing feats by making it all the way to the final, where they lost 2–1 to Nantes of Ligue 1); 13. George Burley (Ipswich Town), Harry Redknapp (Tottenham) and Alan Pardew (Newcastle); 14. Joe Royle was replaced by Kevin Keegan in 2001; 15. Jürgen Klinsmann; 16. Lucas Radebe of Leeds and Mark Fish of Bolton; 17. Danny Graham; Michu; 18. Mario Balotelli in 2011–12 (slightly surprising stat, although the best Italian players tend to stay in Serie A); 19. Ole Gunnar Solskjaer, Ronny Johnsen and Henning Berg; 20. Heart of Midlothian and Hibernian

Quiz 391. Trivia

1. Twiggy; 2. Elizabeth Taylor's husbands (Conrad Hilton Jr, Michael Wilding, Mike Todd, Eddie Fisher, Richard Burton [twice], John Warner and Larry Fortensky); 3. Las Vegas; strip billiards (the perils of fame – 'single bloke in laddish behaviour incident in private rooms' is hardly headline news were someone else the perpetrator); 4. Patsy Kensit and Nicole Appleton; 5. Richard I (they married in Cyprus while Richard was on his way to the Crusades, and she spent most of their marriage in Europe, often raising money for his ransom or his wars); 6. Sony Music (Tommy Mottola); 7. John Alderton; 8. Heidi Klum; 9. Ben Watt; 10. Tess Daly; 11. New York; 12. (c) Bogart; Lauren Bacall; 13. Vidal Sassoon and Gore Vidal; 14. Annette Bening; 15. Johnny Cash; 16. Bryan Ferry; 17. Tommy, the drummer, now a record producer; 18. Oxford Brookes University (Oxford University is wrong); 19. False (the millionaire composer never demurred at the notion of being Lord Lloyd Webber and he sits on the Conservative benches); 20. Prince Harry; Princess Beatrice of York; Princess Anne

Quiz 392. General Knowledge

1. Ronald Reagan; 2. Sweden; 3. Richard Briers; 4. *Book of Kells*; 5. South America takes up 11.9 per cent (Antarctica 9.4 per cent and Europe just 6.7 per cent); 6. (c) a new Tesco; 7. Sinai Peninsula; 8. David Garrick; 9. Damien Hirst; 10. C. L. R. James; 11. *Sun*; 12. (c)

Rather bizarrely, not for Lorraine the dashing Mr Chekhov; 13. Second largest and most northerly of the islands which comprise Japan; 14. None, the prize is eligible only to American authors, just as the Man Booker prize is eligible only to Commonwealth authors writing in English; 15. They hadn't made a will (and interminable wrangling will ensue, from which the main benefactors will be lawyers); 16. Alan Ball (Blackpool, Everton, Arsenal, Southampton); 17. Tatum O'Neal; 18. Billy Connolly; 19. James Bulger; 20. They were ninety pairs of identical twins

Quiz 393. General Knowledge

Part 1

1   What might you expect to see at Giza in Africa?

2   Florence Nightingale earned her legendary status for her care of soldiers during which war?

3   Japan consists of many islands; are there *c*.500, *c*.1,500, or more than 3,000?

4   What was the title of Sprenger and Kramer's fifteenth-century text, dealing with the identification and punishment of witches?

5   Which famous philosopher served as a tutor to the young Alexander the Great?

6   What did South Carolina do in 1860 shortly before ten others did the same?

7   What priceless treasure did the Moghuls discover when they captured the fort at Agra in 1526?

8   Which song sets A. C. Benson's words to music and appears at the end of Elgar's 'Coronation Ode'?

9   What connects Beady Eye and High Flying Birds?

10 Flavio Briatore was once the principal of which Formula 1 team? Which English football club did he also own? (2 pts)

Part 2

11 Which two of the following countries drive on the right: Canada, Australia, Republic of South Africa, Thailand, Argentina and Pakistan (2 pts)

12 Which is the highest of the nine orders of angels, according to standard hierarchy?

13 Who are the only country to lose all three World Cup finals they have reached?

14 What is the name of the hybrid car brought on to the market by Honda to rival the Toyota Prius?

15 Who, according to a popular rhyme, 'took an axe; and gave her mother forty whacks'? (In reality she was found innocent.)

16 Who are the five children who win the golden tickets in *Charlie and the Chocolate Factory* by Roald Dahl? (5 pts)

17 What are the five boroughs of the city of New York? (5 pts)

Total Points: 27. Targets: Novice 14 Pro 20. Your Score:

Quiz 394. London

Boris, buses, bridges and all

Part 1

1　In 2009, Mayor of London Boris Johnson overruled Camden Council and approved the construction of which skyscraper? (a) The Pinnacle (b) Vauxhall Sky Gardens (c) Columbus Tower

2　The Anglican church of St Margaret is situated in the grounds of which larger religious building?

3　In which London square can a monument to Gandhi be found?

4　What was Phyllis Pearsall's contribution to getting around London in 1936?

5　What is to be found at 30 Millbank, London SW1, further down the road from Tate Britain?

6　Canary Wharf is located on which spur of land formed by a loop in the river, once one of London's most derelict areas?

7　Which famous legal institution closed in July 2006 after 271 years?

8　Who left his unusual house at 13 Lincoln's Inn Fields to the nation when he died in 1837? (It remains a public museum.)

9　In which decade was the first Gay Pride march held in London?

10　Which London borough is sandwiched between Southwark and Greenwich south of the River Thames?

Part 2

11 Where in London is the US Embassy located?

12 What sits at 30 St Mary Axe?

13 Which London station has housed the main Eurostar terminus since 2007?

14 What was designed and built by John Nash in 1827 as a monument to the victories at Trafalgar and Waterloo?

15 What is the cable-stayed bridge crossing the Thames between Chelsea Bridge and Battersea Bridge?

16 Kensal Green, Norwood, Highgate, Nunhead, Brompton, Abney Park, Tower Hamlets; what's the connection?

17 Marie Grosholz brought her artworks to a London exhibition in 1802; they would become a permanent exhibition, first in Baker Street and later round the corner in Marylebone Road; what was Marie's married name?

18 In the famous old London rhyme, which two bells ask a question? (2 pts)

19 What are the two blue lines on the London Underground map? (2 pts)

20 What is the Prince of Wales's London residence when he is in town?

Total Points: 22. Targets: Novice 9 Pro 17. Your Score:

Quiz 395. Tourist Attractions

Sun, sea, sand and city breaks

Part 1

1   London is the UK's most popular tourist destination. Which city comes second?

2   Montego Bay lies on the north coast of which Caribbean island?

3   Which edifice did the Moghul Emperor Shah Jahan commission for his Mumtaz ('Jewel')?

4   The Burj Khalifa, the world's tallest free-standing structure at 829.24 metres, is found in which city?

5   Which group of islands includes Tenerife and Lanzarote and in which ocean do they lie? (2 pts)

6   The Radcliffe Camera was designed by whom in which century to house what in which city? (4 pts)

7   Where might you stay in the Bellagio Hotel, with an eleven-acre lake and a singing fountain?

8   Where did the first Disney theme park open in Europe in 1992?

9   What is the large, wildlife-filled trough that runs virtually the length of Kenya from north to south?

10 There are some wonderful old missionary monasteries dating from the early sixteenth century near Popocatépetl; what, and where, is Popocatépetl? (2 pts)

Part 2

11 The Iguazu Falls are protected by national parks on either side belonging to which two South American countries? (2 pts)

12 Rhodes, Lesbos and Chios are all part of which Greek island group close to the Turkish coast? (a) Ionian (b) Dodecanese (c) Cyclades

13 Which Portuguese-influenced state on the west coast of India is a popular tourist destination and the country's wealthiest state?

14 What connects the Paris cathedral on the Île de la Cité and the cathedrals at Reims and Tournai?

15 What is the city about 15 metres from Berlin that was the seat of the Prussian kings and kaisers until the end of the Great War in 1918? (a) Potsdam (b) Lübeck or (c) Mannheim

16 What name is given to the northeast coast of Spain, above Barcelona?

17 The Royal Exhibition Building erected to house an international exhibition in 1880–81 lies in Carlton Gardens in which Australian city? What major political event was hosted in the building in 1901? (2 pts)

18 What are the two autonomous regions of Portugal, both in the North Atlantic and representing the last vestiges of the Portuguese empire? (2 pts)

19 What name is given to the stretch of beaches and resorts on the French Mediterranean coast?

20 Which city boasts the famous sand and surf attraction, Bondi Beach?

Total Points: 28. Targets: Novice 11 Pro 21. Your Score:

Quiz 396. History

A mix of ancient and more recent history

Part 1

1   At the end of the eleventh century, who led armed resistance to the Norman invaders from a base on the island of Ely in the watery fens?

2   The ancient city and empire of Carthage was based in which modern city? (a) Tunis (b) Barcelona (c) Alexandria

3   Which notorious gangster (and later successful author) served as chief enforcer for both Henry Hill and Charlie Richardson?

4   Justinian the Great (527–65) was a significant ruler of which empire?

5   In which city was Tsar Alexander II of Russia assassinated in 1881?

6   In the 1870s Austin and George Bidwell were sentenced to penal servitude for what crime? (a) defrauding the Bank of England of over £100,000 (about £30 million in today's terms) (b) stealing the Queen's art collection from Windsor Castle (c) forging signed copies of works by major authors of the time such as Dickens and Disraeli

7   Who or what were the Khmer Rouge and who was their leader? (2 pts)

8   Elizabeth Garrett Anderson was the first woman to qualify and work as what in the UK in 1859?

9   What was the first commodity to be rationed during World War II?

10 The Great Indian Mutiny of 1857 saw the end of control of India by which organization? The loyalty of which key local army units allowed the British to retain control after more than twelve months of fighting? (2 pts)

Part 2

11 What was the old name of Bangladesh and the adjoining part of India under British colonial rule? And after independence in 1947, to which country was it attached politically, but not geographically? (2 pts)

12 Who was the last British survivor of the World War I trenches, who died, aged 111, in 2009?

13 The Emperor Tiberius was succeeded by his grand-nephew; who was he? (a) Claudius (b) Caligula (c) Nero

14 Muhammad Ali is regarded as the founder of the modern structure of which state?

15 Which modern South American city was founded as the City of the Kings by Spanish General Francisco Pizarro in 1535 and remained the centre of Spanish South America for the next 300 years?

16 What was the burning of art and books by zealots in Florence in 1497 named? And who was the Dominican preacher who instigated it? (2 pts)

17 For what historical event is the meadow of Runnymede, not far from Windsor Castle, best known?

18 Construction of which conduit linking Moscow to the eastern part of the Russian Empire began in 1891?

19 Who led the rebel Nationalists in the Spanish Civil War (1936–9)?

20 Which major figure in the Russian Revolution was the founder of the Red Army in his time as People's Commissar of Military Affairs?

Total Points: 24. Targets: Novice 10 Pro 18. Your Score: [   ]

Quiz 397. Movies

A specialist thriller section and a Mix and Match

Part 1

A section on the master of the genre

1   Which two words made up Alfred Hitchcock's Academy Award acceptance speech in 1967?
2   Which Hitchcock movie has an exciting climax on the face of Mount Rushmore?
3   Name the three films Grace Kelly made with Alfred Hitchcock. (3 pts)
4   Name the four films James Stewart made with Alfred Hitchcock. (4 pts)
5   Name the three films Ingrid Bergman made with Alfred Hitchcock. (3 pts)
6   Name the four films Cary Grant made with Alfred Hitchcock. (4 pts)
7   What, in 1929, was Hitchcock's first 'talkie'? And which movie did he shoot twice, in 1934 and 1956? (2 pts)
8   Which Hitchcock film concerns two men who agree to commit the other's murder?
9   Who plays the exiled Nazi the authorities are trying to trap in *Notorious*? And who is the smooth villain in *North by Northwest*? (2 pts)
10 Which classic 'Hitchcock blonde' did the director cast first in *The Birds* as an unknown in 1963 and then in *Marnie* the following year? Who was her co-star in *Marnie*? (2 pts)

Part 2

Mix and Match: match these thrillers to the author of the source novel from which the film's screenplay derived

1. *The Talented Mr Ripley*; 2. *The 39 Steps*; 3. *The Constant Gardener*; 4. *Layer Cake*; 5. *The Maltese Falcon*; 6. *The Firm*; 7. *The Bourne Identity*; 8. *Savages*; 9. *Get Shorty*; 10. *Patriot Games*

a. Don Winslow; b. Dashiell Hammett; c. Elmore Leonard; d. Patricia Highsmith; e. Tom Clancy; f. John Grisham; g. John Buchan; h. John le Carré; i. J. J. Connolly; j. Robert Ludlum

Your Workings:

Total Points: 33. Targets: Novice 17 Pro 25. Your Score:

Quiz 398. Ashes

By the time this is published they may have changed hands again (let's hope not)

Part 1

1   The inscription on the Ashes urn commemorates an Australian victory in which year?

2   In 1948 Australia brought one of their strongest sides to England and won 4–0: who took twenty-seven wickets apiece as the England batting line-up was consistently routed? (2 pts)

3   Who was the England captain for the infamous Bodyline tour to Australia of 1933?

4   Whose Ashes heroics in 1975 won him the BBC Sports Personality of the Year award?

5   Who took sixteen wickets on his test debut at Lord's in 1972?

6   Which England player hit the only six of the entire 1958–9 Ashes series in Australia?

7   1902 and Australia headed for the last test with a 2–0 lead; who spared England's blushes with a magnificent seventy-seven minute hundred in the final innings, leaving Hirst and Rhodes to 'get 'em in ones' and win the game?

8   Which England captain was the first to bag a pair in an Ashes test, and lost his job after the game?

9   Which formidable Australian opening bowlers destroyed England in 1974–5 as the hosts sauntered to a 4–1 win? (2 pts)

10 Who are the leading run-scorers and wicket-takers for each side in Ashes cricket? And which wicketkeeper has most dismissals? (5 pts)

Part 2

11 1986–7 in Australia: England won 2–1 under Mike Gatting. Which opening
    batsman scored three centuries for the visiting side? Who came into the
    side for the fourth test and was man of the match as he and Botham bowled
    out the Aussies for peanuts? (2 pts)

12 Who took nineteen wickets in an Ashes test in 1956? Who took the other
    one? (2 pts)

13 In 1977 England made three changes for the third test; who came in for his
    test debut, and who made a return to the side and scored a hundred? (2 pts)

14 1997 and England were flattered by a 3–2 margin of defeat at home in a
    six-match series; which two England batsmen put on 288 towards a total
    good enough to win the first test? And who took eleven wickets on a turn-
    ing Oval pitch to win the final dead rubber? Who finished the series with an
    impressive thirty-six wickets on his first tour of England? (4 pts)

15 Which spin bowler scored his test best 95 after going in as a nightwatch-
    man against Australia in 1983?

16 1989 and the start of a miserable decade and a bit for England; which
    Australian ran riot with forty-one wickets in the series, and who took
    twenty-nine more on his debut tour? (2 pts)

17 Which quick bowler, known as the Typhoon, was England's secret weapon
    as they won the 1954–5 Ashes series 3–1 away from home?

18 England won 5–1 in 1978–9 at the height of the Packer defections from test
    cricket; who headed the run scoring for England with 420 (averaging 42) in
    a low-scoring series? Who bowled his heart out for Australia with forty-one
    wickets despite getting little support? (2 pts)

19 Who took nine wickets in the match and scored 52 batting at no. 10 as
    England's women's team made it a double Ashes celebration in 2005?

20 1981 and the Miracle of Headingley; which lower order batsmen shared
    partnerships of 117 and 67 with Ian Botham as England rescued a lost
    cause after following on? And who routed the Aussies in the last innings,
    taking 8–43 in an inspired spell of fast bowling? (3 pts)

Total Points: 36. Targets: Novice 14 Pro 27. Your Score: [   ]

Quiz 399. Musicals

The hills are alive

Part 1

1 Which musical based on the songs of Abba opened in 1999, starting a wave of musicals based on the songs of pop acts?

2 Tim Curry, Anthony Head, Tim McInnerny and Jason Donovan have all appeared as which cult musical character?

3 Which playwright and composer combination turned John Gay's *The Beggar's Opera* into the dark twentieth-century masterpiece *The Three-penny Opera*? (2 pts)

4 A £4.75 million musical adaptation of which classic novel and movie closed three months early in 2008 after terrible reviews?

5 The musical *Jersey Boys* tells the story of which 1960s pop group?

6 Which controversial Franz Wedekind play from 1891 was turned into a 2008 musical, championed by actor Tom Hulce?

7 Which pop star made a successful West End appearance as the MC in a 2012 revival of *Cabaret*?

8 What was the musical with tunes by Benny and Bjorn from Abba and lyrics by Tim Rice?

9 What overtook *Cats* as the longest running musical in the London West End in 2006?

10 *The Million Dollar Quartet* is a musical about which four American singers? (4 pts)

Part 2

11. What was the black musical created by *Wire* star Clarke Peters in 1990? (a) *Stomp* (b) *Five Guys Named Moe* (c) *Dreamgirls*

12 Who wrote both the music and lyrics to *A Funny Thing Happened on the Way to the Forum*, first performed in 1963? Who starred in both the original Broadway run and the film version from 1966? Who first took the lead role of Pseudolus on the West End stage? (3 pts)

13 Who wrote the book and additional lyrics to accompany the songs of Queen in the musical *We Will Rock You*?

14 Who or what connects *Bat out of Hell* to the 1986 Lloyd Webber musical *Whistle down the Wind*?

15 Which celebrated director brought the musical version of *Charlie and the Chocolate Factory* to the West End in 2013?

16 Which 2003 Stephen Schwartz musical is set in parallel to *The Wizard of Oz*, but from the perspective of the bad guys?

17 The Kander and Ebb musical *Cabaret*, a Broadway hit in 1966 and Academy Award-winning film, is based on a novel by which British author?

18 Who won a BAFTA and an Oscar for Best Supporting Actress after an inspired half hour as Fantine in *Les Misérables* (2012)?

19 Which of the following did *not* open as a piece of musical theatre in 2008? (a) *Shane Warne: The Musical* (b) *Gay Bride of Frankenstein* (c) *Satan Ate My Cheese*

20 Which 2011 musical by Trey Parker, Matt Stone and Robert Lopez won nine Tony Awards and opened in the West End in 2013?

Total Points: 26. Targets: Novice 10 Pro 20. Your Score:

Quiz 400. End Games

Deep breath . . . and out . . . last one . . .

Part 1

1   'Either that wallpaper goes, or I do.' The alleged dying words in 1900 of which writer and wit?

2   'The executioner is, I believe, very expert. And my neck is very slender. Oh God have pity on my soul.' Whose rather touching last words on the block?

3   Why was Eric Hollies bowling Don Bradman for a duck at the Oval in a 1948 test match regarded as a cruel end to the great batsman's career?

4   'I am going outside and may be some time.' Whose last words before sacrificing himself for his comrades?

5   Which exciting 1967 debut album had a near twelve-minute closing track called 'The End'?

6   *Sleeping Murder*, published posthumously in 1976, was the last book written by which author? Who was the book's leading character? (2 pts)

7   Which great British statesman is believed to have said, 'I'm so bored with it all', before slipping into a coma and dying nine days later?

8   'Louis, I think this is the start of a beautiful friendship.' Which actor is speaking the final lines in which movie? (2 pts)

9   According to the Book of Revelation, what will be the site of the last battle at the end of days?

10 'When you ain't got nothing, you got nothing to lose / You're invisible now, you got no secrets to conceal.' Which classic folk song ends with this couplet (not including repetition of the chorus)?

Part 2

11   What are the final stops on the Piccadilly Line on the London Underground? (3 pts)

12   '. . . and wondered how any one could ever imagine unquiet slumbers for the sleepers in that quiet earth'. Which overwrought ending to a Victorian novel?

13   What was Charles Dickens's final novel, left unfinished on his death in 1870?

14   Which two 1970s cover versions featured on the double-A side single from Westlife that was the last UK no. 1 of the twentieth century? (2 pts)

15   What is Julius Caesar alleged to have said as he was assassinated by the conspirators on the steps of the Senate?

16   'So we beat on, boats against the current, borne back ceaselessly into the past.' Which American classic ends thus? (Author and title, please.) (2 pts)

17   What quote, taken from a Neil Young song, was found in Kurt Cobain's handwriting on what was taken to be a suicide note?

18   '. . . and drew him down to me so he could feel my breasts all perfume yes and his heart was going like mad and yes I said yes I will Yes.' The last lines of which long, modern classic? (Author and title, please.) (2 pts)

19   'After all, tomorrow is another day!' So ends which famous book and film?

20   Which literary figure's last words are 'The rest is silence . . .'?

Total Points: 27. Targets: Novice 14 Pro 20. Your Score:

Answers Quizzes 393–400

Quiz 393. General Knowledge

1. Pyramids; 2. Crimean; 3. Over 3,000; 4. *Malleus Maleficarum* (allow *Hexenhammer*); 5. Aristotle; 6. Seceded from the Union; 7. The Koh-i-Noor diamond; 8. 'Land of Hope and Glory'; 9. The Gallagher brothers (Liam's new band is Beady Eye while Noel has High Flying Birds); 10. Renault; Queens Park Rangers; 11. Canada and Argentina drive on the right; 12. Seraphim; 13. Netherlands; 14. Honda Insight; 15. Lizzie Borden; 16. Augustus Gloop; Veruca Salt; Violet Beauregarde; Mike Teavee; Charlie Bucket; 17. The Bronx, Brooklyn, Manhattan, Queens, Staten Island

Quiz 394. London

1. (c) Columbus Tower; 2. Westminster Abbey (it serves as the local church for the House of Commons); 3. Tavistock Square; 4. The first *A–Z* map book; 5. Conservative Party head-quarters; 6. Isle of Dogs; 7. Bow Street magistrates' court; 8. Sir John Soane; 9. 1972; 10. Lewisham; 11. Grosvenor Square (no. 24); 12. The Gherkin; 13. St Pancras Eurostar Termi-nal; 14. Marble Arch; 15. Albert Bridge; 16. They are the location of the 'Magnificent Seven' Victorian cemeteries built between 1832 and 1841; 17. Madame Tussaud; 18. Old Bailey ('When will you pay me?') and Stepney ('When will that be?'); 19. Victoria Line and Piccadilly Line; 20. Clarence House (Prince Charles moved from St James's Palace in 2002)

Quiz 395. Tourist Attractions

1. Edinburgh; 2. Jamaica; 3. Taj Mahal; 4. Dubai, UAE; 5. Canary Islands; in the Atlantic, off the southern coast of Morocco; 6. James Gibbs in eighteenth century (1749) to house the Bodleian Library in Oxford; 7. Las Vegas (where else?); 8. Marne-la-Vallée, just outside Paris (accept Paris); 9. The Great Rift Valley; 10. It is a volcano in Mexico, the country's second highest peak; 11. Brazil and Argentina; 12. (b) Dodecanese; 13. Goa; 14. All have the name Cathédrale de Notre-Dame; 15. Potsdam; 16. Costa Brava; 17. Melbourne; the first Australian Parliament; 18. Madeira and the Azores; 19. Côte d'Azur; 20. Sydney, Australia

Quiz 396. History

1. Hereward; 2. (a) Tunis; 3. 'Mad Frankie' Fraser; 4. Byzantine; 5. St Petersburg; 6. (a) along with a master forger they passed forged bills to a huge value after establishing a serviceable line of credit – they were caught because the date was missing from some of the money orders; 7. They were the pro-communist forces in Cambodia who controlled the nation between 1975 and 1979; they were led by Pol Pot; 8. A doctor (she was preceded by Elizabeth Blackwell in the US by ten years); 9. Petrol; 10. The East India Company; the Sikhs; 11. Bengal; Pakistan; 12. Harry Patch; 13. (b) Caligula; 14. Egypt (Muhammad Ali

Pasha became ruler of Egypt in 1805 and instigated huge reforms in his forty-three-year rule); 15. Lima, Peru; 16. The Bonfire of the Vanities; Savonarola; 17. It is where King John met the rebel barons to sign the Magna Carta in 1215; 18. Trans-Siberian Railway; 19. General Franco; 20. Leon Trotsky

Quiz 397. Movies

1. Thank you; 2. *North by Northwest*; 3. *Dial M For Murder*, *Rear Window* and *To Catch a Thief*; 4. *Rope*, *Rear Window*, *The Man Who Knew Too Much*, *Vertigo*; 5. *Spellbound*, *Notorious*, *Under Capricorn*; 6. *Suspicion*, *Notorious*, *To Catch a Thief*, *North by Northwest*; 7. *Blackmail*; *The Man Who Knew Too Much*; 8. *Strangers on a Train*; 9. Claude Rains; James Mason; 10. Tippi Hedren; Sean Connery; Mix and Match 1, d; 2, g; 3, h; 4, i; 5, b; 6, f; 7, j; 8, a; 9, c; 10, e

Quiz 398. Ashes

1. 1882; 2. Ray Lindwall and Bill Johnston; 3. Douglas Jardine; 4. David Steele; 5. Bob Massie; 6. Fred Trueman; 7. Gilbert Jessop; 8. Ian Botham in 1981(the story has a happy ending . . .); 9. Dennis Lillee and Jeff Thomson; 10. Don Bradman and Jack Hobbs; Shane Warne and Ian Botham; Ian Healy; 11. Chris Broad; Gladstone Small; 12. Jim Laker; left-arm spinner Tony Lock; 13. Ian Botham and Geoff Boycott; 14. Nasser Hussain and Graeme Thorpe; Phil Tufnell; Glenn McGrath; 15. Eddie Hemmings (it helped save the match although England still lost the series 2–1); 16. Terry Alderman; Merv Hughes; 17. Frank Tyson; 18. David Gower; Rodney Hogg; 19. Katharine Brunt; 20. Graham Dilley and Chris Old; Bob Willis

Quiz 399. Musicals

1. *Mamma Mia!*; 2. Frank N. Furter in *The Rocky Horror Show*; 3. Bertolt Brecht and Kurt Weill; 4. *Gone with the Wind*; 5. Four Seasons; 6. *Spring Awakening*; 7. Will Young; 8. *Chess*; 9. *Les Misérables*; 10. Elvis Presley, Carl Perkins, Johnny Cash and Jerry Lee Lewis; 11. *Five Guys Named Moe*; 12. Stephen Sondheim; Zero Mostel; Frankie Howerd; 13. Ben Elton; 14. Jim Steinman, who produced the Meat Loaf album and wrote the lyrics for *Whistle Down the Wind*; 15. Sam Mendes; 16. *Wicked*; 17. Christopher Isherwood; 18. Anne Hathaway; 19. *Satan Ate My Cheese* was not a musical; 20. *The Book of Mormon*

Quiz 400. End Games

1. Oscar Wilde; 2. Anne Boleyn; 3. Hollies earned his place in history by denying the great man a career average of over 100; 4. Captain Lawrence Oates, beset by frostbite and not wishing to slow down his colleagues on a disastrous polar expedition in 1912; 5. The Doors; 6. Agatha Christie; Miss Marple (the book was written much earlier, *c.*1941); 7. Winston Churchill; 8. Humphrey Bogart (as Rick Blaine) in *Casablanca*; 9. Armageddon;

10. Bob Dylan's 'Like a Rolling Stone'; 11. Cockfosters, Uxbridge and Heathrow Terminal 5 (be nice, accept Heathrow); 12. Emily Brontë's *Wuthering Heights*; 13. *The Mystery of Edwin Drood*; 14. 'I Have a Dream' and 'Seasons of the Sun'; 15. '*Et tu, Brute?*' ('And you, Brutus?'); 16. *The Great Gatsby* by F. Scott Fitzgerald; 17. 'Better to burn out, than to fade away . . .'; 18. James Joyce's *Ulysses* (you did well if you got that far); 19. *Gone with the Wind*; 20. Hamlet